DAVID BUSCH'S

Nikon® Z9/Z8

GUIDE TO

DIGITAL STILL PHOTOGRAPHY

DAVID D. BUSCH

David Busch's Nikon® Z9/Z8
Guide to Digital Still Photography
David D. Busch

Project Manager: Jenny Davidson
Technical Editor: Darrell Young
Layout: Bill Hartman
Cover Design: Mike Tanamachi
Indexer: Valerie Haynes Perry
Proofreader: Mike Beady

ISBN: 979-8-88814-136-6
1st Edition (2nd printing, December 2024)

Rocky Nook, Inc.
1010 B Street, Suite 350
San Rafael, CA 94901
USA
www.rockynook.com

Distributed in the UK and Europe by Publishers Group UK
Distributed in the U.S. and all other territories by Publishers Group West

Library of Congress Control Number: 2023939495

This book is printed on acid-free paper.
Printed in Korea

rockynook

For Cathy

Acknowledgments

Thanks to everyone at Rocky Nook, including Scott Cowlin, managing director and publisher, for the freedom to let me explore the amazing capabilities of the Nikon Z9 and Z8 cameras in depth. I couldn't do it without my veteran production team, including project manager, Jenny Davidson and technical editor, Darrell Young. Also, thanks to Bill Hartman, layout; Valerie Haynes Perry, indexing; Mike Beady, proofreading; Mike Tanamachi, cover design; and my agent, Carole Jelen, who has the amazing ability to keep both publishers and authors happy.

About the Author

With more than 3 million books in print, **David D. Busch** is the world's #1 selling digital camera guide author, and the originator of popular digital photography series like *David Busch's Pro Secrets* and *David Busch's Quick Snap Guides.* He has written more than four dozen hugely successful guidebooks and compact guides for Nikon digital cameras, dozens of additional user guides for other camera models, as well as many popular books devoted to dSLRs, including *Mastering Digital SLR Photography, Fourth Edition* and *Digital SLR Pro Secrets.* As a roving photojournalist for more than 20 years, he illustrated his books, magazine articles, and newspaper reports with award-winning images. He's operated his own commercial studio, suffocated in formal dress while shooting weddings, and shot sports for a daily newspaper and an upstate New York college. His photos and articles have been published in magazines as diverse as *Popular Photography, Rangefinder, Professional Photographer,* and hundreds of other publications. He's also reviewed dozens of digital cameras for CNet Networks and other CBS publications. His advice has been featured on National Public Radio's *All Tech Considered.*

When About.com named its top five books on Beginning Digital Photography, debuting at the #1 and #2 slots were Busch's *Digital Photography All-In-One Desk Reference for Dummies* and *Mastering Digital Photography.* He's had as many as five of his books listed in the Top 20 of Amazon.com's Digital Photography Bestseller list—simultaneously! Busch's 350-plus other books published since 1983 include bestsellers like *Digital SLR Cameras and Photography for Dummies.*

Busch is a member of the Cleveland Photographic Society (www.clevelandphoto.org), which has operated continuously since 1887. Visit his website at http://www.nikonguides.com or his Facebook group *David D. Busch Photography Guides.*

Contents

CHAPTER 4

Electronic Flash 143

CHAPTER 5

Photo Shooting Menu 187

CHAPTER 11

Retouch and My Menus 377

CHAPTER 12

Introduction to Video 387

APPENDIX A

Firmware Updates 429

Index 437

Preface

The dynamic duo of the Nikon Z9 and Z8 are, without a doubt, the most advanced digital cameras the company has ever produced, with just about every feature the most demanding professional photographer and avid enthusiast could ask for—plus more than a few exciting capabilities most of us never even dreamed of. With no mechanical shutter, both cameras rely on all-electronic shutters that can grab full-frame photos at 20 frames per second, and cropped images at a blazing 120 fps clip. You can even capture action that happened *before* you pressed the shutter release down all the way. Super-responsive autofocus can search for, detect, and lock focus on the eyes, faces, and torsos of people, birds, dogs, cats, animals, and other difficult-to-track subjects, including planes, trains, and motorcycles. Impressive five-axis image stabilization counters camera shake at slow shutter speeds and helps ensure the best image quality from their 46-megapixel sensors.

Best of all, the Z9 and Z8 look and handle like the Nikons we love, with controls and menus that veteran Nikon owners will find comfortably familiar and new users will grow to appreciate as they explore the latest enhancements. Every photo enthusiast will easily master the camera's capabilities, even though the sheer number of features and options can be daunting. The only thing standing between you and pixel proficiency is the lack of a comprehensive manual. Complete instructions for both the Z9 and Z8 are available only online, downloadable as a massive PDF.

Everything you need to know is in there, somewhere, but you don't know where to start, nor how to find the information you really need to master your camera. In addition, the camera manual doesn't offer much guidance on the principles that will help you master digital photography. Nor does it really tell you much about how mirrorless shooting might differ from the kinds of digital photography you may already be used to. If you're like most enthusiasts, you're probably not interested in spending hours or days studying a comprehensive book on digital photography that doesn't necessarily apply directly to the enhanced features of your camera.

What you really need is a guide that explains the purpose and function of the camera's basic controls, available lens options, and most essential accessories from the perspective of mirrorless cameras. It should tell you how you should use them, and *why*. Ideally, there should be information about the exciting features at your disposal, how to optimize image quality, when to use exposure modes like Aperture- or Shutter-priority, and the use of special autofocus modes. In many cases, you'd prefer to read about those topics only after you've had the chance to go out and take a few hundred great pictures with your new camera. Why isn't there a book that summarizes the most important information in its first two or three chapters? This is that book.

If you can't decide on what basic settings to use with your camera because you can't figure out how changing ISO or white balance or focus defaults will affect your pictures, you need this guide. I won't talk down to you, either; this book isn't padded with dozens of pages of checklists telling you how to take a travel picture, a sports photo, or how to take a snapshot of your kids in overly simplistic terms. There are no special sections devoted to "real-world" recipes here. All of us do 100 percent of our shooting in the real world! So, I give you all the information you need to cook up great photos on your own!

Introduction

Judging from the emails I receive daily, there has been an urgent need for a concise—yet comprehensive—manual for Nikon's top-of-the-line cameras since the Nikon Z9 began shipping in late 2021. Thanks to Nikon Professional Services, I received my Nikon Z9 (and, later, my Z8) on the first day they were made available to the public. And since I received them, I've spent a lot of time exploring and discovering how to use these two remarkable cameras. I have planned from Day One to collect what I've learned into a guide, as I've done for virtually every Nikon interchangeable-lens digital camera since my initial D70 book more than two decades ago.

I quickly learned that I'd embarked on a nearly impossible mission. Although ebooks are trending—Nikon's own manuals for the Z9 and Z8 are available only as downloadable PDF files—printed (hard copy) camera manuals that you can flip through while using your camera are still the most efficient way to master these beasts. YouTube videos are a popular short-cut, but vary in quality and force you to stick to the blogger's pace and organizational whims. A 30-minute video generally has less content than a single chapter you can read in a few minutes. For self-paced instruction, most readers still prefer to read—not listen.

The challenge I encountered was finding a way to cover everything that needed to be explained in a book that, in its printed version, wouldn't have been prohibitively expensive and require at least 1,200 pages. Nobody wants to buy an $89 camera reference the size of the *Oxford English Dictionary.* The solution I came up with is the book you hold in your hands, *David Busch's Nikon Z9/Z8 Guide to Digital Still Photography.* The look and feel of this book is similar to my previous guides for Nikon cameras, but with some significant differences:

- **Focus on still photography.** The Nikon Z9 and Z8 are two of the most advanced cameras ever offered for conventional—and unconventional—still photography. It's safe to say that each of you will be using your camera primarily to shoot photos, rather than videos. Indeed, some will never shoot anything other than stills. Even so, the Z9/Z8 are two of the most sophisticated cameras to offer both stills *and* professional-level video capabilities. The video-oriented features are worthy of a separate book at least the size of this one.

  So, I decided to concentrate on the Z9 and Z8's still photography capabilities in this book, while still providing all the information most readers need to capture great video. You'll find a lot of detail about video in this book, including an expanded chapter introducing advanced video concepts, including color grading. But the main thrust is going to be how to master your camera's amazing still photography features.
- **Less hand-holding.** I acknowledge that the audience for a Nikon Z9 or Z8 guide is likely to consist largely of dedicated photo enthusiasts who justify their hefty price tags because they appreciate and need either camera's amazing roster of features.

My previous guides for Z-series models had to address the needs of both beginners eager to learn everything they could about their cameras and photography in general, as well as the interests of more advanced amateurs and pros. It was a balancing act that worked well, because veteran photographers recognized that they were at some point tyros themselves, and had no problem skimming over the material they already had mastered, or using it as a refresher.

I don't leave neophytes high and dry in this book, and do provide information on complex topics such as exposure and autofocus, but really basic content has been excised from the main book, with the most important material included in several free Bonus Chapters available for download (described next).

- **Online bonus chapters.** My previous books had a comprehensive chapter that covered choosing and using lenses. I described the advantages and disadvantages of prime and zoom lenses, how to make best use of wide-angle, normal, telephoto, and special-purpose lenses, and included descriptions of most Z-mount lenses and the most popular F-mount optics that could be used with one of the FTZ adapters.

  You'll find all that information in this book's Chapter 13, which is available for free (to purchasers of the book only) on Rocky Nook's website:

  https://rockynook.com/nikon-z8-z9/

  There you'll also find an additional bonus Chapter 14, "Protection, Prevention, and Troubleshooting," which shows you how to keep your camera safe, diagnose problems, fix some common ills, and, importantly, learn how to avoid them in the future. Finally, as Nikon continues to enhance the Z9 and Z8 through firmware updates, I will eventually be adding a bonus chapter that will bring the printed and ebook versions of this book up to date with the latest features and improvements since the Z9 V. 5.0 and Z8 V. 2.01 firmware current when this book went to press.

- **No heavy IT focus.** Yup, the Z9 has an Ethernet port. Your camera can connect to FTP servers, has its own wireless access point built-in, and can interface with your desktop or laptop computer in multiple ways. Although some problems still exist as smart device operating systems evolve, Nikon will eventually get SnapBridge working reliably.

  However, this is a still photography book, and I'm not going to jump down the information technology rabbit hole. Those who know IT don't need my explanations, and Nikon already provides 85 (Z8) to 109 (Z9) pages of detailed networking instruction in its own PDF manual.

- **No software how-tos.** I don't show you how to use Nikon NX Studio, or discuss working with Adobe Lightroom or Photoshop (other than a few step-by-step instructions for functions like HDR or focus stacking). I've never done this in my books, and software is updated, becomes obsolete, or is discontinued too often, anyway.

- **No filler figures.** I've eliminated figures with superfluous examples used to provide a more attractive layout. Frequently, I combine several figures into a single large illustration that covers everything. I'm not going to show you detailed images of submenus you can easily check out with your camera while reading this book. Illustrations may not show examples of every possible setting. Tightening up the illustrations has left me with significantly more space for explanations of the features and options available to you.

Nikon's own downloadable PDF manual is filled with information, but there's really very little about *why* you should use particular settings or features. Its organization makes it difficult to find what you need. Multiple cross-references send you searching back and forth between two or three sections of the book to find what you want to know. The basic manual is also hobbled by black-and-white line drawings and tiny monochrome pictures that aren't very good examples of what you can do.

I've tried to make *David Busch's Nikon Z9/Z8 Guide to Digital Still Photography* different from your other camera learn-up options. The roadmap sections in Chapter 1 use larger, color pictures to show you where all the buttons and dials are, and the explanations of what they do are longer and more comprehensive. I've tried to avoid overly general advice, including the two-page checklists on how to take a "sports picture" or a "portrait picture" or a "travel picture." You won't find half the content of this book taken up by generic chapters that tell you how to shoot landscapes, portraits, or product photographs. Instead, you'll find tips and techniques for using all the features of your Nikon camera to take *any kind of picture* you want. If you want to know where you should stand to take a picture of a quarterback dropping back to unleash a pass, there are plenty of books that will tell you that. This one concentrates on teaching you how to select the best autofocus mode, shutter speed, f/stop, or flash capability to take, say, a great sports picture under any conditions.

This book is not a lame rewriting of the manual that came with the camera. Some folks spend five minutes with a book like this one, spot some information that also appears in the original manual, and decide "Rehash!" without really understanding the differences. Yes, you'll find information here that is also in the owner's manual, such as the parameters you can enter when changing your camera's operation in the various menus. Basic descriptions—before I dig in and start providing in-depth tips and information—may also be vaguely similar. There are only so many ways you can say, for example, "Hold the shutter release down halfway to lock in exposure." But not *everything* in the manual is included in this book. If you need advice on when and how to use the most important functions, you'll find the information here.

Family Resemblance

If you've owned previous models in the Nikon digital camera line, and copies of my books for those cameras, you're bound to notice a certain family resemblance. Nikon has been very crafty in introducing upgraded cameras that share the best features of the models they replace, while adding new capabilities and options. You benefit in two ways. If you used a previous Nikon camera prior to switching to this latest camera model, you'll find that the parts that haven't changed have a certain familiarity for you, making it easy to make the transition to the newest model. There are lots of features and menu choices of the camera that are exactly the same as those in the most recent models. This family resemblance will help level the learning curve for you.

Similarly, when writing books for each new model, I try to retain the easy-to-understand explanations that worked for previous books dedicated to earlier camera models, and concentrate on expanded descriptions of things readers have told me they want to know more about, a solid helping of fresh sample photos, and lots of details about the latest and greatest new features. Rest assured, this book was written expressly for you, and tailored especially for the camera.

Who Am I?

After spending many years as the world's most successful unknown author, I've become slightly less obscure in the past decade or so, thanks to a horde of camera guidebooks and other photographically oriented tomes. You may have seen my photography articles in the late, lamented *Popular Photography* magazine. I've also written about 2,000 articles for magazines like *Rangefinder*, *Professional Photographer*, and dozens of other photographic publications. You may have attended one of the workshops or presentations I've given at groups ranging from camera clubs to meetings of the Professional Photographers of America organization to which I belong.

But, first, and foremost, I'm a photojournalist who made my living in the field until I began devoting most of my time to writing books. Although I love writing, I'm happiest when I'm out taking pictures, which is why I spend four to six weeks in Florida each winter as a base of operations for photographing the wildlife, wild natural settings, and wild people in the Sunshine State. In recent years, I've spent a lot of time overseas, too, photographing people and monuments. You'll find photos of some of these visual treasures within the pages of this book.

Like all my digital photography books, this one was written by a Nikon devotee with an incurable photography bug who has used Nikon cameras professionally for longer than I care to admit. Over the years, I've worked as a sports photographer for an Ohio newspaper and for an upstate New York college. I've operated my own commercial studio and photo lab, cranking out product shots on demand and then printing a few hundred glossy 8 × 10s on a tight deadline for a press kit. I've served as a photo-posing instructor for a modeling agency. People have actually paid me to shoot their weddings and immortalize them with portraits. I even prepared press kits and articles on photography as a PR consultant for a large Rochester, NY company, which older readers may recall as an industry giant. My trials and travails with imaging and computer technology have made their way into print in book form an alarming number of times, including a few dozen on scanners and photography.

Like you, I love photography for its own merits, and I view technology as just another tool to help me get the images I see in my mind's eye. But, also like you, I had to master this technology before I could apply it to my work. This book is the result of what I've learned, and I hope it will help you master your Nikon camera, too.

In closing, I'd like to ask a special favor: let me know what you think of this book. If you have any recommendations about how I can make it better, contact me directly at questions@dslrguides.com. Or, visit my website at www.nikonguides.com, click on the E-Mail Me tab, and send your comments, suggestions on topics that should be explained in more detail, or, especially, any typos. (The latter will be compiled on the Errata page you'll also find on my website.) I really value your ideas and appreciate it when you take the time to tell me what you think! Most of the organization and some of the content of the book you hold in your hands came from suggestions I received from readers like yourself. If you found this book especially useful, tell others about it. Visit http://www.amazon.com/dp/B0C5TB9PZD and leave a positive review. Your feedback is what spurs me to make each one of these books better than the last. Thanks!

Your Roadmap and Setup Guide

1

If you're a veteran Nikon camera owner, you may find many of the controls and menus of the Z9 or Z8 very similar to what you had with your previous camera, whether it was a Z-series model like the Z7 II or Z6 II, or a traditional dSLR model like the D850, D5, or D6. However, there are lots of powerful new capabilities in these new cameras, so even experienced Nikon photographers can be daunted by the sheer number of features available in the Z9 and Z8.

Initial Setup

Once you've unpacked and inspected your camera, the initial setup of your camera is fast and easy. Basically, you just need to set the clock, charge the battery, attach a lens, and insert a memory card or two. I'll address each of these steps separately, but if you already are confident you can manage these setup tasks without further instructions, feel free to skip this section entirely. While most buyers of a camera of this caliber tend to be experienced photographers, I realize that some readers are ambitious, if inexperienced, and have made a considerable jump into a very advanced camera system. You should, at the minimum, skim the contents of the next section, because I'm going to list a few options that you might not be aware of.

Mastering the Multi Selector and Command Dials

I'll be saving descriptions of most of the other controls used with the Nikon Z9/Z8 for the "Visual Roadmap" sections later in this chapter, which will provide descriptions and use of all the camera's buttons and dials and switches. However, you may need to perform a few tasks during this initial setup process, and most of them will require the MENU button and the multi selector or sub-selector buttons. Figure 1.1 shows the location of the key controls on the Nikon Z9. The Z8's layout is exactly the same. I'll explain the other controls shown later in this chapter.

- **Main and sub-command dials.** The main command dial and sub-command dial are located on the rear and front of the camera, respectively, and located at the top of the figure and within the inset at bottom. The main command dial is used to change settings such as shutter speed, while the sub-command dial adjusts an alternate or secondary setting. For example, in Manual exposure mode, you'd use the sub-command dial to change the aperture, while the main command dial is used to change the shutter speed. (In both cases, the dial is "active" for these adjustments only when the camera's exposure meter is on, until the "Standby Timer" runs out.) The meter will automatically go to sleep after an interval (you'll learn how to specify the length of time in Chapter 7), and you must wake the camera (just tap the shutter-release button) to switch the meter back on and activate the main and sub-command dials.

- **MENU button.** It requires almost no explanation; when you want to access a menu, press it. To exit most menus or to confirm and exit in some cases, press it again.
- **Multi selector pad/directional controls.** This pad may remind you of the similar control found on many point-and-shoot cameras, and other digital cameras. It consists of a thumb-pad-sized button with notches at the up, down, left, right, and diagonal positions.

  The multi selector is used extensively for navigation (for example, to navigate among menus, to advance or reverse display of a series of images during picture review, or to change the kind of photo information displayed on the screen). It can also be used interchangeably with the sub-selector "joystick" (described later) to choose one of the user-selectable focus areas on the viewfinder and LCD monitor displays.

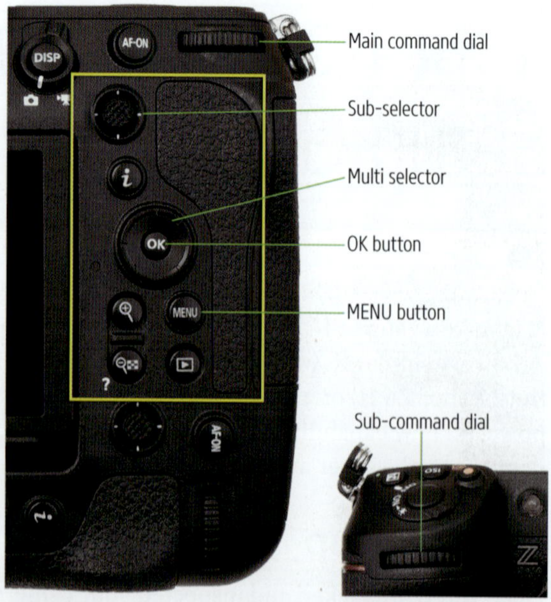

Figure 1.1 Location of the multi selector and command dials.

- **OK (multi selector center) button.** The center button (as well as the right directional button) can be used to select a highlighted item from a menu. (I find pressing the right directional button faster and easier.) The center button also can function as an OK/Enter key.
- **Sub-selector.** The sub-selector can be moved like a joystick or pressed as if it were a button. As a navigational control, the sub-selector joystick's default function is a convenient control for positioning the focus point *only*, as I'll explain in Chapter 3. If you also want to use the joystick for menu navigation scrolling or playback functions, you can add those behaviors using Custom Setting f2: Custom Controls, as described in Chapter 7.

  The sub-selector center button, by default, can be pressed to lock focus or exposure (as an AE/AF lock button), but it can also be redefined to other behaviors with Custom Setting f2.

Touch Screen

The LCD monitor supports a number of touch operations. For example, you can use it to navigate menus or make many settings. However, the touch screen can be especially useful during image playback and when shooting to adjust settings, specify a focus point, or to trip the shutter. You can specify which touch features are available using the Setup menu's Touch Controls entry, as described in Chapter 9. The main gestures you can use with the screen are shown in Figure 1.2.

- **Flick left/right (Playback mode).** Quickly move a single finger a short distance from side to side across the monitor. During playback, a flick to the right or left advances to the next or previous full image. Note that if a second finger or other object is also touching the monitor, it may not respond, or may, instead, cause the image to zoom.

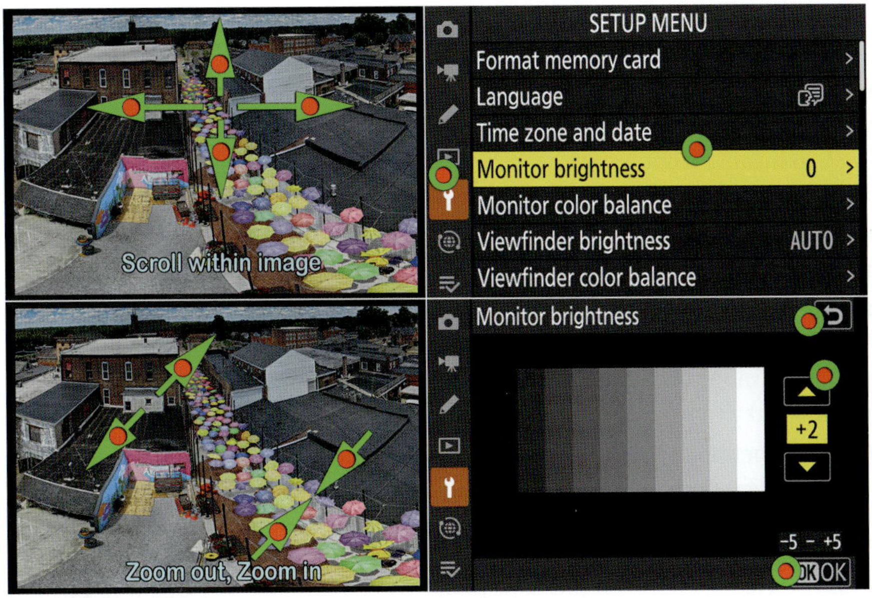

Figure 1.2 Flick or slide your finger across the touch screen to scroll from side to side, up or down (top left). Pinch or spread two fingers to zoom in and out (bottom left). Tap menu tabs, entries, and settings to make adjustments (top and bottom, right).

- **Flick left/right/up/down (magnified playback).** If you've zoomed in during playback, you can scroll around within the image by moving a single finger across the screen in left, right, up, or down directions. (See Figure 1.2, top left.)
- **Finger slide (magnified playback).** Instead of flicking, you can press down on the screen and slowly slide your finger in any direction to move to any area within a magnified image.
- **Double-tap zoom.** During playback, double tap a full image to quickly zoom in the maximum amount. Double tap again to return to full-image view. If you're looking at 4, 9, or 72 thumbnails instead, a double tap jumps immediately to full-image view.
- **Flick up (Playback).** During picture review of a full image, an upward flick can perform any one of five different tasks (or None) using Custom Setting f12 (on the Z8) or Custom Setting f13 (on the Z9): Full-frame Playback Flicks, as described in Chapter 7. They include:

NOTE The numbering of some Custom Settings entries differ between the Z9 and Z8. I'll note the differences in each case.

  - **Rating.** One specific rating, from zero to five stars (or Candidate for Deletion), will be given to the currently displayed image.
  - **Select for Upload to Computer.** The current image will be assigned for transfer using all methods, including FTP.
  - **Select for Upload (FTP).** The current image will be assigned for transfer using FTP.
  - **Protect.** The flicked image will be marked as Protected. A second flick will Unprotect it.
  - **Voice Memo.** The voice memo recorded for the displayed image using the Record Voice Memo option of the Playback version of the *i* menu will be played back.
  - **None.** Upward flicks are ignored.

- **Flick down (Playback).** Custom Setting f12 (Z8)/f13 (Z9) can be used to assign the same tasks available for Flick Up.
- **Flick Advance Direction.** Use this Custom Setting f12 (Z8)/f13 (Z9) option to change from the default left/right gesture to advance to the next image during playback to the reverse (right to left). **Note:** The *labels* in the menu entry both read Left-Right; it is only the *arrows* separating the two words that flip direction.
- **Spread/pinch.** Spread apart two fingers to zoom into an image during playback or pinch them together to zoom out. (See Figure 1.2, bottom left.)
- **Tap.** Touch the screen with a single finger to make a menu adjustment. (See Figure 1.2, top and bottom right.) For example, you can tap an up/down or left/right triangle to increment or decrement a setting, such as monitor brightness. Menu options with only On/Off choices can be toggled by tapping the entry (it's not necessary to hit the on/off icon).

  When Touch Shutter/Touch AF is activated, tapping the screen locates the focus point at the tapped location and takes a picture when you remove your finger from the screen. When Touch Shutter is deactivated, tapping the screen simply relocates the focus point. (You'll find a Touch Shutter icon at the left side of the LCD monitor screen that allows you to cycle among Touch Shutter, Touch Shutter/Touch AF, Position Focus Point, and Off.)

Here's a summary of the things you can do with the touch screen using the gestures described above:

In Playback mode:

- **Navigate among images one by one.** You can flick the left or right screen to advance to the previous or next image during full-frame (non-zoomed) playback.
- **Advance quickly.** In full-frame playback, touch the bottom of the display to produce a frame advance bar, which you can drag to scroll quickly forward and back among your images.
- **Zoom in or out.** Double tap on the touch screen to zoom in or out of an image under review. Use pinch and stretch to zoom in and out.
- **Relocate zoomed area.** You can slide a finger around the monitor to reposition the zoomed area.
- **View thumbnails and movies.** You can navigate among index thumbnails and movies with taps.

In Photo mode (when using the LCD monitor):

- **Select a focus point.** In both Photo and Movie modes, you can tap a location on the touch screen to specify a focus point.
- **Take pictures.** In Photo mode, if the monitor is active, you can tap the touch screen and lift your finger to take a picture without pressing the shutter-release button. A quick tap can set the focus point and capture an image with one gesture. (However, you can't begin video capture with a tap.) The touch focus/shutter functions can be enabled/disabled using the Touch Controls entry in the Setup menu.
- **Adjust settings.** Some settings, such as shutter speed, aperture, ISO sensitivity, and *i* menu adjustments can be activated by tapping their icons or sliders. When adjustments are available, a white rectangle is drawn around the indicator that can be accessed by touch. You will see up/down and left/right triangles used to adjust increments, or other icons for various functions. After you make your change, you can tap OK or a Return arrow to confirm and return to the previous screen.

- **Navigate menus.** Personally, I often find the touch screen a little clumsy for navigating menus. The menu bars and icons are a bit too small on the 3.2-inch screen to be tapped with precision by those with large fingers. You still must press the MENU button to produce the menus, tap the main menu tab at the left of the screen, tap the specific item, and then choose among its options. Most of the time the multi selector directional buttons are a lot faster.
- **Enter text.** When working with a text-entry screen (for example, to enter copyright information in the Setup menu), you can tap the on-screen keyboard to enter your text. That's *much* faster than the alternative—using the directional buttons to tediously move the highlighting from one character to another.

As noted, you can disable touch functions entirely or enable them for playback functions only (and thus disabling touch menu navigation) in the Setup menu, as described in Chapter 9. In addition, you can turn the Touch Shutter/AF feature off by tapping an icon that appears at the left side of the screen during viewfinder and movie shooting.

Because the screen uses static electricity, it may not respond when touched with gloved hands, fingernails, or when covered with a protective film. The Touch Controls screen does have a Glove mode that improves response for winter shooters who don't want to lose fingers to frostbite. I have a GGS glass screen over my Z9 and Z8's monitors and it works just fine; your experience may vary, depending on the covering you use. Don't use a stylus, pen, or sharp object instead of a finger; if your fingers are too large, stick to the physical controls such as the buttons or dials.

A TOUCH OF SCREEN

Throughout this book, when telling you how to use a touch-compatible feature, I'm going to stick to referring to the physical buttons and dials, for the benefit of those who prefer to use the traditional controls and to avoid having to repeat that you can use either the touch screen or the physical controls. From time to time I'll remind you that a particular function can also be accessed using the touch screen.

Menu Anatomy

If you used any Nikon digital SLR or mirrorless camera before you purchased your Z9 or Z8, you're probably already familiar with the basic menu system. The menus consist of a series of screens with entries, as shown in the illustration of the first page of the Photo Shooting menu in Figure 1.3. Navigating among the various menus is easy and follows a consistent set of rules:

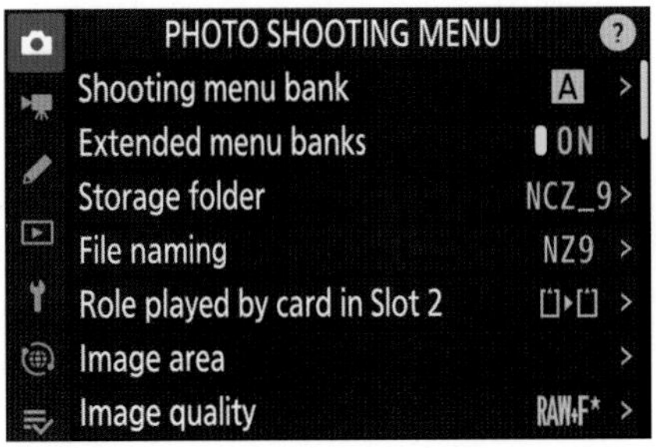

Figure 1.3 The multi selector's navigational buttons are used to move among the various menu entries shown here.

- **View menu.** Press the MENU button on the lower-right corner of the back panel to display the main menu screens.

- **Navigate main menu headings.** Use the multi selector's left/right/up/down directional buttons (or the sub-selector) to navigate among the menu entries to highlight your choice. Moving the highlighting to the left column lets you scroll up and down among the top-level menus. From the top in Figure 1.3, they are Photo Shooting, Video Recording, Custom Settings, Playback, Setup, Network, and My Menu, with Help access (when available) represented by a question mark at the upper right of the screen. (You can access Help by pressing the Zoom Out/Index button.)
- **Choose a top-level menu.** A highlighted top-level menu's icon will change from black-and-white to yellow highlighting. Use the multi selector's right directional button to move into the column containing that menu's choices. The selected top-level menu's icon background will change from yellow to a color associated with that menu (shades of green for Photo Shooting and Video Recording, red for Custom Settings, blue for Playback, orange-brown for Setup, purple for Network, and taupe for My Menu). The currently selected menu option will be highlighted in yellow, as shown in the figure. **Note:** You can also press the OK button of the multi selector (or press the sub-selector) to move into a top-level menu's entries, but it's usually simpler to just press the right directional button, because you'll be using the multi selector's directional buttons to navigate the menus anyway.
- **Select a menu entry.** Use the up/down buttons to scroll among the entries. A scroll bar appears at the far right of the screen, with a position slider showing the relative position of the currently highlighted entry.
- **Choose options.** To work with a highlighted menu entry, press the OK button, the sub-selector button, or, more conveniently, just press the right directional button on the multi selector. Any additional screens of choices will appear. You can move among them using the same controls.
- **Toggle controls.** Nikon has streamlined many entries that have only On or Off options, providing a quick-access toggle, as shown with the Extended Menu Banks command in Figure 1.3. To switch states, you can tap the entry on the touch screen, or highlight the entry and press either the OK or right directional button.
- **Confirm your choice.** You can activate your setting by pressing the OK button or, sometimes, by pressing the left or right directional buttons on the multi selector. Some functions require scrolling to a Done menu choice or include an instruction to set a choice using some other button. If you don't follow the required procedure to exit, you may end up not actually confirming the adjustment you intended to make. For example, when specifying an Auto Bracketing set, after you've chosen Number of Shots and Increment, you *must* press OK to activate the set. Exiting by pressing the left directional button (which works with some menu entries), will result in your changes being ignored.
- **Exit menus.** As noted, pressing the multi selector left button usually backs you out of the current screen and pressing the MENU button again usually does the same thing. You can exit the menu system at any time by tapping the shutter-release button.
- **Returning to an entry.** The camera "remembers" the top-level menu and specific menu entry you were using the last time the menu system was accessed, so pressing the MENU button brings you back to where you left off. So, if you were working with an entry in the Custom Settings

menu's Metering/Exposure section, then decided to take a photo, the next time you press the MENU button the Custom Settings menu and the Metering/Exposure entry you last used will be highlighted. Even better, if you scroll up or down to a different main menu heading, you'll find the entry you last used with that menu highlighted as well.

- **Accessing a frequently used entry.** If you use the same menu items over and over, you can create a My Menu listing of those entries. Or, if you'd rather have a rotating listing of the last 20 menu items you accessed, you can convert My Menu to a Recent Settings menu instead. I'll show you exactly how to do that in Chapter 11.

MENU DISPLAYS

The figures in this book illustrating menu options are for easy reference only, and may not correspond exactly to what you see on your camera's display. The Nikon Z9 and Z8 menus scroll continuously with listings at the bottom of the screen partially cut off, rather than in neat pages. For clarity, I have trimmed the menu screens so that each figure shows a complete set of menu options. In addition, none of the entries are grayed out in any of the figures; in real life, some will conflict with others and cannot be displayed as shown.

Setting the Clock

The camera's clock settings are stored in internal memory powered by a rechargeable battery that's not accessible to the user. It is recharged whenever a removable battery is installed in the battery compartment, and two days of normal use will recharge the internal battery enough to power the clock for about a month. The camera is normally sold without its main battery installed, so you'll probably see a clock icon the first time you power it up. In addition, if you store your camera for a long period without a charged main battery, the "clock" battery may go dead and "forget" your time/date/zone settings. It will recharge when a fresh battery is inserted, and you'll need to set the clock again.

So, when you receive your camera, it's likely that its internal clock hasn't been set to your local time, so you may need to do that first. You'll find complete instructions for setting the four options for the date/time (time zone, actual date and time, the date format, and whether you want the camera to conform to Daylight Savings Time) in Chapter 9. However, most Z9/Z8 users can perform this step without instruction. Just press the MENU button, use the multi selector (that thumb-friendly directional pad I described earlier, located to the immediate right of the back-panel LCD monitor) to scroll down to the Setup menu, press the multi selector button to the right, and scroll down to Time Zone and Date, and press right again. The options will appear on the screen that appears next. Keep in mind that you'll need to reset your camera's internal clock from time to time, as it is not 100 percent accurate. Fortunately, the Z9 has a built-in GPS receiver (but the Z8 does not), and you can ask the Z9 to Set Clock From Satellite using the option in the Location Data (Built-in) entry of the Setup menu.

Battery Included

The Nikon Z9 and Z8 are sophisticated hunks of machinery and electronics, but they need a charged battery to function, so rejuvenating the EN-EL18d lithium-ion battery pack furnished with the Z9, or the EN-EL15c battery supplied with the Z8, is a first step. You have several charging choices:

- **Charge in the camera.** Some batteries can be recharged while still in the Z9 or Z8 camera (or within the Z8's MB-N12 battery grip). (See Figure 1.4, upper left.) The cable supplying the power should be plugged into the USB connector on the left side of the Z9 or the USB Power Delivery connector of the Z8. I'll show you the exact location of both shortly in Figure 1.7.
- **Use the supplied charger.** The Z8 includes the MH-25a charger (see Figure 1.4, top center), while the Z9 comes with the MH-33 charger and EH-7P charging adapter. (Figure 1.4, upper right.)

In addition to the latest incarnations of their respective batteries, earlier versions of the EN-EL18 series and EN-EL15 series can be used and charged, with some differences:

For the Z9:

- **EN-EL18d.** This robust 3300mAh battery can be charged *in the camera*, using the EH-7P charging AC adapter supplied with the Z9, or a third-party USB Power Delivery (PD) charger (if USB Power Delivery is enabled in the Setup menu, as described in Chapter 9). It can also be charged *externally* using the EH-7P adapter to power the included MH-33 battery charger.
- **EN-EL18c.** This 2500mAh battery can be charged exactly like the EN-EL18d, as described above. In addition, it can be charged using the older MH-26 and MH-26a chargers.
- **EN-EL18b.** This 2500mAh battery cannot be charged in the camera, but can be charged with the MH-33 charger, or the older MH-26/26a chargers.
- **EN-EL18a/EN-EL18.** These are 2500/2000mAh batteries (respectively), and can only be charged in the MH-26 or MH-26a chargers.

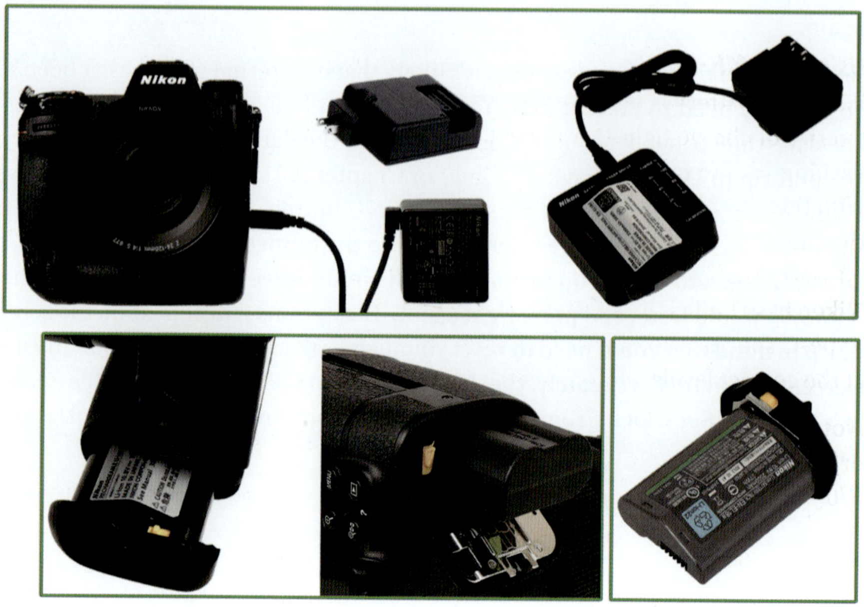

Figure 1.4 Charging options (top); inserting the battery (lower left); using the BL-7 battery chamber cover (lower right).

For the Z8:

- **EN-EL15c/EN-EL15b.** These 2280/1900mAh batteries (respectively) can be charged using the supplied MH-25a charger, or inside the camera with an optional EH-7P/EH-8P adapter kit or a compatible USB Power Delivery charger, if enabled in the Setup menu.
- **EN-EL15a/EN-EL15 (Li-ion20).** These 1900mAh batteries must be charged using the MH-25 or MH-25a charger.
- **EN-EL15 (Li-ion01).** These original batteries were involved in a recall from Nikon, and most of the defective units, subject to overheating, have been replaced. If you have one, you'll need to check the service advisory from Nikon in your country to see if you have an affected unit.

All rechargeable batteries undergo some degree of self-discharge just sitting idle in the camera or in the original packaging. Lithium-ion power packs of this type typically lose a few percent of their charge every few days, even when the camera isn't turned on. Li-ion cells lose their power through a chemical reaction that continues when the camera is switched off. So, it's very likely that the battery purchased with your camera is at least partially pooped out, so you'll want to revive it before going out for some serious shooting.

The batteries slide out of the camera easily for external recharging, and can only be inserted in the correct orientation when you reinstall them. (See Figure 1.4, lower right.)

TIP I own five EN-EL18-series batteries in all, and purchased a BL-7 battery chamber cover for each of them. (See Figure 1.4, lower right.) That means I can twist the tab on the cover a quarter-turn, slide the battery out, and slip in a replacement battery and lock it in with a reverse quarter-turn. Otherwise, I'd have to remove the BL-7 from the old battery and attach it to the new one, which wastes more time than you'd think. I also use the same batteries with my older Nikon D4s, and can set aside one or two for that camera by mounting the appropriate BL-6 covers instead. I have to admit I've never used more than two or three on a typical assignment, but it's nice to have spares, all properly equipped with chamber covers.

Using the MH-33 Charger (Z9)

When the battery is inserted (terminals first) into the MH-33 charger and its EH-7P power source, a series of charge lights illuminate to show the progress of the rejuvenation. When the lamps stop flashing, charging is finished, in about 4 hours for a fully discharged EN-EL18d battery, or 3 hours with the EN-EL18b or c versions. As mentioned earlier, you can also charge the battery while it's in the camera by plugging the EH-7P's USB-C plug into the USB port on the Z9. I have a third-party 60-watt USB-C charger that I have successfully used to power the MH-33 and power/charge the Z9. Nikon hasn't officially approved most such chargers, but the power negotiation protocols of the USB Type-C specification indicate that compatible devices should be able to reliably supply/draw juice at the correct levels.

Note: Nikon says that if the charge lamps flash rapidly, either the battery was inserted incorrectly or the ambient temperature is not within the recommended temperature range (32–104 degrees F/0–40 degrees C).

The MH-33 charger can perform recalibration of the batteries, a process that involves completely discharging the battery and then recharging it while bringing the battery's internal usage monitor circuitry back into sync with the battery's actual charge capabilities. Just press the single button on the charger to begin. Calibration is recommended every 30 cycles to eliminate cumulative errors, and you'll be prompted when it's necessary. Because calibration takes so long, I recommend you do it during downtime, or overnight. If your battery is already nearly depleted when the process begins, it will proceed more quickly.

Using the MH-25a Charger (Z8)

When the battery is inserted into the MH-25a charger properly (it's impossible to insert it incorrectly), a charge light begins flashing, and remains flashing until the status lamp glows steadily indicating that charging is finished, in about 2.5 hours. You can use the supplied connector cable or attach a handy included plug adapter that allows connecting the charger directly to a wall outlet (both shown at top left in Figure 1.4). When the battery is charged, flip the lever on the bottom of the camera and slide the battery in. As noted earlier, you can also charge the battery in the camera using the EH-7P AC adapter (see Figure 1.4, top right). You can check the Setup menu's Battery Info entry to make sure the battery is fully charged. If not, try putting it in the charger again. One of three things may be the culprit: 1.) the actual charging cycle sometimes takes longer than you (or the charger) expected; 2.) the battery is new and needs to be "seasoned" for a few charging cycles, after which it will accept a full charge and deliver more shots; 3.) you've got a defective battery. The last is fairly rare, but before you start counting on getting a particular number of exposures from a battery, it's best to make sure it's fully charged, seasoned, and ready to deliver.

Because Li-ion batteries don't have a memory, you can top them up at any time. However, their capacity when fully charged will eventually change over time. Once in a while, it's a good idea to use a battery until it is fully discharged, and then recharge it beyond the normal charging time. (Don't remove the battery from the charger until the light has gone out *and* the battery has fully cooled down.) It's also best to not store a battery for long periods either fully discharged or completely charged in order to maintain its longevity. If you own several (as you should), you'll probably want to rotate them to even the electronic wear and tear.

Final Steps

Your Nikon camera is almost ready to fire up and shoot. You'll need to select and mount a lens, adjust the viewfinder for your vision, and insert a formatted memory card or two. Each of these steps is easy, and if you've used any Nikon before, you already know exactly what to do. In most of my books I provide step-by-step instructions, which, in the case of a camera like the Z9 or Z8 is almost certainly overkill. The following is a checklist of the procedures I think you'll be able to handle on your own:

- **Diopter correction.** Pull out the button on the right side of the viewfinder housing. Adjustment is available from –4 to +3 correction. If more than one person uses your camera, and each requires a different diopter setting on the camera itself, you can save a little time by noting the number of clicks and direction (clockwise to increase the diopter power; counterclockwise to decrease the diopter value) required to change from one user to the other.

- **Inserting a memory card.** You've probably set up your camera so you can't take photos without a memory card inserted, using the Slot Empty Release Lock entry in the Setup menu. There's a new HOT CARD high-temperature warning label, which those shooting 8K video internally will come to appreciate.
- **Formatting a card.** Always let the Z9 format your memory card using the Setup menu entry to create the correct DCF (Design rule for Camera File system) structure, including the DCIM (Digital Camera Images) folder that can include subfolders for each camera type you use. Format with your computer only as a last resort to revive a card that has failed. You will find more information about formatting a memory card in Chapter 9.

SWITCHING FROM VIEWFINDER TO MONITOR

The camera has a sensor located just above the viewfinder window. When it detects you've brought the camera up to your eye, it switches its display from the LCD monitor to the viewfinder, and then back again when you remove the camera from your eye. You can change this default behavior, as I'll explain in Chapter 9, or manually switch between them using the Monitor Mode button located on the left side of the viewfinder "pentaprism" hump.

Choosing a Release Mode

The release mode determines when and how often a picture is taken, either in single shots, continuously, or after a self-timer has elapsed. If you're a late-comer moving to the interchangeable-lens photography world from a point-and-shoot model, you might have used one that labels these options as drive modes, a term that dates back to the film era when cameras could be set for single shot or "motor drive" (continuous) shooting modes. There are seven release modes, which I'll describe shortly. The Z9 and Z8 access the array of modes in slightly different ways:

With the Z9: Press the release mode dial lock release button on the left shoulder of the Z9, and rotate the release mode dial to select Single Frame, Continuous Low, Continuous High, Self-Timer, or Quick Release Mode Selection. In that farthest right position, C15 (Z9 only), C30, C60, and C120 can be selected by rotating the rear command dial while the Release Mode button is held down.

With the Z8: Hold the Release Mode button down and rotate the rear command dial to select any of the release modes.

- **Single Frame.** In Single Frame mode, one picture is taken each time you press the shutter-release button down all the way. If you press the shutter and nothing happens (which is very frustrating!), you may be using a focus mode that requires sharp focus to be achieved before a picture can be taken. This is called focus-priority and is discussed in more detail under "Choosing a Focus Mode," later in this chapter.
- **Continuous Low-Speed.** This "low-speed" shooting mode (Continuous L) can be set to produce bursts of 1 to 10 frames per second. You can specify the frame rate used:
    - **Z9 Only.** When the Z9's release mode dial is in the Continuous L position, hold down the release mode button and rotate either front or rear command dial to set your frame rate from 1 to 10 frames per second.

- **Z8 Only.** Just hold down the release mode button and rotate the main command dial to highlight Continuous L, then rotate the sub-command dial to choose from 1 to 10 frames per second.
- **Z9 or Z8.** You can also set a default frame rate for Continuous L in Custom Setting d1, as described in Chapter 7.

I use Continuous L when slicing a scene into tiny fragments of time isn't necessary or desirable (say, I'm bracketing in multi-shot bursts, or don't want a zillion versions of a scene that really isn't changing that fast). In Continuous Low-Speed and Continuous High-Speed mode, the viewfinder and LCD monitor update in real time while shooting is underway at shutter speeds of 1/250th second or faster, so you are almost always looking at the actual image you are capturing.

My recommendation: I find Continuous Low-Speed, set to 2 fps, to be particularly useful for street photography and photojournalism applications. Because the speed is so slow, you can use it like Single Frame most of the time and capture a single image by pressing the shutter-release button once and then lifting your finger. But if you find a subject that merits a more rapid-fire approach, you can keep the shutter-release button pressed down, and fire off several shots sequentially. That's faster than switching from single to continuous mode, and you can avoid the intrusive, distracting "machine-gun" approach.

- **Continuous High-Speed.** This mode fires off shots at *up to* 10, 12, 15, or 20 fps. You can select the frame rate used:
  - **Z9 Only.** When the Z9's release mode dial is in the Continuous H position, hold down the release mode button and rotate either front or rear command dial to set your frame rate from 10, 12, 15, or 20 frames per second.
  - **Z8 Only.** Just hold down the release mode button and rotate the main command dial to highlight Continuous H, then rotate the sub-command dial to choose from 10, 12, 15, or 20 frames per second.
  - **Z9 or Z8.** You can also set a default frame rate for Continuous H in Custom Setting d1, as described in Chapter 7.

  Maximum frame rates are achieved in AF-C focus mode, in Manual exposure mode, and shutter speeds of 1/250th second or faster. Speeds may slow in silent mode, when using flash or Photo Flicker Reduction, at slower shutter speeds, and with very small f/stops (typically f/16 or smaller).
- **C15 (Z9 only), C30/C60/C120.** The camera captures images at 30, 60, or 120 frames per second in High-Speed Frame Capture mode. The Z8 can access any of these by holding down the release mode button and rotating the rear command dial. Z9 owners must rotate the release mode dial to the quick release mode selection position first. As you might expect, this ultra-high-speed mode has some limitations:
  - **Touch Shutter.** Using the Touch Shutter feature takes just one image, not a sequence.
  - **Time limit.** Frames are captured in bursts that last no longer than four seconds. Trust me, a 480-shot continuous burst is not something you should look forward to reviewing.
  - **All images are captured in JPEG or HEIF Normal format.** RAW capture is disabled.
  - **Limited Image Area and size.** See the sidebar that follows for the restrictions. A chief limitation of the fastest C120 mode is that image size is restricted to the 4128 × 2752, 11MP Small format.

- **Exposure compensation.** Exposure compensation is limited to –3 to +3 EV; lower/higher settings are ignored.
- **Maximum ISO Sensitivity is 25600.** Higher values will be ignored, and the Minimum Shutter Speed specified for Auto ISO Sensitivity Control is not applied.
- **High-Speed frame capture incompatibilities.** These fastest frame rates cannot be used with modes involving multiple images, such as bracketing, multiple exposures, HDR overlay, interval-timer photography, time-lapse video, or focus shift. In addition, flash photography, flexible program (in Programmed Auto exposure mode), HLG tone mode, and photo flicker reduction are not available.

- **Self-timer.** If you want to set a short delay before your picture is taken, you can use the self-timer. When setting the self-timer you can hold down the Frame Rate button and choose delays of 2s, 5s, 10s, or 20s. You can also choose these parameters in the Self-timer entry, Custom Setting c2 (as described in Chapter 7), as well as the number of shots taken after the delay and the interval between each of those shots.

  Once the self-timer has been selected as the release mode, press the shutter-release button to lock focus and start the timer. In AF-S autofocus mode, if the camera is unable to focus, the timer may not begin. The green self-timer lamp on the front of the camera will blink and the beeper will sound (unless you've silenced it in the menus) until the final two seconds, when the lamp remains on. If you've turned Beep on in the Camera Sounds entry of the Setup menu, an annoying chirp will let you know the timer is active and will increase in speed during the last two seconds.

C15/C30/C60/C120 RESTRICTIONS

- C15, C30: Image Size: Large, Image Area: FX or DX, Shutter Speeds: 1/32000th–1/60th second
- C60: Image Size: Large, Image Area: DX, Shutter Speeds: 1/32000th–1/60th second
- C120: Image Size: Small, Image Area: FX, Shutter Speeds: 1/32000th–1/125th second

  Note: If a DX lens is attached, the camera will use the C60 frame rate and DX Image Area instead.

TIP If you plan to join the scene when working with the self-timer, consider using manual focus so the camera won't refocus on your fleeing form and produce unintended results. (Nikon really needs to offer an option to autofocus at the *end* of the self-timer cycle.) An alternative is to use one of the optional wireless remotes, including the WR-R10/WR-T10, WR-11a, or WR-1, because focus is initiated when you press the button (after you've ensconced yourself safely in the frame). Nikon's SnapBridge app also allows you to control your camera remotely from a smart device app running on your iOS or Android phone.

SHOOTING MOVIES

If you want to get started shooting movies right away, it's easy. Just rotate the Photo/Movie selector switch (located on the back of the camera to the immediate right of the viewfinder window) to the Movie position and press the button with the red dot on the top-right panel, southwest of the shutter-release button. Press the button again to stop shooting. That's it!

Selecting an Exposure Mode

Available exposure modes include four manual and semi-automatic modes, including Programmed auto (or Program mode), Shutter-priority auto, Aperture-priority auto, and Manual exposure mode. These modes allow you to specify how the exposure settings are selected, for greater creative control. Just press the MODE button on the top-left shoulder of the camera and rotate the main command dial to select what Nikon likes to call "Shooting" mode:

- **P (Programmed auto).** This mode allows the camera to select the basic exposure settings, but you can still override those choices to fine-tune your image, while maintaining metered exposure, as I'll explain in Chapter 2.
- **S (Shutter-priority).** This mode is useful when you want to use a particular shutter speed to stop action or produce creative blur effects. Choose your preferred shutter speed by rotating the main command dial when the meter is active, and the camera will select the appropriate f/stop for you. Shutter speeds of up to 1/32000th second are available, although it's unlikely you'll ever need/use anything faster than 1/4000th second.
- **A (Aperture-priority).** Choose when you want to use a particular lens opening, especially to control sharpness or how much of your image is in focus. Specify the f/stop you want using the sub-command dial when the meter is "awake" (tap the shutter-release button to activate the meter, if necessary), and the camera will select the appropriate shutter speed for you.
- **M (Manual).** Select when you want full control over the shutter speed and lens opening, either for creative effects or because you are using a studio flash or other flash unit not compatible with the automatic metering when using an attached electronic flash. Use the main command dial and sub-command dial when the exposure meter is active to specify the shutter speed and f/stop (respectively).

Choosing a Metering Mode

The metering mode determines how exposure is calculated. You might want to select a particular metering mode for your first shots, although the default Matrix metering is probably the best choice as you get to know your camera. I'll explain when and how to use each of the four metering modes later.

There is no default button assigned to change metering modes because, practically speaking, you may not be changing from one metering mode to another very often. The Z9/Z8's Matrix metering will do an excellent job more than 90 percent of the time. There are some exceptions for certain kinds of subjects, as I'll explain in Chapter 3, and those who understand the finer points of exposure may find themselves using Spot metering more frequently than most. But, for the most part, when you do need to set a specific metering mode, it's relatively easy to do from the Meter entry on the Photo Shooting or Video Recording menus.

- **Matrix metering.** The standard metering mode; the camera attempts to intelligently classify your image and choose the best exposure based on readings from the sensor.
- **Center-weighted metering.** The camera meters the entire scene but gives the most emphasis to the central area of the frame, measuring about 12mm (by default; you can choose a smaller 8mm area or full-frame averaging instead, using Custom Setting b5, as I'll describe in Chapter 7).

- **Spot metering.** Exposure is calculated from a smaller 4mm central spot, about 1.5 percent of the image area, centered on the current focus point.
- **Highlight-weighted metering.** Despite its icon (a "spot" accompanied by an asterisk), this is not a spot metering variation. Highlight-weighted metering uses a matrix measuring system to emphasize the highlights of an image, retaining detail in the brightest areas.

Note: If you really need a dedicated Metering Mode button, you can define one. Select a button of your choice, such as Fn4 on the Z9 or Fn3 on the Z8 (both located on the upper-left corner of the back panel), then use Custom Setting f2 to select Metering Mode from the Press + Command Dials list of available behaviors. I'll tell you more about creating customized buttons in Chapter 7.

Choosing a Focus Mode

You can easily switch between automatic and manual focus by moving the A/M, AF/MF, or M-AF/MF switch on your lens (if present). You can select the autofocus mode (*when* the camera measures and locks in focus) and autofocus pattern (*which* of the available autofocus points are used to interpret correct focus). While you can use the *i* menu to specify focus mode, it's faster to work with the dedicated Focus Mode button on the front of the camera. To specify when focus is locked, follow these steps:

1. **Activate autofocus.** Make sure the camera is set for autofocus mode by sliding any A/M switch on the lens, if present, to the A position.
2. **Enter setting mode.** Hold down the Focus Mode button.
3. **Choose AF mode.** Rotate the main dial until AF-S or AF-C (or M if you want Manual focus) is shown in the viewfinder or back-panel color LCD monitor when the information display screen is visible. (Press the button labeled DISP, located above the right corner of the LCD monitor, to produce it.) If you haven't activated autofocus mode, as described in Step 1, you can select AF-S or AF-C, but the focus mode will not change until you set the switch on the lens to A. The available modes are as follows:
   - **(AF-C) Continuous-servo autofocus.** This mode, sometimes called *continuous autofocus*, sets focus when you partially depress the shutter button (or other autofocus activation button), but continues to monitor the frame and refocuses if you or your subject has moved. This is a useful mode for photographing sports and moving subjects. Focus- or release-priority can be specified for AF-C mode using Custom Setting a1.
   - **(AF-S) Single-servo autofocus.** This mode, sometimes called *single autofocus*, locks in a focus point when the shutter button is pressed down halfway (there are other autofocus activation button options, described in Chapter 3), and the focus confirmation light glows at bottom left in the viewfinder. The focus will remain locked until you release the button or take the picture. This mode is best when your subject is relatively motionless. As you'll learn in Chapter 7, you can use Custom Setting a2 to specify that a picture will not be taken unless sharp focus is achieved (*focus-priority*), or so that it will go ahead and snap a photo while still adjusting focus (*release-priority*).

Choosing the Autofocus Area Mode

The Z9 and Z8 use up to 493 different focus points to calculate correct focus. Nikon allows you to choose which points to use with its Autofocus-area mode options. One or more points are selected automatically by the camera or chosen by you. I'll show you exactly where these focus areas are located and tell you how to use them in Chapter 4. While you can use the *i* menu to specify AF-area mode, it's faster to work with the dedicated Focus Mode button on the front of the camera. To choose an AF-area mode, follow these steps:

1. **Enter setting mode.** Hold down the Focus Mode button.
2. **Rotate the sub-command dial.** Rotate the sub-command dial on the front of the camera to highlight one of the Focus Area modes described below.
3. **Choose AF-area mode.** Select one of these modes:
   - **Pinpoint-AF (AF-S only).** The camera uses a small point to calculate focus. Use this for precise focus on a specific area. This mode is not available when shooting movies.
   - **Single-point (AF-S or AF-C).** The camera focuses on a point you select, using the multi selector directional buttons or sub-selector joystick. This mode is good for non-moving subjects.
   - **Dynamic-area (Small/Medium/Large) (AF-C only).** You select the focus point, but if the subject moves from the selected area, it will use information from the surrounding points. It's often the best AF-area mode for moving subjects.
   - **Wide-area AF (Small).** Calculates focus from a larger area than Single-point AF and is best for stationary subjects that occupy more space in the frame.
   - **Wide-area AF (Large).** Calculates focus from an even larger zone and can achieve accurate focus on subjects that may be located in a wider area of the frame.
   - **Wide-area AF (C1/C2).** You can choose the height and width of the area using the up/down and left/right directional buttons, with 20 different combinations available in Still Photography mode, and 12 available for video. I'll show you these in Chapter 3.
   - **3D-tracking (AF-C only).** The camera follows a subject you specify by moving the focus point to the subject and pressing AF-ON or the shutter-release button halfway to start tracking.
   - **Subject-tracking AF (Video only).** The camera follows a subject you specify by moving the focus point to the subject and pressing AF-ON or the shutter-release button halfway to start tracking.
   - **Auto-area AF (AF-S or AF-C).** The camera chooses a focus point without input from you, rapidly detecting likely subject matter, especially humans. If a portrait subject is detected, faces will be indicated by a yellow border.

Adjusting White Balance and ISO

If you like, you can custom-tailor your white balance (color balance) and ISO sensitivity settings. To start out, it's best to set white balance (WB) to Auto$_0$, and ISO to ISO 200 for daylight photos, and to ISO 400 for pictures in dimmer light. (Don't be afraid of ISO 1600 or even higher, however; the camera does a *much* better job of producing low-noise photos at higher ISOs than earlier generations.)

You can set either now:

- **White balance.** Hold down the White Balance button, located on lower edge of the back of the Z9, just under the rear LCD, or positioned on the top-left shoulder of the Z8. Then rotate the main command dial to specify your choice. Additional options are available for some settings with the sub-command dial. I'll explain those in detail later in this chapter.
    - **Auto variations.** When WB A_0, A_1, or A_2 appear, with the WB button still held down, rotate the sub-command dial to select (or retain) A_0 (Keep White/Reduce Warm Colors), which is the default auto white balance setting. The other two partially or fully preserve the warm color cast produced by incandescent lighting, as I'll explain in Chapter 5.)
    - **Natural Light Auto**
    - **Direct Sunlight**
    - **Cloudy**
    - **Shade**
    - **Incandescent**
    - **Fluorescent (Cool-white, Day white, Daylight varieties)**
    - **Flash**
    - **K Choose color temperature**
    - **Preset manual**
- **ISO.** To set ISO, press the ISO button on the top-right shoulder just aft of the On/Off switch, and rotate the main command dial until the ISO value you want is displayed in the viewfinder, monitor, and monochrome control panel. Rotate the sub-command dial to turn Auto ISO on or off.

Reviewing the Images You've Taken

Your camera has a broad range of playback and image review options, including the ability to have all the images in a burst "stacked" so you can review only the first shot in a series rather than pore through them all one by one. I'll cover these in more detail in Chapter 8. For now, you'll want to learn just the basics. Here is all you really need to know at this time, as seen in Figure 1.5:

- **Press the Playback button to review images.** Press the Playback button (marked with a white right-pointing triangle) at the bottom-right corner of the back of the camera to display the most recent image on the LCD monitor. Press the Playback button again, or just tap the shutter-release button to exit playback view.
- **Previous/Next image.** Press the multi selector left or right to review additional images. Press right to advance to the next image or left to go back to a previous image. You can also use the main command dial.
- **Change amount/type of information.** Press the multi selector button up or down or the DISP button to change among overlays of basic image information or detailed shooting information.
- **Zoom In/Zoom Out.** Press the Zoom In button repeatedly to zoom in on the image displayed; the Zoom Out button reduces the image. A thumbnail representation of the whole image appears in the lower-right corner with a yellow rectangle showing the relative level of zoom. At intermediate zoom positions, the yellow rectangle can be moved around within the frame using the multi selector.

- **Press to delete current image.** Some mistakes should never see the light of day. Press the Trash button to erase the currently displayed image. A Delete? message will appear. Press Trash again to confirm, or the Playback button to cancel.
- **Protect an image.** Press the Fn3 (Z8) or Fn4 (Z9) button to protect the current image from accidental deletion. Images will still be removed when the memory card is formatted, however.
- **Access Playback *i* menu.** Summons a quick-access menu that lets you apply ratings to an image, choose pictures to upload to a smart device, sort through images by attributes, define those attributes, record and attach voice memos to an image, retouch pictures, or copy to a different card. I'll address all of these in detail in Chapter 8.

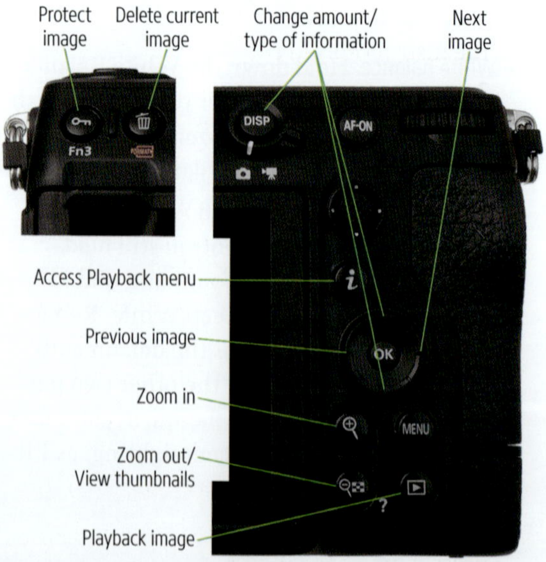

Figure 1.5 Review your images.

Playing Back Images

Reviewing images is a joy, whether you use the big 3.2-inch color LCD monitor or the viewfinder (which is especially handy for viewing images in bright light under which the monitor may tend to wash out).

Here are the basics involved in reviewing images on the camera's displays (or on a television/HDTV screen you have connected with a cable). You'll find more details about some of these functions later in this chapter, or, for more complex capabilities, in the chapters that I point you to. This section just lists the must-know information.

- **Start review.** To begin review, press the Playback button at the lower-right corner of the back of the camera. The most recently viewed image will appear on the display.
- **Playback folder.** If you have more than one folder on your memory card, you can change which folder is used for playback by starting playback with the Playback button, and then pressing the *i* button and selecting Choose Slot and Folder. Press the right directional button, select the slot (any slots containing an empty memory card will be grayed out), and then press the right directional button again to choose from a list of available folders. Press the right directional button again to activate that slot/folder.

  You can also select the active folder using the Playback Folder option (choose NCZ_9/_8, All, or Current) in the Playback menu. You can create and activate a *new* folder (or change the default name to something else) using the Storage Folder entry in the Photo Shooting menu. See Chapter 5 for more information on both options.

- **View thumbnail images.** To change the view from a single image to 4, 9, or 72 thumbnails, follow the instructions in the "Viewing Thumbnails" section that follows.
- **Zoom in and out.** To zoom in or out, press the Zoom In or Zoom Out buttons, following the instructions in the "Zooming the Playback Display" section, next. (It also shows you how to move the zoomed area around using the multi selector pad.)
- **Move back and forth.** To advance to the next image, press the right edge of the multi selector pad; to go back to a previous shot, press the left edge. When you reach the beginning/end of the photos in your folder, the display "wraps around" to the end/beginning of the available shots. **Note:** You can assign a special behavior to the sub-command dial such that rotating it skips ahead either 10 or 50 images, or advance by other parameters, such as rating. See the discussion of Custom Setting f3 (Customize Controls Playback > Sub-dial Frame Advance) in Chapter 7 for more information.
- **See different types of data.** To change the type of information about the displayed image that is shown, press the up and down portions of the multi selector pad.
- **Remove images.** To delete an image that's currently on display, press the Trash button once, then press it again to confirm the deletion. To select and delete a group of images, use the Delete option in the Playback menu to specify particular photos to remove, as described in more detail in Chapter 8.
- **Cancel playback.** To cancel image review, press the Playback button again, or simply tap the shutter-release button.

Zooming the Playback Display

The Playback display zooms in and out of preview images using the procedure that follows:

1. **Zoom in.** When an image is displayed (use the Playback button to start), press the Zoom In button to fill the screen with a slightly magnified version of the image. When viewing on the monitor, you can also press the multi selector center button, tap the touch screen twice, or touch two fingers to the LCD monitor and spread them apart to enlarge the image.
2. **Continue zooming.** A navigation window appears in the lower-right corner of the LCD monitor showing the entire image. Keep pressing to continue zooming in to the maximum of 32X enlargement (with a full-resolution large image in FX format). (Medium and Small images can be enlarged up to 24X and 16X, respectively.)
3. **Zoomed area indicated.** A yellow box in the navigation window shows the zoomed area within the full image. The entire navigation window vanishes from the screen after a few seconds, leaving you with a full-screen view of the zoomed portion of the image.
4. **Move zoomed area around.** Use the multi selector buttons to move the zoomed area around within the image. The navigation window will reappear for reference when zooming or scrolling around within the display. You can also slide one finger around the touch screen to move the zoomed area.

5. **Find faces.** To detect faces, rotate the sub-command dial while an image is zoomed. Up to 35 faces will be detected by the camera, indicated by white borders in the navigation window. Rotate the sub-command dial or tap the on-screen guide to move highlighting to the individual faces.
6. **Review same area on another image.** Use the main command dial or tap the left/right triangles at the bottom of the touch screen to move to the same zoomed area of the next/previous image. This allows you to compare a detail in a series of similar shots. I often use the capability to see if a spot in an image is a dust spot (it shows up in the same place in other images) or just an artifact found in a single image.
7. **Zoom out.** Use the Zoom Out button to zoom back out of the image.
8. **Exit.** To exit zoom in/zoom out display, keep pressing the Zoom Out button until the full screen/full image/information display appears again. Or, just tap the shutter-release button halfway or press the Playback button to exit playback entirely.

Viewing Thumbnails

The camera provides other options for reviewing images in addition to zooming in and out. You can switch between single image view and 4, 9, or 72 reduced-size thumbnail images on a single display.

Pages of thumbnail images offer a quick way to scroll through a large number of pictures quickly to find the one you want to examine in more detail. The camera lets you switch quickly with a scroll bar displayed at the right side of the screen to show you the relative position of the displayed thumbnails within the full collection of images in the active folder on your memory card. The Zoom In and Zoom Out/Thumbnail buttons are used, or you can use the pinch and spread gestures with two fingers on the touch screen to increase or decrease the number of thumbnail indexes shown.

Here's how to work with thumbnail images:

- **Add thumbnails.** To increase the number of thumbnails on the screen, press the Zoom Out button or pinch the touch screen. The camera will switch from single image to 4 thumbnails to 9 thumbnails to 72 thumbnails. (The display doesn't cycle back to single image again.)
- **Reduce number of thumbnails.** To decrease the number of thumbnails on the screen, press the Zoom In button or use the spread gesture on the touch screen to change from 72 thumbnails to 9 thumbnails to 4 thumbnails, to single-image display. Continuing once you've returned to single-image display starts the zoom process described in the previous section.
- **Change folder.** When viewing images, press the *i* button to produce the dialog box that includes an option to choose the folder of the memory card that contains the images you want to view.
- **Switch between thumbnails and full image.** When viewing thumbnails, you can quickly switch between thumbnail view and full-image display by pressing the OK button in the center of the multi selector, or by double-tapping the thumbnail image on the touch screen.
- **Retouch an image/thumbnail.** When an image or thumbnail is viewed, press the *i* button to access the options screen that includes a Retouch option for that image (described in Chapter 11).

- **Change highlighted thumbnail area.** Use the multi selector to move the yellow highlight box around among the thumbnails, or, preferably, use the monitor and a single finger on the touch screen to scroll back and forth or to select a particular thumbnail. Note that *touching* a thumbnail moves the highlighting to that thumbnail, while *tapping* the thumbnail produces a full-screen view of the image.
- **Protect and delete images.** When viewing thumbnails or a single-page image, press the *i* button and choose Protect to preserve the highlighted image against accidental deletion (a key icon is overlaid over the thumbnail image; return to the *i* menu to remove protection).
- **Exit image review.** Tap the shutter-release button or press the Playback button to exit image review. You don't have to worry about missing a shot because you were reviewing images; a half-press of the shutter-release button automatically brings back the camera's exposure meters, the autofocus system, and, unless you've redefined your controls or are using manual focus, cancels image review.

Your Visual Roadmap

If you've used any Nikon dSLR previously, even if this is your first mirrorless camera, you'll find your Z9 or Z8 comfortably familiar in shape and placement of the controls. The only things you really lost in migrating were the mirror and a modest amount of weight and bulk. Your camera has been right-sized to fit in the hand, with all the buttons, dials, and knobs needed for the most frequently adjusted functions arranged for easy access. Another 12 settings can be adjusted from the *i* menu, and you can customize which dozen options appear there to suit your own working habits. (I'll show you how to personalize the *i* menu in Chapter 7.) With so many control choices available, you'll find that the bulk of your shooting won't be slowed down by a visit to the vast thicket of text options called Menu-land.

If you want to operate your camera efficiently, you'll need to learn the location, function, and application of all these controls. What you really need is a street-level roadmap that shows where everything is, and how it's used. But what Nikon gives you in the user's manual is akin to a world globe with an overall view and many cross-references to the pages that will tell you what you really need to know.

You'll also find this "roadmap" section a good guide to the rest of the book, as well. I'll try to provide as much detail here about the use of the main controls as I can, but some topics (such as autofocus and exposure) are too complex to address in depth right away. So, I'll point you to the relevant chapters that discuss things like setup options, exposure, use of electronic flash, and working with lenses with the occasional cross-reference.

FRATERNAL TWINS

If you happen to own both the Z9 and Z8 you probably noticed that the bodies of the two cameras are virtually identical in many respects. For the illustrations in this book I used the Z9 for most shots, as the Z8 body configuration is basically a sub-set of the Z9's, lacking only the Z9's built-in grip and with a component or two (such as the Fn3 button and camera speaker) in slightly different locations. So don't fret if you do not see "your" camera pictured in a particular illustration. In addition to the different layout, there are some differences in some of the menu entries, as well; if the change is relevant, I'll give you a screenshot of both.

Front View

This is the side seen by your subjects as you snap away. For the photographer, though, the front is the surface your fingers curl around as you hold the camera, and there are really only a few buttons to press, all within easy reach of the fingers of your left and right hands. There are additional controls on the lens itself. You'll need to look at several different views to see everything. Figure 1.6 shows the front of the camera with the lens removed. The components are as follows:

- **AF-assist illuminator/Red-eye reduction lamp.** This green LED lights up when needed during focusing under dim lighting to provide some additional illumination that can be helpful when focusing on subjects within a few feet of the camera. It also blinks as a self-timer countdown indicator, and can provide a burst of light to contract your subject's pupils to reduce red-eye effect.
- **Sub-command dial.** This dial is used to change shooting settings. When settings are available in pairs (such as shutter speed/aperture), this dial will be used to make one type of setting, such as aperture, while the main command dial (on the back of the camera) will be used to make the other, such as shutter speed.
- **Electronic contacts.** These 11 contact points mate with matching points on the bayonet mount of the lens itself and allow two-way communication between the camera and lens for functions like aperture size and autofocus information.
- **Sensor shield/Image sensor.** Although the Z9/Z8 do not have a mechanical shutter, they are furnished with a much sturdier shield that can, at your option, be lowered automatically when the camera is powered down, using the Sensor Shield Behavior at Power Off entry of the Setup

Figure 1.6

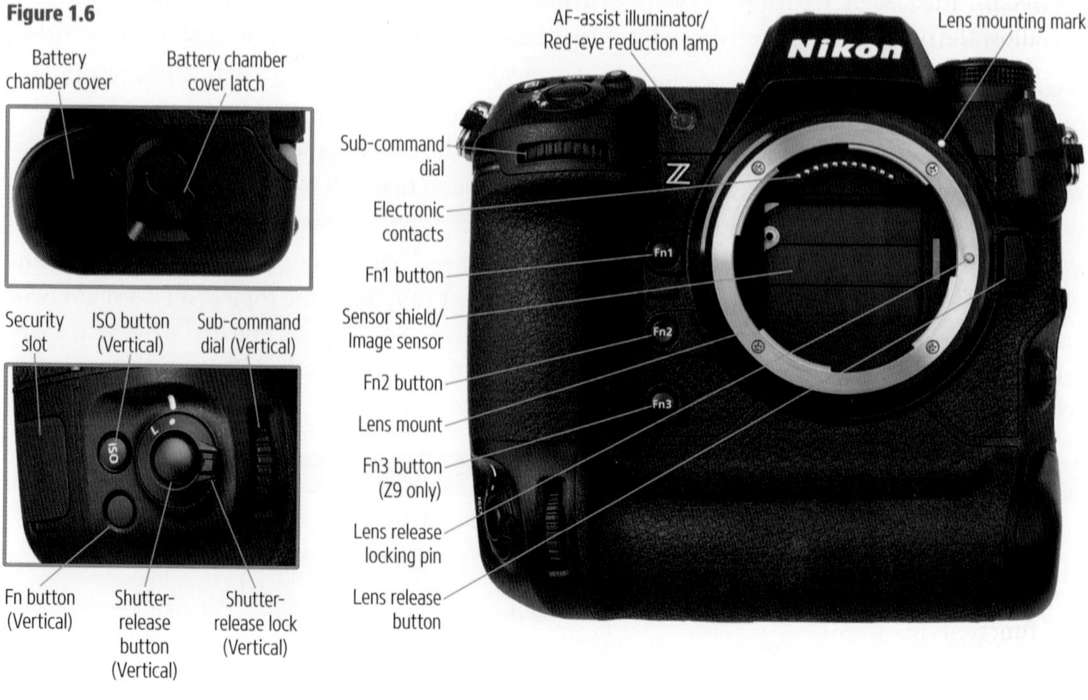

menu. You can also opt to have the camera's sensor fully exposed when switched off, or when cleaning the sensor manually. In any case, you should never touch or press against the sensor shield or the sensor, to avoid damaging the in-body image stabilization system or the protective surface of the sensor itself.

- **Function 1 (Fn1) button.** At the default setting, you can press this button and rotate either command dial to cycle among Shooting Menu Banks A–D. However, using Custom Setting f2, it can be programmed to perform any one of more than 40 different actions when pressed, plus more than 20 additional behaviors when held down while a command dial is rotated. I'll explain how to define a function using Custom Setting f2 in Chapter 7.
- **Function 2 (Fn2) button.** By default, this button cycles among the available image areas when held down while rotating a command dial. This button can be redefined using the same functions offered for the Fn1 button, as discussed in Chapter 7.
- **Function 3 (Fn3) button (Z9 only).** When pressed, this button hides icons and other information in the shooting display, giving you a blank screen that may be less distracting as you compose your image. You can redefine its behavior using Custom Setting f2.

  Note to Z8 owners: The Fn3 button is located on the *back* of the Z8, and has a different function—Picture Control. The Live View Information Display Off function described above is instead invoked by pressing the Video Record button when the Photo/Video selector on the back of the camera is in the Photo position.
- **Lens mount.** This precision bayonet mount mates with the matching mount on the back of each compatible lens. The all-new Z-mount is held on the camera using four screws that provide a secure attachment to the body, but not *too* secure. Their mounting holes are shallow enough to allow the bayonet mount to pop off if you drop the camera on the lens (which avoids even worse damage to the camera body itself). But don't worry, the mount is more than secure enough for everyday use, even with the heaviest lenses.
- **Lens mounting mark.** Align this mark on the camera body with the corresponding mark on the lens when attaching to the camera.
- **Lens release button.** Press this button to retract the locking pin on the lens mount so a lens can be rotated to remove it from the camera.
- **Lens release locking pin.** This pin slides inside a matching hole in the lens to keep it from rotating until the lens release button is pressed.
- **Power connector cover (Z8 only).** This little door, not shown in the figure, is present only on the Z8. It would be located on the inside edge of the handgrip. It flips open to allow plugging a cable from the AC/DC adapter into the battery compartment in the hand grip.
- **Sub-command dial (Vertical).** This dial is built into the Z9's vertical grip/battery compartment. The Z8 version is located in the same position when the optional MB-N12 vertical grip is attached.
- **Shutter-release button (Vertical).** In the inset at lower left, you can see some additional controls built-into the Z9 and available with the Z8's MB-N12 grip. This is the shutter-release button that functions identically to the one on top of the camera.

- **Shutter-release lock (Vertical).** This switch allows you to lock the vertical shutter release to prevent accidentally taking a picture. If you find your camera sometimes snaps off a shot unexpectedly while shooting in horizontal orientation, it's likely that your right hand is accidentally pressing the shutter-release button. Lock it until needed.
- **Fn button (Vertical).** This button does not correspond to Fn1, Fn2, Fn3, or Fn4 and can be assigned its own definition.
- **ISO button (Vertical).** You can conveniently change ISO settings with the camera rotated.
- **Security slot (Z9 only).** This is a standard Kensington slot (K-slot) that can be used to attach a security cable.
- **Battery chamber cover/latch (Z9 only).** The Z9's battery is inserted/removed from this end.

You'll find more controls on the other side of the camera, shown in Figure 1.7. In the illustration, you can see the mode dial on top, and the rubber covers on the side that protect the PC/X flash terminal (Z9 only), ten-pin remote terminal, USB, HDMI, headphone and microphone connectors, and Ethernet terminal (Z9 only). The main points of interest shown include:

- **PC/X flash terminal (Z9 only).** This is a "dumb" connection that hides beneath a flexible cover, along with the 10-pin remote terminal. You can see the two connectors uncovered within the inset at upper left in Figure 1.7. Connect a standard PC/X-contact cable or other accessory to this connector. If you are connecting a non-dedicated flash unit to your Z9 (say, a studio strobe or some other non-automatic non-Nikon flash), it would plug in here.
- **Ten-pin remote terminal.** This is used for a variety of accessories, including cable release cords, remote releases of other types (including radio/IR receivers such as the WR-R10/R11a), GPS receivers (including the Nikon GP-1a), and so forth.
- **Monitor button.** Press this button multiple times to cycle among the available monitor modes, which I'll describe in detail in Chapter 9:
  - **Automatic Display Switch.** The active display always switches from the monitor to the viewfinder when you place your eye or anything else up to the viewfinder and switches to the LCD when the sensor no longer detects an object.
  - **Viewfinder Only.** The monitor is disabled, and the viewfinder is used exclusively for shooting, navigating menus, or image playback.
  - **Monitor Only.** The viewfinder is disabled, and display is directed to the LCD monitor only.
  - **Prioritize Viewfinder 1/2.** With these power-saving options, when you're shooting pictures, the display is directed to the viewfinder exclusively; it turns on when you move your eye to the EVF and turns off when you remove your eye.
- **Focus mode button.** Hold this button and rotate the main command dial to cycle among AF-S, AF-C, or Manual focus (in Photo mode), or AF-S, AF-C, AF-F, or Manual focus (in Video mode). Rotate the sub-command dial to cycle among available AF-area modes.
- **Ethernet connector (Z9 only).** This connector allows a wired RJ45 Ethernet connection to provide direct linking to local area networks.
- **External microphone connector.** Although the camera has built-in microphones on top, if you want better quality (and want to shield your video clip soundtracks from noises emanating from the

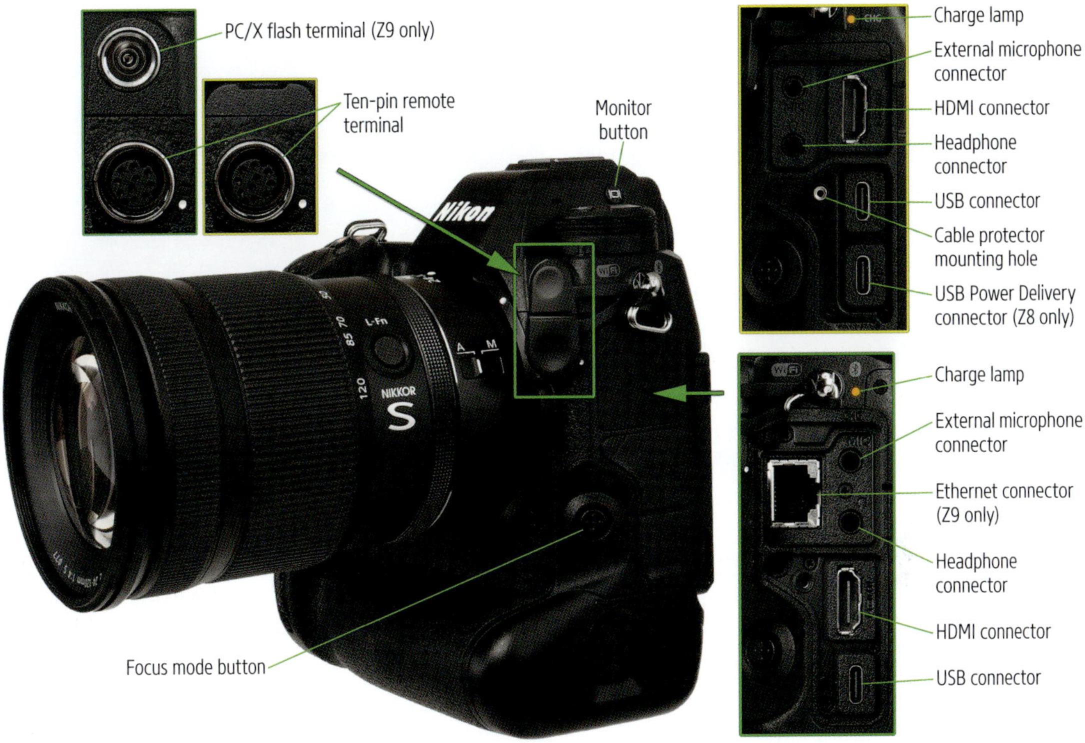

Figure 1.7

camera and/or your handling of it), you can plug in an accessory mic, such as the Nikon ME-1, here.

- **Headphone connector.** Plug in your headphones or other audio device here using a stereo miniplug to monitor your sound as you record, or to listen to the audio when playing back a video clip.
- **HDMI connector.** You need to buy an accessory standard HDMI cable to connect to an external video recorder, monitor, or HDTV, as one to fit this port is not provided with the camera. If you have a high-resolution television or monitor, it's worth the expenditure to be able to view your camera's output in all its glory. And if you want to use a video recorder, a good cable will be worth its weight in gold.
- **USB connector.** Plug in the USB cable included in the box and connect the other end to a USB port in your computer to transfer photos, to upload Picture Control settings, or to upload/download other settings between your camera and computer. This USB 3 Type-C connector is also used for charging the Nikon Z9's battery internally.

  With the Z8, this connector is for data transfer only, and it will not draw power. The Z8 uses the USB PD connector instead, described next.
- **USB Power Delivery connector (Z8 only).** This is an additional USB port specifically for power (non-data) connections. Juice is supplied only when the Z8's battery is inserted, and will power the camera so you can operate it without draining the internal battery. You can specify whether power can be supplied using the USB Power Delivery entry in the Setup menu.

- **Cable protector mounting hole.** Attach the supplied cable protector clip (shown in Figure 1.8) using this threaded socket. An HDMI or USB cable (or both) can be inserted in the clip, which prevents them from accidental detachment. You'll find the cable protector especially useful when shooting video with an external HDMI monitor or recorder or working tethered through a USB connection. "What is this thing for?" seems to be the number one question asked by new Z9 or Z8 owners who have never used these before and haven't read their manual or my book carefully.

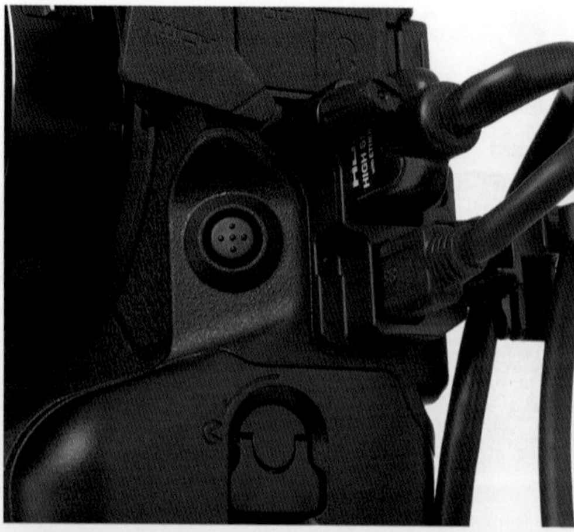

Figure 1.8 HDMI/USB cable protector.

The Business End

The back panels of the Nikon Z9 and Z8 bristle with more than a dozen different controls, buttons, and knobs. That might seem like a lot of controls to learn, but you'll find, as I noted earlier, that it's a lot easier to press a dedicated button and spin a dial than to jump to a menu every time you want to change a setting. Although the back of the Z9 and Z8 are similar, there are some differences. I've color-coded the different parts of the back panel and will describe the components shown in Figure 1.9 separately.

Blue box (upper left of each camera):

- **Fn4/Fn3 button.** This button is labeled Fn4 on the Z9 and Fn3 on the Z8.
  - **In Shooting mode:** Press and hold while rotating the main command dial to select Original, User-defined, or Creative Picture Controls, as described in Chapter 5. When a Creative control is highlighted, you can rotate the sub-command dial to increase/decrease strength of the effect.
  - **In Playback mode:** Press to Protect/Unprotect the current image.
- **Trash button.** Press to erase the image shown on the LCD monitor. A display will pop up on the LCD monitor asking you to press the Trash button once more to delete the photo or press the Playback button to cancel. If you press this button at the same time as the ISO button on the top-right panel for several seconds, the camera will initiate the Format Card procedure.

Cyan box (upper right of each camera):

- **DISP button.** Shows or hides informational displays in the LCD monitor or viewfinder. Press to cycle among the available displays in Photo, Video, and Playback modes.
- **Photo/Video switch.** Switches the camera from Still Photo Shooting mode to Video mode.

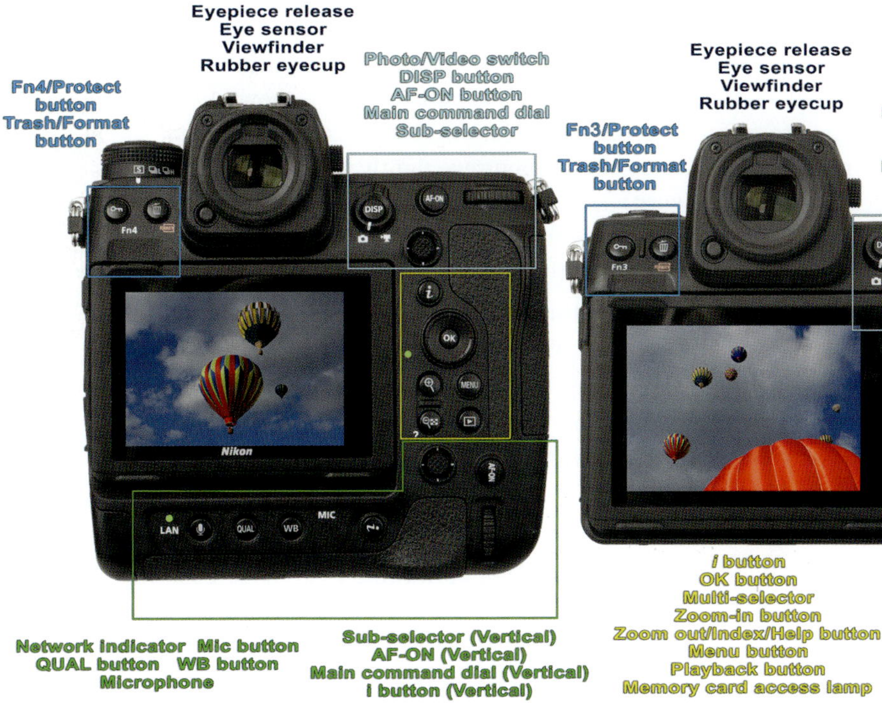

Figure 1.9

- **AF-ON button.** Press this button to activate the autofocus system without needing to partially depress the shutter release. This control, used with other buttons, allows you to lock exposure and focus separately: Lock exposure by pressing the shutter-release button halfway; autofocus by pressing the shutter release halfway or by pressing the AF-ON button. There are lots of cool ways you can use the AF-ON button, and I'll explain them in detail in Chapter 12.
- **Main command dial.** This is the main control dial of the camera, used to set or adjust most functions, such as shutter speed, bracketing sequence, white balance, ISO, and so forth, either alone or when another button is depressed simultaneously. It is often used in conjunction with the sub-command dial on the front of the camera when pairs of settings can be made, such as image formats (main command dial: image format; sub-command dial: resolution); exposure (main command dial: shutter speed; sub-command dial: aperture); or flash (main command dial: flash mode; sub-command dial: flash compensation). You can swap functions of the main and sub-command dials, reverse the rotation direction, choose whether the aperture ring on the lens or the sub-command dial will be used to set the f/stop, and activate the main command dials to navigate menus and images. You'll learn about these Custom Settings menu options in Chapter 7.
- **Sub-selector.** In shooting mode, this joystick-like control can be pressed sideways instead of the multi selector to select a focus point (autofocus is covered in Chapter 3), whereas pressing the sub-selector down (as if it were a button) locks focus and exposure while it's held down. In Playback mode, it behaves the same as the multi selector to scroll around within a zoomed image. Or, you can reprogram it to display the next or previous image instead, using Custom Setting f2, as I'll explain in Chapter 7.

Next, we have the viewfinder and rear LCD monitor located in the center of both cameras:

- **Viewfinder/Rubber eyecup/Eyepiece release.** You can frame your composition by peering into the 3,690,000-pixel (Quad-VGA) OLED electronic viewfinder, which shows 100 percent of your image frame at a generous 0.8 percent magnification. It's surrounded by a soft rubber frame that seals out extraneous light when pressing your eye tightly up to the viewfinder, and it also protects your eyeglass lenses (if worn) from scratching. Your eye can be up to 21mm away from the viewfinder window (the "eyepoint") and still view the entire focus screen area. To allow unscrewing the eyecup, press the eyepiece release button at the 7 o'clock position.
- **Eye sensor.** Detects when your eye (or anything else) approaches the viewfinder window (anything closer than about three inches in my tests).
- **Tilting LCD monitor.** The 3.2-inch LCD monitor has a 2,100,000-dot XGA TFT touch-sensitive screen with a 170-degree viewing angle that allows you to see the screen clearly even from the side or slightly above. It provides a 100 percent view of what the sensor sees. It tilts vertically and horizontally so you can position the camera down low (say, for macro shots of flowers) or up high for a periscope view in both landscape and portrait orientations.

The important navigational/viewing/menu controls of both cameras are located at the right side, highlighted by a yellow box in Figure 1.9:

- **Playback button.** Press this button to review images you've taken, using the controls and options I'll explain in the next section. To remove the image display, press the Playback button again, or simply tap the shutter-release button.
- ***i* button.** The button has dual functions, depending on mode:
    - **Shooting mode.** Pressing this button in Photo or Movie Shooting modes summons the *i* menu, discussed shortly. A total of 12 adjustments can be accessed from the *i* menu, but you can replace any entry you don't use much with another function of your choice, using Custom Setting f1: Customize *i* Menu, as described in Chapter 7. The Video Recording *i* menus can also be customized.
    - **Playback mode.** When reviewing a still image, press the *i* button and choose Manage Series, Rating, Select for Upload to Smart Device, Filtered Playback, Filtered Playback Criteria, Record/Play Voice Memo, Send/Deselect (Smart Device), Retouch, Jump to Copy on Other Card, Choose Slot and Folder, Protect, Unprotect All, IPTC, Side-by-Side Comparison, or Slide Show.

      When a movie clip is displayed during Playback mode, your choices are Rating, Filtered Playback, Filtered Playback Criteria, Volume Control, Trim Video, Choose Slot and Folder, Protect, Unprotect All, and Slide Show.

  Note: The Jump to Copy on Other Card option displays the other image in a pair, say, the original and a backup copy stored on the other slot, or a RAW or JPEG image when you elect to store them on different memory cards.

- **Multi selector.** This joypad-like disk can be shifted up, down, side to side, and diagonally for a total of eight directions. It can be used for several functions, including AF-point selection, scrolling around a magnified image, trimming a photo, or setting white balance bias along the green/magenta and blue/yellow axes. Within menus, pressing the up/down arrows moves the on-screen cursor up or down; pressing toward the right selects the highlighted item and displays its options; pressing left cancels and returns to the previous menu.
- **OK button.** The OK button in the center of the multi selector can be pressed to activate several different default functions, depending on your current mode. Like many other controls, it can be redefined; in this case use Custom Setting f2. I'll explain those options in Chapter 7.
  - **Shooting mode.** Resets focus point to the center of the frame.
  - **Playback mode.** Turns zoom on/off.
  - **Menu mode.** Selects highlighted menu option (same as the right arrow button).
- **Memory card access lamp.** This green LED is located to the left of the multi selector on the Z9 and just to the right of the *i* button on the Z8. When lit or blinking, this lamp indicates that a memory card is being accessed.
- **MENU button.** Summons/exits the menu display. When you're working with submenus, this button also can serve to exit many submenus and return to the main menu.
- **Zoom In button.** This button has separate Playback and Shooting mode functions:
  - **Shooting mode.** In Shooting mode, press to zoom in on the live image, which makes it easier to autofocus or manual focus on a specific area. The zoomed area can be moved around the frame using the directional buttons.
  - **Playback mode.** Press to zoom in on an image when in full-screen view, or to decrease the number of thumbnails when in index view (described next). **Note:** You can also zoom in and out in Playback mode using "pinch" and "spread" gestures on the touch screen, similarly to the techniques used with smartphones. I'll explain zooming and other playback options in an upcoming section.
- **Zoom Out/Index/Help button.** This button has separate Playback and Shooting mode functions:
  - **Shooting mode.** If you've zoomed in on the live view, pressing this button zooms out again. When working with many menu items, if you see a ? icon appear in the bottom-left corner of the screen, pressing this button produces a concise Help screen. The screen includes tips on how to make the relevant setting with the highlighted menu item. The Help screen may have several pages you can scroll through using the up/down buttons. Press this button again to return to the menus.
  - **Playback mode.** Use this button to change from full-screen view to four, nine, or 72 thumbnails. Press the Zoom In button to go the other way back to full-screen and magnified views.

The Nikon Z9's built-in grip has an array of buttons and indicators directly underneath the rear LCD monitor. At the right side of the grip are a set of vertical controls also found on the optional MB-N12 battery grip that can be attached to the Z8:

- **Network indicator.** This LED shows the status of the Z9's Ethernet connection:
  - **Off.** No connection.
  - **Green.** Waiting to connect.
  - **Flashing green.** Connected.
  - **Flashing amber.** Error.
- **Mic button.** Press and hold to record a voice memo; release to end recording. During recording the camera display shows a microphone icon and a countdown of the remaining recording time. If you'd rather press to start recording and press again to stop, you can enable that behavior using the Voice Memo Options in the Setup menu, as described in Chapter 9.
- **QUAL button.** Press and hold while rotating the main command dial (to choose Image Quality) or the sub-command dial (to specify Image Size).
- **WB button.** Hold this button and rotate the main command dial to select from the white balance settings described earlier in this chapter (Auto variations, Natural Light Auto, Direct Sunlight, Cloudy, Shade, Incandescent, Fluorescent, Flash, K [color temperature], and Preset Manual). The multi selector directional buttons can be pressed to fine-tune color, using the up/down buttons to change the green/magenta bias and left/right buttons to adjust blue/amber bias. The sub-command dial can be rotated for additional options with several settings:
  - **Auto variations.** Choose A_0, A_1, or A_2.
  - **Fluorescent.** Select Cool-white, Day white, or Daylight.
  - **K.** Specify 2500K–10,000K
  - **Preset Manual.** Activate Pre_1–Pre_6.
- **Microphone.** Speak into this cluster of four holes when recording a voice memo.
- **Sub-selector (Vertical).** The counterpart to the sub-selector on both the Z9 and MB-N12 grip.
- **AF-ON (Vertical).** The counterpart to the AF-ON button on both the Z9 and MB-N12 grip.
- **Main command dial (Vertical).** The counterpart to the main command dial on both the Z9 and MB-N12 grip.
- ***i* button (Vertical).** This is counterpart to the *i* button on the Z9. The MB-N12 grip lacks this button.

Going Topside

The top surface of your Z9/Z8 has its own set of frequently accessed controls. (See Figure 1.10.)

- **Release mode dial lock release button (Z9 only).** The Z9 has a separate dial for selecting a release mode, seen in the green inset in the upper-left corner of Figure 1.10. Before you can choose any of the release mode dial's settings, you must hold down this button to free the dial so it can rotate.
- **Release mode dial (Z9 only).** Unlock this dial and rotate to select Single shot, Continuous Low, Continuous High, Self-timer, and Quick Release modes. To set options *within* each of the release modes, use the Release Mode button, described next.

- **Release Mode button (Z8).** This button functions slightly differently with the Z9 and Z8. The Z8 uses this button to select release modes and their options. Press and hold the button and rotate the main command dial to select from:
  - **Single Shot.** The camera takes one picture each time the shutter release is pressed all the way. There are no additional options.
  - **Continuous Low.** Rotate the sub-command dial to specify a frame rate from 1 to 10 frames per second.
  - **Continuous High/C30/C60/C120.** Rotate the sub-command dial to specify 10 to 20 frames per second, plus C30, C60, and C120 high-speed rates. The C30 and C60 rates are captured in Large Image Size in FX/DX Image Areas, respectively. C120 images are captured in Small FX format unless a DX lens is attached. You'll find more details in Chapter 5.
  - **Self-timer.** Rotate the sub-command dial to specify 2-, 5-, 10-, or 20-second delays. **Note:** You can specify the number of shots taken when the timer elapses and the interval between those shots using Custom Setting c2, as described in Chapter 7.
- **Release Mode button (Z9).** You have two options:
  - **Release mode dial.** Select a particular release mode using the release mode dial. Once you've locked in a particular mode, you can rotate the main command dial to select frame rates or self-timer settings as described above. The advantage of this method is that you can't accidentally switch from one release mode to another.
  - **Quick-release mode.** Rotate the release mode dial all the way to the Quick-release position. Then, hold down the Release Mode button and rotate the main command dial to select any of the individual release modes, and the sub-command dial to select available options.

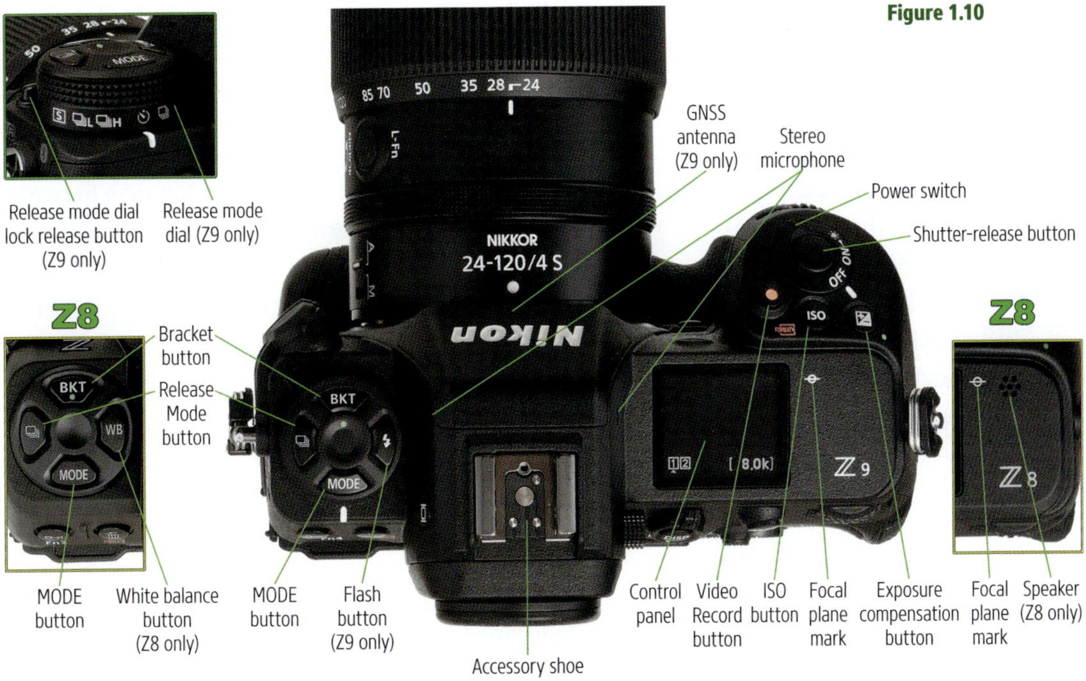

Figure 1.10

- **MODE button.** Hold this button and rotate the main command dial to select Programmed Auto, Shutter-priority, Aperture-priority, or Manual exposure modes.
- **Bracket button.** Press this button and rotate the main command dial to select number of shots in a bracketed set (0, 3, 5, 7, or 9), and the sub-command dial to set exposure changes of 0.3, 0.7, 1.0, 1.3, 1.7, 2.0, 2.3, 2.7, or 3.0 stops (the defaults; you can choose 1/2 EV or 1 EV steps using Custom Setting b2, as described in Chapter 7). You'll learn more about bracketing in Chapter 2.
- **White balance button (Z8 only).** This is the counterpart to the WB button found under the rear LCD on the Z9, described earlier. (See the yellow-boxed inset at left in Figure 1.10.) It operates in the same way: hold down the button and the main command dial to specify your choice:
  - **Auto variations.** When WB A_0, A_1, or A_2 appear, with the WB button still held down, rotate the sub-command dial to select one of these.
  - **Natural Light Auto.**
  - **Direct Sunlight.**
  - **Cloudy.**
  - **Shade.**
  - **Incandescent.**
  - **Fluorescent.** Select Cool-white, Day white, or Daylight.
  - **Flash.**
  - **K.** Specify 2500K–10,000K
  - **Preset Manual.** Activate Pre_1–Pre_6.
- **Flash button (Z9 only).** Hold and rotate the main command dial to choose flash mode (Fill Flash, Red-eye Reduction, Slow Sync, Slow Sync + Red-eye, Rear-curtain Sync, Flash Off). Rotate the sub-command dial to select –3.0 to +1.0 flash exposure compensation. There's more on using electronic flash in Chapter 4.
- **Accessory shoe.** Slide an electronic flash into this mount when you need a more powerful Speedlight. A dedicated flash unit, like the Nikon SB-5000, can use the multiple contact points shown to communicate exposure, zoom setting, white balance information, and other data between the flash and the camera. You can also mount other accessories on this shoe, such as a GPS receiver or stereo microphone.
- **Stereo microphone.** This pair captures sounds when shooting video.
- **GNSS antenna (Z9 only).** The Z9's built-in GPS receiver is located under the Nikon nameplate.
- **Power switch.** Rotate this switch clockwise to turn on the camera.
- **Shutter-release button.** Partially depress this button to activate the exposure meter (and the main and sub-command dials that adjust metering settings), lock in exposure, and focus (unless you've redefined the focus activation button, as outlined in Chapter 7). Press all the way to take the picture. Tapping the shutter release when the camera has turned off the autoexposure and autofocus mechanisms reactivates both. When a review image is displayed on the back-panel color monitor, tapping this button removes the image from the display and reactivates the autoexposure and autofocus mechanisms. You can also tap the button to exit image review and menus, readying the camera to take a picture.

- **Exposure compensation button.** Hold down this button and spin the main command dial to add or subtract exposure when using Program, Aperture-priority, or Shutter-priority modes. (In Manual mode, the exposure remains the same, but the "ideal" exposure shown in the electronic analog display [more on that in the next section] is modified to reflect the extra/reduced exposure you're calling for.) The exposure compensation amount is shown on the monochrome control panel as plus or minus values.

  Values from –5 EV to +5 EV are available in Photo mode, with –3 EV to +3 EV available in Video Recording mode. You can adjust the increment from the default 1/3 stop to 1/2 or 1.0 stops using Custom Setting b2.
- **Focal plane mark.** This indicator shows the *plane* of the sensor, for use in applications where exact measurement of the distance from the focal plane to the subject is necessary. (These are mostly scientific/close-up applications.)
- **Video Record button.** When the Photo/Video switch is in the Video position, you can press this button to begin video capture; press a second time to stop. This button has no default function in Photo mode, but you can assign a behavior using Custom Setting f2, as described in Chapter 7.
- **Control panel.** This useful OLED (organic LED) indicator shows the status of many settings, such as exposure, frames shot/remaining, and other information.
- **ISO button.** Hold this button and rotate the main command dial until the ISO value you want is shown on the top control panel, in the viewfinder, and on the monitor. The sub-command dial turns Auto ISO on or off.
- **Speaker (Z8 only).** Sounds generated by the Z8 emerge here. The speaker on the Z9 is located on the underside of the viewfinder housing.

Underneath Your Camera

There's not a lot going on with the bottom panel of your camera. The Z9 has only a tripod socket and a positioning hole that can be used with some accessories, such as video cages. The socket accepts other accessories, such as quick-release plates that allow rapid attaching and detaching the camera from a matching platform affixed to your tripod.

The Z8 adds a battery compartment door, which can be removed when attaching the optional MB-N12 grip, which provides more juice to run your camera to take more exposures with a single charge and a complete set of vertical controls.

Lens Components

Not all Nikon lenses include all of the features shown in Figure 1.11, but the Nikkor Z 100-400mm f/4.5-5.6 VR S lens shown provides a good example. Components shown in the figure include:

- **Lens hood mounting mark.** Lenses use this the bayonet to mount the lens hood, lining up a matching mark on the hood with this *lens hood alignment indicator,* a dot on the edge showing how to align the lens hood with the bayonet mount.

Figure 1.11

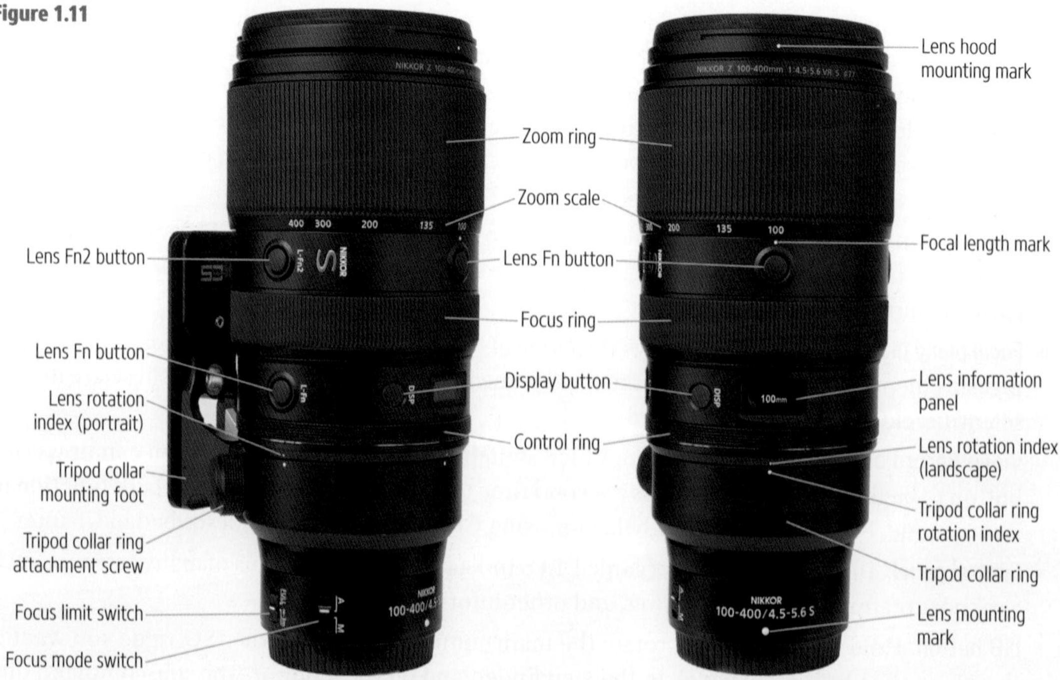

- **Filter thread (not shown).** Most lenses have a thread on the front for attaching filters and other add-ons. Some F-mount lenses, such as the AF-S Nikkor 14-24mm f/2.8G ED lens, have no front filter thread, either because their front elements are too curved to allow mounting a filter and/or because the front element is so large that huge filters would be prohibitively expensive. Some of these front-filter-hostile lenses allow using smaller filters that drop into a slot at the back of the lens.
- **Focus ring.** This is the ring you turn when you manually focus the lens, or fine-tune autofocus adjustment. The amount of focus change per degree of rotation can be fine-tuned using Custom Setting f11, as explained in Chapter 7. The location of the focus ring may vary, depending on the lens.
- **Control ring.** This ring can be assigned the Focus function if you find its position more convenient. By default, it is used to open and close the aperture in Aperture-priority and Manual exposure modes, but a variety of other behaviors are available using Custom Setting f2.
- **Zoom ring/Zoom scale.** Turn this ring to change the zoom setting, using the zoom scale as reference.
- **Lens function ring.** If present, this ring, by default, recalls the last focus position. Custom Setting f2 allows you to define some other behavior, such as Save Focus Position, Switch Eyes, or Aperture control. Separate definitions can be assigned for clockwise and counterclockwise rotation.
- **Lens Function buttons.** Depending on the lens, you may find one or more buttons labeled L-Fn or L-Fn2 which can be assigned specific behaviors. For example, the Nikkor 24-120 f/4 S has just one L-Fn button, while the 100-400mm f/4.5-5.6 VR S has one L-Fn and four L-Fn2 buttons. Separate functions are available for the L-Fn and L-Fn2 buttons. By default, the L-Fn button serves as an AE/AL lock, and the L-Fn2 as an AF-ON button.

- **Lens information panel/Display button.** The OLED (organic light emitting diode) display (if present) illuminates to provide information when mounted and the camera is powered up. Pressing the DISP button cycles among three different info screens:
    - Focus distance, Minimum focus index, Depth-of-field
    - Current focal length
    - Current aperture
- **Tripod collar ring/index/attachment screw.** The tripod collar is a thick rotating ring near the base of the lens, locked at any position with an attachment screw that can be backed all the way out if you want to remove the tripod collar and mounting foot entirely. Lens rotation indexes are guides that mark 90-degree positions for landscape and portrait mode camera orientations. A security slot for attaching an anti-theft cable can be found inside the attachment screw of some lenses.
- **Tripod collar mounting foot.** This foot is used to attach the lens to a tripod or other support, providing a safer mount with better weight distribution than using the tripod socket on the bottom of the camera. Nikon doesn't like to pay royalties for the right to include an Arca-Swiss compatible foot, so the first thing I do when I get a Nikon lens is purchase the Kirk Photo replacement foot, shown in the figure. (Really Right Stuff also makes an excellent replacement.)
- **Focus mode switch.** Allows you to change from automatic focus to manual focus. Note that if you've set manual focus using the camera's controls, the Autofocus setting of this switch will be ignored.
- **Focus limit switch.** Choose Full to allow focusing on subjects from infinity to the lens' closest focus distance. The "Distance" setting (which varies from lens to lens) limits focus from infinity down to a specific distance. For example, that value is 9.85 feet (3 meters) with the 100-400mm f/4.5-5.6 VR S and 16 feet (5 meters) with the Nikkor 70-200mm f/2.8 VR S lens.
- **Electronic contacts (not shown).** These metal contacts pass information to matching contacts located in the camera body, allowing a firm electrical connection so that exposure, distance, and other information can be exchanged between the camera and lens.
- **Rubber lens-mount gasket (not shown).** This seal *helps* (emphasis mine) prevent water or dust from entering the camera when the lens is mounted. It does not make a lens completely water-resistant.

Working with Information Displays

The good news is that mirrorless cameras like your Nikon Z9 or Z8 are able to include a great deal more information in their displays during shooting or image review than their dSLR counterparts. The bad news is that all that data can be obtrusive, especially when you're trying to compose an image in the viewfinder or on the rear LCD monitor. Fortunately, you have a great deal of control over which bits of information are displayed, and you can create your own customized screens that will display as much or as little as you desire, and cycle among them using the DISP button. I'll show you exactly how to do that using the Custom Monitor/Viewfinder Shooting Display options in Chapter 7, and the Playback Display Options entry in Chapter 8.

The next sections will introduce you to the basic displays you can view while composing/capturing still photos, and when reviewing the images you took during playback.

Shooting Mode Displays

In Photo and Video Shooting modes, much of the important shooting status information is shown on the electronic viewfinder and LCD monitor displays. In either Shooting mode, you can press the DISP button to cycle through the available views. As I noted above, you can define four different monitor shooting displays and four unique viewfinder shooting displays, using Custom Settings (d19/d20 for the Z9 and d17/d18 for the Z8).

Keep in mind that while the viewfinder and LCD each have customizable displays, they are *separate* and you are free to define different sets of information icons to each. In addition, the way the icons are displayed is slightly different. The viewfinder display arrays some types of information at black bars at the top and bottom of the screen, rather than overlaid onto the image area of the frame. That gives you a less-cluttered canvas on which to compose your image. The LCD, in contrast, overlays everything on the image frame, as seen in Figure 1.12. That alone provides a good reason for carefully customizing your displays. Note that the figure shows only some of the possible icons that can be displayed, and that not all icons will be visible at all times.

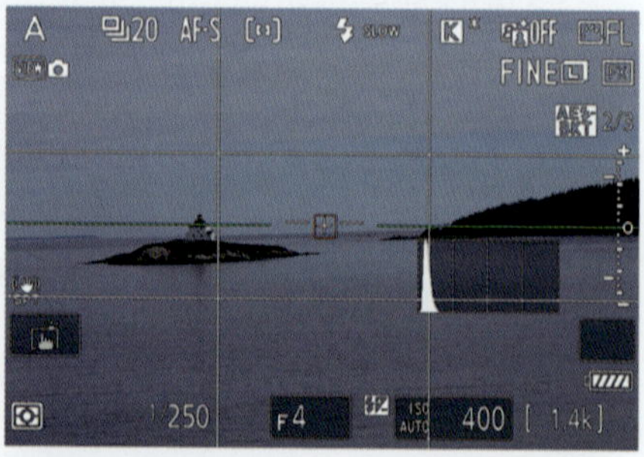

Figure 1.12 Typical Photo mode LCD information display.

One additional text/graphics-only screen is available for the LCD monitor only, and is seen in Figure 1.13. It shows not only exposure information, but, arrayed in two rows at the bottom of the screen are icon indicators that display key settings, such as current picture control, white balance, focus mode, and metering mode. It's often smart to allocate this screen to the LCD monitor as a reference while relying on a different display in the viewfinder. The graphics screen cannot be customized by the user, as it is set up to do triple duty, with three different useful functions:

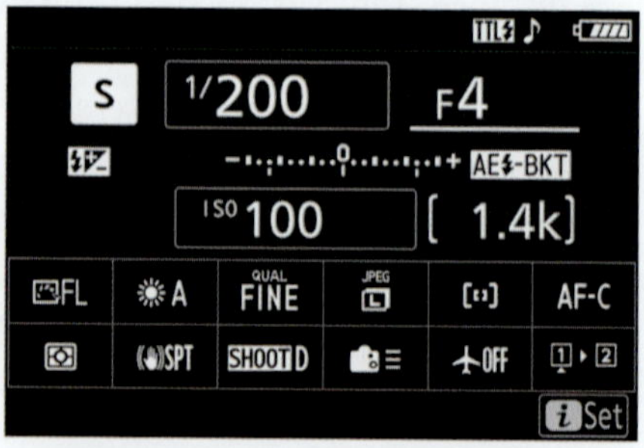

Figure 1.13 The Photo Shooting Information screen is displayed only on the LCD monitor.

- Serve as an informational screen, providing data such as current exposure settings, shooting mode, battery level, and number of exposures remaining, along with the status of the 12 settings available from the *i* menu.
- Allow *changing* the shutter speed and/or aperture, plus ISO sensitivity using the touch screen controls.
- Act as a gateway to the Photo Shooting version of the *i* menu. You can tap the *i* set icon on the touch screen, or press the *i* button to access any of the 12 *i* menu settings. The default indicators and adjustments available are shown in Figure 1.14. After you've highlighted an icon, the command dials can be used to make a setting. You're not locked into those options, however. In Chapter 7, I'll show you how to replace any of the entries with others that you might find more useful.

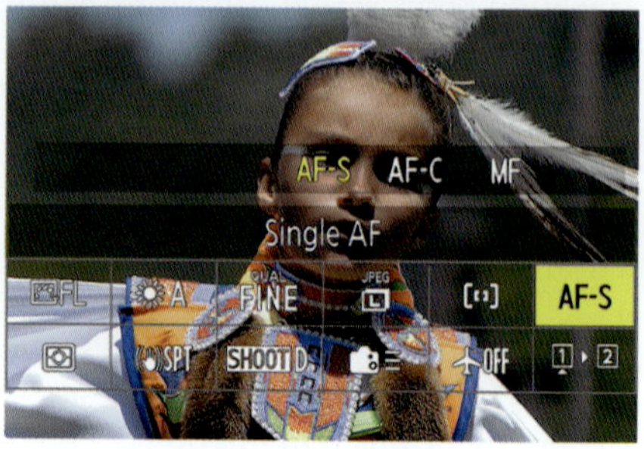

Figure 1.14 The *i* menu allows making adjustments quickly.

A more complete reference for your camera's shooting mode displays can be seen in Figure 1.15, which includes the basic array of icons available for the Nikon Z9's rear LCD monitor. The Z8's screen is virtually identical, with only a few differences, and the viewfinders of each camera icons similar to those displayed on the LCD. Note that the icons re-orient automatically when the cameras are rotated to the vertical position.

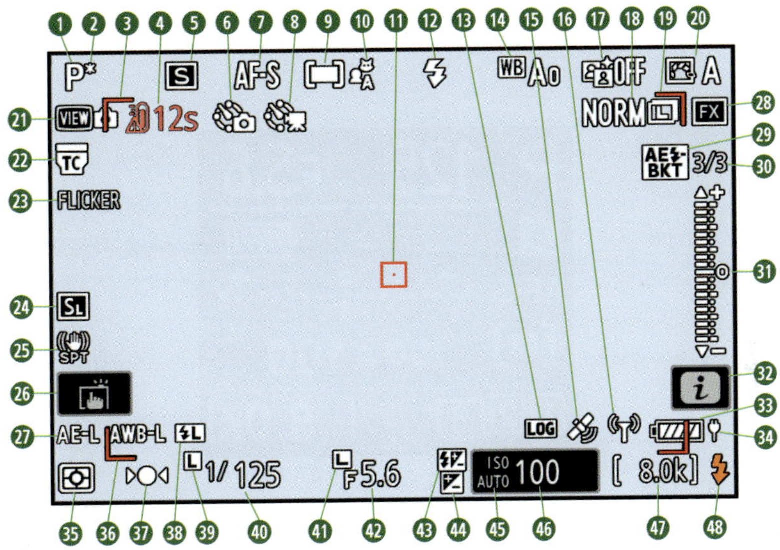

1. Shooting mode
2. Flexible program indicator
3. AF-area brackets
4. Temperature warning
5. Release mode
6. Interval timer indicator
   ⊕ icon
   "No memory card" indicator
   Memory card high-temperature warning
7. Focus mode
8. Time-lapse video recording indicator
9. AF-area mode
10. Subject detection
11. Focus point
12. Flash mode
13. Track log indicator
14. White balance
15. Satellite signal indicator
16. Wi-Fi connection indicator
    Bluetooth connection indicator
    Airplane mode
17. Active D-Lighting
18. Image quality
19. Image size
20. Picture Control
21. View mode
22. "Lens built-in teleconverter enabled" indicator
23. Flicker detection
24. Silent mode
25. Vibration reduction indicator
26. Touch shooting
27. Autoexposure (AE) lock
28. Image area
29. Exposure and flash bracketing indicator
    WB bracketing indicator
    ADL bracketing indicator
    HDR indicator
    Multiple exposure indicator
30. Pre-Release Capture
    Number of shots in exposure and flash bracketing sequence
    Number of shots in WB bracketing sequence
    Number of shots in ADL bracketing sequence
    HDR strength
    Number of shots in multiple exposure
31. Exposure indicator
    Exposure
    Exposure compensation
    Auto bracketing
32. *i* icon
33. Battery indicator
34. USB power delivery
35. Metering
36. Auto white-balance (AWB) lock
37. Focus indicator
38. FV lock indicator
39. Shutter speed lock icon
40. Shutter speed
41. Aperture lock icon
42. Aperture
43. Flash compensation indicator
44. Exposure compensation indicator
45. ISO sensitivity indicator
    Auto ISO sensitivity indicator
46. ISO sensitivity
47. Number of exposures remaining
    Camera control mode
48. Flash-ready indicator

Figure 1.15 LCD Monitor icon reference.

Control Panel Display

The monochrome LCD panel on the top-right shoulder of the Nikon Z8 and Z9 includes more than a dozen indicators that provide information, battery status, focus modes, and other data at a glance. Although the display is highly visible under most lighting conditions, if you rotate the camera's power switch, located concentrically with the shutter-release button, clockwise to its limit, the panel will be back-illuminated for viewing under dimmer lighting. At the same time, buttons on the back and top of the camera will also be lit up. Figure 1.16 shows the top panel and a typical information display.

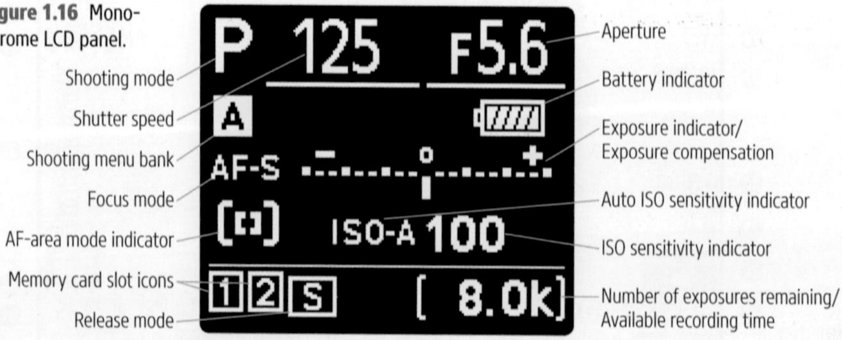

Figure 1.16 Monochrome LCD panel.

Using the Photo Data Displays

When reviewing an image on the viewfinder or monitor displays, your camera can supplement the image itself with a variety of shooting data, ranging from basic information presented at the bottom of the display, to a series of text overlays that detail virtually every shooting option you've selected. There is also a display for GPS data if you're using a GPS device, and two views of histograms. I'll explain how to work with histograms in the discussion on achieving optimum exposure in Chapter 2. However, this is a good place to provide an overview of the kind of information you can view when playing back your photos.

You can change the *types* of information displayed using the Playback Display Options entry in the Playback menu. There you will find checkboxes you can mark for both basic photo information (overexposed highlights and the focus point used when the image was captured) and detailed photo information (which includes an RGB histogram and various data screens). You must mark any unchecked box to enable that type of information display. I'll show you how to activate these info options in Chapter 8 and provide more detailed reasons why you might want to see each type of data when you review your pictures. This section will simply show you the type of information available. Most of the data is self-explanatory.

To change to any of these views while an image is on the screen in Playback mode, press the DISP button or up/down buttons. Figure 1.17 shows how the camera cycles among the various screens, from the File Information screen shown at upper left, to the Picture Only display at lower left, after which the cycle begins again with the File Information screen.

Your options are:

- **File Information screen.** The basic full-image review display is officially called the File Information screen and looks like the screen at upper left in Figure 1.17. Press the DISP button to advance to the next information screen. **Note:** You can also press the multi selector down to move to the next screen, or press the up button to cycle in the other direction.
- **Exposure Data.** You'll next move to this screen, shown in the next panel to the right, with only basic exposure information shown. Keep pressing the DISP button to advance to the screens that follow.

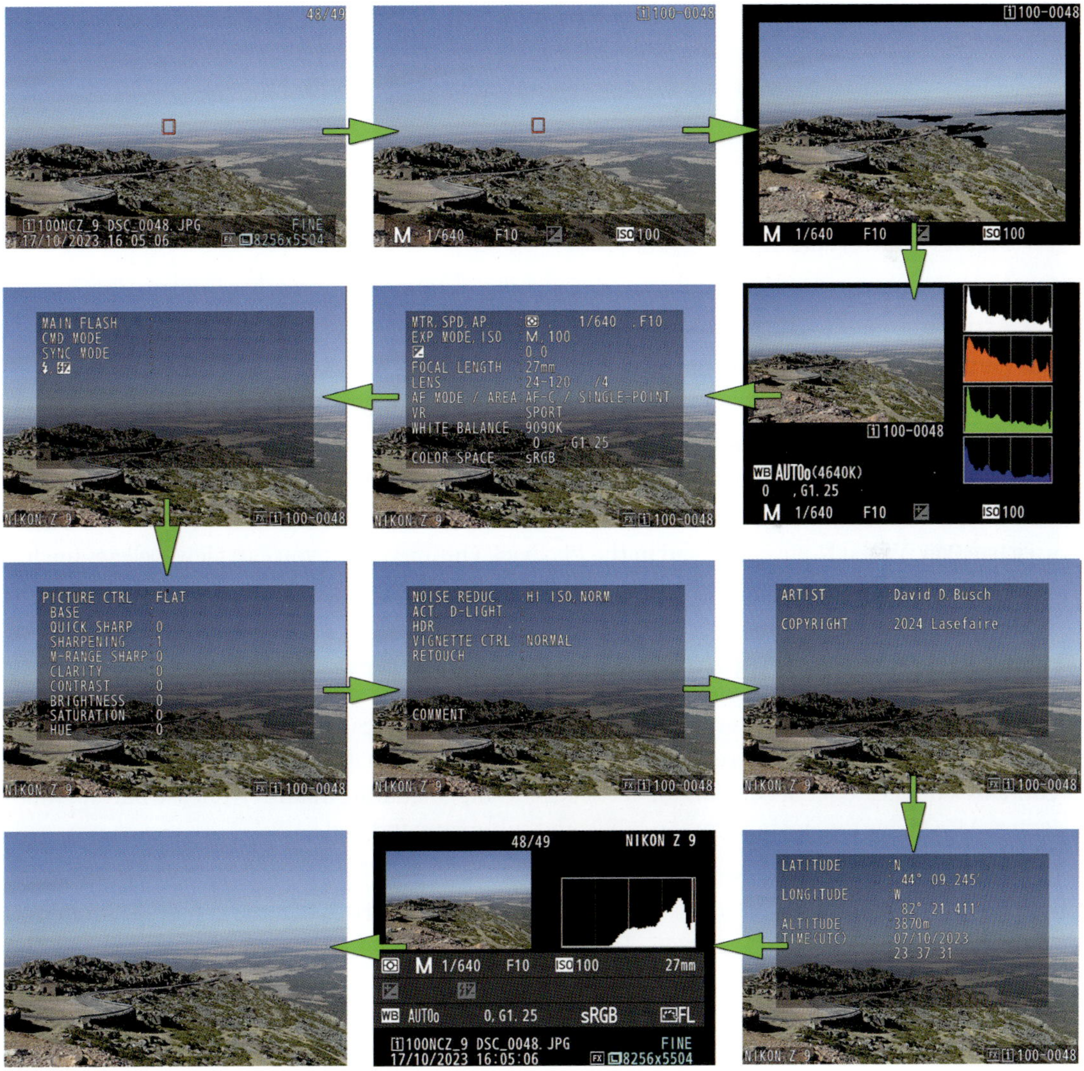

Figure 1.17 The Photo Information screen cycle.

- **Highlights.** When highlights display is active, any overexposed areas will be indicated by a flashing black border. As I am unable to make the printed page flash, you'll have to check out this effect for yourself. You can visualize what these "blinkies" look like in the figure, as they are most easily discerned as the black splotches off in the distance.
- **RGB Histogram.** Another optional screen is the RGB Histogram. I'm going to leave the discussion of histograms for Chapter 2.
- **Shooting Data 1–6.** These are a series of screens that collectively provide everything else you might want to know about a picture you've taken. Note that each screen may not show all the information that can be displayed on that screen, and that all the screens may not appear. Only the data and screens that apply to your image will be shown. For example, the GPS screen appears only if a picture has GPS information embedded in it; the Artist/Copyright screen is shown only if you have chosen to embed that information in your image file. (I'll show you how to do that in Chapter 9.) The six screens include:
  - Exposure, lens, and autofocus/VR information.
  - Flash exposure information.
  - Picture Control adjustments.
  - Noise reduction, Active D-Lighting, Retouching, Comments, and other information.
  - Artist information and copyright notices, if enabled.
  - GPS data is displayed if the image was taken using a GPS device.
- **Overview Data.** This screen, shown at bottom center in the figure, provides a smaller image of your photo, but more information, including a luminance (brightness) histogram, metering mode used, lens focal length, exposure compensation, flash compensation, and lots of other data that's self-explanatory.
- **Picture Only.** When None is selected in the Playback Options entry, you can view a clean, uncluttered screen with no overlays, as seen at bottom left in the figure.

Attaching the MB-N12 Power Battery Pack

The Nikon MB-N12 Power Battery Pack is an optional $350 vertical grip/battery pack accessory. It holds two EN-EL15c batteries (replacing the single battery normally housed in the camera's grip). It contains a duplicate set of controls for vertical shooting, including a shutter-release button, multi selector, AF-ON button, main command dial, and sub-command dial.

Although one of the attractions of the Z8 over the Z9 is its smaller size and lighter weight, many photographers prefer the ergonomics of a vertical grip, particularly when the camera is rotated 90 degrees to shoot in portrait orientation. The MB-N12 is a distinct improvement over some earlier Nikon grips, because it offers that full set of controls, the ability to recharge its batteries while still attached to the camera, and convenient hot-swapping of one of the batteries while the camera is still powered up. The latter two features are great for time-lapse and interval shooting.

To attach the MB-N12 grip, just follow these steps:

1. **Turn off the camera.** Then, remove the camera's battery.
2. **Remove the camera's battery chamber door.** Open the door and tilt it at approximately a 60-degree angle. That will align the two hinge pins with slots, so you can gently slide the door off. The inner chamber with contacts for both battery and control signals can be seen at the bottom of the compartment in Figure 1.18.
3. **Remove contact cap from the grip.** This protects the contacts from damage while the grip is not attached.
4. **Store battery chamber cover.** There is a handy recess in the MB-N12 grip to store the battery door when it's detached from the camera.
5. **Disable controls.** A lock switch is concentric with the grip's shutter-release button. Rotate it to the L position to avoid activating the camera before you are ready to take a picture.
6. **Lower the camera onto the grip.** The extension goes in the battery compartment, and the tripod screw on the attachment wheel mates with the camera's tripod socket.
7. **Secure the grip to the camera.** Rotate the attachment wheel to the right until the grip is firmly attached. The assembly will look like Figure 1.19. The MB-N12 has its own tripod socket on the bottom so you can still mount the camera/grip on a tripod.

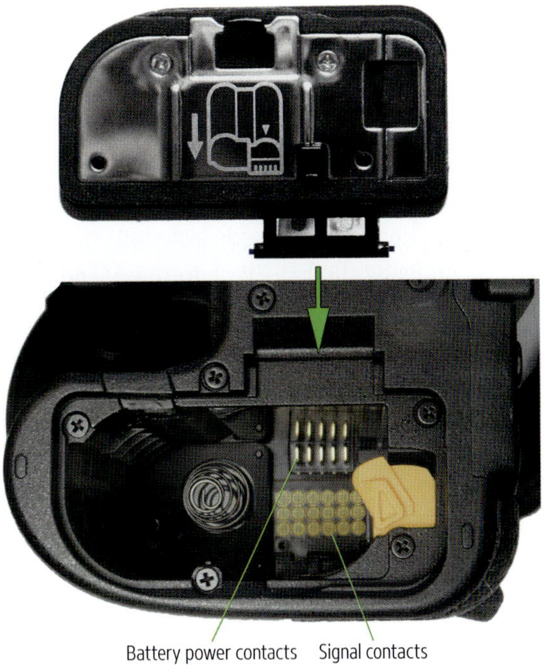

Figure 1.18 Detach the battery compartment door.

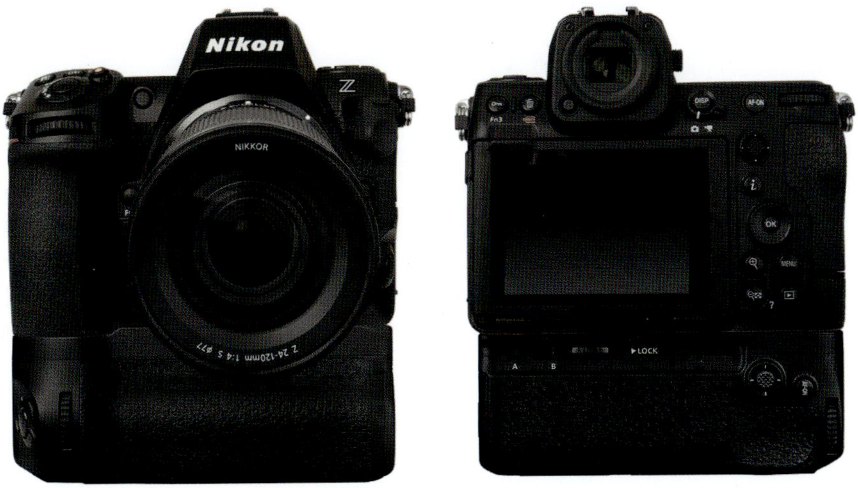

Figure 1.19 The MB-N12 grip attached to the camera.

8. **Open battery holder-chamber cover.** Slide the latch on the end of the grip toward the back of the camera and open the door. Inside, you'll find a slide-out battery holder.
9. **Insert one or two batteries in the holder.** If you are using only one battery, it can be placed in either position. If you are using two batteries, the one in the outermost chamber A will be used first; when it is exhausted, the camera will switch to the battery in the innermost chamber B. You can replace the chamber A battery at any time, even while using the camera continuously.
10. **Recharge batteries in the grip (optional).** The batteries in the grip can be recharged without removing them, using the EH-7P charging AC adapter, which is furnished with the Z9, and an optional accessory for the Z8.

NOTE When using the MB-N12 grip, the status of the battery in use is shown on the shooting display and control panel. The shooting display also shows an icon indicating which battery (A or B) is in use. The Battery Info entry in the Setup menu provides information on battery age and battery level.

Nailing the Right Exposure 2

The Nikon Z8 and Z9 have an exceptional amount of intelligence when it comes to calculating the correct exposure for a wide variety of scenes. Even so, you are smarter—and more creative. The more you shoot, the more ways you'll discover how to improve on your camera's picture-taking decisions and, even when to *ignore* them when you want to create a particular look or effect. For example, when you shoot with the main light source behind the subject, you end up with *backlighting*, which can result in an overexposed background and/or an underexposed subject. The exposure system recognizes backlit situations nicely, and, in most cases, can properly base exposure on the main subject using the default Matrix metering mode, producing a decent photo.

But as a creative photographer there will be many instances where you would rather *not* have automatic correction for backlighting. What if you *want* to underexpose the subject, to produce a silhouette effect? The camera does a poor job of exposing intentional silhouettes and will end up producing unwanted detail in what should have been inky black areas of your image. Fortunately, the camera has metering modes and other exposure options that allow you to produce the image you are looking for. If you're looking for an extensive exposure range, features like the camera's built-in HDR and Active D-Lighting can fine-tune your exposure as you take photos, preserving detail in the highlights and shadows as required. Your camera also has the capability of *fine-tuning* exposure separately for each of the metering modes, so you can consistently add or subtract a little exposure to suit your creative tastes.

In the next few pages, I'm going to give you a grounding in exposure concepts, either as an introduction or as a refresher course, depending on your current level of expertise. When you finish this chapter, you'll understand most of what you need to know to take well-exposed photographs creatively in a broad range of situations.

Getting a Handle on Exposure

> This section explains the fundamental concepts that go into creating an exposure. If you already know about the role of f/stops, shutter speeds, and sensor sensitivity in determining an exposure, you might want to skip to the next section, which explains how the camera calculates exposure.

In the most basic sense, exposure is all about light. Correct exposure brings out the detail in the areas you want to picture, providing the range of tones and colors you need to create the desired image. Poor exposure can cloak important details in shadow or wash them out in glare-filled featureless expanses of white. However, getting the perfect exposure requires some intelligence—either that built into the camera or the smarts in your head—because digital sensors can't capture all the tones we are able to see. If the range of tones in an image is extensive, embracing both inky black shadows and bright highlights, we often must settle for an exposure that renders most of those tones—but not all—in a way that best suits the photo we want to produce.

As the owner of a Z-series mirrorless camera, you're probably well aware of the traditional "exposure triangle" of aperture (quantity of light, light passed by the lens), shutter speed (the amount of time the shutter is open), and the ISO sensitivity of the sensor—all working proportionately and reciprocally to produce an exposure. The trio is itself affected by the amount of illumination that is available to work with. So, if you double the amount of light, increase the aperture by one stop, make the shutter speed twice as long, or boost the ISO setting 2X, you'll get twice as much exposure. Similarly, you can increase any of these factors while decreasing one of the others by a similar amount to keep the *same* exposure.

Working with any of the three controls always involves trade-offs. Larger f/stops provide less depth-of-field, while smaller f/stops increase depth-of-field and decrease sharpness through a phenomenon called diffraction. Shorter shutter speeds do a better job of reducing the effects of camera/subject motion, while longer shutter speeds make that motion blur more likely. Higher ISO settings increase the amount of visual noise and artifacts in your image, while lower ISO settings reduce the effects of noise. (See Figure 2.1.)

To further understand exposure, you need to understand the six aspects of light that combine to produce an image. Start with a light source—the sun, an interior lamp, electronic flash, or the glow from a campfire—and trace its path to your camera, through the lens, and finally to the sensor that captures the illumination.

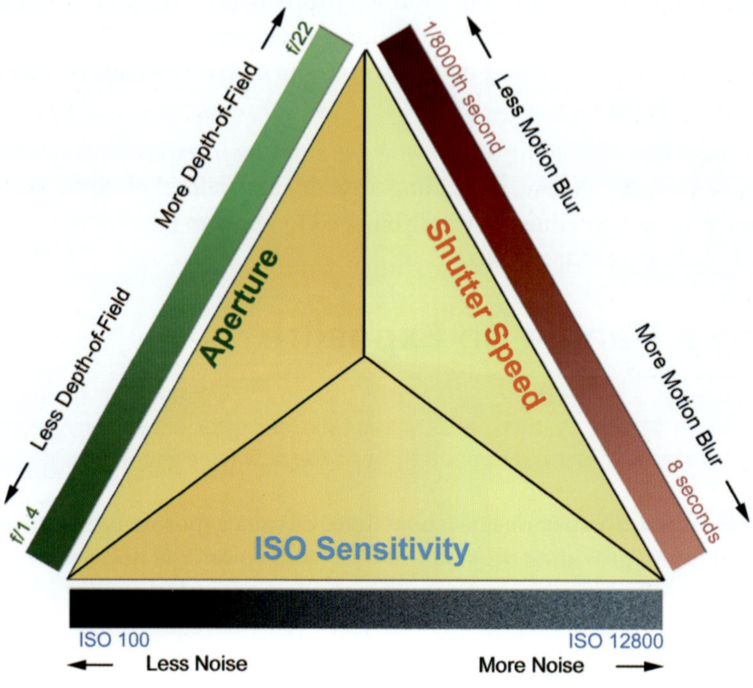

Figure 2.1 The traditional exposure triangle includes aperture, shutter speed, and ISO sensitivity.

Here's a brief review of the things within our control that affect exposure, listed in "chronological" order (that is, as the light moves from the subject to the sensor):

- **Light at its source.** Our eyes and our cameras—film or digital—are most sensitive to that portion of the electromagnetic spectrum we call *visible light.* That light has several important aspects that are relevant to photography, such as color and harshness (which is determined primarily by the apparent size of the light source as it illuminates a subject). But, in terms of exposure, the important attribute of a light source is its *intensity.* We may have direct control over intensity, which might be the case with an interior light that can be brightened or dimmed, or electronic flash output that can be increased or decreased manually or automatically. In other cases, we might have only indirect control over intensity, as with sunlight, which can be made to appear dimmer by introducing translucent light-absorbing or reflective materials in its path.
- **Light's duration.** We tend to think of most light sources as continuous. But, as you'll learn in Chapter 4, the duration of light can change quickly enough to modify the exposure, as when the main illumination in a photograph comes from an intermittent source, such as an electronic flash.
- **Light reflected, transmitted, or emitted.** Once light is produced by its source, either continuously or in a brief burst, we are able to see and photograph objects by the light that is reflected from our subjects toward the camera lens; transmitted (say, from translucent objects that are lit from behind); or emitted (by a candle or television screen). When more or less light reaches the lens from the subject, we need to adjust the exposure. This part of the equation is under our control to the extent we can increase the amount of light falling on or passing through the subject (by adding extra light sources or using reflectors), or by pumping up the light that's emitted (by increasing the brightness of the glowing object).
- **Light passed by the lens.** Not all the illumination that reaches the front of the lens makes it all the way through. Filters can remove some of the light before it enters the lens. Inside the lens barrel is a variable-sized diaphragm that produces an opening called an *aperture* that dilates and contracts to control the amount of light that enters the lens. You, or the camera's autoexposure system, can control exposure by varying the size of the aperture. The relative size of the aperture is called the *f/stop.*
- **Light passing through the shutter.** Once light passes through the lens, the amount of time the sensor receives it is determined by the shutter, which can remain open for as briefly as 1/32000th of a second, or, for as long as 30 seconds—or even longer if you use the Bulb, Time, or Extended shutter speed settings.
- **Light captured by the sensor.** Not all the light falling onto the sensor is captured. If the number of photons reaching a particular photosite doesn't pass a set threshold, no information is recorded. Similarly, if too much light illuminates a pixel in the sensor, then the excess isn't recorded or, worse, spills over to contaminate adjacent pixels. We can modify the minimum and maximum number of pixels that contribute to image detail by adjusting the ISO setting. At higher ISOs, the incoming light is amplified to boost the effective sensitivity of the sensor.

Four of these factors—quantity of light, light passed by the lens, the amount of time the shutter is open, and the sensitivity of the sensor—all work proportionately and reciprocally to produce an exposure. That is, as I mentioned, if you double the amount of light, double the size of the aperture opening, make the shutter speed twice as long, or double the ISO sensitivity, you'll get twice as much exposure. Similarly, you can reduce any of these and reduce the exposure when that is preferable.

As we'll see however, changing any of those aspects in P, A, or S mode does not change the exposure; that's because the camera also makes adjustments when you do so, in order to maintain the same exposure. That's why Nikon provides other methods for modifying the exposure in those modes.

F/STOPS AND SHUTTER SPEEDS

If you're *really* new to more advanced cameras (and I realize that a few ambitious amateurs do purchase the Z9 or Z8 as their first serious camera), you might need to know that the lens aperture, or f/stop, is a ratio, much like a fraction, which is why f/2 is larger than f/4, just as 1/2 is larger than 1/4. However, f/2 is actually *four times* as large as f/4. (If you remember your high school geometry, you'll know that to double the area of a circle, you multiply its diameter by the square root of two: 1.4.)

Lenses are usually marked with intermediate f/stops that represent a size that's twice as much/half as much as the previous aperture. So, a lens might be marked: f/4, f/5.6, f/8, f/11, f/16, with each larger number representing an aperture that admits half as much light as the one before. Of course, you can also set *intermediate* apertures, such as f/6.3 and f/7.1, which fall between f/5.6 and f/8.

Shutter speeds are actual fractions (of a second), but the numerator is omitted, so that 60, 125, 250, 500, 1,000, and so forth represent 1/60th, 1/125th, 1/250th, 1/500th, and 1/1000th second. To avoid confusion, Nikon uses quotation marks to signify longer exposures: 2", 2.5", 4", and so forth representing 2.0-, 2.5-, and 4.0-second exposures, respectively.

Equivalent Exposure

Most commonly, exposure settings are made using the aperture and shutter speed, followed by adjusting the ISO sensitivity, if it's not possible to get the preferred exposure (that is, the one that uses the "best" f/stop or shutter speed for the depth-of-field or action stopping we want).

One of the most important aspects in this discussion is the concept of *equivalent exposure*. This term means that exactly the same amount of light will reach the sensor at various combinations of aperture and shutter speed. Whether we use a small aperture (large f/number) with a long shutter speed or a wide aperture (small f/number) with a fast shutter speed, the amount of light reaching the sensor can be exactly the same. Table 2.1 shows equivalent exposure settings using various shutter speeds and f/stops; in other words, any of the combination of settings listed will produce exactly the same exposure.

TABLE 2.1 Equivalent Exposures

SHUTTER SPEED	F/STOP	SHUTTER SPEED	F/STOP
1/30th second	f/22	1/1000th second	f/4
1/60th second	f/16	1/2000th second	f/2.8
1/125th second	f/11	1/4000th second	f/2
1/250th second	f/8	1/8000th second	f/1.4
1/500th second	f/5.6		

When the camera is set for Programmed-auto (P), the metering system selects the correct exposure for you automatically, but you can change quickly to an equivalent exposure by spinning the main command dial until the desired equivalent exposure combination is displayed, with an asterisk appearing next to the P when you're using this "Flexible Program" feature. You can make Flexible Program adjustments more easily if you remember that you need to rotate the command dial toward the left when you want to increase the amount of depth-of-field (DOF) or use a slower shutter speed; rotate to the right when you want to reduce the depth-of-field or use a faster shutter speed. The need for more/less DOF and slower/faster shutter speed are the primary reasons you'd want to use Flexible Program. This program shift mode does not work when you're using flash.

In Aperture-priority (A) and Shutter-priority (S) modes, you can change to an equivalent exposure, but only by either adjusting the aperture with the sub-command dial in A mode (the camera chooses the shutter speed) or shutter speed with the main command dial in S mode (the camera selects the aperture). I'll cover all these exposure modes later in the chapter.

F/STOPS VERSUS STOPS

In photography parlance, *f/stop* always means the aperture or lens opening. However, for lack of a current commonly used word for one exposure increment, the term *stop* is often used. In the past, EV (Exposure Value) served this purpose, and was used as a measure of the total sensitivity range of a device such as a light meter, but exposure value and its abbreviation have since been inextricably intertwined with its use in describing exposure compensation. In this book, when I say "stop" by itself (no *f/*), I mean one whole unit of exposure, and am not necessarily referring to an actual f/stop or lens aperture. So, adjusting the exposure by "one stop" can mean changing to the next shutter speed increment (say, from 1/125th second to 1/250th second) or the next aperture (such as f/4 to f/5.6). Similarly, 1/3-stop or 1/2-stop increments can mean either shutter speed or aperture changes, depending on the context. Be forewarned.

Calculating Exposure

Although it can make some good guesses based on how the brightness levels vary within a scene, your camera has no way of knowing for sure what it's pointed at. So, it must make some assumptions and calculate the correct exposure based on its internal rules. One parameter is that the brightness of all—or part—of a scene will average down to a so-called middle-gray tone. The conventional wisdom is that this tone is roughly 18 percent gray. Unfortunately, while the traditional 18 percent value is a middle gray in terms of what the eye sees, the camera is actually calibrated for a slightly darker tone. This section explains how your camera decides on an exposure in one of its semi-automatic (non-manual) modes.

The exposure is measured using a specific pattern of exposure measuring areas that you can select (more on that later). Exposure is calculated based on the assumption that each area being measured reflects about the same amount of light as a neutral gray card that reflects a "middle" gray of about 12 to 18 percent reflectance. (The photographic "gray cards" you buy at a camera store have an 18 percent gray tone. Your camera is calibrated to interpret a somewhat darker 12 percent gray; I'll explain more about this later, too.) That "average" 12 to 18 percent gray assumption is necessary, because different subjects reflect different amounts of light. In a photo containing, say, a white cat and a dark gray cat, the white cat might reflect five times as much light as the gray cat. An exposure based on the white cat will cause the gray cat to appear to be black, while an exposure based only on the gray cat will make the white cat washed out.

This is more easily understood if you look at some photos of subjects that are dark (they reflect little light), those that have predominantly middle tones, and subjects that are highly reflective. The next few figures show a simplified scale with a middle-gray 18 percent tone, plus black and white patches, along with a human figure (not a cat) to illustrate how different exposure measurements actually do affect an exposure.

Correctly Exposed

The image shown in Figure 2.2, left, represents how a photograph might appear if you inserted the patches shown at the bottom, and then calculated exposure by measuring the light reflecting from the middle-gray patch, which, for the sake of illustration, we'll assume reflects approximately 12 to 18 percent of the light that strikes it. The exposure meter in the camera sees an object that it thinks is a middle gray, calculates an exposure based on that, and the patch in the center of the strip is rendered at its proper tonal value. Best of all, because the resulting exposure is correct, the black patch at left and white patch at right are rendered properly as well.

When you're shooting pictures, and the meter happens to base its exposure on a subject that averages that "ideal" middle gray, then you'll end up with similar (accurate) results. The camera's exposure algorithms are concocted to ensure this kind of result as often as possible, barring any unusual subjects (that is, those that are backlit, or have uneven illumination). The camera has four metering modes, each of which is equipped to handle certain types of unusual subjects, as I'll outline.

Overexposed

At center in Figure 2.2 you can see what would happen if the exposure were calculated based on metering the leftmost, black patch. The light meter sees less light reflecting from the black square than it would see from a gray middle-tone subject, and so figures, "Aha! I need to add exposure to brighten this subject up to a middle gray!" That lightens the "black" patch, so it now appears to be gray.

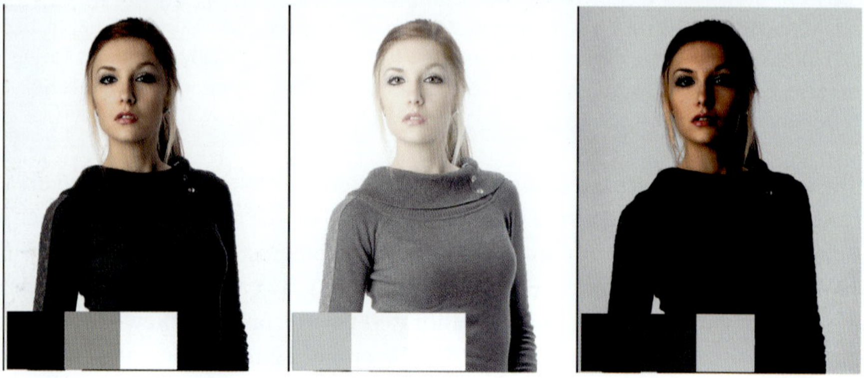

Figure 2.2 1.) Exposure calculated from the middle-gray patch produces a correct exposure for all three patches and the subject. 2.) Exposure measured from the black patch yields an overexposed image. 3.) Exposure calculated from the white patch produces underexposure.

But now the patch in the middle that was *originally* middle gray is overexposed and becomes light gray. And the white square at right is now seriously overexposed and loses detail in the highlights, which have become a featureless white. Our human subject is similarly overexposed.

Underexposed

The third possibility in this simplified scenario is that the light meter might measure the illumination bouncing off the white patch and try to render *that* tone as a middle gray. A lot of light is reflected by the white square, so the exposure is *reduced*, bringing that patch closer to a middle gray tone. The patches that were originally gray and black are now rendered too dark, as you can see at right in Figure 2.2. Clearly, measuring the gray card—or a substitute that reflects about the same amount of light—is the only way to ensure that the exposure is precisely correct.

Metering Mid-Tones

As you can see, the ideal way to measure exposure is to meter from a subject that reflects 12 to 18 percent of the light that reaches it. If you want the most precise exposure calculations, the solution is to use a stand-in. Any mid-tone subject—including green grass or a rich, medium-blue sky—also reflects about 12 to 18 percent of the light. Metering such an area should ensure that the exposure for the entire scene will be correct or close to correct for average subjects.

In some very bright scenes (like a snowy landscape or a lava field), you won't have a mid-tone to meter. Another substitute for a gray card is the palm of a human hand (the backside of the hand is too variable). But a human palm, regardless of ethnic group, is even brighter than a standard gray card, so instead of one-half stop more exposure, you need to add one additional stop. That is, if your meter reading is 1/500th of a second at f/11, use 1/500th second at f/8 or 1/250th second at f/11 instead. (Both exposures are equivalent.)

Or, you might want to resort to using an evenly illuminated gray card mentioned earlier. Small versions are available that can be tucked in a camera bag. Place it in your frame near your main subject, facing the camera, and with the exact same even illumination falling on it that is falling on your subject. Then, use the Spot metering function (described in the next section) to calculate exposure.

ORIGIN OF THE 18 PERCENT "MYTH"

Why are so many photographers under the impression that camera light meters are calibrated to the 18 percent "standard," rather than the true value, which may be 12 to 14 percent, depending on the vendor? You'll find this misinformation in an alarming number of places. I've seen the 18 percent "myth" taught in camera classes; I've found it in books, and even been given this wrong information from the technical staff of camera vendors. (They should know better—the same vendors' engineers who design and calibrate the cameras have the right figure.)

The most common explanation is that during a revision of Kodak's instructions for its gray cards in 1977, the advice to open up an extra half stop was omitted, and a whole generation of shooters grew up thinking that a measurement off a gray card could be used as is. Kodak restored the proviso in 1997, it's said, but by then it was too late.

But the standard Kodak gray card reflects 18 percent of the light while, as I noted, your camera is calibrated for a somewhat darker 12 percent tone. If you insisted on getting a perfect exposure, you would need to add about one-half stop more exposure than the value provided by taking the light meter reading from the card. Of course, in most situations, it's not necessary to do this. Your camera's light meter will do a good job of calculating the right exposure, especially if you use the exposure tips in the next section. But I felt that explaining exactly what is going on during exposure calculation would help you understand how your camera's metering system works.

EXTERNAL METERS CAN BE CALIBRATED

The light meters built into your camera are calibrated at the factory and can only be changed using the Fine-Tune Optimal Exposure option (Custom Setting b6). But if you use a hand-held incident or reflective light meter, you *can* calibrate it, using the instructions supplied with your meter. Because a hand-held meter *can* be calibrated to the 18 percent gray standard (or any other value you choose), my rant about the myth of the 18 percent gray card doesn't apply.

MODES, MODES, AND MORE MODES

Call them modes or methods, the Z9/Z8 seem to have a lot of different sets of options that are described using similar terms. Here's how to sort them out:

- **Metering method.** These modes determine the *parts of the image* within the sensor that are examined in order to calculate exposure. The camera may look at many different points within the image, segregating them by zone (Matrix metering); examining the same number of points, but giving greater weight to those located in the middle of the frame (Center-weighted metering); evaluating only a limited number of points in a limited area (Spot metering); or adjusting exposure to preserve detail in highlights (Highlight-weighted metering).
- **Exposure method.** These modes (Program, Aperture-priority, Shutter-priority, or Manual) determine *which* settings are used to expose the image. The camera may adjust the shutter speed, the aperture, or both, or even ISO setting (if Auto ISO is active), depending on the method you choose.

To meter properly you'll want to choose both the *metering method* (how light is evaluated) and *exposure method* (how the appropriate shutter speeds and apertures are chosen). I'll describe both in the following sections.

Choosing a Metering Method

The camera has four different schemes for evaluating the light received by its exposure sensors: Matrix, Center-weighted, Spot, and Highlight-weighted. Select the mode you want from the *i* menu (or you can assign the metering adjustment function to a custom control using Custom Setting f2, as noted in the sidebar below).

Your camera calculates exposure by measuring the light that passes through the lens and strikes the sensor. These pixels are said to be able to detect light over a range of –3 to +17 EV at ISO 100. That translates into exposures from eight minutes at f/16 to 1/2000th second at f/16.

INSTANT SWITCHING

If you frequently use one metering method, but occasionally like to switch to another method on the fly, you can redefine one of the camera's buttons to shift to your alternate mode with the twirl of a command dial. The button can be programmed to cycle among Matrix metering, Center-weighted metering, Spot metering, or Highlight-weighted metering when a command dial is rotated (as discussed in Chapter 7), using Custom Setting f2.

I've done this as a way to compare the exposure settings of the three metering methods while composing a single image in the viewfinder. I've also found the capability useful when I'm, say, working with Matrix metering and want to zero in on a particular area of the frame temporarily using Spot metering. The indicators in the viewfinder will help you remember what metering mode you've switched to. (See Figure 2.3.)

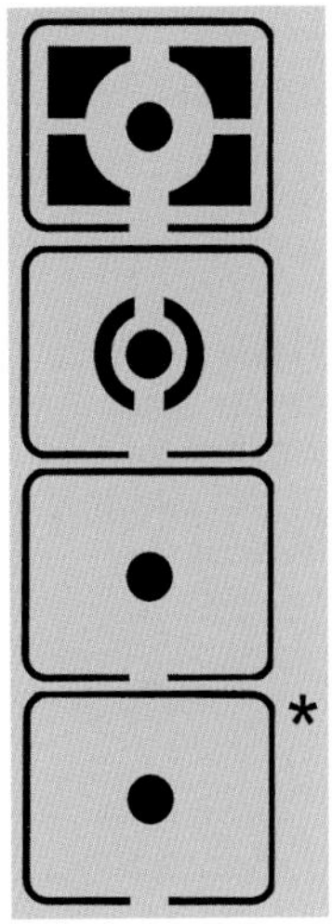

Figure 2.3 Top to bottom: Matrix, Center-weighted, Spot, and Highlight-weighted metering icons.

In everyday terms, 0 EV represents the illumination you might see outdoors at night under a full moon, while the brightest daytime scene you're likely to encounter (a snow scene in full daylight) would be 16 EV. Your camera is able to *detect* photons under an extremely broad EV span—two stops dimmer than full moonlight, and one stop brighter than a daylight snow scene. However, the ability to *capture* images is limited to a much smaller range. Note that the sensor's dynamic range (the tones it can preserve in your final image) is less than the full range of tones it can *detect*. It's easy to get these two separate aspects confused.

Matrix Metering

For Matrix metering mode, the camera reads the light falling on the sensor and compares the brightness of many areas using a matrix array. When Matrix metering is active, an icon indicator appears in the photo information screen, which you can summon by pressing the DISP button until it's shown. Then, the camera evaluates the differences between the many zones, and compares them with a built-in database representing actual images, to make an educated guess about what kind of picture you're taking. For example, if the top sections of a picture are much lighter than the bottom portions, the algorithm can assume that the scene is a landscape photo with lots of sky. However, if there is a lighter area in the center of the frame, and the camera detects skin tones, it will assume that you're shooting a portrait and not a landscape photo and expose for the human subject. A typical image suitable for Matrix metering is shown at top in Figure 2.4.

NOTE The Matrix Metering icon is shown at upper left in Figure 2.4, for reference; it does not appear overlaid on your image or in the viewfinder/monitor display! In addition, the light-gray boxes at left in this figure represent the autofocus zones for the Z9 and Z8.

Matrix metering mode can often recognize many types of bright scenes and automatically increase the exposure to reduce the risk of a dark photo. This will be useful when your subject is a snow-covered landscape or a close-up of a bride in white. Granted, you may occasionally need to use a bit of exposure compensation, but often, the exposure will be close to accurate even without it. In my experience, Matrix metering is most successful with light-toned scenes on bright days and is especially good when humans are in the frame. When shooting in dark, overcast conditions, it's more likely to underexpose a scene of that type.

Exposure meters have long used brightness to calculate correct exposure. The advanced exposure technology uses other information to make more intelligent settings.

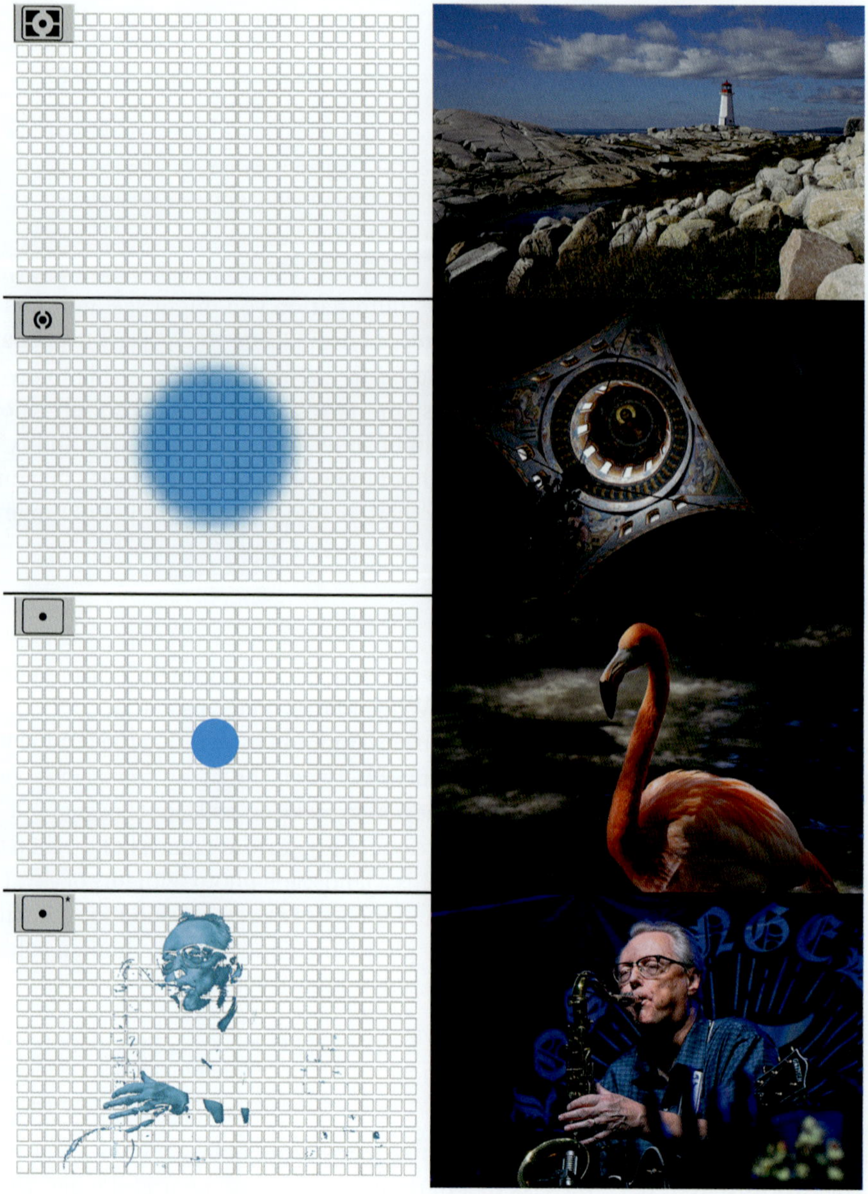

Figure 2.4 Top to bottom: Matrix, Center-weighted, Spot, and Highlight-weighted metering.

These factors include:

- **Patterns.** As mentioned earlier, the camera compares exposure across the entire sensor with a database of tens of thousands of picture types, looking for differences among pixels, and similarities to images in the database. When it finds a match, it uses that information as a basis for its recommended exposure. If the contrast in a scene is high enough that the sensor probably won't be able to preserve detail in both highlights and shadows, in most cases, the camera will favor the highlights. As you'll learn later in this chapter, once highlights are lost, they are gone forever, but it is sometimes possible to retrieve data in shadow areas. If you are shooting RAW, the exposure setting and other adjustments can often boost information in darker areas.
- **Faces.** By default, the Z9 and Z8 adjust their matrix metering calculations when a face is detected within the frame, and will optimize exposure to provide the best rendition of faces, even if the result is an improperly exposed background. You can partially disable this bias by disabling Custom Setting b4 (Matrix Metering Face Detection), but the camera will still use face tones within the frame to set exposure.
- **Colors.** The camera can enhance its readings based on the colors detected in the frame. Large areas of blue in the upper part of the image can be deemed to be sky; greens can be reasonably assumed to be foliage, and the presence of skin tones readily indicate human beings.
- **Autofocus area.** Whether you or the camera selects which autofocus zone is used, the exposure system assumes, logically, that the part of the image that is in focus contains your subject matter.
- **Distance and focal length.** The distance and focal length supplied by your Z-mount lenses is used to better calculate what kind of scene you have framed. For example, if you're shooting a portrait with a longer focal-length lens focused to about 5 to 12 feet from the camera, and the upper half of the scene is very bright, the camera assumes you would prefer to meter for the rest of the image and will discount the bright area. However, if a wide-angle lens is attached and focused at infinity, the camera can assume you're taking a landscape photo and take the bright upper area into account to produce better-looking sky and clouds.

Matrix metering is best for most general subjects, because it is able to intelligently analyze a scene and make an excellent guess of what kind of subject you're shooting a great deal of the time. The camera can tell the difference between low-contrast and high-contrast subjects by looking at the range of differences in brightness across the scene. Because the camera has a fairly good idea about what kind of subject matter you are shooting, it can underexpose slightly when appropriate to preserve highlight detail when image contrast is high. (It's often possible to pull detail out of shadows that are too dark using an image editor, but once highlights are converted to white pixels, they are gone forever.)

CAUTION If you're using a strong filter, including a polarizing filter, split-color filter, or neutral-density filter (particularly a graduated neutral-density filter), you should switch from Matrix metering to Center-weighted, because the filter can affect the relationships between the different areas of the frame used to calculate a Matrix exposure. For example, a polarizing filter produces a sky that is darker than usual, hindering the Matrix algorithm's recognition of a landscape photo. Extra-dark or colored filters disturb the color relationships used for color Matrix metering, too.

Center-weighted Metering

In this mode, the exposure meter emphasizes a zone measuring 12mm in the center of the frame to calculate exposure. This type of metering was the only available option some decades ago, and was considered an upgrade from averaging, which simply based exposure on an average of the illumination of the entire frame.

With Center-weighted metering, you end up with conventional metering without any "intelligent" scene evaluation. (See Figure 2.4, second from the top.) The light meter considers brightness in the entire frame but places the greatest emphasis on a large area in the center of the frame (shown in blue), on the theory that, for most pictures, the main subject will not be located far off-center.

About 75 percent of the exposure is based on the selected 12mm central area, and the remaining 25 percent of the exposure is based on the rest of the frame. So, if the camera reads the center portion and determines that the exposure for that region should be f/4 at 1/250th second, while the outer area, which is a bit darker, calls for f/16 at 1/250th second, it will give the center portion the most weight and arrive at a final exposure on the order of f/5.6 at 1/250th second.

Of course, Center-weighted metering is most effective when the subject in the central area is a midtone. Even then, if your main subject is surrounded by large, extremely bright or very dark areas, the exposure might not be exactly right. (You might need to use exposure compensation, a feature discussed shortly.) However, this scheme works well in many situations if you don't want to use one of the other modes, for scenes like the one shown in the figure. This mode can be useful for close-ups of subjects like flowers, or for portraits. You can adjust the size of the area assigned the greatest weight using Custom Setting b5, as described in Chapter 7.

Your choices include Small (with an 8mm circle), Standard (the default, with a 12mm circle), and Average, which is the same as the old-time full-frame averaging systems. By default, the camera will show a translucent gray circle in the display that represents the size of the center-weighted area in display configurations 1–3 (which cycle through when you press the DISP button). You can disable/enable the circle using the Custom Monitor/Viewfinder Shooting Display entries: d19/d20 for the Z9 and d17/d18 for the Z8.

Spot Metering

Spot metering is favored by those of us who have used a hand-held light meter to measure exposure at various points (such as metering highlights and shadows separately). However, you can use Spot metering in any situation where you want to individually measure the light reflecting from light, midtone, or dark areas of your subject—or any combination of areas. This mode is useful if you have the time to make careful measurements and calculate your exposure based on them. Note that Spot metering is not available in Video Recording mode; Matrix metering will be used instead.

This mode confines the reading to a limited 4mm area in the viewfinder, making up only 1.5 percent of the image, as shown by the blue circle in Figure 2.4 (third set down from the top). The circle is centered on the *current focus point* (which can be *any* of the available focus points, *not* just the center one shown in the figure), *but is larger than the focus point*, so don't fall into the trap of believing that exposure is being measured only within the viewfinder indicators that represent the active focus point. This is the only metering method you can use to specify exactly where to measure exposure within the frame. However, if you have selected Auto-area AF, only the center focus point is used to spot meter.

You'll find Spot metering useful when you want to base exposure on a small area in the frame. If that area is in the center of the frame, so much the better. If not, you'll have to make your meter reading for an off-center subject using an appropriate focus point, and then lock exposure by pressing the shutter release halfway, or by pressing the center of the sub-selector. This mode is best for subjects where the background is significantly brighter or darker.

If you Spot meter a very light-toned area or a dark-toned area, you will get underexposure or overexposure respectively; you would need to use an override for more accurate results. On the other hand, you can Spot meter a small mid-tone subject surrounded by a sky with big white clouds or by an indigo blue wall and get a good exposure. (The light meter ignores the subject's surroundings, so they do not affect the exposure setting.) That would not be possible with Center-weighted metering, which considers brightness in a much larger area.

Using Spot Metering

Matrix and Center-weighted metering basically have few options to worry about. They are both affected by exposure compensation changes and Custom Setting b6: Fine-Tune Optimal Exposure adjustments. Spot metering, on the other hand, can benefit from your input in selecting the spot used. Here are some considerations to keep in mind:

- **Moving the spot.** Remember that you don't move the metering spot itself; the current *focus* spot is used. So, you must be using an AF-area mode that allows changing the AF spot, which happens to be any of the AF-area modes *except* Auto-area AF. In that mode, the center focus point is *always* used as the metering spot, and you cannot change it.
- **Choosing a compatible AF-area mode.** Hold down the Focus mode button and rotate the sub-command dial to change AF-area modes. You can also use the *i* menu to cycle among the AF areas. The modes available differ depending on the focus mode you've chosen. All these AF-area modes will allow you to switch the AF point to any of the available focus areas in the display:
    - **AF-S focus mode:** Pinpoint AF, Single-point AF, Wide-area AF (Small, Large, C1, C2).
    - **AF-C focus mode:** Single-point AF, Dynamic-area AF [Small, Medium, Large], Wide-area AF (Small, Large, C1, C2), 3D-tracking.
    - **Manual focus mode:** Only Single-point selection is available. **Note:** With manual focus, the camera does not autofocus, of course; the position of the focus point is used only for the electronic rangefinder and Spot metering functions. You can find information on all the focus and AF-area modes in Chapter 3.

- **Wrap around.** You'll use the sub-selector or the multi selector's directional buttons to move the AF point around within the display—and the metering spot with it. The focus point's movement will stop at the left/right/top/bottom edges *unless* you've turned on focus point wrap-around in Custom Setting a10.
- **When using Auto-area AF.** If you've selected Auto-area AF, the center focus point will always be used—*even if the camera selects a different point for the autofocus function*. That's actually a positive: since in Auto-area AF mode you don't know what the focus spot will be until you press the shutter release halfway, it's *good* to know that the camera will be using the center spot. While Spot metering is most useful when not using Auto-area AF, it still functions, albeit in a less flexible way.
- **Reminder: when the focus point moves, the spot metering point moves, too.** If you're using Dynamic-area AF and continuous autofocus (AF-C, described in Chapter 3), the camera may move the focus point you originally selected and base focus on the surrounding focus points. *The metering area will tag along.*

A good example of a scene where you might want to use Spot metering is shown in Figure 2.4, third from the top, which shows a flamingo amidst a very dark background. The illumination might have fooled both Matrix and Center-weighted metering (although Center-weighted might have come close), but Spot metering allowed taking a reading directly from the bird's plumage. While I preferred Spot metering in this case, another option might have been Highlight-weighted metering, described next.

Highlight-weighted Metering

In this metering mode, the exposure system examines your entire scene, just as it does using Matrix metering. It is *not* a spot metering mode, despite its icon, which is the same as the Spot icon, with an asterisk added. With this mode, the dual Expeed 7 processors seek out non-specular highlight areas of your image and base exposure on a setting that will keep those highlights from being overexposed. Less emphasis ("weight") is given to non-highlight areas. That's why Highlight-weighted *might* have worked for the flamingo image, but it's actually better suited for images in which the highlights are spread over a larger area of the frame. This metering mode does not use the current focus point as the base point for its calculations.

So, if you're shooting spotlit performers on-stage at a concert or play, the camera is able to calculate the correct exposure using the performers, and ignoring, for the most part, the dark surroundings. You'd have your choice of measuring exposure in Spot mode, as described in the previous section, placing the metering spot on the dancer's face or shirt, or, you could select Highlight-weighted metering and allow the camera to identify the performer when figuring exposure. Your results might be similar with either, depending on how well you "placed" the Spot area and how cleverly the system sorts out your subject from the background. I tend to use Spot metering when the area I want to meter is clearly defined and Highlight-weighted metering when there is a range of highlights that I'd like to preserve, as in the photo of Billy Zoom, from the LA punk band X, shown in Figure 2.4, bottom.

LOCKING EXPOSURE

An important tool when using any metering method is the ability to *lock* exposure once you've set shutter speed, aperture, and ISO to your satisfaction, allowing you to reframe your image before taking a picture. The default behavior of the sub-selector center button is AE-L/AF-L, which locks both exposure and autofocus. However, you can define another control, such as the AF-ON button, for that function using Custom Setting f2: Custom Controls, described in Chapter 7.

Your defined control can be set to function as an AE/AF lock, or AE Lock Only (which is useful if you're using back-button focus, described in the next chapter). The same custom setting can also be used to define a Shutter Speed and Aperture Lock button, which effectively locks exposure by freezing the shutter speed in Aperture-priority mode and aperture in Shutter-priority mode.

Choosing an Exposure Method

You'll find four methods for choosing the appropriate shutter speed and aperture when using the semi-automatic/manual modes. You can choose among Aperture-priority, Shutter-priority, Program, or Manual options by pressing the MODE button on the top-left shoulder of the camera and rotating the main command dial. Your decision on which is best for a given shooting situation will depend on things like your need for lots of (or less) depth-of-field, a desire to freeze action or allow motion blur, or how much noise you find acceptable in an image. Each of the exposure methods emphasizes one aspect of image capture or another. This section introduces you to all four.

Aperture-Priority

In Aperture-priority (A) mode, you specify the lens opening used, and the camera will set a suitable shutter speed appropriate for the aperture and the ISO sensitivity in use. If you change the aperture, from f/5.6 to f/11, for example, the camera will automatically set a longer shutter speed to maintain the same exposure, using guidance from the built-in light meter. (I discussed the concept of equivalent exposure earlier in this chapter and provided the equivalent exposure settings in Table 2.1.)

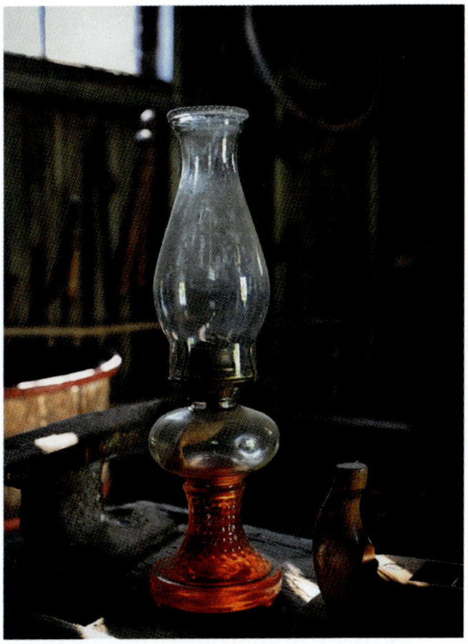

Figure 2.5 Use Aperture-priority to "lock in" a large f/stop when you want to blur distracting elements, or emphasize the main subject in the photo, in this case an antique lantern.

Aperture-priority is especially good when you want to use a particular lens opening to achieve a desired effect. Perhaps you'd like to use the smallest f/stop possible (such as f/22) to maximize depth-of-field (DOF) in a close-up picture. Or, you might want to work with a large f/stop to throw everything except your main subject out of focus, as in Figure 2.5. Maybe you'd just like to "lock in" a particular f/stop because it's the sharpest available aperture with that lens. Or, you might prefer to use, say, f/2.8 on a lens with a maximum aperture of f/1.4, because you want the best compromise between shutter speed and sharpness.

Aperture-priority can even be used to specify a *range* of shutter speeds you want to use under varying lighting conditions, which seems almost contradictory. But think about it. You're shooting a soccer game outdoors with a telephoto lens and want a relatively high shutter speed, but you don't care if the speed changes a little should the sun duck behind a cloud. Set your exposure method to A, and adjust the aperture until a shutter speed of, say, 1/1000th second is selected at your current ISO setting. (In bright sunlight at ISO 400, that aperture is likely to be around f/11.) Then, go ahead and shoot, knowing that your camera will maintain that f/11 aperture (for sufficient depth-of-field as the soccer players move about the field), but will drop down to 1/750th or 1/500th second if necessary, should the lighting change a little.

When the shutter speed indicator in the viewfinder and the top-panel monochrome control panel blink, that indicates that selecting an appropriate shutter speed at the selected aperture is not possible, and that over- and underexposure will occur at the current ISO setting. That's the major pitfall of using Aperture-priority: you might select an f/stop that is too small or too large to allow an optimal exposure with the available shutter speeds. For example, if you choose f/2.8 as your aperture and the illumination is quite bright (say, at the beach or in snow), even your camera's fastest shutter speed might not be able to cut down the amount of light reaching the sensor to provide the right exposure. Or, if you select f/8 in a dimly lit room, you might find yourself shooting with a very slow shutter speed that can cause blurring from subject movement or camera shake. Aperture-priority is best used by those with a bit of experience in choosing settings. Many seasoned photographers leave their camera set on A all the time. The exposure indicator scale in the control panel and viewfinder indicate the amount of under- or overexposure.

When to use Aperture-priority:

- **General landscape photography.** The Z9 and Z8, in particular, are great cameras for landscape photography, of course, because its high resolution allows making huge, gorgeous prints, as well as smaller prints that are filled with eye-popping detail. Aperture-priority is a good tool for ensuring that your landscape is sharp from foreground to infinity, if you select an f/stop that provides maximum depth-of-field, as shown in Figure 2.6.

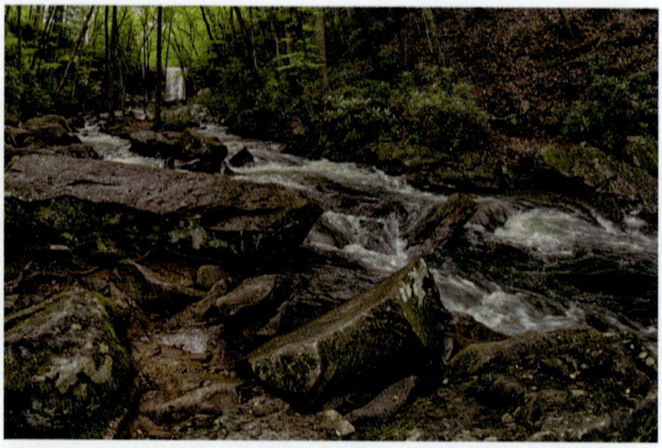

Figure 2.6 Extra depth-of-field came in handy when shooting Cucumber Falls in Ohiopyle, Pennsylvania.

  If you use Aperture-priority mode and select an aperture like f/11 or f/16, it's your responsibility to make sure the shutter speed selected is fast enough to avoid losing detail to camera shake, or that the camera is mounted on a tripod. One thing that new landscape photographers fail to account for is the movement of distant leaves and tree branches. When seeking the ultimate in sharpness, go ahead and use Aperture-priority, but boost ISO sensitivity a bit, if necessary, to provide a sufficiently fast shutter speed, whether shooting hand-held or with a tripod.

- **Specific landscape situations.** Aperture-priority is also useful when you have no objection to using a long shutter speed, or, particularly, *want* the camera to select one. Waterfalls are a perfect example. You can use Aperture-priority mode, set your camera to ISO 100, use a small f/stop, and let the exposure system select a longer shutter speed that will allow the water to blur as it flows. Indeed, you might need to use a neutral-density filter to get a sufficiently long shutter speed. But Aperture-priority mode is a good start.
- **Portrait photography.** Portraits are the most common applications of selective focus. A medium-large aperture (say, f/5.6 or f/8) with a longer lens/zoom setting (in the 85mm to 135mm range) will allow the background behind your portrait subject to blur. A *very* large aperture (I frequently shoot wide open with my Nikkor Z 85mm f/1.8 S lens) lets you apply selective focus to your subject's *face.* With a three-quarters view of your subject, as long as his or her eyes are sharp, it's okay if the far ear or her hair is out of focus.
- **When you want to ensure optimal sharpness.** All lenses have an aperture or two at which they perform best, providing the level of sharpness you expect to find. That's usually about two stops down from wide open, and thus will vary depending on the maximum aperture of the lens.
- **Close-up/Macro photography.** Depth-of-field is typically very shallow when shooting macro photos, and you'll want to choose your f/stop carefully. Perhaps you might want to use a wider stop to emphasize your subject. Or, you might need the smallest aperture you can get away with to maximize depth-of-field. Aperture-priority mode comes in very useful when shooting close-up pictures, too. Because macro work is frequently done with the camera mounted on a tripod, and your close-up subjects, if not living creatures, may not be moving much, a longer shutter speed isn't a problem. Aperture-priority can be your preferred choice.

Shutter-Priority

Shutter-priority (S) is the inverse of Aperture-priority: you choose the shutter speed you'd like to use, and the metering system selects the appropriate f/stop. Perhaps you're shooting action photos and you want to use the absolute fastest shutter speed available; in other cases, you might want to use a slow shutter speed to add some blur to an action photo that would be mundane if the action were completely frozen. Shutter-priority mode gives you some control over how much action-freezing capability your digital camera brings to bear in a particular situation.

Take care when using a slow shutter speed such as 1/8th second or slower, because you'll get blurring from camera shake unless you're using vibration reduction or have mounted the camera on a tripod or other firm support. Very high shutter speeds (the maximum is 1/32000th second!) require a lot of light.

You'll also encounter the same problem as with Aperture-priority when you select a shutter speed that's too long or too short for correct exposure under some conditions. As in Aperture-priority mode, it's possible to choose an inappropriate shutter speed. If that's the case, the shutter speed indicator in the viewfinder and control panel LCD will blink.

When to use Shutter-priority:

- **To reduce blur from subject motion.** Set the shutter speed to a higher value to reduce the amount of blur from subjects that are moving. The exact speed will vary depending on how fast your subject is moving and how much blur is acceptable. You might want to freeze a basketball player in mid-dunk with a 1/1000th-second shutter speed or use 1/200th second to allow the spinning wheels of a motocross racer to blur a tiny bit to add the feeling of motion.
- **To add blur from subject motion.** There are times when you want a subject to blur, say, when shooting waterfalls with a one- or two-second exposure in Shutter-priority mode.
- **To add blur from camera motion when *you* are moving.** Say you're panning to follow a pair of relay runners. You might want to use Shutter-priority mode and set a 1/60th-second shutter speed, so that the background will blur as you pan with the runners. The shutter speed will be fast enough to provide a sharp image of the athletes, while reducing their distracting background to a blur. For Figure 2.7, I was panning to follow the relay runner, and shot at 1/30th second to allow the background to blur.

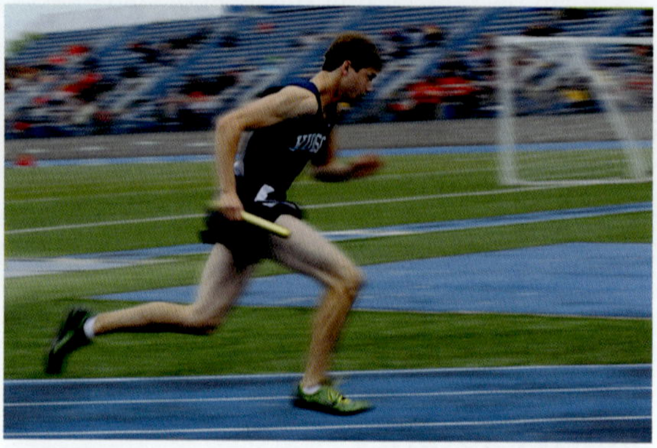

Figure 2.7 Shutter-priority allows you to specify a speed that will render a moving subject like this relay runner reasonably sharp as you pan.

- **To reduce blur from camera motion when *you* are moving.** In other situations, the camera may be in motion, say, because you're shooting from a moving train or auto, and you want to minimize the amount of blur caused by the motion of the camera. Shutter-priority is a good choice here, too.
- **Landscape photography hand-held.** If you can't use a tripod for your landscape shots, you'll still probably want the sharpest image possible, especially when shooting a scene in which gusts of wind may cause foliage to flutter. Shutter-priority can allow you to specify a shutter speed that's fast enough to reduce or eliminate the effects of camera shake. Just make sure that your ISO setting is high enough that the camera will select an aperture with sufficient depth-of-field, too.
- **Concerts and stage performances.** I shoot a lot of concerts with my 70-200mm f/2.8 lens and have discovered that, when vibration reduction is taken into account, a shutter speed of 1/180th second is fast enough—along with vibration reduction—to eliminate camera shake that can result from hand-holding the camera with this lens, and also to avoid blur from the movement of all but the most energetic performers. I use Shutter-priority and set the ISO so the camera will select an aperture in the f/4-5.6 range.

Programmed Auto Mode

Program mode (P) uses the camera's built-in smarts to select the correct f/stop and shutter speed using a database of picture information that tells it which combination of shutter speed and aperture will work best for a particular photo. If the correct exposure cannot be achieved at the current ISO setting, the shutter speed and aperture will blink in the viewfinder and control panel. You can then boost or reduce the ISO to increase or decrease sensitivity.

The recommended exposure can be overridden if you want. Use the EV (exposure value) setting feature to add or subtract exposure from the metered value. And, as I mentioned earlier in this chapter, in Program mode you can rotate the main command dial to change from the recommended setting to an equivalent setting (as shown previously in Table 2.1) that produces the same exposure but using a different combination of f/stop and shutter speed.

This is called "Flexible Program" by Nikon. Rotate the main command dial left to reduce the size of the aperture (going from, say, f/4 to f/5.6), so that the camera will automatically use a slower shutter speed (going from, say, 1/250th second to 1/125th second). Rotate the main command dial right to use a larger f/stop, while automatically producing a shorter shutter speed that provides the same equivalent exposure as metered in P mode. An asterisk appears next to the P in the viewfinder/monitor display, so you'll know you've overridden the default program setting. Your adjustment remains in force until you rotate the main command dial until the asterisk disappears, or you switch to a different exposure mode, or turn the camera off.

MAKING EV CHANGES

Sometimes you'll want more or less exposure than indicated by the metering system. Perhaps you want to underexpose to create a silhouette effect or overexpose to produce a high-key look. It's easy to use the camera's exposure compensation system to override the exposure recommendations. Press the exposure compensation (EV) button on the top panel (just southeast of the shutter release). Then rotate the main command dial left to add exposure, and right to subtract exposure. The EV change you've made remains for the exposures that follow, until you manually zero out the EV setting. The EV plus/minus icon appears in the viewfinder and control panel to warn you that an exposure compensation change has been entered. You can increase or decrease exposure over a range of plus or minus five stops. (If you've activated Easy Exposure Compensation using Custom Setting b3, as described in Chapter 7, you don't have to hold down the EV button; rotating the main or sub-command dials alone changes the EV value when using Program, Aperture-priority, Shutter-priority, or Manual exposure modes.)

When to use Program mode:

- **When you're in a hurry to get a grab shot.** The camera will do a pretty good job of calculating an appropriate exposure for you, without any input from you.
- **When you hand your camera to a novice.** Set the camera to P, hand the camera to your friend, relative, or *trustworthy* stranger you meet in front of the Eiffel Tower, point to the shutter-release button and viewfinder, and say, "Look through here, and press this button."
- **When no special shutter speed or aperture settings are needed.** If your subject doesn't require special anti- or pro-blur techniques, and depth-of-field or selective focus aren't important, use P as a general-purpose setting. You can still make adjustments to increase/decrease depth-of-field or add/reduce motion blur with a minimum of fuss.

Manual Exposure

Part of being an experienced photographer comes from knowing when to rely on your camera's automation (with P mode), when to go semi-automatic (with S or A), and when to set exposure manually (using M). Some photographers actually prefer to set their exposure manually, as the camera will be happy to provide an indication of when its metering system judges your manual settings provide the proper exposure, using the analog exposure scale at the bottom of the viewfinder.

Manual exposure can come in handy in some situations. You might be taking a silhouette photo and find that none of the exposure modes or exposure compensation features give you exactly the effect you want. Set the exposure manually to use the exact shutter speed and f/stop you need. Or, you might be working in a studio environment using multiple flash units. The additional flash units are triggered by receiver devices (gadgets that set off the flash when they sense the light from another flash unit, or, perhaps from a radio or infrared remote control). Your exposure meter doesn't compensate for the extra illumination, so you need to set the aperture manually.

Because, depending on your proclivities, you might not need to set exposure manually very often, you should still make sure you understand how it works. Fortunately, the camera makes setting exposure manually very easy. Just press the MODE button and rotate the main command dial to change to Manual mode, and then turn the main command dial to set the shutter speed, and the sub-command dial to adjust the aperture. Press the shutter release halfway or press your defined AE lock button, and the exposure scale in the viewfinder shows you how far your chosen setting diverges from the metered exposure.

METERING WITH OLDER LENSES

You may use the FTZ adapter to mount older lenses that lack the CPU chip that tells the Nikon camera what kind of lens is mounted. These lenses can still be used with Aperture-priority and Manual exposure modes only, assuming you've entered the Non-CPU Lens Data in the Setup menu, as described in Chapter 9. If the camera knows the maximum aperture of the lens, you can set the aperture using the lens's aperture ring, and, in Aperture-priority mode, it will automatically select an appropriate shutter speed. In Manual mode, you can set the aperture, and the analog exposure scale in the viewfinder will indicate when you've set the correct shutter speed manually.

When to use Manual exposure:

- **When working in the studio.** If you're working in a studio environment, you generally have total control over the lighting and can set exposure exactly as you want. The last thing you need is for the camera to interpret the scene and make adjustments of its own. Use M, and shutter speed, aperture, and (as long as you don't use ISO Auto) the ISO setting are totally up to you.
- **When using non-dedicated flash.** The Nikon Creative Lighting System (CLS) and the new Advanced Wireless Lighting (introduced with the SB-5000 Speedlight) are cool, and can even be used to coordinate use of your camera with external compatible dedicated flash units, like the SB-5000 or SB-910. But if you're working with non-CLS flash units, particularly studio flash plugged into the PC/X flash terminal found on the Z9 (or an AS-15 Sync Terminal adapter attached to the

Z8's hot shoe), the camera has no clue about the intensity of the flash, so you'll have to dial in the appropriate aperture manually.

- **If you're using a hand-held light meter.** The appropriate aperture, both for flash exposures and shots taken under continuous lighting, can be determined by a hand-held light meter, flash meter, or combo meter that measures both kinds of illumination. With an external meter, you can measure highlights, shadows, backgrounds, or additional subjects separately, and use Manual exposure to make your settings.
- **When you want to outsmart the metering system.** Your metering system is "trained" to react to unusual lighting situations, such as backlighting, extra-bright illumination, or low-key images with murky shadows. In many cases, it can counter these "problems" and produce a well-exposed image. But what if you don't *want* a well-exposed image? Manual exposure allows you to produce silhouettes in backlit situations, wash out all the middle tones to produce a luminous look, or underexpose to create a moody or ominous dark-toned photograph.
- **When you want to select shutter speed and aperture.** Aperture- and Shutter-priority give you auto-exposure while allowing you to lock in a preferred shutter speed or aperture—but not both at the same time. Manual exposure makes it possible to specify both and *retain* autoexposure capabilities. All you have to do is activate ISO Auto. The camera will keep the shutter speed and aperture you want but raise or lower the sensitivity setting to provide an appropriate exposure.
- **When you want extra-long exposures.** None of the semi-automatic modes will give you an exposure longer than 30 seconds. In Manual mode, however, you can spin the command dial past 30 seconds to Time or Bulb and achieve exposures as long as you want. For example, I used a three-minute exposure (and an Aurora Aperture PowerND 16-stop neutral-density filter) to capture a Great Lakes shore scene. (See Figure 2.8.) The extended exposure feature, which allows timed shots of up to 900 seconds in Manual exposure mode makes long exposures like this easier and more precise.

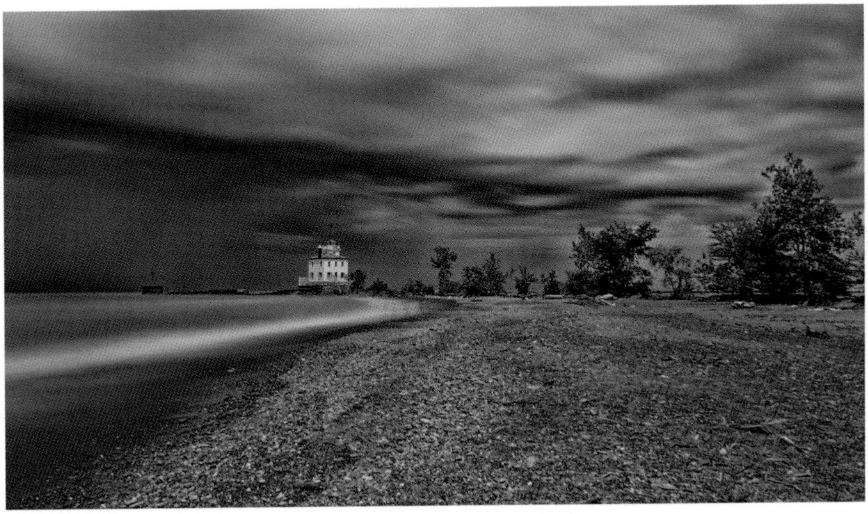

Figure 2.8 A three-minute exposure (using a neutral-density filter) yielded this unusual shot.

Adjusting Exposure with ISO Settings

As I mentioned above, another way of adjusting exposures is by changing the ISO sensitivity setting. Sometimes photographers forget about this option, because the common practice is to set the ISO once for a particular shooting session (say, at ISO 200 for bright sunlight outdoors, or ISO 800 when shooting indoors) and then forget about it. ISOs higher than ISO 200 or 400 are seen as "bad" or "necessary evils." However, changing the ISO is a valid way of adjusting exposure settings, particularly with cameras like the Z9/Z8, which produce good results at ISO settings that create grainy, unusable pictures with some other models.

Indeed, I find myself using ISO adjustment as a convenient alternate way of adding or subtracting EV (Exposure Value—another way of representing one stop of exposure) when shooting in Manual mode, and as a quick way of choosing equivalent exposures when in Program or Shutter-priority or Aperture-priority modes. For example, I've selected a Manual exposure with both f/stop and shutter speed suitable for my image using, say, ISO 200. I can change the exposure in 1/3-stop increments by holding down the ISO button located on the top-right shoulder of the camera, and spinning the main command dial one click at a time. The difference in image quality/noise at ISO 200 is negligible if I dial in ISO 160 or ISO 125 to reduce exposure a little or change to ISO 250 or 320 to increase exposure. I keep my preferred f/stop and shutter speed, but still adjust the exposure. (And, as I noted earlier, if ISO Auto is active, I can even allow the camera to set the exposure automatically using the f/stop and shutter speed I want.)

Or, perhaps, I am using Shutter-priority mode and the metered exposure at ISO 200 is 1/500th second at f/11. If I decide on the spur of the moment I'd rather use 1/500th second at f/8, I can press the ISO button and spin the main command dial to switch to ISO 100. Of course, it's a good idea to monitor your ISO changes, so you don't end up at ISO 6400 accidentally. An ISO indicator appears in the control panel and in the viewfinder to remind you what sensitivity setting has been dialed in.

ISO settings can, of course, also be used to boost or reduce sensitivity in particular shooting situations. The Z9/Z8 have basic ISO settings from ISO 64 to ISO 25600, plus "extended" Lo settings down to Lo 1 (ISO 32 equivalent) and Hi settings up to Hi 2 (ISO 102400 equivalent). Both cameras can also adjust the ISO automatically as appropriate for various lighting conditions. When you choose the Auto ISO sensitivity settings (Auto ISO) in the Photo Shooting menu, as described in Chapter 11, the camera adjusts the sensitivity dynamically to suit the subject matter, based on minimum shutter speed and ISO limits you have prescribed. You should use Auto ISO cautiously if you don't want the camera to use an ISO higher than you might otherwise have selected.

Fortunately, the camera includes several useful wrinkles in its Auto ISO arsenal. You can set limits, specifying both a *maximum sensitivity* (for both ambient exposures and flash) and a *minimum* shutter speed. If Auto ISO is active (it will be indicated in the viewfinder, control panel, and photo information display on the monitor), the camera will never select an ISO you deem to be too high. Moreover, if your exposure will result in a speed slower than the minimum you set (thereby risking blur from subject motion and/or camera movement), the camera will switch to a higher ISO setting to allow using the minimum shutter speed or faster.

However, as I'll explain in Chapter 5, buried in the Photo Shooting menu within the Minimum Shutter Speed option in the Auto ISO sensitivity settings is an additional Auto setting that allows you to specify how quickly the camera reacts to counter that longer shutter speed. Select Slower, and the camera will delay raising the ISO (useful if you want to keep a constant shutter speed, even if slow, to maintain a consistent "look" in a series of photos). Choose Faster, and the camera responds more quickly to reduce the possibility of image blur. Nikon has given enthusiast photographers a useful tool that allows you to fine-tune your camera's behavior, so it works the way you want it to in a wider variety of circumstances.

Dealing with Noise

Visual image noise is that random grainy effect that some like to use as a special effect, but which, most of the time, is objectionable because it robs your image of detail even as it adds that "interesting" texture. Noise is caused by two different phenomena: high ISO settings and long exposures.

High ISO noise commonly appears as you increase your camera's ISO setting, which causes the camera to amplify the base signal (captured at ISO 64). One improvement seen in the camera is the inclusion of a *dual gain signal* amplifier, which provides improved results at higher ISO settings, and, uncommonly, allows retaining top contrast and image quality even when you drop into the sub-base range, down to Lo 1 (ISO 32 equivalent).

In the other direction, you can easily capture relatively low-noise images at ISO 800 and above. However, some noise may become visible at ISO 1600, and is often fairly noticeable at ISO 6400. At ISO 25800 and above, noise is often quite bothersome, although I have used ISO 25600 when photographing subjects that are fairly low in contrast. Nikon tips you off that settings higher than ISO 25600 may be tools used in special circumstances only by labeling them Hi 0.3 through Hi 2. You can expect noise and increase in contrast in any pictures taken at these lofty ratings.

High ISO noise appears as a result of the amplification needed to increase the sensitivity of the sensor. While higher ISOs do pull details out of dark areas, they also amplify non-signal information randomly, creating noise. You'll find a High ISO NR choice in the Photo Shooting menu, where you can specify High, Normal, or Low noise reduction, or turn the feature off entirely. Because noise reduction tends to soften the grainy look while robbing an image of detail, you may want to disable the feature if you're willing to accept a little noise in exchange for more details.

A similar noisy phenomenon occurs during long time exposures, which allow more photons to reach the sensor, increasing your ability to capture a picture under low-light conditions. However, the longer exposures also increase the likelihood that some pixels will register random phantom photons, often because the longer an imager is "hot," the warmer it gets, and that heat can be mistaken for photons. There's also a special kind of noise that CMOS sensors like the ones used in the Z9 and Z8 are potentially susceptible to. CMOS imagers contain millions of individual amplifiers and A/D converters, all working in unison. Because these circuits don't necessarily all process in precisely the same way all the time, they can introduce something called fixed-pattern noise into the image data.

Fortunately, Nikon's electronics geniuses have done an exceptional job minimizing noise from all causes in the camera. Even so, you might still want to apply the optional long exposure noise reduction that can be activated using Long Exp. NR in the Photo Shooting menu, where the feature can be turned On or Off. This type of noise reduction involves the camera taking a second, blank exposure, and comparing the random pixels in that image with the photograph you just took. Pixels that coincide in the two represent noise and can safely be suppressed. This noise reduction system, called *dark frame subtraction,* effectively doubles the amount of time required to take a picture, and is used only for exposures longer than one second. Noise reduction can reduce the amount of detail in your picture, as some image information may be removed along with the noise. So, you might want to use this feature with moderation.

You can also apply noise reduction to a lesser extent using Photoshop, and when converting RAW files to some other format, using your favorite RAW converter, or an industrial-strength product like Noise Ninja (www.picturecode.com) to wipe out noise after you've already taken the picture.

Bracketing

Bracketing is a method for shooting several consecutive exposures using different settings, as a way of improving the odds that one will be exactly right. Alternatively, bracketing can be used to create a series of photos with slightly different exposures (or white balances) in anticipation that one of the exposures will be "better" from a creative standpoint. For example, bracketing can supply you with a normal exposure of a backlit subject, one that's "underexposed," producing a silhouette effect, and a third that's "overexposed" to create still another look.

Before digital cameras took over the universe, it was common to bracket exposures, shooting, say, a series of three photos at 1/125th second, but varying the f/stop from f/8 to f/11 to f/16. In practice, smaller than whole-stop increments were used for greater precision, and lenses with apertures that were set manually commonly had half-stop detents on their aperture rings or could easily be set to a mid-way position between whole f/stops. It was just as common to keep the same aperture and vary the shutter speed, although in the days before electronic shutters, film cameras often had only whole-stop increment shutter speeds available.

The Z9 can bracket exposures much more precisely, and bracket white balance and Active D-Lighting (described later in this chapter) as well. While WB bracketing is sometimes used when getting color absolutely correct is important, autoexposure bracketing is used much more often. When this feature is activated, the camera takes a series of consecutive photos: starting with the metered "correct" exposure, then progressing to shots with less exposure, and additional shots with more exposure, using an increment of +3/–3 stops. In A mode, the shutter speed will change, while in S mode, the aperture will change as the bracketed exposures are made.

Setting up autoexposure bracketing parameters is trickier than it needs to be, but you can follow these steps:

1. **Choose type of bracketing.** First, select the type of bracketing you want to do, using Auto Bracketing Set within the Auto Bracketing entry in the Photo Shooting menu, as explained in Chapter 5. You can select autoexposure and flash, autoexposure only, flash only, white balance only, and ADL bracketing. (See Figure 2.9, left.)

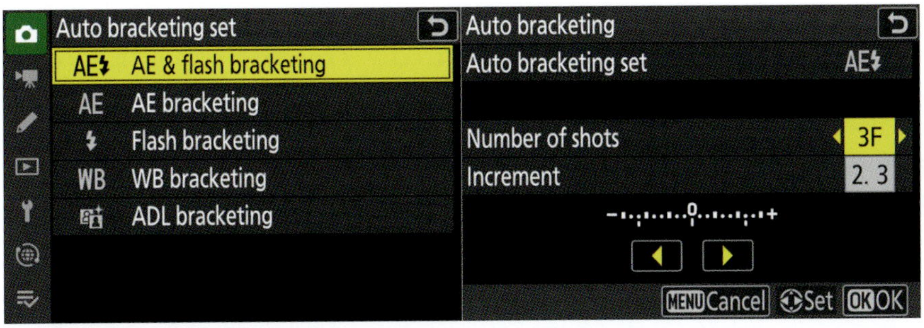

Figure 2.9 Choose bracketing set (left), plus number of shots and increment (right).

2. **Choose bracketing order.** With Custom Setting e7 you can select [Normal] MTR > Under > Over or Under > MTR > Over bracket orders. I prefer the latter (Underexposure, Metered exposure, Overexposure), as it makes certain types of manual HDR exposures easier to work with when the frames are captured in order of increasing exposure.
3. **Select number of bracketed exposures.** In the Auto Bracketing entry of the Photo Shooting menu, select Number of Shots and use the multi selector left/right buttons or touch screen, pressing right to choose the number of shots in the sequence, 0 (which turns bracketing off), 3-, 5-, 7-, or 9-shot bracket sets centered around the metered exposure. (See Figure 2.9, right.)
4. **Choose bracket increment.** Next, select Increment, and use the left/right buttons or touch screen to choose the exposure increment: $1/3$, $2/3$, 1, $1\,1/3$, $1\,2/3$, 2, $2\,1/3$, $2\,2/3$ EV. **Note:** If you select an increment of 2 EV or 3 EV, then the number of shots in the bracketed set that you specified in Step 3 is limited to 5. If you had chosen 7 or 9 shots in Step 3, the camera will automatically change the setting to 5 shots.
5. **Disable Auto ISO.** I always disable Auto ISO when bracketing exposures, in order to limit the adjustments to f/stop and shutter speed using the increments I've selected. If Auto ISO is enabled, bracketing will still take place as directed, but the camera may make an ISO change rather than adjust f/stop or shutter speed, which may not be what you want, as described next.
6. **Choose exposure mode.** If you're using selective focus techniques or producing a set of exposures for later HDR processing, you may want the focus point and aperture to remain constant during the bracket sequence. In that case, Aperture-priority should be your preferred exposure mode. Or, you may want to avoid shutter speeds that are too slow because the scene you are capturing includes moving subjects. Choose Shutter-priority and bracketing will change only the aperture (as long as Auto ISO has been disabled).

   Manual exposure can be used for bracketing, too. If you plan on shooting in Manual exposure mode, you can specify how bracketing is performed using Custom Setting e6. Your choices are flash/shutter speed, flash/shutter speed/aperture, flash/aperture, flash/ISO sensitivity, or flash only. White balance and ADL bracketing are not available in Manual exposure mode.
7. **Frame and shoot.** As you take your photos, the camera will vary exposure, flash level, or white balance for each image, based on the bracketing "program" you selected, and in the order you specified in Custom Setting e7. In Single-frame mode, you'll need to press the shutter-release button the number of times you specified for the exposures in your bracketed burst. I've found it

easy to forget that I am shooting bracketed pictures, stop taking my sequence, and then wonder why the remaining pictures in my defined burst are "incorrectly" exposed. To avoid that, I often set the camera to one of the two continuous shooting modes, so that all my bracketed pictures are taken at once. The camera will stop when the sequence is complete.

8. **Turn bracketing off.** When you're finished bracketing shots, remember to return to the Auto Bracketing entry and change Number of Shots to 0, and the BKT indicator is no longer displayed, as the setting remains in effect when you power down the camera and subsequently turn it on again.

ACTIVATING BRACKETING

Once you've set up the type of bracketing you want to use, as described next, taking a bracketed set of exposures is easy. When bracketing is active, to initiate exposing a set, just press the Bracketing Burst button. (Use Custom Setting f2 as described in Chapter 7 to assign the Bracketing Burst behavior to a button.) Once the button is pressed, all shots in the set will be taken each time you press the shutter-release button once. However, note that if bracketing is initiated using a defined button, the camera will not stop automatically at the end of a sequence. It will continue to capture series of shots until you release the button.

White Balance Bracketing

White balance bracketing is available only when you're not shooting RAW images. One snap, and you get 3, 5, 7, or 9 JPEG at the quality level you specified, bracketed as you directed. Very slick. As you might guess, WB bracketing is applied only to JPEG files; you can't specify WB bracketing if you've chosen RAW or RAW+JPEG. RAW files created are always unmodified and will be converted according to the white balance settings you opted for in the camera when the photo is imported into your image editor (if you make no white balance changes during importation). (At the time this book was written, only the Z8 allowed creating HEIF files instead of JPEGs for many functions, including white balance bracketing.)

White balance bracketing produces JPEG files that vary, not by f/stops (which is the case with exposure bracketing), but by units called *mireds* (micro reciprocal degrees) that are used to specify color temperature. You don't really need to understand mireds at all, other than to know that WB bracketing varies the color temperature of your images by 5 mireds for each shot taken in the bracket set.

Changes are made only in the amber-blue range; bracketing isn't applied to the green-magenta color bias. In addition, if you want to change the relative *color temperature* used for images, you'll need to work with the Choose Color Temperature option in the Photo Shooting/Video Recording menu. I'll go into a little more detail on that later in this chapter.

Meanwhile, to activate White Balance bracketing, just follow these steps:

1. **JPEG/HEIF only.** Make sure you've selected a JPEG-only (or HEIF-only) setting in the Image Quality entry of the Photo Shooting menu.
2. **Specify WB Bracketing.** In the Auto Bracketing entry of the Photo Shooting menu, choose WB Bracketing as your bracketing set.

3. **Choose number of shots.** In the Auto Bracketing screen, after you've chosen WB Bracketing, scroll down to Number of Shots and select how many bracketed exposures you want. Select 0, 3, 5, 7, or 9 (use the right directional button) and the camera will take the specified number of shots, in the amber and blue directions, equally spread on either side of the zero point of the amber-blue scale. For example, if you choose 5 as your number of shots, the sequence will include one neutral shot, plus two biased by 5 and 10 mireds in both amber and blue directions. With 0 as your number of shots, bracketing is disabled, just as it is with exposure bracketing.

ADL Bracketing

To initiate Active D-Lighting bracketing, select it from the Photo Shooting menu's Auto Bracketing Set menu entry and select number of shots and amount, as described next. As with exposure bracketing, you can trigger a burst with one press of the shutter release if you've defined a Bracketing Burst button.

- **0 (Number of shots).** Active D-Lighting bracketing is disabled. Only *bracketing* is turned off. If you've turned basic Active D-Lighting on in the Photo Shooting menu, then each shot you take will have the amount of ADL applied that you specified. Those choices are Auto, Extra High 2 (H2), Extra High 1 (H1), High (H), Normal (N), Low (L), or Off.
- **2 (Number of shots).** Only two shots will be taken, using the option you specify by scrolling down to the Amount box. The available pairs are Off/Auto, Off/Extra High 2, Off/Extra High 1, Off/High, Off/Normal, and Off/Low.
- **3–5 (Number of shots).** You can choose 3, 4, or 5 shots. One will be Off (ADL disabled), and the others will be taken at the settings indicated in the Amount box.
    - **3 shots:** Off, plus Low and Normal. (You cannot change these.)
    - **4 shots:** Off, plus Low, Normal, and High. (You cannot change these.)
    - **5 shots:** You can select either Off, plus Low, Normal, High, and Extra High 1, or Low, Normal, High, Extra High 1, and Extra High 2. (Off is not available.)

As with exposure, flash, and WB bracketing, remember to turn off ADL bracketing when you no longer want to use it. Once set, it is automatically invoked each time you take a picture until disabled.

Flash Bracketing

You can capture bracketed sequences with an external flash attached and powered up. The way in which the flash contributes to the bracketed exposures is determined by the Auto Bracketing Set option in the Photo Shooting menu. There are three choices, shown earlier in Figure 2.9, left:

- **AE & flash bracketing.** During the sequence, both ambient exposure and flash exposure are varied individually to produce the bracketed set. Use this setting if you want the camera to adjust the flash output to match changes in ambient exposure during the sequence.
- **AE bracketing.** Only the ambient exposure is bracketed. The flash output is not changed from shot to shot.
- **Flash bracketing.** Ambient exposure is not bracketed, but the flash output is varied to produce the bracketed set.

Working with HDR

High Dynamic Range (HDR) photography is quite the rage these days, and entire books have been written on the subject. It's not really a new technique—film photographers have been combining multiple exposures for ages to produce a single image of, say, an interior room while maintaining detail in the scene visible through the windows.

It's the same deal in the digital age. Suppose you wanted to photograph a dimly lit room that had a bright window showing an outdoors scene. Proper exposure for the room might be on the order of 1/60th second at f/2.8 at ISO 200, while the outdoors scene probably would require f/11 at 1/400th second. That's almost a 7 EV step difference (approximately 7 f/stops) and well beyond the dynamic range of any digital camera, including the Z9 or Z8.

Until sensors gain much higher dynamic ranges (which may not be as far into the distant future as we think), special tricks like Active D-Lighting and HDR photography will remain basic tools. With the Z9/Z8, you can create in-camera HDR exposures, or shoot HDR the old-fashioned way—with separate bracketed exposures that are later combined in a tool like Photomatix or Adobe's Merge to HDR image-editing feature. I'm going to show you how to use both.

HDR Overlay

I've been surprised at how well Nikon has solved the hand-held auto HDR problem, because there are two stumbling blocks that, at least theoretically, should lead to less-than-awesome results. First, while your camera can generate HDR images for you on the fly, there is the tendency to put the feature to work under non-optimal conditions; specifically, impromptu hand-held situations. If you've done any traditional HDR, you know that the technique works best when the camera is mounted on a tripod, so that the bracketed exposures are virtually identical except for the exposure itself. Although all HDR software can correct for slight camera movement and align images that are slightly out of register, the results I've gotten have not been great. I expected hand-held HDR to be comparable. However, Nikon's implementation does an excellent job.

The second theoretical weakness of the HDR feature is the limitation of combining just two shots to arrive at the final image. The best traditional HDR photos I've produced have involved at least three shots, and more frequently five or more, each separated by a stop of exposure. The camera takes two shots, total, and combines them. Despite these speed bumps, I've been pleased with my results.

Your Nikon Z9/Z8's in-camera HDR feature is simple, not particularly flexible, but still surprisingly effective in creating high dynamic range images. It's also remarkably easy to use. Although it combines only two images to create a single HDR photograph, it can often produce images that are as good as those created using the manual HDR method I'll describe in the section after this one.

It's often tricky to capture detail in both highlights and shadows in a single image, because the number of tones, the *dynamic range* of the sensor, is limited. The human eye has a "dynamic range" of up to 30 stops; typical digital cameras can capture 10 to 12 stops worth of tones in JPEG mode, and up to 14 stops if you're processing RAW files. High-end cameras like the Z9 and Z8 can potentially image tones in a range of up to 17 stops. If you need more tones, HDR is one way of overcoming the inherent limitations of the sensor.

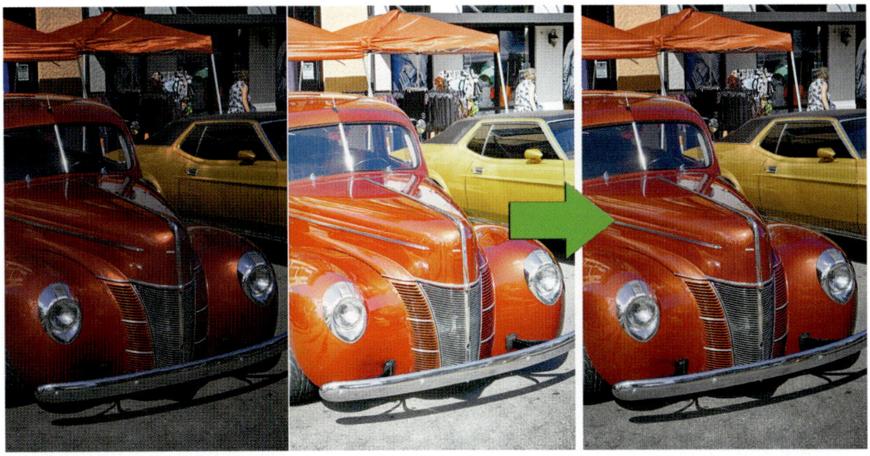

Figure 2.10 The underexposed image (left) can be combined with the overexposed image (center) to produce the merged HDR image (right).

Figure 2.10 illustrates how the two shots that the HDR feature merges might look. There is a three-stop differential between the underexposed image at left, and the overexposed image at center. The in-camera HDR Overlay feature is able to combine the two to derive an image similar to the one shown in Figure 2.10, right, which has a much fuller range of tones.

To use HDR Overlay, just follow these steps. The feature cannot be used simultaneously with photo flicker reduction, bracketing features, multiple exposure, focus shift shooting, interval-timer series, or time-lapse photography. The fastest continuous shooting rates (C30, C60, or C120), as well as Bulb and Time exposures are also incompatible.

1. **Activate the menu.** Press the MENU button and navigate to the Photo Shooting menu, represented by a camera icon.
2. **Scroll down to HDR Overlay.** Press the right multi selector button. A screen appears with three choices: HDR Mode, HDR Strength, and Save Individual Pictures (RAW). (See Figure 2.11, left.)
3. **Turn on HDR.** Choose HDR Mode, press right, and select either On (series) if you want to shoot multiple HDR photos consecutively or On (single photo) to take a single HDR image and then shut the feature off. Choose OFF to disable the feature. Press OK to confirm. (See Figure 2.11, center.)

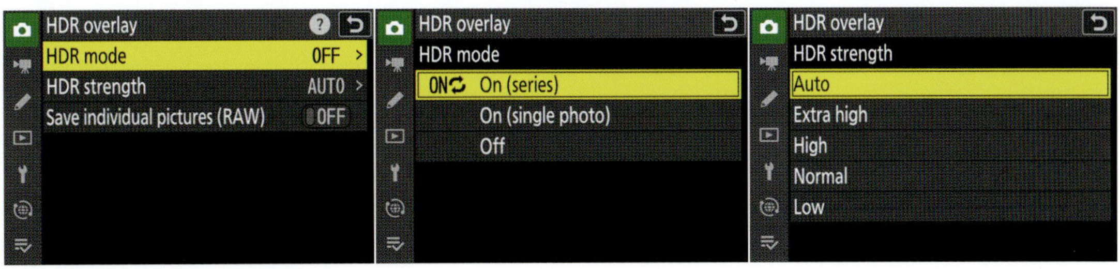

Figure 2.11 Choose HDR parameters.

4. **Set strength.** Choose HDR Strength. Select Auto (the camera chooses the EV differential based on how contrasty it deems your scene to be). Auto is a good choice for your initial experiments if your camera is set for Matrix metering. If you've chosen Center-weighted or Spot metering, the Auto option uses Normal, instead.

   To fine-tune the strength, you can choose Extra High, High, Normal, or Low. Use stronger settings for higher-contrast subjects, and a lower value for lower-contrast subjects. Press OK to confirm. (See Figure 2.11, right.)

   Watch for haloing effects: HDR can cause haloing around the boundaries of areas within an image. If you see this "glowing" look in image review, change to a lower HDR strength.
5. **Save Individual Images (optional).** Ordinarily, the camera captures two images, combines them to produce an HDR shot, and then deletes the individual images. Turn Save Individual Pictures (RAW) on, and the camera will store a Large RAW version of each shot (even if you are in JPEG Only mode and have not selected RAW or Large image quality/size). You'll have the intermediate images available for editing/tweaking on your computer.
6. **Set Aperture-priority mode.** You want exposure to be adjusted by changing the shutter speed, rather than using a different aperture, in order to keep your depth-of-field the same for each shot.
7. **Ready to go.** You'll know the camera is in HDR mode when an indicator (HDR H, HDR A, etc.) appears at the bottom of the viewfinder display and the right side of the LCD screen. If your current display mode doesn't include the indicator, press DISP until it appears. An HDR indicator also appears on the control panel.
8. **Take your shot.** Although you can shoot HDR hand-held, you'll get the best results with the camera mounted on a tripod, and with subjects that don't display a lot of motion. While the two images are combined, the message "Busy" and an HDR indicator will flash in the control panel. Note that because the camera tries to align shots, even if there is slight camera movement, some portion of the images at the edges will be cropped out. You're better off using a tripod for Auto HDR, even though it does a decent job handheld.

Bracketing and Merge to HDR Pro

If your credo is "If you want something done right, do it yourself," you can also shoot HDR manually, without resorting to the camera's HDR mode. Instead, you can shoot individual images either by manually bracketing or using the auto bracketing modes, described earlier in this chapter.

There are stand-alone HDR utilities, such as Photomatix Pro, and most image editors, including Photoshop, have HDR capabilities built-in. Adobe has added similar capabilities to the latest versions of Lightroom Classic, Lightroom Cloud, Lightroom iOS/Android, Adobe Camera RAW, and lightroom.adobe.com. While my goal in this book is to show you how to take great photos *in the camera* rather than how to fix your errors in Photoshop, the Merge to HDR feature in Adobe's flagship image editor is too cool to ignore.

The ability to have a bracketed set of exposures that are identical except for exposure is key to getting good results with this Photoshop feature, which allows you to produce images with a full, rich dynamic range that includes a level of detail in the highlights and shadows that is almost impossible to achieve with digital cameras without HDR image merging.

When you're using Merge to HDR Pro, you take several pictures, some exposed for the shadows, some for the middle tones, and some for the highlights. The exact number of images to combine is up to you. Four to seven is a good number. Then, use the Merge to HDR Pro command to combine all the images into one HDR image that integrates the well-exposed sections of each version. Here's how.

The images should be as identical as possible, except for exposure. So, it's a good idea to mount the camera on a tripod, use a remote release, and take all the exposures in one burst. Just follow these steps:

1. **Set up the camera.** Mount the camera on a tripod.
2. **Set the camera to shoot a bracketed burst with an increment of 2 EV or 3 EV.** This was described earlier in this chapter.
3. **Choose an f/stop.** Set the camera for Aperture-priority and select an aperture that will provide a correct exposure at your initial settings for the series of manually bracketed shots. *And then leave this adjustment alone!* As I noted earlier, you don't want the aperture to change for your series, as that would change the depth-of-field. You want the camera to adjust exposure *only* using the shutter speed.
4. **Choose manual focus.** You don't want the focus to change between shots, so set the camera to manual focus, and carefully focus your shot.
5. **Choose RAW exposures.** Set the camera to take RAW files, which will give you the widest range of tones in your images.
6. **Take your bracketed set.** Press the button on the remote (or carefully press the shutter release or use the self-timer) and take the set of bracketed exposures.
7. **Continue with the Merge to HDR Pro steps listed next.** You can also use a different program, such as Photomatix, if you know how to use it.

DETERMINING THE BEST EXPOSURE DIFFERENTIAL

How do you choose the number of EV/stops to separate your exposures? You can use histograms, described later in this chapter, to determine the correct bracketing range. Take a test shot and examine the histogram. Reduce the exposure until dark tones are clipped off at the left of the resulting histogram. Then, increase the exposure until the lighter tones are clipped off at the right of the histogram. The number of stops between the two is the range that should be covered using your bracketed exposures. You can learn more about histograms in the section following this one.

The next steps show you how to combine the separate exposures into one merged HDR image. The sample images in Figure 2.12 (left) show the results you can get from a three-shot bracketed sequence. The images were taken from a hill above Florence, Italy, in the Piazzale Michelangelo, a square that is actually a glorified parking lot with a fancy name (and a fantastic view).

1. **Copy your images to your computer.** If you use an application to transfer the files to your computer, make sure it does not make any adjustments to brightness, contrast, or exposure. You want the real raw information for Merge to HDR Pro to work with.
2. **Activate Merge to HDR Pro.** Choose File > Automate > Merge to HDR Pro.
3. **Select the photos to be merged.** Use the Browse feature to locate and select your photos to be merged. You'll note a check box that can be used to automatically align the images if they were not taken with the camera mounted on a rock-steady support. This will adjust for any slight movement of the camera that might have occurred when you changed exposure settings.
4. **Choose parameters (optional).** The first time you use Merge to HDR Pro, you can let the program work with its default parameters. Once you've played with the feature a few times, you can read the Adobe help files and learn more about the options than I can present in this non-software-oriented camera guide.
5. **Click OK.** The merger begins.
6. **Save.** Once HDR merge has done its thing, save the file to your computer.

If you do everything correctly, you'll end up with a photo like the one shown in Figure 2.12 (right).

What if you don't have the opportunity, inclination, or skills to create several images at different exposures, as described? If you shoot in RAW format, you can still use Merge to HDR, working with a *single* original image file. What you do is import the image into Photoshop several times, using Adobe Camera Raw to create multiple copies of the file at different exposure levels.

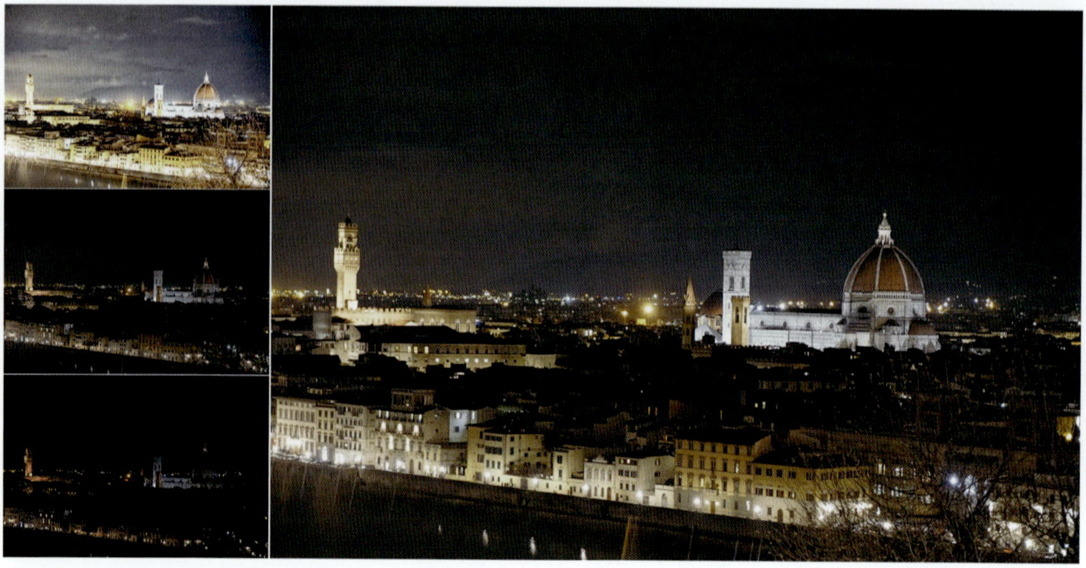

Figure 2.12 Left: Three bracketed photos should look like this. Right: You'll end up with an extended dynamic range photo like this one.

For example, you'd create one copy that's too dark, so the shadows lose detail, but the highlights are preserved. Create another copy with the shadows intact and allow the highlights to wash out. Then, you can use Merge to HDR to combine the two and end up with a finished image that has the extended dynamic range you're looking for. (This concludes the image-editing portion of the chapter. We now return you to our alternate sponsor: photography.)

Fixing Exposures with Histograms

While you can often recover poorly exposed photos in your image editor, your best bet is to arrive at the correct exposure in the camera, minimizing the tweaks that you have to make in post-processing. However, you can't always judge exposure just by simply looking at the preview image on your display before the shot is made, nor the review image in Playback. Ambient light may make the monitor difficult to see, and the brightness level you've set for the monitor and viewfinder in the Setup menu can affect the appearance of the image. The viewfinder and LCD screen aren't designed to provide a 100 percent accurate view.

Instead, you can use a histogram, which is a chart shown on the camera's display that shows the number of tones that have been captured at each brightness level. Histograms are available in real time on your display as you shoot and in the review image during playback, but they are available only when enabled:

- **Photo and Movie modes.** For still and movie shooting, the histogram can be activated by using the Custom Monitor/Custom Viewfinder Shooting Display entries of the Custom Settings menu. I'll explain how to do this in Chapter 7. The histogram appears at lower right in both displays. The LCD screen version is shown at left in Figure 2.13.
- **Playback.** To see histograms during image review, check the Histogram box in the Playback Display Options entry of the Playback menu (discussed in Chapter 8). The camera offers four histogram variations in two screens: one histogram that shows overall brightness levels for an image (see Figure 2.13, center) and an alternate version that also shows brightness (also called *luminance*), but offers additional histograms that separates the red, green, and blue channels of your image into separate graphs (see Figure 2.13, right).

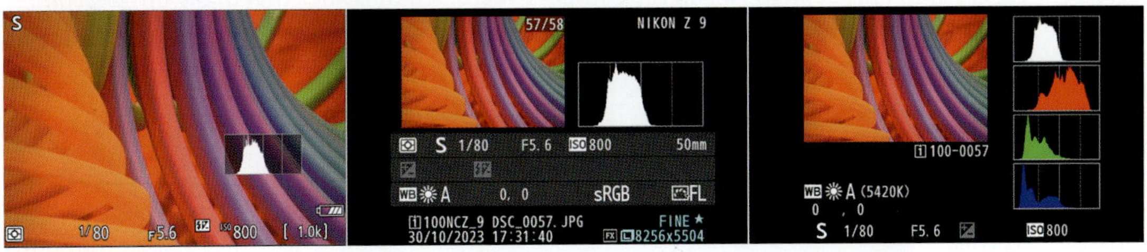

Figure 2.13 In photo and movie shooting modes the histogram appears in your live view image when enabled (left). Histograms are available on two different screens during playback (center and right).

Tonal Range

Histograms help you adjust the tonal range of an image, the span of dark to light tones, from a complete absence of brightness (black) to the brightest possible tone (white), and all the middle tones in between. Because all values for tones fall into a continuous spectrum between black and white, it's easiest to think of a photo's tonality in terms of a black-and-white or grayscale image, even though you're capturing those tones in three separate color layers of red, green, and blue.

Because your images are digital, the tonal "spectrum" isn't really continuous: it's divided into discrete steps that represent the different tones that can be captured. Figure 2.14 may help you understand this concept. The gray steps shown range from 100 percent gray (black) at the left, to 0 percent gray (white) at the right, with 20 gray steps in all (plus white).

Along the bottom of the chart are the digital values from 0 to 255 recorded by your sensor for an image with 8 bits per channel (8 bits of red, 8 bits of green, and 8 bits of blue equal a 24-bit, full-color image). Any black captured would be represented by a value of 0, the brightest white by 255, and the midtones would be clustered around the 128 marker. The actual information captured may be "finer" and record, say, 0 to 4,094 for an image captured with a 14-bits-per-channel NEF (RAW) file.

Grayscale images (which we call black-and-white photos) are easy to understand. Or, at least, that's what we think. When we look at a black-and-white image, we think we're seeing a continuous range of tones from black to white, and all the grays in between. But, that's not exactly true. The blackest black in any photo isn't a true black, because *some* light is always reflected from the surface of the print, and if viewed on a screen, the deepest black is only as dark as the least-reflective area a computer monitor can produce. The whitest white isn't a true white, either, because even the lightest areas of a print absorb some light (only a mirror reflects close to all the light that strikes it), and, when viewing on a computer monitor, the whites are limited by the brightness of the display's LCD or LED picture elements. Lacking darker blacks and brighter, whiter whites, that continuous set of tones doesn't cover the full grayscale tonal range.

The full scale of tones becomes useful when you have an image that has large expanses of shades that change gradually from one level to the next, such as areas of sky, water, or walls. Think of a picture taken of a group of campers around a campfire. Since the light from the fire is striking them directly in the face, there aren't many shadows on the campers' faces. All the tones that make up the *features* of the people around the fire are compressed into one end of the brightness spectrum—the lighter end.

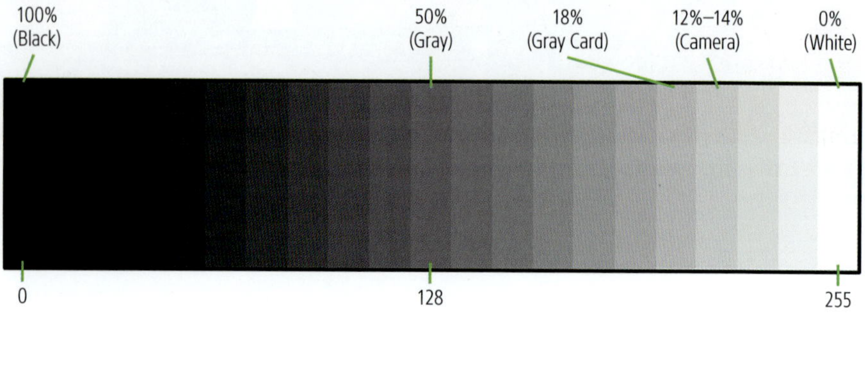

Figure 2.14 A tonal range from black (left) to white (right) and all the gray values in between.

Yet, there's more to this scene than faces. Behind the campers are trees, rocks, and perhaps a few animals that have emerged from the shadows to see what is going on. These are illuminated by the softer light that bounces off the surrounding surfaces. If your eyes become accustomed to the reduced illumination, you'll find that there is a wealth of detail in these shadow images.

This campfire scene would be a nightmare to reproduce faithfully under any circumstances. If you are an experienced photographer, you are probably already wincing at what is called a *high-contrast* lighting situation. Some photos may be high in contrast when there are fewer tones, and they are all bunched up at limited points in the scale. In a low-contrast image, there are more tones, but they are spread out so widely that the image looks flat. Your digital camera can show you the relationship between these tones using a *histogram.*

Histogram Basics

Histograms are a simplified display of the numbers of pixels at each of 256 brightness levels, producing an interesting "mountain range" shape in the graph. Although separate charts may be provided for brightness and the red, green, and blue channels, when you first start using histograms, you'll want to concentrate on the brightness histogram.

Each vertical line in the graph represents the number of pixels in the image for each brightness value, from 0 (black) on the left to 255 (white) on the right. The vertical direction measures that number of pixels at each level. That range isn't a fixed number; it changes to accommodate the scene.

Although histograms are most often used to fine-tune exposure, you can glean other information from them, such as the relative contrast of the image. Figure 2.15, top, is a simplified rendition of the upper half of the Overview screen, with an image having normal contrast. In such an image, most of the pixels are spread across the image, with a healthy distribution of tones throughout the midtone section of the graph. That large peak at the right side of the graph represents all those light tones in the sky. A normal-contrast image you shoot may have less sky area, and less of a peak at the right side, but notice that very few pixels hug the right edge of the histogram, indicating that the lightest tones are not being clipped because the histogram graph is only getting close to the right edge of the histogram window, but has not gone past it.

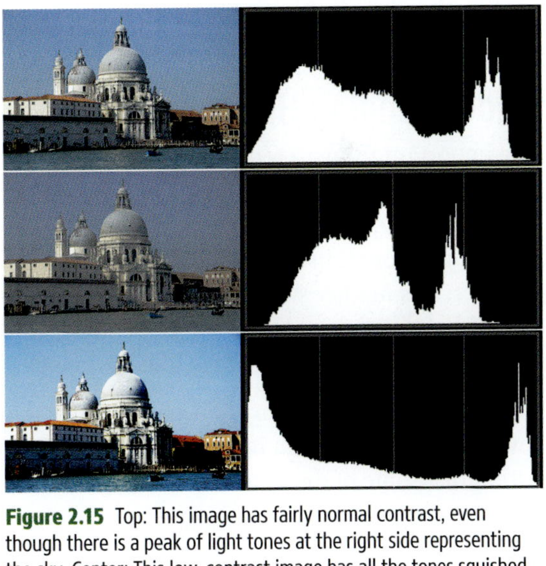

Figure 2.15 Top: This image has fairly normal contrast, even though there is a peak of light tones at the right side representing the sky. Center: This low-contrast image has all the tones squished into one section of the grayscale. Bottom: A high-contrast image produces a histogram in which the tones are spread out.

With a lower-contrast image, like the one shown in Figure 2.15, center, the basic shape of the previous histogram will remain recognizable, but gradually will be compressed together to cover a smaller area of the gray spectrum. The squished shape of the histogram is caused by all the grays in the original image being represented by a limited number of gray tones in a smaller range of the scale.

Instead of the darkest tones of the image reaching into the black end of the spectrum and the whitest tones extending to the lightest end, the blackest areas of the scene are now represented by a light gray, and the whites by a somewhat lighter gray. The overall contrast of the image is reduced. Because all the darker tones are actually a middle gray or lighter, the scene in this version of the photo appears lighter as well.

Going in the other direction, increasing the contrast of an image produces a histogram like the one shown in Figure 2.15, bottom. In this case, the tonal range is now spread over the entire width of the chart, but, except for the bright sky, there is not much variation in the middle tones; the mountain "peaks" are not very high. When you stretch the grayscale in both directions like this, the darkest tones should become darker and the lightest tones should become lighter. But that may not be possible, because shades that might have been gray before can change to fully black or completely white as they are moved toward either end of the scale, and once that happens, they can't become blacker or whiter.

The effect of increasing contrast may be to move some tones off either end of the scale altogether, while spreading the remaining grays over a smaller number of locations on the spectrum. That's exactly the case in the example shown. The number of possible tones is smaller, and the image appears harsher.

Understanding Histograms

The important thing to remember when working with the histogram display in your camera is that changing the exposure does *not* change the contrast of an image. The curves illustrated in the previous three examples remain exactly the same shape when you increase or decrease exposure. I repeat: The proportional distribution of grays shown in the histogram doesn't change when exposure changes; it is neither stretched nor compressed. However, the tones as a whole are moved toward one end of the scale or the other, depending on whether you're increasing or decreasing exposure. You'll be able to see that in some illustrations that follow.

So, as you reduce exposure, tones gradually move to the black end (and off the scale), while the reverse is true when you increase exposure. The contrast within the image is changed only to the extent that some of the tones can no longer be represented when they are moved off the scale.

To change the *contrast* of an image, you must do one of four things:

- **Change the contrast setting** using the menu system. You'll find these adjustments in your camera's Picture Controls menus, as explained in Chapter 5.
- **Use your built-in shadow-tone "booster."** As previously discussed, Active D-Lighting (or plain old D-Lighting applied after the fact from the Retouch menu) can also adjust contrast.

- **Alter the contrast of the scene itself,** for example, by using a fill light or reflectors to add illumination to shadows that are too dark.
- **Attempt to adjust contrast in post-processing** using your image editor or RAW file converter. You may use features such as Levels or Curves (in Photoshop, Photoshop Elements, and many other image editors), or work with HDR software to cherry-pick the best values in shadows and highlights from multiple images.

Of the four of these, the third—changing the contrast of the scene—is the most desirable, because attempting to fix contrast by fiddling with the tonal values is unlikely to be a perfect remedy. However, adding a little contrast can be successful because you can discard some tones to make the image more contrasty. However, the opposite is much more difficult. An overly contrasty image rarely can be fixed because you can't add information that isn't there in the first place.

What you *can* do is adjust the exposure so that the tones *that are already present in the scene* are captured correctly. Figure 2.16, top, shows the histogram for an image that is badly underexposed. You can guess from the shape of the histogram that many of the dark tones to the left of the graph have been clipped off. There's plenty of room on the right side for additional pixels to reside without having them become overexposed. So, you can increase the exposure (either by changing the f/stop or shutter speed, or by adding an EV value) to produce the corrected histogram shown in Figure 2.16, center.

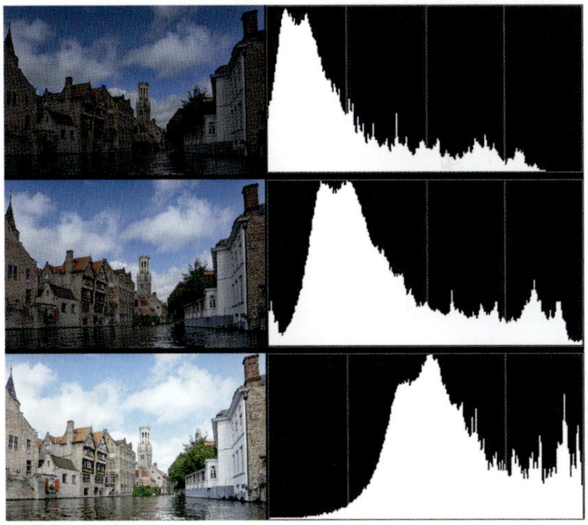

Figure 2.16 Top: A histogram of an underexposed image may look like this. Center: Adding exposure will produce a histogram like this one. Bottom: A histogram of an overexposed image will show clipping at the right side.

Conversely, if your histogram looks like the one shown in Figure 2.16, bottom, with bright tones pushed off the right edge of the chart, you have an overexposed image, and you can correct it by reducing exposure. In addition to the histogram, there is a Highlights option, which, when activated, shows areas that are overexposed with flashing tones (often called "blinkies") in the review screen. Depending on the importance of this "clipped" detail, you can adjust exposure or leave it alone. For example, if all the dark-coded areas in the review are in a background that you care little about, you can forget about them and not change the exposure, but if such areas appear in facial details of your subject, you may want to make some adjustments.

In working with histograms, your goal should be to have all the tones in an image spread out between the edges, with none clipped off at the left and right sides. Underexposing (to preserve highlights) should be done only as a last resort, because retrieving the underexposed shadows in your image editor will frequently increase the noise, even if you're working with RAW files. A better course of action is to expose for the highlights, but, when the subject matter makes it practical, fill in the shadows with additional light, using reflectors, fill flash, or other techniques rather than allowing them to be seriously underexposed.

A traditional technique for optimizing exposure is called "expose to the right" (ETTR), which involves adding exposure to push the histogram's curve toward the right side *but not far enough to clip off highlights.* The rationale for this method is that extra shadow detail will be produced with a minimum increase in noise, especially in the shadow areas. It's said that half of a digital sensor's response lies in the brightest areas of an image, and so require the least amount of amplification (which is one way to increase digital noise). ETTR can work, as long as you're able to capture a satisfactory amount of information in the shadows.

Exposing to the Right

It's easier to understand exposing to the right if you mentally divide the histogram into fifths (unfortunately, the camera's histogram uses quarters instead). And, for the sake of simplicity and smaller numbers, assume you're shooting in 14-bit RAW. Any 14-bit image can record a maximum of 16,383 different tones per red, green, or blue channel. However, each fifth of the histogram does *not* encompass 3,277 tones (one-fifth of 16,383).

Instead, the right-most fifth, the highlights, shown in Figure 2.17, accounts for fully *half* of the different captured tones. Moving toward the left, the next fifth represents one quarter of the available levels, followed by one-eighth, one-sixteenth, and, in the left-most section where the deepest shadows reside, only 1/32nd different tones are captured. When processing your RAW file, there are only roughly 500 tones to recover in the shadows, which is why boosting/amplifying them increases noise. (The effect is most noticeable in the red and blue channels; your sensor's Bayer array has twice as many green-sensitive pixels as red or blue.)

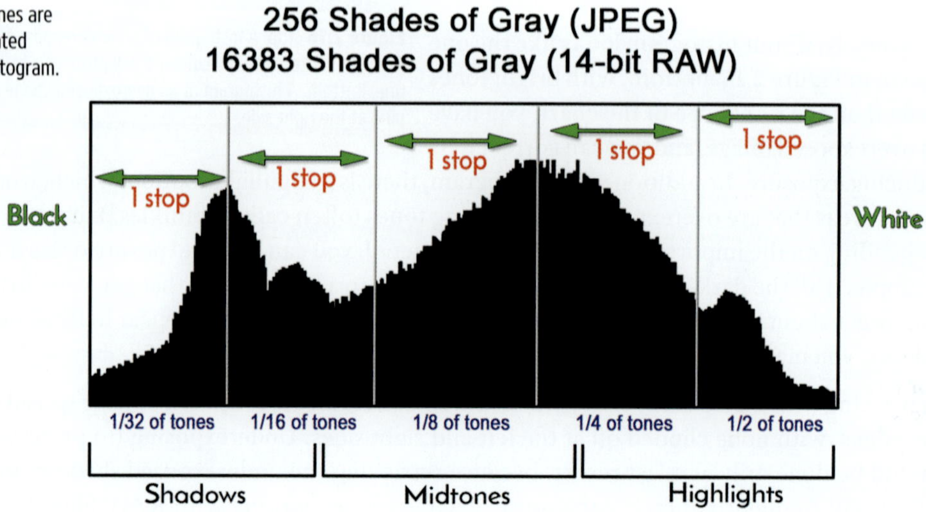

Figure 2.17 Tones are not evenly allocated throughout a histogram.

Instead, you want to add exposure—as long as you don't push highlights off the right edge of the histogram—to brighten the shadows. Because half of the tones are available in the highlights, even if the RAW image *looks* overexposed, it's possible to use your RAW converter's Exposure slider (such as the one found in Adobe Camera Raw) to bring back detail captured in that surplus of tones in the highlights. This procedure is the exact opposite of what was recommended for film of the transparency variety—it was fairly easy to retrieve detail from shadows by pumping more light through them when processing the image, while even small amounts of extra exposure blew out highlights. You'll often find that the range of tones in your image is so great that there is no way to keep your histogram from spilling over into the left and right edges, costing you both highlight and shadow detail. Exposing to the right may not work in such situations. A second school of thought recommends *reducing* exposure to bring back the highlights, or "exposing to the left." You would then attempt to recover shadow detail in an image editor, using tools like Adobe Camera Raw's Exposure slider. But remember, above all, that this procedure will also boost noise in the shadows, and so the technique should be used with caution. In most cases, exposing to the right is your best bet.

Dealing with RGB Channels

The more you work with histograms, the more useful they become. One of the first things that histogram veterans notice is that it's possible to overexpose one channel even if the overall exposure appears to be correct. For example, flower photographers soon discover that it's really, really difficult to get a good picture of a red rose, like the one shown at left in Figure 2.18. The exposure looks okay—but there's no detail in the rose's petals. Looking at the histogram (see Figure 2.18, right) shows why: the red channel is blown out. If you look at the red histogram, there's a peak at the right edge that indicates that highlight information has been lost. In fact, the green channel has been blown, too, and so the green parts of the flower also lack detail. Only the blue channel's histogram is entirely contained within the boundaries of the chart, and, on first glance, the white luminance histogram at top of the column of graphs seems fairly normal.

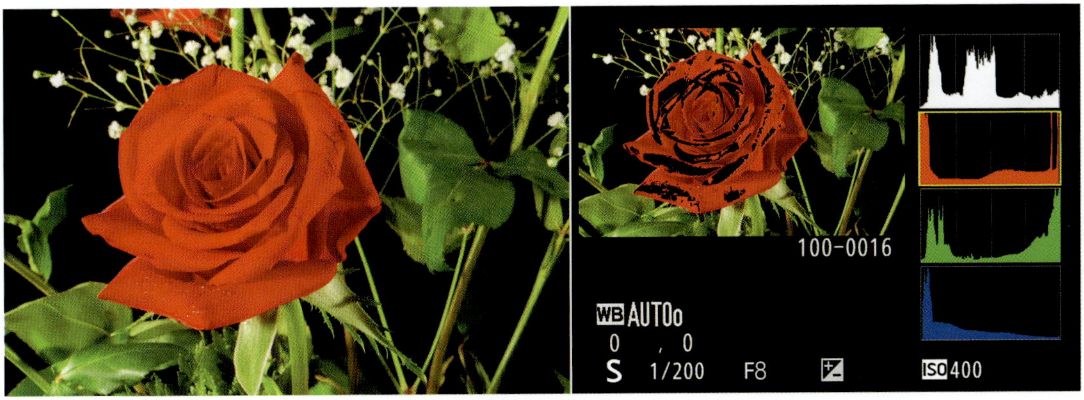

Figure 2.18 It's common to lose detail in bright red flowers because the red channel becomes overexposed even when the other channels are properly exposed (left). The RGB histograms show that both the red and green channels are overexposed, with tones extending past the right edge of the chart (right).

Any of the primary channels—red, green, or blue—can blow out all by themselves, although bright reds seem to be the most common problem area. More difficult to diagnose are overexposed tones in one of the "in-between" hues on the color wheel. Overexposed yellows (which are very common) will be shown by blowouts in *both* the red and green channels. Too-bright cyans will manifest as excessive blue and green highlights, while overexposure in the red and blue channels reduces detail in magenta colors. As you gain experience, you'll be able to see exactly how anomalies in the RGB channels translate into poor highlights and murky shadows.

The only way to correct for color channel blowouts is to reduce exposure. As I mentioned earlier, you might want to consider filling in the shadows with additional light to keep them from becoming too dark when you decrease exposure. In practice, you'll want to monitor the red channel most closely, followed by the blue channel, and slightly decrease exposure to see if that helps. Because of the way our eyes perceive color, we are more sensitive to variations in green, so green channel blowouts are less of a problem, unless your main subject is heavily colored in that hue. If you plan on photographing a frog hopping around on your front lawn, you'll want to be extra careful to preserve detail in the green channel, using bracketing or other exposure techniques outlined in this chapter.

Fine-Tuning Exposure

When all else fails—that is, when you find your camera *consistently* over- or underexposes when using a particular exposure mode—you can recalibrate the camera to produce images more to your liking. This setting is a powerful adjustment that allows you to dial in a specific amount of exposure adjustment that will be applied, invisibly, to every photo you take using each of the metering modes. No more can you complain, "My camera always underexposes by 1/3 stop!" If that is actually the case, and the phenomenon is consistent, you can use this custom menu adjustment to compensate.

Exposure compensation is usually a better idea (does your camera *really* underexpose that consistently?), but this setting does allow you to adjust your camera's behavior yourself. Your dialed-in modifications will survive a two-button reset. However, you have no indication that fine-tuning has been made, so you'll need to remember what you've done. After all, you someday might discover that your camera is consistently *over*exposing images by 1/3 stop, not remembering that you've made the adjustment.

In practice, it's rare that the Z9/Z8 will *consistently* provide the wrong exposure in any of the metering modes, especially Matrix metering, which can alter exposure dramatically based on the camera's internal database of typical scenes. This feature may be most useful for Spot metering, if you always take a reading off the same type of subject, such as a human face or gray card. Should you find that the gray card readings, for example, always differ from what you would prefer, go ahead and fine-tune optimal exposure for Spot metering, and use that to read your gray cards.

To fine-tune your exposure:

1. **Select fine-tuning.** Choose Custom Setting b6: Fine-Tune Optimal Exposure from the Custom Settings menu.
2. **Consider yourself warned.** In the screen that appears, choose Yes after carefully reading the warning that Nikon insists on showing you each and every time this option is activated. The screen shown in Figure 2.19, left, appears.
3. **Select metering mode to correct.** Choose Matrix metering, Center-weighted metering, Spot metering, or Highlight-weighted metering by highlighting your choice and pressing the multi selector right button.
4. **Specify amount of correction.** Press the up/down buttons to dial in the exposure compensation you want to apply. (See Figure 2.19, right.) You can specify compensation in increments of 1/6 stop, half as large a change as conventional exposure compensation. This is truly *fine-tuning.*
5. **Confirm your change.** Press OK when finished. You can repeat the action to fine-tune the other three exposure modes if you wish. To return your settings to your defaults, simply repeat the process and dial in 0 correction for the desired mode.

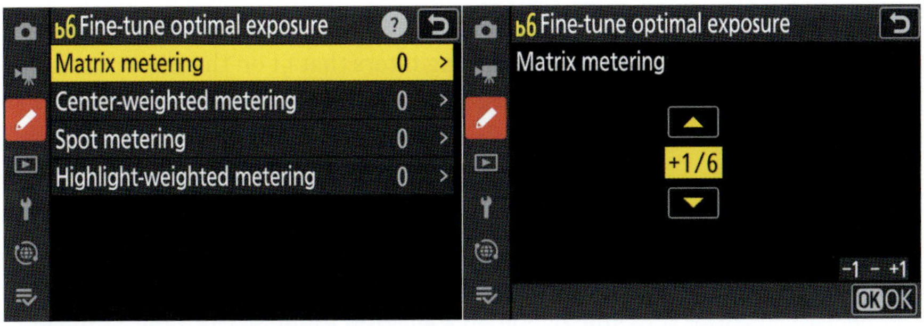

Figure 2.19 Fine-tune optimal exposure.

Living with Color Temperature

Nikon has been valiant in its efforts to help us tame the color balance monster. Some earlier Nikon pro cameras (the last one being the Nikon D2Xs) had a white sensor on their pentaprisms, which measured ambient color temperature. Although this special sensor was abandoned by Nikon long ago, the technology lives on in the form of ExpoDisc filter/caps and their ilk, which allow the camera's built-in custom white balance measuring feature to evaluate the illumination that passes through the disc/cap/filter/Pringle's can lid, or whatever neutral-color substitute you employ. (A white or gray card also works.) To help us tangle with the many different types of non-incandescent/non-daylight sources, Nikon has provided the camera with several presets for cool-white, day white, and daylight fluorescent lamps. If those aren't enough, you can select a specific color temperature, or capture and save up to six white balance settings for retrieval later.

In practical terms, color temperature is how "bluish" or how "reddish" the light appears to be to the digital camera's sensor. Indoor illumination is quite warm, comparatively, and appears reddish to the sensor. Daylight, in contrast, seems much bluer to the sensor. Our eyes (our brains, actually) are quite adaptable to these variations, so white objects don't appear to have an orange tinge when viewed indoors, nor do they seem excessively blue outdoors in full daylight. Yet, these color temperature variations are real, and the sensor is not fooled. To capture the most accurate colors, we need to take the color temperature into account in setting the color balance (or *white balance*) of the camera—either automatically using the camera's smarts or manually using our own knowledge and experience.

The only time you need to think in terms of actual color temperature is when you're making adjustments using the Choose Color Temp. setting in the White Balance entry within the Photo Shooting menu, which, as I'll describe in Chapter 11, allows you to dial in exact color temperatures, if known. You can also shift and bias color balance along the blue/amber and magenta/green axes, and bracket white balance.

In most cases, however, one of the three Auto settings in the Photo Shooting menu's White Balance entry—Keep White (Reduce Warm Colors), Keep Overall Atmosphere, or Keep Warm Lighting Colors—will do a good job of calculating white balance for you. Auto can be used as your choice most of the time. Use the preset values ($Auto_0$, $Auto_1$, or $Auto_2$) or set a custom white balance that matches the current shooting conditions when you need to.

Remember that if you shoot RAW, you can specify the white balance of your image when you import it into Photoshop, Photoshop Elements, or another image editor using NX Studio, Adobe Camera Raw, or your preferred RAW converter. While color-balancing filters that fit on the front of the lens exist, they are primarily useful for film cameras, because film's color balance can't be tweaked as extensively as that of a sensor.

Color Rendering

Faithful color rendition goes beyond color temperature. So-called "white" light is produced by a spectrum of colors that, when added together, provide the neutral color needed for accuracy. Artificial light sources don't necessarily offer the same balanced spectrum found in sunlight. Some portions of the spectrum may be deficient or truncated or include gaps with certain wavelengths missing entirely. Astronomers use their knowledge of which elements absorb which colors of light to calculate the makeup of distant stars using spectrographs. In photography, the analysis of spectra is used to calculate the color rendering index, which measures how accurately colors are presented.

All artificial light sources have a color rendering index (CRI). That figure is calculated by rating eight different colors on a scale of 0 to 100, based on how natural the color looks compared to a perfect or "reference" light source at a particular color temperature. A CRI of 80-plus is considered acceptable; for critical applications like photography, a CRI higher than 93 is best. Incandescent and halogen bulbs typically have a CRI of 100 compared to a reference light source at the same color temperature. Standard LED lamps are rated at 83, although some can have CRIs as high as 98. Many types of fluorescent lights fall into the CRI 50 to 75 range.

Vendors, such as GE and Sylvania, may actually provide a figure known as the color rendering index on the packaging using a scale of 0 (some sodium-vapor lamps) to 100 (daylight and most incandescent lamps). Daylight fluorescents and deluxe cool white fluorescents suitable for photography might have a CRI of about 79 to 95, which is perfectly acceptable for most photographic applications. Less desirable are warm white fluorescents, which may have a CRI of 55. White deluxe mercury vapor lights are even less suitable with a CRI of 45, while low-pressure sodium lamps can vary from CRI 0–18. If you're using such a source not intended for photography, it may be worth your while to determine its color rendering index before you shoot. The figure is often supplied on the packaging of the light source.

Making color temperature adjustments are the only times you're likely to be confused by a seeming contradiction in how color temperatures are named: warmer (more reddish) color temperatures (measured on the Kelvin scale) are the *lower* numbers, while cooler (bluer) color temperatures are *higher* numbers. It might not make sense to say that 3,400K is warmer than 6,000K, but that's the way it is. If it helps, think of a glowing red ember contrasted with a white-hot welder's torch, rather than fire and ice.

The confusion comes from physics. Scientists calculate color temperature from the light emitted by a mythical object called a black body radiator, which absorbs all the radiant energy that strikes it, and reflects none at all. Such a black body not only *absorbs* light perfectly, but it *emits* it perfectly when heated (and since nothing in the universe is perfect, that makes it mythical).

At a particular physical temperature, this imaginary object always emits light of the same wavelength or color. That makes it possible to define color temperature in terms of actual temperature on the Kelvin scale that scientists use (which doesn't use degrees like Celsius and Fahrenheit scales do). Incandescent light, for example, typically has a color temperature of 3,200K to 3,400K. Daylight might range from 5,500K to 6,000K. Each type of illumination we use for photography has its own color temperature range—with some cautions.

The common types include:

- **Daylight.** Daylight is produced by the sun, and so is moonlight (which is just reflected sunlight). Daylight is present, of course, even when you can't see the sun. When sunlight is direct, it can be bright and harsh. If daylight is diffused by clouds, softened by bouncing off objects such as walls or your photo reflectors, or filtered by shade, it can be much dimmer, less contrasty, and more flattering for subjects such as people.

  Daylight's color temperature can vary quite widely. It is highest in temperature (most blue) at noon when the sun is directly overhead, because the light is traveling through a minimum amount of the filtering layer we call the atmosphere. The color temperature at high noon may be 6,000K. At other times of day, the sun is lower in the sky and the particles in the air provide a filtering effect that warms the illumination to about 5,500K for most of the day. Starting an hour before dusk and for an hour after sunrise, the warm appearance of the sunlight is even visible to our eyes when the color temperature may dip to 5,000K–4,500K.
- **Incandescent/Tungsten/Halogen Light.** The term incandescent or tungsten-halogen illumination is usually applied to the direct descendants of Thomas Edison's original electric lamp. Such lights consist of a glass bulb that contains a vacuum, or is filled with a halogen gas, and contains a tungsten filament that is heated by an electrical current, producing photons and heat. Tungsten-halogen lamps are a variation on the basic light bulb, using a more rugged (and longer-lasting)

filament that can be heated to a higher temperature, housed in a thicker glass or quartz envelope, and filled with iodine or bromine ("halogen") gases. The higher temperature allows tungsten-halogen (or quartz-halogen/quartz-iodine, depending on their construction) lamps to burn "hotter" and whiter. Although popular for automobile headlamps today, they've also been used for photographic illumination.

Although incandescent illumination isn't a perfect black body radiator, it's close enough that the color temperature of such lamps can be precisely calculated and used for photography without concerns about color variation (at least, until the very end of the lamp's life). As I noted, the color rendering index of such lamps tends to be very high, so you need to account only for the color temperature.

Of course, old-style tungsten lamps are virtually obsolete in the United States and most other countries. They were at first replaced either by compact fluorescent lights (CFL) or newer, more energy-efficient (and expensive) tungsten and halogen lights, and, eventually by LED illumination. It appears that LED illumination is on track to supplant all of these for most applications in the near future.

- **Fluorescent Light/LEDs.** Fluorescent light has some advantages in terms of illumination, but some disadvantages from a photographic standpoint. This type of lamp generates light through an electro-chemical reaction that emits most of its energy as visible light, rather than heat, which is why the bulbs don't get as hot. The type of light produced varies depending on the phosphor coatings and type of gas in the tube. So, the illumination fluorescent bulbs produce can vary widely in its characteristics.

  That's not great news for photographers. Different types of lamps have different "color temperatures" that can't be precisely measured on the Kelvin scale, because the light isn't produced by heating. Worse, fluorescent lamps have a discontinuous spectrum of light that can have some colors missing entirely. A particular type of light source can lack certain shades of red or other colors, which is why fluorescent lamps and other alternative technologies such as sodium-vapor illumination can produce strange hues and ghastly looking human skin tones. Their spectra can lack the reddish tones we associate with healthy skin and emphasize the blues and greens popular in horror movies. Their color rendering indexes are far from ideal.

  Compact fluorescent lights (CFLs) are those spiraling bulbs that became popular as old-school tungsten bulbs were phased out. However, CFLs don't work in all fixtures and for all applications, such as dimmers (even if you purchase special "dimmable" CFLs), electronic timer or "dusk-to-dawn" light controllers, some illuminated wall switches, or with motion sensors. Only certain types of CFLs (cold cathode models) operate outside in cold weather; they emit IR signals that can confuse the remote control of your TV, air conditioner, etc.

  Today, the future of illumination is solidly in the realm of LED light sources, particularly for movies, in the form of compact units that clip onto the camera and provide a continuous beam of light to fill in shadows indoors or out, and/or to provide the main illumination when shooting video inside. Several vendors have introduced LED studio lights that are bright enough for general-purpose shooting. It's become obvious that LED illumination will soon become the most widely used continuous light source. They've already made dramatic inroads in the automotive industry for taillights, headlights, and interior illumination.

Getting Crafty with Exposures

Your Nikon Z9/Z8 has an interesting array of special automated and semi-automated exposure and shooting modes that deserve special attention. I'm saving the multiple exposure facilities for Chapter 5, in which I detail all the Photo Shooting menu entries. Focus shift shooting, more commonly known as "focus stacking," isn't an exposure mode, so I'll be covering it in Chapter 3, which deals with autofocus, manual focus, subject detection, and other interesting topics. I'm going to finish off this chapter with a discussion of interval and time-lapse photography, and show you how to create a series of images over time for artistic expression, movie applications, and documentation—including star trails.

The Z9 and Z8 are capable of both interval photography (for still pictures) and time-lapse video, both available from the Photo Shooting menu. Humans have been capturing still photos as documentation for ages. A series of still photos taken from the same vantage point at specific intervals is called *interval photography.* Displaying all those images continuously as a motion picture results in a *time-lapse video* that shows in a few seconds or minutes of action that actually takes place over the course of hours, days, or months.

Doing Interval Photography

There are two ways to capture a series of photos at intervals: manually, and using the Z9/Z8's automatic interval photography mode. As you might expect, the manual method is labor-intensive and time-consuming. If you have the patience and motivation, you can take individual photos from approximately the same location at intervals of days, weeks, or months. One project I've started is to take photos at different times of the year, creating a series of landscape images that show the same scene in spring, summer, fall, and winter.

Construction sites also make interesting subjects for shots captured manually to document the work in progress. They can move at a snail's pace for large structures, or quite quickly in the case of home construction. For best results, try for a consistent viewpoint. It's likely you'll want a set of images taken from the same perspective so you can easily compare the progress of the construction. That can be tricky, and it requires some planning. You'll need to record the position of your camera so you can replicate it on subsequent visits.

Choose an appropriate time of day. For "progress" shots, sunny weather at midday will provide the most contrast, with shadows helping to make the details of the construction clearly visible. Early morning and late afternoon shots produce long shadows that can either be distracting or part of the composition if you want to use them creatively. Keep in mind that the weather may not always cooperate. At times, there may be no sunny days at critical times.

Automated interval photography is generally the most practical for sequences of a few hours to a day. For Figure 2.20, I pointed my camera out my office window in Florida, hoping to use Interval Timing Shooting to catch some manatees. I left the camera running for hours, capturing the three images shown in the figure. I've also used interval shooting for images of sunsets. Typically, I aim the camera at the horizon and set it to shoot a three-shot bracket with a 3.0-stop increment. Then, I set the interval to capture an image every 10 seconds.

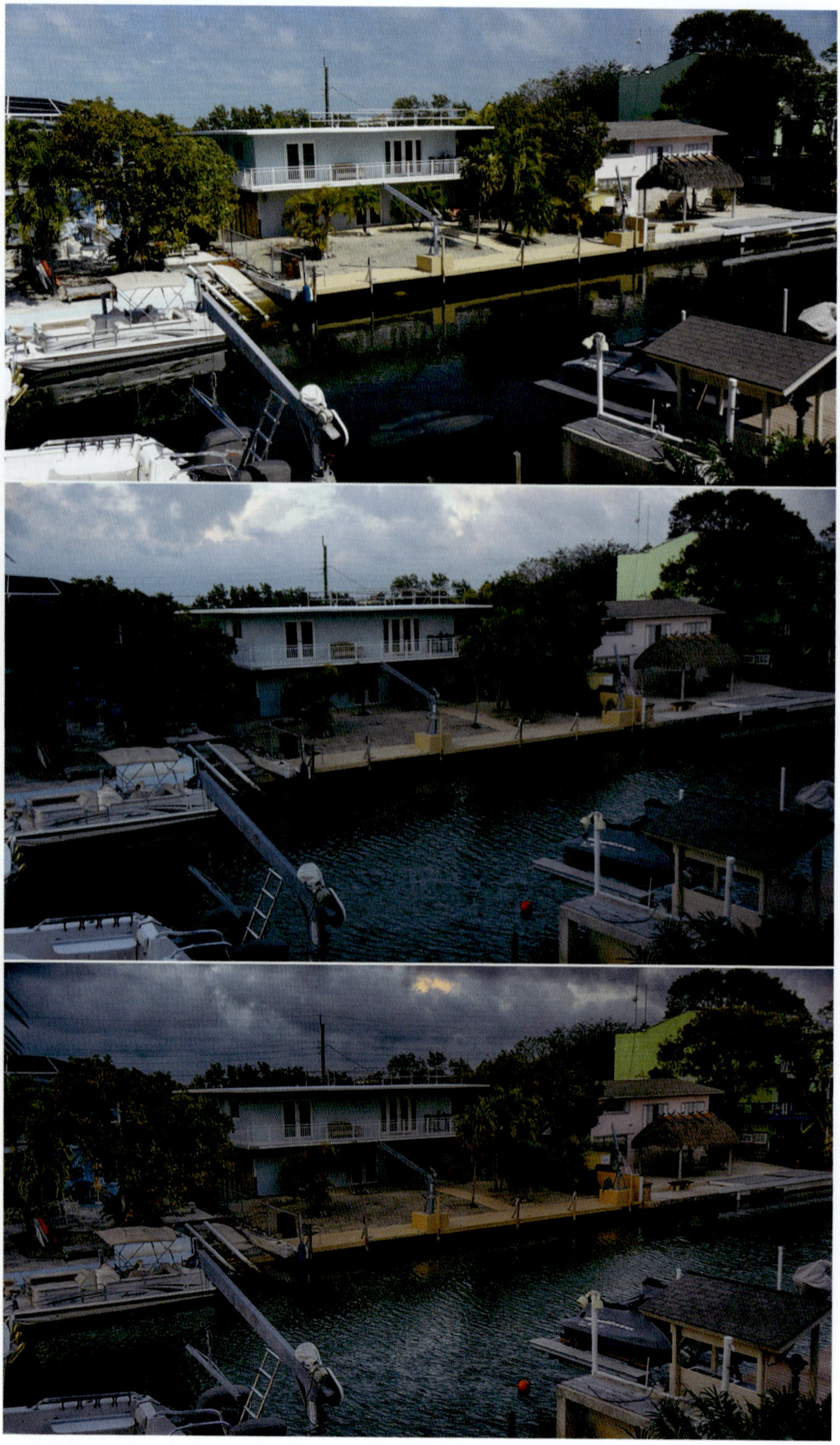

Figure 2.20 One of my time-lapse photos captured a mother manatee and her calf swimming by (top); the other exposures produced interesting variations on a static scene.

The camera's built-in interval photography feature allows you to take pictures for up to 9999 intervals in bursts of as many as nine shots, with a delay of up to 24 hours between shots/bursts, and an initial start-up time of as long as 24 hours from the time you activate the feature. That means that if you want to photograph a rosebud opening and would like to photograph the flower once every two minutes over the next 16 hours, you can do that easily. If you like, you can delay the first photo taken by a couple hours, so you don't have to stand there by the camera waiting for the right moment.

This next section will tell you everything you need to know to capture images using the camera's built-in intervalometer—whether you intend to use the resulting still photos as such, or plan to combine them into a home-brewed time-lapse movie, as described shortly. To set up interval timer shooting, just follow these steps.

Before you start:

1. **Check your time.** The camera uses its internal clock to activate, so make sure the time has been set accurately in the Setup menu before you begin.
2. **Check release mode.** You don't need to set the camera for continuous shooting. The camera will take the specified number of shots at each interval regardless of release mode setting, with one exception: if Self-timer is selected, the sequence will be unable to start.
3. **Turn off bracketing.** You can certainly bracket exposures while performing interval photography—but it's *not* done with the Photo Shooting menu's Auto Bracketing feature. You must set up bracketing using the Interval Timer Shooting entries options. If conventional auto bracketing is enabled, that feature will be *disabled* for interval shooting.
4. **Position camera.** Mount the camera on a tripod or other secure support.
5. **Fully charge the battery.** You might want to connect the camera to an external power source if you plan to shoot long sequences. Although the camera more or less goes to sleep between intervals, some power is drawn, and long sequences with bursts of shots can drain power even when you're not using the interval timer feature.
6. **Make sure the camera is protected** from the elements, accidents, and theft.

When you're ready to go, set up the camera for interval shooting:

1. **Access feature.** Choose Interval Timer Shooting from the Photo Shooting menu. The screen shown in Figure 2.21 will appear. Although Start is the option at the top, save it for last. Unless you're simply repeating an interval sequence you have already set up, you'll need to make the settings listed below first.
2. **Specify a starting time.** Highlight Choose Start Day/Time and press the right directional button. A screen appears allowing you to choose either Now (to begin interval shooting immediately after you finish making your settings and select Start) or Choose Day/Time. (See Figure 2.22, upper left.)

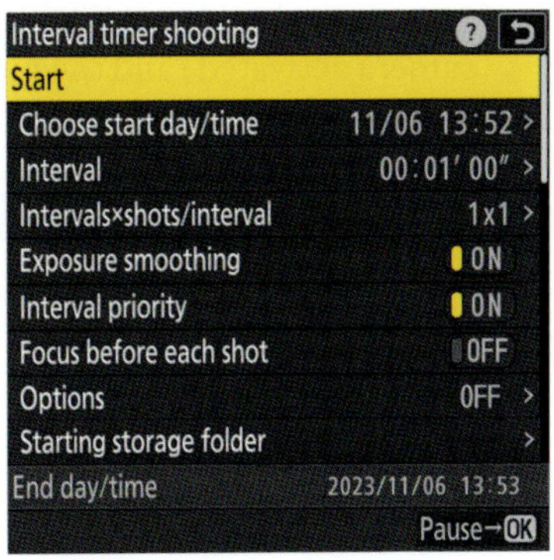

Figure 2.21 Interval timer shooting options.

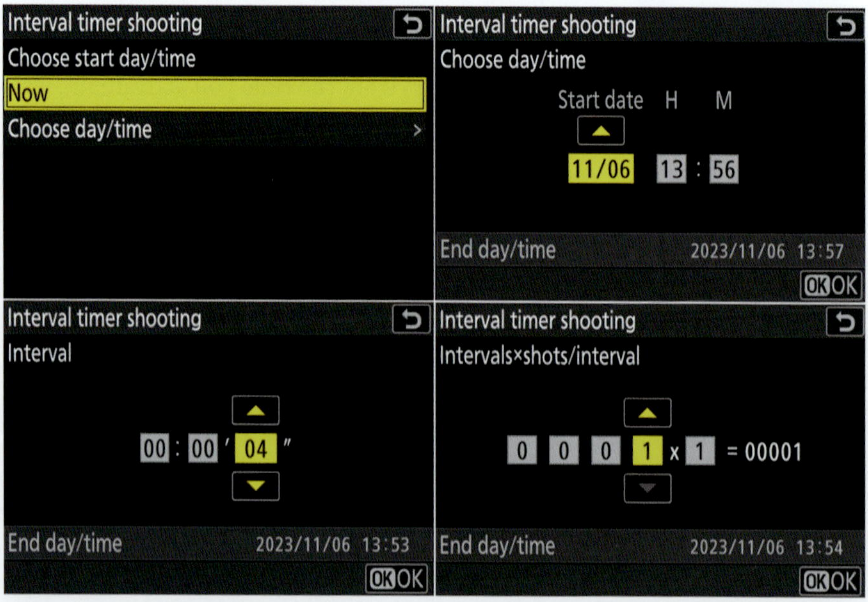

Figure 2.22 Choose starting day/time (top). Select interval and shots per interval (bottom).

To set a start time in the future, highlight Choose Day/Time, and press the right directional button. A screen appears that allows entering a Start Date, H (Hour), and M (Minute). (See Figure 2.22, upper right.) You can set the current date, or up to seven days in the future. Hours are available in 24-hour format. Press OK when you've specified the start time.

3. **Set the interval between exposures.** Scroll down to the Interval entry and press the right directional button to produce the screen shown in Figure 2.22, lower left. Use the left/right directional buttons to move among hours, minutes, and seconds, and use the up/down directional buttons to choose an interval from one second to 24 hours. Press the OK button when finished to move back to the main screen.
4. **Select the spacing and number of shots.** Highlight Intervals × Shots/Interval and press the right directional button to access the screen shown at lower right in Figure 2.22. Use the left/right directional buttons to highlight the number of intervals (that is, how many times you want the camera activated) and the number of shots taken after each interval has elapsed (as many as nine images taken at each activation). The total number of shots to be exposed overall will be shown at far right once you've entered those two parameters. You can highlight each number column separately, so that to enter, say, 250 intervals, you can set the 100s, 10s, and 1s columns individually (rather than press the up button 250 times!). You can select up to 9,999 intervals, and 9 shots per interval for a maximum of 89,991 exposures with one interval shooting cycle. Press OK to return to the main screen. **Tip:** Your memory card won't hold 89,991 exposures at full resolution!

NOTE The interval cannot be shorter than the shutter speed; for example, you cannot set one second as the interval if the images will be taken at two seconds or longer.

5. **Specify Exposure Smoothing.** You can turn this feature on or off. When activated, the camera will adjust the exposure of each shot to match that of the previous shot in P, S, or A mode. So, if you want the shutter speed to remain the same for each image (and don't care if the aperture is adjusted), use Shutter-priority mode. If you'd rather lock in your selected aperture (say, to keep the same depth-of-field), use Aperture-priority mode. Smoothing can also be used in Manual mode, but, of course, the camera won't vary either the shutter speed *or* aperture. You must have set ISO Sensitivity to Auto to allow the camera to conform exposures by adjusting the ISO instead. Press OK to confirm.
6. **Set Interval Priority.** Interval Priority can be set to On or Off. This parameter handles situations in which the shutter speed automatically selected in Program or Aperture-priority ends up being longer than the interval between shots. Perhaps you're shooting outdoors, and daylight has waned into night and a shutter speed of, say, 2 seconds is required even though your selected interval is one second.
   - **Interval Priority On:** The camera takes the picture at the specified interval anyway, even though the image may be taken at a shorter shutter speed and, therefore, underexposed. You can avoid the underexposure by activating Auto ISO Sensitivity, and selecting a minimum shutter speed that is shorter than the interval time. In that case, the camera will increase the ISO setting (if necessary) to produce the correct exposure using the automatically selected shutter speed.
   - **Interval Priority Off:** The chosen interval is lengthened to allow a correct exposure.
7. **Focus Before Each Shot.** Choose On to tell the camera to focus before each new exposure. Use this option if your subject is likely to move or, more commonly, a different subject is in the frame for some or all exposures. For example, if you were recording passersby on a busy street, some might be closer to the camera than others. **Note:** The camera will use Release Priority for AF-S or AF-C focus, regardless of your Custom Setting a1 or a2.
8. **Options.** Additional options are available here, as seen in Figure 2.23, left. They include Auto-exposure Bracketing and Time-Lapse Video. You can choose one or the other, then follow the steps listed in Step 9a and 9b. The default is Off, which disables both.

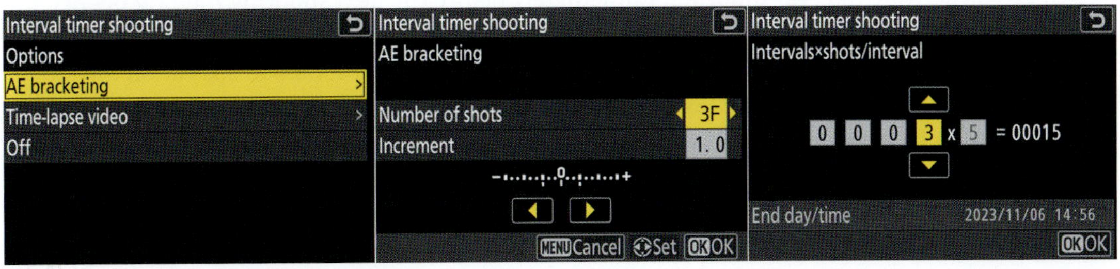

Figure 2.23 Autoexposure bracketing settings.

9a. **AE Bracketing (optional).** As I noted earlier, you must set up exposure bracketing for interval shooting here, rather than using the Photo Shooting menu's Auto Bracketing entry. Two parameters are available, as seen in Figure 2.23, center:

- **Number of shots.** The number of shots in each bracket sequence is set as with Auto Bracketing. You can choose three or two shots bracketed either under or over the metered exposure (–3/+3 and –2/+2), or 3, 5, 7, or 9 shots with the exposures spread equally between under and over exposure. The exposure scale at the bottom of the screen shows the distribution of the exposures.
- **Increment.** Select an increment of 0.3, 0.5, 0.7, 1.0, 1.3, 1.5, 1.7, 2.0, 2.3, 2.5, 2.7, or 3.0 stops. (If you choose 7 or 9 shots, the increments are limited to 0.3 to 1.7 on the Z9 and 0.3 to 1.0 on the Z8.) The exposure scale at the bottom of the screen will display the relative size of the increment selected. Once you've defined your bracketed set, the Intervals × Shots/Interval display (as in Figure 2.22, lower right) will change to reflect the number of shots taken at each interval. (See Figure 2.23, right.)

9b. **Time-lapse Video (optional).** The camera will save the still photos captured in your interval sequence *and also assemble a time-lapse movie.* The movie options for Interval Timer shooting are similar to those used with the Time-lapse Video entry, and I'll describe them in the next section.

10. **Starting Storage Folder.** Highlight New Folder and press the right directional button to tell the camera to create a new folder for each time-lapse sequence. This allows you to easily keep your sequences separate in their own folders. If you've chosen New Folder, you can also activate Reset File Numbering, which resets the numbering of each sequence to 0001 when a new folder is created. It's handy to have each sequence numbered separately.

11. **Activate shooting.** When all the parameters have been entered, scroll to the Start option at the top of the menu and press OK. If you've selected Now under Start Options, then interval shooting will begin immediately. If you chose a specific date/time instead, the appropriate delay will elapse before recording begins. Leave your camera turned on (and connected to an external power source if necessary).

    Once you activate interval shooting, immediately before the next shooting interval begins, the shutter speed display shows the number of intervals remaining and the aperture display shows the number of shots remaining in the current interval. A "timer" icon will appear on the monochrome control panel and the viewfinder/LCD displays. Between intervals, you can view that information by pressing the shutter-release button halfway; when you release the button, the data appears until the standby timer expires.

PAUSE OR CANCEL INTERVAL SHOOTING

While interval shooting is underway, you can review the images already taken using the Playback button. The monitor will clear automatically about four seconds before the next interval begins. Press the OK button between intervals (but not when images are still being recorded to the memory card) or choose the Interval Timer Shooting menu entry and select Pause. Interval shooting can also be paused by turning the camera on or off. To resume the Interval Timer Shooting menu again, press the multi selector right button, and choose Restart. You may also select Off to stop the shooting entirely.

Time-Lapse Video

Time-lapse cinematography is relatively new. Invented in the early 1950s by John Ott, the technique caught the public eye when he used it for a sequence in an Academy Award–winning nature film by Walt Disney. A film documenting the building of Disneyland in California was probably the first use of time-lapse photography to picture construction progress in movie form. Who today hasn't marveled at a time-lapse photograph of a flower opening, a series of shots of the moon marching across the sky, or one of those extreme time-lapse picture sets showing something that takes a very, very long time, such as a building slowly under construction?

The Z9 and Z8 provide three different ways to capture time-lapse video rather than just a series of still pictures. One requires a little work on your part, but the other two are highly automated. I'll explain the differences between them, and then show you how to use either of the two automated methods.

- **Do it yourself.** You gain more flexibility and some options if you capture the individual frames using the camera's Interval Timer, and then combine them in a video editor to produce a finished movie. Depending on the power of your video editor, you may be able to crop and manipulate your images to create a professional-level video with up to 8K resolution.
- **Interval sequence plus video.** Interval Timer Shooting is fully capable of automatically creating a video from the sequence frames you capture, using Step 9b as described above. Use that mode when you want stills and a video. It's convenient for shorter video clips to accompany the individual frames, as the interval timer retains all the shots you capture *and* creates a .MOV or .MP4 video clip.
- **Video only.** If all you want is video, the Z9/Z8's Time-Lapse Video entry is in some ways simpler to use. You don't (can't) stipulate a start time, and instead of specifying a particular number of shots, you indicate the desired length of the finished video. In addition, you can choose either FX (full frame) or DX (cropped) image areas. I'll provide a more detailed description of this method next.

If you've mastered interval photography, shooting time-lapse video to allow the camera to capture the individual frames and assemble them into a movie for you is a snap! The settings screen is similar to the one for interval shooting, with some additional options. The key entries, shown in Figure 2.24, include:

- **Start.** Unlike the similar Interval Timer shooting entry, Time-Lapse Video has no Start Options. Make your other settings, select Start, and time-lapse photography will begin automatically about three seconds later. Be sure to double-check your settings before triggering the camera.

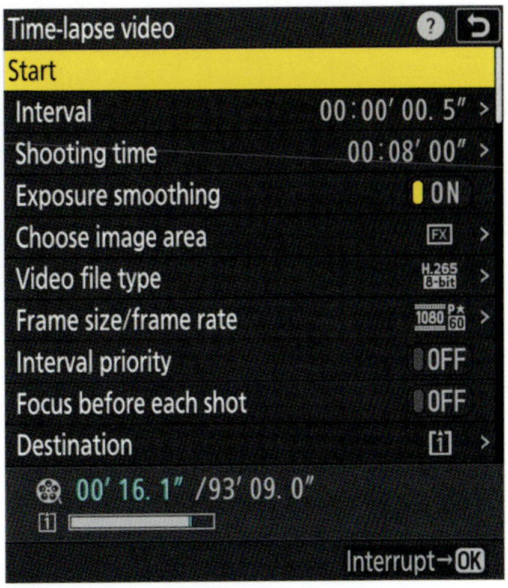

Figure 2.24 Time-lapse video options.

- **Interval.** Select an interval between frames; use a longer value for slow-moving action, such as a flower bud unfolding. You might want to experiment and choose a time between shots of one minute or longer. Some blooms mature faster than others. Use a shorter value for movies, say, depicting humans moving around at a comical pace for a Charlie Chaplin–like effect. This parameter can be set from 1 second to 10 minutes.
- **Shooting Time.** You can specify how long the camera will continue to capture frames at the interval you specified. The shortest time you can select is one minute, while the longest period you can capture is 23 hours, 59 minutes. That should be plenty for most applications. Andy Warhol's 1963 flick *Sleep* was only 5 hours, 20 minutes long!

  The information bar (seen at the bottom of Figure 2.24) displays the length of your finished movie (in cyan) and the maximum length possible given the remaining capacity of your memory card in gray. A graphic below the text represents the Slot number of your current card and the amount of storage left. If the movie length is displayed in red instead of cyan, there is not enough space on the memory card for a video of that length.
- **Exposure Smoothing.** You can turn exposure smoothing on or off. When activated, the camera adjusts the exposure of each frame to match that of the previous frame in P, S, or A mode. That avoids sudden changes in exposure modes other than Manual exposure (which, of course, will remain at your manual settings throughout). Smoothing can also be used in Manual mode, but, of course, the camera won't vary either the shutter speed *or* aperture. You must have set ISO Sensitivity to Auto to allow the camera to compensate appropriately for changes in brightness. Press OK to confirm.
- **Choose Image Area.** You can select FX-based movie format or DX-based movie format (both cropped to the 16:9 aspect ratio of HD video, of course).
- **Video File Type.** You can choose to create your video in 8-bit .MOV format or 8-bit .MP4 format. I'll explain the difference between the two in Chapter 12, but the most important one here is that .MP4 allows creating *only* Full HD (1920 × 1080) resolution videos. (See Figure 2.25, left.)

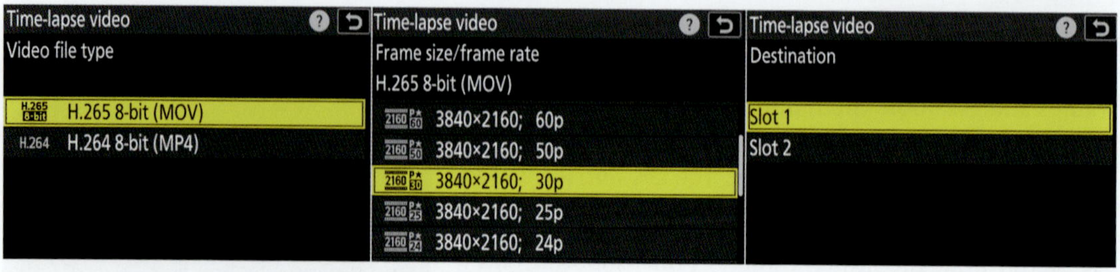

Figure 2.25 Choosing video file type, frame size/rate, and file destination.

- **Frame Size/Frame Rate.** Here you can select the frame size and frames per second setting for your time-lapse movie. As noted, only 1920 × 1080 videos at 60/50p, 30/25p, and 24p frame rates are available for .MP4 movies. If you've selected .MOV as your file type, then FHD (1920 × 1080) and 4K (3840 × 2160) resolutions are available at 60/50p, 30/25p, and 24p frame rates, and 8K (7680 × 4320), at 30/25p, and 24p frame rates. (See Figure 2.25, center.)
- **Interval Priority.** This setting is similar to its intervalometer counterpart, as explained previously. It takes care of situations in which the shutter speed automatically selected in Program or Aperture-priority ends up being longer than the interval between shots. When enabled, the camera captures the movie frame at the specified interval, giving it priority even though the image may be taken at a shorter shutter speed and underexposed.

  To compensate, activate Auto ISO Sensitivity, and select a minimum shutter speed that is shorter than the interval time. The camera will boost ISO to allow exposure at the correct interval. When disabled, the camera increases the interval you specified to allow correct exposure. However, with some subjects, the increased time may be visible in the finished movie as a jump or delay.
- **Focus Before Each Shot.** Choose On to tell the camera to focus before each new exposure. Use this option if your subject is likely to move or, more commonly, a different subject is in the frame for some or all exposures. For example, if you were recording passersby on a busy street, some might be closer to the camera than others.
- **Destination.** Select the memory card slot used to store your video. The Z9 labels your choices as Slot 1 and Slot 2 (as seen in Figure 2.25, right) while the Z8 labels them CFexpress/XQD Card Slot/SD Card Slot.

Star Trails

Star trails are another great application for both long exposures and interval shooting. You can shoot the night sky using long exposures with your camera mounted on a tripod. However, because of the rotation of the Earth, longer exposures will record the apparent motion of the celestial objects through the sky, producing a light trail. If you use a very, very long exposure, the light trail will record as continuous streaks, centered around the Polaris (the North Star) in the northern hemisphere and Sigma Octantis (which is, unfortunately, too dim to be easily seen with the naked eye) in the southern hemisphere. If you activate Extended Shutter Speeds, you can record night shots as long as 15 minutes.

Such long exposures can result in excessive noise and sensor overheating, so it's more common for photographers to take a series of individual exposures and combine them to produce a single star trail image. If you want your stars to appear as reasonably sharp points, you'll need to keep the exposure short enough that their movement in the sky isn't apparent. Fortunately, there's a simple formula you can use to calculate that exposure time, the "500 Rule." Divide 500 by the focal length of your lens to determine the longest exposure (in seconds) before stars start to produce a blurred trail. For example, with a 50mm lens, the longest exposure would be 10 seconds (500 divided by 50). Capturing the complete canopy of stars generally requires a wider viewing perspective. With the 16mm wide-angle setting, exposures could be as long as roughly 30 seconds.

For Figure 2.26, I set my camera to ISO 200, and used a basic exposure of 30 seconds at f/5.6. I selected an interval of 32 seconds and 170 total exposures, which totals about 90 minutes. Noise reduction was OFF! Then, I followed these steps, using Photoshop:

1. **Transfer files to a folder.** Select a folder on your computer and copy all your files to that location.
2. **In Photoshop:** Choose Files > Scripts > Load Files into Stack.
3. **Browse to folder.** Click the Browse button and navigate to the folder where your images are stored.
4. **Click OK.** Photoshop will create a file with one layer for each of your captured images.
5. **Select All layers.** Then click Layer Blending Options from the Layers palette and choose Lighten.
6. **Flatten image.** You'll want to flatten your image (the multi-layer file will be huge!). You'll end up with an impressive star trail image.

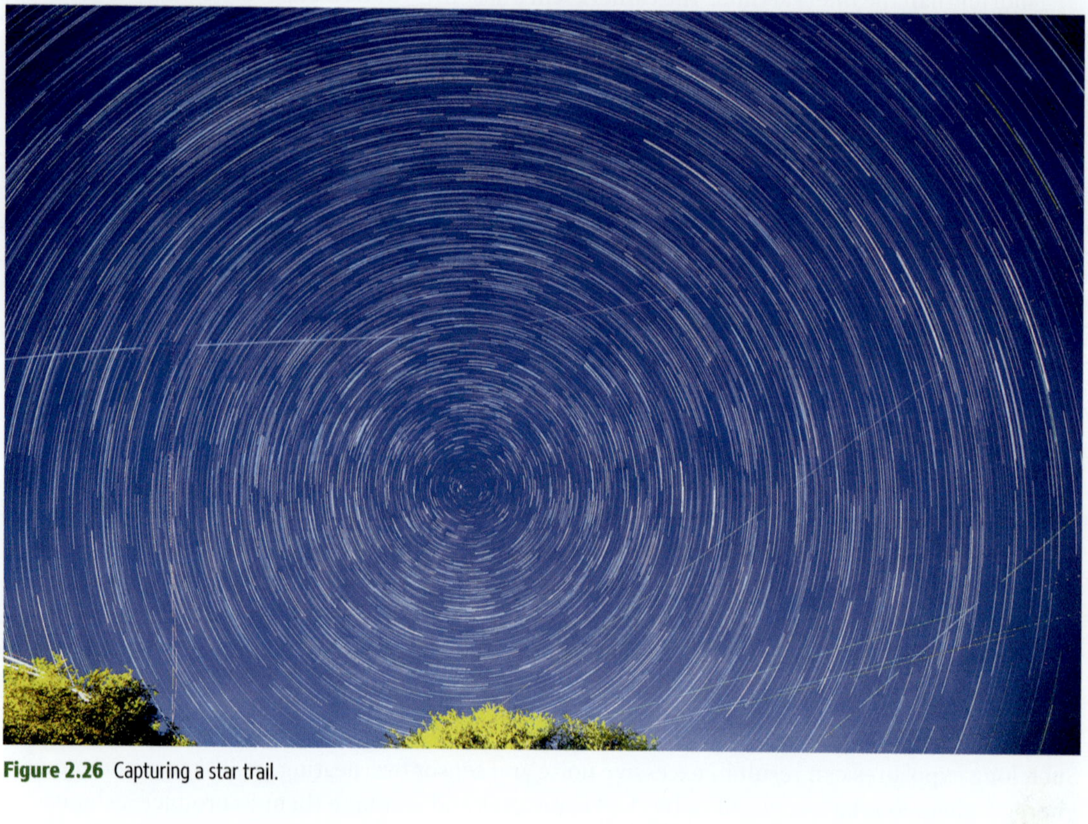

Figure 2.26 Capturing a star trail.

Mastering the Mysteries of Focus

3

How far we've come! My first professional job was as a reporter/sportswriter/photographer for a daily newspaper (back when a backslash really *meant* something). Focusing to achieve a sharp image was a manual process accomplished by turning a ring or knob on the camera or lens until, in one's highly trained professional judgment, the image was satisfactorily in focus. Manual focus was particularly challenging when shooting sports.

Today, modern digital cameras like the Z9 and Z8 can identify potential subject matter, lock in on human faces, animals, birds, vehicles, and airplanes (if present), and automatically focus faster than the blink of an eye. Usually. Of course, sometimes a camera's AF will zero in on the *wrong* subject, become confused by background pattern, or be totally unable to follow a fast-moving target like a bird in flight.

While autofocus *has* come a long way in the last decades, it's still a work-in-progress that relies heavily on input from the photographer, and, it seems, frequent firmware updates from Nikon as the company continues to fine-tune the capabilities of its mirrorless cameras.

One key problem is that the camera doesn't have any way of determining, for certain, what subject you want to be in sharp focus. It may select an object and lock in focus with lightning speed—even though the subject is not the one that's the center of interest of your photograph. Or, the camera may lock focus too soon, or too late. While Nikon has given us faster and more precise autofocus systems, with many more choices, it's common for the sheer number of options to confuse even the most advanced photographers. So, even though your Z9/Z8 has the potential to calculate and set focus for you quickly and with a high degree of accuracy, you still need to make a few settings that provide guidance on three Ws of autofocus: *what* (which includes subject detection), *where* (what areas of the frame should be considered), and *when* (at which points in time should autofocus begin and stop). Your decisions in how you apply those choices supplies a fourth W: *why* (how the other criteria are applied to achieve your creative goals).

This chapter is going to concentrate on the information you need to master to put all of the Ws to work. However, you'll find discussions of some manual/automatic focus features elsewhere in this book. Nikon has scattered focus-oriented settings among three different top-level menus. I've found that separating the "how to" lessons like those in this chapter from the reference material has proved to be the best way to explain complex topics. Nobody likes to be bogged down in 100-page chapters that try to cover everything in a convoluted way.

Here's a quick guide to the information you need:

- **Autofocus/Manual Focus features.** I'm going to introduce your camera's long roster of focus options in this chapter. I'll cover how focus works, how to use all the individual focus and focus point modes, tracking, subject detection, and available focus aids. I'm also going to describe useful techniques like trap focus, back-button focus, and focus stacking.
- **Focus feature reference.** In Chapter 5, you'll find more detail about the menu options for the AF Subject Detection (*what*), AF-area mode (*where*), and Focus method (*when*) trio of functions, which are all located in the Photo Shooting menu. There's also a description of Auto Capture, a related feature which you can use to have the camera automatically triggered to focus and then capture a sequence of still images or a video if it detects subjects that fulfill size, position, motion, and other parameters you specify.
- **Custom Settings reference.** Chapter 7 contains comprehensive listings of the fourteen autofocus/manual focus options in the Custom Settings menu.
- **Setup Fine Tuning.** AF Fine-tuning and retaining focus position are addressed in Chapter 9's Setup Menu discussions.

How Focus Works

Simply put, focus is the process of adjusting the camera so that parts of our subject that we want to be sharp and clear are, in fact, sharp and clear. We allow the camera to focus for us, automatically, or we can rotate the lens's focus ring manually to achieve the desired focus. Manual focusing is especially problematic because our eyes and brains have poor memory for correct focus. That's why your eye doctor conducting a refraction test must shift back and forth between pairs of lenses and ask, "Does that look sharper—or was it sharper before?" in determining your correct prescription. Too often, the slight differences are such that the lens pairs must be swapped multiple times.

Similarly, manual focusing involves jogging the focus ring back and forth as you go from almost in focus, to sharp focus, to almost focused again. The little clockwise and counterclockwise arcs decrease in size until you've zeroed in on the point of correct focus. What you're looking for is the image with the most contrast between the edges of elements in the image.

Your autofocus mechanism, like all such systems found in modern cameras, also evaluates these increases and decreases in sharpness, but it is able to remember the progression perfectly, so that autofocus can lock in much more quickly and, with an image that has sufficient contrast, more precisely. Unfortunately, while the autofocus system finds it easy to measure degrees of apparent focus at each of the focus points in the viewfinder, it doesn't really know with any certainty *which object* should be in sharpest focus. Is it the closest object? The subject in the center? Something lurking *behind* the closest subject? A person standing over at the side of the picture? Using autofocus effectively involves telling the camera exactly what it should be focusing on.

Learning to use a modern autofocus system is easy, but you do need to fully understand how it works to get the most benefit from it. Once you're comfortable with autofocus, you'll know when it's appropriate to use the manual focus option, too.

As the camera collects focus information from the sensors, it then evaluates it to determine whether the desired sharp focus has been achieved. The calculations may include whether the subject is moving, and whether the camera needs to "predict" where the subject will be when the shutter-release button is fully depressed, and the picture is taken. The speed with which the camera is able to evaluate focus and then move the lens elements into the proper position to achieve the sharpest focus determines how fast the autofocus mechanism is. Although the AF system will almost always focus more quickly than a human eye, there are types of shooting situations where that's not fast enough. For example, if you're having problems shooting a sport with many fast-moving players because the autofocus system manically follows each moving subject, a better choice might be to switch Autofocus modes, or shift into Manual and prefocus on a spot where you anticipate the action will be, such as a goal line or soccer net.

You'll be using a *hybrid* autofocus system, using two technologies called contrast-detection autofocus (CDAF) and phase-detection autofocus (PDAF). I'm going to provide a quick overview of contrast detection first, and then devote much of the rest of this chapter to the complexities of phase detection.

Contrast Detection

This is a slower, but potentially more accurate mode, best suited for static subjects, and was originally the only kind of autofocus available for mirrorless cameras and for dSLRs when shooting in their Live View and Video modes. The recent innovation of adding phase-detection abilities to the sensor itself (as I'll describe shortly) made contrast detection a fine-tuning option for hybrid autofocus systems that combined CDAF and PDAF.

Contrast detection is very easy to understand, and is illustrated by Figure 3.1, a close-up of some weathered wood. At top in the figure, the transitions between the edges found in the image are soft and blurred because of the low contrast between them. Whether the edges are horizontal, vertical, or diagonal doesn't matter in the least; the focus system looks only for contrast between edges, and those edges can run in any direction at all.

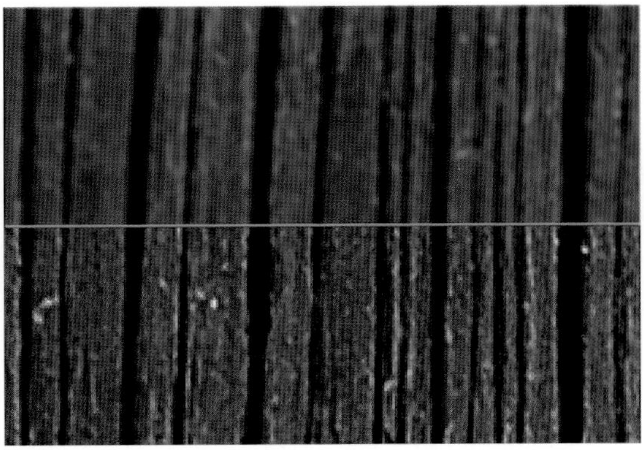

Figure 3.1 Focus in contrast-detection mode evaluates the increase in contrast in the edges of subjects, starting with a blurry image (top) and producing a sharp, contrasty image (bottom).

At the bottom of Figure 3.1, the image has been brought into sharp focus, and the edges have much more contrast; the transitions are sharp and clear. Although this example is a bit exaggerated so you can see the results on the printed page, it's easy to understand that when maximum contrast in a subject is achieved, it can be deemed to be in sharp focus. Although achieving focus with contrast detection is generally quite a bit slower, there are several advantages—and disadvantages—to this method.

Those advantages and disadvantages are:

- **Works with more image types.** Any subject that has edges will work with CDAF.
- **Focus on any point.** With contrast detection, any portion of the image can be used to focus: you don't need dedicated AF sensors. Focus is achieved with the actual sensor image, so focus point selection is simply a matter of choosing which part of the sensor image to use. It's easy to move the focus point around to virtually any location. Because a smaller area of the sensor can be used to focus, the camera uses contrast detection to confirm focus when the autofocus area mode is set to Pinpoint AF. (I'll explain AF-area modes later in this chapter.)
- **Potentially more accurate.** Contrast detection is clear-cut. The camera can clearly see when the highest contrast has been achieved, as long as there is sufficient light to allow it to examine the image produced by the sensor. However, some "hunting" may be necessary. As the camera seeks the ideal plane of focus, it may overshoot and have to back up a little, then re-correct if the new focus plane is not optimal. However, once CDAF settles on the ideal focus plane, the results are generally very accurate. Contrast detection is an excellent way of fine-tuning focus that has been achieved through PDAF. As noted, the Z9 and Z8 can use contrast detection when the AF-area mode is Pinpoint AF, especially in AF-S focus mode, or under low-light conditions.

Phase Detection

Phase detection is easily much more rapid than contrast detection. The challenge is to make its operation as accurate as possible. Digital SLRs, like the Z9 and Z8's sibling the D780, have always used PDAF. Such dSLR systems include an array of tiny autofocus sensors, located in the "floor" of the mirror box, with a small portion of the illumination directed downward to the autofocus sensor array.

The separate AF sensor of the dSLR is replaced by a very large number of phase-detect autofocus points embedded in the Z9/Z8's imaging sensor. They can be found in every twelfth row, and are aggregated to produce 493 selectable focus points (or 405 focus points in Auto-area mode). There are roughly four million autofocus pixels overall; your camera groups them together into the 493 focus positions in the 17 by 29 array you can specify in Single-point AF-area mode, as seen in Figure 3.2.

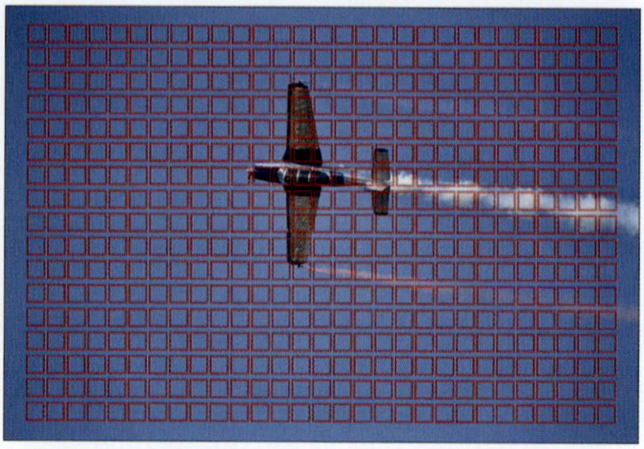

Figure 3.2 The boxes represent the 493 selectable AF areas when using Single-point autofocus.

The phase-detection pixels in the camera's sensor have a mask covering half of the pixel on one side, with a nearby laterally displaced phase-detection pixel masked on the opposite side. The effect is to create two different "views," each arriving from opposite sides of the lens. This pair of images functions exactly like the rangefinders used for surveying and in rangefinder-focusing cameras like the venerable Leica M series. The two images are separated when out of focus, and then gradually brought together to achieve sharp focus, as shown from top to bottom in Figure 3.3. **Note:** Using some photosites as AF sensors doesn't rob your camera of resolution; the phase-detect sensors are actually *dual-pixel* photosites and are used to collect *both* autofocus and image information. In addition, your Z9 and Z8 cameras have 46 *million* pixels available to create an image; assigning some to double duty has no effect on image quality.

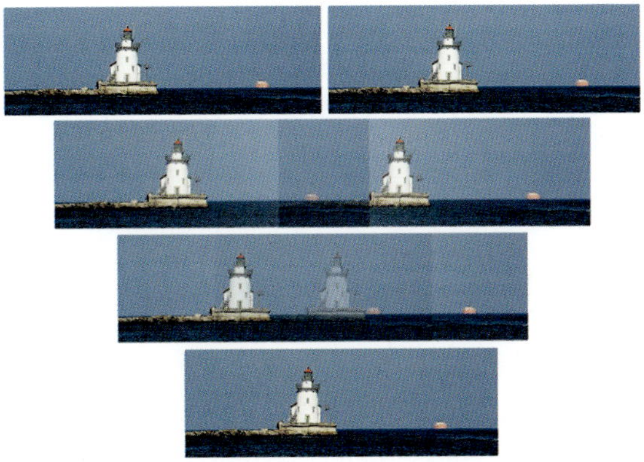

Figure 3.3 In phase detection, parts of an image are split in two and compared (top). When the image is in focus, the two halves of the image align, as with a rangefinder (bottom).

This process determines when the image pair are "in phase" and aligned. The rangefinder approach of phase detection indicates exactly how out of focus the image is, and in which direction (focus is too near, or too far) thanks to the amount and direction of the displacement of the split image. The system can quickly and precisely snap the image into sharp focus and match the lines.

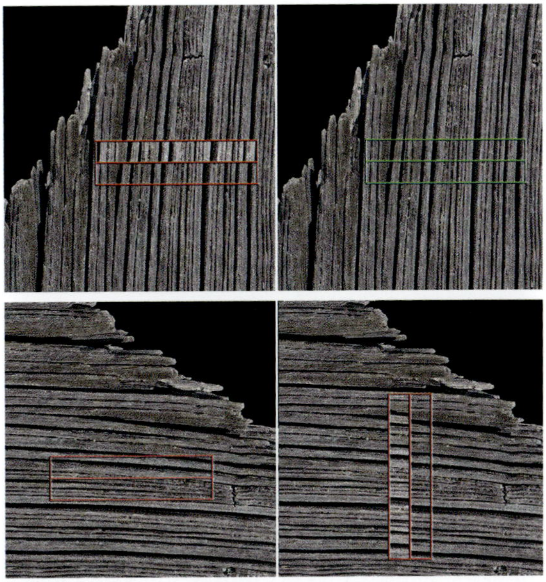

Figure 3.4 When an image is out of focus, the split lines don't align precisely (top left). Using phase detection, the camera is able to align the features of the image and achieve sharp focus quickly (top right). Horizontal lines aren't ideal for horizontally oriented sensors (bottom left) and require vertically oriented AF sensors (bottom right).

The PDAF sensors are all *line sensors,* which means they work best with features that transect the sensor either perpendicularly or at an angle, as visualized in Figure 3.4, top left and right. It's easy to detect when the two halves of the vertical lines of the weathered wood—actually a 19th century outhouse—are aligned. However, when the same sensor is asked to measure focus for, say, horizontal lines that don't split up quite so conveniently, or, in the worst case, subjects such as the sky (which may have neither vertical nor horizontal lines), focus can slow down drastically, or even become impossible. One such scenario is pictured in Figure 3.4, bottom left. A possible solution is to incorporate vertically oriented AF sensors, which can easily focus horizontal subject matter (see Figure 3.4, bottom right), or sensors that are sensitive in both horizontal *and* vertical orientations. Such sensors are called "cross-type" sensors.

However, none of Nikon's mirrorless models have cross sensors; the company uses a different approach. Once the focus plane has been achieved using the line sensors of the phase-detect system, the camera is able to use contrast detection to fine-tune focus, if necessary. The combination provides the speed of PDAF with the accuracy of CDAF.

All dSLRs perform autofocus using the lens's largest f/stop, which means that lenses with a maximum aperture smaller than f/5.6 or f/8 can't use autofocus at all. Your Z9/Z8 doesn't have that limitation: it always autofocuses at the *aperture you've set* if it is f/5.6 or wider. That reduces the possibility of focus shift that can result from focusing at one aperture and taking the actual photo at a different aperture (and different depth-of-field characteristics). However, if your selected f/stop is smaller than f/5.6, the Z9/Z8 will use f/5.6 anyway.

TIP If you find the horizontal line AF sensors (which are most sensitive to vertical lines) have difficulties focusing on a subject that is predominated by horizontal features, rotate the camera at least 45 degrees and lock focus, then return to your previous orientation. Obviously, this works best with subjects that aren't moving.

Your Z9/Z8's phase-detect system offers one final bonus: reducing/eliminating the need for AF fine-tuning (although the option still exists in the Setup menu). The dSLR's separate AF mechanism has a half-dozen different components that can potentially be out of alignment; with mirrorless cameras only the lens/lens mount and sensor planes need to be perfectly lined up.

Adding Circles of Confusion

You know that increased depth-of-field brings more of your subject into focus. But more depth-of-field also makes autofocusing (or manual focusing) more difficult because the contrast is lower between objects at different distances. So, autofocus with a 200mm lens (or zoom setting) may be easier than at a 28mm focal length (or zoom setting) because the longer lens has less apparent depth-of-field. By the same token, a lens with a maximum aperture of f/1.8, such as the Z-mount 50mm f/1.8 and 35mm f/1.8 optics, will be easier to autofocus (or manually focus) than one of the same focal length with an f/4 maximum aperture, such as the Nikkor Z 24-70mm f/4 zoom, because the f/4 lens has more depth-of-field *and* a dimmer view at a particular focal length.

To make things even more complicated, many subjects aren't polite enough to remain still. They move around in the frame, so that even if the camera is sharply focused on your main subject, it may change position and require refocusing. An intervening subject may pop into the frame and pass between you and the subject you meant to photograph. You (or the camera) have to decide whether to lock focus on this new subject or remain focused on the original subject. Finally, there are some kinds of subjects that are difficult to bring into sharp focus because they lack enough contrast to allow the camera's AF system (or our eyes) to lock in. Blank walls, a clear blue sky, birds-in-flight, or other subject matter may make focusing difficult.

If you find all these focus factors confusing, you're on the right track. Focus is, in fact, measured using something called a *circle of confusion* (see Figure 3.5). An ideal image consists of zillions of tiny little points, which, like all points, theoretically have no height or width. There is perfect contrast between the point and its surroundings. You can think of each point as

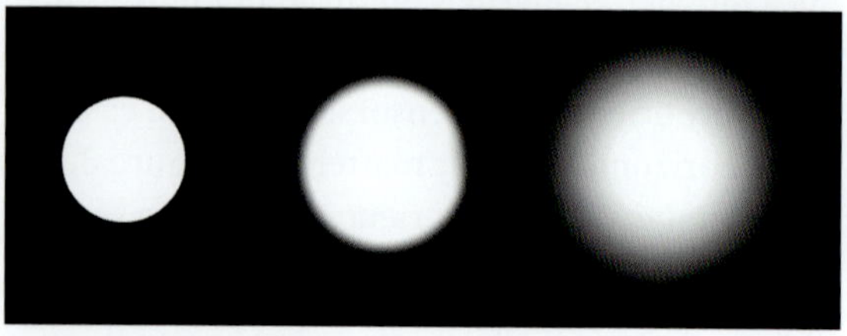

Figure 3.5 When a pinpoint of light (left) goes out of focus, its blurry edges form a circle of confusion (center and right).

a pinpoint of light in a darkened room. When a given point is out of focus, its edges decrease in contrast and it changes from a perfect point to a tiny disc with blurry edges (remember, blur is the lack of contrast between boundaries in an image).

If this blurry disc—the circle of confusion—is small enough, our eye still perceives it as a point. It's only when the disc grows large enough that we can see it as a blur rather than a sharp point that a given point is viewed as out of focus. You can see, then, that enlarging an image, either by displaying it larger on your computer monitor or by making a large print, also enlarges the size of each circle of confusion. Moving closer to the image does the same thing. So, parts of an image that may look perfectly sharp in a 5 × 7–inch print viewed at arm's length, might appear blurry when blown up to 11 × 14 and examined at the same distance. Take a few steps back, however, and it may look sharp again.

To a lesser extent, the viewer also affects the apparent size of these circles of confusion. Some people see details better at a given distance and may perceive smaller circles of confusion than someone standing next to them. For the most part, however, such differences are small. Truly blurry images will look blurry to just about everyone under the same conditions.

Technically, there is just one plane within your picture area, parallel to the back of the camera (or sensor, in the case of a digital camera), that is in sharp focus. That's the plane in which the points of the image are rendered as precise points. At every other plane in front of or behind the focus plane, the points show up as discs that range from slightly blurry to extremely blurry. In practice, the discs in many of these planes will still be so small that we see them as points, and that's where we get depth-of-field. Depth-of-field is just the range of planes that include discs that we perceive as points rather than blurred splotches. The size of this range increases as the aperture is reduced in size and is allocated roughly one-third in front of the plane of sharpest focus, and two-thirds behind it. The range of sharp focus is always greater behind your subject than in front of it. (See Figure 3.6.)

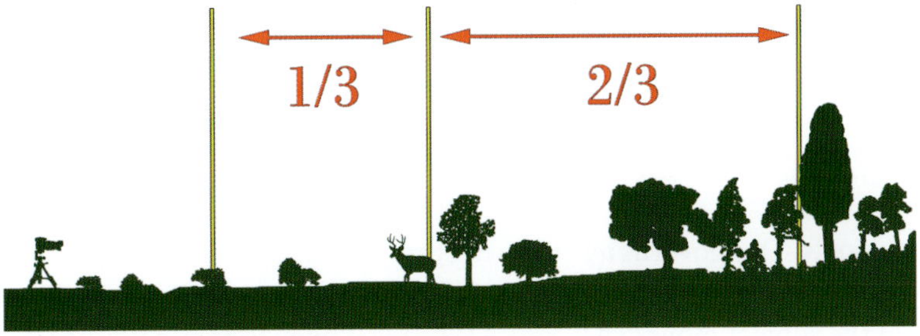

Figure 3.6 The range of sharp focus is greater behind your subject than in front of it.

Working with Autofocus

Autofocus can sometimes be frustrating for the new digital photographer. That's because correct focus plays a greater role among your creative options with a digital camera, even when photographing the same subjects. Most point-and-shoot digital cameras and smartphones have sensors that are much tinier than the sensor in the camera. Those smaller sensors require shorter focal length lenses and zoom settings, which have, effectively, more depth-of-field.

The bottom line is that with the average point-and-shoot camera or smartphone, *everything* is in focus from about one foot to infinity and at virtually every f/stop. Unless you're shooting close-up photos a few inches from the camera, the depth-of-field is prodigious, and autofocus is almost a non-factor. Of course, some of the latest phones have multiple lenses, extra-large f/stops (with reduced depth-of-field), and intelligent algorithms that can process images to produce selective focus effects and blurry backgrounds.

Your Z9/Z8 needs no special tricks to achieve similar effects, because, as full-frame models, they use longer focal length lenses, so there is less depth-of-field. That's a *good* thing, creatively, because you have the choice to use selective focus to isolate subjects. But it does make the correct use of autofocus more critical. To maintain the most creative control, you have to choose three attributes:

- **How much is in focus.** Generally, by choosing the f/stop used, you'll determine the *range* of sharpness/amount of depth-of-field. The more extensive the DOF, the "easier" it is for the autofocus system's locked-in focus point to be appropriate (even though, strictly speaking, there is only one actual plane of sharp focus). With less depth-of-field, the accuracy of the focus point becomes more critical, because even a small error will result in an out-of-focus shot.
- **What subject is in focus.** The portion of your subject that is zeroed in for autofocus is determined by the autofocus zone that is active, and which is chosen either by you or by the Nikon camera (as described next). For example, when shooting portraits, it's actually okay for part of the subject—or even part of the subject's face—to be slightly out of focus as long as the eyes (or even just the *nearest* eye) appear sharp.
- **When focus is applied.** For static shots of objects that aren't moving when focus is applied it doesn't matter as much. But when you're shooting sports, or birds in flight, or children, the subject may move within the viewfinder as you're framing the image. Whether that movement is across the frame or headed right toward you, timing the instant when autofocus is applied can be important.

Bringing the AF System into Focus

There are three aspects of autofocus that you need to understand to use this essential feature productively:

- **Autofocus mode and priority.** This governs *when* during the framing and shooting process autofocus is achieved. Should the camera focus once when activated, or continue to monitor your subject and refocus should the subject move? (AF-S or AF-C?) Is it okay to take a picture even if sharp focus isn't yet achieved, or should the camera lock out the shutter release until the image is sharp?
- **Autofocus point selection.** This aspect controls how the camera selects which areas of the frame are used to evaluate focus. Point selection allows the camera (or you) to specify a subject and lock focus in on that subject. Choosing the right AF-area mode is the key here.
- **Autofocus activation.** When should the autofocus process *begin*, and when should it be locked? This aspect is related to the autofocus mode but uses controls that you can specify to activate and/or lock the autofocus process.

As the camera collects information from the sensors, it then evaluates the data to determine whether the desired sharp focus has been achieved. The calculations may include whether the subject is moving, and whether the camera needs to "predict" where the subject will be when the shutter-release button is fully depressed, and the picture is taken.

The speed with which the camera is able to evaluate focus and then move the lens elements into the proper position to achieve the sharpest focus determines how fast the autofocus mechanism is. Although your camera will almost always focus more quickly than a human, there are types of shooting situations where that's not fast enough. For example, as I mentioned, if you're having problems shooting sports because the camera's autofocus system follows each moving subject, a better option might be to switch autofocus modes or shift into manual and prefocus on a spot where you anticipate the action will be, such as a goal line. At night football games, for example, when I am shooting with a telephoto lens almost wide open under dim lighting, I sometimes focus manually on one of the referees who happens to be standing where I expect the action to be taking place (say, a halfback run or a pass reception).

Focus Mode and Priority

Choosing the right focus mode (AF-S, AF-C, or Manual) is another key to focusing success. (Your camera also has an additional focus mode, AF-F—full-time autofocus in Video mode, as explained in Chapter 12.) To save battery power, when shooting stills, your camera doesn't start to focus the lens until you partially depress the shutter release or press the AF-ON button on the back of the camera (unless you've reprogrammed the button for some other function or have specified another control to activate autofocus, as described in Chapter 12). But, autofocus isn't some mindless beast out there snapping your pictures in and out of focus with no feedback from you after you press that button. There are several settings you can modify that return at least a modicum of control to you. Your first decisions should be whether you set the camera to AF-S, AF-C, or manual focus, and whether to use focus-priority or release-priority (described shortly).

You can easily specify AF-S, AF-C, or Manual focus: just press the Focus Mode button on the front of the camera and rotate the main command dial. Or press the *i* button and access Focus Mode, located by default at the far right in the top row of the *i* menu. If you have a lot of time on your hands, use the Focus Mode entry in the Photo Shooting or Video Recording menus. The AF mode appears at the top-left edge of the viewfinder or on the monitor screen as you make the adjustments.

Autofocus Mode

This choice determines *when* your camera starts to autofocus, and what it does when focus is achieved. In still photo mode, automatic focus is not something that happens all the time when your camera is turned on. As I mentioned, to save battery power, your camera generally doesn't start to focus the lens until you partially depress the shutter release or another button assigned that behavior, such as the AF-ON button.

Single-Servo Autofocus (AF-S)

In this mode, also called *Single Autofocus*, focus is set once and remains at that setting until the button is fully depressed, taking the picture, or until you release the shutter button without taking a shot. The Z9/Z8 focuses very quickly, relying only on phase detection. As mentioned earlier, contrast-detection correction is applied only when using the Pinpoint-AF area mode, or when the camera's low-light AF feature (see the sidebar below) is enabled.

> **LOW-LIGHT AF**
>
> All digital cameras find autofocusing in low-light environments a challenge. One aid is Custom Setting d10/d11 (Z8/Z9): Starlight View (Photo Lv). Autofocus may take longer. You may also be able to improve autofocus performance for subjects that are within the range of about three feet to nearly 10 feet (1 to 3 meters) with the built-in AF-assist illuminator lamp on the front of the camera, which is activated by default but may be disabled using Custom Setting a12.

For non-action photography, this setting may be your best choice, as it minimizes out-of-focus pictures (at the expense of spontaneity). The drawback here is that you might not be able to take a picture at all while the camera is seeking focus; you're locked out until the autofocus mechanism is happy with the current setting. As described in Chapter 5, you can set AF-S mode to use either focus-priority (the default) or release-priority using Custom Setting a2.

A red indicator shows the user-selected focus area, which you can move around within the frame using the directional controls. In Auto-area AF mode, red brackets (which you cannot move) are displayed at the outer edges of the frame, representing the location of the 493 individual PDAF focus points. When sharp focus is achieved, the user-specified focus point (or the points selected by the camera in Auto-area AF mode) will turn green. You'll hear a beep (if not disabled using Beep Options in the Setup menu, as described in Chapter 9) and the camera is set to focus-priority. By keeping the shutter button depressed halfway, you'll find you can reframe the image while retaining the focus (and exposure) that's been set. You can also use your defined AE-L/AF-L button (by default the sub-selector button). If the camera is unable to focus, the focus point will flash red. Because of the small delay while the camera zeroes in on correct focus, you might experience slightly more shutter lag. This mode uses less battery power.

Using the directional controls, you can select any of the available focus areas in this AF mode when your Autofocus Area setting (described shortly) is set to Single-point AF, any of the four variations of Wide-area AF, or virtually anywhere within the focus area encompassed by the boxes in Figure 3.2 when Pinpoint-area AF is active. AF-S is the mode to use if you want to place the focus point within your frame with accuracy. One advantage is that you can place your subject within the focus area (no matter where it is in the frame), then press the shutter release halfway to lock focus, and then reframe, and focus will remain at the plane you focused on.

Continuous-Servo Autofocus (AF-C)

This is the mode to use for sports and other types of photography with fast-moving subjects. In this mode, once the shutter release is partially depressed, the camera sets the focus but continues to monitor the subject, so that if it moves or you move, the lens will be refocused to suit. Focus and exposure aren't really locked until you press the shutter release down all the way to take the picture. You'll find that AF-C produces the least amount of shutter lag of any autofocus mode when set to release-priority: press the button and the camera fires, even if sharp focus has not quite been achieved. It also uses the most battery power, because the autofocus system operates as long as the shutter-release button is partially depressed.

When using AF-C, the active focus areas are shown in red, as with AF-S mode. However, when you press the shutter release halfway down (or press a defined AE-L/AF-L button such as the sub-selector button), when the camera achieves sharp focus, by default you won't see a green box or hear a beep as confirmation. That can be a *good* thing. If that were the case, since AF-C constantly refocuses as long as the shutter release is held down halfway (or AE-L/AF-L button is depressed), you'd be treated by a barrage of beeps and constantly flickering green indicator until the picture is taken. If you see your subject has gone out of focus and the camera doesn't quickly recover, just release the button and press again to restart the focusing process. If you'd prefer to see the green focus confirmation indicators, you can activate it using Custom Setting a11: Focus Point Display > AF-C In-Focus Display. You'll learn how to customize focus point display for manual focus, Dynamic-area AF assist, and 3D-tracking, too, in Chapter 7.

Continuous-servo autofocus uses a technology called *predictive focus tracking*, which allows the camera to calculate the correct focus if the subject is moving toward or away from the camera at a constant rate. It uses either the automatically selected AF point (in Auto-area AF mode) or the point you select manually to set focus. As described in Chapter 7, you can set AF-C mode to use release-priority (the default) or focus-priority using Custom Setting a1.

Focus-Priority versus Release-Priority

One autofocus aspect that's often misunderstood is the concept of *priority*. The camera allows you to choose either focus-priority or release-priority, which determine whether it delays taking a picture until sharp focus is achieved when the shutter release is pressed down all the way, or whether it takes a picture immediately. You can use Custom Settings a1: AF-C Priority Selection and a2: AF-S Priority Selection to specify your choice.

- **Focus-priority.** This is the default setting for the AF-S autofocus mode. When enabled, the camera will not take a picture when you press the shutter release down all the way until focus is confirmed. This may cause a slight delay, *but only if the camera has not yet finished the autofocus process*. In practice, there are three possibilities:
  - **In AF-S mode:** If you've already pressed the shutter release halfway to lock in focus, the camera will go ahead and take your photo with no further delay.
  - **In AF-S mode:** If you haven't pressed the shutter release halfway—say you press down all the way in one continuous motion—there may be a delay until the camera confirms focus. This delay may be very short if your subject can be easily focused using your current AF-area mode, or somewhat longer if achieving sharp focus (say, with a subject that's low in contrast against its background) is problematic. Note that focus-priority can reduce continuous shooting frame rates while the camera waits for the AF system.

- **In AF-C mode:** If you've set AF-C mode to focus-priority (which I don't recommend), the camera will continuously focus and refocus as long as the shutter release is held down halfway. That will usually translate into only a minimal delay when the shutter button is finally fully depressed to take the picture.

- **Release-priority.** This is the default setting for AF-C autofocus mode. When active, the camera will take a picture as soon as the shutter release is pressed down all the way, *even if sharp autofocus has not been confirmed.* Sports, action, and wildlife photographers use release-priority almost exclusively, because capturing the decisive moment takes precedence over getting the sharpest possible photo. But don't make the mistake of thinking that release-priority will produce a large number of slightly out-of-focus photos. The majority of the time, this setting will produce sharp photos even though the AF system has not yet been able to *confirm* focus.

  I like to stick with release-priority for AF-C mode, because it has less impact on continuous shooting speeds. In general, AF-C will lock in focus for the first shot in a continuous sequence and subsequent exposures in the series won't really require much adjustment of focus. You could use focus-priority in AF-C mode when *not* shooting continuously and the sharpest focus possible was required. Release-priority provides no special advantages for AF-S mode (especially if you prefocus by pressing the shutter button halfway), so I don't use it.

- **Focus+Release.** Nikon actually has the name for this option backward: priority is given to *release* (not focus) initially, but under dim lighting or with low contrast subjects, the Z9/Z8 will shift to focus-priority for the first shot in a sequence, then continue in release-priority mode. Use this for continuous shooting, so the camera will take a little extra time focusing for the first shot. It will then capture the remaining images in the sequence using the same focus point, but will refocus, as necessary, if it can.

Full-time Autofocus (AF-F) (Movie Mode Only)

This mode is available only in Movie mode. You don't need to activate focus with a button: the camera adjusts focus continually as your subject moves. Focus locks only when the shutter release is pressed halfway. You can turn off continuous focusing temporarily by holding down the AF-ON button. Obviously, this mode uses the most juice. Because changing the focus plane while capturing video can be intrusive, AF-F is slower; but focus speed and tracking can be fine-tuned using Custom Settings g6 and g7.

Manual Focus

Set manual focus by sliding the focus mode switch on a lens to the M position (if it has such a switch), or by using the Focus Mode button, *i* menu, or Photo Shooting/Video Recording menu options. (F-mount lenses attached to the camera using the FTZ adapter may use a variation on the M position, which I'll explain later.) There are some advantages and disadvantages to using manual focus. While your batteries will last slightly longer in manual focus mode, it will take you longer to focus the camera for each photo, a process that can be difficult for some types of subjects. Modern digital cameras depend so much on autofocus that the viewfinders are no longer designed for optimum manual focus. Pick up any legacy film camera and you'll see a bigger, brighter viewfinder with a focusing screen that's a joy to focus on manually. I'll tell you more about manual focus later in this chapter.

Choosing an Autofocus Area Mode

If your camera isn't focusing on the correct subject, autofocus speed and activation are pretty much wasted effort. As you've learned, the camera has up to 493 different points on the screen that can be individually selected to determine the active focus zone.

You can choose *which* of those points is used by selecting an AF-area mode. As with Focus mode, you can select the AF-area mode from the *i* menu, Photo Shooting/Video Recording menus, or by holding down the Focus Mode button and rotating the sub-command dial. The *i* menu is your best choice, as it also allows you to choose AF subject detection options, as I'll describe shortly. The camera has six main AF-area modes for focus point selection, with several variations for two of them (plus Subject-tracking AF mode, available when shooting video). I'm going to describe each of the modes and explain how to use them.

NOTE With all AF-area modes (except for Auto-area AF and 3D-tracking), a dot appears in the middle of the focus point when it is located in the center of the frame. You can return the focus point to the center of the frame by pressing the OK button. If you find yourself using the sub-selector rather than the directional buttons to adjust the focus point location, you might want to be able to press the sub-selector button inward to return the focus point to the center of the frame. If that's the case, you can assign Select Center Focus Point to the button using Custom Setting f2: Custom Controls, as explained in Chapter 7.

Pinpoint AF

This mode is available only in Single AF (AF-S) focus mode. In this mode, you always select the focus point manually, using the sub-selector joystick *or* the multi selector (which, helpfully, will respond to your thumb presses not only in the left/right and up/down directions, but diagonally, as well). As I mentioned, you can return the focus point to the center at any time by pressing the OK button.

The focus point is represented by the tiny red box shown at left in Figure 3.7. You have an extraordinary amount of freedom in placing the focus area, which is roughly one-quarter the size of that used for Single-Point AF (described next). Pinpoint AF uses phase detection first, and then confirms focus using contrast detection within the selected area; it's not limited by the positions represented by the larger gray boxes.

Obviously, selecting an AF point so precisely can be time-consuming, as it takes 28 presses of the left/right buttons to move from one side of the frame to the other. (The focus point will wrap around

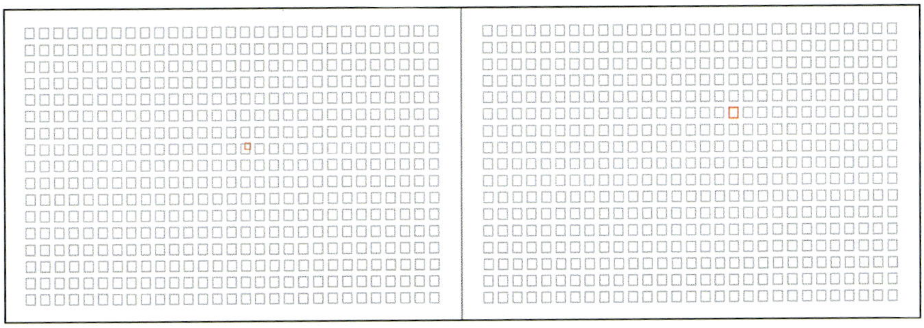

Figure 3.7 The Pinpoint AF selection box can be moved in tiny increments virtually anywhere within the area represented by the AF point boxes (left). By default, Single-point AF allows you to choose from all available focus zones (right).

to the other side if you've enabled that behavior using Custom Setting a10.) Pinpoint AF is best suited for subjects that don't move. It's especially good for macro work and any photography undertaken with the camera mounted on a tripod.

Single-Point AF

As with the other user-selectable area modes, you can select the focus point manually, using the sub-selector joystick *or* the multi selector. The camera evaluates focus based solely on the point you select from among the 493 available, making this another good choice for subjects that don't move much. Single-Point AF is excellent for achieving focus on a subject that might otherwise blend in with its background.

TIP You can speed up the AF point's traverse using Custom Setting a14: Focus Point Selection Speed and Custom Setting a4: Alternating Points, as described in Chapter 7. The Alternating Points mode allows much faster positioning of your focus zone. I use it a lot for sports, because I plan on filling as much of the frame as possible with players and can usually estimate where they will appear in the frame. (That's usually off center, closer to the edge where I expect them to enter the frame.) However, the Alternating Points setting does not affect the number of focus points used with Pinpoint AF or with Wide-area AF (Small or Large), which I'll describe shortly.

Dynamic-area AF

In this mode, available only when AF-C is active, you still select the *primary* focus point yourself from among those available using the multi selector or sub-selector controls. The camera will focus on that point in most cases, but if the subject departs from the selected area, the camera uses information from the surrounding areas. However, if the user-selected primary focus point isn't suitable for focusing, the camera will use one of the secondary focus points instead. That might be the case if the selected focus point is on an area of low contrast, such as the sky, or the subject is too small (perhaps a distant object).

You can choose from three different Dynamic-area sizes: Small, Medium, and Large, shown in Figure 3.8. The red-highlighted points surrounding the main focus box show the active focus points. You can dispense with the extra points by setting Custom Setting a11: Focus Point Display > Dynamic-area AF Assist to Off. You can move the grouping to any of the other 493 points, but when the grouping reaches the top border or corners, some of the potential points are outside the array, effectively giving you fewer points to work with.

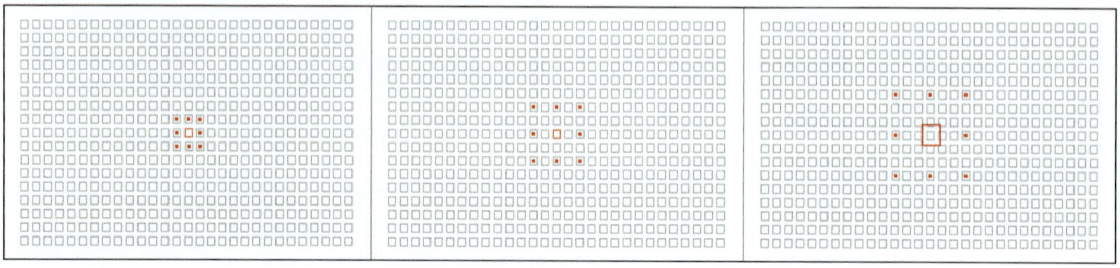

Figure 3.8 You can select a primary focus point with Dynamic-area AF, but adjacent points will also be used if your subject moves outside the primary area. Small, Medium, and Large areas (left to right).

Dynamic-area AF is a more sophisticated version of Single-point AF. You can select the *initial* focus point, and then trust the camera's smarts to continue focusing on a moving subject as long as that subject remains within the Dynamic-area's autofocus frame pattern. That frees you to concentrate on framing your composition rather than worrying about whether your subject remains in focus.

This setting is excellent for slow-moving subjects, as seen in Figure 3.9, left, but flexible enough to follow subjects that move erratically from side to side (say, a child at play or a basketball player moving around the court on defense), because the camera can use the distance information to differentiate the original subject from objects that are closer or farther away, especially human subjects (see Figure 3.9, right). However, many photographers also use this setting for birds in flight. Very rapid motion may call for the camera's tracking feature, described shortly.

TIP In Pinpoint AF, Single-point AF, or Dynamic-area AF, if you want to lock the focus point you've selected for a series of shots, you can temporarily lock the focus point by partially depressing and holding the shutter release or pressing and holding the AE-L/AF-L button (by default the sub-selector button). Press the multi selector center button to move the single focus point back to the center of the frame quickly.

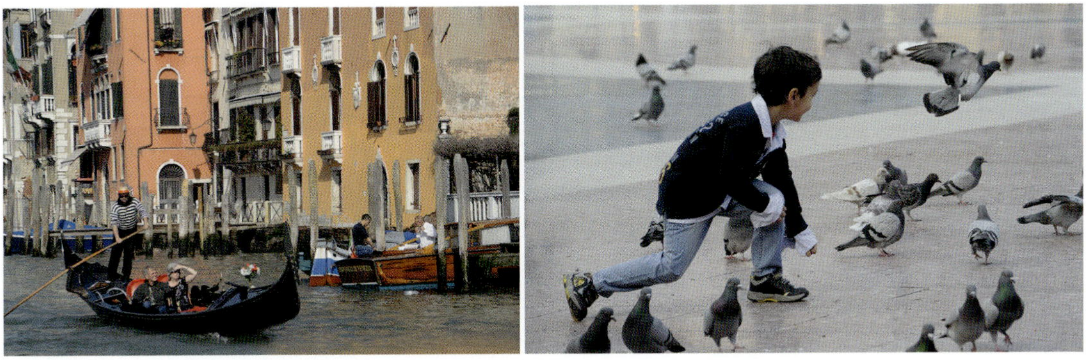

Figure 3.9 Focus on slow-moving subjects with Dynamic-area AF (left). More erratic subjects (right) can work too but may require using the camera's tracking feature.

Wide-area AF (Small and Large; C1, C2)

This mode uses the focus points within zones you can move around the display. Two zones are defined for you. Choose either the smaller of the wide-area zones (one is shown outlined in red in Figure 3.10, left), or an even larger zone, (like the one seen outlined in red in Figure 3.10, right). Two additional customizable modes are available, labeled C1 and C2, each with 20 possible configurations with dimensions in any combination of 1, 5, 9, 13, or 19 zones wide by 1, 3, 7, or 11 zones tall. (The zones in Movie mode are limited to 1, 5, 9, 13 wide by 1, 3, 7 zones tall.)

I use the customizable zones C1 and C2 a lot, as they are especially good for subjects that occupy a predictable region of the frame. Although I was shooting the basketball game shown in Figure 3.11 with a 14mm lens, I hoped to capture some exciting action under the hoop. I set my Wide-area AF (C1) zone to a tall rectangle that encompassed the area around the basket, and my Z9 tended to ignore players at the periphery, even if they ventured close to the baseline.

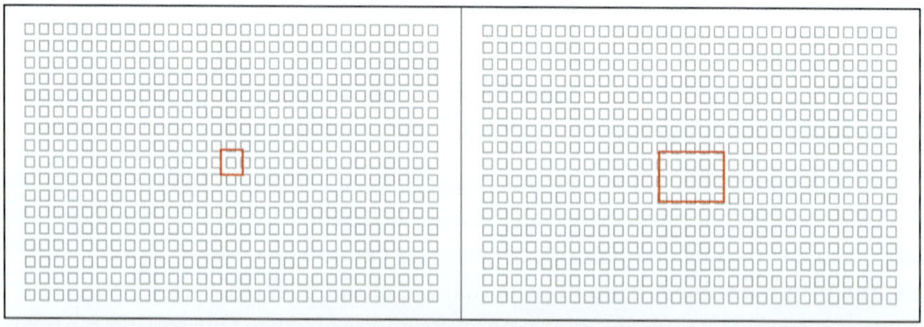

Figure 3.10 Wide-area AF zones Small (left) and Large (right) cannot be redefined.

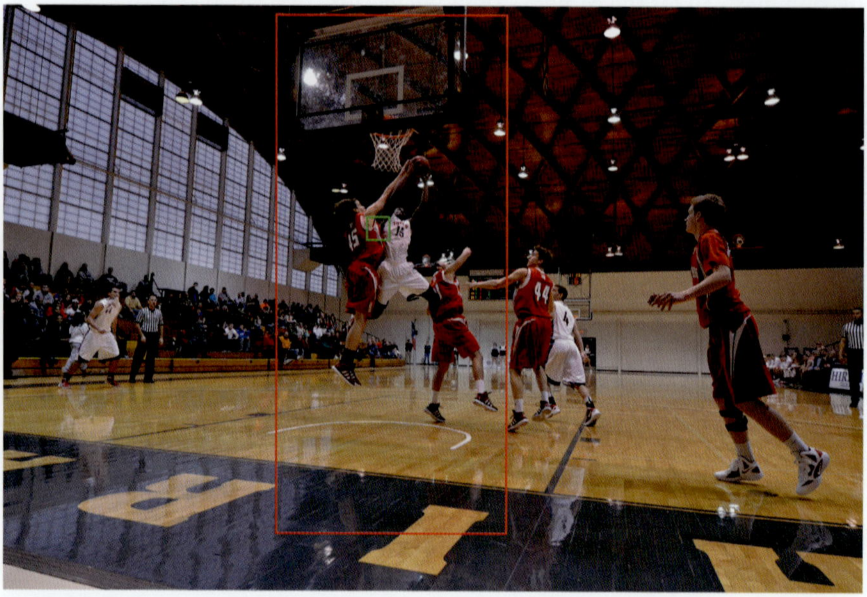

Figure 3.11 A custom Wide-area AF zone can be tailored to concentrate on a specific area of the frame.

3D-Tracking

This AF option, available only in AF-C mode, tells the Z9/Z8 to lock in focus on a subject you specify, and then follow it as that subject moves within the frame (or you move the camera). The camera identifies the subject using several qualities, such as color, the pattern of the subject (including shape and size), and, if active and appropriate, subject detection. It works best when these aspects are clearly distinct from the subject's surroundings. The 3D-tracking mode might do a great job following a rooster around a chicken coop, but might get easily confused if you tried to track a single chick scuttling around within a flock. If your target happens to be one included in the camera's subject-detection algorithms, tracking performance can be further enhanced. Keep in mind, though, that in this mode, subject detection may not be given top priority. One advantage of 3D-tracking is that it works with *all kinds* of moving objects, and it isn't limited to the defined subject-tracking categories (people, animals, birds, vehicles, or airplanes).

When in 3D-tracking mode, you can activate tracking by placing the displayed focus point over your subject and pressing the AF-ON button (or by pressing the shutter-release button down halfway). The Z9/Z8 will then focus on the subject and continue to track/focus as it moves within the frame. Release the AF-ON or shutter button if you want to recompose with a different subject. If your subject moves too quickly, leaves the frame or is blocked by other objects, is too similar to other subjects in the frame, or changes in appearance, tracking may fail. **Note:** A similar function, Subject-tracking AF, is available in video mode, using the OK, AF-ON, or shutter release as the trigger to begin following a selected subject.

Automatic-area AF

With Auto-area AF, autofocus point selection is out of your hands; the camera performs the task for you using its own intelligence. It will work with the distance information supplied by the lens and, if enabled, its subject detection technology to distinguish humans, animals, vehicles, etc., from their background. In that case, a prioritized subject at the side of the frame will be detected and used to evaluate focus, while the camera ignores the background area in the frame.

In AF-S mode, the active focus points, all located within the red brackets shown in Figure 3.12, are highlighted with green boxes that illuminate as you hold the shutter release down halfway; until that happens, you have no idea where in the frame the camera will be focusing. In AF-C mode, red boxes appear around the focused area, highlighted in that color to indicate that the current focus point is only tentative and won't be locked in until you press the shutter release down all the way. If you'd rather see which points are being used for focus in green, use Custom Setting a11: Focus Point Display > AF-C In-Focus Display, as described earlier.

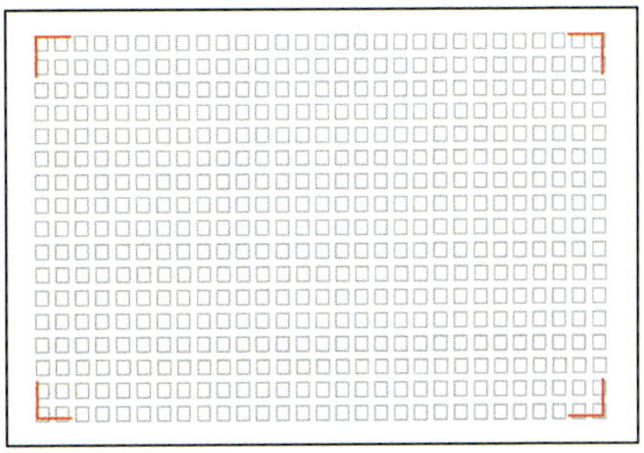

Figure 3.12 The red brackets show the area covered in Automatic-area AF.

Birds in flight—one of the most difficult of all autofocus targets—can often be grabbed using Automatic-area AF in combination with the Z9/Z8's avian-oriented subject-detection option. Subject detection and tracking features merit a more detailed discussion of their own, which I'll provide in an upcoming section.

REDUCING YOUR OPTIONS

If you find yourself using only certain AF-area modes, you can tell the camera to "hide" the modes you do not work with. Custom Setting a8: Limit AF-Area Mode Selection allows you to enable or disable any of the AF-area modes (except Single-point AF, which is mandatory). If you need more help activating this option, I'll explain it for you in Chapter 7.

Reach Out and Touch Something

I described the powerful touch-screen features of the Z9 and Z8 in Chapter 1. They are especially useful when applied to achieving focus and (optionally) taking a picture with little more effort than a gesture. You can activate touch options using the Touch Controls entry in the Setup menu, enabling them for playback only (if you want to avoid unintentional activation), or for both playback and shooting functions. A Touch icon appears at the left edge of the LCD monitor screen. Tap it to cycle among these behaviors:

- **Touch AF.** The camera positions the focus point where you touch the screen. If you are using Auto-area AF or Subject-tracking AF in video mode, when you lift your finger, the camera will track your subject as it or the camera moves. Press OK to cancel tracking, or when you want to reposition the focus point. This option is most useful in AF-C mode, because it allows you to select a focus point and focus with one tap.
- **Position Focus Point.** The Z9/Z8 will position the focus point you indicate on the screen, but will not *focus or take a picture*. However, like Touch AF, if you are using Auto-area AF or Subject-tracking AF in video mode, when you lift your finger, the camera will track your subject as it or the camera moves. Use this mode when you want to decide when to initiate focus in both AF-C and AF-S focus modes.
- **Touch Shutter/Touch AF.** Tap the screen, and the camera will *immediately* focus on that point and take a picture when you lift your finger. It works in both AF-C and AF-S modes. This is a great option. For example, if you unexpectedly see some action taking place, you can tap the touch screen to take a photo right away, and then continue to shoot (if you like) with the camera continuing to track the subject you just shot.
- **Off.** Touch focus/shutter is disabled.

Subject Detection

Improvements in subject detection have gone a long way toward fixing one of the most significant limitations of autofocus: the camera doesn't really know which of the many objects within the frame you want to focus on. Previous systems tended to lock onto the closest objects, or use information from the Matrix metering system to identify likely subjects (usually humans, due to the tell-tale coloring of their faces). Adding patterns and textures to the features provided some improvements. Things really became interesting when Nikon (as well as other vendors) added enough intelligence to their image-processing algorithms to allow cameras to discern human bodies, individual faces, then eyes.

The latest iterations, improved through firmware updates since these cameras were introduced, have added the ability to identify people, animals, birds, vehicles, and even airplanes. Today's cameras can find torsos and limbs, differentiate between race cars and passenger vehicles, and tell the difference between large birds and aircraft. This technology is possible because mirrorless cameras collect their autofocus information directly from the sensor at higher resolutions than were possible with the AF components embedded in the floor of the mirror box of dSLR cameras.

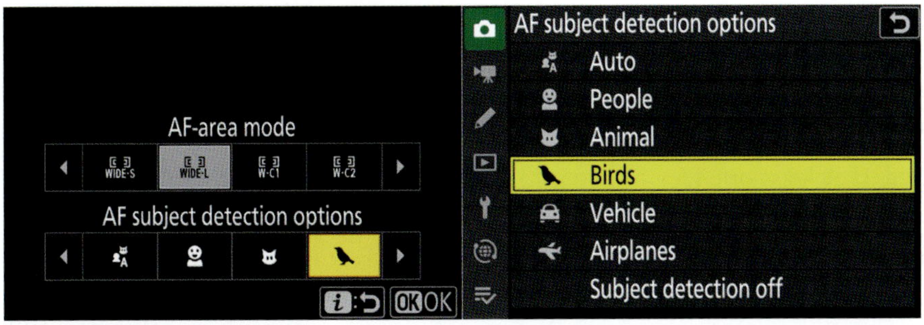

Figure 3.13 Choose both AF-area mode and subject-detection options from the *i* menu (left). Subject-detection options can also be specified in the Photo Shooting menu (right).

As I noted earlier, the *i* menu AF-area option lets you choose an AF-area mode and subject-detection type (or turn subject detection off) from a single screen (see Figure 3.13, left). You can also choose your subject from the AF Subject Detection Options entry of the Photo Shooting menu—but then you'll need to use the separate AF-area mode to specify area. (See Figure 3.13, right.)

Subject detection can be used to assign focus-priority with any of the Wide-area AF modes or Auto-area AF, and may also be used with 3D-tracking AF (but may be overridden by the camera). When active, the Z9/Z8 will first look for large identifiable components, such as the shape of vehicles or airplanes, or the bodies of humans, animals, and birds. If the subject is large enough within the frame, the system will next zero in on a major component, such as the front end of vehicles or the face or head of a living creature. When enough detail is available, focus can use the eyes or other small components. Once locked in on a likely subject, the AF system can ignore the background or other objects in the scene.

The appearance of the AF indicator boxes provides a clue to how the camera is calculating focus. A single large, medium, or small square box indicates the Z9/Z8 has detected a torso, face, or eye of a living creature, respectively (or the equivalent-size part of a non-animate subject). A triangle next to a box indicates more than one face or eye has been found and you can use the left/right directional controls to move to the next face or eye. A dancing array of tiny boxes shows that subject detection is not being used and the camera will search subjects that are close, large, and/or high in contrast.

You'll get the best results when your subjects are facing the camera directly; the features become less accurate as the face turns away from the camera toward a profile view. The camera will look for both human faces and eyes and attempt to focus on the nearest eye. If the camera cannot positively identify an eye, it will switch to Face-detection mode automatically. This mode is the most versatile when your subjects are relatively close to the camera, as eyes will be relatively larger and easier to detect. Face detection alone will work well for groups, or when your subject is farther away from the camera.

If you're shooting animals or birds, the camera will try to detect animal bodies, faces, and eyes and focus on them. Remember to turn this option off if no animals are present, as the feature sometimes "finds" the face of a dog or cat in unlikely places, such as shrubbery that happens to resemble a furry friend.

You can't directly select the focus zone yourself (although you can narrow it down considerably by defining a very small zone using Wide-area AF (C1 or C2). Instead, a box will be displayed on the display when the camera detects a likely subject. You don't need to press the shutter release to activate this behavior—in this mode, the camera starts looking for faces immediately. Several faces may be detected, with a box aligned with the selected face (usually, the face that is closest to the camera) or the selected eye (if eye detection is active). When a human or animal face or eye is detected, you have several options at your disposal:

- **Face or eye detected.** If at least one face or eye is found, a box will appear around the detected feature.
- **Multiple faces/eyes.** If more than one face or eye is present, the box will include one or two triangles indicating that you can use the left or right directional controls to move the highlighting to the next face or eye. Figure 3.14 shows what the screen looks like when two eyes are detected (left), or when multiple faces are found (right).

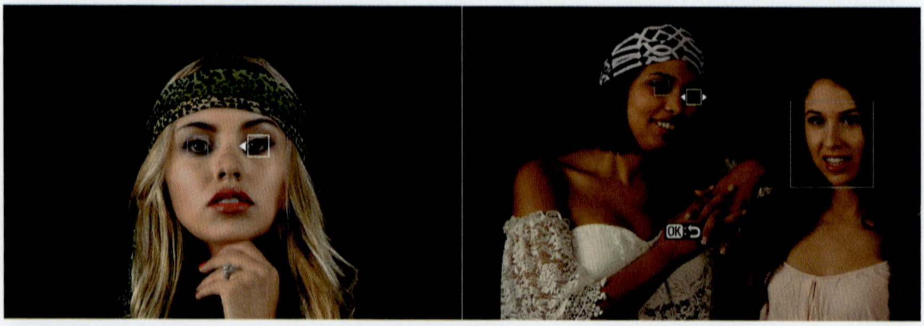

Figure 3.14 When an eye or face is detected, a box appears around the eye or face.

- **Select different face/eye.** Use the directional controls to switch to a different face or eye. If touch operation is enabled, you can tap a face with your finger and the camera will focus on that face (and take a picture immediately when you remove your finger from the screen if you've activated Touch Shutter/Touch AF).
- **Tracking.** If the subject with the highlighted face moves or you reframe the image, the camera will track and follow the selected face or eye.
- **Locking focus.** In AF-S mode, when you press down the shutter release halfway, the camera attempts to focus the face or eye. As sharp focus is achieved, the border turns green. If the camera is unable to focus, the border blinks red. Focus may also be lost if the subject turns away from the camera and is no longer detectable. In AF-C mode, the focus continues to concentrate on the selected face/eye until the shutter release is pressed down all the way to take the picture.

3D-Tracking

The useful 3D-tracking autofocus feature is one of those capabilities that can be confusing at first, but once you get the hang of it, it's remarkably easy to use. In fact, it's available only when you're using AF-C focus mode and the Photo/Video selector switch is set to the Photo position. (The video equivalent is Subject-tracking AF, described in Chapter 12.)

The Z9/Z8 intelligently use the color, shape, size, and patterns found within your subject to track its movement within the frame, and does the best job when these features are distinct from other objects in view. If subject detecting is turned on, the camera will use that information, too.

Here are my recommended steps for using this feature:

1. **Choose refocus delay.** Navigate to Custom Setting a3: Focus Tracking with Lock-on. Choose the Blocked Shot AF Response value from 1 (Quick) to 5 (Delayed). This determines how quickly the camera refocuses when an intervening object passes in front of the subject you have chosen to track. With Quick, the camera will wait only a short moment, then refocus on the new object. With the maximum Delayed setting, the interrupting subject matter will be ignored for a period of time.

   You'll want to use a delay setting when shooting sports in which players or officials are likely to pass in front of the camera unexpectedly. A Quick setting will work well when shooting continuously, allowing the camera to refocus rapidly.

   You can also specify whether the subject motion is relatively steady—say a race car—or moving erratically, like the bucking bull shown in Figure 3.15.

2. **Specify focus point display.** A focus point box is displayed on the screen in this mode. You have two settings to make using Custom Setting a11: Focus Point Display:
   - **Activate AF-C Point Display.** Select AF-C In-focus Display and set to On. The Z9/Z8 will then change the active focus points to green when they are in focus. This setting applies to all focus modes, not just 3D-Tracking.
   - **3D-Tracking Focus Point Color.** You can select an appropriate contrasting color (red or white) for the focus box as you move it around the screen using the multi selector or sub-selector.

3. **Select your subject.** Move the red or white focus box within the frame to "aim" the camera until the subject you want to focus on and track is located within the border. Because you can select at any time, if, say, you're shooting sports, you can wait until just before some action is going to begin, and then choose your subject. To specify a subject for tracking, hold down the AF-ON button, or press the shutter release down halfway.

4. **Change subject.** If your subject leaves the frame or you decide to track a different subject, release the AF-ON or shutter-release button, and resume at Step 3.

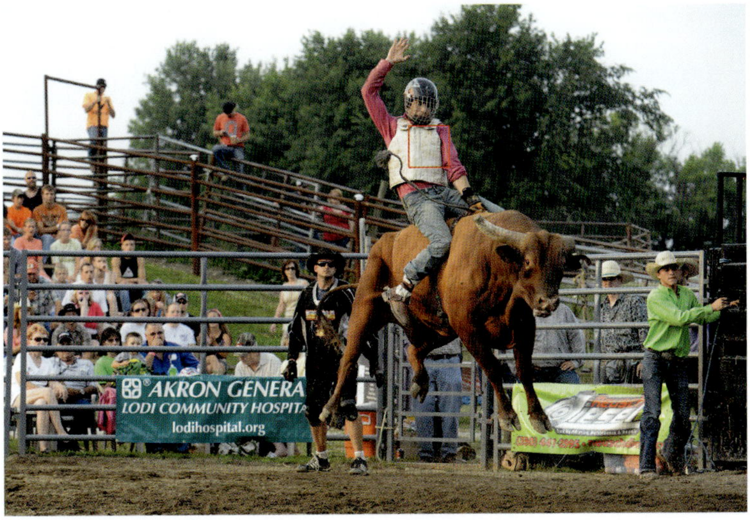

Figure 3.15 Press OK to produce a frame you can use to select an object to track.

5. **Focus.** When the tracked subject is brought into focus, the active focus points turn green, seemingly take on a life of their own, and will "follow" your subject around on the LCD as you reframe your image. (In other words, the subject being tracked doesn't have to be in the center of the frame for the actual photo.) Best of all, if your subject moves, the camera will follow it as required. You can reframe as desired.
6. **Tracking continues.** The only glitches that may pop up might occur if your subject is small and difficult to track, is too close in tonal value to its background, or if the subject approaches the camera or recedes sufficiently to change its relative size on the LCD significantly. The camera may also be unable to track subjects that leave the frame, are moving too fast, are too large/small, or too bright/dark. Because tracking uses subject distance, color, any patterns present, and brightness, it works best when used with subject matter that differs in colors/patterns and brightness from its surroundings.
7. **Take your picture.** Press the shutter release down all the way.
8. **Or exit.** To cancel focus tracking, release the shutter release or AF-ON button.

Store by Orientation

Some types of shooting call for different ways of choosing a focus point's orientation. For example, say you're shooting a sport like basketball that lends itself to both horizontal and vertical framing. You may rotate your camera constantly as the action unfolds but want the focus point to remain in the upper portion of your horizontal or vertical frame. That won't happen if you are shooting with a camera in its default mode. Your chosen focus point will stay fixed relative to the other points and "rotate" along with the camera, as shown at top in Figure 3.16.

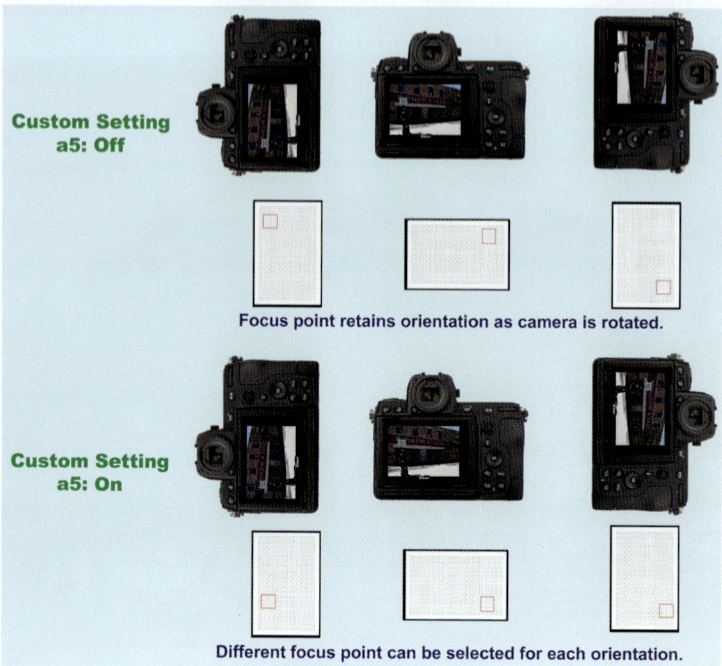

Figure 3.16 Store AF points by orientation—or not.

The same focus point in the camera's array is used regardless of the camera's orientation. If you've set your focus point for the basket or net when the camera is rotated in one direction vertically (that is, the top of the vertical frame), the focus point will encompass the right side of the frame when the camera is in the horizontal position and evaluate the floor if you happen to rotate it vertically in the other direction.

However, you have another option, tucked away in Custom Setting a5: Store Points by Orientation. When either Focus Point or Focus Point and AF-area Mode are selected, the focus point does not shift as the camera is rotated, as shown in the upper half of Figure 3.16. This feature allows *different* focus points to be selected for each of the three likely camera orientations (ignoring the possible, but less likely, upside-down horizontal position, which simply inverts the normal position in which you hold the camera). If you've chosen Focus Point and AF-area Mode, you may specify a different AF-area mode for each orientation in addition to the focus point position.

When Store Points by Orientation is activated, simply rotate the camera to any of the three configurations, and select the focus point you want. Repeat, if you like, for the other two. (It's best to do this during a lull in the action, although you can re-select points on the fly if you like.) Then, as you shoot, you'll notice the focus point shifting in the viewfinder as you rotate the camera. You don't need to keep the point in the same relative position in the frame (as I just described). You can select any focus point for any of the three orientations if, for example, you're shooting architecture and want to focus on a different position in the frame as you vary camera orientation.

Manual Focus

The Nikon Z9 and Z8 supply you with powerful manual focusing aids. You can zoom in to your subject to manually focus on an enlarged image, view color-coded cues that show you which parts of the image actually *are* in focus, or check an electronic "rangefinder" that alerts you when a given subject is in focus. There is even a split-screen display zoom option that allows you to evaluate focus on two different areas of the frame. These manual focus aids are great features. Indeed, the switch to mirrorless technology has actually revived interest in old-school manual focus. There are five reasons why manual focus is being used more by creative photographers:

- **WYSIWYG.** What you see (in the viewfinder or LCD monitor) is what you get, in terms of sharp focus when focusing manually with the camera, or you're evaluating the exact same sensor image that will be captured when you press the shutter release. Traditional single-lens reflex (SLR) cameras use a mirror to direct the image to a separate focusing screen (when not in live view), which can be coarser, not as bright, and possibly out of alignment.
- **WYSIWYW.** Focusing manually can mean that *what you see is what you want,* that is, *you* can select the precise plane of focus you desire for, say, a macro photo or portrait, rather than settle for what the camera *thinks* you want. Your camera doesn't have any way of determining, for certain, what subject you *want* to be in sharp focus. It can't read your mind (at least, not yet). Left to its own devices, the camera may select a likely object—often the one nearest the camera—and lock in focus with lightning speed, even though the subject is not the one that's the center of interest of your photograph.

- **Less confusion.** Nikon has given us faster and more precise autofocus systems, with many more options, and it's common for the sheer number of these choices to confuse even the most advanced photographers. If you'd rather not wade through the AF alternatives for a given shot, switch to manual focus and shoot. You won't have to worry about whether the camera locks focus too soon, or too late, or has been set to give special priority to animals or airplanes.
- **Focus aids.** As I noted earlier, you can zoom in on the sensor image as you focus manually, use split-image comparison of two parts of the image simultaneously, and use a feature called *focus peaking* to accentuate in-focus areas with distinct colored outlines. I'll explain all these options later.
- **More lenses.** All mirrorless cameras—and not just the Nikon Z-series—had a limited number of lenses available when they were originally introduced. Happily, Nikon has been filling in the gaps quickly. Meanwhile, the reduced flange-to-sensor distance offers plenty of room to insert an adapter that allows mounting an extensive number of existing lenses, including those from manufacturers other than Nikon. Many of those third-party optics are inexpensive manual focus lenses, or lenses intended for other camera platforms which function only in manual focus on the Z-series models. A whole generation of enthusiast photographers who grew up using nothing but autofocus have discovered that focusing manually is a reasonable tradeoff for access to this wide range of optics.

Of course, manual focus does require judgment and fast reflexes (if your subject is moving). On the one hand, autofocus does save time and allows us to capture subjects (particularly fast-moving sports) that are difficult to image sharply using manual focusing (unless you have training and know certain techniques). On the other hand, learning to apply the Nikon camera's autofocus system most effectively also requires a bit of study and some practice. Then, once you're comfortable with autofocus, you'll know when it's appropriate to use the manual focus option, too.

The important thing to remember is that focus isn't absolute. For example, some things that look in sharp focus at a given viewing size and distance might not be in focus at a larger size and/or closer distance. In addition, the goal of optimum focus isn't always to make things look sharp. Not all of an image will be or should be sharp. Controlling exactly what is sharp and what is not is part of your creative palette. Use of depth-of-field characteristics to throw part of an image out of focus while other parts are sharply focused is one of the most valuable tools available to a photographer. But selective focus works only when the desired areas of an image are in focus properly. For the digital photographer, correct focus can be one of the trickiest parts of the technical and creative process.

As I've noted several times, some subjects lend themselves to manual focus, especially close-up or *macro* photography, in which AF can be a creative hindrance. If you're photographing a flower, why let the camera decide which leaf or petal should be sharpest—particularly if you are using a relatively large aperture and selective focus as an effect? A mirrorless camera's live view is especially useful when focusing manually because you have extra tools at your disposal to focus precisely and quickly.

Here are the basic steps for quick and convenient setting of focus manually with the camera:

- **Activate manual focus.** Switch to manual focus by sliding the switch on the lens to the M position, or by selecting Manual focus using the *i* menu.
- **Aim at your subject and turn the control/focusing ring on the lens.** Turn the control/focusing ring until your subject appears to be in the sharpest possible focus. While you can redefine the focus/control ring's function (as described in Chapter 7), in Manual focus mode it can *only* be used to adjust focus. Note that some lenses, such as the Z 24-70mm f/4 S optic, lack a control ring and have only a focus ring.
- **If you have difficulty focusing.** If you are unable to focus precisely, you have three options: zooming, magnification, and focus peaking. The first two give you a larger image to focus but have their own advantages and disadvantages. The third is a relatively new feature in the Nikon product line, gaining in popularity since more and more photographers are depending on live view (with dSLRs) or the full-time live view provided by mirrorless cameras.
    - **Zooming in optically.** If you are using a zoom lens (rather than a fixed focal length *prime* lens), you can zoom in on your subject using the longest available focal setting. Even if you plan to take a wide-angle photo, the reduced depth-of-field at a telephoto setting can make it easier to see the exact effect of slight changes in focus while zoomed in. With most lenses, when you zoom back out to take the picture, the center of interest will still be in sharp focus. However, some lenses (generally less expensive optics) can change focus as they zoom. The most blatant of these are called *varifocal* lenses. Sticklers refer to lenses that *don't* change focus as they zoom as "true" zoom or *parfocal* lenses. However, even a true zoom can change focus slightly when zooming.
    - **Magnification.** To magnify a portion of the image and enhance your ability to focus, press the Zoom In button located to lower right of the LCD monitor. As you press the button repeatedly, to enlarge the view to eight different levels of magnification, a navigation window, seen at lower right in Figure 3.17, displays a yellow box at the approximate location within the overall frame of the magnified view. You can relocate the zoomed area using the multi selector or sub-selector joystick. Press the center button at any time to restore the zoom window to the center of the frame.

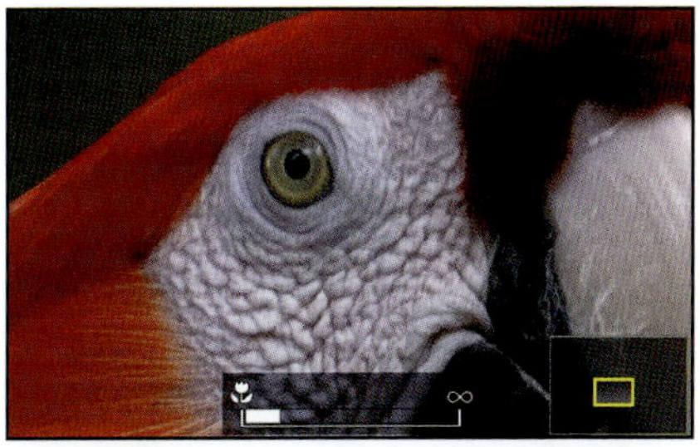

Figure 3.17 You can magnify the image to make manual focusing easier.

-
    - **Focus peaking.** Activate this feature using the instructions for Custom Setting a13: Focus Peaking in Chapter 7. Focus peaking provides a colored overlay around edges within your image that are sharply focused. As the color fades or becomes stronger, it is easier to determine when your subject is precisely focused. Choose Peak 1 (low sensitivity), Peak 2 (standard sensitivity), or Peak 3 (high sensitivity), depending on the contrast of your subject,

as seen in Figure 3.18. The flowers shown tended to blend in with the background, so I selected high sensitivity. The default peaking highlight color of red was fine in this case, but you can change it to yellow, blue, or white. The alternate hue may be needed to provide a strong contrast between the peaking highlights and the color of your subject. Yellow might be the best choice to focus on, say, a red rose. Access the Focus Peaking Highlight Color option to adjust the color.

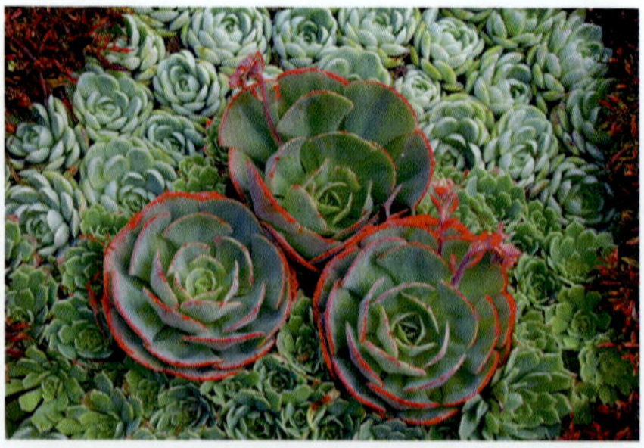

Figure 3.18 With Peaking Highlights activated, in-focus areas are highlighted in color.

- **Use the electronic rangefinder.** Position the focus point over the subject and rotate the focus ring until sharp focus is achieved using the electronic rangefinder feature. The focus point will change to green and the in-focus indicator at lower left in the display will change according to the symbols shown in Figure 3.19. Note that while the electronic rangefinder appears when in manual focus or manual focus override, it shows the direction in which you should rotate the ring, with *most* lenses. Some lenses, especially those from third parties, rotate in the opposite direction, however.

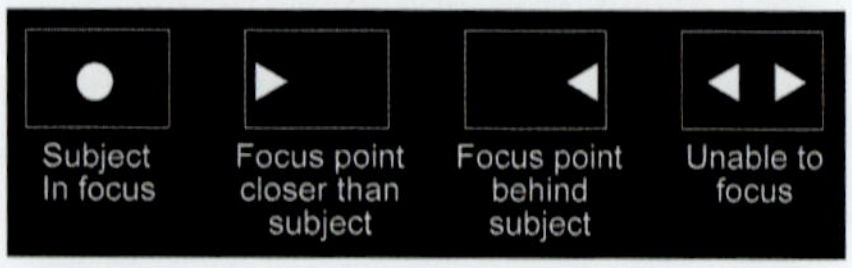

Figure 3.19 The electronic rangefinder in the lower-left corner of the display shows manual focus status.

- **Preview depth-of-field.** Your Z9/Z8 doesn't have a Pv (Preview) button by default, but you can define one for, say, Fn1 or Fn2 in Custom Setting f2: Custom Controls. Then, when you press the defined Pv button, the lens will stop down to the aperture selected by you (in Manual mode) or by the camera (in Aperture-priority mode). (This doesn't work in Program or Shutter-priority mode, because the aperture isn't determined in either mode until you lock exposure or take a photo.) To open the aperture to maximum again, release the button.
- **Split-screen display zoom.** Like depth-of-field preview, this feature isn't available by default. You must add it to the *i* menu, using Custom Setting f1: Customize *i* Menu. I'll describe this capability next.

Split-Screen Display Zoom

Split-screen Display Zoom is most useful when the camera is mounted on a tripod. To use it, you must assign the Split-screen Display Zoom behavior to the *i* menu, using Custom Setting f1: Customize *i* Menu, as described in Chapter 7. When you activate this feature, the live view LCD display is divided into two boxes, each showing a separate area of the frame side-by-side. To use this capability, just follow these steps:

1. **Split the screen.** Press the *i* button and scroll to the icon representing the Split-screen Display Zoom function that you have added to the customized *i* menu. Press OK to activate.

2. **Areas are indicated by a navigation window.** The screen will split into two areas, shown next to each other. The relative positions of the two areas are shown in a magnification window, seen at lower right in Figure 3.20.
3. **Zoom in or out of the split display.** Use the Zoom In and Zoom Out buttons to magnify or reduce magnification of both portions of the image.
4. **Choose one of the two sides of the frame.** Press the OK button to select one of the two sides of the frame.
5. **Move selected area horizontally.** You can use the left/right buttons to scroll that box's selected area from side to side.

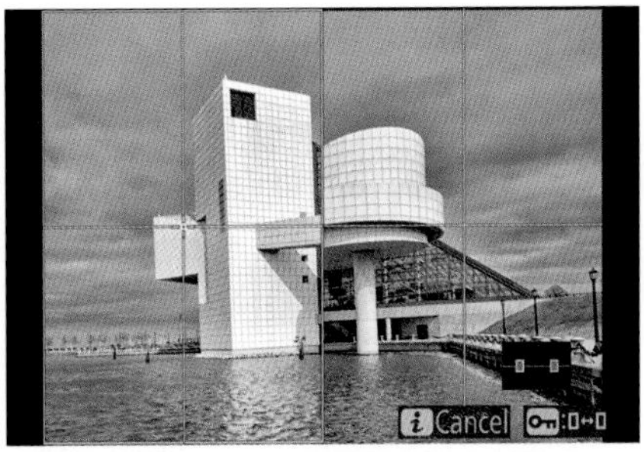

Figure 3.20 Split-screen display in live view.

6. **Move both areas vertically.** Press the up or down buttons to scroll *both* areas up or down simultaneously. In other words, the split-screen images will always match horizontally, but you can adjust either of their positions left or right. Landscape photographers have already noted that they'd like the ability to change the locations in both horizontal and vertical directions.

NOTE Because the split screen shows areas on opposite sides of the frame, you can also use it to horizontally align the image, so that the horizon or any buildings that span the image are oriented at the same angle. I'll describe additional applications next.

7. **Focus on selected area.** When either box is selected, you can focus the image on *that* area by pressing the shutter-release button halfway.
8. **Exit.** Press the *i* button again to exit the split-screen display.

You're probably wondering what else this feature is useful for—unless you're way ahead of me. Here are some typical applications. These are all fairly technical in nature, and likely to be needed only for specialized types of photography, particularly in the architectural and landscape fields. But if you do need the split-screen feature, you'll really need it.

- **Check horizontal alignment.** Some subjects lend themselves to symmetrical compositions (or, *demand* such treatment, in the case of buildings or other bi-laterally symmetrical scenes that look weird if the camera has been placed slightly to one side or the other). Use the split screen to view comparable parts of the same image simultaneously to see if the camera is aligned appropriately.
- **Check front/back tilt.** Sometimes you unintentionally lean the camera forward or back slightly, which can produce fall-back or fall-forward effects when shooting very tall or very deep subjects (*pitch*) or rotate the camera around its base (imagine a line running vertically through, say, the tripod socket; that's *yaw*). You might also *roll* the camera by rotating it along the axis that runs through the center of the lens.

  When these rotations are severe, you'll probably notice it visually; lean way back to take in the top of a building, and you'll see the effect on the screen. However, less drastic tilting may escape your attention. You can use the split-screen feature in conjunction with the live view virtual horizon to ensure the camera is completely level. The virtual horizon's indicators will show you when the camera is rotated around the axis running through the center of the front element of the lens or pitched forward or back. The split-screen capability can help you counter yaw by comparing the two magnified sides of the image.

- **Control perspective and focus.** The split screen allows you to check the focus of different parts of a scene, which landscape photographers will like. Those using shift-tilt lenses will like the feature even more. These specialized lenses can be tilted without changing the position of the camera, providing control over which part of subjects photographed at an angle are in focus. The split screen can be used to select either side of the image and focus on the side that you want to be rendered most sharply. These lenses can also be shifted side to side, say to allow photographing the top of a building while keeping the focal plane of the camera parallel to the structure. In such cases, you can use the camera in portrait orientation (in which case the screen will be split top and bottom, rather than side to side), and then view both parts of the image before making additional shift adjustments for the best perspective control.

Using the Focus/Control Ring

The focusing controls of the Nikon Z-series mirrorless cameras add some new wrinkles that can take some getting used to, whether you are a neophyte photographer or an old hand. One innovation found on certain lenses is the addition of a *control ring* to replace the familiar single *focus ring* used on traditional lenses and continuing to be used on some Z-mount lenses, while the second involves the Z-series' dependence on a technology called *focus-by-wire* to perform the actual focus adjustments.

When focusing manually, the control ring can function like a traditional focus ring in many ways. As you rotate the ring to the right, the plane of focus moves farther away, bringing more distant subjects into focus; after the focus plane reaches "infinity" further rotation has no effect. Rotate the ring to the left, however, and the camera focuses closer and closer until the minimum focus distance is reached. A helpful indicator bar, with the icon of a flower at left and an infinity symbol at right, is displayed along the bottom of the screen. So far, manual focus with your camera is pretty much the same as with any Nikon camera you've used. A very few older Nikon lenses and some other vendors reverse the left/right directions, much to the consternation of those who switch platforms.

The cool new feature is that you can redefine the behavior of the control ring from its default of manual override of autofocus and fully manual focusing, with other customizable functions, including step-less aperture control, exposure compensation, and ISO sensitivity adjustment. The most popular of these options is probably the step-less (no-click) aperture setting for video capture, which allows changing the f/stop silently while capturing video. Some like the ability to add/subtract exposure compensation quickly, or the option to change ISO sensitivity on the fly with a single twist of the control ring. Just remember that when you're using an F-mount lens on the camera with the FTZ adapter, any control ring behaviors you've specified don't apply.

The second innovation comes from the focus-by-wire functions. Ordinarily, a lens, like those used in F-mount optics, has a mechanical linkage between the traditional focusing ring and the lens elements that move during focus adjustment. So, during manual focus, your rotation of the ring is translated into changes in focus. Motors built into a lens given the AF-S or AF-I designation (or those within the camera body with older AF lenses) take over to adjust the lens elements during autofocus, which is why the ring doesn't rotate when the camera is handling the focus chores. Focus override, which allows fine-tuning focus during the AF process, requires a special arrangement within the lens to allow the focus ring to assume control when the photographer wants to make adjustments without exiting to manual focus. Not all lenses include this capability, indicated by an A/M-M or MA-M switch on the side of the lens, and the focus ring can't be moved during AF without potentially damaging the mechanical components.

Thanks to focus-by-wire these shenanigans aren't necessary. With all Z-mount lenses, rotating the focus ring or the control ring (when it's set to function as a focus ring) delivers an electrical signal to the built-in motors. So, overriding the AF system is as simple as rotating the ring any time you want. That's cool enough all by itself. However, focus-by-wire enables the camera to adjust the "throw" of the lens during manual focus to match the speed with which you turn it.

In ancient times, it was common to require a *lot* of rotation of a focusing ring to focus from the minimum focus distance to infinity. The need to rotate, say, almost a full turn of the ring allowed for precise manual focus, which was a semi-great idea back in the day when autofocus didn't exist. However, when autofocus began to replace manual focus for the most part, lens designers began to produce lenses that required a reduced amount of throw to focus, so that each degree of rotation covered a larger portion of the focus distance from minimum to infinity. That led to faster focus, while making accurate manual focus more difficult.

Focus-by-wire, however, allows the AF operation to *adapt* to the rotational speed of the focus/control ring. Rotate rapidly, and the throw is relatively short—you may need to turn the ring only one-third of the way around to make a focus adjustment. Slow down your focusing motion, though, and each movement becomes more precise. You may have to rotate the ring all the way around to make the same adjustment that required only a one-third turn when done rapidly. You can easily see how this feature makes manual focus both more convenient and more precise. Your options, described in more detail in Chapter 7, include:

- **Custom Setting f9: Focus Ring Rotation Range.** With compatible Z lenses, you can adjust how dramatically focus changes with a given twist of the focus ring.
- **Custom Setting f10: Control Ring Response.** Adjusting the responsiveness of a focus lens ring isn't exclusively the province of manual focus adjustments. The "bonus" control ring introduced with Nikon's Z-mount optics can also be given High or Low response profiles.
- **Custom Setting f11: Switch Focus/Control Ring Roles.** If your lens includes both a focus ring and Control Ring you may find it more convenient to use the innermost or outermost rings for either focus or the custom behavior. This setting allows you to reverse the functions. Set to Off, the focus ring focuses, and the Control Ring performs its defined function. Select On, and the two rings trade functions.

Focus Summary

So far, this chapter has provided a detailed overview of how to use the various automatic and manual focusing options available for the Nikon Z9 and Z8. You'll find detailed descriptions of the focusing options available in the Custom Settings menu in Chapter 7. Here's a summary for reference:

- **a1 AF-C Priority Selection.** Options: Release (default), Focus+Release, Focus
- **a2 AF-S Priority Selection.** Options: Release, Focus (default)
- **a3 Focus Tracking with Lock-on.** Options: Blocked Shot AF Response: 5 (Delayed), 4, 3 (default), 2, 1 (Quick); Subject motion: Steady, Erratic
- **a4 Focus Points Used.** Options: All points (default), Alternating points
- **a5 Store Points by Orientation.** Options: Focus Point, Focus point and AF-area mode, Off
- **a6 AF Activation.** Options: Shutter/AF-ON (default); AF-ON Only: Out-of-focus release, Enable (default), Disable
- **a7 Focus Point Persistence.** Options: Auto (default), Off
- **a8 Limit AF-Area Mode Selection.** Options: Pinpoint, Single-point AF, Dynamic-area AF (Small, Medium, Large), Wide-area AF (Small, Large, C1, C2), 3D-tracking, Auto-area AF (Default is all available)
- **a9 Focus Mode Restrictions.** Options: Single AF, Continuous AF, Manual Focus, No restrictions (default)
- **a10 Focus Point Wrap-Around.** Options: Off (default), On
- **a11 Focus Point Display.** Options: Manual Focus Mode: On (default), Off; Dynamic-area AF assist: On (default), Off; AF-C in-focus display: On, Off (default); 3D-tracking focus point color: White (default), Red
- **a12 Built-in AF-Assist Illuminator.** Options: On (default), Off
- **a13 Focus Peaking.** Options: Focus peaking display: On, Off (default); Focus peaking sensitivity: 3 (high sensitivity), 2 (standard) (default), 1 (low sensitivity); Focus Peaking Highlight Color: Red (default), Yellow, Blue, White
- **a14 Focus Point Selection Speed.** Options: Low, Normal (default), High
- **a15 Manual Focus Ring in AF Mode.** Options: On (default), Off

Trap (Auto) Focus

This technique comes in handy when you know where the action is going to take place (such as at the finish line of a horse race), but you don't know exactly *when*. The solution is to prefocus on the point where the action will occur, and then tell your camera not to take the photo until something moves into the prefocus spot (see Figure 3.21). It's a good technique for sports action when you know that, say, a runner is going to pass by a certain position. You can also use trap focus for hand-held macro shots—set focus for a particular distance and then move the camera toward your subject. The shutter will trip automatically when your subject comes into focus.

Trap focus in Viewfinder mode isn't as difficult as you might think. The key is to decouple the focusing operation from the shutter release function. Just follow these steps:

1. **Confirm AF-ON button.** First, access Custom Setting f2 and make sure the definition for the AF-ON button is set to its default value, AF-ON, and not some other behavior. You want the AF-ON button to activate autofocus.
2. **Confirm AF-S Focus Priority.** Make sure Custom Setting a2 is set to Focus. The shutter will trip only when your subject is in focus when using AF-S.
3. **Disable Out-of-Focus Release.** By default, Custom Setting a6: AF Activation is set to Shutter/AF ON, which means the shutter release button initiates exposure metering *and* autofocus. You want to start autofocus separately, using the AF-ON button only. Highlight AF-ON Only and press the right button to reveal the Out-of-Focus Release option, and choose Disable. Press OK.

   Henceforth, pressing the shutter release halfway down does *not* activate autofocus. That happens *only* when you press the AF-ON button, and focus locks will occur *only* when something occupies the preset plane you specify in Step 7.
4. **Set focus mode to AF-S.**
5. **Set your point selection mode to Single-point AF.**
6. **Make sure your lens is set to autofocus (either A or M/A).**
7. **Prefocus on the spot where the action will occur, or an equivalent distance.** Use the focus ring on your lens. I like to manually focus on that point to make sure it is the exact position I want to capture. For Figure 3.21, I focused on a plane between the third and fourth hurdles, which were located 30 feet apart (the standard for men's hurdle events). You can also press the AF-ON button to focus on that point, and then release the button. In either case, further AF activity will cease. The prefocused distance is the "trap" you've set for your pending subject.

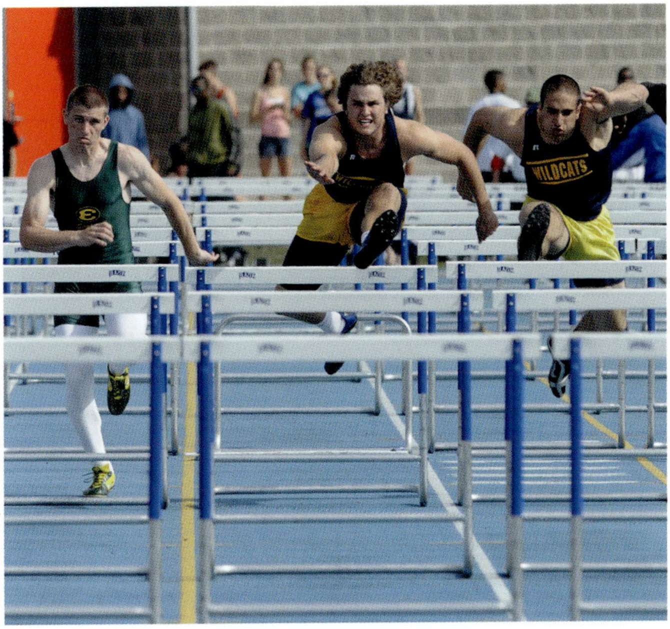

Figure 3.21 By prefocusing on a point between two of the hurdles, trap focus captured this athlete the instant he moved into the point of focus.

8. **Reframe your picture, if necessary, so that nothing is at the prefocused distance.** If an object occupies that spot, the camera will take the photo immediately when you press the shutter release.
9. **Press and hold down the shutter release all the way.** The camera will not refocus, because you've disconnected the autofocus function from the shutter release.
10. **Trap sprung!** The picture will be taken when a subject moves into the prefocused area. Note that trap focus may not work well with some subjects, particularly when using small f/stops. Increased depth-of-field may cause the camera to take the photo when your subject has barely entered the trap and not yet perfectly in the preselected focus plane. Even so, trap focus is a very useful technique.

If you like what trap focus does, you should consider Auto Capture, available with the Z9 but not the Z8. As explained in Chapter 5, Auto Capture allows you to set up criteria the camera will use to trigger the shutter for a sequence of shots (or a video clip) when the camera detects a subject at a given distance, of a particular size, moving at a given speed or in a certain direction. You could easily choose one of the hurdles shown in Figure 3.21 as a target distance and Auto Capture would take a sequence of shots when an athlete reaches that position. Combine that with Pre-Release Capture, and you can grab shots from just *before* the hurdle is reached, too.

DANGER, WILL ROBINSON!

If you don't use trap focus often, or don't work with the AF-ON button as your primary autofocus start control regularly, don't make the mistake I did. One time I forgot that I had followed the steps above. The next time I picked up my camera, it "refused" to autofocus—at least when I pressed the shutter release halfway. Much consternation followed until I remembered what I had done a few days earlier, pressed the AF-ON button, and found that the AF function was just fine. I had simply "turned off" the shutter release as an AF start control.

Back-Button Focus

Once you've been using your camera for a while, you'll invariably encounter the terms *back focus* and *back-button focus* and wonder if they are good things or bad things. Actually, they are *two different things,* and are often confused with each other. *Back focus* is a bad thing and occurs when a particular lens consistently autofocuses on a plane that's *behind* your desired subject. This malady may be found in some of your lenses, or all your optics may be free of the defect. The good news is that if the problem lies in a particular lens (rather than a camera misadjustment that applies to *all* your lenses), it can be fixed. I'll show you how to do that at the end of this chapter.

Back-button focus (often just referred to as BBF), on the other hand, is a tool you can use to separate two functions that are commonly locked together—exposure and autofocus—so that you can lock in exposure while allowing focus to be attained at a later point, or vice versa. It's a *good* thing, although using back-button focus effectively may require you to unlearn some habits and acquire new ways of coordinating the action of your fingers.

As you have learned, the default behavior of your Nikon camera is to set both exposure and focus (when AF is active) when you press the shutter release down halfway. When using AF-S mode, that's that: both exposure and focus are locked and will not change until you release the shutter button or press it all the way down to take a picture and then release it for the next shot. In AF-C mode, exposure is locked and focus set when you press the shutter release halfway, but the camera will *continue to refocus* if your subject moves for as long as you hold down the shutter button halfway. Focus isn't locked until you press the button down all the way to take the picture.

What back-button focus does is *decouple* or separate the two actions, as you did with trap focus, described above. You can retain the exposure lock feature when the shutter is pressed halfway but assign autofocus *start* and/or autofocus *lock* to a different button. So, in practice, you can press the shutter button halfway, locking exposure, and reframe the image if you like (perhaps you're photographing a backlit subject and want to lock in exposure on the foreground, and then reframe to include a very bright background as well).

But, in this same scenario, you *don't* want autofocus locked at the same time. Indeed, you may not want to start AF until you're good and ready, say, at a sports venue as you wait for a ballplayer to streak into view in your viewfinder, or when you're photographing a garden and expect a butterfly to alight somewhere nearby. With back-button focus, you can lock exposure on the spot where you expect the athlete or insect to be and activate AF at the moment your subject appears. Your camera gives you a great deal of flexibility, both in the choice of which button to use for AF, and the behavior of that button. That's where the learning of new habits and mind-finger coordination comes in. You need to learn which back-button focus techniques work for you, and when to use them.

Back-button focus lets you avoid the need to switch from AF-S to AF-C when your subject begins moving unexpectedly. You retain complete control. It's great for sports photography when you want to activate autofocus precisely based on the action in front of you. It also works for static shots. You can press and release your designated focus button, and then take a series of shots using the same focus point. Focus will not change until you once again press your defined back button. (See Figure 3.22.)

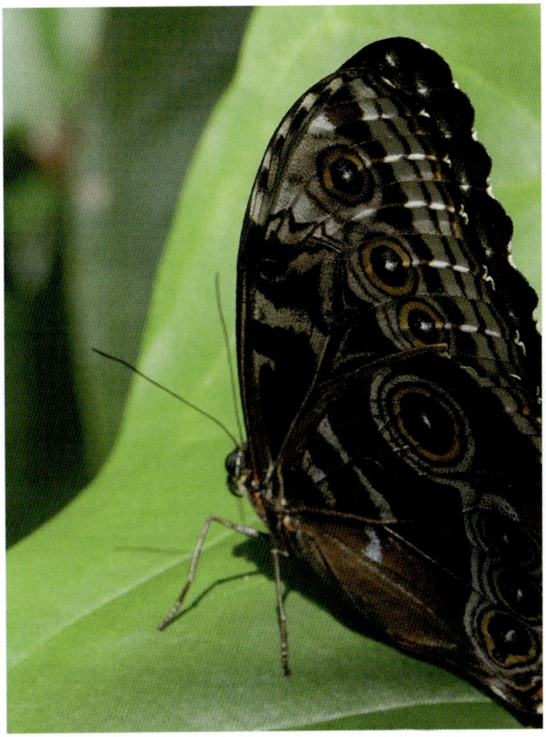

Figure 3.22 Lock your exposure for the garden by pressing the shutter release halfway; then activate autofocus when the butterfly decides where to land.

Want to focus on a spot without moving the focus point within your frame? Use back-button focus to zero in focus with the current focus area—no need to move it—then reframe. Focus will not change. Don't want to miss an important shot at a wedding on a photojournalism assignment? If you're set to *focus-priority* there may be a delay in taking a picture until the focus is optimum; in *release-priority* there may still be a slight delay. With back-button focus you can focus first and wait until the decisive moment to press the shutter release and take your picture. The camera will respond immediately and not bother with focusing at all. Back-button focus can also save battery power. Constantly refocusing in AF-C mode can consume a lot of power.

Activating Back-Button Focus

Here's how to set up back-button focus. Just follow these steps:

1. **Assign AF activation to AF-ON function only.** As with trap focus, you want to initiate autofocus only with the AF-ON button. Navigate to Custom Setting a6: AF Activation. There, the options are Shutter/AF-ON or AF-ON only. With the former option, pressing the shutter release halfway *or* the AF-ON control will enable *both* autoexposure and autofocus. Instead, select AF-ON Only to decouple the two functions, so that AF activation starts *only* when you press your designated AF-ON button. However, for back-button focus, you'll want to press the right directional button and *enable* Out-of-Focus Release.
2. **Assign AF-ON function.** Most users of BBF prefer to use the AF-ON button to initiate autofocus. However, if you'd rather use a different button, Custom Setting f2: Custom Controls can assign the AF-ON button to the button of your choice. In all cases, if you've followed these steps, the defined button is used to *initiate* autofocus. The shutter-release button cannot be used to initiate autofocus.
3. **Set Focus Mode to AF-C.**
4. **Confirm Release Priority.** Make sure Custom Setting a1 is set to Release.
5. **Activate Focus.** As you frame your subject, wait until you want to initiate focus, then press the AF-ON button, and your AF-C focus mode will kick into action. You then have two options:
    - **Release the AF-ON button.** When you release the button, focus will be locked and you can reframe as needed (just as with AF-S).
    - **Track focus.** Continue to press the AF-ON button and AF-C mode will continue to operate as necessary to keep your subject in focus. With the button held down, you can take pictures by pressing the shutter release fully.

Fine-Tuning the Focus of Your Lenses

Theoretically, at least, there should be little or no need at all to fine-tune the focus of native Z-mount lenses. With a traditional dSLR, the autofocus mechanism is a separate component located in the floor of the mirror box. There are a number of different components that can be slightly misaligned in relationship to the lens and the dSLR's optical manual focusing screen. AF Fine-tune can correct for that error. The Z9 and Z8, in contrast, calculate autofocus using the actual sensor image, and so should "see" any misalignment between the lens and sensor planes and correct for it automatically.

However, Nikon, in its wisdom, has included an AF Fine-tune feature for those who need it. You can use it with both native Z-mount lenses as well as F-mount lenses attached using the FTZ adapter. In this section, I'll show you how to calibrate your lenses using the AF Fine-tune feature.

Why is the focus "off" for some lenses in the first place? There are lots of factors, including the age of the lens (an older lens may focus slightly differently), temperature effects on certain types of glass, humidity, and tolerances built into a lens's design that all add up to a slight misadjustment, even though the components themselves are, strictly speaking, within specs. A very slight variation in your lens's mount can cause focus to vary slightly. Finally, focus planes can shift slightly with some lenses, especially at smaller apertures.

With any luck (if you can call it that) a lens that doesn't focus exactly right will at least be consistent. If a lens always focuses a bit behind the subject, the symptom is *back focus.* If it focuses in front of the subject, it's called *front focus.* There are products available, such as Reikan FoCal ($89), a tool for both PCs and Macs that comes with software and a focusing target. The popular LensAlign MkII Focus Calibration system is no longer widely available. You can fine-tune your autofocus system manually. The key tool you can use to fine-tune your lens is the AF Fine-Tuning Options entry in the Setup menu, shown in Figure 3.23. You'll find the process easier to understand if you first run through this quick overview of the menu options:

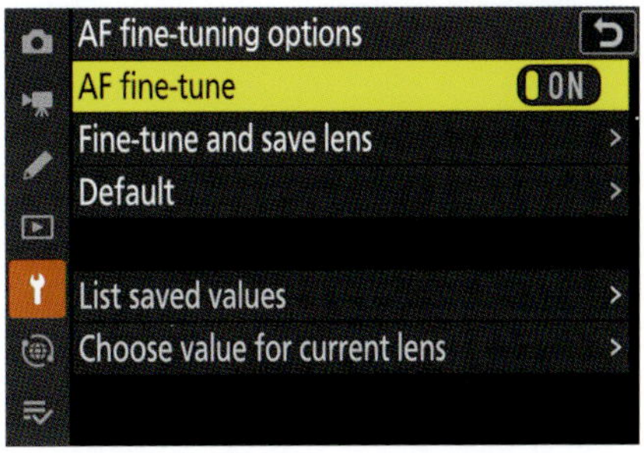

Figure 3.23 The AF Fine-Tuning Options menu.

- **AF Fine-tune (On/Off).** This option enables/disables autofocus fine-tuning for all the lenses you've defined using the menu entry. If you discover you don't care for the calibrations you make in certain situations (say, it works better for the lens you have mounted at middle distances but is less successful at correcting close-up focus errors), you can deactivate the feature as you require. You should set this to On when you're doing the actual fine-tuning.
- **Fine-tune and Save Lens.** This setting lets you tune the autofocus calibration for the current Z-mount and CPU-chipped F-mount lenses (virtually all Nikon-brand autofocus lenses) mounted on the camera. When you first fine-tune a lens, the default saved value will be 0 (zero). You can press the multi selector up/down buttons to choose a value between +20 and –20 for both wide-angle and telephoto positions of a zoom lens. Only a single +20 or –20 adjustment can be made for prime lenses.

  Positive numbers move the focal point farther from the camera and would be used if your lens consistently suffers from front-focus problems. Negative numbers move the focal point closer to the camera and would be used if your lens is plagued with consistent back focus. The value is relative and doesn't correlate to any particular distance or percentage.
- **Default.** This entry often confuses. It is a value that is applied to *every* lens mounted on the camera that doesn't already have a customized saved value associated with it. That is, if your camera has consistent front- or back-focus problems with *all* lenses, you can enter a value here, and the camera will apply the correction to each CPU lens you use. This default setting can be overridden by saved values you've stored for particular lenses. So, you can change the default focal plane for all lenses, and still further fine-tune specific lenses that need more autofocus correction. My recommendation is that if your camera and lenses are so out of whack that you need global correction and individual fine-tuning, you *really* ought to consider shipping the whole kit off to Nikon for proper calibration.

- **List Saved Values.** This screen shows you the saved fine-tuning values for all lenses. If the currently mounted lens has a stored value, it will be marked with a solid black box icon. You can delete lenses from this list by highlighting them and pressing the Trash button. You can also change the number or apply an alphanumeric name that can be used to identify a particular lens.
- **Choose Value for Current Lens.** Your camera can differentiate between different lenses of the same type, and even record/display the serial number of a particular lens. So, it's possible to store multiple fine-tuning values for more than one lens of the same type. This entry becomes available so you can choose which of the available values to use if you have fine-tuned multiple lenses of the same type.

Evaluating Current Focus

The first step is to capture a baseline image that represents how the lens you want to fine-tune autofocuses at a particular distance. You'll often see advice for photographing a test chart with millimeter markings from an angle, and the suggestion that you autofocus on a particular point on the chart. Supposedly, the markings that actually *are* in focus will help you recalibrate your lens. The problem with this approach is that the information you get from photographing a test chart at an angle (like the one shown in Figure 3.24) doesn't actually tell you what to do to make a precise correction. So, your lens back focuses three millimeters behind the target area on the chart. So what? Does that mean you change the saved value by –3 clicks? Or –15 clicks? Angled targets are a "shortcut" that don't save you time.

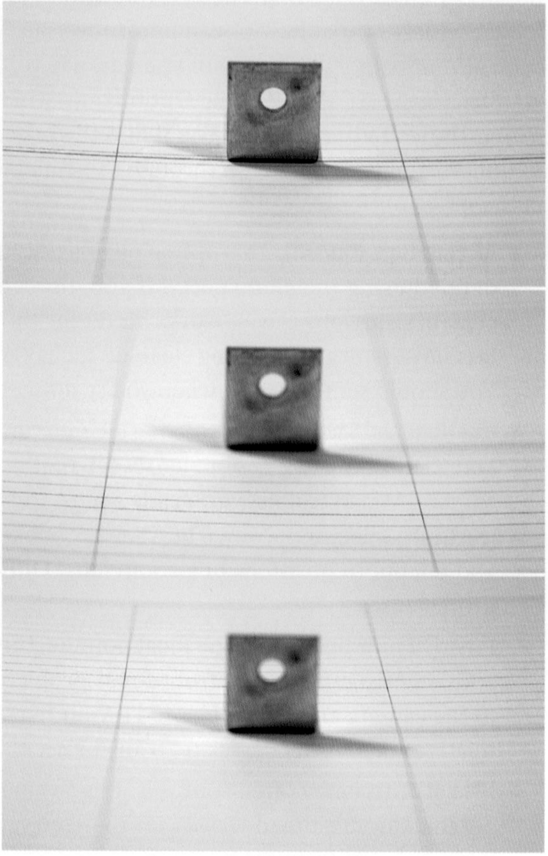

Figure 3.24 Shooting a chart at an angle may reveal front- or back-focus, but won't tell you how much correction is needed.

Instead, you'll want to photograph a target that represents what you're actually trying to achieve: a plane of focus locked in by your lens that represents the actual plane of focus of your subject. For that, you'll need a flat target, mounted precisely perpendicular to the sensor plane of the camera. Then, you can take a photo, see if the plane of focus is correct, and if not, dial in a bit of fine-tuning in the AF Fine-Tuning menu, and shoot again. Rinse, lather, and repeat until the target is sharply focused.

You can use the focus target shown in Figure 3.25, or you can use a chart of your own, as long as it has contrasty areas that will be easily seen by the autofocus system, and without very small details that are likely to confuse the AF. Download your own copy of my chart from www.nikonguides.com/FocusChart.pdf (*the URL is case-sensitive*). Then print out a copy on the largest paper your printer can handle. (I don't recommend just displaying the file on your monitor and focusing on that; it's unlikely you'll have the monitor screen lined up perfectly perpendicular to the camera sensor.) Then, follow these steps:

1. **Position the camera.** Place your camera on a sturdy tripod, positioned at roughly eye-level at a distance from a wall that represents the distance you want to test for. Keep in mind that autofocus problems can be different at varying distances and lens focal lengths, and that you can enter only *one* correction value for a particular lens. So, choose a distance (close-up or mid-range) and zoom setting with your shooting habits in mind. You'll use a remote release/control to trigger the shutter.
2. **Set the autofocus mode.** Choose the autofocus mode (AF-C or AF-S) you want to test.
3. **Level the camera (in an ideal world).** If the wall happens to be perfectly perpendicular, you can use a bubble level, plumb bob, or other device of your choice to ensure that the camera is level to match. Many tripods and tripod heads have bubble levels built in. Avoid using the center column if you can. When the camera is properly oriented, lock the legs and tripod head tightly.
4. **Level the camera (in the real world).** If your wall is not perfectly perpendicular, use this old trick. Tape a mirror to the wall, and then adjust the camera on the tripod so that when you look through the viewfinder at the mirror, you see directly into the reflection of the lens. Then, lock the tripod and remove the mirror.
5. **Mount the test chart.** Tape the test chart on the wall so it is centered in your viewfinder. You should place the chart roughly 30X to 40X the focal length of the lens setting you'll be testing. For example, for a 100mm lens, place the chart 3,000mm from the camera (roughly 9.8 feet).
6. **Photograph the test chart.** Choose an appropriate exposure (manually or in Aperture-priority mode) with the lens set one stop from maximum aperture. Lighting should be similar to what you'll be using most frequently for your actual photography (i.e., daylight, incandescent, etc.). Focus and take a test photo, using the remote release to avoid shaking or moving the camera. It makes sense to take multiple photos, at least a half dozen, with fine-tuning turned on and off so you can compare them to see if there is a difference.
7. **Evaluate the images.** If you have the camera connected to your computer with a USB cable or Wi-Fi, so much the better. You can view images after transfer to your computer. Otherwise, *carefully* open the card door, slip the memory card out, and copy the image(s) to your computer.
8. **Evaluate focus.** If the image is not sharply focused, you may need to make a fine-tuning adjustment and photograph the target again. To perform the fine-tuning, just follow the instructions in the next section. I've separated the fine-tuning adjustments from these steps because some people may want to just tweak the focus at a later time without going through all these evaluation steps.

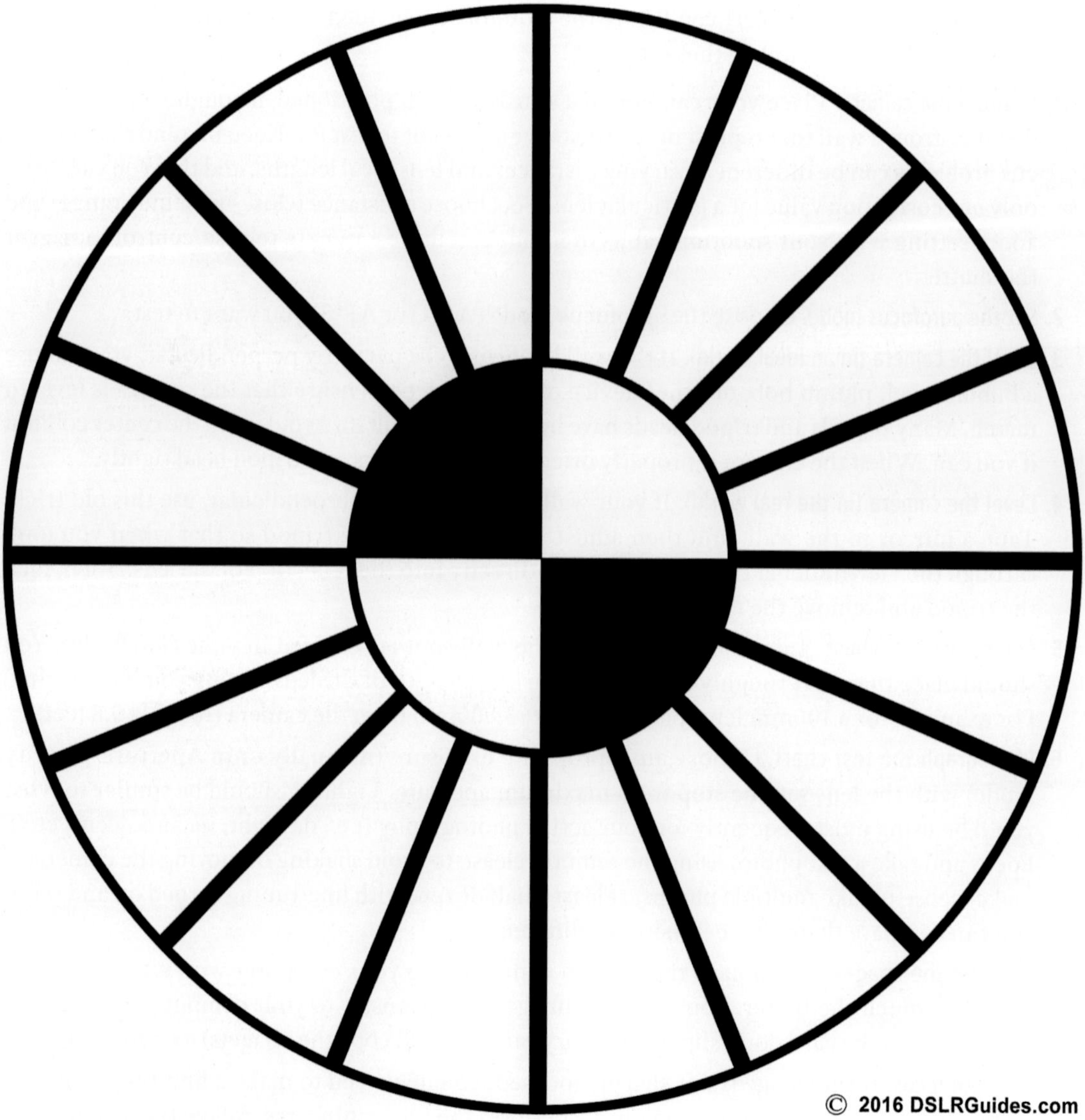

Figure 3.25 Use this focus test chart or create one of your own.

Changing the Fine-Tuning Setting

Adjust the fine-tuning for the lens you have mounted by following these steps:

1. **Mount lens.** If you haven't been running the test described previously, mount the Z-mount or F-mount CPU-equipped lens (with FTZ adapter) you want to fine-tune. The camera will automatically recognize the lens you are using during the "calibration" process and display its name on the screen.
2. **Activate fine-tuning.** If you haven't already done so, choose AF Fine-Tune (On/Off) and turn it ON.
3. **Select Fine-Tune and Save Lens.** A screen similar to the one shown in Figure 3.26 will appear.
4. **Highlight Wide or Tele scales (Zoom lenses only).** If you're calibrating a zoom lens, dual scales will appear labeled Wide and Tele. Use the up/down controls to switch between the two scales. Prime (non-zoom lenses) will display only a single scale.
5. **Adjust focus.** Press the left/right directional controls to adjust the autofocus from +20 (move the focal point away from the camera to fix front-focus problems) to –20 values (move the focal point toward the camera to fix back focus). Make your change for both wide and tele scales if you're working with a zoom lens. In practice, your adjustments will tend to be +5/–5 or larger. Smaller adjustments don't provide much difference.
6. **Confirm adjustment.** Press OK when the value(s) you want are entered. You may have to run the test described above several times and use some trial and error to determine the correct adjustment.
7. **View saved values.** Choose List Saved Values to see the names of the lenses you've fine-tuned. (See Figure 3.27.) Highlight the lens you'd like to assign a number or alphanumeric name to and press the right directional button to produce the screen shown in Figure 3.28.
8. **Assign a label.** Choose a lens identifier, which can be a number or an alphanumeric name, using the standard camera text-entry screen. You can use a label of up to 22 characters. This identifier can be used to differentiate a particular lens from other lenses of the same type, if you own, say, some duplicate lenses. You can define fine-tuning parameters for up to 40 different lenses.

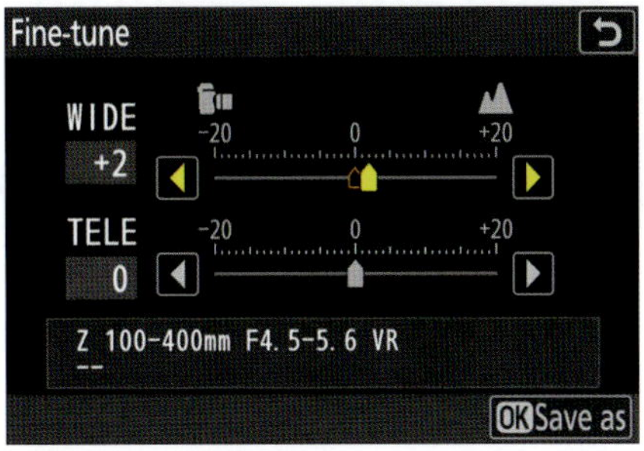

Figure 3.26 Fine-tune values.

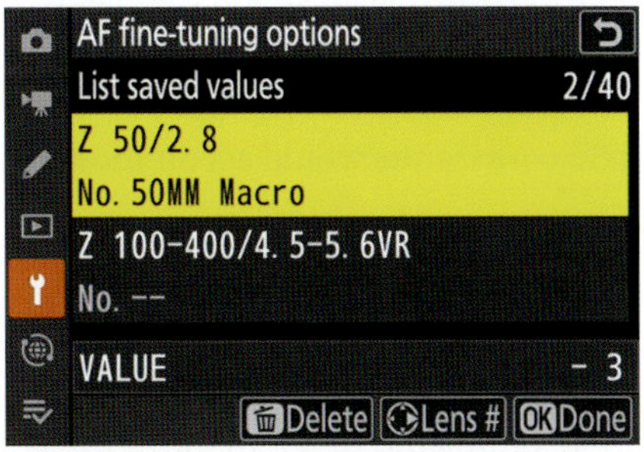

Figure 3.27 List the saved values you've stored.

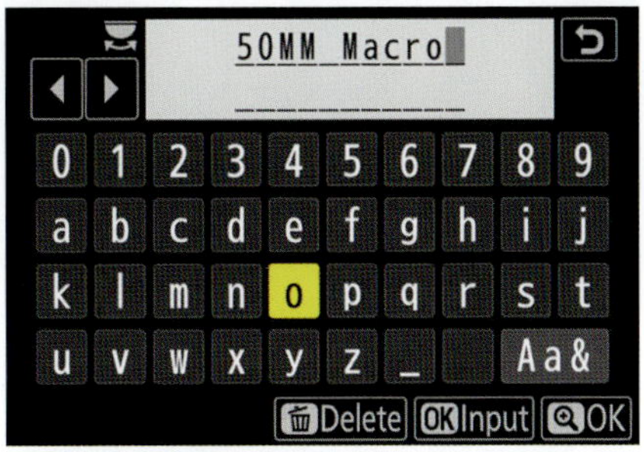

Figure 3.28 Assign an identifier, if necessary, to differentiate a particular lens from other lenses of the same type you may use.

That's not as far-fetched as you might think. Some organizations, such as newspapers, allow their photographers to use their favorite lenses exclusively, but they may need to share other specialized optics among several photographers. If you don't know which of the pooled 600mm lenses you'll be using on any particular day, you can calibrate your camera separately for each of them.

9. **Confirm.** Press the Zoom In button to confirm and return to the Choose Lens Number screen.
10. **Exit.** Press MENU to exit.

Focus Shift Shooting

Focus stacking—which Nikon calls Focus Shift shooting—is commonly used as a way of increasing the narrow depth-of-field commonly encountered when doing macro (close-up) photography of flowers or other small objects at short distances. In some cases, depth-of-field will be so narrow that it's impossible to keep the entire subject in focus. Although having part of the image out of focus can be a pleasing effect for a portrait of a person, it is likely to be a hindrance when you are trying to make an accurate photographic record of a flower, or small piece of precision equipment.

In a sense, Focus Shift shooting can be considered like HDR translated for the world of focus—taking multiple shots with different settings, and, using software, combining the in-focus areas of each image in order to make a whole that is better than the sum of the parts. Focus stacking requires a non-moving object, so some subjects, such as flowers, are best photographed in a breezeless environment, such as indoors. You can do focus stacking outdoors, and it can be a useful tool for deep-focus landscape images with important content much closer to the camera than conventional depth-of-field constraints would accommodate.

With the Z9/Z8's Focus Shift shooting feature, the camera takes a series of pictures starting at a focus point you specify. The camera then adjusts the focus slightly between each image, refocusing from closest to your subject to infinity. You end up with a series of images that can be combined using two simple Photoshop commands, which I will describe shortly. Figure 3.29 can help you visualize what's going on. At left in the figure is a close-up of a box of crayons captured at f/2.8 and focused on

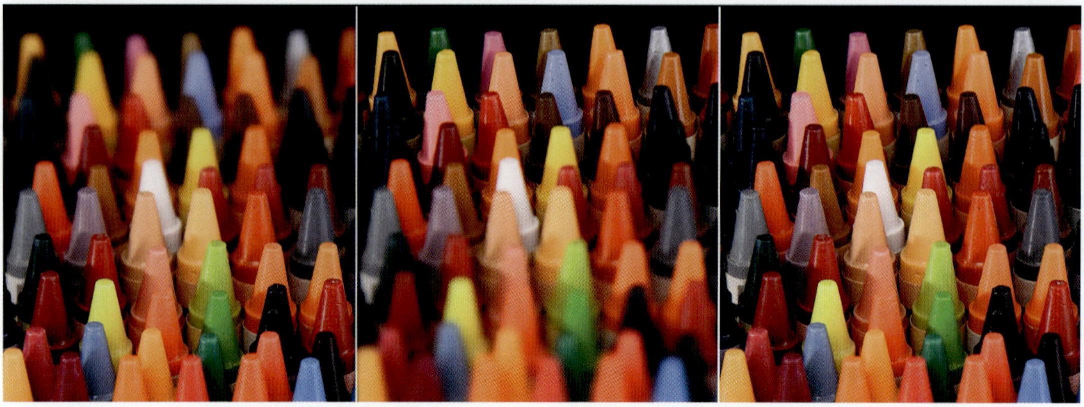

Figure 3.29 Images focused at the nearest focus planes (left) are combined with others at increasing distances, to a most distant point (center), and then merged to produce an image with extreme depth-of-field (right).

the front rows. The center image shows the same crayons, but with the focus on the back rows. Focus Shift takes as many as 300 separate exposures at different focus points in-between, and then merges them in a way that uses only the *sharpest* pixels in each individual image, as seen at right in the figure.

It's a shame, but most of the discussions you see about focus stacking don't really explain the full potential and advantages of this powerful technique. Here's a summary:

- **Focus stacking increases depth-of-field.** Everybody knows this; it's the first thing associated with the technique. The second thing they think of is macro photography. But the process can be used for many other types of static subjects, including landscape and architectural photography.
- **Focus stacking makes the best use of your lens' sharpness.** Yes, you can increase DOF without focus stacking just by stopping down your lens to a smaller aperture. However, every lens has an optimum, sharpest, aperture. If you use a smaller f/stop you will lose sharpness due to *diffraction effects,* as I explain in Chapter 5. So, the increased *range* of sharpness comes at the cost of some definition. Apertures *wider* than a given lens' best f/stop will be less sharp due to uncorrected aberrations and other effects that are reduced at the optimum aperture.

  But with focus stacking, each and every exposure in the stack can be made using the *sharpest* aperture setting available with that lens.
- **Focus stacking can alleviate image noise effects.** You don't always have absolute control over the lighting you use, especially if you're working with electronic flash. So, if you shoot at f/32 to get maximum depth-of-field you may have to boost your Z9/Z8's ISO sensitivity to compensate, potentially to the point of increasing noise levels in your image. A single image shot at f/32 and ISO 1000 might have depth-of-field similar to a stack-focus one exposed at f/5.6 and ISO 100, but pixel-peepers may find the sharpness and noise qualities to be very different.
- **Focus stacking provides unprecedented control over focus range.** You can choose exactly what areas of your image are in sharp focus, including some ways I discovered that are impossible to achieve under normal conditions.

  With focus shift shooting, you have dozens or hundreds of individual images to work with, each with a narrow plane of focus. You can, then, pick and choose exactly where your depth-of-field begins and ends with remarkable precision. If, for creative reasons, you want everything a millimeter in front of your main subject to be blurry, and everything a millimeter or more behind it to blur, you can do that, while keeping your subject tack sharp. When stacking your final image, all you have to do is not merge any of the frames in the area you want to be out of focus. This can lead to the extraordinary effect I describe in the next section.

Freaky Focus

I'd never seen this effect until I figured out how to do it, and it tends to blow people's minds at presentations I give. The three images shown in Figure 3.30 were all extracted from the same series of 100 shots created with a Focus Shift sequence. Not all the results are what you might expect to see.

- At top is an image of some pottery, created using 100 images in a Focus Shift sequence. As you can see, each of the four pieces is in sharp focus. I discarded the shots focused behind and in front of the pottery, so those areas of the seamless background are blurred. The green arrows point to components that are in focus.

- For the center image, I discarded the frames shot of the bowl in the rear, so it ended up out of focus, while the four pieces in front of it are sharp. This demonstrates one way to control the extent of the sharply focused area.
- I got a little weird for the image at the bottom of the figure, discarding all the well-focused shots for the two pieces in the middle. This is a view you'll never, ever see in real life: a tableau of five elements with the *front* and *rear* pieces sharply focused, while the pieces in the middle are blurry. While you can do some nifty tricks with shift/tilt lenses, the only way you can achieve this particular effect (outside of tedious compositing) is by creatively manipulating sets of focus stacked images.

I plan on playing with this some more. My next project is to set up some chess pieces so that alternating rows are in focus, while the rest of the rows are sharp.

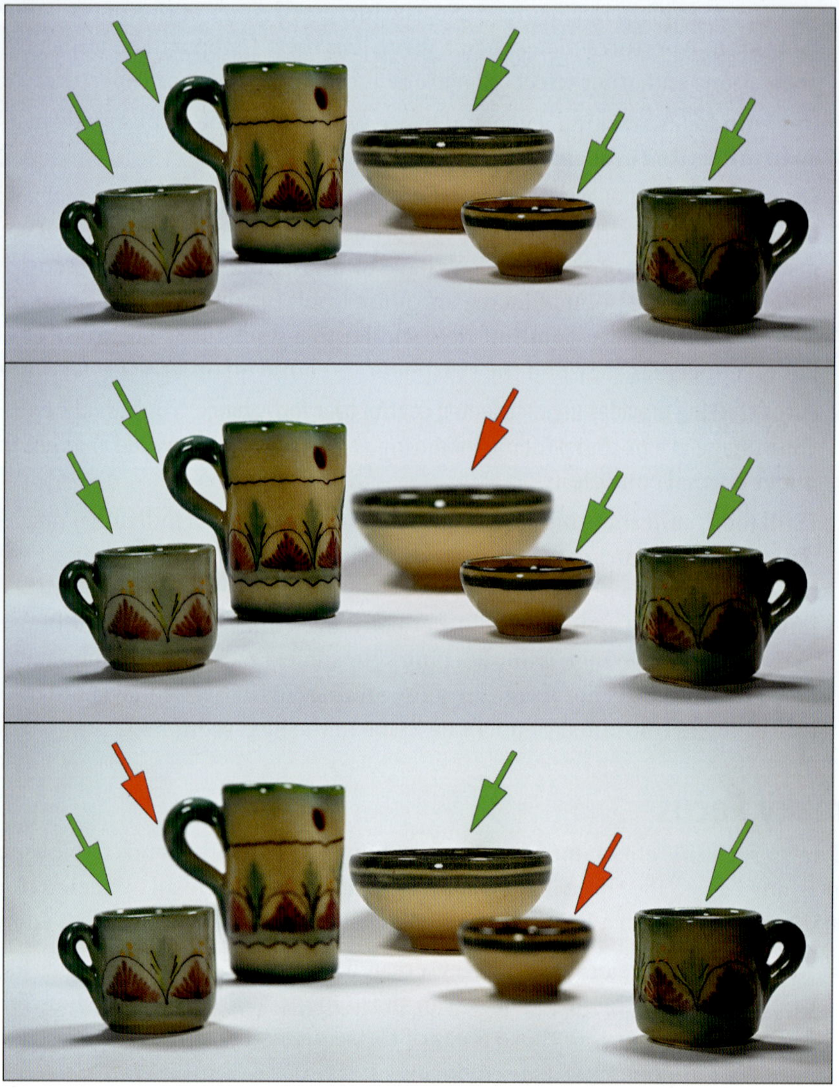

Figure 3.30 Freaky fun with Focus Shift.

Focus Shift How-To

Fortunately, producing a conventional focus-stacked image doesn't require my variety of unhinged thinking if all you want is enhanced depth-of-field. Here are the detailed steps you can take to use Focus Shift Shooting for your own deep-focus images:

1. **Set the camera firmly on a solid tripod.** A tripod or other equally firm support is absolutely essential for this procedure. You don't want the camera (or the subject) to move at all during the exposures.
2. **Use a remote release, if desired.** It's probably best if you trigger the camera without moving it. However, the procedure does pause for a short period of time once you activate it, perhaps giving your tripod/camera time to settle down even if you begin by poking the OK button with your finger.
3. **Attach a lens with an appropriate focus range.** Focus Shift Shooting uses the lens's built-in autofocus motor, and so will not work with lenses that do not autofocus on the Z9 or Z8.
4. **Set the focus modes.** Press the Focus Mode button and rotate the main command dial to choose AF-S (single focus) and the sub-command dial to choose Single-point AF.
5. **Set the quality of the images to JPEG FINE *.** Use the Photo Shooting menu to make this adjustment.
6. **Set the exposure, ISO, and white balance manually.** Use test shots, if necessary, to determine the best values. None of the Hi ISO settings can be used.
    - **Maintain exposure.** Indoors, when lighting conditions are stable, by turning off autoexposure, Auto ISO, and Auto White Balance, you can prevent visible variations from arising among the multiple shots that you'll be taking. When shooting indoors, you don't want the camera to change exposure, the ISO setting, or white balance between shots. However, if you're *outdoors* where lighting may change, you may need to use Aperture-priority to keep a constant exposure.
    - **Avoid wide apertures, too.** As I said above, even though you'll be effectively increasing depth-of-field through focus stacking, you should still avoid the *widest* apertures of your lens, as well as the smallest, as they are rarely the sharpest f/stops. In addition, because wide apertures do have less DOF, if you shoot at f/2.8, say, instead of f/5.6, the camera will need to capture more shots.
    - **Close down a few stops.** I always close down at least 1.5 f/stops. Shutter speed is not as important (and less so if you're using flash). Since the camera is on a tripod, ambient light exposures won't add any blur from camera movement, but I tend to avoid very slow speeds anyway to keep the process speedy and efficient. You can manually set a slightly higher ISO sensitivity, if needed, to obtain the shutter speed/aperture combination you want to use.
7. **Avoid conflicting features.** Disable vibration reduction, even with lenses that can detect being mounted on a tripod; if your lens has VR and an on/off switch, slide the VR switch to Off. Make sure Photo Flicker Reduction and High Frequency Flicker Reduction are turned off. The self-timer cannot be used to start the sequence. If Picture Control is set to Auto, change it to Standard. You may also use one of the other "original" Picture Controls (as described in Chapter 5) if you want to apply that control's effect to your stack.

8. **Set focus point to nearest point.** Use the directional buttons to position the red focus box on the subject nearest the camera lens that you want to include. The less of the foreground you include in your set, the fewer shots you'll need to complete your sequence. Focus *slightly in front of that subject.* It's safer to include some of the out-of-focus foreground and discard those images.
9. **Access the Focus Shift Shooting menu.** It's shown in Figure 3.31. Select an appropriate setting for each of the following six parameters, using my guidelines:

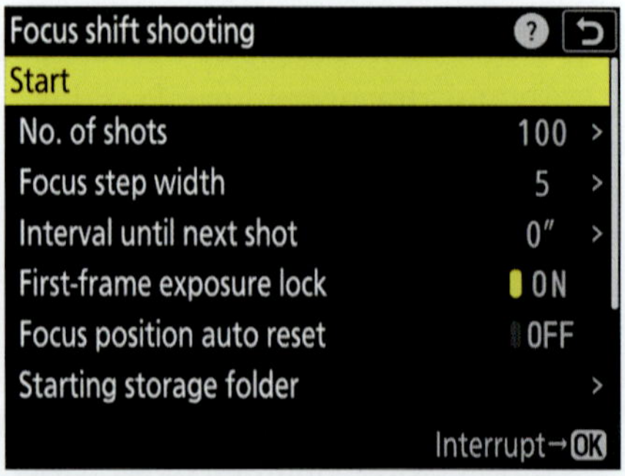

Figure 3.31 Focus Shift Shooting options.

- **No. of Shots.** You can choose from 1 to 300 individually refocused shots. The number of images captured will depend on how finely you want to have the camera change focus between shots (and you'll combine this with the step width option described next). For a subject with a lot of fine detail and depth (such as a macro shot of an insect), you'll want lots of images, a hundred or more, to record focus at many different planes. For architectural or landscape scenes taken with a wide-angle lens, you'll need fewer.
- **Focus Step Width.** You can specify values from 1 (a narrow slice per adjustment) to 10 (a much wider focus change). Nikon does not specify how much each increment changes the focus, for a very good reason: it *can't.* Depending on the focal length of your lens and your f/stop, the effective plane of apparent focus may vary from narrow, to very narrow, to super-narrow in macro shooting environments. (If you're confused, see "Circles of Confusion" earlier in this chapter.)

  You may need some trial-and-error to choose the correct number of shots and focus step width. For example, with 50 shots and a wide focus step, the first 10 may encompass your entire subject and the last 40 may be wasted on completely out-of-focus images. It's often worthwhile to take a test shot, view a slide show of all your images, and decide whether to increase/decrease the number of shots and/or focus step width.

  As a guideline, you should consider using a step width of 4 or 5 for distant subjects (e.g., landscapes) and smaller steps (1 or 2) for macro photos, because the changes in focus are large between steps with close-ups.
- **Interval Until Next Shot.** You can select 00 seconds to 30 seconds. At 00 seconds, the camera will take all the photos consecutively at a rate of up to 5 frames per second in Single Shot or Continuous mode. (You can't use the self-timer release mode.) The 00-second setting works well when shooting by ambient light that doesn't change. However, you can use flash, too. Just specify an interval that is greater than the maximum recycle rate of your flash. **Note:** Also consider how much your flash heats up when fired at brief intervals, particularly when the full power of the flash is needed for each shot. Multiple shots at close-range in macro mode can work fine, because only a fraction of the flash's power is used for each exposure.
- **First-Frame Exposure Lock.** Choose On and the camera will lock exposure at the settings calculated for the first shot. You'll use this most of the time, as you will get the best results if the illumination does not change between shots. Select Off to tell the camera to recalculate

exposure for each frame. You might do that when shooting landscapes on a day with intermittent clouds. Your results may not be as good as if the lighting was kept consistent, however.

- **Focus Position Auto Reset.** When set to On, after the Focus Shift sequence is finished, the Z9/Z8 will refocus at the specified starting position. If you're shooting tests or simply want to try again after making some other adjustment, this allows you to repeat your previous focus settings. It can be a time-saver. If set to Off, focus remains at the position of the final shot. I haven't been able to think of a reason why you'd want this, but Nikon, in their wisdom, probably came up with something.
- **Starting Storage Folder.** Choose New Folder, and each time you shoot a sequence, the camera will create a fresh folder. I can't think of a reason you would not want to do that. Select Reset File Numbering, and the file numbering is reset each time a new folder is created, which makes it easier to differentiate between the first, last, and in-between images of your set.

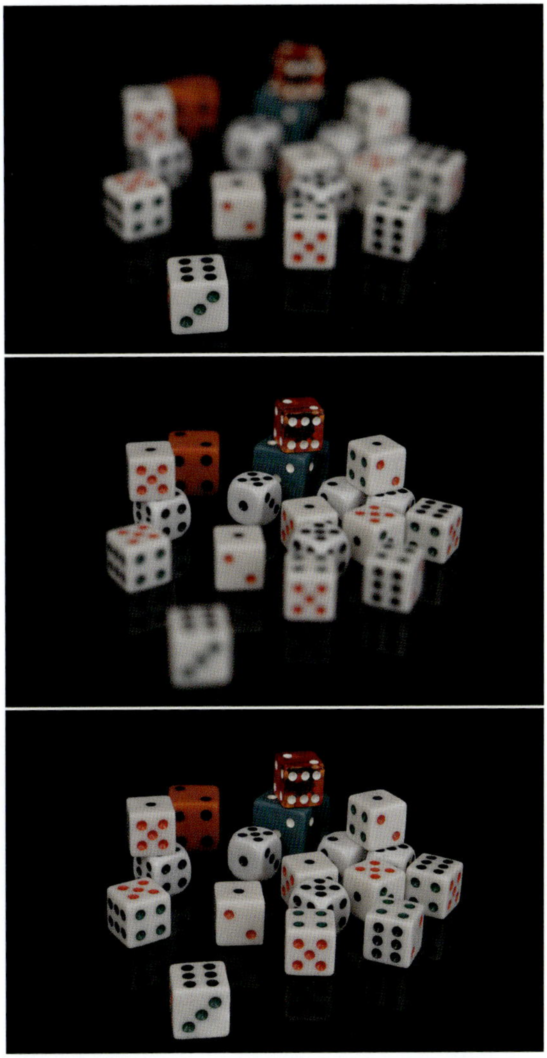

Figure 3.32 Closest point of sharp focus (top); furthest point of sharp focus (center), merged image (bottom).

10. **Capture images.** When all the parameters are locked in, highlight Start and press the OK button. The LCD monitor displays a "Preparing..." message and then commences the capture within about three seconds. Don't worry; the Standby Timer is disabled and your camera will not shut off, as long as your battery has sufficient power to complete the series. The sequence ends when the number of shots you requested have been taken *or* focus reaches infinity. So, you may end up with many "extra" shots—or not—depending on your settings.

    Note that Focus Shift is not "sticky." Once you've grabbed a sequence, the feature is turned off and you must Start again to repeat, or change parameters and Start anew.

    As your shots are taken, the camera will refocus from the closest point you specified (as in Figure 3.32, top) to the farthest point (Figure 3.32, center) and then on to infinity (see Figure 3.32, bottom).
11. **Combine your images.** I'll describe the steps for that next.

The next step is to process the images you've taken in Photoshop. Transfer the images to your computer, and then follow these steps:

1. In Photoshop, select File > Scripts > Load Files into Stack. In the dialog box that then appears, navigate on your computer to find the files for the photographs you have taken, and highlight them all.
2. At the bottom of the next dialog box that appears, check the box that says, "Attempt to Automatically Align Source Images," then click OK. The images will load; it may take several minutes for the program to load the images and attempt to arrange them into layers that are aligned based on their content.
3. Once the program has finished processing the images, go to the Layers panel and select all the layers. You can do this by clicking on the top layer and then Shift-clicking on the bottom one.
4. While the layers are all selected, in Photoshop go to Edit > Auto-Blend Layers. In the dialog box that appears, select the two options, Stack Images and Seamless Tones and Colors, then click OK. The program will process the images, possibly for a considerable length of time.
5. If the procedure worked well, the result will be a single image made up of numerous layers that have been processed to produce a sharply focused rendering of your subject. (See Figure 3.32, bottom.) If it did not work well, you may have to take additional images the next time, focusing very carefully on small slices of the subject as you move progressively farther away from the lens.
6. You'll want to flatten the final image before saving it. Given the 46MP resolution of the Z9/Z8, the stack of individual shots will easily be more than 2GB, which exceeds the maximum file size of some older storage media and/or OS file systems.

Although this procedure can work very well in Photoshop, you also may want to try it with programs that were developed more specifically for focus stacking and related procedures, such as Helicon Focus (www.heliconsoft.com), PhotoAcute (www.photoacute.com), or CombineZM (https://combinezm.informer.com/).

Electronic Flash

4

The Nikon Z9 and Z8 are compatible with a long list of Nikon SB-series Speedlights, dating back to the company's original professional-level flash unit, the SB-800, which was introduced in 2003. All Speedlights introduced since then use the Nikon Creative Lighting System (CLS), which allows efficient through-the-lens metering of flash exposures and wireless off-camera strobes for versatile multi-flash lighting. Although virtually everything else about the Z-series cameras were developed specifically for that platform—from sensor to lens mount—they all benefit from the availability of these mature, well-tested array of electronic flash options, including the latest SB-5000 unit, which can be triggered remotely through optical or radio links.

Some consider electronic flash a necessary evil, providing supplementary illumination that is often harsh or less natural looking, as well as difficult to use. However, what they are deriding is *bad* flash photography, as applied by photographers who don't understand how to use strobes properly or are too lazy to fully apply the creative versatility flash offers. They may feel that Speedlights are too expensive.

Fortunately, it's easy to become adept at using electronic flash. Working with one or multiple off-camera flash wirelessly is easier than ever, thanks to Nikon's *unified flash control* for its SB-300, SB-400, SB-500, and SB-5000 units. You can adjust duplicated settings with the Z9/Z8's menus, using controls on the flash unit itself, or remotely with software like the optional Camera Control 2 utility. As you do so, the adjustments are automatically made on the other device. You don't have to worry about accidentally overriding your own settings.

USING OLDER FLASH

Don't worry, your older Nikon flash units can still be used with your Z9 or Z8. However, you won't have full control of their features from your camera's menu, and will need to use controls on the flash themselves. If you own an SB-800, SB-900, or SB-910 (which have all been discontinued by Nikon) they are fully compatible with Nikon's Creative Lighting System, iTTL automatic flash exposure system, and optical wireless communication. As well, the SB-700, SB-R200 flash, and SU-800 Wireless Speedlight Commander are still being sold and can be used the with Z9/Z8 even though they don't conform to the unified flash control protocols.

Electronic Flash Basics

Electronic flash has become the studio light source of choice for many pro photographers because it's more intense (and its intensity can be varied to order by the photographer using the strobe's power adjustment features) and freezes action. Flash frees you from the need for a tripod (unless you want to use one to lock down a composition), and has a snappy, consistent light quality that matches daylight. (While color balance changes as the flash duration shortens, some Nikon flash units can communicate the exact white balance provided for that shot.) And even pros will cede that an external flash needn't be used in direct-flash mode, and has essential applications as an adjunct, particularly to fill in dark shadows or to serve as a wireless trigger for additional, off-camera strobes.

But electronic flash isn't as inherently easy to use as continuous lighting. Electronic flash units do require a modest investment, don't show you exactly what the lighting effect will be (unless you use a second source or mode called a *modeling light* for a preview), and the exposure of electronic flash units is more difficult to calculate accurately.

Electronic flash illumination is produced by photons generated by an electrical charge that is accumulated in a component called a *capacitor* and then directed through a glass tube containing xenon gas, which absorbs the energy and emits the burst of light. In automatic mode (which Nikon calls *iTTL*), the main flash is preceded by one or more mini-bursts, which Nikon dubs "monitor preflash," that allow gauging how much light is bouncing back from your subject and background, and to communicate with other external flash units linked wirelessly. In practice, external strobes can be linked to the camera in several different ways:

- **Camera-mounted/hardwired external dedicated flash.** Units offered by Nikon or other vendors that are compatible with Nikon's Creative Lighting System—CLS—can be clipped onto the accessory "hot" shoe or linked through a wired system such as the Nikon SC-28/SC-29 cables. I'll describe CLS later in this chapter.
- **Wireless dedicated flash.** A CLS-compatible unit can be triggered by signals produced by a preflash (before the main flash burst begins), which offers two-way communication between the camera and flash unit. The triggering flash can be a CLS-compatible flash unit in Master mode, or a wireless non-flashing accessory, such as the Nikon SU-800, which does nothing but "talk" to the external flashes.
- **Wired, non-intelligent mode.** The Z9 has a dedicated old-style PC/X connector built in, and the Z8 does not, but you can add one easily by sliding the Nikon AS-15 Sync Terminal adaptor into the hot shoe. The PC/X connector is a non-intelligent camera/flash link that sends just one piece of information, one way: it tells a connected flash to fire. There is no other exchange of information between the camera and flash. The PC/X connector can be used to link non-dedicated/non-CLS-friendly strobes, which can be studio flash units, manual non-CLS flash, flash units from other vendors that can use a PC cable, or even Nikon-brand Speedlights that you elect to connect in a non-CLS, "unintelligent" mode.
- **Radio/Infrared transmitter/receivers.** Another way to link flash units to the camera is through a radio transmitter/receiver system, using either a dedicated radio-compatible flash unit, such as the Nikon SB-5000 (see Figure 4.1, left), or an add-on wireless infrared or radio *transmitter*, like the

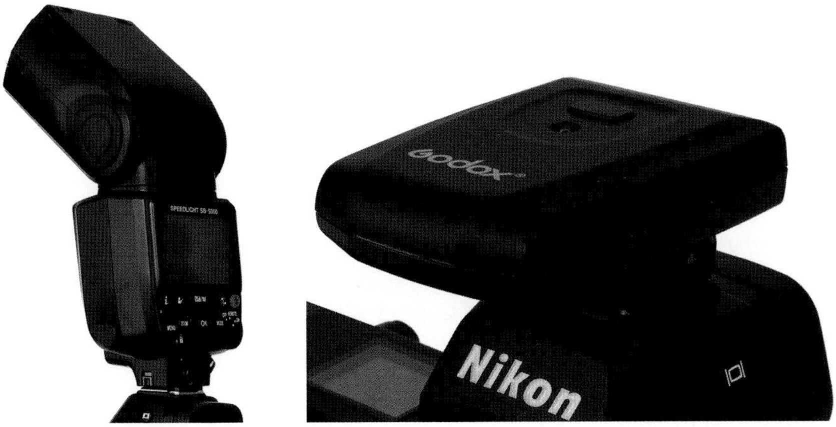

Figure 4.1 The Nikon SB-5000 offers radio control (left). Third-party add-ons also can use radio transmission to trigger electronic flash units (right).

Nikon WR-R11a/WR-T10, PocketWizard, Radio Popper, a Paul C. Buff CyberSync trigger, or the Godox device shown in Figure 4.1, right. These are generally mounted on the accessory shoe and emit a signal when the camera sends a command to fire through the hot shoe. The simplest of these function as a wireless PC/X connector, with no other communication between the camera and flash (other than the instruction to fire). However, sophisticated units have their own built-in controls and can send additional commands to the receivers when connected to compatible flash units. I use one to adjust the power output of my Alien Bees studio flash from the camera, without the need to walk over to the flash itself.

- **Simple optical connection.** In the days before intelligent wireless communication, the most common way to trigger off-camera, non-wired flash units was through something called a *slave* unit, although the term has fallen into disuse. These remote units can be small external triggers connected to the remote flash (or built into the flash itself) and set off when the optical sensor detects a burst initiated by a flash connected to the camera. When it "sees" the main flash, the off-camera flash units are triggered quickly enough to contribute to the same exposure. The main problem with this type of connection—other than the lack of any intelligent communication between the camera and flash—is that the receiver unit may be fooled by any preflashes that are emitted by the other strobes, and fire too soon. Modern triggers have a special "digital" mode that ignores the preflash and fires only from the main flash burst.

The Moment of Exposure

Traditional cameras have a vertically traveling physical shutter that consists of two curtains. Just before the flash fires, the front curtain opens and moves down to the opposite side of the frame, at which point the shutter is completely open. The flash can be triggered at this point (so-called front-curtain sync), making the flash exposure. Then, after a delay that can vary from 30 seconds to 1/200th second (or faster when high-speed sync, discussed later, is used), a rear curtain begins moving down the sensor plane, covering up the sensor again. If the flash is triggered just before the rear curtain starts to close, then rear-curtain sync is used. In both cases, though, a shutter speed of 1/200th second is the maximum that can be used to take a photo, unless you're using the 1/250 s (Auto FP) or 1/200 s (Auto FP) high-speed sync settings.

Your Z9/Z8 does much the same thing when using flash, but with one notable change. Neither camera relies on an actual physical shutter, but instead uses an all-electronic "virtual" shutter to perform the same functions. Figure 4.2 is a fanciful illustration of a how your electronic shutter works (your camera's shutter does *not* look like this!)

Here's how an exposure takes place:

1. **Current image "dumped."** Prior to pressing the shutter release down all the way, you are viewing the sensor image using the Z9/Z8's electronic viewfinder or rear LCD monitor. Before the exposure begins, the camera dumps the current image from the sensor, leaving it in what you can think of as a blank, inactive state, represented at top left in Figure 4.2.
2. **Sensor becomes active.** The actual exposure commences when the electronic shutter activates part of the sensor, starting from the top edge. Several rows are captured at a time as the camera simulates an electronic first curtain that moves down the frame. Figure 4.2, top center, represents this "movement" as more and more of the sensor becomes active.
3. **The shutter "opens" fully.** The virtual first curtain continues to descend, so that more and more of the sensor responds to light. Figure 4.2, top right and bottom left represent this "movement" of the first curtain.
4. **The entire sensor is active.** Within roughly 3.7 milliseconds (which is about 1/270th second) from the beginning of the exposure—the transit time—the whole sensor surface is active. (See Figure 4.2, bottom center.) It responds to light until the end of the exposure, and the flash, if used, can be triggered during this interval. The exact moment when that occurs is important, as I'll explain next.
5. **The exposure ends.** When the exposure is finished, the electronic shutter "turns off" the sensor, starting at the top, again, several rows at a time, as if a physical second, rear curtain were dropping. (See Figure 4.2, bottom right.)

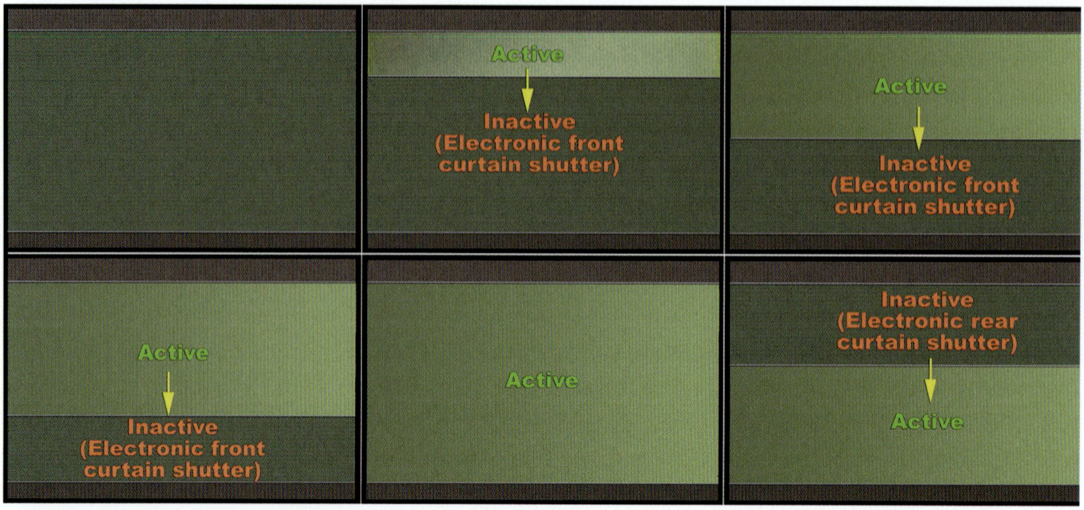

Figure 4.2 How an electronic shutter works.

Here's a more detailed look at what transpires when you take a photo using electronic flash, all within a few milliseconds of time. The following list assumes you are using iTTL exposure mode:

1. **Flash sync mode.** After you've selected a shooting mode, choose the flash sync option.

   With the Nikon Z9, press the Flash Mode/Flash Compensation button (with the lightning bolt icon) on the left shoulder of the camera and rotate the main command dial. With the Z8, access the Flash Mode entry in the Photo Shooting menu. If you change flash sync mode frequently, you can add it to the *i* menu, or define a button to summon the adjustment using Custom Setting f1 and f2 settings, respectively, as described in Chapter 7. I'll explain your sync options shortly.
2. **Metering method.** Choose the metering method you want, from Matrix, Center-weighted, Spot, or Highlight-weighted metering.
3. **Activate flash.** Mount an external flash (or connect it with a cable) and turn it on. A ready light appears in the viewfinder and on the back of the dedicated flash when the unit is ready to take a picture (although the flash might not be *fully* charged when the indicator first appears).
4. **Check exposure.** Select a shutter speed when using Manual, Program, or Shutter-priority modes; select an aperture when using Aperture-priority and Manual exposure modes.
5. **Preview lighting.** If you want to preview the lighting effect, assign the Preview behavior to a button. (Fn1 or Fn2 are the traditional choices.) Then enable modeling flash using Custom Setting e5, as described in Chapter 7. Press the defined Preview button to produce a modeling flash burst.
6. **Lock flash setting (if desired).** Optionally, if the main subject is located significantly off-center, you can frame so the subject is centered, lock the flash at the exposure needed to illuminate that subject, and then reframe using the composition you want. Lock the flash level using the Flash Value (FV) Lock button you designate (many assign the Fn1 or Fn2 button to this function, using Custom Setting f2). Press the FV lock button, and the flash will emit a monitor preflash to determine the correct flash level, and then flash will be locked at that level until you press the FV lock button again to release it. FV lock icons appear in the display.
7. **Take photo.** Press the shutter release down all the way.
8. **Distance data received.** Z-mount lenses, as well as F-mount and E-, D-, or G-series lenses attached using an adapter, now supply focus distance to the camera.
9. **Preflash emitted.** The external flash sends out several preflash bursts. One series of bursts can be used to control additional wireless flash units in Commander mode, while another is used to determine exposure. The preflashes happen in such a brief period before the main flash that they are virtually undetectable.
10. **Exposure calculated.** The preflash bounces back and is measured at the sensor. It calculates brightness and contrast of the image to determine exposure. If you're using Matrix metering (more on metering modes shortly), the camera evaluates the scene to determine: whether the subject may be backlit (for fill flash), whether a subject requires extra ambient light exposure to balance the scene with the flash exposure, or whether the camera classifies the scene in some other way. The camera-to-subject information as well as the degree of sharp focus of the subject matter is used to locate the subject within the frame. If you've selected Spot metering, only standard i-TTL (without balanced fill flash) is used. (See the sidebar i-TTL Flash Control.)

i-TTL FLASH CONTROL

CLS-compatible flash units include up to several Flash Control modes, depending on the model. (I'll explain them all later in this chapter.) With the one you'll use most often, TTL mode, the camera calculates and sets flash exposure (but applies any flash exposure compensation you dial in, as explained later). In Manual mode, you adjust the output level of the flash.

In TTL mode, the camera selects one of two variations:

- **i-TTL balanced fill flash (TTL BL).** The camera analyzes the preflash reflection from all areas of the frame and adjusts the output to provide a balance between the main subject of your image and the background lighting.
- **Standard i-TTL fill flash.** The brightness of the background is not considered in setting the flash output. This mode tends to emphasize the main subject, even if some background detail is lost. You can force the camera to select Standard i-TTL fill flash by switching to Spot metering mode. Use flash exposure compensation to adjust the main subject/background balance as required.

11. **Exposure begins.** The exposure by ambient light begins when the electronic front curtain has fully exposed the sensor.
12. **Flash fired.** At the correct triggering moment (depending on whether front- or rear-curtain sync is used), the camera sends a signal to one or more flashes to start flash discharge. The flash is quenched as soon as the correct exposure has been achieved.
13. **Shutter closes.** The electronic rear curtain "descends" to conclude the exposure, and the live view from the sensor resumes. You're ready to take another picture. Remember to press the defined FV lock button (if used) again to release the flash exposure if your next shot will use a different composition.
14. **Exposure confirmed.** Ordinarily, the full charge in the flash may not be required. If the flash indicator in the viewfinder blinks for about three seconds after the exposure, that means that the entire flash charge was required, and it *could* mean that the full charge wasn't enough for a proper exposure. Be sure to review your image on the monitor to make sure it's not underexposed, and, if it is, make adjustments (such as increasing the ISO setting) to remedy the situation.

A Tale of Two Exposures

Calculating the proper exposure for an electronic flash photograph is a bit more complicated than determining the settings for continuous light. The right exposure isn't simply a function of how far away your subject is (which the camera can figure out based on the autofocus distance that's locked in just prior to taking the picture). Various objects reflect more or less light at the same distance so, obviously, the camera needs to measure the amount of light reflected back and through the lens.

That measurement is complicated by two things: a picture taken using flash is actually *two separate exposures*: the exposure produced by the flash itself, and the exposure that results from the continuous, ambient light that is also illuminating your subject. If the calculations are correct, the plane in which your main subject resides will be properly exposed. However, anything more than slightly in *front of* or *behind* that plane will be overexposed or underexposed (respectively), thanks to the inverse square law I mention in Chapter 8. To summarize, the intensity of the light is inversely proportional to the square of the distance. In practice, that means a light source that is 12 feet away from a subject provides only one-quarter as much illumination as the same source located 6 feet away. In f/stop terms, you need to open up two stops whenever the distance doubles. (See Figure 4.3.)

So, as you shoot, you need to consider "depth-of-light" (the range in which a subject is acceptably illuminated in front of and behind the plane used to calculate the exposure) in addition to depth-of-field. Fortunately, in many flash photography situations, the main subject is the closest thing to the lens, so there often won't be a problem with overexposed foreground objects.

Backgrounds, however, are another story. In daylight situations, balancing the flash and ambient illumination more or less takes care of itself automatically. Photographers generally let the daylight provide most of the exposure and use the flash only to fill in shadows.

However, if you're photographing indoors or at night, the background, not illuminated by the flash, will appear darker than the foreground subject. Fortunately, every flash picture consists of *two* exposures, the exposure produced by the flash, and a second exposure that results from the background illumination. For the flash exposure, the shutter speed is more-or-less irrelevant, as long as you're using a shutter speed slower than the synchronization speed—1/200th second in the case of both the Z9 and Z8. The f/stop selected, and the power output of the flash determine the exposure.

The ambient light exposure is more "normal," using both the shutter speed and aperture. Slower shutter speeds allow more ambient light to reach the sensor, and higher shutter speeds allow less. If you want to *minimize* the ambient portion of the exposure, use a higher shutter speed, up to 1/200th second when not using High-Speed Sync (discussed later in this chapter). To *maximize* the ambient exposure, use a slower shutter speed. The camera has a special Slow Sync shutter setting that automatically uses these slower speeds to balance flash/ambient exposures, but you can also use Custom Setting e2: Flash Shutter Speed to specify the slowest/fastest shutter speed used under normal conditions.

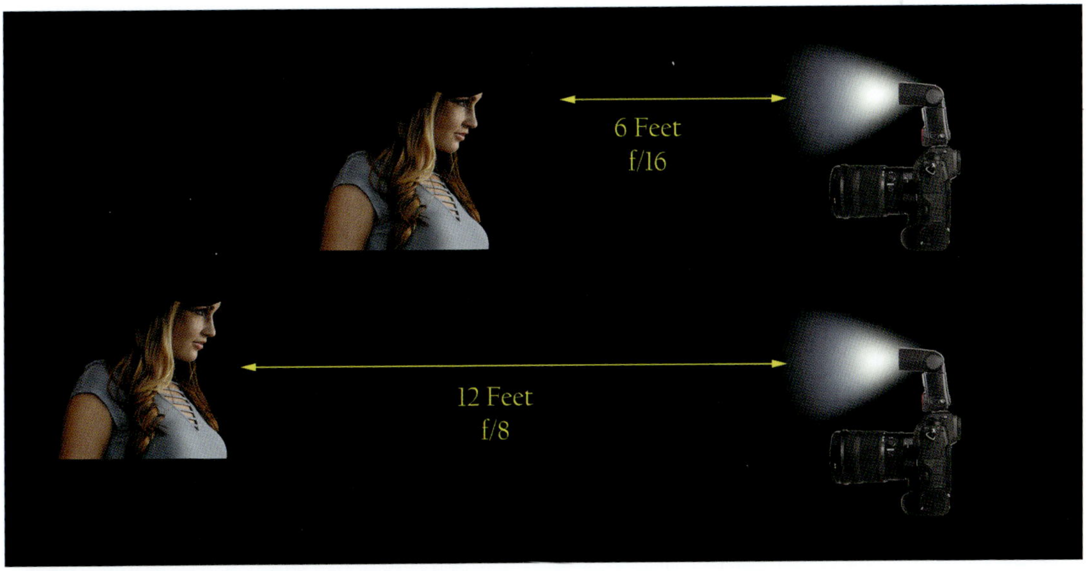

Figure 4.3 A light source that is twice as far away provides only one-quarter as much illumination.

There are several complications involved in balancing flash and ambient light exposures. So-called "mixed" lighting is one of them. Your flash is balanced for daylight, while ambient light is often incandescent or some other "warm" illumination. This mixture is exaggerated in Figure 4.4, which shows the Plaza Mayor in Segovia, Spain, with the city's cathedral in the background lit by incandescent lamps, with the foreground illuminated by flash. The solution in this case would be to install an orange-tinted "warming" filter on the flash (many Nikon Speedlights include them) to balance the flash illumination with the incandescent background.

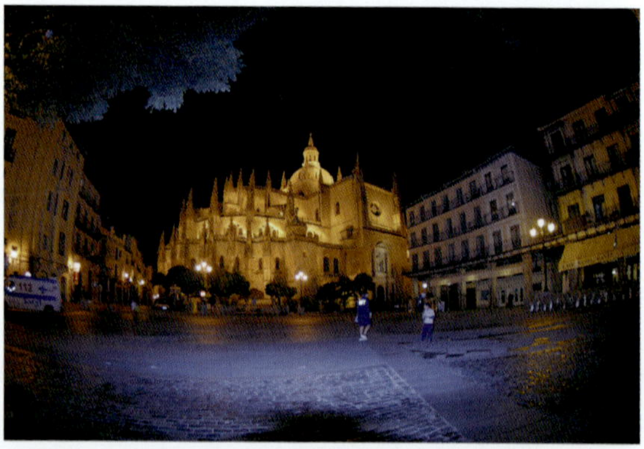

Figure 4.4 Electronic flash illuminated the foreground, and incandescent lighting illuminated the background in this mixed-lighting example.

The second problem that arises stems from the fact that while the flash exposure is concluded in an instant (typically 1/1000th to 1/50,000th of a second), the ambient light continues for the entire time the shutter is open. So, you end up with *two* images produced by the *dual* exposures. If the subject is moving, the additional ambient light exposure produces a "ghost" image. The best way of handling that conundrum is to adjust the sync setting, and I'm going to explain how to do that shortly.

Measuring Exposure

By this time, you should be wondering how flash is measured, as the flash burst isn't available for evaluation until it's triggered when you press the shutter release down all the way to take the picture. The solution is to fire the flash multiple times. The first pulse is a *monitor preflash* that can be analyzed, then followed virtually instantaneously by a series of pulses (if required) to communicate wirelessly with any optically triggered remote flash units. (You'll find more on advanced wireless lighting later in this chapter.) Only then is the main flash triggered, which (when shooting in auto-flash mode) emits exactly the calculated intensity needed for a correct exposure. (All these pulses happen so quickly that they may appear to you to be a single burst.)

Because of the exposure calculations, the primary flash may be longer in duration for distant objects and shorter in duration for closer subjects, depending on the required intensity for exposure. This default through-the-lens evaluative flash exposure system is called i-TTL BL (for intelligent Through The Lens, Balanced Fill Flash) and can operate whenever you have attached a Nikon-dedicated flash unit. There are additional modes that will be discussed later, and not all modes are available with every flash unit, but all the modes are listed in Table 4.1. These modes are set using your particular electronic flash's controls, as described in your unit's manual.

The amount of light emitted by the flash is changed in an interesting way—interrupting the flash as the charge flows from the capacitor through the flash tube. When full power is required, either to supply the correct exposure in automatic modes or because you're using the flash in Manual mode at the full-power (1/1) setting, then all the energy in the capacitor flows through the flash tube.

TABLE 4.1 Flash Modes

MODE	METERING MODES AVAILABLE	FUNCTION
TTL BL	Matrix, Center-weighted	Balanced Fill Flash.
Standard TTL	Spot	Only flash output used in exposure calculation.
TTL BL FP	Matrix, Center-weighted	Balanced Fill Flash, shutter speeds higher than 1/200th second available.
TTL FP	Spot	Flash and ambient illumination not balanced, shutter speeds higher than 1/200th second available.
AA (Auto Aperture)	N/A	Exposure measured by sensor on flash. Uses ISO and aperture information supplied by camera.
Automatic	N/A	Exposure measured by sensor on flash. Uses ISO and aperture information input to flash by user.
Manual	N/A	Exposure calculated by user.

However, if less than full power is needed, the energy is stopped partway through the exposure by opening the circuit with a solid-state switch. In the olden days, this was always done using a component called a *thyristor,* but today a component called an *insulated-gate bipolar transistor,* or IGBT, is more common.

Because the current is interrupted before the full power of the capacitor is used, the resulting burst becomes shorter as the power output is reduced. For example, with some Nikon flash units you might see a burst lasting about 1/1000th second at full power, but only a little longer than 1/10,000th second at 1/16th power, or 1/40,000th second at 1/128th power. (The SB-5000 adds a 1/256th power option, providing a 1/30,800th-second exposure.) This behavior is nifty when you want to freeze really fast action, such as falling water droplets—just use a lower power output level and/or work extremely close to your subject.

Because the full contents of the capacitor are not used with these partial flashes, the Speedlight is able to recycle more quickly, or even use the retained energy to fire multiple times in Repeating flash mode (described later in this chapter). The only downside is that shorter flash exposures tend to take on a bluish tinge as the duration decreases. That's because the burst starts out with a very cool color temperature and ends up much warmer at the end of the burst, averaging out to a hue that's pretty close to daylight in color balance. When you trim off the reddish end of the flash, your resulting image may be noticeably more blue. That's why the Flash color balance setting doesn't always produce a pleasing color rendition. You may have to fine-tune the white balance, as described in Chapter 11, or shoot RAW and correct in your image editor.

Those of you using studio flash units may be interested to know that your non-automatic strobes produce their varying power levels in a different way. With the typical studio flash, the capacitor is *always* fully discharged each time you take a picture and then recharged *to the level you specify* for the next shot. It happens very quickly because you're using AC power or a high-voltage battery pack instead of low-capacity alkaline or rechargeable cells.

If you set the flash for 1/2 power, the capacitor (or capacitors—studio flash may use several of them) is charged only halfway; at 1/4 power it's only replenished to 25 percent of its capacity. Then, when you take the photo, the full contents of the capacitor are sent through the flash tube. That's why you need to "dump" your studio flash when you reduce the power output from a higher level. The capacitor retains the charge that was in there before and can't fire at the reduced capacity you want until the existing power is dumped and then replenished to the level you specify. Because of the way studio flash store and release their power, they can be designed to be more consistent at different power levels than your typical Nikon flash unit. Of course, wild color variations from flash units aren't a huge problem, but just something you should be aware of.

So, to summarize, with CLS-compatible flash units, your automatic exposure is calculated by measuring a preflash and determining an appropriate exposure from that. There are other exposure modes than i-TTL available from Nikon external flash units, and I'll get into them later in this chapter, but this section has described the process in a nutshell.

Caveats

By now you're aware that calculating exposure—either using the camera's features, or manually—is different when using flash. You're free to use Aperture-priority, Shutter-priority, Programmed Auto, or Manual exposure (for the ambient light) and the Z9/Z8 will generally adhere to the ISO and aperture settings you specify, plus the shutter speeds you desire, as long as your shutter speed doesn't conflict with the camera's sync requirements.

Another exception can be found in the available apertures when using Programmed Auto mode. At any given ISO setting, the *largest* aperture may be constrained. For example, you might assume that at ISO 100 the Z9 or Z8 might take advantage of your super-fast 135mm f/1.8 Plena tele and let you shoot fairly distant subjects with that f/1.8 aperture in Program mode. Not so. The *widest* f/stop available at ISO 100 is f/4, and if your flash isn't powerful enough to illuminate your subject at f/4, you'll end up with an underexposure. As a result, since Program mode can't use all your available apertures, and Shutter-priority mode has limits in which speeds are available, Aperture-priority is almost always your best autoexposure mode. The available f/stops at various ISO values is shown in Table 4.2.

TABLE 4.2 Available Apertures for Programmed Auto

ISO VALUE	MAXIMUM APERTURE	ISO VALUE	MAXIMUM APERTURE
ISO 64	f/3.5	ISO 800	f/7.1
ISO 100	f/4	ISO 1000	f/7.1
ISO 125	f/4.5	ISO 1250	f/8
ISO 160	f/4.5	ISO 1600	f/8
ISO 200	f/5	ISO 2000	f/9
ISO 250	f/5	ISO 2500	f/9
ISO 320	f/5.6	ISO 3200	f/10
ISO 400	f/5.6	ISO 4000	f/10
ISO 500	f/6.3	ISO 5000	f/11
ISO 600	f/6.3	ISO 6400	f/11

Guide Numbers

Guide numbers, usually abbreviated GN, were originally developed as a way of calculating exposure manually, but today are more useful as a measurement of the power of an electronic flash unit. A GN is usually given as a pair of numbers for both feet and meters that represent the range at ISO 100. For example, the Nikon SB-5000 has a GN in i-TTL mode of 34.5/113 (meters/feet) at ISO 100 when using the coverage needed for a 35mm lens (the flash has a *zoom head* to spread/narrow the light for a range of focal lengths). To calculate the right exposure at that ISO setting, you'd divide the guide number by the distance to arrive at the appropriate f/stop.

So, if you wanted to shoot a subject at a distance of 10 feet, you'd use f/11.3 (or f/11). At 5 feet, an f/stop of f/22 would be used. Some quick mental calculations with the GN will give you any particular electronic flash's range. Many years ago, Nikon offered a 45mm GN lens that could couple the f/stop setting of the lens with the focus distance. You specified the guide number of the flash using a scale on the lens itself, and as you focused closer or farther away the f/stop was reduced or increased to match. Today, guide numbers are most useful for comparing the power of various flash units, rather than actually calculating what exposure to use.

Choosing a Flash Sync Mode

In addition to the flash modes mentioned earlier, the Z9 and Z8 have five *flash sync modes,* plus a sixth (High-Speed Sync, described later) that comes into play in some circumstances. The five main modes, plus Off (which disables the flash) are selected using the Flash Mode/Compensation button (Z9) or the Photo Shooting menu's Flash Mode entry (Z8). (See Figure 4.5 for the icons.) Those modes (which I've listed in logical order, so the explanation will make more sense, rather than the order in which they appear during the selection cycle) are as follows:

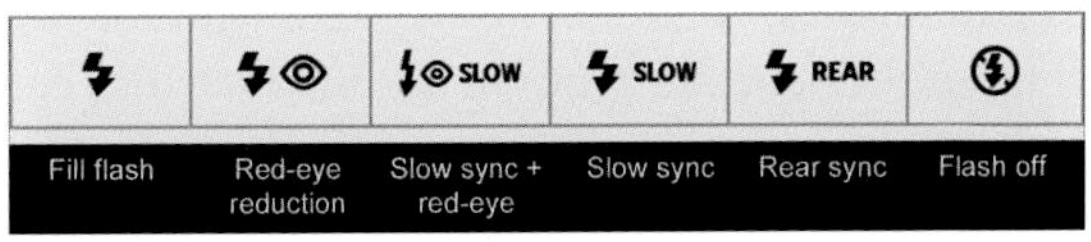

Figure 4.5 Icons for flash sync modes include fill flash/front-curtain sync, red-eye reduction, slow sync + red-eye, slow sync, rear-curtain sync, and flash off.

- **Fill flash/Front-curtain sync (available in Auto and PSAM modes).** This setting, available in all exposure modes, should be your default setting. In this mode, the flash fires as soon as the electronic front curtain opens completely. The electronic shutter then remains open for the duration of the exposure, until the electronic rear curtain closes. If the subject is moving and ambient light levels are high enough, the movement will cause that secondary "ghost" exposure that appears in front of the flash exposure.
- **Rear-curtain sync (available in PSAM modes).** With this setting, which can be used with Program, Shutter-priority, Aperture-priority, or Manual exposure modes, the front curtain opens completely and remains open for the duration of the exposure. Then, the flash is fired and the electronic rear curtain closes. If the subject is moving and ambient light levels are high enough, the movement will cause a secondary "ghost" exposure that appears behind the flash exposure (trailing it). You'll find more on "ghost" exposures next.

In Program and Aperture-priority modes, this setting tells the camera to combine rear-curtain sync with slow shutter speeds (just like slow sync, discussed below) to balance ambient light with flash illumination. (It's best to use a tripod to avoid blur at these slow shutter speeds.)

- **Red-eye reduction (available in Auto and PSAM modes).** In this mode, there is a one-second lag after pressing the shutter release before the picture is actually taken, during which the attached flash unit's red-eye reduction feature is used, causing the subject's pupils to contract (assuming they are looking at the camera), and thus reducing potential red-eye effects. With the SB-5000 and SB-500 Speedlights, three short flash bursts are emitted just before the main burst for exposure. Other Nikon flash units cause the camera's green AF-illuminator light to glow for a second before the main burst. Don't use red-eye reduction with moving subjects or when you can't abide the delay.
- **Slow sync (available in P or A modes).** This setting allows Program and Aperture-priority modes to use shutter speeds as slow as 30 seconds with the flash to help balance a background illuminated with ambient light with your main subject, which will be lit by the electronic flash. You'll want to use a tripod at slower shutter speeds, of course.
- **Slow-sync + Red-eye (available in Auto and PA modes).** This mode combines slow sync with the external flash's red-eye reduction behavior when using Program or Aperture-priority modes.
- **Flash off (available in Auto and PSAM modes).** The flash does not fire, even if powered on.

Ghost Images

The difference might not seem like much, but whether you use front-curtain sync (the default setting) or rear-curtain sync (an optional setting) can make a significant difference to your photograph *if the ambient light in your scene also contributes to the image.* At faster shutter speeds, particularly 1/200th second, there isn't much time for the ambient light to register, unless it is very bright. It's likely that the electronic flash will provide almost all the illumination, so front-curtain sync or rear-curtain sync isn't very important.

However, at slower shutter speeds, or with very bright ambient light levels, there is a significant difference, particularly if your subject is moving, or the camera isn't steady. In any of those situations, the ambient light will register as a second image accompanying the flash exposure, and if there is movement (camera or subject), that additional image will not be in the same place as the flash exposure. It will show as a ghost image and, if the movement is significant enough, as a blurred ghost image trailing in front of or behind your subject in the direction of the movement.

As I mentioned earlier, when you're using front-curtain sync, the flash goes off the instant the shutter opens, producing an image of the subject on the sensor. Then, the electronic shutter remains open for an additional period (which can be from 30 seconds to 1/200th second). If your subject is moving, say, toward the right side of the frame, the ghost image produced by the ambient light will produce a blur on the right side of the original subject image. That makes it look as if your sharp (flash-produced) image is chasing the ghost (see Figure 4.6, top), which looks unnatural to those of us who grew up with lightning-fast Justice League-style superheroes who always left a ghost trail *behind them* (see Figure 4.6, bottom).

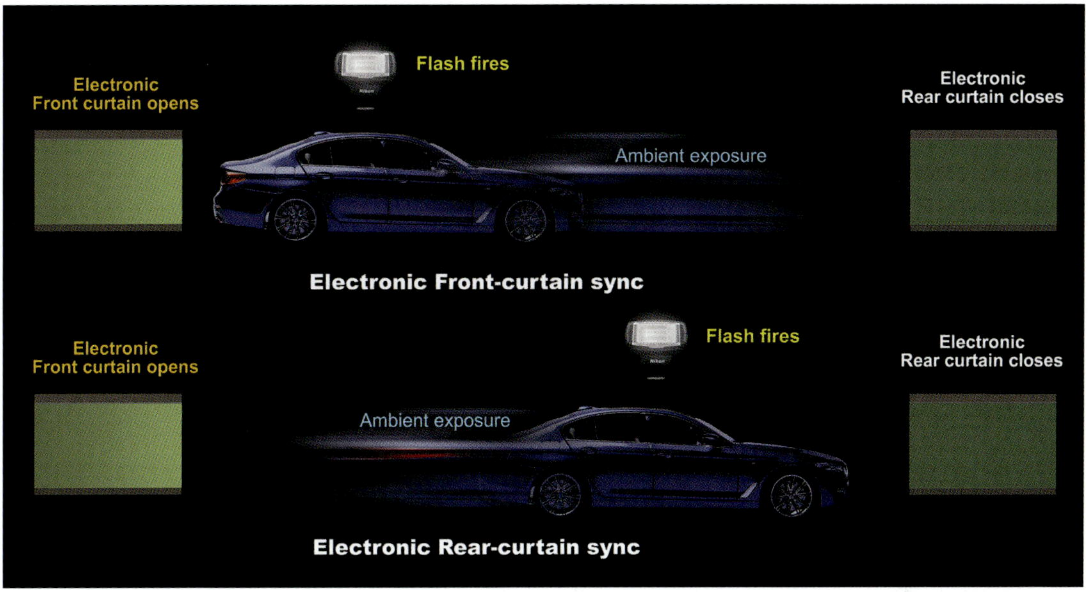

Figure 4.6 Front-curtain sync produces an image that trails in front of the flash exposure (top), while rear-curtain sync creates a more "natural-looking" trail behind the flash image (bottom).

So, Nikon provides rear-curtain sync to remedy the situation. In that mode, the electronic shutter opens, as before. The shutter remains open for its designated duration, and the ghost image forms. If your subject moves from the left side of the frame to the right side, the ghost will move from left to right, too. *Then*, about 1.3 milliseconds before the rear shutter curtain closes, the flash is triggered, producing a nice, sharp flash image *ahead* of the ghost image.

EVERY WHICH WAY, INCLUDING UP

Note that, although I describe the ghost effect in terms of subject matter that is moving left to right in a horizontally oriented composition, it can occur in any orientation, and with the subject moving in *any* direction. (Try photographing a falling rock, if you can, and you'll see the same effect.) Nor are the ghost images affected by the fact that modern shutters travel vertically rather than horizontally. Secondary images are caused between the time the front curtain fully opens and the rear curtain begins to close. The direction of travel of the shutter curtains, or the direction of your subject, does not matter.

Avoiding Sync Speed Problems

Using a shutter speed faster than 1/200th second can cause problems. Triggering the electronic flash only when the virtual shutter is completely open makes a lot of sense if you think about what's going on. To obtain shutter speeds faster than 1/200th second, *only part of the sensor is exposed at one time*, by starting the second curtain to "descend" before the first curtain has completely opened, as shown in Figure 4.7. That effectively provides a briefer exposure as a slit of the shutter passes over the surface of the sensor. If the flash were to fire during the time when the front and rear curtains partially obscured the sensor, only the slit that was actually open would be exposed.

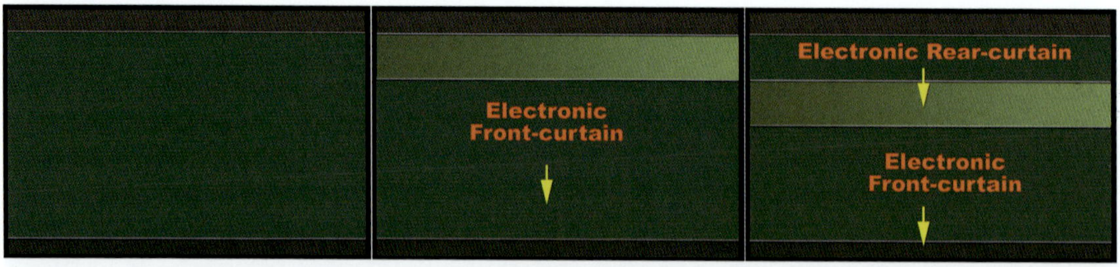

Figure 4.7 A closed shutter (left); partially open shutter as the front curtain begins to move downward (middle); only part of the sensor is exposed as the slit moves (right).

You'd end up with only a narrow band, representing the portion of the sensor that was exposed when the picture is taken. For shutter speeds *faster* than 1/200th second, the rear curtain begins moving *before* the front curtain reaches the bottom of the frame. As a result, a moving slit, the distance between the front and rear curtains, exposes one portion of the sensor at a time as it moves from the top to the bottom. Figure 4.7 shows three views of our typical (but imaginary) focal plane shutter. At left represents a "closed" electronic shutter; the live view image has been dumped and the exposure has not yet begun. At center in the figure, the front curtain has moved down about 1/4 of the distance from the top; and in the right-hand version, the electronic rear curtain has started to "chase" the front curtain across the frame toward the bottom.

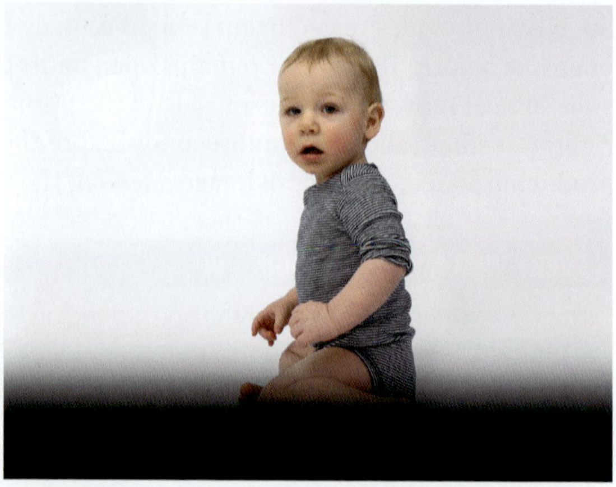

Figure 4.8 If a shutter speed faster than 1/200th second is used, you can end up photographing only a portion of the image.

If the flash is triggered while this slit is moving, only the exposed portion of the sensor will receive any illumination. You end up with a photo like the one shown in Figure 4.8. Note that a band across the bottom of the image is black. That's the area obscured by the rear electronic curtain, which had started to "move" when the flash was triggered. Sharp-eyed readers will wonder why the black band is at the *bottom* of the frame rather than at the top, where the rear curtain begins its journey. The answer is simple: your lens flips the image upside down and forms it on the sensor in a reversed position. You never notice that, because the camera is smart enough to show you the pixels that make up your photo in their proper orientation during picture review. But this image flip is why, if your sensor gets dirty and you detect a spot of dust in the upper half of a test photo, if cleaning manually, you need to look for the speck in the *bottom* half of the sensor.

I generally end up with sync-speed problems only when shooting in the studio, using studio flash units rather than my Nikon-dedicated Speedlights. That's because if you're using "smart" flash (like one of the Nikon Speedlights), when a strobe is attached any unintentional goof in shutter speed settings is corrected. If you happen to set the shutter to a faster speed in S or M mode and are not using High-Speed Sync, it will automatically be adjusted down to 1/200th second as soon as you turn on the flash (or prevent you from choosing a faster speed if the flash is already powered up). In A or P modes, where the camera selects the shutter speed, it will never choose a shutter speed higher than 1/200th second when using flash. In P mode, shutter speed is automatically set from 1/60th to 1/200th second when using flash.

But when using a non-dedicated flash, such as a studio unit plugged into an adapter mounted on the accessory shoe, the camera has no way of knowing that a flash is connected, so shutter speeds faster than 1/200th second can be set inadvertently. To avoid that problem with studio flash, I strongly recommend using Manual exposure and the 1/200th-second shutter speed (or slower, which may be required by some studio flash units).

SILENCE ISN'T GOLDEN

One oddity you need to be aware of is that you can't use electronic flash if you've activated the Z9 or Z8's Silent Mode in the Setup menu. Instead, use the Camera Sounds entry of the Setup menu and set Shutter Sound and Beep to Off.

High-Speed Sync

Note that the Z9 and Z8 can use a feature called *high-speed sync* that allows shutter speeds faster than 1/200th second with certain external Nikon flash units. When using Auto FP high-speed sync, the flash fires a continuous series of bursts at reduced power for the entire duration of the exposure, so that the illumination is able to expose the sensor as the slit moves. High-speed sync (HSS) is set using the controls that adjust the compatible external flash. You don't need to make any special settings on the flash, as I'll describe in this section.

As I said earlier, triggering the electronic flash only when the shutter is completely open makes a lot of sense if you think about what's going on. To obtain shutter speeds faster than 1/200th second, only part of the sensor is exposed at one time, by starting the rear curtain on its journey before the front curtain has completely opened. That effectively provides a briefer exposure as a slit of the shutter passes over the surface of the sensor. If the flash were to fire during the time when the front and rear curtains partially obscured the sensor, only the area defined by the slit that was actually open would be exposed.

This technique is most useful outdoors when you need fill-in flash but find that 1/200th second is way too slow for the f/stop you want to use. For example, at ISO 200, an outdoors exposure is likely to be 1/200th second at, say, f/14, which is perfectly fine for an ambient/balanced fill-flash exposure if you don't mind the extreme depth-of-field offered by the small f/stop. But, what if you'd rather shoot at 1/1600th second at f/5.6? High-speed sync will let you do that, and you probably won't mind the reduced flash power, because you're looking for fill flash, anyway. This sync mode offers more flexibility than, say, dropping down to ISO 100.

High-speed sync is also useful when you want to use a larger f/stop to limit the amount of depth-of-field for selective focus techniques. Select a shutter speed higher than 1/200th second, and the faster sync speed automatically reduces the effective light of the flash, without other intervention from you.

To use Auto FP high-speed sync with units like the Nikon SB-5000, SB-910/SB-900, SB-700, SB-500, SB-R200, and a few discontinued Speedlights like the SB-800 and SB-600, there is no setting to make on the flash itself. You need to use Custom Setting e1 to specify 1/200 s (Auto FP) or 1/250th s (Auto FP). When using P or A exposure modes, the shutter speed will be set to 1/200th–1/250th second when a compatible external flash is attached. Higher shutter speeds than 1/200th–1/250th second—all the way up to 1/8000th second—can then be used with full synchronization, at reduced flash output. There are also situations in which you might want to set flash sync speed to *less* than 1/200th second, say, because you *want* ambient light to produce secondary ghost images in your frame. You can choose the following settings:

- **1/200 s (Auto FP)/1/250th s (Auto FP).** These similar settings allow using the compatible external flash units with high-speed synchronization at 1/200th or 1/250th second or faster and activates Auto FP sync when the camera selects a shutter speed of 1/200th–1/250th second or faster in Programmed and Aperture-priority modes. Other flash units will be used at speeds no faster than 1/200th second.
- **1/200 s.** At this default setting, only shutter speeds up to 1/200th second can be used with flash. You'd use this when working with "dumb" studio flash units.
- **1/200 s–1/60 s.** You can also specify a specific shutter speed from the range of speeds 1/200th second to 1/60th second to be used as the synchronization speed for external flash units. Forcing a slower shutter speed produces a "slow-sync" effect. For example, when 1/60th second has been set as the maximum flash shutter speed, ambient light is more likely to contribute to the exposure. (See Figure 4.9.) That can help balance the flash exposure with available light falling on the background. That slow shutter speed can generate ghost images when you *want* to create a feeling of motion; or, *unintentionally* as shown by the motion blur of the "older" actor's free hand at right in the figure. You may need to use a tripod or VR to minimize ghost images.

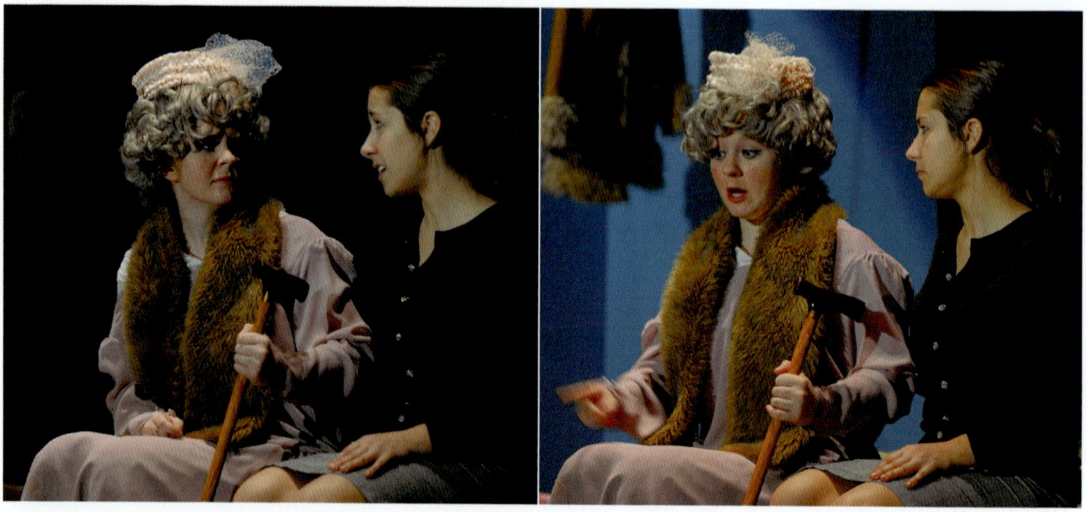

Figure 4.9 With a shutter speed of 1/200th second, the background is dark (left). At 1/60th second, the ambient light behind the actors provided detail in the background (right).

Using External Flash

In this section, we'll deal with the Nikon Creative Lighting System (CLS), which was introduced in July 2003, when the company unveiled the SB-800 Speedlight, a flash unit compatible with early professional digital SLRs, such as the Nikon D2h/D2hs, and, within a few months, more affordable models like 2004's Nikon D70 and all subsequent digital cameras from the company. CLS has the following features, although not all of these are supported by every Nikon camera:

- **i-TTL.** Intelligent through-the-lens exposure control calculates exposure based on a monitor preflash that is fired a fraction of a second before the main burst, and then evaluated by the same RGB exposure sensor used for continuous light measurements. The system's intelligence allows sophisticated adjustments, such as balancing the flash exposure with the ambient light exposure, say, when you shoot in full daylight to fill in the shadows.
- **Advanced wireless lighting.** AWL is a system that uses the same preflash concept to communicate triggering and exposure information to external flash units that aren't physically linked to the camera and located within a reasonable distance (say, about 30 feet). You may be able to divide multiple flash units into up to three different "groups," and communicate with them using your choice of any of four "channels" (to avoid having your flash units triggered by the master flash of another Nikon photographer in the vicinity). I'll explain AWL in more detail later.
- **FV Lock.** A *flash value* locking system allows you to fix in place the current flash exposure so that you can, for example, measure flash exposure for a subject that is not in the center of the frame, and then reframe while using that value for subsequent exposures. You can define an Fn button to perform this function, as described in Chapter 7. When FV lock is activated, the camera meters only a center area of the frame even if Matrix metering has been selected, when the flash is mounted in the hot shoe. In wireless modes, metering is done using the average of the entire frame
- **Auto FP high-speed sync.** Focal plane HS sync allows synchronizing an external flash while using shutter speeds faster than 1/200th second. With a compatible flash and camera, shutter speeds up to 1/8000th second can be used, although only a part of the flash's illumination is used, and flash range is reduced (sometimes to as little as a few feet).
- **Focus assist.** Although focus assist illumination is built-in, the CLS system also allows including wide-area AF-assist illumination to be built into the front of the flash unit, or into a flash connecting cable. Auxiliary focus assist illumination offers wider and/or more distant coverage.
- **Zoom coverage.** Some CLS-compatible flash units have a powered zoom head built in to allow changing the area covered by the flash to match the focal length of the lens in use, as communicated by the camera to the flash itself. Zooming can also be done manually.
- **Flash color information communication.** The exact color temperature of the light emitted by a CLS-compatible flash can vary, based on the duration of the flash burst. The flash is initially rather blue in color and becomes redder as the burst continues. The Speedlight is able to send information to the camera to allow adjusting white balance in AWB mode based on the true color information of the flash exposure.

If you want to temporarily disable a flash that's attached and powered up, a handy way to do this is to assign the Flash Disable/Enable function to the Fn1 or Fn2 buttons, using Custom Setting f2, as described in Chapter 7. Then, when you press the button, any external flash attached and powered up will not fire while the button is held down. This is useful if you want to temporarily disable the flash, say, to take a picture or two by available light, and then return to normal flash operation.

Using Flash Exposure Compensation

If the exposure produced by your flash isn't satisfactory, you can manually add or subtract exposure to the flash exposure calculated by the camera. You can use the Flash Compensation entry in the Photo Shooting menu or assign Flash Mode/Flash Compensation to a button, such as Fn1, using Custom Setting f2: Custom Controls, as explained in Chapter 7. When assigned to a button, you can adjust Flash Mode by pressing the button and rotating the main command dial, and Flash Compensation by holding the button and rotating the sub-command dial. You can make adjustments from –3 EV to +1 EV in 1/3 EV increments.

As with ordinary exposure compensation, the adjustment you make remains in effect until you zero it out by pressing the button assigned to flash mode/flash compensation and rotating the sub-command dial until 0 appears on the monochrome control panel and in the viewfinder. To view the current flash exposure compensation setting, press the defined button. When compensation is being used, an icon will be shown in the display.

As also described in Chapter 7, you can use Custom Setting e3: Exposure Compensation for Flash to balance ambient light and flash exposure over the entire frame, or just take into account the background. The option specifies how the flash level is modified when you apply exposure compensation. (The camera has separate ambient light exposure compensation and flash exposure compensation settings.) You can adjust one or the other, or both if you are using flash. Custom Setting e3 affects only *exposure compensation* (the ambient kind) when you are also using flash. It determines how ambient exposure compensation is applied when some of the illumination will also come from a flash unit.

- **Entire frame.** When you apply ambient exposure compensation (press the exposure compensation (EV) button on the top panel to the right of the ISO button and rotate the main command dial), both ambient *and* flash exposure compensation are adjusted over the entire frame. That balances the exposure for the two elements.
- **Background only.** When this option is selected *only* ambient exposure compensation is changed when you apply it; flash exposure compensation is unaffected. So exposure compensation is applied only to the background areas of your image, which are typically illuminated by ambient light. Flash exposure compensation is not affected but can be set separately if you've assigned Flash Mode/Compensation to a button using Custom Setting f2, as described earlier. If that's the case, just rotate the sub-command dial to adjust flash compensation.

EXPOSURE COMPENSATION COMBINES

An important thing to remember is that any ambient light and flash exposure compensation you specify *are combined*. So, if you select +2 EV using the Exposure Compensation button on the top panel (to the right of the ISO button), and then choose +2 flash exposure compensation, you end up with +4 EV added and, probably, an overexposed image.

Specifying Flash Shutter Speed

This is another way of specifying the shutter speed used when working with flash. Unlike Custom Setting e1: Flash Sync Speed described earlier, this setting determines the *slowest* shutter speed that is available for electronic flash synchronization when you're not using a "slow-sync" mode. When you want to avoid ghost images from a secondary exposure, you should use the highest shutter speed that will synchronize with your flash. This setting prevents Programmed or Aperture-priority modes (which both select the shutter speed for you) from selecting a shutter speed that captures ambient light along with the flash.

With Custom Setting e2: Flash Shutter Speed, select a value from 30 s to 1/60 s, and the camera will avoid using speeds slower than the one you specify with electronic flash if you don't override that decision by deliberately choosing slow sync, slow rear-curtain sync, or red-eye reduction with slow sync. If you think you can hold the camera steady, a value of 1/30 s is a good compromise; if you have shaky hands, use 1/60 s or higher. Those with extraordinarily steady grips or who are using vibration reduction can try the 1/15 s setting. Remember that this setting only determines the slowest shutter speed that will be used, not the default shutter speed, which is set with Custom Setting e1.

Previewing Your Flash Effect

The Nikon camera's compatible external units, including the SB-5000, SB-910, SB-700, and some earlier models, can simulate a modeling light, in the form of a set of repeated bursts of light that allow you to pre-visualize the effect the strobe will provide when fired for the main exposure. This modeling flash, turned on or off using Custom Setting e5, is not a perfect substitute for a real incandescent or fluorescent modeling lamp, as it lasts only for a short period of time and is not especially bright. However, it does assist in seeing how your subject will be illuminated, so you can spot any potential problems with shadows.

When this feature is activated, if you've assigned the Preview (depth-of-field) behavior to a function button (Fn1–Fn4), pressing that control briefly triggers the modeling flash for your preview. Selecting Off disables the feature. You'll generally want to leave it On, except when you anticipate using the depth-of-field preview button for depth-of-field purposes (imagine that) and do *not* want the modeling flash to fire when the flash unit is charged and ready. Some external flash units, such as the SB-5000 and SB-910, have their own modeling flash buttons.

Flash Control

As I noted earlier, newer Nikon electronic flash units, such as the Nikon SB-5000, SB-500, SB-400, or SB-300 Speedlights are compatible with the unified flash control system and can be adjusted by the Flash Control setting in the Photo Shooting menu. All other Nikon electronic flash units, including the SB-600, SB-700, SB-800, SB-900, and SB-910 must be adjusted using the controls *on the flash itself.* Not all of the options can be accessed by every one of the Speedlights listed. For example, with the SB-400, you can only choose between TTL and Manual exposure, plus manual output levels. Unavailable options will be grayed out. To use the Flash Control menu entry, the flash must be mounted on the hot shoe, powered up, and not set in a Remote mode.

The exact options available from the Flash Control screen will vary, depending on the capabilities of the flash unit you are using. I'll discuss each of the adjustments available, whether they are chosen from the Flash Control menu or using the flash unit's own controls, in the sections that follow. Consult your flash unit's manual for the exact procedures used to make the adjustments described.

Working with Nikon Flash External Units

Nikon offers a wide range of external flash units that are compatible with CLS, ranging from the top-of-the-line SB-5000 to the entry-level SB-300, and will probably introduce more Speedlights during the life of this book. In addition, there are a number of older units that have been officially or unofficially discontinued, such as the SB-500, SB-600, SB-400, SB-800, and SB-910/SB-900, which are still available, in both new and used condition. I'm going to concentrate on the most recent in the following sections. Unfortunately, it's not possible to cover available third-party flash units, although Nissin, Profoto, and Godox provide excellent options.

Nikon SB-300

This entry-level Speedlight is the smallest and most basic of the Nikon series of Speedlights. The SB-300 has a limited, easy-to-use feature set suited for point-and-shoot photography and some slightly more advanced techniques. Do note however that it does not support wireless off-camera flash. The SB-300 has a moderate guide number of 18/59 at ISO 100. Its main advantage, then, is to provide some additional elevation of the flash above the camera to provide an improved coverage angle and less chance of red-eye effects. Its flash head tilts up to 120 degrees, with click stops at 120, 90, 75, and 60 degrees when the flash is pointed directly ahead. It has a zoom flash head. The SB-300 is lighter in weight at 3.4 ounces than the SB-400 it replaces and uses two AAA batteries.

Nikon SB-400

Recently discontinued, but still widely available new from many retailers, this entry-level Speedlight was, until the SB-300 was unveiled, the smallest and most basic of the series. The SB-400 has a limited, easy-to-use feature set suited for point-and-shoot photography and some slightly more advanced techniques. Do note however that, like the SB-300, it does not support wireless off-camera flash. The 4.5-ounce SB-400 has a moderate guide number of 21/69 at ISO 100 when the zooming head (which can be set to either 18mm or 27mm) is at the 18mm position. It tilts up to 90 degrees, allowing you to bounce the light off of a ceiling, but it cannot be rotated to the side.

Nikon SB-500

This Nikon flash unit has a permanent place in my bag, because it's small enough to justify carrying it around even when I have no expectation of needing a flash unit. It has a guide number of 24/79 at ISO 100, a speedy recycle time of about 3.5 seconds, and runs on 2 AA batteries for up to 140 flashes. It includes a built-in LED video light with three output levels and can also be used for still photography as fill light, especially at the brightest setting. It's perfect for wireless mode, with four wireless channels and two groups available in Commander mode. The SB-500's head tilts up to 90 degrees, with click-stops at 0, 60, 75, and 90. It rotates horizontally 180 degrees to the left and right, for flexible bounce-flash lighting. If you need a zoom head to adjust flash output to better distribute light at various focal lengths, you're better off with the SB-700 even with its limited zoom range (described next); this unit lacks zooming capabilities.

Nikon SB-700

This affordable unit has a guide number of 28/92 (meters/feet) at ISO 100 when set to the 35mm zoom position. It has many of the top-model SB-910's features, including zoomable flash coverage equal to the field of view of 24-120mm settings with a full-frame camera, and extra-wide 14mm coverage with a built-in diffuser panel. It has a built-in modeling flash feature, and a wireless Commander mode.

But the SB-700 lacks some important features found in the SB-910 and SB-5000. Depending on how you use your Speedlight, these differences may or may not be important to you. They include:

- **No repeating flash mode.** You can't shoot interesting stroboscopic effects with the SB-700 as you can with the SB-5000 or older SB-910/900 units.
- **No port for external power pack.** Using an external battery pack, like those available from Quantum and others, can be important for wedding and event photographers who want to fire off a bunch of shots quickly, while avoiding frequent changes of the AA batteries the SB-700 uses. An external pack has another benefit: more exposures before the Speedlight slows down to prevent overheating. External batteries don't generate heat inside the flash as internal batteries do.
- **No external PC/X sync socket.** This option, not found on the SB-700, is of limited use for those who want to attach an off-camera flash to any camera which does have a PC/X contact.
- **Limited zoom range.** The SB-700's zoom head is limited to 24-120mm, plus 14mm with the diffuser panel. The ability to match the zoom head to the focal length you're using can match the coverage to the field of view, so the flash's output isn't wasted illuminating areas that aren't within the actual frame.

Nikon SB-R200

One oddball flash unit in the Nikon line is the SB-R200. This unit is a specialized wireless-only flash that's especially useful for close-up photography and is often purchased in pairs for use with the Nikon R1 and R1C1 Wireless Close-Up Speedlight systems. Its output power is low at 10/33 (meters/feet) for ISO 100 as you might expect for a unit used to photograph subjects that are often inches from the lens. It has a fixed coverage angle of 78 degrees horizontal and 60 degrees vertical, but the flash head tilts down to 60 degrees and up to 45 degrees (with detents every 15 degrees in both directions). In this case, "up" and "down" has a different meaning because the SB-R200 can be mounted on the SX-1 Attachment Ring mounted around the lens, so the pair of flash units are on the sides and tilted toward or away from the optical axis. It supports i-TTL, D-TTL, TTL (for film cameras), and Manual modes.

Nikon SB-910

The Nikon SB-910 was the flagship of the Nikon flash lineup until the SB-5000 model was unveiled. However, the SB-910 remains one of the most-used Nikon flash units (along with its predecessor, the SB-900), so I'll continue to include it in my coverage of Speedlights for the foreseeable future. It's still widely available used and has a guide number of 34/111.5 (meters/feet) when the "zooming" flash head (which can be set to adjust the coverage angle of the lens) is set to the 35mm position. It includes Commander mode, repeating flash, modeling light, and selectable power output, along with some extra capabilities.

The SB-910 was basically a slight reboot of the older SB-900, which gained a bad reputation for overheating and then shutting down after a relatively small number of consecutive exposures (as few as a dozen or so shots). The SB-910 also can overheat but features a different thermal protection system. Instead of disabling the flash as it begins warming up, the SB-910 increases the recycle time between flashes, giving the unit additional time to cool a bit before the next shot. While this "improvement" is not a real fix, it does encourage you to slow your shooting pace a bit to stretch out the number of flashes this Speedlight produces before it must be shut down for additional cooling.

Nikon estimates that you should be able to get 190 flashes from the SB-910 when using AA 2600 mAh rechargeable batteries, if firing the Speedlight at full output once every 30 seconds, with a minimum recycling time of 2.3 seconds (which gradually becomes longer as the flash heats up and the thermal protection kicks in). To get the maximum number of shots from your batteries, Nikon figures that AF-assist illumination, power zoom, and the LCD panel illumination are switched off.

There are some improvements, such as illuminated buttons and a restyled soft case, but, in general, the SB-910 is very similar to the SB-900 that we Nikon photographers have learned to know and fear. For example, you can angle the flash and rotate it to provide bounce flash. It includes additional, non-through-the-lens exposure modes, thanks to its built-in light sensor, and can "zoom" and diffuse its coverage angle to illuminate the field of view of lenses from 8mm to 200mm.

The SB-910/SB-900 also has its own powerful focus assist lamp to aid autofocus in dim lighting and has reduced red-eye effects simply because the unit, even when attached to the hot shoe and not used off-camera, is mounted in a higher position that tends to eliminate reflections from the eye back to the lens.

Nikon SB-5000

This Speedlight is currently the flagship of the Nikon flash lineup, and is likely to remain so for a while, as there are rumors that Nikon has ceased developing new Speedlights and has handed the reins over to a third-party manufacturer. Since we've already seen the company selling Nikon-branded lenses made by Tamron, that move is entirely plausible.

While it resembles the SB-910 and has a virtually identical guide number (34.5 meters, 113 feet), it more or less solves the overheating problem that plagued its top-line predecessors. A novel internal cooling system purportedly allows up to 90 consecutive shots, or 120 shots at five-second intervals without overheating. (Wedding photographers will love this.)

However, the big news is the addition of radio control to the optical triggering available with previous Nikon flash units that could be operated wirelessly. Radio control allows triggering the flash from a distance of nearly 100 feet—without requiring a line-of-sight connection. Best of all, you don't need to purchase two of these to use the SB-5000 wirelessly. Nikon already has a radio trigger in its product line, the WR-R10/WR-R11a wireless remote receiver that I have been using for years as a remote shutter release. As a trigger-only device, the WR-R10/WR-R11a has a longer range than the SU-800 commander used for optical wireless operation. The SB-5000 retains compatibility with Nikon's earlier optical wireless system, so your current flash units can be used with it in non-radio mode.

I power my SB-5000 (and all my other Speedlights) with Panasonic (formerly Sanyo) Eneloop AA nickel metal hydride batteries. These are a special type of rechargeable battery with a feature that's ideal for electronic flash use. The Eneloop cells, unlike conventional rechargeable batteries, don't self-discharge over relative short periods of time. Once charged, they can hold onto most of their juice for a year or more. That means you can stuff some of these into your Speedlight, along with a few spares in your camera bag, and not worry about whether the batteries have retained their power between uses. There's nothing worse than firing up your strobe after not using it for a month and discovering that the batteries are dead.

Note that the SB-5000 and many other Nikon flash units contain firmware that can be updated. The Custom Settings readouts on the flash itself will tell you what firmware version you currently have. If an update is required, you'll need to download the firmware module from the Nikon website. Load it onto a memory card, and then mount the flash on your camera and power it up. You'll find a fourth entry in the Firmware section of the Setup menu, marked S (for Speedlight or Strobe). The SB-910's firmware can be updated through the camera/flash connection just like the camera's own firmware.

Figure 4.10 shows the SB-5000 fastened to the optional Nikon SK-7 bracket and linked to your Z9 or Z8 through the available SC-28 cable. There are a couple advantages to this configuration. First, the side-mounting moves the flash even farther from the axis of the lens, providing additional red-eye protection. You can still tilt the flash for bounce effects. I find this setup easier to hold, and not as awkward because you don't have a top-heavy flash unit mounted above the camera.

But, best of all, it's easy to uncouple the flash/SC-28 from the bracket and use both off-camera. There's no need to fuss with wireless modes, channels, groups, or other settings; the flash thinks that it's still connected directly to the camera—which it is, of course. Another nine-foot cable, the SC-29, is available and has a built-in focus assist illuminator. I own both, but I like having the SC-29's focus-assist lamp on top of the camera, so that it is aimed at my subject should the camera need a bit of extra illumination for focusing. Although the SB-5000 has its own focus lamp, it may or may not be pointed at your subject when it comes time to use it.

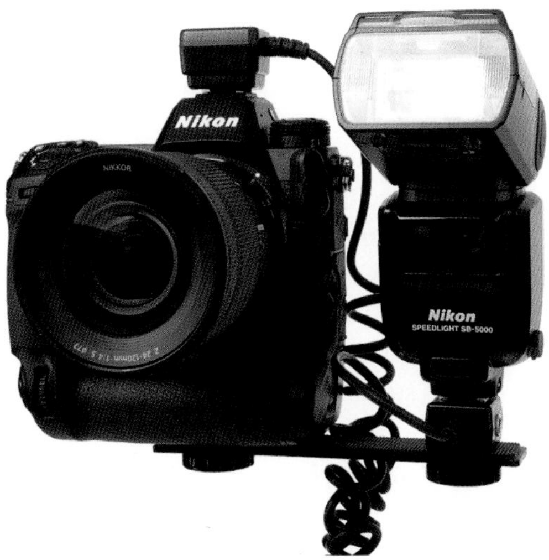

Figure 4.10 The Nikon SB-5000 attached to an optional bracket.

Light Modifiers

The top-of-the-line Speedlights have a better array of included light-modifying tools than other Speedlights in the Nikon line. The standard pop-up white "card" slides out of the flash head, as shown in Figure 4.11, left. The card reflects a little fill illumination toward your subject when the flash is tilted to bounce off a ceiling or rotated and tilted to bounce off a wall or other surface. A wide-angle diffuser also slides out and rotates to cover the front of the flash and spread the light to cover lenses with focal lengths as wide as 12mm. The included diffuser dome (see Figure 4.11, center) provides softer illumination for direct flash, with the flash pointed at your subject, or something of a "bare bulb" effect when pointed upward. (The "bare bulb" concept dates back to film days when an electronic flash, flashbulb (!), or even an incandescent lamp was used without a reflector or shade to provide a flood of soft illumination that spread out in all directions from the source.)

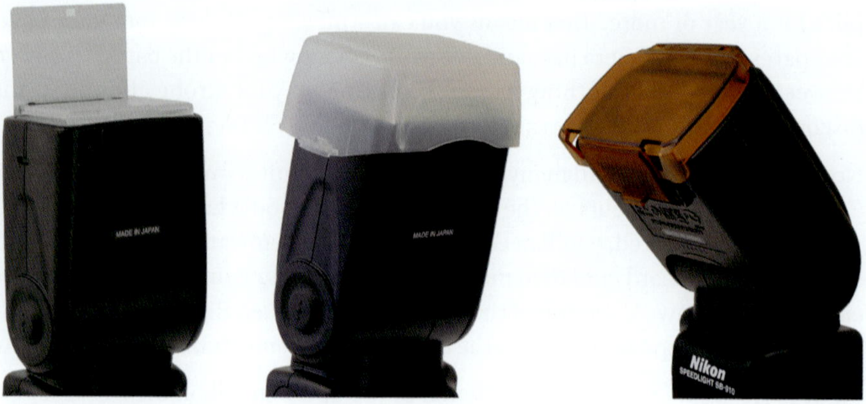

Figure 4.11 Left: The slide-out bounce card adds a kicker of light to fill in shadows or provide a catch light in the eyes of humans (or others). Center: The included diffuser dome produces a soft, flattering light. Right: The SZ-2TN incandescent filter warms the flash's illumination to match tungsten lighting.

Various filters are available for Nikon strobes to change the color of the light source. Two are included with the SB-910 and SB-5000, the SZ-2TN incandescent filter (shown in Figure 4.11, right) and the SZ-2FL fluorescent filter. The incandescent filter is most useful, because it changes the Speedlight's illumination to match typical indoor lamps, so you can use both to light a scene without encountering a nasty mixed-lighting situation. The nifty thing about the SZ-series filters is that they include a type of bar code that can be read by a sensor underneath the unit's flash head, so the strobe (and your camera) "knows" that a particular filter has been fitted.

Other Accessories

The top-end flash units come with the AS-21 Speedlight Stand, which lets you give the strobe a broad "foot" that can rest on any flat surface when working in wireless mode. The stand has a tripod-type socket underneath, so you can also mount the flash on a tripod or light stand without needing to purchase a special adapter.

Using Zoom Heads

External flash zoom heads can adjust themselves automatically to match lens focal lengths in use reported by the camera to the flash unit, or you can adjust the zoom head position manually if you want to use a setting that doesn't correspond to the automatic setting the flash will use. With older flash units, like the discontinued SB-600, automatic zoom adjustment wastes some of your flash's power, because the flash unit assumes that the focal length reported comes from a full-frame camera. Because of the 1.5X crop factor when DX mode is used, the flash coverage when the flash is set to a particular focal length will be wider than is required by the cropped image.

You can manually adjust the zoom position yourself, using positions built into the flash unit that more closely correspond to your lens' field of view when using the SB-5000, SB-910, and SB-900 (which do not automatically take into account the difference between FX/full-frame and DX/APS-C coverage).

Flash Modes

External flash units have various flash modes included. With units supporting unified flash control, you can choose the flash mode using the Flash Control menu, as seen in Figure 4.12.

- **TTL.** Through-the-lens metering is the standard mode for flash photography. Your Nikon Z9 and Z8 support several iTTL modes:
    - **iTTL Automatic Balanced Fill Flash (TTL BL).** In both Matrix and Center-weighted exposure modes, the camera and flash balance the exposure so that the main subject and background are well-exposed. A TTL BL indicator appears on the LCD. However, if you switch to Spot metering, the flash switches to standard iTTL, described next.
    - **Standard iTTL (TTL).** In this mode, activated when Spot metering is selected (or if you've selected it using the MODE button on the flash, or fixed the flash exposure using FV Lock), the exposure is set for the main subject, and the background exposure is not taken into account. *Only* the flash exposure is measured and used to determine exposure. A TTL indicator appears on the LCD. In either iTTL Automatic Balanced Fill Flash or Standard iTTL modes, if the full power of the flash is used, the ready-light indicator on the flash and in the viewfinder will blink for three seconds. This is your cue that perhaps even the full power of the flash might not have been enough for proper exposure. If that's the case, an EV indicator will display the amount of underexposure (–0.3 to –3.0 EV) on the LCD while the ready-light indicator flashes.
    - **High-speed TTL (TTL BL/TTL FP).** This TTL FP variation is enabled when you've set Custom Setting e1 to 1/200 s (Auto FP) or 1/250 s (Auto FP). When active, it changes the TTL Fill Flash and Standard modes so that higher shutter speeds can be used. I don't recommend using the 1/250 s (Auto FP) version, as banding can occur.

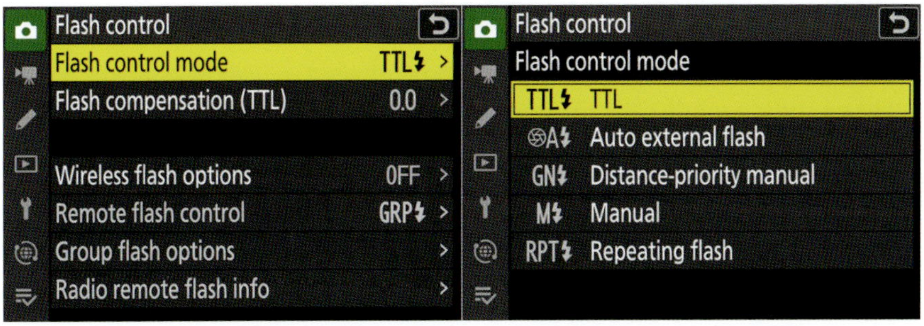

Figure 4.12 Select Flash Control Mode from the Flash Control menu.

- **AA: Auto Aperture flash.** An A indicator next to an icon representing a lens opening/aperture is shown on the LCD when this mode is selected. The SB-5000, SB-800, or SB-910/SB-900 use a built-in light sensor to measure the amount of flash illumination reflected back from the subject and adjusts the output to produce an appropriate exposure based on the ISO, aperture, focal length, and flash compensation values set on the camera. This setting on the flash can be used within Program or Aperture-priority modes. Like the A and GN modes described next, this option is a hold-over to provide compatibility with some older Nikon cameras, and not really useful.
- **A: Non-TTL auto flash.** In this mode, the Speedlight's sensor measures the flash illumination reflected back from the subject and adjusts the output to provide an appropriate exposure, without the feedback about the aperture setting that's used with AA mode. This setting on the flash can be used when the camera is set to Aperture-priority or Manual modes. You can use this setting to manually "bracket" exposures, as adjusting the aperture value of the lens will produce more or less exposure; the flash has no idea what aperture you've changed to.
- **GN: Distance priority manual.** You enter a distance value, and the SB-5000 or SB-910/SB-900 adjusts light output based on distance, ISO, and aperture to produce the right exposure in either Aperture-priority or Manual exposure modes. You can choose this option from the Flash Control menu with the SB-5000. With the SB-910/SB-900, press the MODE button on the flash and rotate the selector dial until the GN indicator appears (the GN option appears only when the flash is pointed directly ahead, or is in the downward bounce position). Then press the OK button to confirm your choice. After that, you can specify a shooting distance by pressing the Function 2 button, and then rotating the selector dial until the distance you want is indicated on the LCD. Press the OK button to confirm. The SB-5000 or SB-910/SB-900 will indicate a recommended aperture, which you then set on the lens mounted on the camera in Manual exposure mode.
- **M: Manual flash.** The flash fires at a fixed output level. Press the MODE button and rotate the selector dial until M appears on the LCD panel. Press the OK button to confirm your choice. Choose the power output level you want, down to 1/256th power with the SB-5000 and 1/128th power with most other Nikon Speedlights. Calculate the correct f/stop to use, either by taking a few test photos with a flash meter or by the seat of your pants. Then, choose Aperture-priority or Manual exposure and select the f/stop you've decided on.
- **RPT: Repeating flash.** The flash fires repeatedly to produce a multiple flash strobing effect. To use this mode, set the exposure mode to Manual. Then set up the number of repeating flashes per frame, frequency, and flash output level.

With Speedlights that *do not* support unified flash control, you will need to use the controls on the flash itself. The SB-700 has a sliding mode selector switch to the left of the Speedlight's LCD with positions for TTL, Manual, and GN settings. Those are the only modes available with that flash when you're using it as a master. However, when the SB-700 is used as a remote flash triggered by a master commander flash, it can operate in Repeating mode. Consult the manual for your particular flash.

The SB-5000 also allows you to set flash mode using the flash unit's buttons and dials, and any changes you make will also be reflected in the Flash Control menu.

Just follow these steps:

1. Press the Wireless Setting button (shown in Figure 4.13) to choose single flash unit mode.
2. Press the right edge of the rotary multi selector wheel to highlight the flash mode indicator in the upper-left corner of the screen.
3. Rotate the wheel to cycle among the available flash modes.
4. Press OK to confirm and exit.

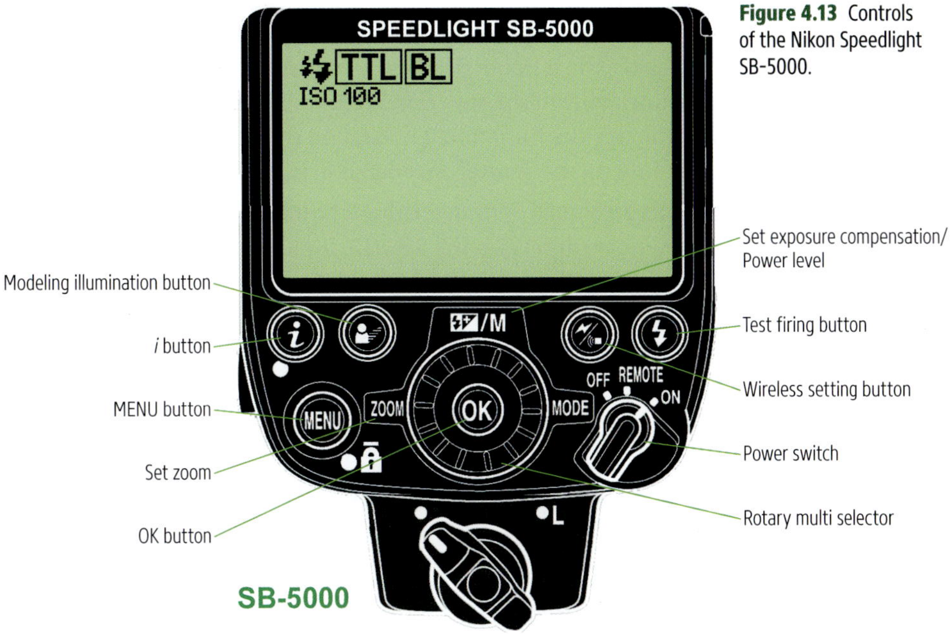

Figure 4.13 Controls of the Nikon Speedlight SB-5000.

Repeating Flash

Repeating flash is a function that can be used with external flashes like the SB-5000, SB-910, and SB-900. Check your manual for the exact buttons to press to make the following settings using Manual exposure mode:

1. **Set flash for RPT mode.** Steps 2–4 can be performed using the Flash Control menu with the SB-5000, as shown in Figure 4.14. If you're using the SB-910/SB-900 you can activate the repeating function using the flash's controls: Press the MODE button and rotate the selector dial until RPT is shown at upper left on the LCD. Then press the OK button to confirm.
2. **Choose Flash Output Level.** With these flash units, you must specify the power level of the flash. That level will determine the range of the number of flashes you can expect from the capacitor's charge. Use the options in the Flash Control menu to set the output level for the SB-5000. With the SB-910/SB-900, press the Function 2 button (on the SB-910) or the Function 1 button (on the SB-900) until the number of flashes is highlighted on the LCD (to the immediate right of the RPT indicator), and rotate the selector dial. Choose a power level from 1/8th to 1/128th power.

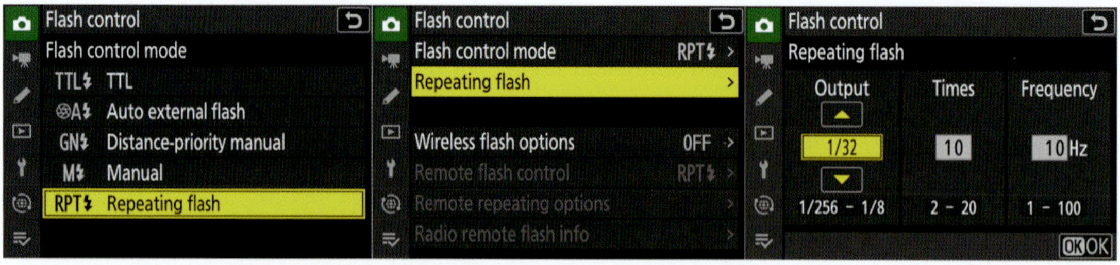

Figure 4.14 Menu options for repeating flash with the SB-5000.

3. **Select number of shots.** Next, choose the number of shots in your series. With the SB-5000, use the Times setting to determine how many flashes to emit. With the SB-910, highlight the option by pressing the Function 3 button; it's the Function 2 button on the SB-900. The number of shots you can specify varies depending on the shutter speed and firing frequency (specified next).
4. **Choose frequency: how many shots per second.** This determines how quickly the series is taken. With the SB-5000, use the Frequency setting. With the SB-910, highlight the option by pressing the Function 3 button; it's the Function 2 button on the SB-900.

The maximum number of shots in a series varies, depending on the shutter speed, output level, and frequency you select. The multiple flashes can be emitted only while the electronic shutter is completely open, so a faster shutter speed limits the number of bursts that can be fired off at a given frequency. High output levels and high frequency settings both deplete the capacitor more quickly. So, the number of possible bursts will depend on the combination you choose. With the SB-910 or SB-5000, the maximum number of shots you can expect is about 90 (at 1/64th or 1/128th power), and frequencies of from 1 to 3 bursts per second. That's a large number of firings over a long period of time (30 seconds or more).

If you want very rapid bursts, expect fewer total flashes: the SB-5000 and SB-910 will give you 24 firings at 1/128th power and 20 to 100 firings per second. Still, that's quite a bit of flexibility if you think about it. You can get 24 bursts in just a bit more than one second at the 20Hz setting, or over five seconds at the 100Hz setting. I needed only four bursts to capture the plummeting lime seen in Figure 4.15. One thing you'll notice is that as moving objects slow or speed up, the distance between one "shot" in a series varies.

BURN OUT

When using repeating flash with the SB-910/SB-900, SB-700, SB-5000, or *any* large number of consecutive flashes in any mode (more than about 15 shots at full power), allow the flash to cool off (Nikon recommends a 10-minute time out) to avoid overheating the flash. The SB-5000 increases the recycling time to extend the useful period, while the SB-910/SB-900, SB-700, or SB-500 will signal you when it's time for a cooling-off period. The flash will actually disable itself, if necessary, to prevent damage.

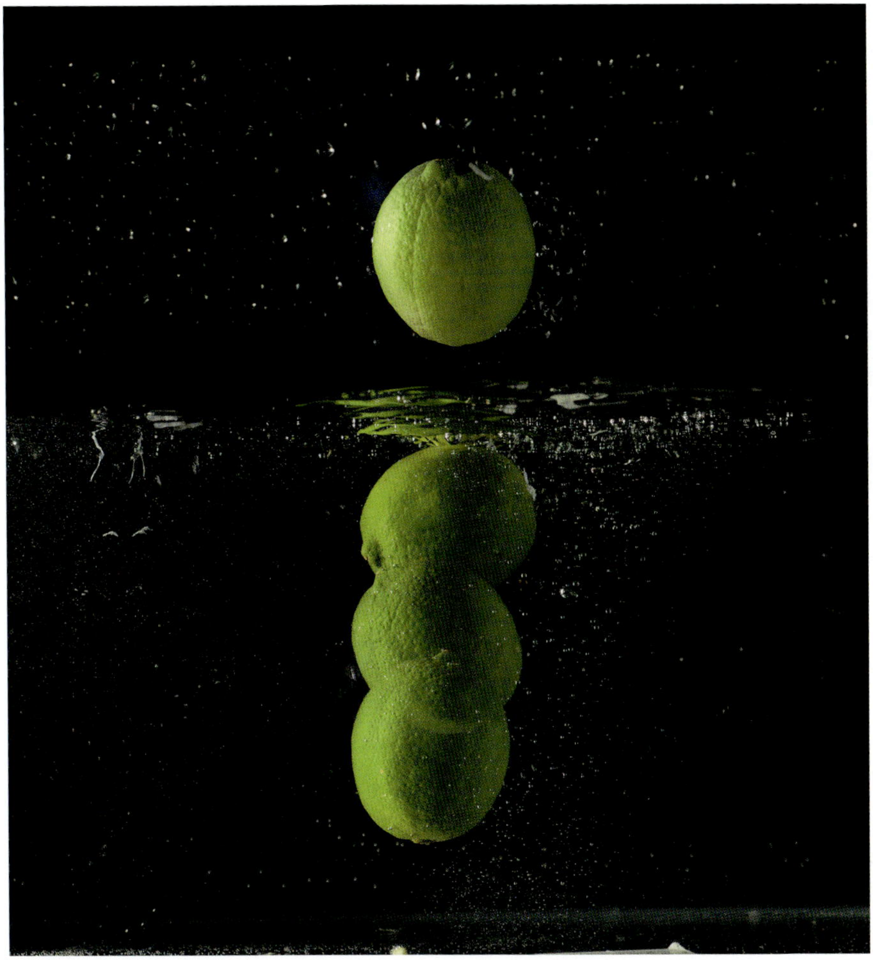

Figure 4.15 Capturing a lime as it plunges into a half-filled fish tank.

Introducing Wireless and Multiple Flash

An on-camera flash is most useful for fill light or as a master flash to trigger other units; the real key to effective flash photography is to get the flash off the camera, so its illumination can be used to paint your subject in interesting and subtle ways from a variety of angles.

Nikon shooters have long had wireless flash capabilities, ever since the creation of the Nikon Creative Lighting System, described earlier. Like the i-TTL exposure system, the Advanced Wireless Lighting (AWL) system (both Optical and Radio versions) uses preflashes that fire before the main exposure to transmit triggering and exposure information to external flash units that aren't physically connected to the camera. Depending on whether you're using the SB-5000 or one of the older flash units, you may be able to divide multiple flash units into as many as three different "groups" (six with the SB-5000) and communicate with them using your choice of any of up to four "channels" (to avoid interference from other Nikon photographers within range of your flash units who might be using the same channel).

It's not possible to cover every aspect of wireless flash in one chapter. There are too many permutations involved. For example, you can use external flash like the SB-700 or SB-5000, an SU-800 wireless trigger, or a PocketWizard-type device as the master. You may have one external "receiver" flash or use several. It's possible to control all your wireless flash units as if they were one multi-headed flash, or you can allocate them into "groups" that can be managed individually. You may select one of four "channels" to communicate with your strobes. These are all aspects that you'll want to explore as you become used to working with the camera's wireless capabilities.

What I hope to do in the following sections is provide the introduction to the basics so that you'll have the information you need to understand the step-by-step instructions for your Speedlight using the detailed manual supplied with the unit. Once you learn how to operate the camera's wireless capabilities, you can then embark on your own exploration of the possibilities.

Elements of Wireless Flash

Here are some of the key concepts to electronic flash and wireless flash that I'll be describing in this chapter:

- **Master flash.** The *master* is the flash (or other device) that commands each of the additional flashes when using Commander mode.
- **Remote flashes.** For wireless operation, you need at least one flash unit not mounted on the camera, in addition to the master device (which can be another flash or a transmitter unit).
- **Channels.** Nikon's wireless flash system offers users the ability to determine on which of four possible channels the flash units can communicate.
- **Groups.** Nikon's wireless flash system lets you designate multiple flash units in separate groups (as many as three groups, or six groups with the SB-5000). You can then have flash units in one group fire at a different output level than flash units in another group. This lets you create different styles of lighting for portraits and other shots.
- **Lighting ratios.** You can control the power of multiple off-camera Speedlights assigned to each group, in order to adjust each unit's relative contribution to the image, for more dramatic portraits and other effects.
- **Control system.** The SB-5000, whether used alone or with other flashes, can use either the existing optical/infrared control system deployed with earlier Speedlights or the newer radio control offered with the SB-5000 flash or with the WR-R10 or WR-R11a as a radio trigger.

Master Flash

The master flash is the commander that tells all the other units in a setup what to do, including when to fire, and at what intensity. It communicates with your camera, and then, when the firing parameters are determined by the camera (or you, manually), passes along the information to the individual remote flash units.

Your master can be one of the following:

- **An external flash with Commander capabilities.** Use a Nikon SB-5000, SB-910, SB-700, SB-500, or compatible earlier units to communicate with the remote Speedlights using optical or, with the SB-5000, radio control. When used as a master flash, the external strobe must be physically connected to the camera. You can mount the flash on the camera's accessory hot shoe, or mount it on a cable, such as the SC-28 or SC-29, and then connect the other end of the cable to the camera's accessory shoe. (See Figure 4.16, left.) The master flash can be set so that it does or does not contribute to the exposure, although, because it can be used off-camera, the latter mode offers more advantages.
- **The Nikon SU-800.** This device is an expensive non-flash (about $250) that does nothing but serve as an optical commander for CLS-compatible flash units (see Figure 4.16, center and right). It mounts on the hot shoe of the camera and emits infrared signals (rather than monitor pre-flashes) to trigger the remote flash units. It otherwise functions exactly like a "real" master flash, communicating to groups of Speedlights over the same channels, and allowing i-TTL exposure control. It has two main uses. One application is as a commander for Nikon's wireless "macro" lights, the SB-R200 units. In that mode, it's ideal for any Nikon dSLR, as it serves as a trigger for models without a built-in flash, including the Z-series cameras, plus dSLRs like the D850, D810/D800, D6, D5, D4, D4s, D3, D3s, or D3x, and some earlier models. It's also a more convenient close-range substitute for an attached master because it emits no light to cast shadows.

  I like to use my SU-800 for off-camera flash with no need to fuss with a cable connection or camera-mounted master flash unit. The Abraham Lincoln re-enactor was standing in the shade, and the diffused light was not harsh (which is the most common reason for adding flash fill). However, the difference in illumination between him *and* the background was significant, making it impossible to set an exposure that would capture both him and the structures behind him (Figure 4.17, left). I set the SB-500 to Manual exposure and 1/4 power, held it off to the left, and shot at 1/200th second and f/16 to get the photo at right. The SU-800's infrared control has an impressive 66-foot range under these conditions (that is, not under direct sunlight). (See Figure 4.17, right.)

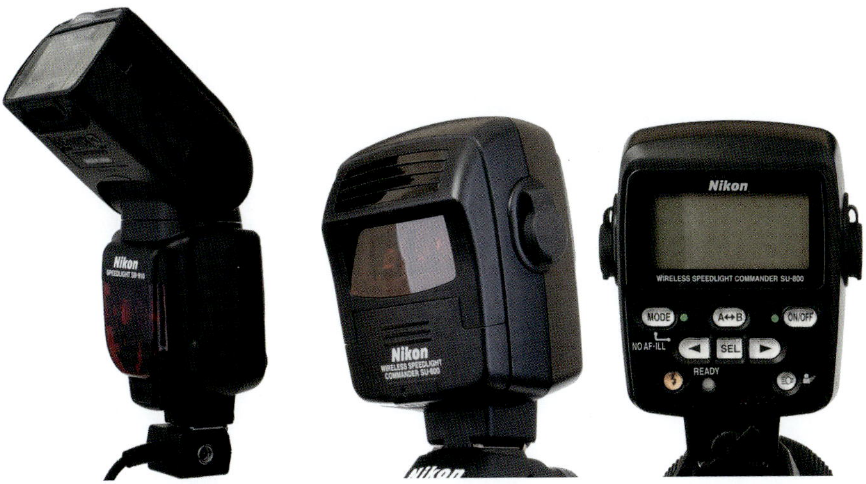

Figure 4.16 An external flash can be used as an off-camera master when connected to a cable that links it to the camera (left). The Nikon SU-800 can serve as a master unit (center and right).

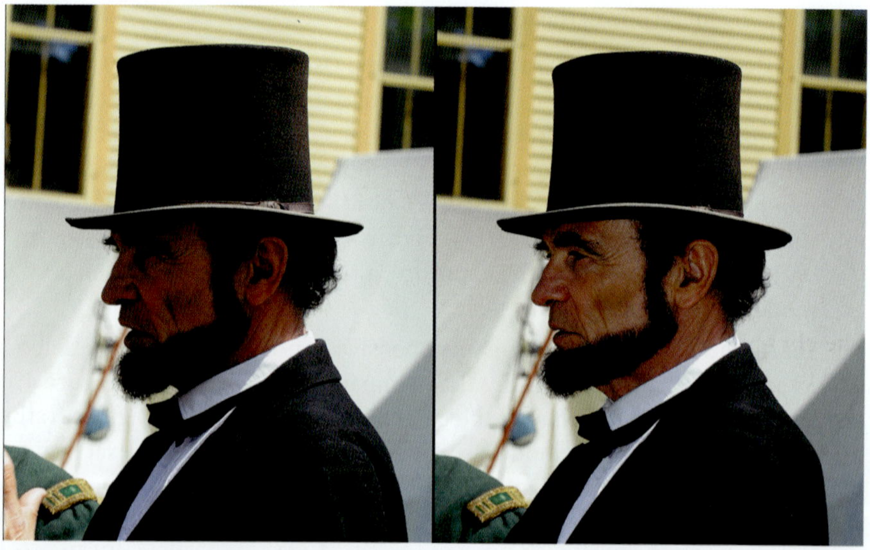

Figure 4.17 A flash can provide pleasing fill illumination outdoors in the shade.

- **Nikon WR-R10/WR-R11a.** When working with the SB-5000 in radio control mode, this device, plugged into the 10-pin connector on the front of the Z9/Z8, can serve as a master controller. It can also be used with the WR-T10 transmitter as a remote release for the camera when you're *not* using radio control flash.

  Note: The discontinued WR-R10 requires the WR-A10 adapter that allows it to be connected to the Z9/Z8's 10-pin terminal. In addition, if you have an older WR-R10 unit, you may need to send it to Nikon for a firmware upgrade to Version 3.00 to allow flash control. The firmware upgrade cannot be performed by the user. To see if your WR-R10 requires an upgrade, attach it to the camera, navigate to the Firmware Version entry in the Setup menu, and view the WR firmware notification.
- **Compatible third-party triggering devices.** These include models from PocketWizard, Radio Popper, and Godox. The advantage of these devices is that, unlike the optical system used by Nikon's CLS products (limited to about 30 feet), third-party devices use radio control to extend your remote "reach" to as far as 1,500 feet or more. Their transmitters/receivers can work in concert with your own master flash, which controls the remote flashes normally when they're in range, with the radio control taking over when the transmitter senses that the remote flash isn't responding to the master's instructions.

To use the Advanced Wireless System, you'll want to work with at least one remote flash unit. The remote flash for optical control can be any unit compatible with the Creative Lighting System, including the current SB-5000 and SB-700, or simpatico discontinued models, such as the SB-910/SB-900, SB-800, or SB-600. (Of these, the SB-600 can't function as a master flash on its own.) You'll need to set the auxiliary Speedlights to remote mode. For radio control mode, at this writing only the SB-5000 is compatible as a remote.

Channels

Channels are the discrete lines of communication used by the master flash to communicate with each of the remote units. The pilots, ham radio operators, or scanner listeners among you can think of the channels as individual communications frequencies.

If you're working alone, you'll seldom have to fuss with channels. Just remember that all the Speedlights you'll be triggering must be using the same channel, exactly like a CB radio or walkie-talkie. (Google these terms if you're younger than 40.) If every flash isn't set for the same channel, they will be unable to "talk" to each other, good buddy. I'll show you how to adjust channels shortly.

The channel ability is most important when you're working around other photographers who are also using the same Nikon CLS system. Each photographer sets his or her flash units to a different channel as to not accidentally trigger other users' strobes. (At big events with more than four photographers using Nikon flash, you may need to negotiate.)

Personally, I think it's unfortunate that Nikon was able to include only four channels when using optical control. Radio control is much more flexible; third parties with CLS-compatible systems offer many more channels. Godox, for example, provides 32 discrete channels and allows up to 99 different wireless ID settings, which makes signal interference highly unlikely no matter how many similar setups are in use simultaneously at a given venue. Radio control with the SB-5000 or WR-R10/WR-R11a offers just three channels (Ch5, Ch10, and Ch15), but the flash units are linked using pairing or a PIN code, which effectively increases the number of non-interfering connections. Don't worry about Canon or Sony photographers at the same event. Their wireless flash systems use different communication systems that won't interfere with yours.

It's always a good idea to double-check your flash units before you set them up to make sure they're all set to the same channel, and this should also be one of your first troubleshooting questions if a flash doesn't fire the first time you try to use it wirelessly.

Groups

Each flash unit can be assigned to one of three groups, labeled A, B, and C. (The SB-5000 has additional groups, D, E, and F.) All the flashes in a single group perform together as if they were one big flash, using the same output level and flash compensation values. That means you can control the relative intensity of flashes in each *group*, compared to the intensity of flashes assigned to a *different* group. A group needs at least one flash unit but can have more.

For example, you could assign one (or more) flash to Group A and use it as the main light in your setup. Group B could be used as the fill light and Group C designated as a hair or background light. The power output of each group could be set individually, so your main light(s) in Group A might be two or three times as intense as the light(s) in Group B (used for fill), while another power level could be set for the Group C auxiliary lights. You don't *have* to use all three groups, but it is an option.

But there's a lot more you can do if you've splurged and own two or more compatible external flash units. Some photographers own five or six Nikon Speedlights, including me, who has one of each model Nikon has offered, starting with the SB-800. As I mentioned, Nikon wireless photography lets you collect individual strobes into *groups* and control all the Speedlights within a given group together. You can operate as few as two strobes in two groups or three strobes in three groups, while controlling more units if desired. You can also have them fire at equal output settings versus using them at different power ratios. Setting each group's strobes to different power ratios gives you more control over lighting for portraiture and other uses.

This is one of the more powerful options of the Nikon wireless flash system. I prefer to keep my Speedlights set to different groups normally. I can always set the power ratio to 1:1 if I want to operate the flash units all at the same power. If I change my mind and need to make adjustments, I can just change the wireless flash controller and then be able to manipulate the different groups' output as desired.

Remember that with whatever equipment you are using, outdoors if you are using optical triggering, you must have a clear line-of-sight between the master flash or SU-800 unit and sensors on the front of the remote flash units. Indoors, this requirement isn't as critical because the preflash and IR signals bounce off walls and other surroundings. Radio control has a longer 98-foot (30 meter) range.

Lighting Ratios

Lighting ratios are the relative proportions of the illumination among the groups, as I just described. To get the most from the CLS system, you'll want to understand how ratios work. That's a topic that deserves a chapter of its own, but many Nikon camera owners will already be familiar with the concept. If not, there are plenty of good books and online tutorials available.

Using Ratios

When lighting a subject, you can use several electronic flash units, as shown in the highly simplified arrangement in Figure 4.18. In this case, the main flash is an external unit placed to the left of the subject, and slightly behind her. An additional flash mounted on the hot shoe provides less intense illumination to fill in the shadows. A third flash illuminates the background, providing separation between it and the subject. All three flashes are set to the same channel, and are assigned to different groups: A, B, and C.

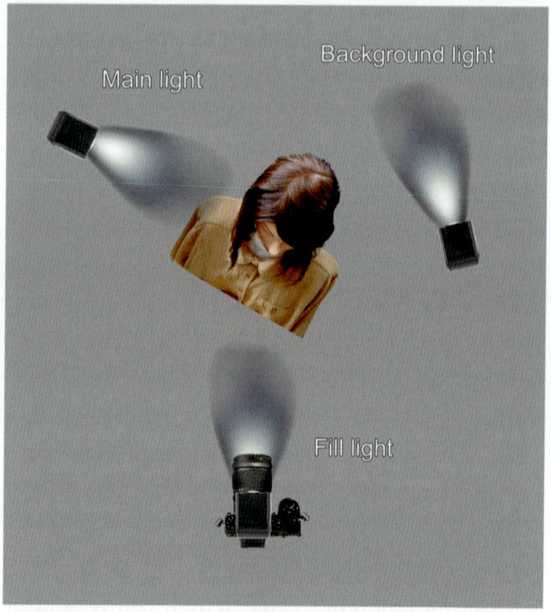

Figure 4.18 Multiple electronic flash units can be set to different intensities.

That setup makes it possible to specify Manual flash mode, in which you control the intensity of the flash, instead of TTL mode, in which the camera interprets the light from the preflash and adjusts output automatically. In Manual mode you can specify a different intensity to each group, with, say, the main light (Group A) firing at full power, the fill light (Group B) at 1/4 power, and the background light (Group C) at 1/8 power. The most common way to balance lights set to different power outputs is to use ratios, which are easy to calculate by setting (or measuring, with an external light meter) the exposure of each light source alone. Once you have the light calculated for each source alone, you can figure the lighting ratio.

For example, suppose that the main light for the portrait setup in Figure 4.18 provides enough illumination that you would use an f/stop of f/11. The fill light you'll be adding is less intense, set to 1/4 power, and also located farther away from the subject (or is diffused, say, with an umbrella reflector). If the fill light produces an exposure, all by itself, of f/5.6, that translates into two f/stops' difference or, putting it another way, the main light source is four times as intense as the fill light. You can express this absolute relationship as the ratio 4:1. Because the main light is used to illuminate the highlight portion of your image, while the secondary light is used to fill in the dark, shadow areas left by the main light, this ratio tells us a lot about the lighting contrast for the scene.

In practice, only the lighting ratio produced by illumination falling on the main subject "counts." The light illuminating the background is just supplementary light and, in most cases, need not be taken into account in calculating the lighting ratio.

In practice, a 4:1 lighting ratio (or higher) is quite dramatic and can leave you with fairly dark shadows to contrast with your highlights. For portraiture, you probably will want to use 3:1 or 2:1 lighting ratios for a softer look that lets the shadows define the shape of your subject without cloaking parts in inky blackness.

If you use electronic flash equipped with a modeling light feature (or incandescent lighting), you will rarely need to calculate lighting ratios while you shoot. Instead, you'll base your lighting setups on how the subject looks, making your shadows lighter or darker depending on the effect you want. If you use electronic flash without a modeling light, or flash with modeling lights that aren't proportional to the light emitted by the flash, you can calculate lighting ratios. If you do need to know the lighting ratio, it's easy to figure by measuring the exposure separately for each light and multiplying the number of f/stops difference by two. A two-stop difference means a 4:1 lighting ratio; two-and-a-half stops difference adds up to a 5:1 lighting ratio; three stops is 6:1; and so forth. Figure 4.19 shows an example of 2:1, 3:1, 4:1, and 5:1 lighting ratios. I'll show you how to adjust the intensity of your Nikon Speedlights to achieve ratios shortly.

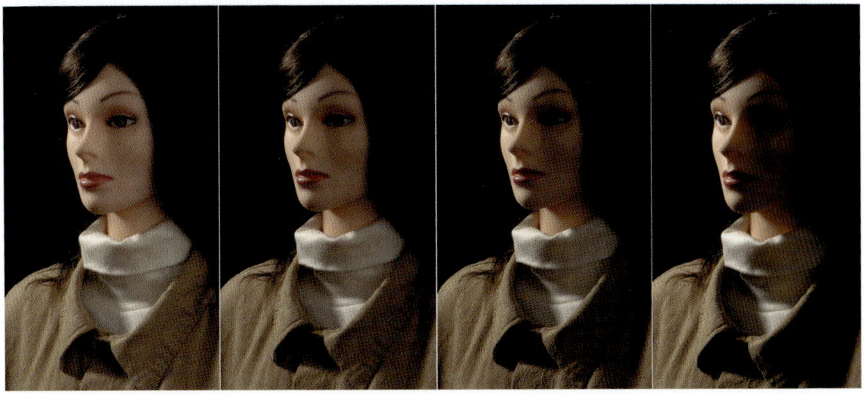

Figure 4.19 Left to right: Lighting ratios of 2:1, 3:1, 4:1, and 5:1.

Setting Your Master Flash

Nikon's wireless flash system gives you a number of advantages that include the ability to use directional lighting, which can help bring out detail or emphasize certain aspects of the picture area. It also lets you operate multiple strobes and establish lighting ratios, as described above, although most of us won't own more than two Nikon Speedlights. You can set up complicated portrait or location lighting setups. Since the top-of-the-line Nikon SB-5000 (and former champ SB-910) pump out a lot of light for a shoe-mount flash, a set of these units can give you near studio-quality lighting. Of course, the cost of these high-end Speedlights approaches that of some studio monolights—but the Nikon battery-powered units are more portable and don't require an external AC power source or battery pack.

Since it's necessary to set up both the camera and the strobes for wireless operation, this guide will help you with both, starting with prepping the camera. To configure your camera for wireless flash, just follow these steps. I'm going to assume that you're using an external flash connected to the camera as a master strobe. I'll use the SB-5000 in the example that follows.

NOTE In the sections that follow, I'm going to provide an overview for setting up some basic features of some the most popular Nikon Speedlights. Covering everything these powerful strobes can do would take an entire book; indeed, the SB-5000 itself is furnished with its own hefty 120-page manual. You'll want to consult the guide that came with your Speedlight to discover all the features available to you.

Setting Commander Mode for the SB-5000

If you're using an SB-5000 as your master flash, setting it for Commander mode for automatic, through-the-lens (TTL) exposure calculation can be done using the Flash Control entry in the Photo Shooting menu. Just follow these steps:

1. Mount the SB-5000 flash on the accessory shoe and power it up. The Flash Control entry in the Photo Shooting menu is grayed out if a compatible flash unit is not mounted and turned on.
2. Navigate to the Flash Control entry. As with all menu functions, you can press OK or press the right directional button to select this and the following entries.
3. The Flash Control screen will look like Figure 4.20, upper left. If you have not been using your flash as a wireless master, the Wireless Flash Options choice will be set to OFF.
4. When wireless flash is disabled, you can access the Flash Control Mode entry and switch among TTL, Auto External Flash, Guide Number (Distance Priority Manual), Manual, and Repeating Flash. (See Figure 4.20, upper right.)
    - Set the TTL Flash Control Mode if you want the camera to calculate flash exposure for the main Commander flash and remote flash units.
    - Set the TTL Flash Control Mode to Manual if you want to set the output levels for your electronic flash yourself, rather than allow the camera to set the output automatically. (See "Lighting Ratios," above.)

5. In the Flash Control screen, select the Wireless Flash Options choice, shown at lower left in Figure 4.20.
6. In the next screen, shown at lower right in Figure 4.20, select Optical AWL.
7. Next, select Remote Flash Control, as seen in Figure 4.21, upper left.
8. Select Group Flash from the screen shown in Figure 4.21, upper right.

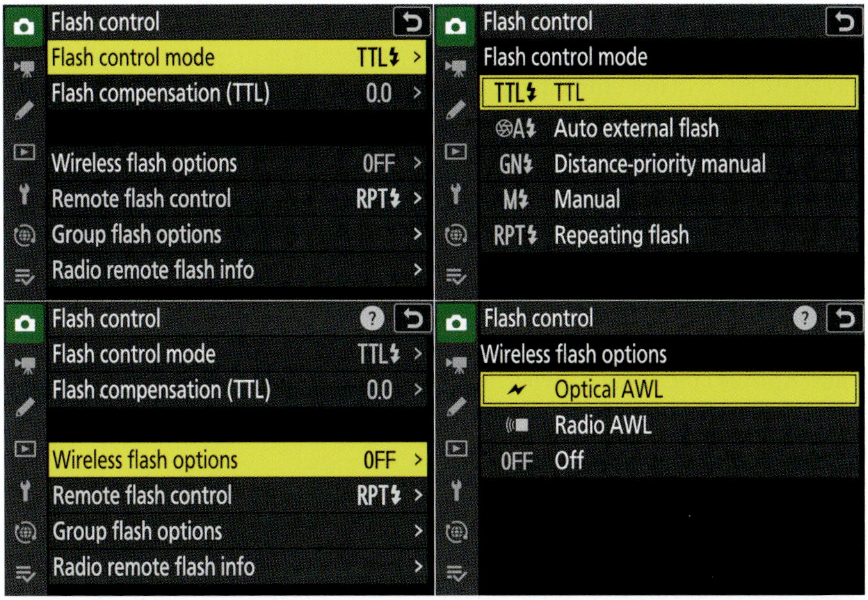

Figure 4.20 Set Flash control mode (top) and activate Optical AWL (bottom).

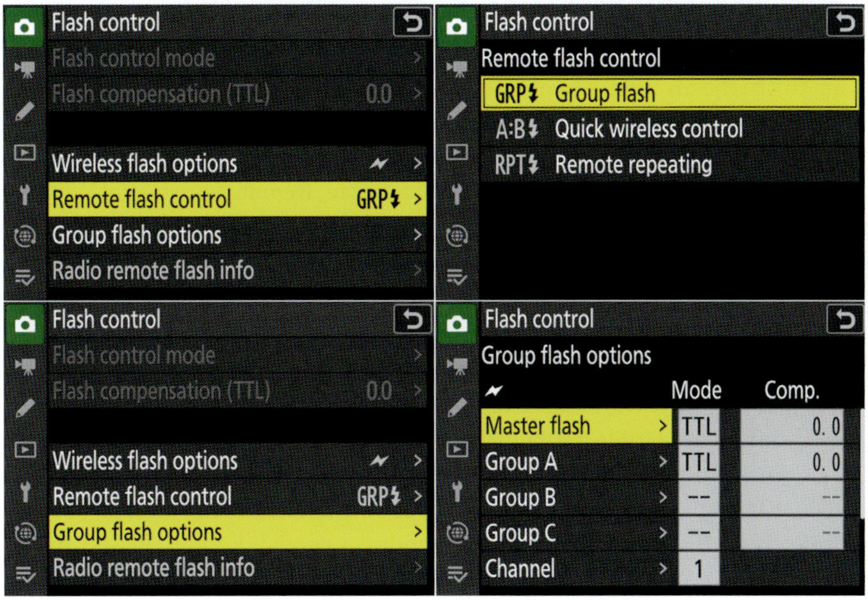

Figure 4.21 Set Group Flash mode (top), and Group Flash options, including mode, output level, and channel (bottom).

9. You will need to specify a group, mode, and output level. Select Group Flash Options, as seen at bottom left in Figure 4.21. If you're working in TTL mode, the screen at bottom right in the figure appears.
   - Master Flash sets the current flash as a Commander.
   - Group A, Group B, and Group C settings specify the mode of the individual groups. (Groups D and E are available in Radio control mode with the SB-5000.) Choose from TTL, AA, M, or --. If you select -- for any flash or Group, that flash or Group will not contribute to the exposure. (For example, you can set your Master Commander flash to -- and it will trigger other flashes wirelessly but will not emit a burst during the exposure.)
10. The term *Comp.* is misleading; it actually refers to output level. In the Comp. column you can specify flash exposure compensation (for TTL mode) or flash power level (for M mode).
11. Specify a Channel, selecting from available channels numbered 1–4. (Not all Nikon flashes can use all four channels.)

Wireless Flash Options

All adjustments of an SB-5000, SB-500, SB-400, or SB-300 mounted on the camera can be made using the camera's menus. And, as I mentioned earlier, SB-910, SB-900, SB-800, SB-700, and SB-600 flash can be adjusted *only* using the controls on the flash units themselves. Under Wireless Flash Options, you can select three wireless modes:

- **Optical AWL.** Optical Advanced Wireless Lighting is the traditional wireless triggering method, available when using a master flash, such as the SB-5000 mounted on the camera.
- **Radio AWL.** Radio AWL can be chosen when the SB-5000 is mounted on the camera *or* you have the WR-R10/WR-R11a unit attached to the camera and are using a radio-compatible off-camera flash (currently only the SB-5000). Your two AWL choices were shown earlier at lower right in Figure 4.20.

  Note that if you want to use the SB-5000 as a radio-controlled master flash, before attaching it to your camera, you should use the flash's controls to specify radio-controlled master flash mode. Just press the Wireless Setting button (second button from the right on the back of the SB-5000, and shown earlier in Figure 4.13) to cycle through Optical Remote, Remote Direct, and Wireless Remote settings. Then press the SB-5000's Menu button and choose group or remote repeating flash. Then, turn the flash off, attach the SB-5000 to the camera, and power it up again. You will then be able to adjust the SB-5000 using the camera's Flash Control menu, or with the controls on the flash itself.
- **Optical/Radio AWL.** This option does not appear on the camera's menu. It combines both modes, allowing you to use a WR-R10/WR-R11a unit attached to the camera to trigger radio-compatible flashes, and an additional compatible flash unit mounted on the camera to trigger non-radio off-camera flash as a Commander using Optical AWL. The camera-mounted optical master can be the SB-910/SB-900, SB-800, SB-700, or SU-800 flash controller, and the combined mode is activated automatically. Note that when the combined mode is selected, Remote Flash Control (described in the list following this one) is set to Group Flash automatically.

Under the Remote Flash Control entry (shown earlier in Figure 4.21, upper right), these are your choices:

- **Group flash.** I described flash Groups earlier in this chapter. This entry allows you to specify separate flash control modes and flash levels for each group of remote units. When working with Optical AWL or Optical/Radio AWL, you can select the channel flashes used to communicate.
- **Quick wireless control.** This option is a fast way to specify flash ratios by adjusting the balance between Groups A and B, with the exposure being determined by TTL metering. That is, the camera determines the intensity of the flash units in Groups A and B, and you specify the ratio between them, with, say, Group A twice as powerful as Group B. Flash compensation for Groups A and B can also be set to add or subtract from the TTL-metered exposure.

  You can also set the output for any Group C flashes you use manually, perhaps to provide fill light. As with Group flash, if you're using Optical AWL or Optical/Radio AWL, you can select the channel used for communication.
- **Remote repeating.** This option is the multi-flash version of Repeating flash, which I explained earlier in this chapter. It is available only when using SB-5000 Speedlights. As with the single-flash version, you can choose flash output level, maximum number of flashes (Times), and Frequency (flashes per second). As with the previous two modes, if you're using Optical AWL or Optical/Radio AWL, you can select the channel used for communication.

Note: If you are using radio control, a Radio Remote Flash Info entry appears, and the flash units currently being managed are shown instead. The next step is to set up each of your off-camera flashes as a remote. That's done using controls on the flash units themselves. I'll get to that after I've explained how to set Commander modes for some other Speedlights.

Setting Commander Modes for the SB-910 or SB-900

Setting Commander modes for the SB-910/SB-900 has been greatly simplified, compared to some previous Nikon Speedlights. If you'd rather use an attached flash as the master, just rotate the On/Off/Remote/Master mode switch to the Master position.

You'll want to tell the SB-910/SB-900 which channel it is using to communicate with the other Speedlights. You'll need to do this separately for each of the SB-910/SB-900 units you are working with if you're using more than one. Here are the steps to follow. (I recommend doing several dry runs to see how setting up multiple flashes works before trying it "live.")

1. **Set master flash to Commander mode.** On the master flash, rotate the power switch to the Master position, holding down the center lock release button of the switch so that it will move to the Master position. (This extra step is needed because Nikon knows you won't want to accidentally change from Master to Remote.)
2. **Access Mode.** Press the Function 2 button (Function 1 button on the SB-900) to highlight M on the LCD. (**Note:** M in this case stands for Master, not Manual.)

SB-910/900 FUNCTION BUTTONS

The steps are almost identical between the SB-910 and SB-900 (shown at the bottom of Figure 4.22), differing primarily in the Function buttons used. In each case, the buttons numbered 1 through 3 are the three buttons just south of the LCD panel starting from left to right.

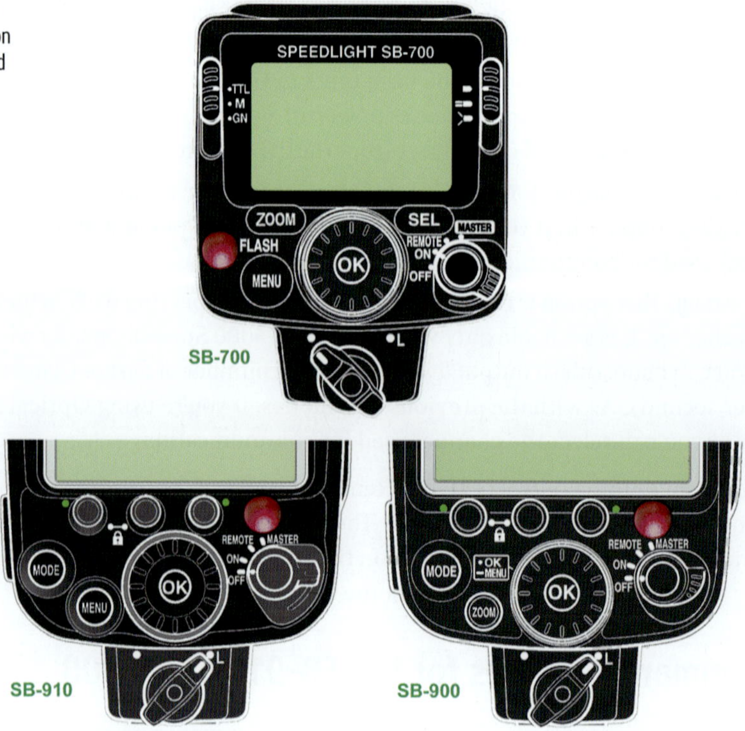

Figure 4.22 Location of the control buttons on the SB-700, SB-910, and SB-900 Speedlights.

3. **Select Mode.** Press the MODE button repeatedly to cycle to the flash mode you want to use for that flash unit, from among TTL, A (Auto Aperture), M (Manual), or - -. Then, press OK.

TIP At the - - setting, the master flash is disabled; it will trigger the other units, but its flash won't contribute to the exposure—except if you're shooting very close to the subject using a high ISO setting, because the monitor preflash may be bright enough to influence the exposure. If an external flash is the master, try tilting or rotating the flash head away from your subject to minimize this spill-over effect.

4. **Set Flash Exposure Compensation.** Press the Function 3 button (Function 2 button on the SB-900) and rotate the selector dial to choose the flash compensation level (–3 to +3) or manual power level (1/1 to 1/128). The amount of exposure compensation (EV correction) appears at the right side of the display, opposite the master flash's mode indicator.
5. **Specify group.** Press the Function 2 button (Function 1 button on the SB-900) to move on to the Group Selection option. Press OK to choose Group A or rotate the selector dial to choose Group B or C, then press OK to confirm the group you've chosen.

6. **Set modes for group.** Once a group is highlighted, select the mode for that group. Press the MODE button and then spin the selector dial to choose the flash mode you want to use for that flash unit, from among TTL, A (Auto Aperture), M (Manual), or - -. Then, press OK.
7. **Set Flash Exposure Compensation for group.** Press the Function 3 button (Function 2 button on the SB-900) and rotate the selector dial to choose the flash compensation level for the current group as you did in Step 3. The amount of EV correction appears at the right side of the display, opposite the group's mode indicator.
8. **Repeat for other groups.** If you're using Group B and Group C, repeat steps 4 to 7 to set the mode and Flash Exposure Compensation for the additional groups.
9. **Specify channel.** Once the modes and compensation for all the groups have been set on the master flash, press the Function 3 button (Function 2 button on the SB-900) and rotate the selector dial to set a channel number that the master flash will use to control its groups.
10. **Set up remote flashes.** Now take each of the remote flash units and set the correct group and channel number you want to use for each of them. I'll describe this step later.

Setting Commander Modes for the SB-700

Setting Commander modes for the SB-700 is similar in concept to the settings for the SB-910 or SB-900. The controls for the SB-700 are shown at top in Figure 4.22. If you want to use an attached SB-700 as the master flash, follow these steps:

1. **Set master flash to Commander mode.** On the master flash, rotate the power switch to the Master position, holding down the center lock release button of the switch so that it will move to the Master position.
2. **Choose mode.** There's a sliding switch on the left side of the SB-700. You can choose TTL, M (Manual), or GN modes.
3. **Set Flash Exposure Compensation.** Press the SEL button to select the master flash, then choose a flash compensation value/output level using the selector dial. Press OK to confirm.
4. **Specify group.** Press the SEL button to move on to the Group Selection option. Press OK to choose Group A or rotate the selector dial to choose Group B. (Group C is not available with the SB-700.) Set the flash exposure compensation value for each group using the selector dial. Then press OK to confirm.
5. **Specify channel.** Once the modes and compensation for all the groups have been set on the master flash, press the SEL button to highlight the Channel, then rotate the selector dial to set a channel number that the master flash will use to control its groups.
6. **Set up remote flashes.** Now take each of the remote flash units and set the correct group and channel number you want to use for each of them.

Setting Commander Modes for the SB-500

Setting Commander modes for the SB-500 is similar in concept to the settings for the SB-5000. If you want to use an attached SB-500 as the master flash, follow these steps:

1. **Mount the SB-500 on the camera and turn on the power.** Rotate the SB-500's power switch, located on the lower-right corner of the back of the unit, to the lightning bolt icon.
2. **Navigate to the Flash Control entry on your camera.** Under the Flash Control entry, choose TTL mode and press OK.
3. **Select Wireless Flash Options.** Choose Optical AWL.
4. **Specify group.** In the Group Flash Options entry, choose Group A or Group B. (Group C is not available with the SB-500.) Choose the exposure mode and flash exposure compensation value for each group using the entries in the second and third columns. (The screen is similar to the one shown in lower right in Figure 4.21, earlier.)
5. **Specify channel.** Once the modes and compensation for all the groups have been set on the master flash, choose a Channel. The mode indicator lamp (CMD) on the flash illuminates when settings are made on the camera.
6. **Set up remote flashes.** Now take each of the remote flash units and set the correct group and channel number you want to use for each of them. I'll describe this step next.

Setting Remote Modes

Each of the external remote flash units must be set to Remote mode. With the SB-5000, that's as easy as rotating the On/Off switch to the Remote position. Then press the wireless setting button located at the 11 o'clock position above the switch (and shown earlier in Figure 4.13) and choose optical, direct remote, or radio control remote modes. (I'm covering only optical triggering here.)

Here's how to set up the Nikon SB-500, SB-700, SB-900, and SB-910 Speedlights as remote flash units. Note that you don't need to specify compensation/output level; that's handled by the master/commander flash. You just need to set the flash to Remote, then choose Group, Channel, and Zoom head function.

1. **Switch flash to remote mode.** With the SB-900/SB-910 or SB-700, rotate the power switch to the Remote position, holding down the center lock release button of the switch so that it will move to the Remote position. If you're using the SB-500, you'll set remote mode in Step 2.
2. **Select group.** With the SB-500, rotate the power switch to A or B to correspond with the remote flash group you selected for the master flash. With the SB-910, press the Function 2 button (Function 1 button on the SB-900) and choose Group A with the selector dial, and press OK. With the SB-700, press the SEL button to highlight the group, then press OK. Repeat for Group B or (with the SB-900/SB-910 only) Group C.
3. **Set channel.** With the SB-500, the remote flash channel is automatically Channel 3 (the only one available with that unit). With the SB-900/SB-910, press the Function 2 button to highlight the channel. If you're using the SB-700, press the SEL button until the channel is highlighted. Then, rotate the selector dial to choose the channel number. Make sure you choose the same channel number you set earlier on the master flash. Press OK to confirm.

4. **Choose zoom head position.** With the SB-910, press the Function 1 button (or the Zoom button on the SB-900 or SB-700) to highlight Zoom Head Position, and choose a zoom head setting with the selector dial. Press OK to confirm. With the SB-900 and SB-700, push the Zoom button multiple times to change zoom settings. The SB-500 does not have a zoom head.
5. **Repeat for each remote flash.** If you're using more than one remote flash, repeat Steps 1 to 4 for each of the additional CLS-compatible units.

QUICK WIRELESS CONTROL

You can choose the balance between groups A and B and set the output for Group C manually.

Radio Control

Radio control for all flashes used with Nikon dSLR and mirrorless cameras is still in its infancy. At the time I write this, only the expensive SB-5000 flash unit can be triggered by radio signals, and the only way to trigger an off-camera SB-5000 using radio control is with another SB-5000 or the Wireless Remote Controller WR-R10/WR-R11a. So, you'll end up spending at least $1,000 for a two-flash radio-controlled setup. Fortunately, Nikon allows you to mix optically and radio-controlled flash units. You do gain three extra groups (Groups D, E, and F, if you can afford flashes to populate them with), but only three groups (A, B, and C) can be used with Nikon's Quick Wireless Control setup. As always, I recommend consulting Nikon's 120-page guide to the SB-5000 if you want to sort out all the configurations and features of this complex flash. I can provide only an overview here, rather than a detailed how-to that explains all the available combinations.

TIP As I mentioned earlier, a more affordable radio control system is available from vendors like Godox. You can purchase inexpensive receivers/transceivers (around $70) and some less pricey Godox flash units and retain TTL exposure calculation and control of the flash output levels right at the transmitter. Unfortunately, third-party solutions are updated more frequently than Nikon's own products (the SB-700, introduced in 2010, is still a current Nikon offering), so it's not practical to cover them in detail in a book like this. That's why I stick to describing Nikon's more stable product line almost exclusively.

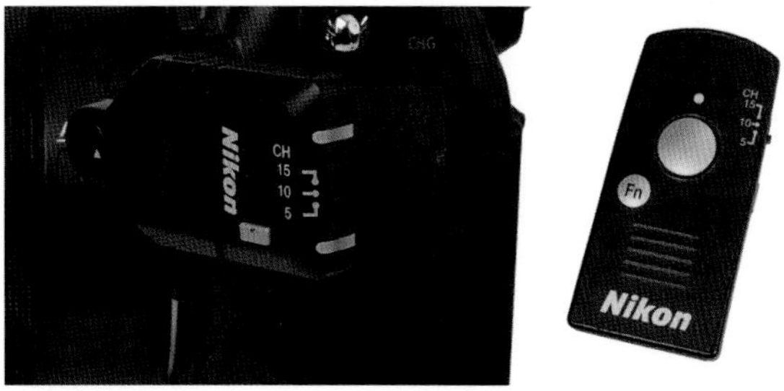

Figure 4.23 The WR-R10 or WR-R11a plugs into the 10-pin accessory port on the front of the camera.

The WR-R10/WR-R11a plugs into the 10-pin port on the front of the camera, as seen in Figure 4.23. (The original WR-R10 is shown; the newer version looks almost identical.) You'll need to set the channel for this controller to the same channel used for your SB-5000, from Channel 5, 10, or 15. Then, you'll need to link the controller using the Wireless Remote (WR) Options entry in the Setup menu. You can connect using pairing (the most common, and easiest) or with a PIN, which is more secure and generally used only by professionals to avoid interference in environments in which there are multiple cameras being used with this same system.

Once you've set the channel on the WR-R10/WR-R11a, press the MENU button on the SB-5000 (it's at lower left of the unit's back panel). Select CHANNEL and press the right button on the SB-5000's rotary multi selector to set the same channel as the WR-R10 or WR-R11a. Then press the OK button on the SB-5000's multi selector.

NOTE You *must* update the older WR-R10's firmware to Version 3.0 to use radio control with your SB-5000. The update cannot be done by the user; you'll have to mail in your unit to Nikon's repair service in your country, as I did.

From the SB-5000's menu, select Link Mode and choose either Pairing or PIN, to match the setting you specified in the camera's Setup menu. Press the SB-5000's OK button to confirm. You can select PAIR > EXECUTE and press the SB-5000's OK button to commence pairing. Once the SB-5000 and WR-R10/WR-R11a have been paired, you won't have to do it again. However, you can pair with a second WR-R10/WR-R11a if you have multiple cameras or multiple WR-R10/WR-R11a controllers.

Concurrent use of optical control and radio control is tricky. You must use a Speedlight *other* than the SB-5000 (such as the SB-910) as an optical master flash mounted in the hot shoe and set to trigger optically controlled remote Speedlights in Groups A, B, C, and *also* have the WR-R10/WR-R11a attached to the camera so it can trigger additional radio-controlled SB-5000 flashes in Groups D, E, and F. It's unlikely that you'll have such a need (or even own the appropriate flash units). This mode could come in handy if you have a complex setup and need to control some flashes at a greater distance (which radio control provides, and optical control may not).

However, when using radio control, the distance between masters and remotes should be 98 feet (30 meters) or less. Up to 18 remote flash units can be used. Keep in mind that in radio control remote mode, the camera's normal Standby Timer is disabled, overriding any setting you've made in the camera. It's easy to run down your battery with extensive use, or if you forget to turn the flash or camera off.

Photo Shooting Menu

5

Your Nikon Z9/Z8 includes an array of convenient direct-access buttons (such as the ISO button on the top-right panel of the camera), several customizable Fn (function) buttons, and a user-configurable *i* (info) menu screen that appears when you press the *i* button. However, many adjustments and settings require a trip to the camera's extensive menu system, which has dozens of individual top-level entries and many additional options tucked away in sub-menus. But under that thicket of choices is the kind of versatility that makes your camera one of the most-tweakable, and fine-tunable cameras ever offered. If your camera doesn't behave in exactly the way you'd like, chances are you can make a small change in the menus that will tailor it to your exact needs.

However, just telling you what your options are and what they do doesn't really give you the information you need to use your camera to its fullest. What you really want to know is *why* you would want to choose a particular option, and *how* making a particular change will help improve your photographs in a given situation. That's a big job, and I'm going to devote a large portion of this book to demystifying the menu choices for you.

I'm not going to waste a lot of space on some of the more obvious menu choices in these chapters. For example, you can probably figure out what the Format Card entry in the Setup menu does, and it has only a few options: specifying which memory card slot to use and whether you want a full or quick format. In this chapter, I'll devote no more than a paragraph or two to the blatantly obvious settings and concentrate on the more confusing aspects of the camera setup. If you need a refresher on menu navigation, you'll find it in Chapter 1. You'll find a description of Pixel Shift shooting in the Firmware Update section beginning on Page 429.

DIFFERENT STROKES

You'll find that the menu systems of the Z9 and Z8 are identical—until they aren't. When this book was written, the Nikon Z9 had a few features that the Nikon Z8 lacked. At the same time, the Z8, as the newer of the two models, had a few features not (yet) included in the Z9. It's very likely that future firmware updates will align the menu systems of the two cameras even more closely, but in putting this book together I had to stick with what I had to work with.

As a result, in this chapter and others covering menu entries in detail, you'll find some labeled (Z9 only) or (Z8 only). In other cases, the entry *names* are slightly different even when the options are identical. So keep in mind that it's likely some of the "Z9/Z8 only" labels may not apply to your camera if you're running firmware updates that weren't available to me.

Photo Shooting Menu Options

The Photo Shooting menu entries and a few options differ slightly between the Z9 and Z8. I've listed them below, noting which ones appear *only* in the Z8. **Reminder:** As I noted earlier in this chapter, future firmware updates may align the entries more closely. This section explains the options of the Photo Shooting menu and how to use them. You might make such adjustments as you begin a shooting session, or when you move from one type of subject to another.

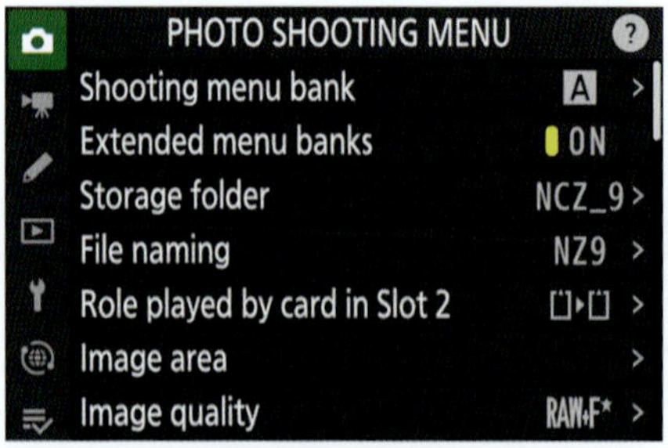

Figure 5.1 Common shooting settings can be changed in the Photo Shooting menu.

Nikon makes accessing these changes very easy.

- Shooting Menu Bank
- Extended Menu Banks
- Storage Folder
- File Naming
- Primary Slot Selection (Z8 Only)
- Role Played by Card in Slot 2 (Z9 Only)/Secondary Slot Function (Z8 Only)
- Image Area
- Tone Mode (Z8 Only)
- Image Quality
- Image Size Settings
- RAW Recording
- ISO Sensitivity Settings
- White Balance
- Set Picture Control
- Manage Picture Control
- Set Picture Control (HLG) (Z8 Only)
- Color Space
- Active D-Lighting
- Long Exposure NR
- High ISO NR
- Vignette Control
- Diffraction Compensation
- Auto Distortion Control
- Skin Softening
- Portrait Impression Balance
- Photo Flicker Reduction
- High Frequency Flicker Reduction
- Metering
- Flash Control
- Flash Mode (Z8 Only)
- Flash Compensation (Z8 Only)
- Focus Mode
- AF-Area Mode
- AF Subject Detection Options
- Vibration Reduction
- Auto Bracketing
- Multiple Exposure
- HDR Overlay
- Interval Timer Shooting
- Time-lapse Video
- Focus Shift Shooting
- Auto Capture
- Pixel Shift Shooting

Shooting Menu Bank

Options: Banks: A, B, C, D; Rename; Copy

My preference: N/A

The Nikon Z9/Z8's Shooting menu banks are four groups named, initially, A, B, C, and D that store specific collections of Photo Shooting menu settings that you can recall at any time by switching to the bank containing the preferences you want to use. These banks are one of the primary reasons why your camera is more versatile than Nikon's entry-level dSLRs, which lack the ability to change shooting specifications *en masse* using a simple menu command. The Shooting menu banks A, B, C, and D should not be confused with the four similarly named Custom settings banks A, B, C, and D, which provide similar, but *separate* storage of your Custom Settings. You can use your Shooting menu banks and Custom settings banks in any combination. That is, you can be using Shooting menu bank A, and Custom settings bank C at the same time.

In addition to the standard menu banks, the Z9/Z8 has the ability to store additional information in what Nikon calls Extended menu banks. They aren't really different banks; when you activate extended banks, the A, B, C, and D banks simply include additional settings information in those banks, as I'll explain in the section that follows this one.

The camera uses bank A by default. The very fastest way to switch among menu banks is to use the default behavior of the Fn1 button. Press and hold the button and rotate the main command dial to cycle among the four banks. To switch to another bank using this menu entry:

- **Navigate to the Photo Shooting menu.** Press MENU and select the Photo Shooting menu.
- **Choose the menu bank option.** Scroll to Shooting Menu Bank and press the multi selector right button.
- **Select the bank to activate.** Scroll to the bank you want to use with the multi selector up/down buttons, and either press OK to confirm your choice or press the multi selector right button to rename or copy the menu bank.
- **Exit menus.** The Photo Shooting menu appears again. Press the MENU button to back out of the menu, or simply tap the shutter release.

Any changes you make to one menu bank do not affect the other banks, except for the following: changes made to Interval Timer Shooting, Multiple Exposure, Time-Lapse Video, Focus Shift Shooting, White Balance Presets, and Extended Menu Banks settings carry across *all* four menu banks. All other Photo Shooting menu changes you make are confined *only* to the bank that is active when you make those adjustments. For example, if you change Image Quality to RAW in bank A, then the Image Quality setting in bank B will not be modified.

Because the settings for each bank are more or less independent of the others, you can set each one up with the settings you like to use in particular situations. For example, you could use bank A for sports, bank B for landscapes, bank C for portraits, and bank D for general shooting. Or, if you're a specialist, one bank could be dedicated to indoor sports (with high ISO settings and tungsten or fluorescent light balance) and another for outdoor sports (normal ISO and daylight white balance), with both specifying JPEG FINE capture only, because RAW or RAW+JPEG can slow down continuous shooting. You could even tailor a camera's operation using parameters other than typical shooting sessions. For example, a wedding photography studio that shares a pool of Nikon Z9/Z8 cameras among several photographers could have one bank named Peter, another named Paul, and a third dedicated to shooter Mary. The currently selected bank is indicated in the monochrome control panel, and in the shooting information display.

TWO FOR ONE

You may have noticed that the Video Recording menu (described in Chapter 6), also boasts a set of four Shooting menu banks. *They are the same banks!* Any changes you make to one, including resets, renaming, or copying, is transferred to the other. The only reason for having the Shooting Menu Bank entry appear in both is to allow you to make adjustments within either, presumably because you may already be specifying other options in the Photo Shooting or Video Recording menus.

Managing Menu Banks

You can create a customized name of up to 20 characters to replace the generic A, B, C, and D designations, and, if you like, copy the settings you've made for one bank to another. The latter capability can come in handy when the alternate bank will share many of the same settings; you'll only need to make changes accounting for the differences in the destination bank.

To manage your menu banks, highlight the bank you want to manage in the Shooting Menu Bank screen, and the screen shown at left in Figure 5.2 appears. Highlight Rename to produce the Z9/Z8 text-entry screen (seen at right in the figure), or choose Copy to duplicate that bank's settings in a different bank. Press the right directional button to proceed.

Use the standard Nikon text-entry screen to specify the name you want to use. Now is a good time to master text entry, because you can use it to enter comments, rename folders, and perform other functions. The Nikon Z9/Z8 uses a fairly standardized text-entry screen to name files, Picture Controls, create new folder names, enter image comments, and other text. You'll be using text entry with other functions that I'll describe later in this book. The screen looks like the one shown at left in Figure 5.2, with some variations (for example, some functions have a less diverse character set, or offer more or fewer spaces for your entries).

Once the text-entry screen appears, you can use the touch screen (highly recommended) to name a menu bank, or just use the navigational controls (such as the multi selector keys or sub-selector joystick) to scroll around within the array of alphanumerics. Then, enter your text:

- **Highlight a character.** Use the touch screen or navigational controls to move within the array of characters. The box in the lower-right corner of the bottom row can be selected to change the "keyboard" from all caps to lowercase or special characters.
- **Insert highlighted character.** Tap the screen or press OK to insert the highlighted character. The cursor will move one place to the right to accept the next character.
- **Non-destructively backspace.** Either command dial can be used to move the cursor left or right. This allows you to backspace and replace a character without disturbing the others you've entered.
- **Erase a highlighted character.** To remove a character you've already input, move the cursor to highlight that character, and then press the Trash button.
- **Confirm your entry.** When you're finished entering text, press the Zoom In button to confirm your entry, then press the left button twice to return to the Photo Shooting menu, or just tap the shutter release to exit the menu system entirely.

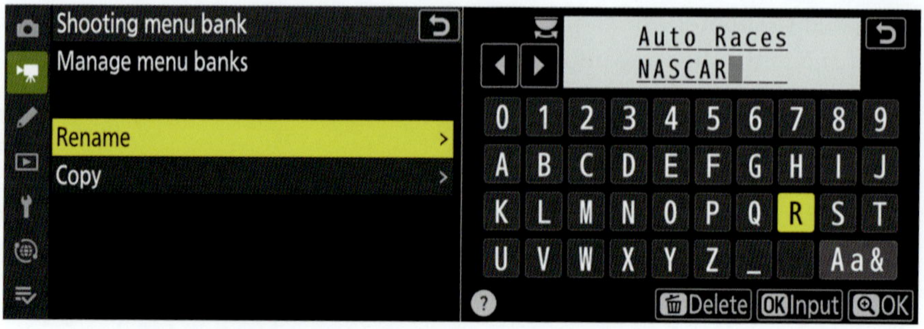

Figure 5.2 Choose Rename or Copy (left); enter text here (right).

As you work with menu banks, keep in mind that while changes you make to a particular bank don't affect the other banks, they are "sticky" within that bank once you've made them. That is, if you've set up a "sports" menu bank to use a high ISO sensitivity setting, and then during a session change the value to ISO 200, that's what you'll get the next time you access that menu bank (unless you remember to change it back to your preferred value at the end of the session). So, at best, your customized banks are preset for you *only* to the extent that you don't change those settings while you use them.

Resetting Your Camera

If you want to return settings to their factory defaults, you can do that. In fact, your Nikon Z9 and Z8 give you *four* different ways to reset parameters. Restoring the A, B, C, and D banks in the Photo Shooting and Video Recording menus to their defaults is just one of them. While this chapter deals primarily with the Photo Shooting menus, it's appropriate to discuss all your reset options here. They include:

- **Shooting menu reset.** Simply highlight the menu bank you want to reset, as described earlier, and press/tap the Trash button to reset the current bank, and *only that bank*. You must reset each bank *individually*, and the reset applies to *both* entries in the Shooting menu banks as well as their counterparts in the linked Video Recording menu (which is the subject of Chapter 6).

  Use this option to reset the values of the currently selected Shooting menu bank to their default values (with a few exceptions noted below). When you press the Trash button in the Shooting menu bank screen, your choices are Yes and No.

  Exception 1: The Shooting menu reset affects the active bank's settings *except for Storage Folder and Manage Picture Control parameters*, which remain at their current values. **Exception 2:** Some settings cannot be assigned to an individual bank; once set, they are the same regardless of whether you are using Bank A, B, C, or D. These nonblank-specific entries include Preset manual white balance settings (D–1 to D–6), Extended menu banks status (on or off), along with multiple exposure, time-lapse video, focus shift shooting, and interval timer shooting settings. A Shooting menu reset has no effect on the settings noted above.
- **Custom Settings menu reset.** This option, which I'll describe in Chapter 7, is used to reset any of the four Custom settings banks. It has no effect on other camera settings or Shooting menu banks.
- **Setup menu reset.** This option restores the factory default values of nearly every setting in the camera, and should be used with caution. The only exceptions are the Language and Time Zone and Date entries of the Setup menu. I use this reset most often when experimenting with various settings and discover I've hopelessly misconfigured my camera, or can't figure out what setting is interfering with another menu entry.

  If you perform this reset, you'll find that some of your most important tweaks have been erased. For example, Image Quality is set to JPEG Normal and RAW Recording to High Efficiency*, neither of which are likely to be your own personal preference. In Chapter 9, I'll show you how to Save/Load settings to quickly restore your favorite settings.

The official Nikon Z9 and Z8 manuals have nearly three dozen pages detailing all the factory-set values of the menu items that are reset using this option. I won't squander valuable space duplicating tables you may not need and can easily access from the official Nikon reference guides. Instead, I'll specify the defaults in this and the other chapters where they are most useful: in the descriptions of individual menu entries. If you need to view the actual defaults for the Photo Shooting menu en masse, you can find them in the Nikon Z9 and Z8 manuals.

- **Two-button reset.** The Nikon Z9/Z8's two-button reset is activated by holding down the EV (exposure compensation) button on the right shoulder of the camera and the BKT button on the left shoulder for about two seconds. (The two are marked with a green dot.) This will *not* reset your Custom settings banks, and it will not reset all your Shooting menu banks; only the settings listed in Tables 5.1 to 5.4 in the current bank will be set to their defaults. The two-button reset is a quick way of returning the parameters shown in each table to their factory settings.

Extended Menu Banks

Options: On, Off (default)

My preference: N/A

The Nikon Z9/Z8 has the ability to include several additional parameters—shooting mode, flash mode, shutter speed, and aperture—to the values stored in a particular menu bank listed in the Photo Shooting or Video Recording menus. So, if you have a Sports mode especially for action photography and always begin a sports session using Shutter-priority and a shutter speed of 1/1000th second, you can include that information in each of your Shooting menu banks. Or, perhaps you have a bank set up for portraits, and you like to use Aperture-priority with an f/stop of f/5.6 to reduce depth-of-field. The Extended menu banks can keep that information on file, too.

When would you *not* want to use Extended menu banks? You'd probably want to switch this feature off if you change exposure modes frequently and don't care (or don't want) a particular shutter speed or aperture to be preset for you when you change to a particular menu bank. (Keep in mind that, once a bank has been loaded, you can always change to a different mode or setting, and that your new setting will become the default for that bank when you reload it in the future.)

With Extended menu banks set to Off (the default), the camera will not store shooting mode, f/stop, or shutter speed in a menu bank. If you select On, then exposure mode *will* be stored. If the exposure mode that is stored is Shutter-priority or Manual, then the shutter speed will be remembered as well. If the exposure mode is Aperture-priority or Manual, the aperture will be remembered. If you turn Extended menu banks off again, the settings that were in effect before On was selected are restored.

TABLE 5.1 Two-button Reset Defaults—Photo Shooting Menu

OPTION	DEFAULT
ISO Sensitivity Settings	
ISO Sensitivity	100
Auto ISO Sensitivity Control	On
Maximum Sensitivities	25600
Maximum Sensitivity with Flash	Same as without flash
Minimum Shutter Speed	Auto
White Balance	Auto > Keep white
Fine-tune	A-B:0, G-M:0
Set Picture Control	Auto
Active D-Lighting	Off
Photo Flicker Reduction	Off
Metering	Matrix metering
Focus Mode	Single AF
Auto Bracketing	Off
Multiple Exposure	Off
HDR Overlay	Off

TABLE 5.2 Two-button Reset Defaults—Video Recording Menu

OPTION	DEFAULT
ISO Sensitivity Settings	
Maximum Sensitivity	25600
Auto ISO Sensitivity Control	On
ISO Sensitivity	100
White Balance	Same as Photo Shooting menu settings
Set Picture Control	Same as Photo Shooting menu settings
HLG Quality	
Quick Sharp	0
Contrast	0
Saturation	0
Hue	0
Active D-Lighting	Off
Metering	Matrix metering
Focus Mode	Full-time AF
AF-area Mode	Single-point AF
Electronic VR	Off

TABLE 5.3 Two-button Reset Defaults—Custom Settings Menu

OPTION	DEFAULT
a9 Focus Mode Restrictions	No restrictions
d10/d9 View Mode (Photo Lv) (Z9/Z8)	Show effects of settings
d11/d10 Starlight View (Photo Lv) (Z9/Z8)	Off
d12/d11 Warm Display Colors (Z9/Z8)	Off
e2 Flash Shutter Speed	1/60th second
f4 Control Lock	
Shutter Speed Lock	Off
Aperture Lock	Off
Focus-point Lock	Off
g3 Control Lock	
Shutter Speed Lock	Off
Aperture Lock	Off
Focus-point Lock	Off
g5 Focus Mode Restrictions	No restrictions

TABLE 5.4 Two-button Reset Defaults—Other Settings

OPTION	DEFAULT
Focus Point	Center
Preset Focus Point	Center
Shooting Mode	P
Flexible Program	Off
Exposure Compensation	Off (0.0)
AE Lock (Hold)	Off
Flash Mode	Fill Flash
Flash Compensation	Off (0.0)
FV Lock	Off

Storage Folder

Options: Rename: NCZ_9/NCZ_8 (default); Select Folder by Number: 100 (default); Select Folder from List

My preference: I use the Select Folder by Number option frequently to organize images by topic or time frame.

If you want to store images in a folder other than the one most recently created and selected by the camera, you can switch among available folders on your memory card or create your own folder. Remember that any folders you create will be deleted when you reformat your memory card.

Storage folders are always created within the top-level DCIM (Digital Camera Images) folder on your memory card. If you happen to use the same memory card in more than one camera, even if it is from a manufacturer other than Nikon, the other camera's image folders will reside amicably in the same DCIM folder. The "foreign" folders will use their own nomenclature; if you spot one named 100MSDCF, for example, it might have been created there by, say, a Sony camera. You generally won't need to access or use any other top-level folders, such as NIKON (which stores saved user settings, Picture Controls, and IPTC [International Press Telecommunications Council] information). The MISC folder and a top-level file with a name like NIKON001.DSC are used for housekeeping and not typically accessed.

Why create your own folders? Perhaps you're traveling and have a high-capacity memory card and want to store the images for each day (or for each city that you visit) in a separate folder. Maybe you'd like to separate those wedding photos you snapped at the ceremony from those taken at the reception. As I mentioned earlier, the camera automatically creates a folder on a newly formatted memory card with a name like 100NCZ_9, and when it fills with 5,000 images (an increase from the limitation of 999 images in most previous Nikon cameras) or a picture numbered 9999, it will automatically create a new folder with a number incremented by one (such as 101NCZ_9).

Folders are always identified using a three-digit number, followed by a five-character folder name. Although the default characters are NCZ_9 or NCZ_8, you can specify a name of your choice. To create your own folder or select an existing folder:

1. **Access active folder entry.** Choose Storage Folder in the Photo Shooting menu and press the right multi selector button.
2. **Choose function.** Three options are listed: Rename, Select Folder by Number, and Select Folder from List.
    - **Rename.** Highlight and select Rename and you'll be taken to a screen similar to the one shown at right in Figure 5.2, but with only five spaces to enter information for the naming scheme. Only numbers from 0 to 9, uppercase alpha characters, and an underline can be selected. Note that you can only change the name of your folder scheme—existing folders cannot be renamed. I like to name my folders using the scheme "NIKZ9" or "NIKZ8." It does not provide any *extra* information beyond that of the default NCZ_9/NCZ_8," but switching from the default value does make it very easy to differentiate between photos taken with *my* camera, and those taken by another camera (most likely another photographer). Sometimes image files from several photographers are submitted to the same destination, and I want to be able

to tell mine from those captured by everybody else who happens to own a Z9 or Z8. See the section, "Entering Text" for a primer on using the on-screen keyboard.

- **Select Folder by Number.** If you've chosen this option, a screen appears with three digits representing the possible folder numbers from 100 to 999. Use the left/right multi selector buttons to move between the digits, and the up/down buttons to increase or decrease the value of the digit. If a folder already exists with the number you dial in, an icon appears showing the folder is empty, partially full, or it has 5,000 images or a picture numbered 9999 (and can contain no more images).

  Press OK to create the new folder and make it the active folder. You'd want to use this option to create a new folder *or* when you don't know whether a folder by a particular number already exists. If a folder with that number already resides on the memory card, you can use it (if it is not full); if it doesn't exist, you can create it.
- **Select Folder from List.** From among the available folders shown, scroll to the one that you want to become active for image storage and playback. I sometimes do this to "sort" my images in the camera when traveling. I could enable a particular folder when I am taking photos of landscapes, and switch to a different folder when shooting urban scenes. This feature is handy when you want to display a slide show located in a particular folder. Use this option if you know that the folder you want to use already resides on the memory card. Press OK to confirm your choice and make the folder active.

3. **Exit menus.** Press the MENU button or tap the shutter release to exit.

Entering Text

As mentioned, our camera offers several opportunities to enter text, so you can change folder names, insert your name as "Artist," or provide copyright information. The camera uses a fairly standardized text-entry screen to name files, rename Picture Controls, create new folder names, and enter image comments and other text. You'll be using text entry with other functions that I'll describe later in this book. The screen looks like the one shown earlier in Figure 5.2, right, with some variations (for example, some functions have a less diverse character set, or offer more or fewer spaces for your entries). To enter text, just use the touch screen to "type" your characters or, alternatively, use the multi selector navigational buttons to scroll around within the array of alphanumerics. (I invariably use the touch screen for this, unless I am outdoors, wearing gloves, and really, really need to enter text.)

- **Highlight a character.** Use the touch screen or multi selector keys to scroll around within the array of characters.
- **Insert highlighted character.** Tap the character or press the multi selector OK button to insert the highlighted character. The cursor will move one place to the right to accept the next character.
- **Non-destructively move forward/backspace.** Use the main command dial to move the cursor within the line of characters you've entered. This allows you to skip ahead or backspace and replace a character without disturbing the others you've entered. Although it's a bit more difficult for the ham-handed, you can also tap the left/right triangles on the screen located to the immediate left of the text-entry area to move the cursor.

- **Erase a highlighted character.** To remove a character you've already input, move the cursor to highlight that character, and then press the Trash button or tap the trash can icon at the bottom of the screen.
- **Confirm your entry.** When you're finished entering text, press the Zoom In button to confirm your entry, then press the MENU button to return to the Photo Shooting menu, or press the MENU button a second time (or just tap the shutter release) to exit the menu system entirely.

File Naming

Options: Choose three-letter prefix, DSC (default)

My preference: NZ8, NZ9

The camera automatically applies a name like _DSC0001.jpg or DSC_0001.nef to your image files as they are created. You can use this menu option to change the names applied to your photos, but only within certain strict limitations. In practice, you can change only three of the eight characters, the *DSC* portion of the filename. The other five are mandated either by the Design Rule for Camera File System (DCF) specification that all digital camera makers adhere to or to industry conventions.

DCF limits filenames created by conforming digital cameras to a maximum of eight characters, plus a three-character extension (such as .jpg, .nef, or .wav in the case of audio files) that represents the format of the file. The eight-plus-three (usually called 8.3) length limitation dates back to an evil and frustrating computer operating system that we older photographers would like to forget (its initials are D.O.S.), but which, unhappily, lives on as the wraith of a file-naming convention.

Of the eight available characters, four are used to represent, in a general sense, the type of camera used to create the image. By convention, one of those characters is an underline, placed in the first position (as in _DSCxxxx.xxx) when the image uses the Adobe RGB color space (more on color spaces later), and in the fourth position (as in DSC_xxxx.xxx) for sRGB and RAW (NEF) files. That leaves just three characters for the manufacturer (and you) to use. Nikon, Sony, and some other vendors use DSC (which may or may not stand for Digital Still Camera, depending on who you ask), while Canon prefers IMG. The remaining four characters are used for numbers from 0000 to 9999, which is why your camera "rolls over" to DSC_0000 again when the 9999-number limitation is reached.

When you select File Naming in the Photo Shooting menu, you'll be shown the current settings for both sRGB and Adobe RGB. Press the right multi selector button, and you'll be taken to the (mostly) standard Nikon text-entry screen described above and allowed to change the DSC value to something else. In this version of the text-entry screen, however, only the numbers from 0 to 9 and characters A to Z are available; the filename cannot contain other characters. As always, press the Zoom In button to confirm your new setting.

Because the default DSC characters don't tell you much, don't hesitate to change them to something else. I use NZ9 or NZ8. However, if you don't need or want to differentiate between different camera models, you can change the three characters to anything else that suits your purposes, including your initials (DDB_ or JFK_, for example), or even customize for particular shooting sessions (EUR_, GER_, FRA_, and JAP_ when taking vacation trips). You can also use the filename flexibility to partially overcome the 9999-numbering limitation. You could, for example, use the template Z91_ to represent the first 10,000 pictures you take with a Z9 camera, and then Z92_ for the next 10,000, and Z93_ for the 10,000 after that.

That's assuming you don't rename your image files in your computer. In a way, filenaming verges on a moot consideration, because they apply *only* to the images as they exist in your camera. After (or during) transfer to your computer, you can change the names to anything you want, completely disregarding the 8.3 limitations (although it's a good idea to retain the default extensions). If you shot an image file named DSC_4832.jpg in your camera, you could change it to Paris_EiffelTower_32.jpg later. Indeed, virtually all photo-transfer programs allow you to specify a template and rename your photos as they are moved or copied to your computer from your camera or memory card.

I usually don't go to that bother (I generally don't use transfer software; I just drag and drop images from my memory card to folders I have set up) but renaming can be useful for those willing to take the time to do it.

Primary Slot Selection (Z8 Only)

Options: CFexpress/XQD card slot (default), SD card slot

My preference: CFexpress/XQD card slot

This Z8-only menu entry allows you to choose one of the two card slots as the location of your preferred memory card. In most cases, you'll want to specify the slot containing your fastest and/or largest memory card. That will generally be the CFexpress/XQD slot; if you are using a CFe card, it will almost always be faster than any SD card you own. However, if you happen to own many SD cards, particularly fast cards with 64GB or 128GB (or more) capacity, you may prefer to use those cards as your primary media until you acquire CFexpress cards. I stopped purchasing XQD cards entirely when the Z9 and Z8 were introduced, as the faster CFexpress media are now about the same price, and much more future-proof. My existing XQD cards are relegated to the Nikon D4s I still use in my studio.

Role Played by Card in Slot 2 (Z9)/Secondary Slot Function (Z8)

Options: Overflow (default), Backup, RAW Primary—JPEG Secondary

My preference: Overflow for everyday shooting; Backup when traveling

Although the menu entry name differs between cameras, the functions are virtually identical. It allows you to specify the function of the second memory card slot, choosing to use the secondary slot to accept overflow images when the primary card fills up; create a backup of all the files stored on the primary card; or to split your RAW+JPEG files between primary and secondary slots. The Video Recording menu's Destination entry (discussed later in this chapter) offers a fourth option: you can select which slot is used to store your video clips (and can therefore choose the largest memory card or fastest memory card for your videos). Keep in mind that if you have only one card inserted, the camera will ignore the options you specify here. The Slot 2 (Z9) and Secondary Slot (Z8) functions are these:

Overflow

In this case, when the memory card in the primary slot fills up, the camera automatically switches over to the card in the secondary slot. The changeover happens quickly, and you're not even likely to notice, unless you have your eye on the "slot" indicators on the display, as the camera provides no notification of the switchover. There are many ways to use this capability:

- **"Limitless" capacity.** My standard operating procedure is to put one 128GB or 256GB memory card in each slot. As a practical matter, that means I can shoot all day (or, sometimes all week) without changing memory cards, even if I am shooting landscapes and bracketing everything (either to optimize exposure, or, when the camera is mounted on a tripod, to capture files for later HDR processing). Or, I might be shooting sports/photojournalism, where the common practice is to change memory cards when your media is 80 percent full to eliminate the possibility of missing anything important due to a card change at an inopportune time. To be honest, I have yet to encounter a shoot (or even a single *trip*) in which I have filled up two 128GB or larger cards in a single session. But if you're using smaller cards and doing a lot of shooting, this capability can be a lifesaver.
- **Small/fast—with backup.** For some sports, if you are shooting continuously, you may want your fastest memory card in the primary slot to maximize write speed out of the camera's buffer, but the real speed demons in the memory card world can be expensive. So, instead of an affordable 64GB medium-speed card, you may put a (per gigabyte) more expensive 64GB high-speed card in the primary slot, and back it up with a slower (and cheaper) 128GB card. You can capture images with the fastest card you've got, yet not have to worry about missing shots, because you have a backup card installed in the secondary slot.
- **Put smaller cards to use.** If you don't think you'll need the overflow capacity, but still want to have it just in case, put a smaller card that you don't use much anymore in the secondary slot. Z8 users may run into that situation with their collection of old 32GB (or even smaller!) SD cards. If your large card that you didn't think would fill *does* come up short, you won't lose any shots. They'll be directed to that old 32GB SD card you put in the secondary slot for insurance. I sometimes do this when I am using several cameras and have a limited number of large cards at my disposal. For example, I often shoot with both my Z9 and Z8 cameras in the same session. I'll save the biggest cards for primary use and use smaller CFe and SD cards in the secondary slot, knowing that any overflow shots will be stored on the small backup cards if necessary.
- **Stretch your budget.** After spending an arm and a leg for your Z8, you'd like to avoid replacing your old fast-but-limited-capacity 32GB SD memory cards for a little while. With one card in each slot (and your older SD card in the secondary slot), you can double your shooting before it's time to swap cards.

Backup

In this case, each photograph you take is recorded on the memory cards in both the primary and secondary slot. The write process takes slightly longer (so it may not be your best option when shooting sports), but it's otherwise a seamless way to create a backup copy of every image you take. If you're shooting RAW+JPEG, both files associated with each image are recorded on both slots. I absolutely love this feature.

Here are some of my favorite applications:

- **Critical shots backed up instantly.** When I was a photojournalist, a lot of the images I took, particularly of news events, were literally once-in-a-lifetime shots that couldn't be duplicated under any circumstances. I also shot weddings, and while it was sometimes possible to restage a particular setup or pose, that was never a satisfactory option, even if done on the day of the nuptials. So, there was always a degree of trepidation until the film was processed or digital files backed up. With dual-slot backup capabilities, backup files can be made instantly, as you shoot. What a relief!
- **Great when there's No-Fi.** Many pros (and more than a few amateurs) rely on in-camera Wi-Fi or Bluetooth connectivity to beam backups to a nearby laptop computer for safekeeping, or, at events, so that an assistant can process some images while photography continues. But, sometimes that's not possible, or, perhaps, you don't own the necessary equipment. Making a backup in your camera is a great alternative when wireless capabilities are unavailable or impractical. You can even shuttle the secondary slot card to an assistant at intervals while retaining the "main" copy of your images in the camera.
- **Leave your personal storage device or computer at home.** When I travel overseas, I like to pack light, with only a carry-on bag that holds my shooting gear and some of my clothing, with the rest of my apparel relegated to the second tote that qualifies as a "personal" item. But I've always carried a laptop so I can make backup copies of my images while I travel. I've found that my dual-card Nikon cameras can easily replace the external backup options if I want to travel *extra* light on shorter trips. I can back up each image as it's shot automatically or shoot on one card (to allow faster capture) and make a duplicate with a card-to-card copy back in my hotel room in the evening. Or I can use the Copy Image(s) feature to make an extra copy of only the images I want. On a recent cross-country trip along the old Route 66, I had a 1TB CFe card ensconced in Slot 2, and copied each day's shooting before turning in for the night.
- **Instant copy to share.** Want to give a traveling companion copies of all the images you shoot? Create a backup as you take the photos and hand over the copy on the spot. (Again, if you want to share only *some* of your pictures, you can use the Copy Image(s) feature instead.) If you're using a Z8, this procedure can make good use of a large collection of old, cheap SD cards.
- **Segregate your images.** I've managed to accumulate a collection of 16GB and 32GB memory cards that I use in my Z8. I sometimes put these to work in travel photography applications on long trips. Each day I put one of these old SD cards in my Z8, specify Backup mode, and shoot the images for that day. The next day, I insert a different SD card for backup. I've got copies of each day's shots and have segregated them onto separate memory cards for simple day-by-day organization.

RAW Primary—JPEG Secondary (Z8)/RAW Slot 1—JPEG Slot 2 (Z9)

In this mode, if you've used the Image Quality setting (discussed shortly) to specify RAW+JPEG, the RAW files are saved to the card in the primary slot, and the JPEG files are saved to the card in the secondary slot. If you've selected RAW or JPEG only (rather than both), the images are stored in the primary slot, until that card fills; then the photos overflow to the secondary slot. (This is effectively the same as the Backup option.)

You'll find this mode useful under the following conditions:

HEIF NOTE

At the time this was written, the Z8 (only) had a Tone entry in the Photo Shooting menu that allowed substituting the HEIF (High Efficiency Image File) format for JPEG. I'll explain the Tone entry and HEIF in more detail later in this chapter, but confine most descriptions to JPEG, which will be used almost exclusively by the vast majority of readers of this book.

- **Separate RAW and JPEG.** Perhaps you like to store your RAW and JPEG files in separate locations. This mode makes it easy to do that. Copy the card containing the RAW files to one destination on your computer, and the JPEG files from the other card to a second destination. The only complication is that the memory card in the primary slot is likely to fill up more quickly than the card with the smaller JPEG files in the secondary slot, so if you shoot to the capacity of the card in the primary slot, you'll need to replace it more often than you will the card with the JPEG files. Or, if you want the two cards to be mirror images of each other (but in different formats), you can swap them both out at the same time, with the secondary slot card only partially full. If you're short on memory cards, you could alternatively temporarily switch the Secondary/Slot 2 function to Overflow, and continue shooting with both RAW and JPEG images recorded on the same card until it, too, fills up.
- **Faster backup of RAW+JPEG.** If you shoot RAW+JPEG, using the Backup option means that you're saving *four* files each time you press the shutter release. That can slow you down in some situations if you're rapid-firing a sequence of images. Storing RAW files on one card and JPEG files on the other is a faster way of capturing a backup, because only two files are saved per click. If you have a problem with one of your JPEG files, you can easily produce a new JPEG from the RAW file. The reverse is not true, however. If your NEF file gets munged, your RAW information is lost forever, even though you still have the JPEG version. So, use this option carefully if your RAW files are especially important for a particular shooting session.

NOTE If you're using the Multiple Exposure or HDR Overlay options (described later in this chapter) and have selected Save Individual Pictures (RAW) for either, the camera will save RAW images even in a JPEG-only mode. The RAW files will be stored on both memory cards *in addition to* the combined JPEG multiple exposure or HDR version.

JPEG Primary—JPEG Secondary (Z8)/JPEG Slot 1—JPEG Slot 2 (Z9)

This is an interesting option that allows you to save *two* JPEG versions. The one stored in the primary slot will have the compression and size characteristics you specify in the Image Quality and Image Size entries, while an additional version will be saved in the other slot using space-saving Basic compression and an image size you specify here.

In other words, you can specify a "main" image stored in the primary slot in JPEG Fine, Normal, or Basic (or their extra-quality variations marked with an asterisk) in Large, Medium, or Small sizes. Then, you can choose to save a second copy of the JPEG in Large, Medium, or Small size, but using *only* Basic compression. This entry operates only when using JPEG-only mode. If you're shooting in RAW (only) or RAW+JPEG the camera defaults to Backup mode, as described above.

This capability might come in handy if you wanted to capture a reduced-size or lower-resolution version, say to transfer to your smartphone or tablet for posting on social media or for emails.

Image Area

Options: Image Area: FX (36 × 24) (default); DX (24 × 16); 1:1 (24 × 24); 16:9 (36 × 20); DX Crop Alert: On, Off

My preference: FX (36 × 24), On

Using Image Area, you can manually specify the image area to be used, which the camera will apply regardless of what type of lens is mounted. Use this option to force the image area issue (as when you're using a DX-format lens that the camera can't detect automatically), or to use a particular image area for all your shots in a session. Your choices include:

- **FX (36 × 24).** This is the full FX image-format area, roughly 36mm × 24mm, producing a 24MP image when Large is selected using the Image Size Settings entry described shortly.
- **DX (24 × 16).** This fills the image frame with the image in the center 24mm × 16mm of the sensor, creating a 1.5X *crop factor.* Your final image will be about 19.5MP in Large size.
- **1:1 (24 × 24).** An image cropped to a square may be useful to emphasize a centered image, such as a close-up of a flower, when you want to direct the eye to the middle of the frame, rather than have it roam around within your image. The resulting 30MP photo still has outstanding resolution even though you're discarding pixels at left and right of the frame.
- **16:9 (36 × 20).** This is a useful cropping that allows you to take still photos using the same 16:9 proportions as a high-definition video frame. I like this crop when I'm producing storyboards for video productions, as my still image compositions will match the aspect ratio of the videos.

If you activate DX Crop Alert, a DX icon will flash in the upper-right corner of the display. I always enable this warning. Unlike dSLR cameras, which maintain the same image in the optical viewfinder with crop mark overlays, your Z8 or Z9 enlarges the cropped image to fill the display. It's easy to overlook the difference in the image area and capture a large number of images with a crop you really didn't intend to use. You may have specified the DX crop to get a little extra "reach" when shooting sports.

Tone Mode (Z8 Only)

Options: SDR, HLG

My preference: Use as needed

This entry allows you to depart from the familiar standard dynamic range (SDR) world to the tonal realm of hybrid log gamma (HLG). An additional Tone mode, Nikon-log (N-Log) can be chosen within the Video File Type entry of the Video Recording menu. Still photographers will be concerned primarily with the choice between SDR and HLG; if you specify SDR here, the camera will save its non-RAW images in JPEG format. Choose HLG instead, and HEIF images will be saved instead. You'll find more information about HEIF in the next section.

Image Quality

Options: RAW+JPEG/HEIF (Fine*, Fine, Normal*, Normal, Basic*, Basic), RAW, JPEG/HEIF (Fine*, Fine, Normal*, Normal [default], Basic*, Basic)

My preference: RAW+JPEG Fine* for everyday shooting; JPEG Fine* for sports

This setting allows you to choose to capture images in RAW format, in JPEG format, or both simultaneously. The entry also allows you to choose the amount of image compression applied to images. You can use this menu entry or opt for the quickest way by pressing the *i* button, selecting the Image Quality entry, and either rotating the command dial or pressing the OK button to select quality from a screen of choices.

HEIF OPTIONS

As this book was being written, the Z8 (only) also includes support for selecting the HEIF format as an alternative to JPEG, using the Tone Mode entry. I expect the Z9 to add that capability via a firmware update by the time this book reaches the shelves. However, as a practical matter for most users, HEIF differs from JPEG only in image quality relative to file size and the ability to create a type of extended dynamic range image. I'll explain HEIF in more detail shortly. However, I'm going to use JPEG as the default non-RAW image file format in most discussions throughout this book. If you are working with the Z8 (or with the Z9 when it gains support for HEIF), you can apply virtually all of my descriptions to HEIF files, too, as appropriate.

When selecting a file format, you can choose RAW only, RAW+ six different JPEG quality levels (Fine*, Fine, Normal*, Normal, Basic*, and Basic), or any of those six JPEG (or HEIF) quality levels alone (with no RAW captured). When you elect to store only JPEG/HEIF versions of the images you shoot, you can save memory card space as you bypass the larger RAW files. Or, you can save your photos as RAW files, which consume more than twice as much space on your memory card. Or, you can store both at once as you shoot.

Many photographers choose to save *both* JPEG and a RAW, so they'll have a JPEG version that might be usable as-is, as well as the original "digital negative" RAW file in case they want to do some processing of the image later. You'll end up with two different versions of the same file: one with a .jpg extension, and one with the .nef extension that signifies a Nikon RAW file.

To choose the combination you want using the menu system, access the Photo Shooting menu, scroll to Image Quality, and select it. Screens similar to the one shown in Figure 5.3 (left and right) will appear. Scroll to highlight the setting you want, and either press OK or push the multi selector right button to confirm your selection.

In practice, you'll probably use the JPEG Fine* and RAW+JPEG Fine* (with the "extra quality" star) selections most often. Why so many choices, then? There are some limited advantages to using some of the higher compression and lower resolution options. Settings that are less than max allow stretching the capacity of your memory card so you can shoehorn quite a few more pictures onto a single memory card. That can come in useful when on vacation and you're running out of storage, or when you're shooting non-critical work that doesn't require 45 megapixels of resolution (such as photos taken for real-estate listings, web page display, photo ID cards, or similar applications).

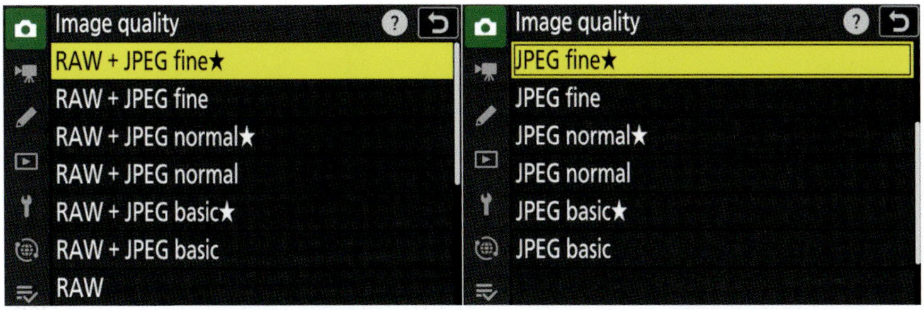

Figure 5.3 You can choose RAW, JPEG, or RAW+JPEG formats here. Nikon is adding the ability to substitute HEIF for JPEG.

Some photographers like to record RAW+JPEG Basic so they'll have a moderate-quality JPEG file for review only and no intention of using for editing purposes, while retaining access to the original full-resolution/uncompressed RAW file for serious editing.

For most work, using lower resolution and extra compression is false economy. You never know when you might need that extra bit of picture detail. Your best bet is to have enough memory cards to handle all the shooting you want to do until you have the chance to transfer your photos to your computer or a personal storage device.

Optimal Quality or Optimal Size?

Nikon has merged the JPEG-oriented "Optimal Quality" and "Optimum Size" options offered with previous cameras into the Image Quality entry. The difference:

- **Optimal Quality (marked with a star).** Choose this option if you want to maintain the best image quality possible at a particular JPEG setting and don't care if the file size varies. Because the camera will use only the minimum amount of compression required at each JPEG setting, file size will vary depending on scene content, and your buffer may hold fewer images during continuous shooting. If you're not shooting continuously, this setting will provide optimum image quality.

  At the Fine * setting, the camera will apply a 4:1 compression ratio; use 8:1 at the Normal * setting, and a rigorous 16:1 compression ratio at Basic *. Figure 5.4 shows a cropped portion of an image recorded with Optimal Quality (top) and one in which Size Priority was used to provide extra compression (bottom).

- **Size Priority (no star).** When this option is selected, the camera will create files that are fairly uniformly sized JPEG images. The camera will first compress the images according to the ratios I described above for Optimal Quality images. It will then apply whatever *additional* compression is required to reduce the size of the image file to the target size. Because some photos have content that is more easily compressible (for example, plain areas of sky can be squeezed down more than areas filled with detail), to maintain the standard file size more compression must be applied to some images, and less to others.

  As a result, there may be a barely noticeable loss of detail in the more heavily compressed images. The uniform file size also means that the camera's buffer will hold the maximum number of shots during continuous shooting, allowing you to shoot longer sequences without the need to pause and wait for some images to be written to the memory card. In practice, you may find you can shoot continuously until the memory card fills.

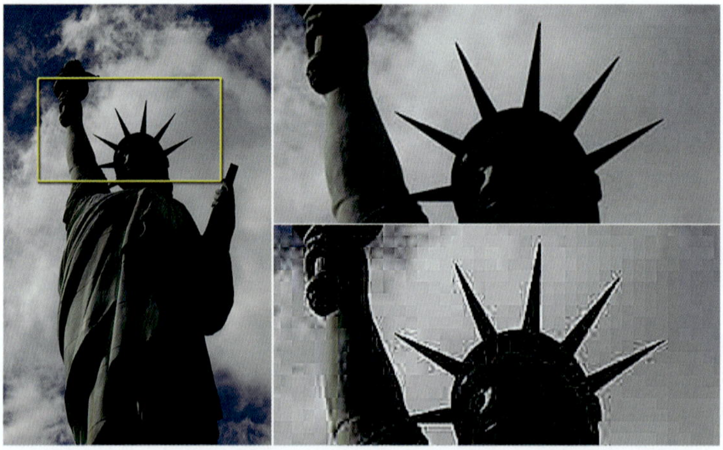

Figure 5.4 At low levels of JPEG compression, the image looks sharp even when you enlarge it enough to see the actual pixels (top); when using extreme JPEG compression (bottom), an image obviously loses quality.

HEIF vs. JPEG

The discussion above applies to both the Nikon Z9 and Z8 when you're using the RAW format alone, RAW+JPEG/HEIF, or JPEG or HEIF formats alone. As I mentioned earlier, if your camera supports the HEIF format, you can choose to capture images in that format instead of JPEG when working with virtually all commands that manipulate a JPEG image.

NOTE The Image Quality menu options appear to be the same in either case; the format (JPEG or HEIF) is enabled using a separate entry, Tone Mode, described earlier. When Tone Mode is set to SDR (Standard Dynamic Range), the JPG format will be used; if HLG (Hybrid Log Gamma) is selected instead, the still images will be saved in HEIF format, with a .HIF extension.

Unless you're using an iPhone and are deep into its features, you probably don't know much about the relatively recent HEIF format. Apple's iOS 11 operating system for its smart devices was the first consumer product to use the HEIF format. Canon was the first digital camera company to support it, with Sony following thereafter.

In a nutshell, HEIF images use an advanced compression scheme to produce files with higher image quality that may be only half the size of JPEGs, and have more features, including transparency and 16-bit color. The downside is that, as I write this, no browser supports it natively, and many software applications as well as operating systems like Windows 10 and Android need updates to accommodate HEIF. Macs need macOS High Sierra or later to interpret HEIF images. If you're using a recent iPhone with HEIF, it can convert your images to JPEG automatically when you export them but will use the format to deploy special features internally (say, for Live images). So, while HEIF may eventually replace JPEG (last updated in 1994) the transition will take many years.

JPEG DEFAULT

As I noted earlier, because HEIF is such a new format that has yet to build a solid following, I expect most of you will work with JPEGs for nearly all of your work when not using RAW. So, I will for the most part use JPEG as an example for many functions. You can assume that in nearly all cases HEIF can be substituted even if I don't use "JPEG/HEIF" terminology every time. If JPEG or HEIF *only* apply, I will point that out.

JPEG vs. RAW

You'll sometimes be told that RAW files are the "unprocessed" image information your camera produces before it's been modified. That's nonsense. RAW files are no more unprocessed than film is after it's been through the chemicals to produce a negative or transparency. A lot can happen in the developer that can affect the quality of a film image—positively and negatively—and, similarly, your digital image undergoes a significant amount of processing before it is saved as a RAW file. Nikon even applies a name (EXPEED 7) to the digital image processing (DIP) chips used to perform this magic.

A RAW file is more similar to a film camera's processed negative. It contains all the information obtained from the Z9 or Z8's photosites *after* it has been run through the camera's analog-to-digital converter algorithm, which makes several adjustments, including white balance and suppression of hot pixels in longer exposures. The data, captured in 14-bit channels per color (and stored in a 16-bit space), has no sharpening or application of any special filters or other settings you might have specified when you took the picture. Those settings are *stored* with the RAW file so they can be applied when the image is converted to a form compatible with your favorite image editor. However, using RAW conversion software such as Adobe Camera Raw or Nikon NX Studio, you can override those settings and apply settings of your own. You can select essentially the same changes there that you might have specified in your picture-taking options.

RAW exists because sometimes we want to have access to all the information captured by the camera before the camera's internal logic has processed it and converted the image to a standard file format like JPEG. Having that data available can provide slightly more resolution (especially if you're applying noise reduction to your JPEG images), and the ability to tweak things like white balance and exposure settings.

So, why don't we always use RAW? Some photographers avoid using Nikon's RAW NEF files on the misguided conviction that they don't want to spend time in post-processing, forgetting that, if the camera settings you would have used for JPEG are correct, each RAW image's default attributes will use those settings and the RAW image will not need much manipulation. Post-processing in such cases is *optional*, and overwhelmingly helpful when an image needs to be fine-tuned.

Although some photographers do save *only* in RAW format, it's more common (and frequently more convenient) to use RAW plus one of the JPEG options, or, if you're confident about your settings, just shoot JPEG and eschew RAW altogether. In some situations, working with a RAW file can slow you down a little. RAW images take longer to store on the memory card and must be converted from RAW to a format your image editor can handle, whether you elect to go with the default settings in force when the picture was taken or make minor adjustments to the settings you specified in the camera.

As a result, those who depend on speedy access to images or who shoot large numbers of photos at once may prefer JPEG over RAW. Wedding photographers, for example, might expose several thousand photos during a bridal affair and offer hundreds to clients as electronic proofs for inclusion in an album. Wedding shooters take the time to make sure that their in-camera settings are correct, minimizing the need to post-process photos after the event. Given that their JPEGs are so good, there is little need to get bogged down shooting RAW.

Sports photographers also avoid RAW files. I recently photographed an air show that was an all-day affair, and, to make sure I didn't miss any peak moments as the aircraft flyovers, military sky-divers, and other action unfolded, I set my camera at the maximum rate and fired away. I managed to shoot 7,200 photos in a single day. I certainly didn't have any plans to do post-processing on very many of those shots, so carefully exposed and precisely focused JPEG images were my file format of choice that day.

JPEG was invented as a more compact file format that can store most of the information in a digital image, but in a much smaller size. JPEG predates most digital SLRs and was initially used to squeeze down files for transmission over slow dial-up connections. Even if you were using an early dSLR with 1.3MP files for news photography, you didn't want to send them back to the office over the telephone line communications that were common before high-speed Internet links became dominant.

But, as I noted, JPEG provides smaller files by compressing the information in a way that loses some image data. JPEG remains a viable alternative because it offers several different quality levels. At the highest quality Fine level, you might not be able to tell the difference between the original RAW file and the JPEG version.

In my case, I shoot virtually everything at RAW+JPEG Fine*. Most of the time, I'm not concerned about filling up my memory cards as I usually have multiple 128GB and 256GB cards with me. I also use a MacBook Air with an external 4TB hard drive. When shooting sports, I'll shift to JPEG Fine (with no RAW file) to squeeze a little extra speed out of my camera's continuous shooting mode, and to reduce the need to wade through eight-photo bursts taken in RAW format.

HIDDEN JPEGS

You may not be aware that your RAW file contains an embedded JPEG file, hidden inside the JPEG Basic format. It's used to provide thumbnail previews of JPEG files, which is why you may notice an interesting phenomenon when loading a RAW image into a program like Adobe Lightroom. When the software first starts interpreting the RAW image, it may immediately display this hidden JPEG view which has, as you might expect, all the settings applied that you dialed into the camera. Then, as it finishes loading the RAW file, the application (Lightroom in particular) uses its own intelligence to fine-tune the image and display what it thinks is a decent version of the image, replacing the embedded JPEG. That's why you may see complaints that Lightroom or another program is behaving oddly: the initial embedded JPEG may look better than the final version, so it looks as if the application is degrading the image quality as the file loads. Of course, in all cases, once the RAW file is available, you can make your own changes to optimize it to your taste.

There is a second use for these hidden JPEG files. If you shoot RAW without creating JPEG files and later decide you want a JPEG version, there are dozens of utility programs that will extract the embedded JPEG and save it as a separate file. (Google "JPEG extractor" to locate a freeware program that will perform this step for your Mac, PC, or other computer.)

Image Size Settings

Options: JPEG: Large (default), Medium, Small; Enable DX Image Sizes: Off (default), On; Image Size (DX), Large (default)

My preference: Large

The next menu command in the Photo Shooting menu (see Figure 5.5), lets you select the resolution, or number of pixels captured in JPEG (Large, Medium, and Small) in full frame or any of the crop modes when using a single-frame release mode or continuous-shooting release mode of 20 frames per second or slower. This entry has one option that can be a bit confusing, so read the following clarification carefully:

- **Image Size.** By default, this entry allows you to specify the image size for *all* of the camera's image area modes. That is, when you specify Large, Medium, or Small here, that size is applied to FX (full frame), DX, 1:1, and 16:9 crops. This is the behavior we are all used to. The resolutions of each are shown in Table 5.5.
- **Enable DX Image Sizes.** On first glance, this seems like an entry that could be used to disable selecting the DX crop mode entirely. Not so! What it actually does is activate the ability to specify a *separate* image size when using DX mode, as described next.
- **Image Size (DX).** If, and *only if*, the option above is set to ON, you can choose to specify Large, Medium, or Small image sizes that will be applied *only* in DX mode. That size will override the setting you made above under Image Size that will continue to be used with FX, 1:1 and 16:9 sizes. This gives you the ability to mix and match image sizes and crops. You could, for example, automatically capture DX images in a space-saving Small format each time you selected the DX crop (or the camera switched to DX mode automatically when a mounted DX lens is detected), while using Large format with any other mode.

Select image sizes using this menu entry or by pressing the *i* button and accessing the Image Size Settings option. Rotate either command dial or press OK to select size from a screen.

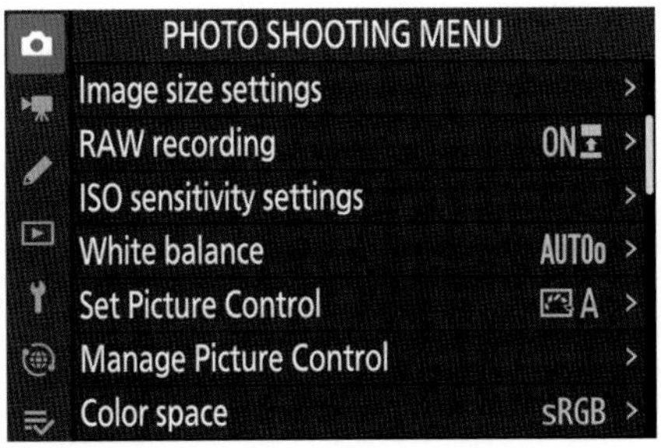

Figure 5.5 The next seven entries in the Photo Shooting menu.

TABLE 5.5 Image Size Settings Options

IMAGE AREA	SIZE	RESOLUTION	MEGAPIXELS
FX (36mm × 24mm)	Large	8256 × 5504	45.4MP
	Medium	6192 × 4128	25.6MP
	Small	4128 × 2752	11.4MP
DX (24mm × 16mm)	Large	5392 × 3592	19.4MP
	Medium	4032 × 2688	10.8MP
	Small	2688 × 1792	4.8MP
1:1 (24mm × 24mm)	Large	5504 × 5504	30.3MP
	Medium	4128 × 4128	17.0MP
	Small	2752 × 2752	7.6MP
16:9 (36mm × 20mm)	Large	8256 × 4640	38.3MP
	Medium	6192 × 3480	21.5MP
	Small	4128 × 2320	9.6MP

Image Size Restrictions

You may find this menu entry grayed out completely if you've set your camera to shoot continuously at 30, 60, or 120 frames per second:

- **30 fps (C15/C30).** All images are shot at Large Image Size, but you can choose either FX (36 × 24) or DX (24 × 16) Image Areas. JPEG Normal compression is used. Shutter speeds are limited to 1/32000–1/60th second.
- **60 fps (C60).** All images are shot at Large Image Size using the DX (24 × 16) crop, at JPEG Normal compression. Shutter speeds are limited to 1/32000–1/60th second.
- **120 fps (C120).** All images are captured at the reduced Small Image Size, using the FX (36 × 24) Image Area (unless a DX lens is attached, in which case the DX (24 × 16) Image Area is used). As with the other settings, JPEG Normal compression is applied. Shutter speeds are restricted to 1/32000 to 1/125th second.

RAW Recording

Options: Lossless Compression, High Efficiency*, High Efficiency

My preference: Lossless Compression

When you've selected any RAW setting for Image Quality, you can choose the type (amount) of compression applied to RAW files as they are stored on your memory card. The default values for type (Lossless compressed) works best for most situations, but there are times when you might want to use one of the other compression choices, High Efficiency and High Efficiency*, as I'll explain later in this section. (See Figure 5.6.)

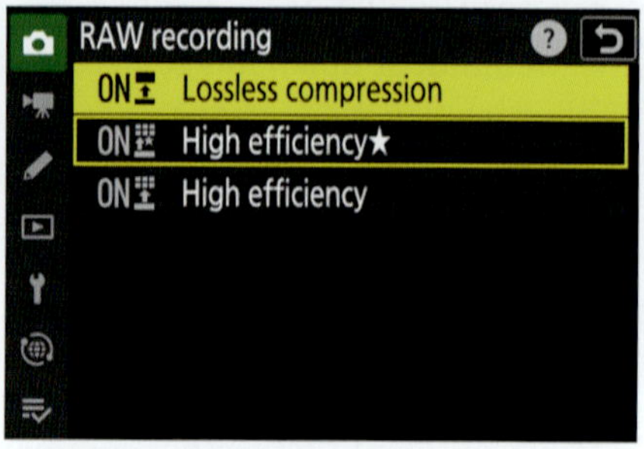

Figure 5.6 RAW recording options.

Compression is a mathematical technique for reducing the size of a collection of information (such as an image; but other types of data or even programs can be compressed, too) in order to reduce the storage requirements and/or time required to transmit or transfer the information. Some compression algorithms arrange strings of bits that are most frequently used into a table, so that a binary number like, say, 1001011011100111 (16 digits long) doesn't have to be stored as two 8-bit bytes every time it appears in the image file. Instead, a smaller number that points to that position in the table can be used. The more times the pointer is used rather than the full number, the more space is saved in the file. Such a compression scheme can be used to reproduce exactly the original string of numbers, and so is called *lossless* compression. Your camera's Lossless Compression setting uses a more advanced algorithm than what I've just described, but the effect is the same: an image file that has been made smaller without discarding any information.

Other types of compression are more aggressive and actually discard some of the information deemed to be redundant from a visual standpoint, so that, theoretically, you won't *notice* that details are missing, and the file can be made even more compact. Nikon calls them "visually" or "virtually" lossless. The RAW storage routines can use this kind of size reduction, which is called *lossy* compression, to reduce file size by up to about half with very little effect on image quality.

You can select from:

- **Lossless Compression.** This is the default setting and uses what you might think of as reversible algorithms that discard no image information, and provide significantly smaller RAW files. The size varies depending on the particular image, but will average around 55MB. That's still more than double the size of the typical 24MB Large JPEG Fine file. As I noted, the squeezed file can always be restored to its original size precisely, with no effect on image quality.
- **High Efficiency*.** Use this setting if you want to store more images on your memory card and are willing to accept a tiny potential loss in image quality in the highlights, after significant editing. The resulting RAW files can be 33 percent or more smaller than Lossless Compressed images, typically producing a 33MB file. The difference may show up only if you perform certain types of extensive post-processing on an image, such as heavy image sharpening or some types of tonal corrections.
- **High Efficiency.** This is the most highly compressed setting, producing files that are around 60 percent smaller than Lossless Compression: roughly 22MB—about the same as a Large JPEG Fine image. You may see a noise increase in shadows with underexposed images, and some color changes at higher ISO settings.

As a practical matter, you will probably want to use Lossless Compression nearly 100 percent of the time, resorting to either of the High Efficiency options only when you are shooting a lot of long continuous sequences and may exceed your camera's buffer capacity, or when you have only limited memory card storage available for some reason. (Shame on you!) The buffers of the Nikon Z9 and Z8 can store 79/81 frames at the Lossless Compression setting (respectively), which should be plenty for typical applications. But if you are shooting at very fast frame rates, the compression algorithms used for both High Efficiency settings are able to process images even more quickly, with room for 685/599 frames (Z9/Z8) at High Efficiency* and *more than* 1,000 frames with both cameras using the more-compressed High Efficiency option. Effectively, you can shoot until your memory card fills or your trigger finger wilts from fatigue.

ISO Sensitivity Settings

Options: ISO sensitivity: 64–25600, plus Lo 1.0 to Lo 0.3 and Hi 0.3 to Hi 2.0; Auto ISO Sensitivity Control: On, Off; Maximum Sensitivity: 100–25600, plus Hi 0.3 to Hi 2.0; Maximum Sensitivity with Flash: 100–25600, plus Same as Without Flash; Minimum Shutter Speed: Auto, 1/16000th–30 seconds

My preference: Varies by subject type

You can make direct ISO settings without resorting to this menu entry. Just press the ISO button, located just south of the shutter release, and then rotate the sub-command dial to switch between Auto ISO and fixed ISO settings, and the main command dial to select specific fixed ISO values.

This menu entry has two parts, which give you more flexibility through its ISO Sensitivity and Auto ISO Sensitivity Control adjustments. The top line, ISO Sensitivity, produces a screen that allows you to specify a fixed ISO setting, just as you would by spinning the main command dial while holding down the ISO button on the top-right panel of the camera. The available settings range from Lo 1 (ISO 32) to ISO 64 through ISO 25600, and thence up to Hi 2 (ISO 102400 equivalent). The available settings are determined by the size of the increment you've specified in Custom Setting b1: 1/3- or 1-step values. Use the ISO Sensitivity menu when you find it more convenient to set ISO using the color LCD monitor.

The Auto ISO Sensitivity Control menu entries at the bottom half of the screen let you specify how and when the camera will adjust the ISO value for you automatically under certain conditions. This capability can be potentially useful, although experienced photographers tend to shy away from any feature that allows the camera to change basic settings like ISO that have been carefully selected. But you needn't fear Auto ISO. You can set some firm boundaries so the camera will use this adjustment in a fairly intelligent way.

When Auto ISO is activated, the camera can bump up the ISO sensitivity, if necessary, whenever an optimal exposure cannot be achieved at the current ISO setting. Of course, it can be disconcerting to think you're shooting at ISO 400 and then see a grainier ISO 6400 shot during LCD review. While the camera provides a flashing ISO-Auto alert in the display, the warning is easy to miss.

As you choose one of Auto ISO options, you'll want to keep in mind how Auto ISO makes its adjustments. In Program and Aperture-priority modes, the camera will first attempt to set an exposure using a shutter speed of 1/16000th second down to the Minimum Shutter Speed value you specify below. It will then begin increasing the ISO rather than use a slower speed. In Shutter-priority mode, the shutter speed you select will always be used, but if the smallest or largest apertures aren't sufficient, the camera will raise or lower the ISO setting. In Manual exposure mode, your selected shutter speed and aperture are always used, and the camera will increase or decrease ISO sensitivity as needed to produce the correct exposure. In effect, Auto ISO gives you automatic exposure in Manual exposure mode.

Here are the important considerations to keep in mind when using the options available for Auto ISO:

- **Off.** Set Auto ISO Sensitivity Control to Off, and the ISO setting will not budge from whatever value you have specified, and the entries below will be grayed out and unavailable. Use this setting when you don't want any ISO surprises, or when ISO increases are not needed to counter slow shutter speeds. For example, if the camera is mounted on a tripod, you can safely use slower shutter speeds at a relatively low ISO setting, so there is no need for a speed bump. On the other hand, if you're hand-holding the camera and the camera, set for Program (P) or Aperture-priority (A) mode, wants to use a shutter speed slower than, say, 1/30th second, it's probably a good idea to increase the ISO to avoid the effects of camera shake. If you're using a longer lens, a shutter speed of 1/125th second or higher might be the point where an ISO bump would be a good idea. In that case, you can turn the automatic ISO sensitivity control on, or remember to boost the ISO setting yourself.

- **Maximum Sensitivity/Maximum Sensitivity with Flash.** Use these parameters to indicate the highest ISO setting you're comfortable having the camera set on its own. You can choose the max ISO setting the camera will use from ISO 100 up to ISO 25600, plus the four "expanded" settings all the way up to Hi 2. Use a low number if you'd rather not take any photos at a high ISO without manually setting that value yourself. Dial in a higher ISO number if getting the photo at any sensitivity setting is more important than worrying about noise. When using the Maximum Sensitivity with Flash setting, you can specify Same As Without Flash, so the camera will perform similarly both with and without an optional flash.

  I've gotten surprisingly good results at ISO 25600; you should try it out yourself before ruling out this seemingly extreme ISO setting. Note that if you've selected an ISO setting that is *higher* than the Maximum Sensitivity you specify here, the camera will use the higher ISO value instead.
- **Minimum Shutter Speed.** This setting allows you to tell the camera how slow the shutter speed must be before the ISO boost kicks in, within the range of 30 seconds to 1/16000th second. The default value is Auto. When Auto is highlighted, press the right multi selector button, and a screen appears allowing you to fine-tune Auto to respond Slower or Faster.

  If you set a value manually, 1/30th second is a good choice, because for most shooters in most situations, any shutter speed longer than 1/30th is to be avoided, unless you're using a tripod, monopod, or looking for a special effect. That shutter speed, coupled with the available vibration reduction features, will generally produce images with minimal blur from camera/photographer shake.

  If you have a great deal of confidence in vibration reduction, steady hands, or the camera is partially braced against movement (say, you're using that monopod), a slower shutter speed, down to 1 full second, can be specified. Similarly, if you're working with a telephoto lens and find even a relatively brief shutter speed "dangerous," you can set a minimum shutter speed threshold of 1/250th second. When the shutter speed is faster than the minimum you enter, Auto ISO will not take effect.

  Your camera is smart in Auto ISO mode. For example, if you accidentally set a minimum shutter speed that is faster or slower than you've specified in Custom Setting e1: Flash Sync Speed or Custom Setting e2: Flash Shutter Speed, the camera will instead use a minimum shutter speed that is within the range set by e1 and e2. (You'll find more on these Custom Settings in Chapter 7.)

  You'll recall that Program and Aperture-priority modes can adjust the shutter speed. When Auto ISO is active, the camera will adjust the ISO setting *only* if the minimum shutter speed specified here would produce underexposure. In all other cases, the camera will simply adjust the shutter speed to produce an appropriate exposure and not touch the ISO setting.

  In addition, when Minimum Shutter Speed is set to Auto, the exposure system is clever enough to try to use faster shutter speeds with telephoto lenses (which are more subject to camera-motion blur). It will use the traditional 1/focal length rule of thumb. This feature works only with autofocus lenses; older manual focus lenses not equipped with a CPU chip are not compatible with this extra function.

White Balance

Options: Auto: $AUTO_0$ Keep White (default), $AUTO_1$ Keep Overall Atmosphere, $AUTO_2$ Keep Warm Lighting Colors; Presets: Natural Light Auto, Direct Sunlight, Cloudy, Shade, Incandescent, Fluorescent (three types), Flash, Choose Color Temperature, Preset Manual

My preference: $AUTO_0$ Keep White

This setting lets you tweak the white balance setting applied to JPEG images, and which is embedded in the RAW image for interpretation by your image editor when the RAW file is imported. Your camera has a bewildering array of white balance settings, including three Auto modes, and, in practice, all of them are, at best, a little bit wrong. However, many are close enough that you may not notice the difference; all the presets can be adjusted by you using white balance fine-tuning and, when importing RAW files, you have even greater flexibility.

In addition to three varieties of full Auto white balance, this menu entry allows you to choose Natural Light Auto, Direct Sunlight, Cloudy, Shade, Incandescent, three types of Fluorescent illumination, Flash, a specific color temperature of your choice, a preset value taken from an existing photograph, or a measurement you make. Some of the settings you make here can be duplicated using the WB button located just under the rear LCD monitor on the Z9 and on the left shoulder of the Z8, using the main and sub-command dials, but this menu entry can often be easier to use until you become familiar with your camera. Your white balance settings can have a significant impact on the color rendition of your images, as you can see in Figure 5.7, a shot of Clint Maedgen of the Preservation Hall Jazz Band.

As I noted, the fastest way to change white balance settings is to use direct setting controls. Hold down the WB button, then rotate the main command dial to choose one of the main settings. Your choices appear on the LCD monitor as you dial. When Auto, Fluorescent, K (Choose Color Temperature), or PRE (Preset Manual) are shown, you can also select a sub-option by holding down the

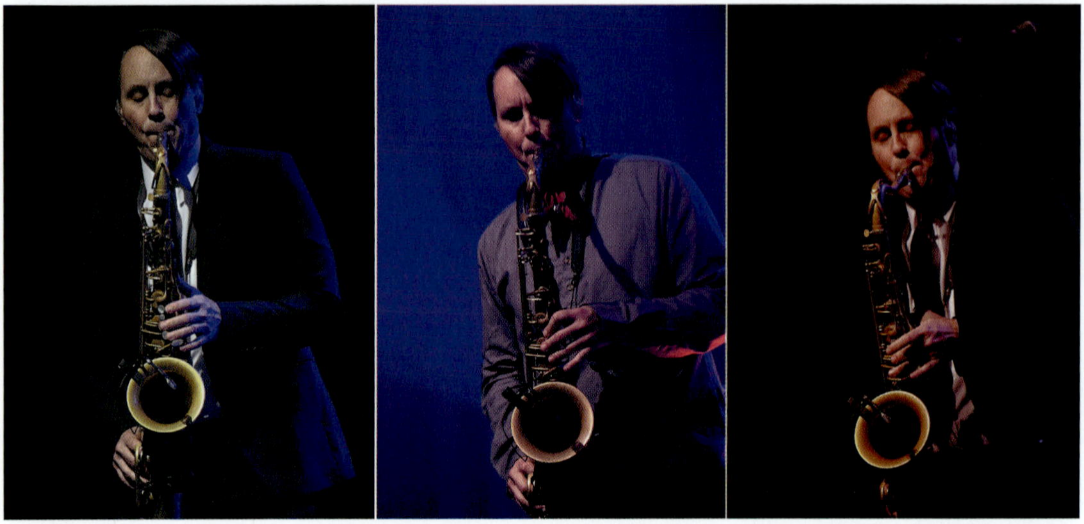

Figure 5.7 Adjusting color temperature can provide different results of the same subject at settings of 3400K (left), 5000K (middle), and 6500K (right).

WB button while rotating the sub-command dial. You can also press the *i* button, select the White Balance icon (by default the second entry from the left of the top row), and rotate the main command dial and sub-command dial, as described above. I'll explain your options next.

This menu entry offers additional options, including fine-tuning presets and the ability to capture and store custom preset color temperatures. Select the White Balance entry on the Photo Shooting menu, and you'll see an array of choices like those shown in Figure 5.8. If you choose Fluorescent, you'll be taken to another screen that presents three different types of lamps, Cool-White, Day White, and Daylight fluorescent. If you know the exact type of non-incandescent lighting being used, you can select it, or settle on a likely compromise.

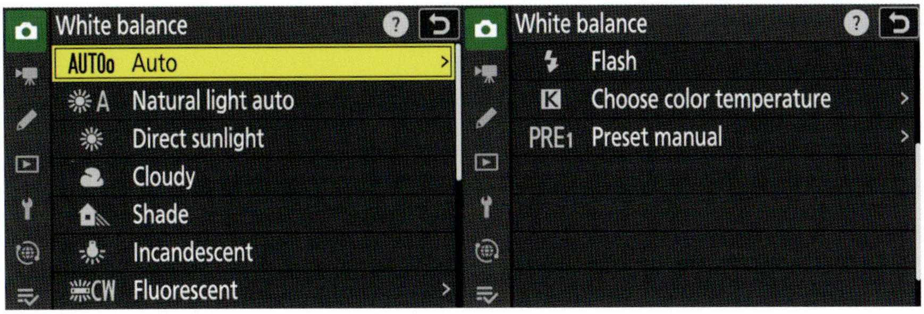

Figure 5.8 The White Balance menu has predefined values, plus the option of setting color temperature and presets you measure yourself.

The K Choose Color Temperature selection allows you to select from an array of color temperatures in degrees Kelvin (more on this in Chapter 8) from 2500K to 10000K, and then further fine-tune the color bias using the fine-tuning feature described below. Select Preset Manual to record or recall custom white balance settings suitable for environments with unusual lighting or mixed lighting, as described later in this section.

For all other settings, highlight the white balance option you want, then press the multi selector right button to view the fine-tuning screen shown in Figure 5.9. The screen shows a grid with two axes, an amber-blue axis extending left/right, and a green-magenta axis extending up and down the grid. By default, the grid's cursor is positioned in the middle, and a readout to the right of the grid shows the cursor's coordinates on the A-B axis (yes, I know the display has the end points reversed) and G-M axis at 0,0.

You can use the multi selector's up/down and right/left buttons to move the cursor to any coordinate in the grid, thereby biasing the white balance in the direction(s) you choose. The amber-blue axis makes the image warmer or colder (but not actually yellow or blue). Similarly, the green-magenta axis preserves all the colors in the original image but gives them a tinge biased toward green or magenta. When you've fine-tuned white balance, either using the Photo Shooting menu options or the defined WB button, an asterisk appears in the white balance section of the display to remind you that this tweaking has taken place.

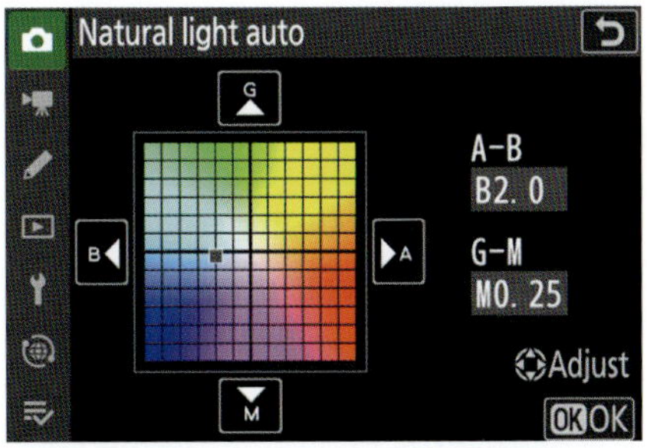

Figure 5.9 Specific white balance settings can be fine-tuned by changing their bias in the amber-blue, magenta-green directions—or along both axes simultaneously.

Why Color Varies

Color temperature—how "bluish" or how "reddish" the light appears to be to the digital camera's sensor—is the main factor you'll have to contend with. Indoor illumination is quite warm, comparatively, while daylight, in contrast, seems much bluer to the sensor. Our eyes (our brains, actually) are quite adaptable to these variations, so white objects don't appear to have an orange tinge when viewed indoors, nor do they seem excessively blue outdoors in full daylight. Yet, these color temperature variations are real, and the sensor is not fooled.

Fortunately, the only time you need to think in terms of *actual* color temperature is when you're making adjustments using the Choose Color Temp. setting in the White Balance entry within the Photo Shooting menu, which allows you to dial in exact color temperatures, if known, as described earlier. You can also shift and bias color balance along the blue/amber and magenta/green axes, and bracket white balance.

So-called "white" light is produced by a spectrum of colors that, when added together, provide the neutral color needed for accuracy. Artificial light sources don't necessarily offer the same balanced spectrum found in sunlight. Some portions of the spectrum may be deficient or truncated or include gaps with certain wavelengths missing entirely. As a result, all artificial light sources are assigned a color rendering index (CRI), which compares the source with a perfect "reference" light source at a particular color temperature.

With the decline in use of traditional incandescent and halogen bulbs, CRI has become more important. A CRI of 80-plus is considered acceptable; for critical applications like photography, a CRI higher than 93 is best. Daylight fluorescents and deluxe cool white fluorescents suitable for photography might have a CRI of about 79 to 95, which is perfectly acceptable for most photographic applications. Less desirable are warm white fluorescents, which may have a CRI of 55. White deluxe mercury vapor lights are even less suitable with a CRI of 45, while low-pressure sodium lamps can vary from CRI 0–18. If you're using such a source not intended for photography, it may be worth your while to determine its color rendering index before you shoot. The figure is often supplied on the packaging of the light source.

To recap, your chief tools for getting correct color in your images are these:

- **"Canned" presets.** Nikon does give you a wide range of pre-defined adjustment types to choose from when you need a quickie solution. You can choose from four kinds of Auto white balance settings, and six illumination categories (with three fluorescent variations). Strictly speaking, in any given situation, all of them are likely to be wrong to some extent. All versions of Nikon's Auto settings lose accuracy with light sources cooler than 3500K. Even "daylight" can vary widely, depending on local conditions or even how far you are from the equator.
- **Visual evaluation.** If you've set Custom Setting d10/d8 to Show Effects of Settings, your camera will display the scene using the current white balance parameters. An image on the display may look too blue or too red if your WB specs are way off. Unfortunately, this is not a precise tool, as neither the LCD monitor nor viewfinder are able to reproduce colors with 100 percent accuracy, and our eyes tend to adapt to color variations so that colors look "right" to us, even when they are not.

- **White balance bracketing.** I included white balance bracketing, which is not available when you're shooting a RAW file, in my explanation of bracketing in Chapter 2, and won't repeat that discussion here. With WB bracketing the camera captures up to nine images at an increment spread you specify, from 1 to 3. The range of color temperatures is actually measured in *mireds* (micro-reciprocal degrees). The actual range covered varies, depending on the number of different shots you want to capture. If you choose 9 shots, the adjustments will range from –60 to +60 mired. You should know that mired values aren't linear; five mireds at 2500K produces a much stronger effect than five mireds at 6000K.

  The bracketing adjustments are made only on the amber/blue axis (no bracketing in the magenta/green bias is possible), but you can select whether the bracketed shots are spread in the blue *or* amber directions (that is, each one bluer/less blue or yellower/less yellow) or balanced to provide both blue- and amber-oriented brackets.
- **Specific color temperatures.** If you know or have an estimate of the scene's color temperature, you can enter that directly, as described earlier.
- **Manual Presets.** You can tell the camera to measure the color temperature of a given scene, and then store that value in one of the six PRE slots, as described next.

Using Preset Manual White Balance

If automatic white balance or one of the predefined settings available aren't suitable, you can set a custom white balance using the Preset Manual menu option. You can apply the white balance from a scene, either by shooting a new picture on the spot and using the resulting white balance (Direct Measurement) or using an image you have already shot (Copy from Existing Photograph). You can use an existing preset or perform direct measurement from your current scene using a reference object (preferably a neutral gray or white object).

To use an existing white balance setting you've already stored, just follow these steps:

1. **Scroll to Preset Manual in the White Balance menu.** Press the right directional button. The screen shown in Figure 5.10 appears.
2. **Select preset.** Use the directional controls to highlight the "slot" containing the value you stored earlier.
3. **Confirm.** Press OK to confirm and exit back to the Photo Shooting menu.
4. **Exit.** Press MENU twice to exit the Photo Shooting menu.

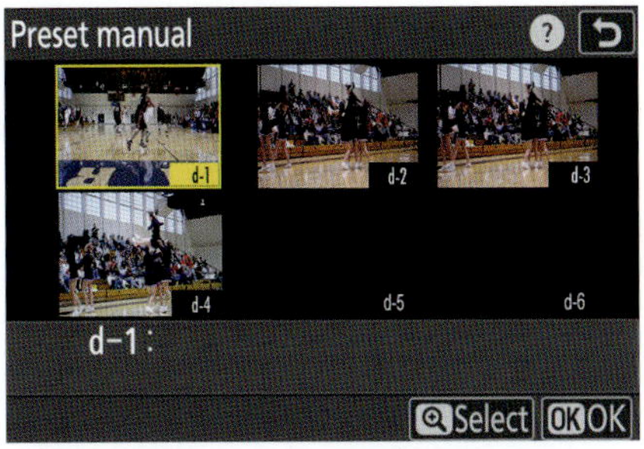

Figure 5.10 When you capture a scene's white balance, it will be stored in the selected slot.

You can also select an existing preset using the *i* menu:

1. **Press the *i* button.** Highlight the White Balance option in the top row.
2. **Select Preset.** Rotate the command dial until the Preset option (PRE) appears.
3. **Choose your preset.** Rotate the sub-command dial until the preset (numbered 1 to 6) appears.
4. **Exit.** Press the *i* button twice to confirm and exit.

To capture a white balance setting, just follow these steps:

1. **Use gray or white reference.** Place the neutral reference, such as a white piece of paper or a gray card, under the lighting you want to measure. You can also use one of those white balance caps that fit on the front of your lens like a lens cap.
2. **Choose Preset Manual.** Press the *i* button, choose White Balance, and rotate the main command dial until Preset Manual (PRE) is selected.
3. **Select "slot."** Rotate the sub-command dial until the slot (d–1 to d–6) you want to use as your white balance register is shown. Press OK. The screen shown in Figure 5.11, left, appears.
4. **Activate Measure mode.** Press and hold the OK button until the screen shown at right in Figure 5.11 appears. In my illustration I've set up a gray card with a green border.
5. **Measure White Balance.** Tap the touch screen at the point where your gray or white reference appears or use the multi selector to move the target frame over that area. (Note that you can't relocate the frame if a flash is attached.) Then press OK again *or* press the shutter release down all the way.
6. **Success?** If the white balance information was captured, a message Data Acquired appears. If it was unable to measure white balance, you'll be asked to try again. (Try using a different target if you fail on successive attempts.)

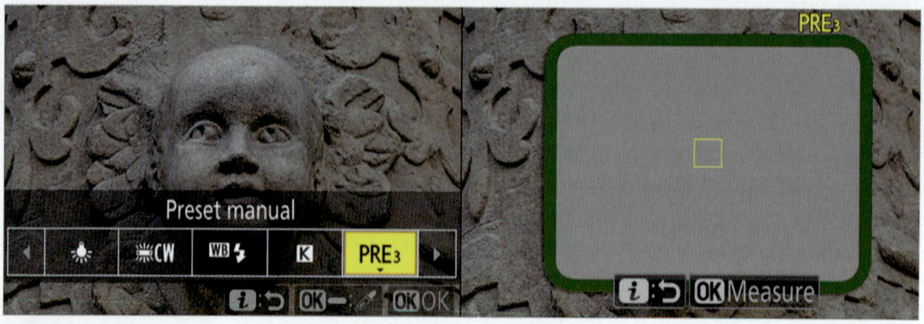

Figure 5.11 To define a new preset, highlight the PRE, left, and rotate the sub-command dial to choose a slot (d1 to d6). Then capture a neutral white or gray target (right).

The preset value you've captured will remain in the slot until you replace that white balance with a new captured value. It can be summoned at any time (use the *i* button menu or the WB button) and when PRE is chosen with the main command dial, select your preset by rotating the sub-command dial until the desired white balance slot is displayed. You can also choose an existing image or protect a captured white balance from being overwritten:

1. Choose Preset Manual from the White Balance menu.
2. A screen of thumbnails appears, showing the six "slots" numbered d–1 to d–6. Use the multi selector buttons to highlight one of the thumbnail slots and press the Zoom In button.

3. The next screen that appears (see Figure 5.12) has four options: Fine-tune, Edit Comment, Select Picture, and Protect.
    - Choose Fine-tune to fine-tune the amber/blue/magenta/green/white balance of an image already stored in one of the four user slots.
    - Choose Edit Comment to add or change the comment applied to d–1 to d–6. The comment can be used as a label to better identify the white balance information in the slot, with terms like Gymnasium Daytime or Rumpus Room. (The standard text-editing screen shown earlier in this chapter appears.)
    - Choose Select Image to view the standard image-selection screen and highlight and choose the existing image you want to use. Press the Zoom In button to confirm your choice and copy the white balance of the selected image to the slot you selected in Step 2. Note that the image must be taken with your current camera—you can't "recycle" the white balance of favorite shots captured with a different model.
    - Choose Protect to lock the white balance setting currently stored in the selected slot. Use this to preserve a captured white balance setting.
4. Press OK to confirm your white balance setting.

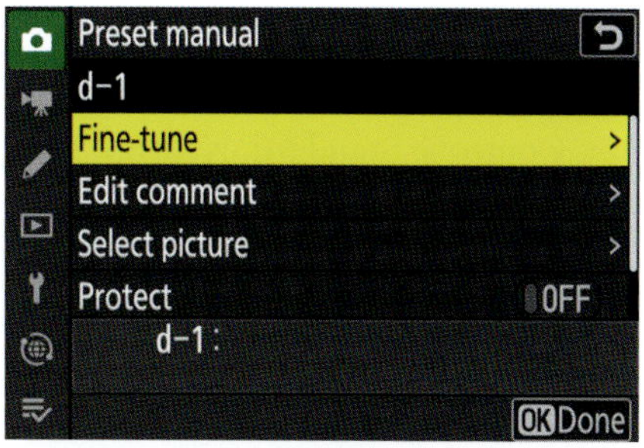

Figure 5.12 The Preset Manual screen lets you fine-tune preset white balance settings, label them with a comment, select an image to use as a white balance reference, and protect captured settings.

A WHITE BALANCE LIBRARY

Consider dedicating a memory card to stow a selection of images taken under a variety of lighting conditions. If you want to "recycle" one of the color temperatures you've stored, insert the card and load one of those images into your choice of preset slots d–1 to d–6, as described above. Large memory cards are a bit pricey to make a dedicated memory card, but I have some old 32GB XQD cards that I use for this.

Set Picture Control

Options: Auto (default), Standard, Neutral, Vivid, Monochrome, Flat Monochrome (Z8), Deep Tone Monochrome (Z8), Portrait, Rich Tone Portrait, Landscape, Flat; Creative Picture Controls (01–20): Dream, Morning, Pop, Sunday, Somber, Dramatic, Silence, Bleached, Melancholic, Pure, Denim, Toy, Sepia, Blue, Red, Pink, Charcoal, Graphite, Binary, and Carbon

My preference: Neutral: I can select other styles during RAW processing. Flat when extended dynamic range without HDR processing is needed.

Nikon has considerably expanded its Picture Control roster in recent years, adding 20 Creative Picture Controls that add special effects to your images as you shoot. The Picture Control styles allow you to choose your own sharpness (in three different ways, as I'll explain shortly), plus adjust contrast, color saturation, and hue settings applied to your images when using P, S, A, and M modes.

NOTE When Tone Control, described earlier, is set to HLG, this Set Picture Control entry is grayed out; use the Set Picture Control (HLG) entry that follows instead. In video mode, use the HLG Quality setting in the Video Recording menu.

The three types of Picture Controls available:

- **Original Picture Controls.** Your camera has seven predefined styles, which it calls Original Picture Controls: Standard, Neutral, Vivid, Monochrome (including Flat Monochrome and Deep Tone Monochrome with the Z8), Portrait, Landscape, and Flat. There is also an Auto setting, which examines your image and applies one of these seven controls as appropriate. Flat is a relatively new option, with an extended, low-contrast dynamic range that lends itself to fine-tuning in an image editor. Video shooters who plan to process their clips also love the versatility of the Flat setting, which allows preserving detail in highlights and shadows when correcting (or "grading") video in advanced video-editing software.

  Note that each of the seven predefined styles has its own default settings for Sharpening (with four variations), along with Contrast, Brightness, Saturation, and Hue. (Monochrome does not have Saturation or Hue settings.) For example, the default Sharpening is +4 for Vivid and Landscape; +3 for Standard and Monochrome; +2 for Neutral and Portrait; and +1 for Flat. Even more interesting, the effects of each increment aren't consistent between Picture Controls. A +1 sharpening applied to the Standard control isn't the same as the +1 applied to the Neutral control. Each of the other parameters available for the preset styles have their own defaults. Any changes you make are *edits* of the default values defined for that particular style.
- **Creative Picture Controls.** These are 20 new special-effects styles, each assigned a number from 1 to 20. Nikon has given a fanciful name to each Creative Picture Control that more or less provides a hint to how the effect modifies your image. The available creative styles include Dream, Morning, Pop, Sunday, Somber, Dramatic, Silence, Bleached, Melancholic, Pure, Denim, Toy, Sepia, Blue, Red, Pink, Charcoal, Graphite, Binary, and Carbon. These 20 additional Creative Picture Controls offer the same parameter adjustments as Original Picture Controls, plus an Effect Level slider for specifying the *amount* of the special effects provided, on a scale from 0 to 100 in increments of 10 steps. You can edit the parameters of these Picture Controls, too. I'll explain Creative Picture Controls shortly.
- **User Controls.** You can define up to nine Picture Controls of your own, numbered C–1 to C–9. Each User Control is based on one of the 28 predefined styles (any of the 8 Original or 20 Creative Controls). You'll use the Manage Picture Control entry, described in the next section.

While all the canned Original and Creative Picture Controls have their preset parameters, their most valuable trait is your ability to *edit* the settings of any of those 28 styles, so they better suit your taste. You can adjust the existing styles, in which case an asterisk appears next to their name in the menus, or save your adjustments as a User Control. But wait, there's more! You can *copy* these styles to a memory card, edit them on your computer, and reload them into your camera at any time. So, effectively, you can have several sets of custom Picture Control styles available: those currently in your camera, as well as a virtually unlimited library of user-defined styles that you have stored on memory cards.

As I've noted, using and fully managing Picture Control styles is accomplished using two different menu entries. This entry, Set Picture Control, has two functions: it allows you to *choose* an existing Original or Creative style and to *edit* any predefined styles. The Photo Shooting menu entry that follows this one, Manage Picture Control, gives you the capability of creating and editing user-defined styles, using one of the canned Original or Creative Picture Controls as a foundation.

PHOTO/VIDEO PICTURE CONTROLS OVERLAP

As you'll learn in Chapter 6, the Video Recording menu has its own Set Picture Controls entry with the same styles available. However, you have the choice of editing and saving a separate version of each individual control, or selecting the Same As Photo Settings option, which will mean the settings you make here will be automatically applied to its Video Recording counterpart.

Choosing a Picture Control Style

To choose from one of the predefined Original or Creative styles or to select a user-defined style you've created (numbered C–1 to C–9), follow these steps:

1. Choose Set Picture Control from the Photo Shooting menu. The screen shown in Figure 5.13 appears. Remember that Picture Controls that have been modified from their standard settings have an asterisk next to their name.
2. Scroll down to the Picture Control you'd like to use. The ones shown in the figure are followed by the last Original Control, Flat, and then the Creative Controls, and, at the tail end of several screens, any User Controls you have created.

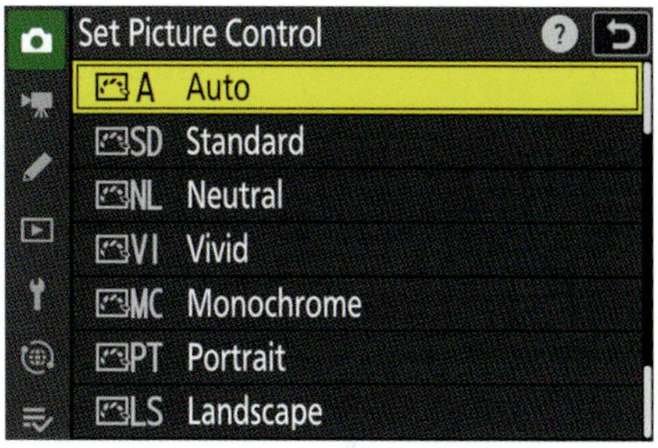

Figure 5.13 You can choose from Auto or the predefined Picture Controls shown here, as well as the Flat predefined control, the Creative Picture Controls, and the User Controls located farther down the scrolling list.

3. Press OK to activate the highlighted style. (Although you can usually select a menu item by pressing the multi selector right button, in this case, that button activates editing instead.)
4. Press the MENU button or tap the shutter release to exit the menu system.

Editing a Picture Control Style

You can change the parameters of any of Nikon's predefined Original Picture Controls (including Auto), Creative Picture Controls, or any of the (up to) nine user-defined styles you create. You are given the choice of using the quick-adjust/fine-tune facility to modify a Picture Control with a few sliders. You can edit these controls using this Set Picture Control entry in the Photo Shooting menu, and you can also edit them when you access a style from the *i* menu. To make quick adjustments to any Picture Control except the Monochrome style and Creative Picture Controls 13–20, follow these steps:

1. Choose Set Picture Control from the Photo Shooting menu.
2. Scroll down to the Picture Control you'd like to edit.
3. Press the multi selector right button to produce an adjustment screen similar to the one shown in Figure 5.14.

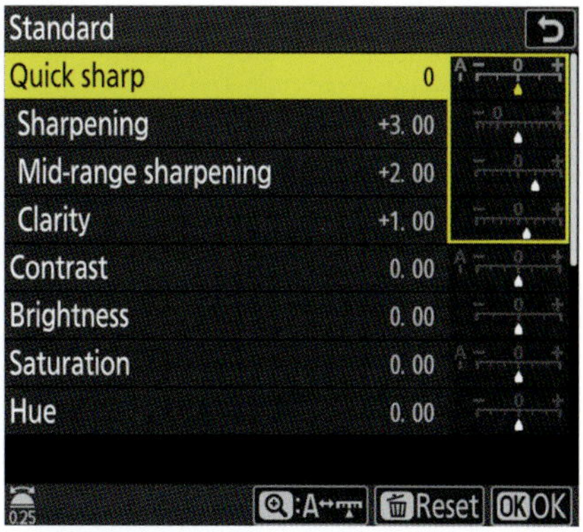

Figure 5.14 Sliders can be used to make quick adjustments to your Picture Control styles.

4. Use the Quick Sharp slider and the left/right directional controls to change the three individual Sharpening adjustments (Sharpening, Mid-Range Sharpening, and Clarity) simultaneously. Alternatively, scroll down to each of those three adjustments and tweak Sharpening, Mid-Range Sharpening, or Clarity independently. (See the next section, "Super Sharpness," for an explanation of the latter parameter.)
5. Next, scroll down to the Contrast, Brightness, Saturation, and Hue sliders with the up/down directional controls, then use the left/right directional controls to decrease or increase the effects. A gray triangle will appear under the original setting in the slider as you make a change. (Saturation and Hue cannot be adjusted for Monochrome or Creative Picture Controls 13–20.)

TIP You can adjust the Auto Picture Control, but each of your modifications are applied *on top of* the Auto adjustments. That is, in Auto Picture Control mode, the camera will automatically adjust, say, Contrast, and then apply any contrast adjustments you have specified, in the range Auto-2 to Auto+2. Because the Auto Picture Control's adjustments may vary depending on what your camera "decides" the image needs, you should edit with caution.

6. Instead of making changes with the slider's scale, when you're working with the Contrast and Saturation adjustments, you can move the cursor to the far left and choose A (for Auto) and the camera will adjust these parameters automatically, depending on the type of scene it detects.
7. Press OK to save your adjustments, or press the Trash button to reset the values to their defaults.

PICTURE CONTROLS WITH THE *i* MENU

You can also perform the exact same functions just described using the *i* menu. Just press the *i* button, navigate to the Set Picture Control icon (located, by default, as the first icon on the left in the top row) and rotate the main command dial if all you want to do is select a Picture Control from a scrolling list. If you'd like to *edit* the control, press OK. The scrolling list appears as at left in Figure 5.15. When you've highlighted the control you want to edit, press the down button to produce a screen like the one seen in Figure 5.15, right. The column at the far right contains all the parameters listed in Steps 4 and 5 above, while the adjustment slider for the currently highlighted parameter appears at the bottom. Once you've made your edits, press OK to confirm and exit, or the *i* button to exit without making changes.

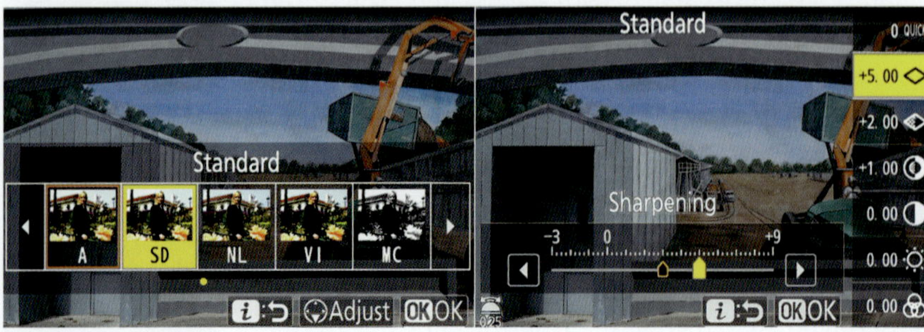

Figure 5.15 Picture Controls can be accessed and edited from the *i* menu.

Editing Picture Controls in the camera is fairly easy, but if you intend to make a lot of changes, or want to get creative and build a roster of custom controls, you may find the free downloadable Picture Control Utility 2 useful. The interface (shown in Figure 5.16) is fast and straightforward to use and offers the option to save your edited controls to a file (for storage/archiving), to a memory card for transfer to your camera, or launch Nikon NX Studio, Capture NX-D, or View NXi, and apply it immediately to an image.

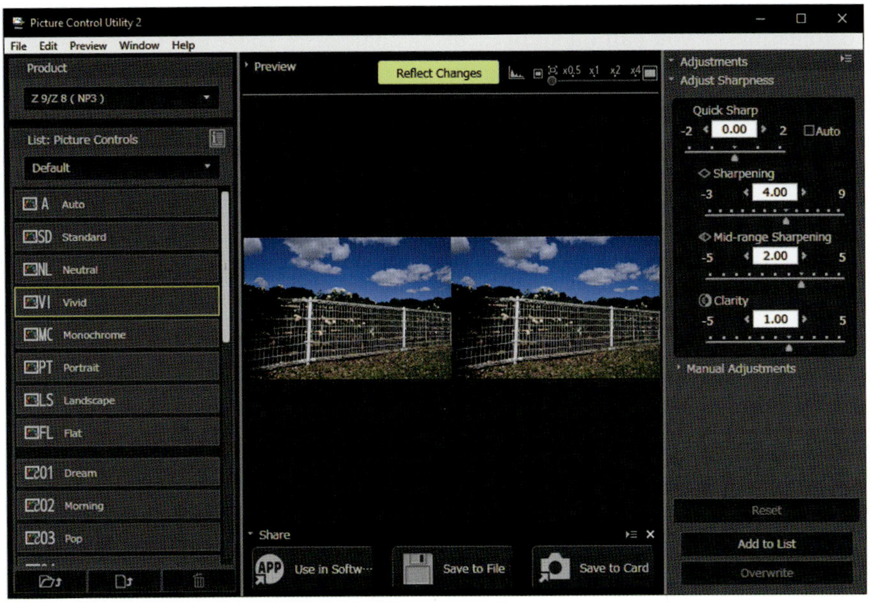

Figure 5.16 The Picture Control Utility 2.

If you plan to use a Picture Control in a camera other than your Nikon Z9 or Z8, you should know that Nikon has used three different file structures over the years, reducing the seamless compatibility previously available. The Edit > Add Product entry on the utility allows you to add dSLR, mirrorless, and Coolpix cameras, or specify which of the three file types (with .NCP, .NP2, .NP3 extensions) is appropriate for your camera.

CUSTOM CURVES

Nikon has thrown you a curve ball by adding an additional customizable parameter that you *can't* edit in the camera. You can add a Photoshop- or Lightroom-like Curve/Tone Curve (respectively) to a User-created Picture Control concocted on your computer with the Picture Control Utility. When creating/editing a User control in the utility, you can select Manual Adjustments, click the Use Custom Curve box, and adjust the tone curve exactly as you would in your image editor. Once saved as a User setting and copied to your camera using the Manage Picture Controls entry discussed next, that curve will be applied to your images when the custom User setting is active. Should you try to edit that control in-camera, you'll see the Contrast and Brightness parameters are grayed out, and their values labeled USER.

SUPER SHARPNESS

Amateur photographers like to be told that their pictures will be "clear and sharp," a simplification of picture quality that is likely to satisfy most of them. As an enthusiast, you know that many other factors also are part of image quality, including color, tonal range, and contrast. Indeed, sharpness itself is more complex than you might expect. Other parameters, such as Contrast, Brightness, Saturation, and Hue are virtually self-explanatory, because you've probably worked with them many times in Photoshop or another image editor.

When it comes to the adjustments you can make in terms of sharpness, there are three different parameters, and multiple ways of controlling them. The Picture Controls have separate sliders for all three, plus a fourth slider, Quick Sharp, which adjusts all three simultaneously. Here's a breakdown:

- **Sharpening.** This control affects the appearance of fine details and patterns because it modifies the sharpness of the contours (edges) of your subjects. The lower the number, the softer those outlines will be; higher numbers produce more distinct details.
- **Mid-range sharpening.** Adjusts overall sharpness according to the fineness of patterns and lines in the mid-tones adjusted by the Sharpening and Clarity controls. In Video mode, this parameter works only when Video Quality has been set to High in the Video Recording menu. Keep in mind that increasing sharpness also increases contrast, so you'll want to use this control judiciously when capturing high-contrast scenes.
- **Clarity.** This adjusts the overall sharpness of the image and the sharpness of thicker outlines without affecting brightness or dynamic range. Think of Clarity as a type of sharpening/enhancing effect applied to the mid-tones of an image. While sharpening generally adjusts only the contours of your subject matter, Clarity makes details sharper while maintaining the gradation of highlight and shadow areas. High values produce contrasty and vivid images with darkened colors and improved detail in the midtones. Low values reduce midtone detail and flatten colors. You might want to apply Clarity to make hazy or fog-clouded subjects look clearer without losing details, or when you want to soften hard-edge subjects. Conversely, if your scene already is contrasty, use Clarity with caution, just as I advised for Mid-range Sharpening. Your best bet is to play with the control to see how you like the results. The camera applies +1 Clarity by default to Standard, Vivid, Landscape, and Monochrome Picture Controls.

Editing the Monochrome Picture Control

Editing the Monochrome styles or the Creative Picture Controls 13–20 is similar to customizing the other styles, except that the parameters differ slightly. Sharpening, Contrast, and Brightness are available, but, instead of Saturation and Hue, you can choose a filter effect (Yellow, Orange, Red, Green, or none) and a toning effect (black-and-white, plus seven levels of Sepia, Cyanotype, Red, Yellow, Green, Blue Green, Blue, Purple Blue, and Red Purple). (Keep in mind that once you've taken a JPEG photo using one of these styles, you can't convert the image back to full color.)

To adjust Filters or Toning:

1. Choose Set Picture Control from the Photo Shooting menu.
2. Scroll down to the Monochrome Picture Control or to one of the Creative Picture Controls that have Filter and Toning options, numbered 13 through 20.
3. Press the multi selector right button to produce an adjustment screen similar to the one shown in Figure 5.17.
4. Set Sharpening, Contrast, and Brightness exactly as you would with the other Picture Controls.
5. Optionally, scroll down to Filter Effects or Toning (which appears after Filter Effects in the scrolling list and is shown at the bottom of the figure).
6. When Filter Effects is highlighted, you can choose Off, Yellow, Orange, Red, or Green. Press OK to finish or Trash to reset to the original values.
7. When Toning is highlighted, you can press the left/right directional controls to choose a tone: Black/White, Sepia, Cyanotype, Red, Yellow, Green, Blue Green, Blue, Purple Blue, or Red Purple. Once you've selected a tone (other than Black/White), press the down button to move to the intensity control, then use the left/right buttons to set a toning strength from +1 to +7. Press OK to confirm, or Trash to reset.

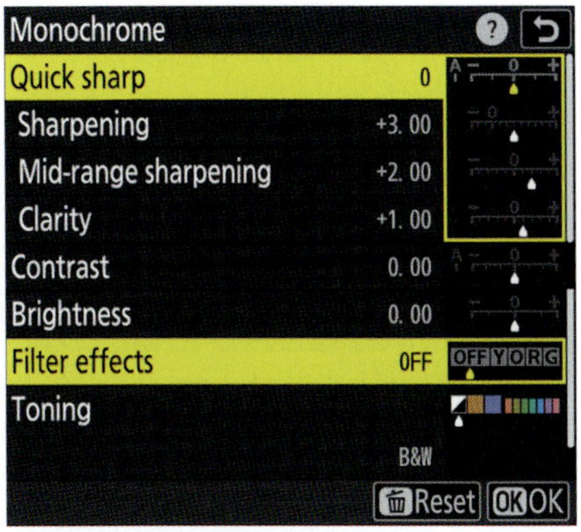

Figure 5.17 Editing Monochrome Picture Style parameters.

FILTERS VS. TONING

Although some of the color choices seem to overlap, you'll get very different looks when choosing between Filter Effects and Toning. Filter Effects add no color to the monochrome image. Instead, they reproduce the look of black-and-white film that has been shot through a color filter. That is, Yellow will make the sky darker and the clouds will stand out more, while Orange makes the sky even darker and sunsets more full of detail. The Red filter produces the darkest sky of all and darkens green objects, such as leaves. Human skin may appear lighter than normal. The Green filter has the opposite effect on leaves, making them appear lighter in tone. Figure 5.18 at left shows the same scene shot with no filter, then Yellow, Green, and Red filters.

The Sepia, Blue, Green, and other toning effects, on the other hand, all add a color cast to your monochrome image. Use these when you want an old-time look or a special effect, without bothering to recolor your shots in an image editor. Toning is shown at right in Figure 5.18.

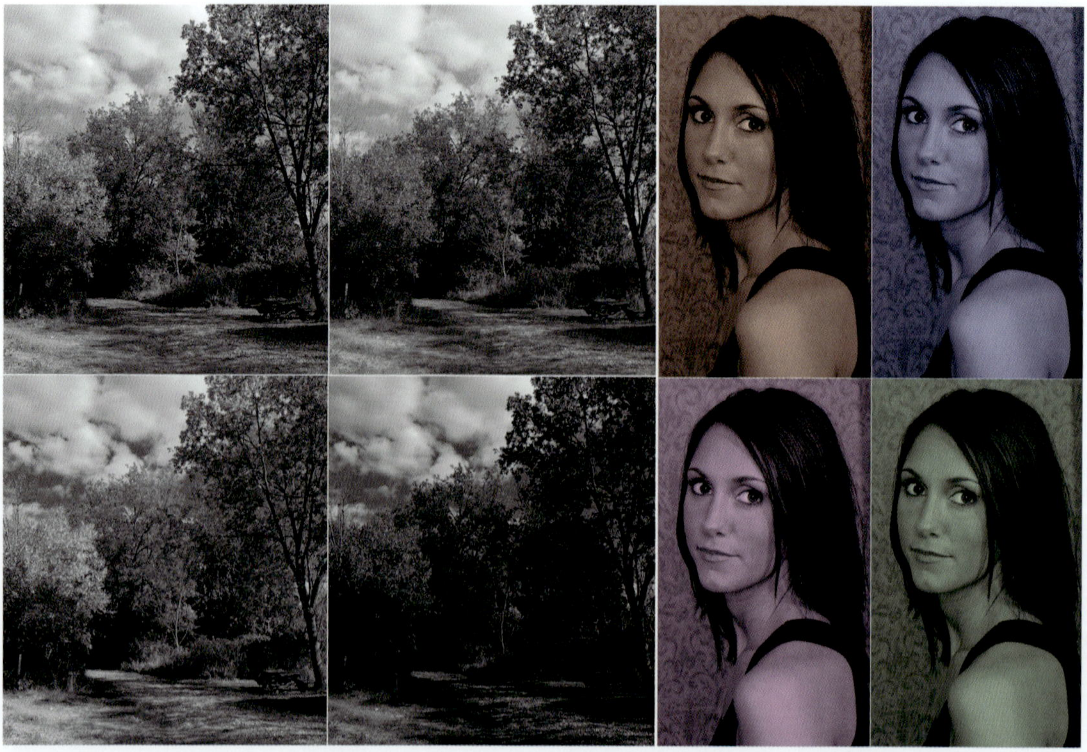

Figure 5.18 Left: Color filter effects: No filter (upper left); yellow filter (upper right); green filter (lower left); and red filter (lower right). Right: Toning effects: Sepia (upper left); Purple Blue (upper right); Red Purple (lower left); and Green (lower right).

Editing Creative Picture Controls

The Creative Picture Controls are located farther down the scrolling list after the predefined controls (see Figure 5.19). They have approximately the same adjustments found in the Original Picture Controls. However, you'll probably find adjusting them to be trickier, because it can be difficult to see how a particular parameter applies to a particular special effect. For example, you know that the Vivid original style emphasizes color saturation but what, exactly, goes into making, say, the Dream creative style? Simply looking at samples with a particular effect applied may not help, as you can see in Figure 5.20. The differences between many of the controls is subtle. Charcoal, Graphite, Binary, and Carbon may differ primarily in amount of contrast, for example.

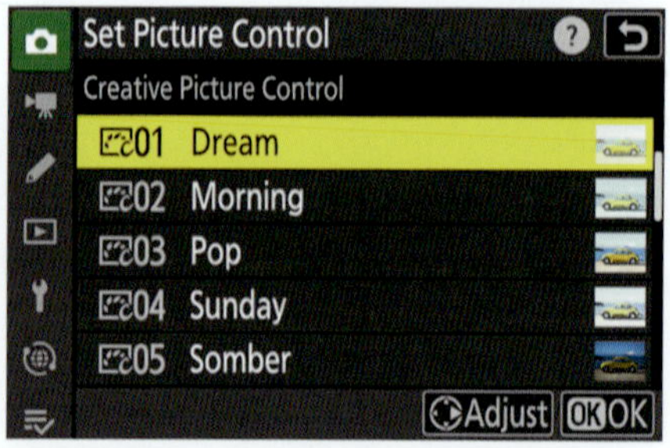

Figure 5.19 The Creative Picture Controls are numbered for easy reference.

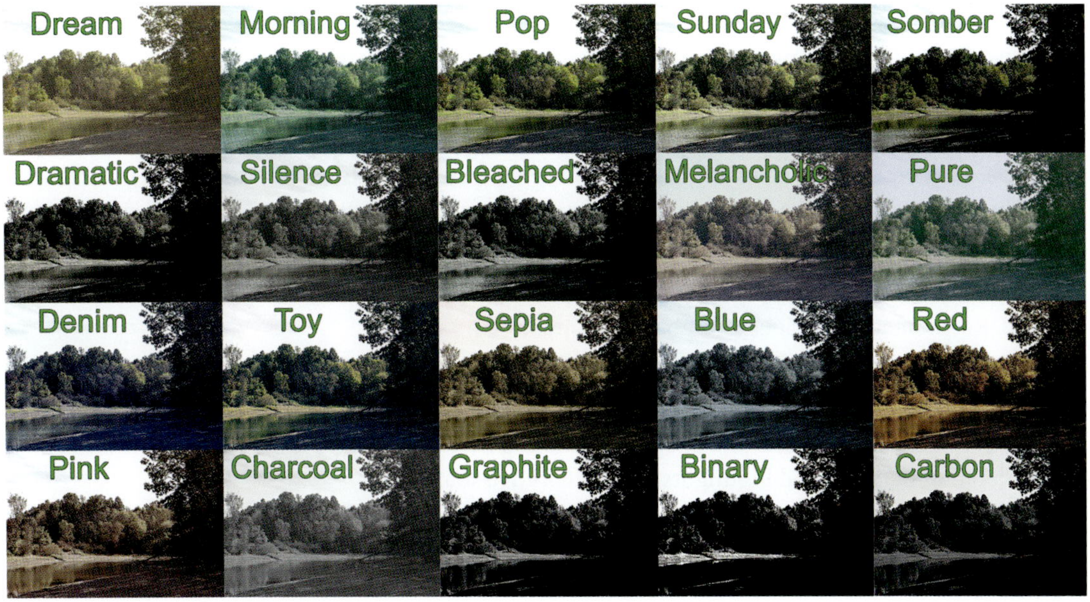

Figure 5.20 Creative Picture Controls.

Nikon provides some simplified descriptions, which may seem a little vague, like a New Age song title, forcing us poor users to evoke our own mental images with only fuzzy visual references. Nikon's summaries are along these lines (for what it's worth):

- **Dream.** Lightness, warmth, pale sepia-like orange brightening darker areas with smooth edges and a soft appearance.
- **Morning.** Atmosphere of fresh morning air, dark areas brightened, with bluish/cyan tones with a sense of transparency. Refreshing image.
- **Pop.** Highest degree of saturation for more colorful tones and textures, even with brighter images.
- **Sunday.** Open atmosphere as if the image were captured on a Sunday afternoon. Increased contrast, blown highlights, for a stronger impression.
- **Somber.** Melancholic, calm atmosphere, like after a rain, with increased saturation and suppressing brightness with compressed tones.
- **Dramatic.** Profound expression emphasizing light and shade at high contrast (like the bleach filter in some image editing plug-ins), suitable for dramatic expression of light.
- **Silence.** Transient and lonely contemplative feeling; tranquil, soft images with reduced saturation.
- **Bleached.** Serious impression with greenish, low-saturation images and metallic feel. Minutely rendered details with tasteful silvery tone.
- **Melancholic.** Retro expression with slightly melancholic atmosphere, magenta tinged, restrained sharpness and reduced saturation.

- **Pure.** Soft image, as if viewed through a veil, with soft blue-green tone, tranquil ambience.
- **Denim.** Deep tone, strong blue shifted toward cyan, high saturation.
- **Toy.** Inspired by toy cameras, but deeper and calmer impression, with high saturation, blue shifted toward indigo.
- **Sepia.** First of the true "color-influenced" Creative Picture Controls, provides sepia images with faded colors, similar to a colorized monochrome picture. This control and the next seven all have Filter Effects and Toning options, as described above.
- **Blue.** Yet more melancholy, this time with a quiet, bluish tone, similar to cyanotypes.
- **Red.** Retro images with heavy amber-red tone.
- **Pink.** No relation to Alecia Beth Moore (P!nk), but still able to deliver a soft, gentle romantic tone with a pinkish atmosphere.
- **Charcoal.** Gentle, monochrome images resembling black-and-white drawings with minimal loss of detail in shadows and highlights, but softer edge sharpness.
- **Graphite.** Sharpened edges and lustrous blacks with crisp, accentuated contrast.
- **Binary.** Two-tone images for crisp black-and-white.
- **Carbon.** Stable, deep, dignified images with less contrast than Graphite, producing strong, black-based gradation.

As the names and descriptions of each of these 20 Creative Picture Controls don't adequately describe their effects, my recommendation is to evaluate each individually, and use the controls to tweak them to your preferences. You'll notice an additional slider, Effect Level, which simply specifies how strongly the effect is applied to the image, on a scale of 0 (zero effect) to 100 (maximum effect). This allows you to attenuate the amount of the effect, or to mix an Original control with a Creative control. For example, if you set the Creative control to 80, the camera will apply the default Original control using the remaining amount. The Dream style controls are shown in Figure 5.21, as an example. You can always adjust these styles and save them under a new name as a User Control, as I'll describe in the Manage Picture Control section that follows.

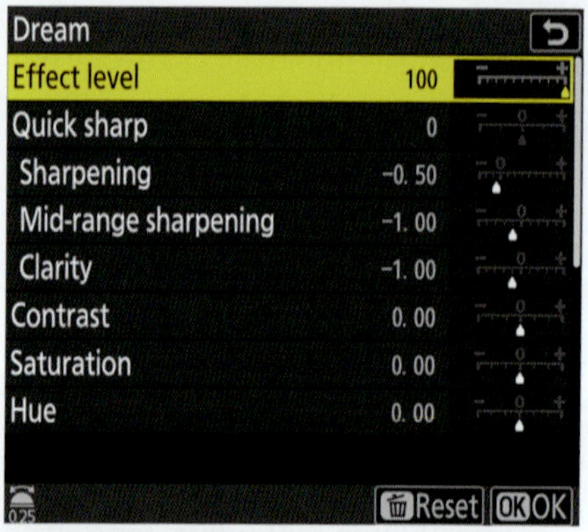

Figure 5.21 Adjusting Creative Picture Controls.

Manage Picture Control

Options: Save/Edit, Rename, Delete, Load/Save

My preference: N/A

The Manage Picture Control menu entry can be used to create new styles, edit existing styles, rename or delete them, and store/retrieve them from the memory card. Here are the basic functions of this menu item, which can be found on the Photo Shooting menu directly below the Set Picture Control entry:

- **Make a copy.** Choose Save/Edit (see Figure 5.22, left), select from the list of available Picture Controls, and press OK to store that style in one of the user-defined slots C-1 to C-9 (with slots C-1 to C-2 shown already occupied in Figure 5.22, right).
- **Save an edited copy.** Choose Save/Edit, select from the list of available Picture Controls, and then press the multi selector right button to edit the style, as described in the previous section. Press OK when finished editing, and then save the modified style in one of the user-defined slots C-1 to C-9.
- **Rename a style.** Choose Rename, select from the list of user-defined Picture Controls (you cannot rename the default styles), and then enter the text used as the new label for the style, using the standard text-entry screen shown earlier in this chapter in Figure 5.2. You may use up to 19 characters for the name.
- **Remove a style.** Select Delete, choose from the list of user-defined Picture Controls (you can't remove one of the default styles), press the multi selector right button, then highlight Yes in the screen that follows, and press OK to remove that Picture Control.
- **Store/retrieve style on card.** Choose Load/Save, then select Copy to Camera to locate a Picture Control on your memory card and copy it to the camera, Delete from Card to select a Picture Control on your memory card and remove it, or Copy to Card to duplicate a style currently in your camera onto the memory card. This last option allows you to create and save on your Slot 1 card Picture Controls in excess of the nine that can be loaded into the camera at one time, for a maximum of 99 custom Picture Controls. Once you've copied a style to your memory card, you can modify the version in the camera, give it a new name, and, in effect, create a whole new Picture Control.

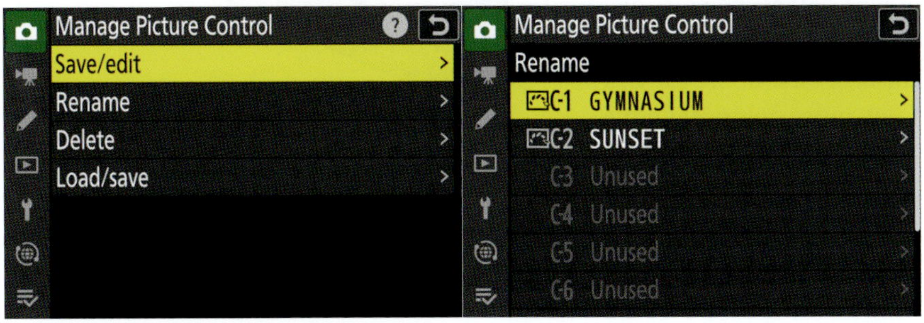

Figure 5.22 You can save, edit, rename, delete, or load and save Picture Controls (left). Picture Controls that you define can be stored in your camera's settings (right).

Set Picture Control (HLG) (Z8 Only)

Options: Standard, Monochrome, Flat

My preference: N/A

As noted, when Tone mode, described earlier, is set to HLG to enable creating HEIF files and HLG video, the conventional Picture Control entry is grayed out. Only Standard, Monochrome, and Flat HLG Picture Controls can be selected from this menu entry. You can adjust the parameters as with the conventional controls described earlier, with the exception that new Highlights and Shadows sliders are available. The extended dynamic range of HEIF files allows making adjustments to bring out or preserve detail in the highlights and shadows to a greater extent than would have been available with JPEG images.

Color Space

Options: sRGB (default), Adobe RGB

My preference: Adobe RGB

The Color Space option gives you two different color spaces (also called *color gamuts*), named Adobe RGB (because it was developed by Adobe Systems in 1998), and sRGB (supposedly because it is the *standard* RGB color space). These two color gamuts define a specific set of colors that can be applied to captured images.

You're probably surprised that the camera doesn't automatically capture *all* the colors we see. Unfortunately, that's impossible because of the limitations of the sensor and the filters used to capture the fundamental red, green, and blue colors, as well as that of the phosphors used to display those colors on the LEDs in your camera and computer monitors. Nor is it possible to *print* every color our eyes detect, because the inks or pigments used don't absorb and reflect colors perfectly. On the other hand, the camera does capture quite a few more colors than we need. A 14-bit RAW image has even more possible colors—16,384 per color channel, or 4.4 *trillion* hues.

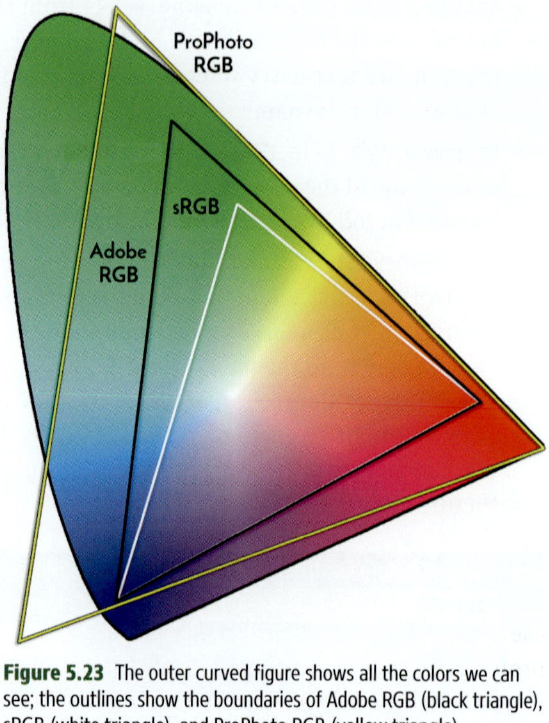

Figure 5.23 The outer curved figure shows all the colors we can see; the outlines show the boundaries of Adobe RGB (black triangle), sRGB (white triangle), and ProPhoto RGB (yellow triangle).

The set of colors, or gamut, that can be reproduced or captured by a given device (scanner, digital camera, monitor, printer, or some other piece of equipment) is represented as a color space that exists within the larger full range of colors. That full range is represented by the odd-shaped splotch of color shown in 5.23, as defined by scientists at an international organization back in 1931. The colors possible with Adobe RGB are represented by the black triangle in the figure, while the sRGB gamut is represented by the smaller white triangle. The location of the corners of each triangle represent the position of the primary red, green, and blue colors in the gamut.

A third color space, ProPhoto RGB, represented by the yellow triangle in the figure, has become more popular among professional photographers as more and more color printing labs support it. While you cannot *save* images using the ProPhoto gamut with your camera, you can convert your photos to 16-bit ProPhoto format using Adobe Camera RAW when you import RAW photos into an image editor. ProPhoto encompasses virtually all the colors we can see (and some we can't), giving advanced photographers better tools to work with in processing their photos. It has richer reds, greens, and blues, although, as you can see from the figure, its green and blue primaries are imaginary (they extend outside the visible color gamut). Those with exacting standards need not use a commercial printing service if they want to explore ProPhoto RGB: many inkjet printers can handle cyans, magentas, and yellows that extend outside the Adobe RGB gamut.

Regardless of which triangle—or color space—is used, you end up with some combination of 16.8 million different colors that can be used in your photograph. (No one image will contain all 16.8 million!) But, as you can see from the figure, the colors available will be *different.*

Adobe RGB, like ProPhoto RGB, is an expanded color space useful for commercial and professional printing, and it can reproduce a wider range of colors. It can also come in useful if an image is going to be extensively retouched, especially within an advanced image editor, like Adobe Photoshop, which has sophisticated color management capabilities that can be tailored to specific color spaces.

The downside is that Adobe RGB images tend to look less saturated on your Z8 or Z9's display and your computer monitor and when viewed on those devices, is likely to be significantly different from what you will get if you output the photo to a printer. The best solution is to *profile* your monitor for the Adobe RGB color space to improve your on-screen rendition using widely available color-calibrating hardware and software. Your camera display can't be profiled, but is not ideal for evaluating color while shooting anyway.

Of course, because Adobe RGB has that wider color gamut than sRGB, it can be your best choice if you will be printing JPEG images on an inkjet printer or a high-end digital printer. You should use the same color space setting in your image-editing software, typically using a color management profile. To that end, you'll need to investigate the wonderful world of *color management,* which uses hardware and software tools to match or *calibrate* all your devices, as closely as possible, so that what you see more closely resembles what you capture, what you see on your computer display, and what ends up on a printed hardcopy. Entire books have been devoted to color management, and most of what you need to know doesn't directly involve your camera, so I won't detail the nuts and bolts here.

While both Adobe RGB and sRGB can reproduce the exact same 16.8 million absolute colors, Adobe RGB spreads those colors over a larger portion of the visible spectrum, as you can see in the figure. Think of a box of crayons (the jumbo 16.8 million crayon variety). Some of the basic crayons from the original sRGB set have been removed and replaced with new hues not contained in the original box. Your "new" box contains colors that can't be reproduced by your computer monitor, but which work just fine with a commercial printing press. For example, Adobe RGB has more "crayons" available in the cyan-green portion of the box, compared to sRGB, which is unlikely to be an advantage unless your image's final destination are the cyan, magenta, yellow, and black inks of a printing press.

If you're not fussy about color fidelity, you can go ahead and use sRGB, as that color space is fine for images that will be output locally on the user's own printer, as this color space matches that of the typical inkjet printer fairly closely. You might actually prefer sRGB as it is well suited for the range of colors that can be displayed on a computer screen and viewed over the Internet. If you plan to take your image file to a retailer's kiosk for printing, sRGB is your best choice, because those automated output devices are calibrated for the sRGB color space that consumers use.

BEST OF BOTH WORLDS

If you plan to use RAW+JPEG for most of your photos, go ahead and set sRGB as your color space. You'll end up with JPEGs suitable for output on your own printer, but you can still extract an Adobe RGB version from the RAW file at any time. It's like shooting two different color spaces at once—sRGB and Adobe RGB—and getting the best of both worlds.

Active D-Lighting

Options: Auto, Extra High 2, Extra High 1, High, Normal, Low, Off (default)

My preference: Off

This is the first entry on the next section of the Photo Shooting menu (see Figure 5.24). Active D-Lighting is a feature that improves the rendition of detail in highlights and shadows when you're photographing high-contrast scenes. It's closely related to, and should not be confused with, *D-Lighting*, which is a "non-active" internal retouching option located in the Retouch options in the Playback version of the *i* menu (and described in Chapter 8). (Retouch was a top-level menu tab in earlier Nikon Z-series cameras, up through the Z7 II and Z6 II.)

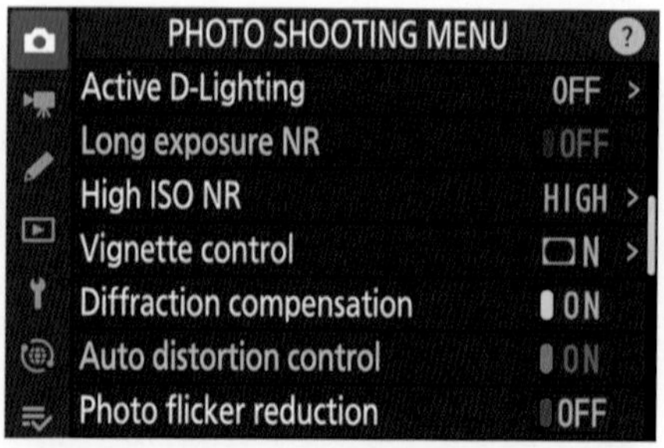

Figure 5.24 The next section of the Photo Shooting menu.

Active D-Lighting, unlike Retouch menu D-Lighting post-processing, applies its tonal improvements *while you are actually taking the photo.* That's good news and bad news. It means that, if you're taking photos in a contrasty environment, Active D-Lighting can automatically improve the apparent dynamic range of your image as you shoot, without additional effort on your part. However, you'll need to disable the feature once you leave the high-contrast lighting behind, and the process does take some time. You wouldn't want to use Active D-Lighting for continuous shooting of sports subjects, for example.

This entry gives you seven choices: Auto, Extra High 2, Extra High 1, High, Normal, Low, and the default, Off. (**Note:** the Retouch version has only High, Normal, and Low options.) You may need to experiment with the feature a little to discover how much D-Lighting you can apply to a high-contrast image before the shadows start to darken objectionably. Note that when this feature is activated, brightness and contrast Picture Control settings cannot be changed. Figure 5.25 shows a "before-and-after" example of Active D-Lighting applied to improve shadow detail. By the time the sample images shown have been half-toned and rendered to the printed page, the differences may be fairly subtle.

For best results, use the Matrix metering mode, so the Active D-Lighting feature can work with a full range of exposure information from multiple points in the image. Active D-Lighting works its magic by subtly *underexposing* your image so that details in the highlights (which would normally be overexposed and become featureless white pixels) are not lost. At the same time, it adjusts the values of pixels located in midtone and shadow areas, so they don't become too dark because of the underexposure. Highlight tones will be preserved, while shadows will eventually be allowed to go dark more readily. Bright beach or snow scenes, especially those with few shadows (think high noon, when the shadows are smaller) can benefit from using Active D-Lighting.

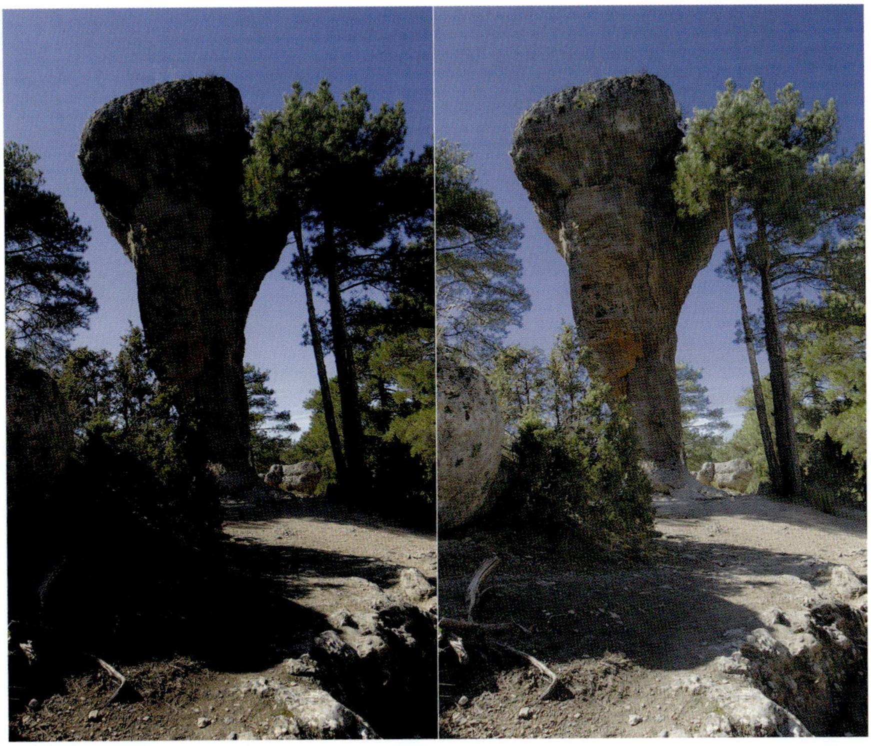

Figure 5.25 No D-Lighting (left); and Extra High 1 (right).

It's important to *always* keep in mind that Active D-Lighting not only adjusts the contrast automatically of your image, it modifies exposure for both existing light and flash as well, as I've noted. The amount of exposure adjustment varies, depending on the level you select, as shown in Table 5.6.

TIP Active D-Lighting cannot be used at ISO Hi 0.3–Hi 2.0. Nikon warns that its use may create noise as random bright pixels, fog, or lines, with uneven shading sometimes visible. In Manual exposure mode, the Auto mode just applies –1/3 and –2/3 stop adjustments to ambient and flash (respectively).

Nikon gives you a lot of flexibility in using Active D-Lighting. You can choose the setting yourself, or let the camera *vary* the amount of tweaking by using Active D-Lighting Bracketing, as described in Chapter 2. You'll find this is a useful feature, if used with caution.

TABLE 5.6 Active D-Lighting Adjustments

SETTING	AMBIENT EXPOSURE ADJUSTMENT	FLASH EXPOSURE ADJUSTMENT
Auto	Exposure calculated based on Matrix metering	Exposure calculated based on Matrix metering
Extra High 2	–1 2/3 stops	–1 stop (or more)
Extra High 1	–1 stop	–1 stop (or more)
High	–2/3 stop	–1 stop
Normal	–1/3 stop	–2/3 stop
Low	No adjustment	–1/3 stop

Long Exposure NR

Options: Off (default), On

My preference: Off. I prefer to apply noise reduction when processing the RAW file.

Visual noise is that awful graininess caused by long exposures and high ISO settings, and which shows up as multicolored specks in images. This setting helps you manage the kind of noise caused by lengthy exposure times. In some ways, noise is like the excessive grain found in some high-speed photographic films. However, while photographic grain is sometimes used as a special effect, it's rarely desirable in a digital photograph. There are easier ways to add texture to your photos.

Some noise is created when you're using shutter speeds longer than one second to create a longer exposure. Extended exposure times allow more photons to reach the sensor but increase the likelihood that some photosites will react randomly even though not struck by a particle of light. Moreover, as the sensor remains switched on for the longer exposure, it heats up, and this heat can be mistakenly recorded as if it were a barrage of photons. This menu setting can be used to activate the long exposure noise-canceling operation performed by the EXPEED 7 digital signal processors.

Here are your options:

- **Off.** This default setting disables long exposure noise reduction. Use it when you want the maximum amount of detail present in your photograph, even though higher noise levels will result. This setting also eliminates the extra time needed to take a picture caused by the noise reduction process. If you plan to use only lower ISO settings (thereby reducing the noise caused by ISO amplification), the noise levels produced by longer exposures may be acceptable. For example, you might be shooting a waterfall at ISO 100 with the camera mounted on a tripod, using a neutral-density filter and a long exposure to cause the water to blur. (Try exposures of 2 to 16 seconds, depending on the intensity of the light and how much blur you want.) (See Figure 5.26.) To maximize detail in the non-moving portions of your photos for the exposures that are one second or longer, you can switch off long exposure noise reduction.
- **On.** When exposures are longer than one second, the camera takes a second, blank exposure to compare that to the first image. Noise (pixels that are bright in a frame that *should* be completely black) in the "dark frame" image is subtracted from your original picture, and only the noise-corrected image is saved to your memory card. Because the noise-reduction process effectively doubles the time required to take a picture, you won't want to use this setting when you're rushed. A message [Performing Noise Reduction] appears on the display and Job NR flashes on the control panel during the process. **Reminder:** If you're using Interval Timer Shooting, make sure your interval between shots is longer than your exposure time to avoid interrupting the noise reduction. Moreover, if you turn off the camera before processing is finished, noise reduction will be canceled and only the unprocessed image will be saved.

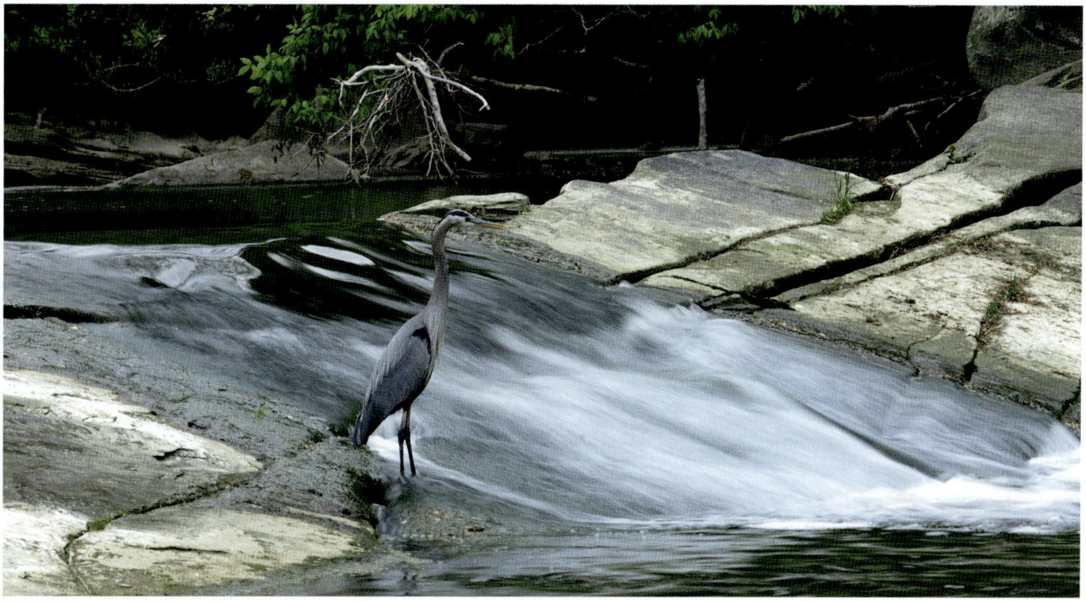

Figure 5.26 A long exposure with the camera mounted on a tripod produces this traditional moving-water photo.

High ISO NR

Options: High, Normal (default), Low, Off

My preference: Normal

Noise can also be caused by higher ISO sensitivity settings. The camera offers direct settings up to ISO 25600 and extended settings that go even higher, up to Hi 2 (the equivalent of ISO 102400). Although it costs you some detail, High ISO noise reduction, which can be set with this menu option, may be a good option in many cases. You can choose Off when you want to preserve detail at the cost of some noise graininess, and the camera will apply high ISO NR only at the highest settings. Or, you can select Low, Normal, and High noise reduction.

The effects of high ISO noise are something like listening to a CD in your car, and then rolling down all the windows. You're adding sonic noise to the audio signal, and while increasing the CD player's volume may help a bit, you're still contending with an unfavorable signal-to-noise ratio that probably mutes tones (especially higher treble notes) that you really want to hear.

The same thing happens when the analog image signal is amplified: You're increasing the image information in the signal but boosting the background fuzziness at the same time. Tune in a very faint or distant AM radio station on your car stereo. Then turn up the volume. After a certain point, turning up the volume further no longer helps you hear better. There's a similar point of diminishing returns for digital sensor ISO increases and signal amplification as well.

As the captured information is amplified to produce higher ISO sensitivities, some random noise in the signal is amplified along with the photon information. Increasing the ISO setting of your camera raises the threshold of sensitivity so that fewer and fewer photons are needed to register as an exposed pixel. Yet, that also increases the chances of one of those phantom photons being counted among the real-life light particles, too.

Fortunately, the stacked CMOS sensor and its dual-channel EXPEED 7 digital-processing chip are optimized to produce low noise levels, so ratings as high as ISO 6400 can be used routinely (although there will be some noise, of course), and even ISO 12800 can generate good results. I regularly shoot concerts at ISO 3200, and indoor sports at ISO 6400. I've even been impressed with results I get at ISO 25600 when High ISO NR is applied. Some kinds of subjects may not require this kind of noise cancellation, particularly with images that have a texture of their own that tends to hide or mask the noise.

Vignette Control

Options: High, Normal (default), Low, Off

My preference: Normal

Some lenses may not be up to the challenge of covering the frame evenly, producing darkening in the corners of your images at certain focal lengths, which is called *vignetting*. If you consistently encounter vignetting, this option may help. You can choose from High, Normal, Low, and Off. It's difficult to quantify exactly how much corner-brightening each setting provides. Your best bet is to shoot some blank walls of a single color with lenses that seem to have this problem and try a few at each of the settings. Then select the value that best seems to counter vignetting with your particular lenses. Results with zoom lenses will vary depending on your focal length setting. Only JPEG images are automatically corrected, but the adjustments can also be applied to RAW files during import.

Diffraction Compensation

Options: On (default), Off

My preference: On

Diffraction is a phenomenon that reduces the sharpness of your image when working at smaller f/stops, especially f/22 or f/32 (if your lens has those apertures available). It can be especially acute with cameras, like the Z9 and Z8, that have exceptionally high resolution. This feature attempts to counteract that effect and works well enough that I leave it enabled by default. Unfortunately, Nikon doesn't deign to tell you what diffraction actually is, or how much it affects your photographs.

Introductory photo courses hammer into budding photographers the idea that smaller f/stops increase sharpness by extending depth-of-field and optimizing the optical effects of particular lenses. In practice, while few lenses are their sharpest wide open, most achieve their maximum sharpness stopped down two or more f/stops; beyond that, diffraction kicks in, and can actually help *reduce* apparent sharpness, due to scattering and interference of individual photons as they pass through smaller lens openings. In effect, the edges of your lens aperture affects proportionately more photons as the f/stop grows smaller. The relative amount of space available to pass freely decreases, and the number of collisions of photons with the edges of the aperture increases.

So, an f/stop of f/11 may produce a slight loss of overall sharpness compared to an opening of f/8 (although depth-of-field will increase); and f/16 will be less sharp than f/11. Images are softened by an almost undetectable amount at every aperture—including wide open—but diffraction becomes more noticeable only at f/stops smaller than f/11. The difference is very slight.

Theoretically, this limit on sharpness should be independent of the resolution of the sensor, or the size of the sensor. The effects of diffraction *should* be the same at, say, f/11, regardless of what type of sensor is being used. However, in practice, smaller pixels do show the effects of diffraction more readily. The diffraction produces a multi-ringed pattern called an *airy disk* (it has nothing to do with air; the phenomenon was named after scientist George Airy), and when the peak area of this disk is large enough, compared to the pixel size of the sensor, or if two disks overlap, an effect may be visible in the image.

Typically, this happens at a particular f/stop with a particular pixel size, and that f/stop is said to be the diffraction limit for that camera/sensor. Point-and-shoot cameras, with their tiny sensors, may begin to show diffraction effects at f/5.6; a cropped-sensor camera at f/11; a lower-resolution full-frame camera (like the 21MP Nikon D6) at f/16; and a camera with *extremely* small pixels, like the Z9 or Z8 at f/11.

Is the sharpness lost to diffraction more objectionable than the reduced *range* of sharpness produced by less depth-of-field at wider apertures? That's up to you. For example, most of the "product" shots of the Z9 and Z8 in this book were taken with my old Nikon D4s at f/22 or f/32, even though that camera's pixels also are prone to diffraction effects. Given the size the images are reproduced in these pages, I felt that the increased depth-of-field of the smaller apertures was worth the possible loss of sharpness from diffraction. In other words, even though more of my subjects were in focus, the overall sharpness of the sharpest parts of the image may be less.

The photons striking the edges of the diaphragm are disrupted from their paths and begin to interfere with those passing through the center of the lens. While this phenomenon takes place at all apertures, it is most pronounced at smaller f/stops.

The best analogy I can think of is a pond with two floating docks sticking out into the water, as shown in Figure 5.27. Throw a big rock in the pond, and the ripples pass between the docks relatively smoothly if the structures are relatively far apart (top). Move them closer together (bottom), and some ripples rebound off each dock to interfere with the incoming wavelets. In a lens, smaller apertures produce the same effect.

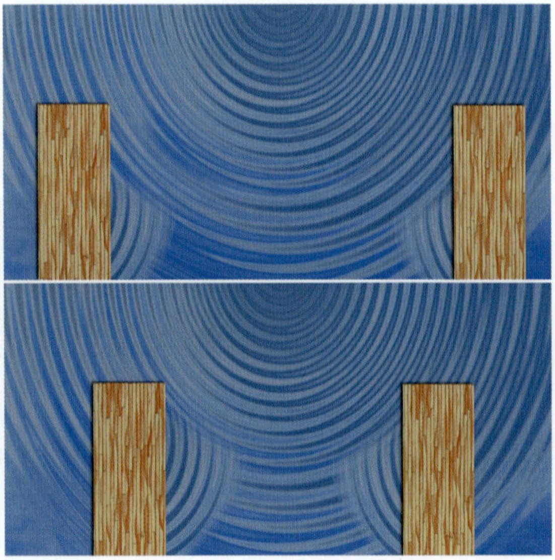

Figure 5.27 Diffraction interference can be visualized as ripples on a lake.

Other than the Diffraction Compensation algorithms Nikon has included in the camera, there's no "cure" for diffraction-limited images, other than to use larger f/stops, or to apply some sharpening of the image in your editor (which is likely to be a losing cause). It is important, then, to be aware of the effects of diffraction on images captured with the camera and take them into account before choosing a small aperture.

Auto Distortion Control

Options: On (default), Off

My preference: On

Wide-angle lenses are prone to barrel distortion, in which straight lines appear to bow outward, especially near the edges of the frame. Telephoto lenses often have the opposite problem: lines may bend inward, producing pincushion distortion. Both of these types of distortion can be easily corrected in your image editor, but your camera's digital image processing chip has similar algorithms built in and can do the job for you. Your choices are easy: just select On or Off to enable or disable this feature. Note that if you have a Z-mount lens attached, On is chosen by default and this menu entry is grayed out and unavailable; it is used primarily with the FTZ adapters.

For the process to work, the lenses must be of a type that can communicate electronically with the camera to let the camera know what type of lens it is working with. All Z-mount lenses can supply the needed information (so turning the feature off is disabled), but if you're using a non-Z-mount lens with an FTZ adapter, you should be working with a G- or D-type optic. The camera will warp the photo before saving it to your memory card, cropping a bit if necessary, to exclude some areas of the image.

Skin Softening

Options: High, Low, Normal, Off (default)

My preference: N/A

Nikon is putting your camera's face recognition prowess to work with an optional complexion-flattering feature than removes texture from portrait shots of humans. The camera can detect and process up to three subjects, using High, Normal, or Low levels of softening. You can also disable the feature by selecting Off. You can specify one level here for stills, and a different level in the Video Recording menu for videos.

When enabled, a gray focus point appears over each subject. You don't need to select People or Auto under the AF Subject Detection options entry (discussed later in this chapter). If you let the camera choose the focus point by selecting Auto-area AF as your AF-area mode, left and right triangles will flank the focus point chosen. The left/right directional controls can be used to move from one subject to another.

Portrait Impression Balance

Options: Mode 1, Mode 2, Mode 3, Off (default)

My preference: Use as needed

This entry allows you to create up to three separate profiles that specify magenta/amber color bias (greens and blues are not affected) and set a brightness level to be used when shooting portraits. To create a specific balance, just follow these steps.

1. **Access this entry.** Navigate to the Portrait Impression Balance entry in the Photo Shooting menu.
2. **Select Mode 1, 2, or 3.** Highlight the mode you want to use/define and press the right directional button. (See Figure 5.28, left.)
3. **Adjust color bias and/or brightness.** When the screen shown in Figure 5.28, right, appears, use the directional controls to move the setting point from the center. Up/down adjusts brightness, while left/right moves the point along the magenta/amber-yellow axis.
4. **Exit.** Press OK to confirm and exit, or the Trash button to cancel your adjustments. Modes that have been changed from the default value will be marked with an asterisk on the display.

This feature is not available when Monochrome or Creative Picture Controls are active, nor when Monochrome is selected for Set Picture Control (HLG), as described earlier.

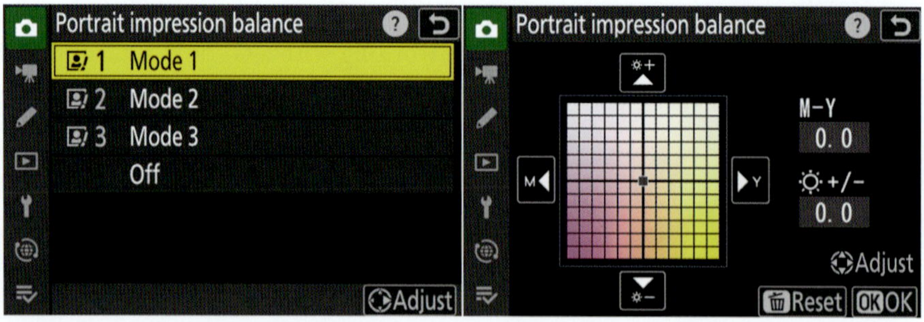

Figure 5.28 Customizing a Portrait Impression Balance.

Photo Flicker Reduction

Options: On, Off (default)

My preference: Use as needed

You've been living with flickering artificial illumination all your life, and never noticed it. Old-fashioned incandescent lights using 60 Hz (Hertz) circuits flicker at 100 to 120 cycles per second, but change their intensity only by a few percent. That's generally not enough to cause discomfort or affect photography. Other types, such as fluorescent and mercury-vapor sources, however, can produce banding, flickering, or alternate light/dark exposures.

Novice sports photographers often ask me why shots they take in certain gymnasiums or arenas have inconsistent exposure, wildly varying color, or banding. The answer is that certain types of artificial lighting have a much more pronounced blinking cycle at 120 Hz in the US and 100 Hz in most other countries. That more extreme flickering is still virtually imperceptible to the eye, but can be captured by the camera if you take a picture using a shutter speed faster than 1/125th second.

This setting, when enabled, detects the light source's blinking frequency (it's optimized for 100 Hz to 120 Hz), and takes the picture at the moment when the flicker has the least effect on the final image. If you've been using digital cameras for a long time, you may remember there was a nagging problem called *shutter lag,* the delay between when the shutter release was pressed all the way down and when the picture was actually taken. Flicker reduction brings shutter lag back, but for a positive reason.

This flicker reduction feature uses the exposure meter to detect light flicker in the 100 Hz and 120 Hz frequencies. When enabled, the camera delays shutter release timing a tiny bit to avoid the "dim" cycle of the light source and giving you a frame that's evenly lit and fully illuminated. If you're taking photos continuously (a common mode when capturing sports), the camera adjusts both the release timing and frame rate so you can capture each shot during the light source's maximum output. You may experience that slight shutter release time lag as the camera "waits" for the proper instant, and your Continuous Low-Speed shooting rate may be reduced, which makes this setting a necessary evil for sports and other activities involving action.

When flicker is detected, a green dot will appear next to the Flicker icon in the shooting display, which will briefly go dark when the shutter is triggered. There is an exception for Continuous

High-Speed modes when in AF-C focus mode and Custom Setting a1 (AF-C Priority Selection) is set to Release; the display will darken only after the first shot in a sequence, and the frame rate will be prioritized.

The feature may not work well for scenes with dark backgrounds, decorative or especially bright lighting, and is not effective when making Bulb or Time exposures (make sure you haven't selected C30, C60, or C120 extended exposures).

High-Frequency Flicker Reduction

Options: On (Shutter speed fine tuning), Off (default)

My preference: Off

This is the first entry on the next screen of the Photo Shooting menu (see Figure 5.29). While the Photo Flicker Reduction entry described above does a good job with most light sources, some newer types of lighting, including higher-quality LED lamps, flicker with lower intensities and much higher frequencies, and require more advanced correction. This setting allows fine-tuning the shutter speed in Shutter-priority or Manual exposure modes so that it syncs up with the cycle of flickering light sources to reduce or eliminate those undesirable banding effects.

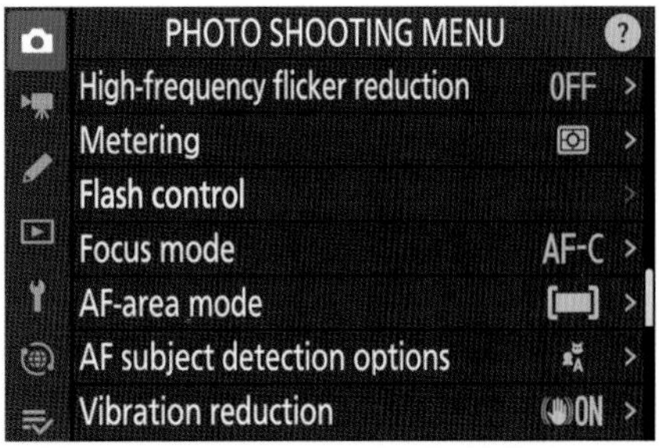

Figure 5.29 The next screen of the Photo Shooting menu.

If you want to store a fine-tuned shutter speed that works for a particular light source, you can store it for instant recall using the Custom Setting f2: Custom Controls (Shooting) entry. Choose either the Recall Shooting Functions or Recall Shooting Functions (Hold) behavior for your custom button. Select Shutter Speed as one of the functions to be saved. Then, when you press the custom button, previously stored settings will be retrieved and you can restore your original settings by pressing the button a second time. I'll explain custom controls in more detail in Chapter 8.

Here's how to use High-Frequency Flicker Reduction:

1. **Enable High-Frequency Flicker Reduction.** If you suspect your scene has LED illumination and want to use S or M exposure modes, navigate to this entry and turn this feature on. The Z9 allows defining up to four presets.
2. **Take sample image.** Capture a sample image and review it in magnified Playback mode and look for banding.
3. **Fine-tune shutter speed.** Examine your scene through the viewfinder, pressing the Magnify button to zoom in.
4. **Adjust shutter speed.** Rotate the command dial until the banding disappears. The shutter speed display will change in smaller 1/96th-stop increments. For example, instead of switching from 1/250th to 1/320th second, successive clicks will take you to 1/250.5 to 1/252.3 to 1/254.2 to 1/256 second, and so on. You can fine-tune your shutter speed in the range between 1/8000th to 1/30th second.

5. **Take new sample image.** Confirm that your adjustment has worked by taking and examining a new sample image of your scene.
6. **Adjustment is "sticky."** Your new shutter speed will remain if you turn the camera off and on again. Should you switch to an exposure mode other than M or S, normal shutter speed increments will return in those modes, but your fine-tuned setting will be restored when you switch back to M or S. Turn High-Frequency Flicker Reduction off to revert to normal speed selection in those modes.

Metering

Options: Matrix (default), Center-weighted, Spot, Highlight-weighted metering

My preference: Matrix

This menu entry is a slower alternative to setting the metering mode using the Z9's *i* menu. It exists primarily so you can assign this menu entry to a custom key using the Custom Setting f2: Custom Controls menu entry (explained in Chapter 7).

For example, if you tend to change metering mode frequently, even a visit to the *i* menu can be bothersome. Define, say, a button to Metering, and each time you press that button you'll be able to rotate the command dial to flip among the four choices. Note that you can also define a button to immediately switch to a specific metering mode, so you can, for example, set Matrix metering as your default mode, then toggle to Spot metering while holding down the defined button.

I explained how to use each of these metering modes in Chapter 2 and won't repeat that information here.

Flash Control

Options: Flash control mode, Flash compensation (TTL), Wireless Flash options, Remote flash control, Group flash options, Radio remote flash info.

My preference: N/A

This entry is available only when a "unified flash control" flash is attached and powered up. Compatible flashes include the Nikon SB-5000, SB-500, SB-400, or SB-300 Speedlights. I explained how to use the available options in Chapter 4 and will not duplicate that information here. All other Nikon electronic flash units, including the SB-600, SB-700, SB-800, SB-900, and SB-910 must be adjusted using the controls on the flash itself.

Before you howl "planned obsolescence!" you should know that *all* Nikon pro bodies that lacked a built-in flash have *always* required making most settings on the optional flash. The Flash Control feature is a relatively recent addition to the Nikon line, made possible by features built into the (fairly) recent flash units cited, so you're actually gaining capability. If you connect any of the other Speedlights (I own all of them, and I tried), the Flash Control entry is grayed out.

Flash Mode (Z8 Only)

Options: Fill Flash (default), Red-eye Reduction, Slow Sync, Slow Sync+Red-eye, Rear-curtain Sync, Flash Off

My preference: N/A

This setting, available only in the Z8's menu system, specifies whether the camera uses fill flash, red-eye reduction, rear-curtain sync, or disables the flash entirely. To set these same flash modes with the Z9, press the button with the Flash icon on the left shoulder of the camera and rotate the command dial to cycle through these options. I explained when and why to use each of these in Chapter 4 and won't repeat that information here.

Flash Compensation (Z8 Only)

Options: -3.0 to +1.0 stops of exposure; Default: 0.0

My preference: N/A

As I write this, the Z8 has a separate entry for setting flash exposure compensation. You can use flash exposure compensation to adjust the flash output to balance the brightness of the main subject illuminated by the flash, compared to the background. Don't confuse this entry with Custom Setting e3: Exposure Compensation for Flash (described in Chapter 7), which tells the camera to apply flash exposure compensation to the background only, or to the entire frame. The two options work together to let you effectively balance your flash output between the two.

Focus Mode

Options: AF-S (default), AF-C, MF

My preference: N/A

This entry is a slower alternative to using the *i* menu to switch from one focus mode to another, as explained in Chapter 3. It can be assigned to a custom key if you need fast access to this setting.

AF-Area Mode

Options: Pinpoint AF, Single-point AF (default), Dynamic-area AF (Small, Medium, Large), Wide-area AF (Small, Large, C1, C2), 3D-tracking, Auto-area AF

My preference: N/A

You can choose the AF-area mode to be used. I described AF-area selection in Chapter 3 and won't repeat my advice here. Like several entries discussed above, it duplicates its *i* menu counterpart, and can be assigned to a custom key for direct access. This menu entry is a slower alternative to using the *i* menu to switch from one focus mode to another.

AF Subject Detection Options

Options: Auto (default), People, Animal, Birds, Vehicle, Airplanes, Subject detection off

My preference: Auto

You can set the priority for the type of subject the camera will look for during autofocus, using an amazing range of types. Subject detection is possible when any of the Wide-Area AF modes (Small, Large, Custom 1, Custom 2), Pinpoint AF, Single-point AF, 3D-tracking, or Auto-area AF are active. You can set separate priorities for detection in the Photo Shooting and Video Recording menus. I explained subject detection in detail in Chapter 3 and won't duplicate that information here.

Vibration Reduction

Options: On (or Normal) (default), Spt (Sport), Off

My preference: N/A

Use this setting to enable vibration reduction, a great feature that counters camera/photographer shake. The VR options may vary depending on which lens you are using. Some optics contain their own vibration reduction technology, which can integrate with, and improve on, the results you get from the in-body image stabilization (IBIS) alone.

When VR is enabled, an indicator appears at the left side of the viewfinder or LCD monitor when using the main shooting screen. Use On (or Normal; the nomenclature varies depending on the lens) for subjects that are not moving to counter camera shake or photographer jitteriness. The Sport setting is recommended for fast and unpredictably moving subjects, especially if you're panning the camera to follow their movements. In that case, in Sport mode the camera's vibration reduction ignores side-to-side movement and corrects only camera shake in other directions. Sport mode also doesn't re-center the VR elements between shots, allowing for faster response.

Use Off if the camera is locked down on a tripod, or if you don't need it and want to conserve the 10 percent reduction in battery life that VR produces. If you will be swiveling the camera on the tripod or using a monopod, then turning VR off is not required. If you use this setting frequently, you can assign the function to an *i* menu position using Custom Setting f1: Customize *i* menu.

While the camera has on-sensor in-body image stabilization, and some Z-mount lenses also have VR, you can also use F-mount lenses with an FTZ adapter, which themselves may include their own vibration reduction. When using an adapted lens without VR, use this menu entry to make VR adjustments for the camera. If the adapted lens does have VR, then the switches on the adapted lens overrides any setting you make here. If the adapted VR lens has Off, Normal, and Sport settings (the same as found in this menu entry) then VR adjustments can only be made using the lens switches. If the adapted lens has an Active setting (useful for countering tiny, sharp movements, say from a moving vehicle), and you set the lens switch to Active, the camera uses the Normal VR setting instead.

Image stabilization/vibration reduction can take many forms, and Nikon has expertise in all of them. *Electronic IS*, used in video cameras (and also available in the Z9 and Z8 while shooting videos)

involves shifting pixels around from frame to frame so that pixels that are not moving remain in the same position, and portions of the image that *are* moving don't stray from their proper path. *Optical image stabilization*, which Nikon calls vibration reduction (VR), is built into many Nikon F-mount lenses, and some Z-mount lenses as well, particularly the S-line telephoto zooms and primes. This type of vibration reduction involves lens elements that shift in response to camera movement, as detected by motion sensors included in the optics.

The final type of VR technology is called *in-body image stabilization* (IBIS) and is built-into the Z9/Z8. It adjusts the position of the sensor carriage itself to counteract movement. Nikon claims 5-axis VR, as seen in Figure 5.30, and the effective improvement can range from 3 stops to 6 stops or more, depending on which F-mount or Z-mount lens you're using. The results can be spectacular–with a 5-stop improvement, a photograph taken at 1/30th second should have the same sharpness (at least in terms of resistance to camera shake) as one shot at 1/1000th second. In practical terms, you probably won't experience such a dramatic gain, however.

Of course, no amount of vibration reduction can eliminate blur from moving subjects, but you should find yourself less tied to a tripod when using longer lenses, or when working with wide-angle lenses under dim lighting conditions than in the past. If you're taking photos in venues where flash or tripods are forbidden, you'll find the camera's image stabilization invaluable.

How It Works

As I mentioned, IBIS uses gyroscope-like motion sensors to detect camera motion. When such motion is sensed, the carriage holding the sensor is shifted a precise amount in the opposite direction. Movement can occur along one of five different axes, as shown in Figure 5.30:

- **X and y axes.** These movements occur when the camera shifts in the x and y directions; that is, the camera moves from side to side or up and down within the plane of the sensor. Shifts in the x and y directions are likely to occur when shooting macro images hand-held but can take place any time. This motion is very easy for the IBIS to detect.

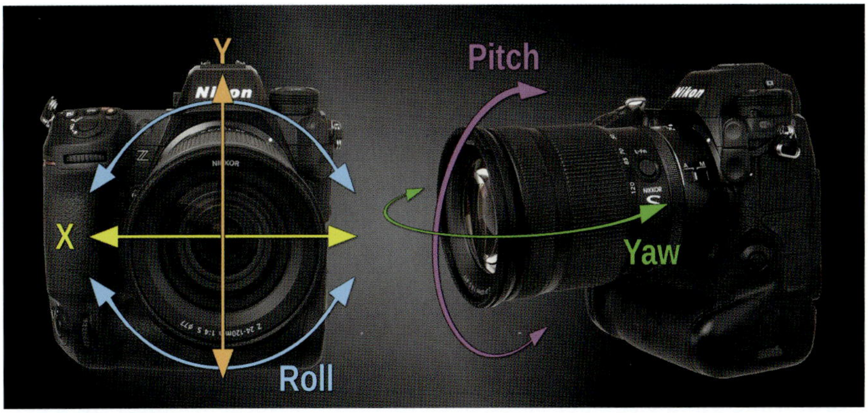

Figure 5.30 The five axes of vibration reduction stabilization.

- **Roll.** This is the rotation of the camera along an axis passing through the center of the front of the lens, or an axis parallel to it. It's easiest to picture the rotational point as the center of the lens, but it may be located closer to your hand as you grip the camera body. Roll happens when you, say, align the horizon while shooting a landscape. There may be a tendency to continue to "correct" for the horizon as you shoot, producing vibration along the roll axis. Roll is especially noticeable in video clips because it's easy to see straight lines changing their orientation during a shot. This type of motion can also be easily handled by IBIS.
- **Pitch.** This type of movement happens when the camera shake is such that the lens is tilted up or down, often because the lens itself is a front-heavy telephoto lens. The magnification of the tele only serves to exaggerate the changes in pitch. Pitch movement tends to be less critical with wide-angle lenses. The camera's in-body image stabilization is less adept at countering this type of movement. It's one case in which vibration reduction built into the lens potentially provides superior correction. That's what happens when you use either an F-mount or Z-mount lens that includes VR; the pitch (and roll) compensation is passed off to the lens itself. Nikon calls this integration *Synchro VR*.
- **Yaw.** Telephotos are also a major contributor to *yaw* vibrations, in which the camera pivots slightly as if you were shooting a panorama—even when you're *not*. VR built into Z-mount lenses (or any F-mount lenses attached with the FTZ adapter) provide higher degrees of correction.

Best of Both Worlds

While it's true that IBIS can do a great job correcting for camera shake, VR built into the lens can potentially do a *better* job for some types of motion. As I noted, in-body stabilization is best for countering movement in the x and y directions, and for compensating for roll; the camera's mechanism can detect side-to-side, up-and-down, and rotational movement of the sensor extremely well. IBIS is slightly less adept at detecting the motion of front-heavy telephoto lenses as they tilt up or down or rotate along a vertical axis. The magnification of the tele only serves to exaggerate the changes in pitch and yaw.

Fortunately, that's where vibration reduction built into lenses and Nikon's Synchro VR capabilities shine. If you are using a lens that does have VR—either a native Z-mount lens or one of the many F-mount lenses that include the feature—the camera uses the two technologies in tandem, allowing the lens to correct for pitch and yaw, while the built-in vibration reduction—in-body IS (IBIS)—compensates for x, y, and roll movements. That makes a lot of sense, because in correcting for x, y, and roll, the camera is able to keep the sensor in the exact same plane to preserve precise focus and simply move the sensor carriage up, down, or slightly rotated to nullify the movement.

However, not all non-stabilized lenses benefit in identical ways from Nikon's stabilization technology. For best results, the system needs to know both focal length and focus distance to provide optimum stabilization. That's an advantage of VR: stabilization built into the lens always knows exactly what focal length setting and focus distance is being used. Focal length information is needed to correct for pitch and yaw, while x and y compensation need to know the focal distance. (Roll correction needs neither type of data and can do its thing just from what IBIS sees happening on the sensor.) However, when all the data is available, the full array of the camera's IS capabilities can be used to correct on all five axes.

Here's a quick summary of some things you should keep in mind:

- **Tripod use.** For best results, turn off vibration reduction when the camera is mounted on a tripod.
- **Vibration reduction doesn't stop action.** Please don't forget this! No type of stabilization is a panacea to replace the action-stopping capabilities of a faster shutter speed. If you need to use 1/1000th second to freeze a high jumper in mid-air, VR doesn't help you.
- **Stabilization might slow you down.** The process of adjusting the sensor to counter camera shake takes time, just as autofocus does, so you might find that VR adds to the lag between when you press the shutter and when the picture is taken. Sport mode is faster than Normal mode. In a situation where you want to capture a fleeting instant that can happen suddenly, image stabilization might not be your best choice.
- **Give vibration reduction a helping hand.** When you simply do not want to carry a tripod all day and you'll be relying on the IBIS system, brace the camera or your elbows on something solid, like the roof of a car or a piece of furniture. Remember that an inexpensive monopod can be quite compact when not extended; brace one against a rock, a bridge abutment, or a fence and you might be able to get blur-free photos at surprisingly long shutter speeds.

Auto Bracketing

Options: Auto Bracketing Set (default: AE & Flash Bracketing), Number of Shots (default: 0F), Increment (default: 1.0), Amount (ADL bracketing only)

My preference: N/A

This entry is the first on the next section of the Photo Shooting menu. (See Figure 5.31.) It allows you to set up bracketing, a useful technique explained in detail in Chapter 3. I won't repeat the step-by-step instructions here. To recap, your options are as follows:

- **Auto Bracketing Set.** Autoexposure and Flash bracketing, Autoexposure Bracketing (only), Flash bracketing (only), White balance bracketing, Active D-Lighting bracketing.
- **Number of Shots.** Use the left/right directional controls or the touch screen to specify the number of shots in your bracket set (or 0F to disable bracketing entirely). Up to nine shots can be selected (0F–9F).
- **Increment.** From 0.3- (one-third stop) to 3.0-stop increments between bracketed exposures.
- **Amount (ADL bracketing only).** If you're doing Active D-Lighting bracketing, you can select up to five shots, which will determine the amount of ADL applied to each in the range Off, Low, Normal, High, and High*.

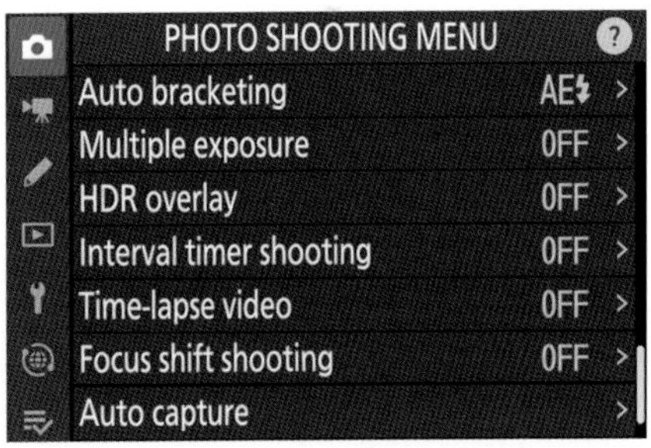

Figure 5.31 The next part of the Photo Shooting menu.

Multiple Exposure

Options: Multiple Exposure Mode: On (Series), On (Single Photo), Off; Number of Shots: 2 to 10; Overlay Mode: Add, Average, Lighten, Darken; Save Individual Pictures (RAW): On, Off; Overlay Shooting (On); Select First Exposure (RAW)

My preference: Multiple Exposure Mode: On (Series); Number of Shots/Overlay Mode, varies

This option lets you combine from 2 to 10 exposures into one image without the need for an image editor such as Photoshop, and it can be an entertaining way to return to those thrilling days of yesteryear, when complex photos were created in the camera itself. In truth, prior to the digital age, multiple exposures were a cool, groovy, far-out, hep/hip, phat, sick, fabulous way of producing composite images. Today, it's more common to take the lazy way out, snap two or more pictures, and then assemble them in an image editor like Photoshop.

Your Nikon Z9 and Z8's Retouch features, available from the Playback version of the *i* menu, can serve as an in-camera replacement for Photoshop, allowing you to combine two images using the Overlay mode (Add) option. As many as 10 shots can be combined using the Motion Blend option in the Playback *i* menu. The advantage of post-processing in the camera is that you can preview your effect before creating a final image. However, the "live" features of the Multiple Exposure entry are more versatile.

You can turn the Multiple Exposure feature off, direct the camera to continue taking multiple exposures until you turn it off (Series), or revert to non-multiple exposure mode after taking one picture (Single Photo). You can elect to keep all exposures, or discard all but the combined multiple exposure, and use a RAW image on your memory card as the base photo on which subsequent pictures are overlaid.

You should keep in mind that some of Nikon's previous implementations of multiple exposure allowed you to choose between combining the exposures of each image to produce the final shot or dividing the exposures equally among the shots. The Z9 and Z8 have additional options and calls the array of choices "Overlay mode," described below.

Once you've selected an Overlay mode, you can turn the use of overlays on or off using the Overlay Shooting option in the sub-menu. The camera has one additional feature, Save Individual Pictures (RAW), which, as you might expect, tells the camera to save the individual photos used to create the multiple exposure in separate RAW files.

This capability can be useful in several ways. First, you may find that one specific frame of your multiple exposure might have made an excellent stand-alone image in its own right. When Save Individual Pictures (RAW) is active, you can retrieve that frame and use it as you like. In addition, having all the shots of the multiple exposure available means you can use them to create your own multi-shot image in Photoshop or your favorite image editor. I do this most often when I discover that one frame doesn't "work" for a given multiple exposure image, but the others meld together well. I can create my own version manually, adjusting brightness, contrast, or other parameters as I go, to "fine-tune" what started out as an automated multiple exposure.

Also useful is the Select First Exposure (RAW) option. If you want to overlay all your subsequent multiple exposures on top of an existing image already on your memory card (say, a background that you'd like to merge with your sequence), you can choose this setting. You'll be taken to the camera's standard image selection screen and offered the choice of any RAW image available on your card. This is a cool way of replacing boring one-color backgrounds with something more interesting.

To take your own multiple exposures, just follow these steps (although it's probably a good idea to do a little planning and maybe even some sketching of a layout on paper first, if that's possible):

1. **Choose capture sequence.** There are two ways to capture multiple exposure images in sequence:
   - **Individual frames.** Each image in the sequence is taken one at a time when you specify, either by pressing the shutter release in Single shot mode, or by using the self-timer. You'd want to use this mode to combine subjects precisely as you frame them individually.
   - **With one press of shutter release.** Use Continuous Low or Continuous High release modes and the camera will expose all images in the sequence one after another. You'd use this mode to track a moving subject.
2. **Activate the feature.** Choose Multiple Exposure from the Photo Shooting menu. (See Figure 5.32.)
3. **Choose Multiple Exposure mode.** Select Multiple Exposure mode. A submenu appears with three choices:
   - **On (series).** The Multiple Exposure feature remains active even after you've taken a complete set of exposures for the number of shots you specified. Use this if you want to shoot several multiple exposures in a row. Remember to turn it off when you're done.
   - **On (single photo).** Once you've taken a single set of multiple exposures, the feature turns itself off. In this mode, when using Continuous Low or Continuous High, the camera will capture one sequence, and then return to non-multiple exposure mode.
   - **Off.** Use this option to cancel multiple exposures.

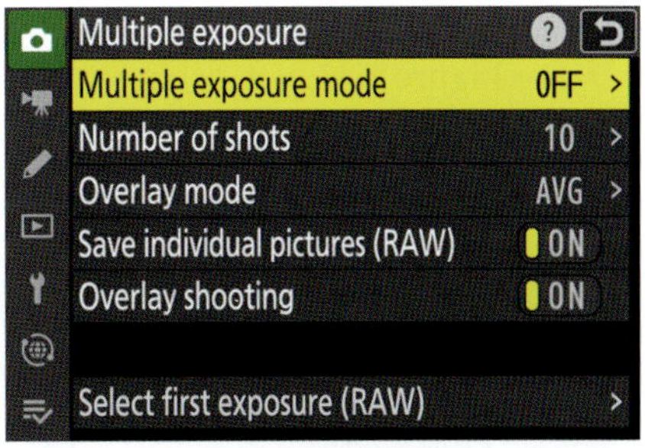

Figure 5.32 The Multiple Exposure menu.

4. **Choose exposures per frame.** Select Number of Shots, choose a value from 2 to 10 with the directional controls, and press OK.
5. **Specify ratio of exposure between frames.** Choose Overlay Mode and select Add, Average, Lighten, or Darken.
   - **Add.** In this mode, each new exposure is added to the previous shots. I use this when photographing a subject that is moving against a dark background. A series of renditions, each fully exposed, appears in the overlaid image to track the subject's movement. (See Figure 5.33, left.)
   - **Average.** In this mode, the camera divides the overall exposure by the number of shots in the series and gives each shot that fraction of the overall exposure. That is, for a four-shot multiple series, the specified exposure for each is set at 1/4 of the total amount. I use this when shooting subjects with a great deal of overlap. (See Figure 5.33, right.)

- **Lighten.** The camera compares pixels in the same position in each exposure and uses only the brightest. This effect is similar to the Lighten blending mode in Photoshop, Lightroom, and other image-editing software. Use this to allow the lightest tones of each shot in the series to show through, such as multiple bursts in a fireworks show. The sky will remain dark, but the pyrotechnics will be captured perfectly. You may have to experiment with this setting until you become familiar with what it does to your images.
- **Darken.** Similar to the Lighten blending mode, only just the darkest pixels are saved. You'd use this in situations that are the opposite of those typical of the Add selection. That is, if the background is light, and a darker subject is moving across that background, Darken would provide separate images.

6. **Confirm setting.** Press OK to set the Overlay mode exposure ratio.
7. **Save Individual Pictures (RAW).** Ordinarily, the camera combines all the shots into a single exposure. However, you can ask the camera to save *all* the individual images in the series as RAW files by choosing On in the Save Individual Pictures (RAW) entry. **Note:** The camera is smart enough to save RAW images as requested *even if Image Quality is currently at a JPEG-only setting.* You'll end up with a combined JPEG image, plus the desired RAW versions.
8. **Overlay Shooting.** This setting shouldn't be confused with Overlay mode, described above. If you select On, then each subsequent exposure is superimposed in the previous images on the LCD display as you shoot. That's particularly useful when you're capturing each image individually. For Figure 5.33, left, I shot two images of saxophonist Todd Cooper of the Alan Parsons Project individually, moving the camera slightly between shots to create a collage of sorts. It was easy to do in Live View mode using this overlay feature.

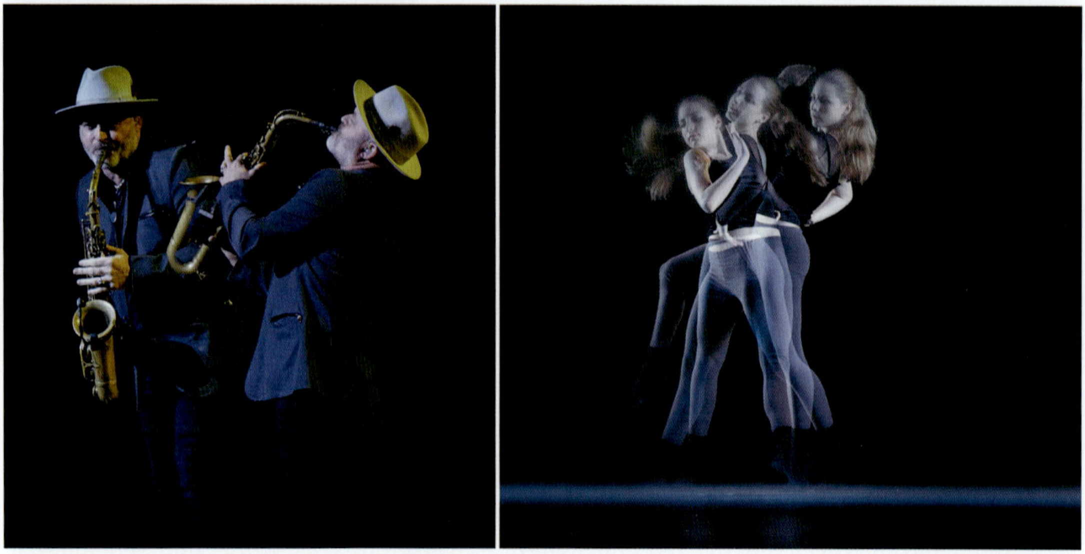

Figure 5.33 Add overlay mode (left) and Average overlay mode (right).

9. **Select First Exposure (RAW).** This is a great feature! You can select an existing RAW image on your memory card and use that as the background for your subsequent multiple exposures. As you capture the individual shots, they will be blended with the background image using the Overlay mode you've selected.
10. **Shoot your multiple exposure set.** In Single shot mode, capture the photo by pressing the shutter-release button multiple times until all the exposures in the series have been taken. When using Continuous Low or Continuous High, the entire series will be shot in a single burst as you hold down the shutter-release button. As each exposure is made, the remaining exposures indicator in the lower-right corner of the frame will indicate which frame is being captured, counting down from r10 to r00, for example. A blinking multiple exposure icon at the right edge of the display vanishes when the series is finished. **Reminder:** you'll need to deactivate the Multiple Exposure feature once you've finished taking a set in On (series) mode, as the setting remains even after the camera has been powered off.

Keep in mind if you wait longer than 30 seconds between any two photos in the series, the sequence will terminate and combine the images taken so far. If you want a longer elapsed time between exposures, go to the Playback menu and make sure On has been specified for Picture Review, and then extend the Standby Timer using Custom Setting c3: Power Off Delay to an appropriate maximum interval. The camera will grant you an additional 30 seconds beyond that. The Multiple Exposure feature will then use the monitor-off delay as its maximum interval between shots.

HDR Overlay

Options: HDR mode: On (Series), On (Single Photo), Off (default); HDR Strength: Auto (default), Extra High, High, Normal, Low; Save Individual Pictures (RAW)

My preference: HDR mode: On (Series); HDR Strength: Auto

I was surprised at how well Nikon has solved the hand-held auto HDR problem, because there are two stumbling blocks that, at least theoretically, should lead to less-than-awesome results. First, when your camera can perform HDR for you on the fly, there is the tendency to put the feature to work under non-optimal conditions; specifically, impromptu hand-held situations. If you've done any traditional HDR, you know that the technique works best when the camera is mounted on a tripod, so that the bracketed exposures are virtually identical except for the exposure itself. Although all HDR software can correct for slight camera movement and align images that are slightly out of register, the results I've gotten have not been great. I expected hand-held HDR to be comparable. However, Nikon's implementation does an excellent job.

The second theoretical weakness of the HDR feature is the limitation of combining just two shots to arrive at the final image. The best traditional HDR photos I've produced have involved at least three shots, and more frequently five or more, each separated by a stop of exposure. The camera takes two shots, total, and combines them. Despite these speed bumps, I've been pleased with my results. I outlined the steps for using HDR Overlay in Chapter 2 and won't repeat them here.

Interval Timer Shooting

Options: Start; Start Options: Now, Choose Start Day and Start Time; Interval; Intervals × Shots/Interval; Exposure Smoothing: On/Off; Interval Priority: On/Off; Focus Before Each Shot: On/Off; Options: AE Bracketing, Time-lapse Video, Off; Starting Storage Folder: New Folder, Reset File Numbering

My preference: N/A

The Z9/Z8's built-in time-lapse photography feature allows you to take pictures for up to 999 intervals in bursts of as many as nine shots, with a delay of up to 23 hours and 59 minutes between shots/bursts, and an initial start-up time of as long as 23 hours and 59 minutes from the time you activate the feature. That means that if you want to photograph a rosebud opening and would like to photograph the flower once every two minutes over the next 16 hours, you can do that easily. If you like, you can delay the first photo taken by a couple hours, so you don't have to stand there by the camera waiting for the right moment.

Or you might want to photograph a particular scene every hour for 24 hours to capture, say, a landscape from sunrise to sunset to the following day's sunrise again. I will offer two practical tips right now, in case you want to run out and try interval timer shooting immediately: *use a tripod, and for best results over longer time periods, plan on connecting your camera to an external power source!*

As you can see from the Options listing above and Figure 5.34, the available parameters are numerous, with many additional settings nested in submenus. I described them in detail in Chapter 2, and won't recap here.

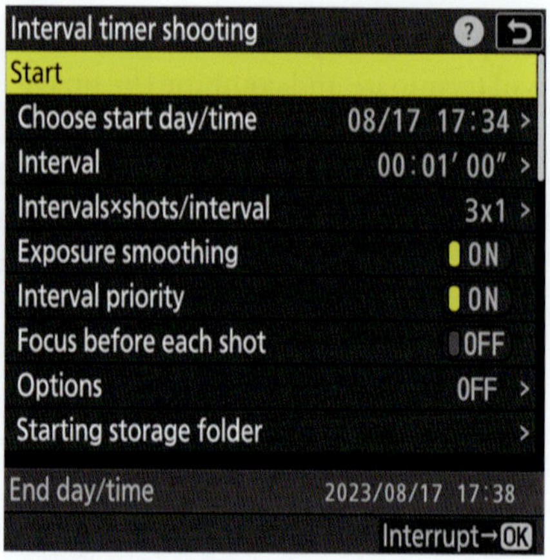

Figure 5.34 Interval timer shooting options.

Time-Lapse Video

Options: Start, Interval, Shooting Time, Exposure Smoothing, Choose Image Area, Video File Type, Frame Size/Frame Rate, Interval Priority, Focus Before Each Shot, Destination

My preference: None

As I said in Chapter 2, time-lapse videos correspond to interval timer shooting, described previously, but allow shooting video clips instead of still photographs (or a series of still photographs). The camera automatically creates a silent time-lapse video at the frame resolution and rate you've selected in the Video Recording menu. Nikon recommends using a white balance other than Auto, and covering the eyepiece opening to prevent light from entering the viewfinder and affecting exposure. And, of course, you'll want to use a tripod and either a fully charged battery or optional AC adapter or other power source.

The options are very similar to those of interval timer shooting:

- **Start.** Unlike the similar Interval Timer Shooting found in the Photo Shooting menu, Time-Lapse Video has no Start Options. Make your other settings, select Start, and time-lapse video will begin about three seconds later.
- **Interval.** Select an interval between frames; use a longer value for slow-moving action (such as a flower bud unfolding), and a shorter value for videos, say, depicting humans moving around at a comical pace. You can select an interval from one second to 10 minutes.
- **Shooting Time.** You can specify time-lapse video duration.
- **Exposure Smoothing.** You can turn exposure smoothing on or off. When activated, the camera adjusts the exposure of each frame to match that of the previous frame in P, S, or A mode. Smoothing can also be used in Manual mode, but, of course, the exposure system won't vary the shutter speed *or* aperture. You must have set ISO Sensitivity to Auto. Press OK to confirm.
- **Choose Image Area.** Select FX-based video format or DX-based video format. You can also turn Auto DX crop on or off, so the camera will recognize DX lenses and crop appropriately.
- **Video File Type.** You can choose H.265 8-bit .MOV-format video or H.264 8-bit .MP4 video. The .MOV format makes 4K and 8K video available, as described next.
- **Frame Size/Frame Rate.** Here you can select the frame size and frames per second setting for your time-lapse video. If you chose H.265 8-bit .MOV video format above, you can select from 7680 × 4320, 30/25/24p; 3840 × 2160, 60/50/30/25/24p; and 1920 × 1060, 60/50/25/24p frame rates. The four 1920 × 1080 combinations are the only ones available if you opt for H.264 8-bit .MP4 video.
- **Interval Priority.** This setting is similar to its intervalometer counterpart, as explained previously. It takes care of situations in which the shutter speed automatically selected in Program or Aperture-priority ends up being longer than the interval between shots. When enabled, the camera captures the video frame at the specified interval, even if a shorter shutter speed must be used, causing underexposure. You can activate Auto ISO Sensitivity Control and select a minimum shutter speed that is shorter than the interval time. When disabled, the camera increases the interval you specified to allow correct exposure.
- **Focus Before Each Shot.** Choose On to tell the camera to focus before each new exposure. Use this option if your subject is likely to move or, more commonly, a different subject is in the frame for some or all exposures. For example, if you were recording passersby on a busy street, some might be closer to the camera than others.
- **Destination.** Choose Slot 1 or Slot 2. Scroll down to see this last option.

Focus Shift Shooting

Options: Start, Number of Shots, Focus Step Width, Interval until Next Shot, First-Frame Exposure Lock, Focus Position Auto Reset, Starting Storage Folder

My preference: N/A

Focus shift/stacking is a great technique that allows combining a series of photos each taken using a different plane of focus, so that they can be combined in an image editor to produce a single image with greatly enhanced depth-of-field. Macro photographers (in particular) have long used focus stacking in their work. The Focus Shift Shooting feature greatly simplifies capture of the individual shots, which can include up to 300 different images. I covered this feature in detail in Chapter 3 and will not repeat that information here.

Auto Capture

Options: Start; Select User Preset (P–1 to P–5)

My preference: N/A

If you liked the concept of trap focus (discussed in Chapter 3), with which the camera can wait until your subject reaches a certain point before automatically taking a picture, you'll absolutely love Auto Capture. In this mode, the camera will constantly evaluate a scene, and then shoot a burst of images or record a video only when a subject is found in the frame at a certain range of distances and moving in a particular direction. You don't have to be vigilant—or even present! In a sense, this option turns the camera into a very expensive game camera which can be set to capture a deer or, perhaps, a pesky raccoon that has been raiding your garbage can. You can define up to five sets of conditions with appropriate settings for a variety of situations:

1. **Review/choose existing preset.** Within the first Auto Capture screen, if you already have a preset defined, highlight Select User Preset (see Figure 5.35, left), highlight one of the five user presets (see Figure 5.35, center), and choose view the current settings (see Figure 5.35, right). Press OK if you're satisfied with them. You can also rename (using up to 19 characters) or copy a preset to another slot.
2. **Define a new preset.** If you haven't pre-defined a preset, you'll need to do that now. Choose Start.
3. **Enter criteria.** There are six auto capture criteria arrayed along the bottom of the screen that appears at upper left in Figure 5.36. You can enter values for some or all, as required.

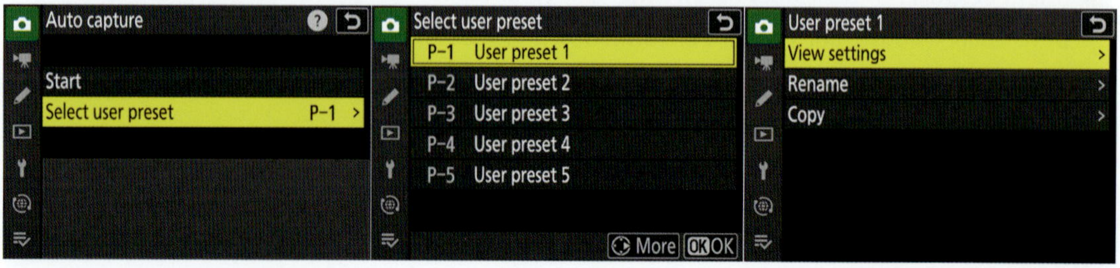

Figure 5.35 Selecting an existing preset.

4. **Motion (Basic).** From the Motion screen you can checkmark Motion, Detection (Subject Detection), and Distance in any combination. (See Figure 5.36, upper right.) You will further refine each of the attributes you selected next.
5. **Motion (Advanced).** If you checked the Motion box, you can specify relative subject speed and size (on scales of 1–5) using the main and sub-command dials, respectively. (See Figure 5.36, center left.) Use this to fine-tune capture for subjects large and small, fast or slow. A value of 1 will trigger capture for subjects that take about 5 seconds to cross the frame; the 5 setting will spot speedy subjects that dart across the scene in a second or less. Size settings vary from 1 (2.5 percent coverage of the frame) to 5 (20 percent or more).

   You can also press the Zoom Out button while viewing this screen to produce the options shown in Figure 5.36, center right, and indicate seven different directions of motion in the left/right, up/down, and inward diagonal directions.
6. **Subject Detection (Advanced).** If you checked the Detection box, you can choose the type of subject to look for, such as people, animals, or vehicles. You can also choose Auto and let the camera decide. (See Figure 5.36, lower left.) A red frame appears around the frame if a subject is detected; a yellow frame, if not.

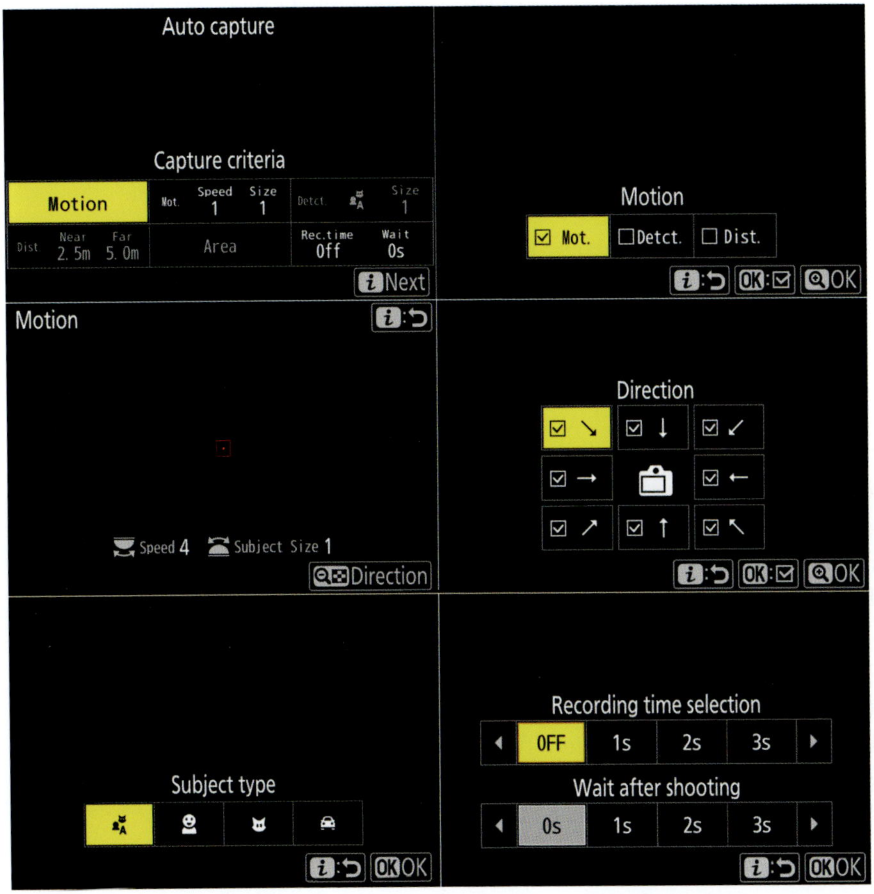

Figure 5.36 Choose your trigger criteria.

7. **Advanced (Distance).** If you checked the Distance box, you can specify a range of distances at which the presence of a subject will start auto capture, and continue for as long as the subject remains in that range. Use the main command dial to specify the near point, and sub-command dial to set the most distant point.

   If you don't know or don't want to estimate (or are not comfortable with meters), you can also set the distance using the camera's AF features. Just place the red Focus Point target square in the center of the frame over something at the closest distance you want to use and press AF-ON. Then move the square to the most distant point and press the shutter release down halfway.

8. **Area.** You can specify the focus points used for Auto-area AF. It is not available if you've selected a different AF-area mode. A display appears with all 493 focus areas shown in a grid. Move the yellow highlight box to select an area and press OK to register it. Pressing the Zoom Out button will select all the boxes.

   Auto capture will start if the subject meets the other criteria and is located within any of the specified focus points. Nikon recommends using this facility for disabling focus points that should be ignored because there are obstacles or unwanted objects.

9. **Timing Options.** You can use Recording Time Selection to specify how long the camera will continue to record images. Note that if your trigger criteria are no longer met, recording will continue for the time you specify. The Wait After Shooting delay tells the camera not to begin again for a specified period. This is useful if you prefer to record several consecutive events that are spaced out rather than continuous. For example, you might want to capture several different birds at your feeder, rather than a single bird that makes multiple visits within a short time. Delays of as long as 30 minutes can be programmed. (See Figure 5.36, lower right.) Press the Protect button if you want to choose Start Day/Time.

10. **Initiate Auto Capture.** When you've finished setting criteria, press the *i* button to move to the next step. A confirmation screen appears. To activate auto capture, press the Video Record button, or the Trash button to exit. A-CAP will be displayed on the control panel and flash in the shooting display. If your release mode is C15, C30, C60, or C120, the Custom Setting d4: Pre-Release Capture options will be in effect.

11. **Continue/End/Restart** While your camera is lurking, the video-record button icon appears on the display. You can press the video record button to end the auto capture session and return to the confirmation screen where you can choose to start again, or end the session.

12. **Settings saved.** Your current settings can be copied to a preset using the Copy option shown earlier. The settings in any preset can be viewed from the Select User Preset screen. (See Figure 5.37.)

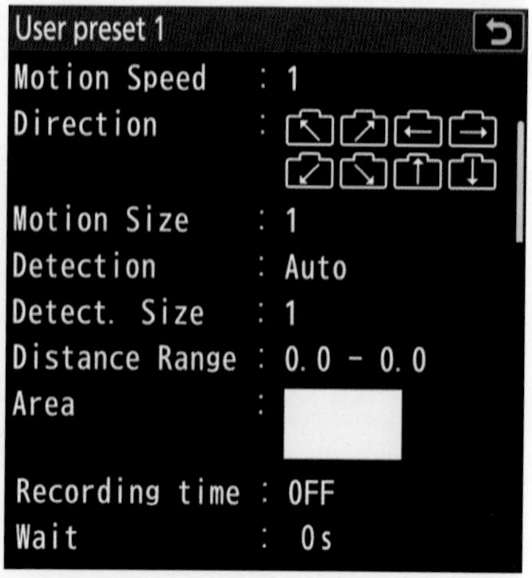

Figure 5.37 Stored settings can be reviewed from this screen.

Video Recording Menu

6

As I noted in the introduction, the focus of this book is entirely on mirrorless still photography. That's because the awesome video capabilities of the Nikon Z9 and Z8 deserve an in-depth book of their own with at least as many pages as this one. Even so, I do include basic coverage of both cameras' video features as a reference and introduction. This chapter provides an overview of the entries in the Video Recording menu. You'll find longer explanations of key options in Chapter 12.

Video Recording Menu

Some of the Video Recording menu's entries duplicate the entries in the Photo Shooting menu but apply specifically to video shooting. Others are unique to movie making. For entries that overlap those used for still photography, I'll simply refer to the relevant description that I included in Chapter 5.

- Shooting Menu Bank
- Extended Menu Banks
- Storage Folder
- File Naming
- Destination
- Video File Type
- Frame Size/Frame Rate
- Video Quality (N-RAW)
- Image Area
- Extended Oversampling
- ISO Sensitivity Settings
- White Balance
- Set Picture Control
- Manage Picture Control
- HLG Quality
- Active D-Lighting
- High ISO NR
- Vignette Control
- Diffraction Compensation
- Auto Distortion Control
- Skin Softening
- Portrait Impression Balance
- Video Flicker Reduction
- High-frequency Flicker Reduction
- Metering
- Focus Mode
- AF-Area Mode
- AF Subject Detection Options
- Vibration Reduction
- Electronic VR
- Microphone Sensitivity
- Attenuator
- Frequency Response
- Wind Noise Reduction
- Mic Jack Plug-in Power
- Headphone Volume
- Timecode
- External Recording Control (HDMI)
- High-Res Zoom
- Auto Capture

Shooting Menu Bank

Options: Banks: A, B, C, D; Rename; Copy

My preference: N/A

This is the first entry in the Video Recording menu (see Figure 6.1). As I noted in Chapter 5, the Nikon Z9 and Z8 have one single complement of Shooting menu banks, labeled, initially, A, B, C, and D, with the entry used to manage them appearing in both the Photo Shooting and Video Recording menus. They are the same bank; you can use this entry, which is found in both the Photo Shooting and Video Recording menus to switch between and manage them. I won't duplicate the detailed description from Chapter 5 here. You can find everything you need to know there.

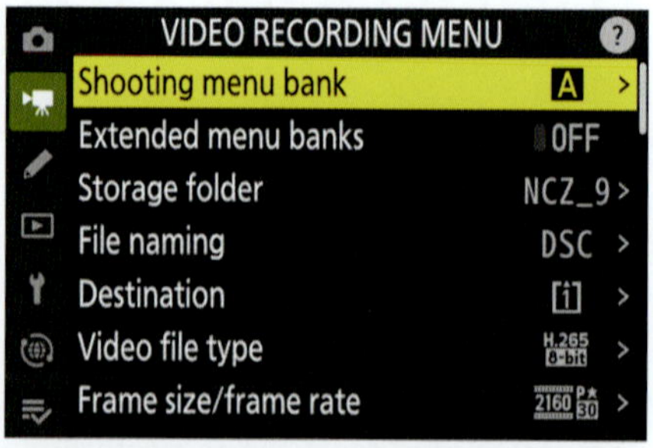

Figure 6.1 The first page of Video Recording menu entries.

Extended Menu Banks

Options: On, Off (default)

My preference: N/A

The Nikon Z9/Z8 has the ability to include several additional parameters in its menu banks, as explained in Chapter 5. For video, those settings are shooting mode, the shutter speed set for Manual exposure, and the aperture specified for Aperture-priority and Manual exposure modes. Still photo settings, such as flash modes, are not relevant for video shooting. If you turn Extended menu banks off, the settings that were in effect before On was selected are restored.

Storage Folder

Options: Rename: NCZ_9/NCZ_8 (default); Select Folder by Number: 100 (default); Select Folder from List

My preference: I use the Select Folder by Number option frequently to organize files by topic or time frame.

You can specify the name used for folders on your memory card. This entry functions exactly as described in Chapter 5, and changes here will be reflected in the Photo Shooting menu. Basically, this is a duplicate of the still photo shooting version.

File Naming

Options: Choose three-letter prefix, DSC (default)

My preference: NZ8, NZ9

The prefix used for video files (only) can be specified here. This entry functions exactly as described in Chapter 5, but in this case, the prefix you create here will be used only for video files. Any file name you've entered in the Photo Shooting menu will not be affected.

Destination

Options: Slot 1, Slot 2 (Z9); CFexpress/XQD Card Slot, SD Card Slot (Z8)

My preference: N/A

You can select which card slot will be used to store your videos. When you access this entry, the camera will display the length of the video that can be recorded on each card using the current frame size and frame rate settings. Neither the Z9 or Z8 offer the additional behavior options (such as overflow or backup) available in the Photo Shooting menu.

Video File Type

Options: N-RAW 12-bit (NEV), ProRes RAW HQ 12-bit (MOV), ProRes 422 HQ 10-bit (MOV), H.265 10-bit (MOV), H.265 8-bit (MOV), H.264 8-bit (MP4); Choice of SDR/N-Log tone modes for N-RAW, ProRes, and H.265 10-bit file types, plus HLG for H.265

My preference: N/A

Here you can choose from among an array of video file types, color depths, tone modes, and file formats. There's a lot of alphabet soup here, but I'll explain the differences among Nikon's RAW (NEV), MOV, and MP4; explain the three tone modes; and discuss the other video-file-type parameters in more detail in Chapter 12.

Frame Size/Frame Rate

Options: Choose 8K (FX): 60/50p, 30/25p, 24p; 4K (FX): 120/100p, 60/50p, 30/25p, 24p; 5.4K (DX): 60/50p, 30/25p, 24p; 3.8K (2.3X): 100/120p; 1920 × 1080: 120/100p, 60/50p, 30/25p, 24p; 1920 × 1080 (Slow-Motion): 30/25p, 24p

My preference: N/A

The options listed are the frame resolutions (8K, 4K, 5.4K, 3.8K, and Full HD [1920 × 1080]) and frame rates (120/100p, 60/50p, 30/25p, 24p, plus two slow-motion settings) available with the various video file types shown under the Video File Type entry above. The particular sizes and rates available vary, depending on the file type. For example 8K (actually 8.3K if you're picky) video can only be captured when using N-RAW, while slow-motion video can be specified only when video file type is set to H.264 8-bit (MP4). You'll find more information on these in Chapter 12, along with a table showing the available video file types.

Video Quality (N-RAW)

Options: High Quality, Normal

My preference: N/A

This is the first entry on the next page of the Video Recording menu entries (see Figure 6.2). It allows you to choose the image quality—determined by the amount of compression needed to achieve the designated bit transfer rate to the storage media—when shooting with Nikon's N-RAW format. High quality employs faster transfer rates than Normal quality (5780 Mbps vs 3470 Mbps with 8K 60p video, for example). Lower-resolution video needs less ambitious transfer rates; 4K 60p video requires 1740 Mbps at High quality and 880 Mbps at Normal quality.

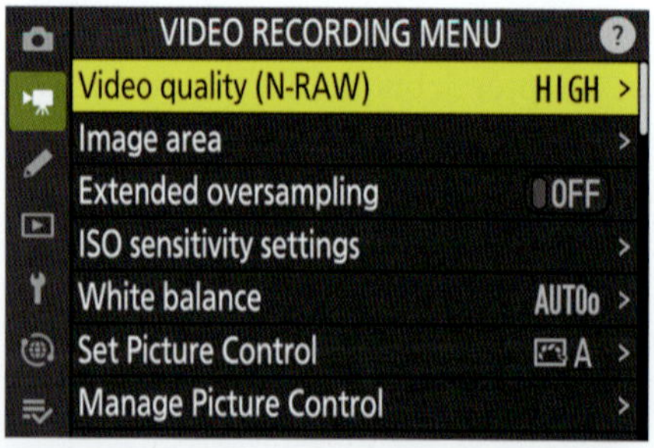

Figure 6.2 The next page of Video Recording menu entries.

As you'll learn in Chapter 12, Nikon's proprietary N-RAW format allows capturing extended dynamic range video internally, without the need for an external recorder. The file sizes are about half the size of ProRes RAW. As video is recorded, the camera also stores a Full HD (1920 × 1080) H.264 .MP4 proxy file which can be edited, then replaced with the RAW file when it is time to do the color grading. That's an enormous advantage for those shooting high-resolution 8K video, which produces massive files.

Although this book concentrates on still photography tools and techniques, I'll tell you more about color grading, transfer rates, high dynamic range videography, and other aspects in Chapter 12.

Image Area

Options: Choose Image Area: FX (default), DX; DX Crop Alert: On, Off

My preference: FX, On

Although high-definition video has been traditionally shot using a 16:9 aspect ratio, you can tell the Z9/Z8 to either shoot using the full-frame area, or use a 1.5X (DX) or 2.3X crop. The DX crop is *automatically* applied when the camera detects a DX-type lens has been mounted. These crops produce the apparent "magnification" or "lens multiplier" effect, providing, say, a 100mm lens with the same field of view as a 150mm or 230mm telephoto. If you activate DX Crop Alert, an icon will appear in the display whenever a cropped image area has been selected. The crops you choose here will be ignored when the video file type is N-RAW 12-bit (NEV) or ProRes RAW. In addition, 8K video is always shot at 8K resolution, except when a DX lens is mounted and 4K resolution is used instead.

Extended Oversampling

Options: On (default), Off

My preference: On

Pro videographers will be the likely users of extended oversampling, which can improve video quality while increasing battery drain. It provides 2:1 oversampled 4K 50/60p video from 8K capture. Oversampling is the process of using the full resolution of a sensor, and then scaling it down to a lower resolution, which can result in better image quality. Just keep in mind that very, very fast media is needed to capture all this information.

ISO Sensitivity Settings

Options: Maximum sensitivity: 200–25600, Hi 0.3 to Hi 2.0; Auto ISO Control (Mode M); ISO Sensitivity (Mode M): 64–25600, plus Lo 1.0 to Lo 0.3 and Hi 0.3 to Hi 2.0

My preference: Varies by subject type

This entry operates much like its Photo Shooting menu counterpart, except that you cannot make direct ISO settings here for Programmed Auto, Aperture-priority, or Shutter-priority exposure modes, for which Auto ISO is *always* enabled. (Auto ISO can be turned off only in Manual exposure mode.)

- **Maximum sensitivity.** Use this parameter to indicate the highest ISO setting you're comfortable having the camera set on its own. You can choose the max ISO setting the camera will use from ISO 200 up to ISO 25600, plus the four "expanded" settings all the way up to Hi 2.0. Use a low number if you'd rather not take any photos at a high ISO without manually setting that value yourself. Dial in a higher ISO number if getting the video at any sensitivity setting is more important than worrying about noise.
- **Auto ISO control (Mode M).** As I noted above, Auto ISO can be disabled *only* in Manual exposure mode. It is on by default, but you can turn it off, here.
- **ISO sensitivity (Mode M).** You can specify a particular ISO Sensitivity setting for Manual exposure in the range ISO 64–Hi 2.0.

White Balance

Options: Same as Photo Settings; Auto: $AUTO_0$ Keep White (default), $AUTO_1$ Keep Overall Atmosphere, $AUTO_2$ Keep Warm Lighting Colors; Presets: Natural Light Auto, Direct Sunlight, Cloudy, Shade, Incandescent, Fluorescent (three types), Flash, Choose Color Temperature, Preset Manual

My preference: N/A

As with many of the Video Recording menu entries in this chapter, you can choose to share settings with the entry's Photo Shooting menu counterpart by choosing Same as Photo Settings here. However, if, as is likely for serious video work, you need to use different white balance parameters when shooting video, you can specify your settings here. When Same as Photo Settings is *not* chosen, this entry's white balance adjustments stand alone and do not affect those in the Photo Shooting menu.

Making the adjustments is done as described in Chapter 5; I won't repeat that information here.

Set Picture Control

Options: Same as Photo Settings; Auto (default), Standard, Neutral, Vivid, Monochrome, Flat Monochrome, Deep Tone Monochrome, Portrait, Rich Tone Portrait, Landscape, Flat; Creative Picture Controls (01–20): Dream, Morning, Pop, Sunday, Somber, Dramatic, Silence, Bleached, Melancholic, Pure, Denim, Toy, Sepia, Blue, Red, Pink, Charcoal, Graphite, Binary, and Carbon

My preference: Neutral works well for video, too, if you don't need the extended dynamic range of the Flat setting.

Choose Same as Photo Settings to share Picture Controls between still photo and video shooting. Or, specify Picture Controls here to be used only when shooting video. The settings can be adjusted as described in Chapter 5. **Note:** The Set Picture Control menu item will be grayed out and unavailable when HLG Tone mode is selected under Video File Type, described above. The only "Picture Control" available for HLG video capture is the HLG Quality setting, as described in the section after next.

Manage Picture Control

Options: Save/Edit, Rename, Delete, Load/Save

My preference: N/A

The Manage Picture Control menu entry can be used to create new styles, edit existing styles, rename or delete them, and store/retrieve them from the memory card. The adjustments will be applied to the Picture Controls used by the Video Recording menu—either the same controls as the Photo Shooting menu or the specific controls specified for video use. The functions are the same as described in Chapter 5.

HLG Quality

Options: Quick Sharp, Sharpening, Mid-Range Sharpening, Clarity, Contrast, Saturation, Hue

My preference: N/A

This is the next page of the Video Recording menu settings (see Figure 6.3). This entry gives you control over the only Picture Control that can be used for HLG video. It is grayed out until you change the Video File Type to H.265 10-bit (MOV) as described above, and specify the HLG Tone mode. (See Figure 6.4, left and center.) You can then navigate to this entry to view the screen seen at right in the figure.

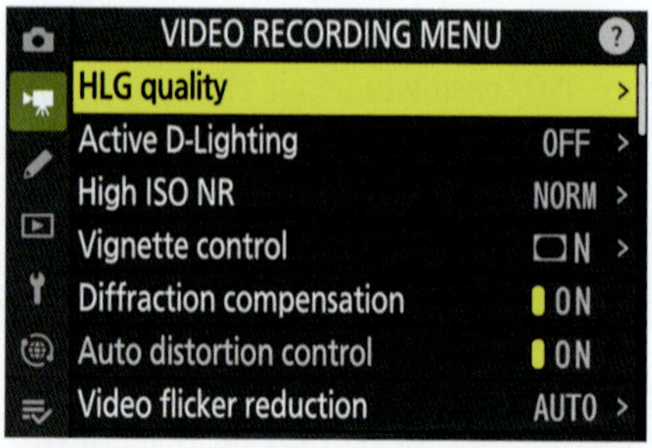

Figure 6.3 The next page of Video Recording menu entries.

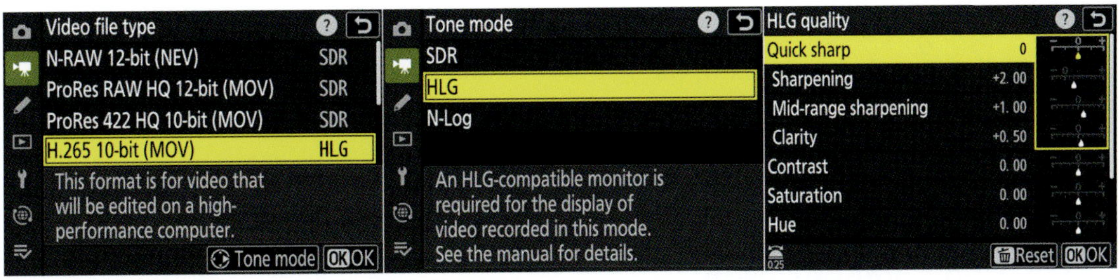

Figure 6.4 When HLG video is enabled (left, center), the HLG Quality Picture Control can be modified (right).

Then, make your adjustments:

1. Use the Quick Sharp slider and the left/right directional controls or the sub-command dial to change the three individual Sharpening adjustments (Sharpening, Mid-Range Sharpening, and Clarity) simultaneously. Alternatively, scroll down to each of those three adjustments and tweak Sharpening, Mid-Range Sharpening, or Clarity independently.
2. Next, scroll down to the Contrast, Saturation, and Hue sliders with the up/down directional controls, then use the left/right directional controls or the sub-command dial to decrease or increase the effects. A yellow triangle will appear under the original setting in the slider as you make a change.
3. Press the Trash button to reset the values to their defaults.
4. Press OK when you're finished making adjustments.

Active D-Lighting

Options: Extra High, High, Normal, Low, Off

My preference: Off

Use this entry to specify the Active D-Lighting parameters used for video (only). Adjustments you make here are not reflected in the Photo Shooting menu counterpart; the two entries are separate. The settings function as described in Chapter 5, except that Auto and Extra High 2 are not available for video.

High ISO NR

Options: High, Normal (default), Low, Off

My preference: Normal

Use this entry to specify the High ISO noise reduction applied when shooting video; these settings correspond to those in the Photo Shooting menu, but are separate and do not affect the other menu's parameters.

Vignette Control

Options: High, Normal (default), Low, Off

My preference: Normal

The Video Recording and Photo Shooting menus share a single Vignette Control setting, so any changes made in either are reflected in the other. I explained this feature in detail in Chapter 5.

Diffraction Compensation

Options: On (default), Off

My preference: On

As described in Chapter 5, diffraction is a phenomenon that reduces the sharpness of your image when working at smaller f/stops, especially f/22 or f/32 (if your lens has those apertures available). Settings made here are carried over to this entry's counterpart in the Photo Shooting menu.

Auto Distortion Control

Options: On (default), Off

My preference: On

This is another entry that adjusts a single set of parameters shared by the Video Recording menu and Photo Shooting menu. You can read more information about Auto Distortion Control in Chapter 5.

Skin Softening

Options: Same as Photo Settings, High, Low, Normal, Off (default)

My preference: N/A

Nikon is putting your camera's face recognition prowess to work with an optional complexion-flattering feature than removes texture from portrait shots of humans. The camera can detect and process up to three subjects, using High, Normal, or Low levels of softening. You can also disable the feature by selecting Off. You can specify one level here for Video Recording, and a different level in the Photo Shooting menu for stills.

When enabled, a gray focus point appears over each subject. You don't need to select People or Auto under the AF Subject Detection options entry (discussed later in this chapter). If you let the camera choose the focus point by selecting Auto-area AF as your AF-area mode, left and right triangles will flank the focus point chosen. The left/right directional controls can be used to move from one subject to another.

Portrait Impression Balance

Options: Mode 1, Mode 2, Mode 3, Off (default)

My preference: Use as needed

This entry, like its Photo Shooting menu counterpart, allows you to create up to three separate profiles that specify magenta/amber color bias (greens and blues are not affected) and set a brightness level to be used when shooting portraits. **Note:** Your setting here applied to video can be different from the one used for stills in the Photo Shooting menu. To create a specific balance, just follow these steps:

1. **Access this entry.** Navigate to the Portrait Impression Balance entry in the Video Recording menu.
2. **Select Mode 1, 2, or 3.** Highlight the mode you want to use/define and press the right directional button.
3. **Adjust color bias and/or brightness.** Use the directional controls to move the setting point from the center. Up/down adjusts brightness, while left right moves the point along the magenta/amber-yellow axis.
4. **Exit.** Press OK to confirm and exit, or the Trash button to cancel your adjustments. Modes that have been changed from the default value will be marked with an asterisk on the display.

Video Flicker Reduction

Options: Auto (default), 50 Hz, 60 Hz

My preference: Use as needed

This is the same entry as the Photo Flicker Reduction option in the Photo Shooting menu described in Chapter 5, and the changes made in either menu apply to the other.

High-Frequency Flicker Reduction

Options: On (Shutter speed fine tuning), Off (default)

My preference: Off

As I noted in Chapter 5, while the Video/Photo Flicker Shooting entries do a good job with most light sources, some newer types of lighting, including higher-quality LED lamps, flicker with lower intensities and much higher frequencies, and require more advanced correction. This setting, (the first entry in Figure 6.5), allows fine-tuning the shutter speed in Shutter-priority or Manual exposure modes so that it syncs up with the cycle of flickering light sources to reduce or eliminate those undesirable banding effects. **Note:** The setting you make here is separate from its counterpart in the Photo Shooting menu.

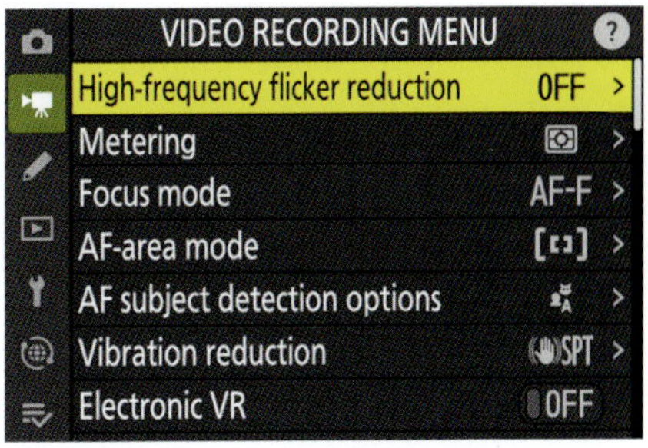

Figure 6.5 The next group of Video Recording menu options.

Metering

Options: Matrix (default), Center-weighted, Highlight-weighted metering

My preference: Matrix

This menu entry, also described in Chapter 5, is a slower alternative to setting the metering mode using the *i* menu. It exists primarily so you can assign this menu entry to a custom key using the Custom Setting g2: Custom Controls menu entry. Note that Spot metering is not available in video mode.

Focus Mode

Options: AF-S (default), AF-C, AF-F, Manual Focus

My preference: N/A

This entry is separate from its Photo Shooting menu counterpart, and includes AF-F (Full-time AF), which tells the Z9 and Z8 to focus continually during video shooting and is not available in still photography mode. I'll explain focus modes for video in more detail in Chapter 12.

AF-Area Mode

Options: Single-point AF (default), Wide-area AF (Small, Large, C1, C2), Subject-tracking AF, Auto-area AF

My preference: N/A

AF-area modes for video can be specified in exactly the same way as described in Chapter 5, but settings you make here are independent of the ones selected in the Photo Shooting menu for still photography. This entry's chief difference between its Photo Shooting menu counterpart is that Pinpoint, 3D-tracking, and Dynamic-area AF are not available for video shooting, but Subject-tracking AF can be used to lock in on a subject and continue focusing on it as it moves within the frame.

AF Subject Detection Options

Options: Subject Detection: Auto (default), People, Animal, Birds, Vehicle, Airplanes, Subject detection off; AF when subject not detected: On (default), Off

My preference: Auto

You can set the priority for the type of subject the camera will look for during autofocus, using an amazing range of types. Subject detection is possible when any of the Wide-Area AF modes (Small, Large, Custom 1, Custom 2), or Auto-area AF are active. You can set separate priorities for detection in the Photo Shooting and Video Recording menus. I explained subject detection in detail in Chapter 3 and won't duplicate that information here.

Vibration Reduction

Options: Same as Photo Settings, On (or Normal) (default), Spt (Sport), Off

My preference: N/A

You can choose a vibration reduction mode, as described in Chapter 5, for video use only, or set the camera to use the same options selected in the Photo Shooting menu.

Electronic VR

Options: On, Off (default)

My preference: Off

As I noted in Chapter 5, electronic VR is a type of anti-shake technology that has long been provided in pro and amateur camcorders. It's automatically disabled when using the N-RAW 12-bit (NEV) or ProRes RAW HQ 12-bit (MOV) video file types; when shooting 8K (7680 × 4320) video, or using 120/100p frame rates. You'll find a detailed discussion of electronic VR in Chapter 12.

Microphone Sensitivity

Options: Auto (default), Manual, Microphone Off

My preference: Varies

This is the first entry in the next group of Video Recording menu options shown in Figure 6.6. It has three options that control your camera's built-in microphone or any external microphone you attach. You can choose Auto Sensitivity; Manual Sensitivity, to set recording levels yourself (with a handy volume meter on screen showing the current ambient sound levels); or turn the microphone off entirely if you're planning to record silent video, use another sound recording source, or add sound in post-production.

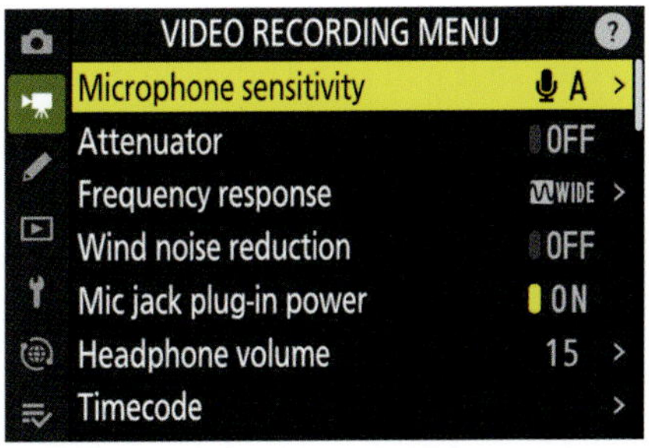

Figure 6.6 The next group of Video Recording menu options.

Attenuator

Options: On, Off (default)

My preference: Varies

When working in noisy environments, choose Enable to reduce the microphone gain and minimize audio distortion from background sounds.

Frequency Response

Options: Wide Range (default), Vocal Range

My preference: Varies

Select from Wide Range frequency response to record a broad range of sounds, or Vocal Range to optimize audio recording for vocals. You'll find an entire section on recording sound in Chapter 12.

Wind Noise Reduction

Options: On, Off (default)

My preference: Varies

Wind blowing across your microphone can be distracting. This setting reduces wind noise (and may also affect other sounds, so use it carefully) for the built-in microphones *only.* Your external microphone, like the Nikon ME-1, may have its own wind noise reduction filter on/off switch.

Mic Jack Plug-in Power

Options: On (default), Off

My preference: Varies by microphone

Some microphones require power from the camera to operate; some do not. If you consult your manual and find that your mic does not require power from the camera, you should set this option to Off. That will avoid possible noise from the power supply that can occur. The plug-in Nikon ME-1 microphone does draw power from the camera, but many third-party mics do not.

Headphone Volume

Options: 15 (default), Values 0–30

My preference: N/A

Use this entry in Video mode to adjust the volume of headphones you've plugged into the camera's headphones jack.

Timecode

Options: Record Timecodes: On, On with HDMI Output, Off; Count-up Method: Record Run, Free Run; Timecode Origin: Reset, Enter Manually, Current Time; Drop Frame: On, Off

My preference: N/A

Advanced video shooters find SMPTE (Society of Motion Picture and Television Engineers)-compatible time codes embedded in the video files to be an invaluable reference during editing. To oversimplify a bit, the time system provides precise *hour:minute:second:frame* markers that allow identifying and synchronizing frames and audio. The time code system includes a provision for "dropping" frames to ensure that the fractional frame rate of captured video (remember that a 24 fps setting actually yields 23.976 frames per second while 30 fps capture gives you 29.97 actual "frames" per second) can be matched up with actual time spans.

As I noted in the introduction to this book, I won't be covering the most technical aspects of movie shooting in great detail (including detailed use of time codes, raw HDMI streaming, etc.). If you're at the stage where you're using time codes, you don't need a primer, anyway. However, the Time Code submenu does include the following options:

- **Record Timecodes.** Turn timecodes off or on. You can select On, or On with HDMI Output to append the time code to the HDMI video output, or Off to not use timecodes.
- **Count Up Method.** Choose Rec Run, in which the time code counts up only when you are actually capturing video, or Free Run (also known as Time of Day), which allows the time code to run up even between shooting clips. The latter is useful when you want to synchronize clips between multiple cameras that are shooting the same event. When using Free Run, even if the cameras record at different times, you'll be able to match the video that was captured at the exact same moment during editing. When Free Run is selected, the time code will always be recorded to the movie file, except for high frame rate (120/100 fps) clips.
- **Timecode Origin.** Normally, the camera uses its internal clock to specify the hours:minutes:seconds, with frames set to :00 when you begin shooting. This entry allows you to manually enter any hour:minute:second:frame of your choice, or to Reset the start time to 00:00:00:00.
- **Drop Frame.** The 30 fps setting yields 29.97 actual frames per second, 60 fps gives you 59.95 frames per second, and 120 fps provides 119.9 fps, causing a discrepancy between the actual time and the time code that's recorded. Enable and the camera will skip some time code numbers in drop-frame mode at intervals to eliminate the discrepancy. When disabled (non-drop frame mode), you may notice a difference of several seconds per hour.

External Recorder Control (HDMI)

Options: On, Off (default)

My preference: N/A

This is the first entry on the last page of the Video Recording menu (shown in Figure 6.7). Use it to allow your camera's controls to stop and start recording on a compatible external recorder.

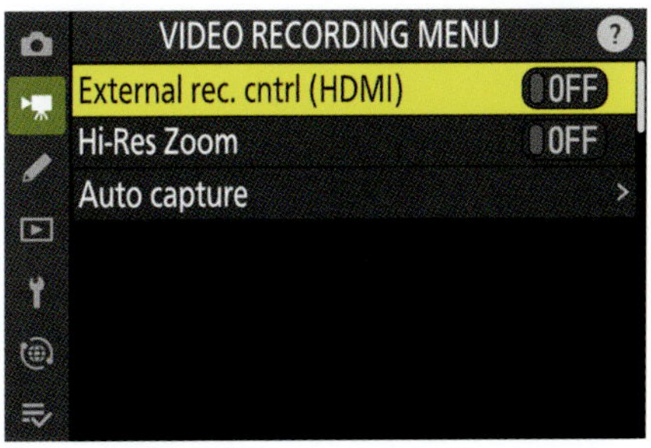

Figure 6.7 The last group of Video Recording menu options.

Hi-Res Zoom

Options: On, Off (default)

My preference: N/A

This is a cool setting that uses your camera's extra resolution to provide a high-quality digital zoom effect—even to prime lenses, which have a fixed focal length, of course. When active, you can zoom in and out by pressing the Fn1 or Fn2 buttons, or by rotating the lens control ring. To start zooming, just follow these steps:

1. **Assign zooming controls.** By default, you can use the sub-selector or left/right directional buttons to zoom in or out. If you prefer, you can go to Custom Setting g2: Custom Controls (*not f2: Custom Controls [Shooting!]*) and assign Hi-Res Zoom + to the Fn1 button, and Hi-Res Zoom – to the Fn2 button. (You cannot assign these controls to any other button.) Alternatively, you can delegate zooming to the lens control ring (if your lens has one) with a separate Custom Control definition.
2. **Enable Hi-Res Zoom.** Set this entry to On.
3. **Select zoom speed.** Visit Custom Setting g8: High-Res Zoom Speed, and select a slower, faster, or standard zooming speed.
4. **Choose Video File type.** You must be shooting 4K or Full HD (1920 × 1080) video with the FX Image Area, so you should select a Video File Type from among ProRes 422 HQ 10-bit (MOV), H.265 10-bit (MOV), H.265 8-bit (MOV), or H.264 (MP4), as described earlier in this chapter. The Frame/Size rate must be 30/25p or 24p for 4K (3840 × 2160) resolution, or 1920 × 1080 at 120/100p, 60/50p, 30/25p, or 24p.
5. **Switch to Video mode.** This zoom is not available in Photo mode. Your AF-area mode is automatically set to Wide-are AF (Large), and Electronic VR is turned off.
6. **Zoom, zoom.** As you zoom in and out, a zoom display bar appears at the bottom of the screen showing the amount of zoom from 1X to 2X.

Auto Capture

Options: Start; Set User Preset (P–1 to P–5)

My preference: N/A

This function is the same as the Auto Capture entry described in Chapter 5, and I won't repeat that information here.

Custom Settings Menu

7

Unlike the Photo Shooting and Video Recording menu options, which you are likely to modify frequently as your picture-taking environment changes, Custom Settings are slightly more stable sets of preferences that let you tailor the behavior of your camera in a variety of different ways for longer-term use.

Some options are minor tweaks useful for specific shooting situations or convenience. Perhaps you'd like to assign a frequently used feature to one of the Fn buttons or turn on the grid display to make it easier to align vertical or horizontal shapes.

Best of all are the settings that improve the way your camera operates. Custom Setting b6, for example, provides a way to fine-tune the exposures your camera calculates for each of the metering modes: Matrix, Center-weighted, Spot, and Highlight-weighted. If you find that one or the other consistently over- or underexposes more than you like, it's easy to dial in a permanent correction. Should you feel that the camera is taking a few pictures that are out of focus, Custom Settings a1 and a2 can be used to tell it not to fire until optimum focus is achieved.

This chapter concentrates on explaining all the options of the Custom Settings menu and, most importantly, when and why you might want to use each setting.

Custom Settings Menu Layout

There are more than four dozen different Custom Settings, arranged in seven different categories, as shown in Figure 7.1: Focus, Metering/Exposure, Timers/AE Lock, Shooting/Display, Bracketing/Flash, Controls, and Video. Some of those may seem to be an odd match. What does bracketing have to do with flash? Oh, wait! You can *bracket* flash (as well as non-flash) exposures. The category system does have an advantage. Once you're familiar with what settings are available within each category, you can select the Custom Settings menu, scroll down to the specific category you want, press the multi selector right button, and enter the Custom Settings system at that point, skipping the other entries.

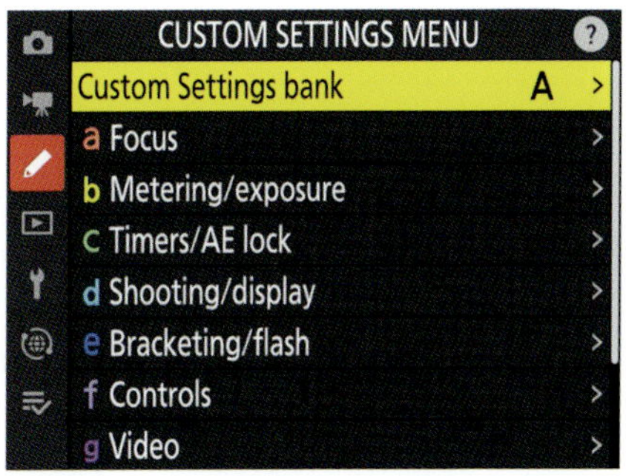

Figure 7.1 Entries are allocated among seven categories in the Custom Settings menu.

However, once you get past the main Custom Settings screen, the entries are one long scrolling list, so if you've guessed wrong about where you want to start, you can enter the list at any point and then scroll up or down until you find the entry you want. Or, press the multi selector left button to get back to the main screen, then move down to another entry point and re-enter. The Custom Settings menu items are all color- and letter-coded: **a** (red) for focus functions; **b** (yellow) for metering/exposure; **c** (green) for timers and AE lock features; **d** (light blue/cyan) for shooting/display functions; **e** (dark blue) for bracketing/flash; **f** (purple) for adjustments to the controls; and **g** (magenta) to adjust Video mode functions.

For simplicity, in this book I have been consistently referring to the Custom Settings menu entries by their letter/names, so that you always know that when I mention Custom Setting a5, I am describing the fifth entry in the Focus menu: Store Points by Orientation. That terminology makes it easy to jump quickly to the specific entry. Note that for simplicity's sake, in the figures that illustrate each of the separate Custom Settings categories in this chapter, that category's entries are shown on as few screens as possible. In practice, as you scroll through the listings, the entries for a category may be spread over several different screens.

You can select a Custom Settings function as you do any menu entry, by pressing the multi selector right button, and navigating through the screen that appears with the up/down (and sometimes left/right) buttons. Confirming an option is usually done by pressing the OK button, pushing the multi selector right button, or sometimes by choosing Done when a series of related options have been chosen.

At the top level, you'll see these entries:

- Custom Settings Bank
- a. Focus
- b. Metering/Exposure
- c. Timers/AE Lock
- d. Shooting/Display
- e. Bracketing/Flash
- f. Controls
- g. Video

Custom Settings Bank

Options: Choose Bank; Manage: Rename, Copy; Reset

My preference: N/A

The Custom Settings banks function similarly to the Photo Shooting and Video Recording banks. You can choose which bank to activate, name/rename each bank individually, and copy the contents of one bank to another when you want to use some/most of the source bank's settings as a starting point. You can also reset each of the bank's settings to their factory defaults. You'll find the defaults for each option listed with the description of each individual entry. You can find tables with the default values in your camera's respective Reference Guides.

a. Focus

The red-coded Focus options deal with some of the potentially most vexing settings. After all, incorrect focus is one of the most damaging picture killers of all the attributes in an image. You may be able to compensate for bad exposure, partially fix errant color balance, and perhaps even incorporate motion blur into an image as a creative element. But if focus is wrong, the photograph doesn't look right, and no amount of "I meant to do that!" pleas are likely to work. The focus options enable you to choose how and when autofocus is applied (using the AF-S or AF-C focus mode you selected on the camera body), the controls used to activate the feature, and the way focus points are selected from the available zones. Figure 7.2 shows the first seven entries in the Custom Settings: Focus section.

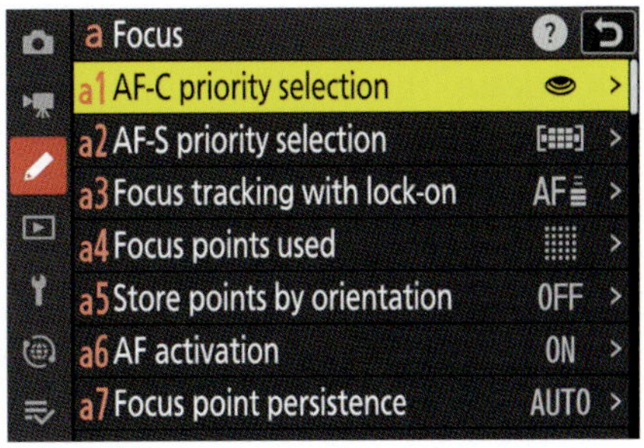

Figure 7.2 The first seven Autofocus options.

a1 AF-C Priority Selection

Options: Release (default), Focus+Release, Focus

My preference: Release

As you learned in Chapter 3, when not shooting movies, the Z9 and Z8 have two primary autofocus modes, continuous autofocus (AF-C) and single autofocus (AF-S). (Video mode adds a third: Full-time autofocus [AF-F].) This menu entry allows you to specify what takes precedence when you press the shutter release all the way down to take a picture: focus-priority or release-priority. You can choose from:

- **Release.** When this option is selected (the default), the shutter is activated when the release button is pushed down all the way, even if sharp focus has not yet been achieved. Because AF-C focuses and refocuses constantly when autofocus is active, you may find that an image is not quite in sharpest focus. Use this option when taking a picture is more important than absolute best focus, such as fast action or photojournalism applications. (You don't want to miss that record-setting home run, or the protestor's pie smashing into the Governor's face.) Using this setting doesn't mean that your image won't be sharply focused; it just means that you'll get a picture even if autofocusing isn't quite complete. If you've been poised with the shutter release pressed halfway, the camera probably has been tracking the focus of your image.
- **Focus+Release.** Choose this option when you want an intermediate priority setting between release-priority and focus-priority (discussed next). It's a good choice for continuous shooting, as the slight pause before focus is locked in gives the camera a little extra time to achieve sharp focus for the first frame of a sequence, while retaining that focus setting for subsequent shots.
- **Focus.** The shutter is not activated until sharp focus is achieved. This is best for subjects that are not moving rapidly. AF-C will continue to track your subjects' movement, as long as it remains within the active focus area, but the camera won't take a picture until focus is locked in. You might miss a few shots, but you will have fewer out-of-focus images.

a2 AF-S Priority Selection

Options: Release, Focus (default)

My preference: Focus

This is the counterpart setting for single autofocus mode.

- **Release.** The shutter is activated when the button is depressed all the way, even if sharp focus is not quite achieved. Keep in mind that, unlike AF-C, the camera focuses only *once* when AF-S mode is used. So, if you've partially depressed the shutter release, paused, and then pressed the button down all the way, it's possible that the subject has moved, and release-priority will yield more out-of-focus shots than release-priority with AF-C.
- **Focus.** This default prevents the camera from taking a picture until focus is achieved and the in-focus indicator in the viewfinder glows steadily. If you're using single autofocus mode, this is probably the best setting. Moving subjects really call for AF-C mode in most cases.

a3 Focus Tracking with Lock-on

Options: Blocked Shot AF Response: 5 (Delayed), 4, 3 (default), 2, 1 (Quick); Subject Motion: Steady, Erratic

My preference: 3, Steady

Sometimes new subjects interject themselves in the frame temporarily. The classic example used is a football game, when a referee dashes in front of your camera briefly just as a receiver is about to make a catch. This setting lets you specify how quickly the camera reacts to these transient interruptions that would cause relatively large changes in focus before refocusing on the "new" subject matter. Fickle focus can be especially vexing when relying on AF-C to preserve focus while shooting continuously. At other times, you *want* the camera to identify and lock onto a new subject that enters the frame. You were tracking that receiver, but the ball is intercepted and capturing the cornerback's run is now your goal. This entry gives you two tools to help you tame both sluggardly and fidgety autofocus.

Using the Blocked Shot AF Response slider shown in Figure 7.3, you can specify a long delay, so that the interloper is ignored, or a shorter delay, so that the camera immediately refocuses when a new subject moves into the frame. A setting of 5 (Delayed) causes the camera to ignore the intervening subject matter for a significant period of time. Use this setting when shooting subjects, such as sports, in which focus interruptions are likely to be frequent and significant. You can also choose a setting of 1 (Quick), which tells the camera to wait only a moment before refocusing.

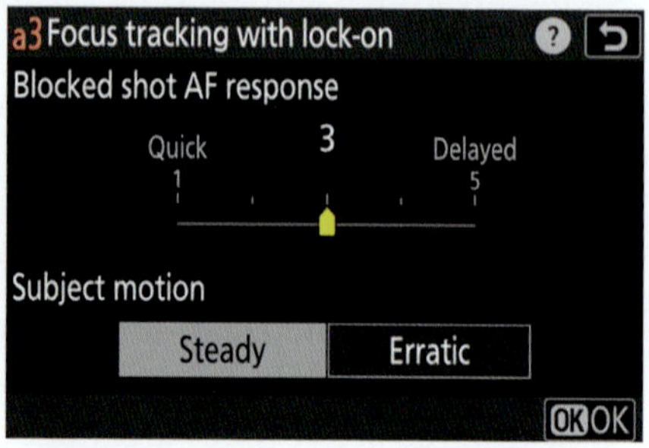

Figure 7.3 Options for Focus Tracking with Lock-on.

Very high continuous frame rates may work better when you allow refocusing to take place rapidly, without a lock-on delay. Intermediate settings from 2 to 4 provide different amounts of delay. The middle value, 3, offers an intermediate delay before the camera refocuses on the new subject.

It's often the best choice when shooting sports in either of the continuous shooting modes, as the long delay can throw off autofocus accuracy at higher frames-per-second settings. The Nikon Z9 and Z8 *always* use the value of 3 when the AF-area mode is set to 3D-tracking. If the AF-area mode is set to Auto-area AF, the camera will ignore "Quick" settings of 1 or 2 you may have made (and use 3 instead), but will happily respond to the delayed settings of 4 or 5 if you've selected them here.

Your second focus lock-on tool is found at the bottom of the screen in the Subject Motion section. You can choose Steady if your subject is moving at a constant speed and direction. Select Erratic if your subject may be stopping, starting, and moving erratically. You'll encounter the latter situation quite frequently when shooting basketball or volleyball. You might also use Erratic, if *you* are moving unpredictably, say when shooting from an off-road vehicle.

a4 Focus Points Used

Options: All Points (default), Alternating Points

My preference: Depends on subject

You can choose the number of focus points available when you manually select a zone using the multi selector up/down and left/right buttons or the sub-selector. You have two choices:

- **All.** This is the default. Up to 493 positions are available for manual selection when your AF-area mode is not Auto-area AF. The exact number used varies by the active AF-area mode.
- **Alternating Points.** This option does *not* disable 75 percent of the AF sensors; they remain active and functional. What it does do is limit the number of positions you can *select* to alternating points and rows, allowing you to move the position of the selected focus point more quickly. This can be the best choice for faster focus point selection when taking pictures of relatively large, evenly illuminated subject matter such that manually choosing the precise initial focus point/zone is not particularly beneficial.

  I often use Single-point AF and enable the Alternating Points option—the available focus areas are plenty and can be set quickly as action moves around the floor when photographing basketball games. The exceptions? When using Pinpoint AF the available focus points remain exactly the same when single-pressing the directional control even though you have selected this option. However, if you *hold down* the directional control, the camera will soon begin jumping in larger increments.

a5 Store Points by Orientation

Options: Focus Point, Focus Point and AF-area Mode, Off (default)

My preference: Focus Point and AF-area Mode

Here you can choose whether separate focus points can be selected for landscape and portrait orientations of the camera, and whether you can select a different AF-area mode for each orientation, as explained in detail in Chapter 3.

When you choose Off, the focus point will maintain the same relative position as you rotate the camera, and the AF-area mode will remain the same. Select Focus Point, and you can choose a different focus point when the camera is set to horizontal orientation, rotated 90 degrees clockwise from horizontal, or rotated 90 degrees counterclockwise from horizontal. With focus point and AF-area mode enabled, your AF-area setting will be preserved as well. In all cases, an upside-down orientation is not supported.

If you're shooting birds in flight or other wildlife or scenic vistas (it's called landscape mode for a reason), you can stick with the default value, Off. The focus point and AF-area mode choices are especially useful for portraits, fashion, sports, photojournalism, and street photography.

a6 AF Activation

Options: Shutter/AF-ON (default), AF-ON Only: Out-of-focus Release: Enable (default), Disable

My preference: AF-ON Only: Out-of-focus Release: Disable (recommended for anyone proficient in back-button focus, described in Chapter 3)

You can specify whether the camera focuses when the shutter release is pressed halfway or disable that behavior. You'd want to disable shutter release AF activation if you elect to use *back-button focus*. Your choices are as follows:

- **Shutter/AF-ON.** Pressing the shutter release halfway, pressing the AF-ON button, *or* a different button you have defined for AF activation (as described under Custom Controls later in this chapter) always activates autofocus.
- **AF-ON Only.** Pressing the shutter release halfway does not activate autofocus. Instead, you can activate AF by pressing the AF-ON button or other button you've defined for that behavior using the Custom Controls commands described later, and in Chapter 3 under the back-button focus section. **Note:** You can bypass the AF-ON button by tapping the screen when Touch Focus is enabled.

  The camera allows additional fine-tuning of your AF-ON Only setting. When this option is highlighted, you can press the multi selector right button and choose from two Out-of-Focus Release options:

  - **Enable.** The camera can take photos when the shutter release is pressed all the way down, even if you have not pressed the AF-ON button and focus has therefore *not* taken place. Effectively, this is release-priority. You might find this useful to enable grab shots that take place without warning, and you want a photo even if it may not be in perfect focus. You still have the option of activating AF by pressing the AF-ON button before you press the shutter release all the way, but if you do not, the photo will still be captured.

    Warning: This is a dangerous setting, and when you choose AF-ON Only, Enable is the *default* behavior. It works well if you are using back-button focus and gotten into the habit of pressing the AF-ON button to initiate autofocus. However, if you are *not* using back-button focus and choose AF-ON Only, *be sure to select disable* (described next) to avoid unwanted out-of-focus photos that may result if you forget to press the AF-ON button before pushing the shutter release down all the way.

- **Disable.** If the image is not in focus, pressing the shutter release down all the way *will not* take a picture (effectively focus-priority). You *must* activate AF by pressing the AF-ON button before using the shutter release to take a picture. It keeps the camera from taking a picture until after autofocus has been activated. This option applies only when focus-priority has been chosen for AF-C or AF-S and you are using an AF-area selection mode that allows the user to select the focus area or zones (in other words, all AF-area modes other than Auto-area AF).

  This option will prevent you from accidentally taking out-of-focus pictures if you forget you are using AF-ON to activate autofocus and press the shutter release without remembering to initiate AF.

a7 Focus Point Persistence

Options: Auto (default), Off

My preference: Auto

This is an esoteric setting that some will find useful. Choose Auto, and the focus point selected by the camera in Auto-area AF or Wide-area AF modes remains in effect when you change to one of the modes in which the focus point is selected by the user. Select Off, and the focus point last chosen by you is restored. This setting comes into play when you:

- **Press a button that changes AF-area mode.** You've assigned AF-area mode, AF-area mode+AF ON, Recall Shooting Functions, or Recall Shooting Functions (Hold) behavior to that button.
- **Press shutter release halfway.** You are changing AF-area mode while focusing with the shutter button half-pressed.
- **Change from auto point selection to manual point selection.** You are switching from an AF-area mode in which the camera chooses the focus point to one that is selected manually. It would apply, for example, if you're switching from Auto-area AF or one of the Wide-area AF modes to Single-point AF or any other mode in which the user chooses the focus point.

Make sure Auto is enabled when you want to let the camera choose the focus point, then lock in that point because you want to switch to 3D-tracking to follow an erratic or fast-moving subject. If set to Off, the camera will change to your last focus point instead.

a8 Limit AF-Area Mode Selection

Options: Pinpoint, Single-point AF, Dynamic-area AF (Small, Medium, Large), Wide-area AF (Small, Large, C1, C2), 3D-tracking, Auto-area AF (default is all available)

My preference: N/A

This is the first entry in the next group of AF settings. (See Figure 7.4.) The fastest way to switch AF-area modes is to press the focus-mode button and rotate the sub-command dial. If there are certain AF-area modes that you don't use, you can disable them using this menu item. That will enable you to switch AF-area modes more quickly. Indeed, some

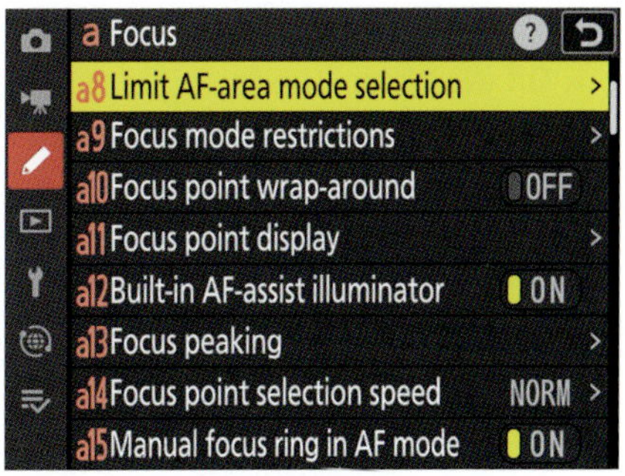

Figure 7.4 The next page of the Focus menu.

shooters use only two or three modes, and can dispense with the others. **Note:** The AF-area modes available from the *i* menu are not changed, and remain available should you decide you need to use one of them.

Single-point AF-area mode is always available and cannot be disabled. However, you can highlight any of the others and press the multi selector right button to remove the check box next to that mode's label to disable it. You can thus enable Single-point AF, plus any combination of the other AF-area modes. I explained this feature in Chapter 3.

a9 Focus Mode Restrictions

Options: Single AF, Continuous AF, Manual Focus, No Restrictions (default)

My preference: No Restrictions

This entry allows you to lock in one particular focus mode so that it can't be changed accidentally or intentionally. You can choose to set the camera so that your choice of AF-S, AF-C, or Manual focus is mandatory for a given session. Most of the time you'll want to use the default, No Restrictions. You might want to use this in a critical situation where it's important to avoid switching focus mode, or when your camera may be used/handled by someone else and you don't want them messing with your setting.

a10 Focus Point Wrap-Around

Options: Off (default), On

My preference: Off

This setting is purely a personal preference parameter. When you press the directional controls to choose a focus point, the camera can be told to stop when the selection reaches the edge of the array, or, it can continue, wrapping around to the opposite edge, like Pac-Man leaving the playing area on one side or top/bottom to re-emerge on the other. (I hope I'm not revealing my age, here.) Your choices are simple; decide which behavior you prefer:

- **On (Wrap).** Pressing the left/right or up/down buttons when you've reached the edge of the focus point display wraps the selection to the opposite side, still moving in the same direction. If you find yourself frequently needing to scoot from one side of the frame to the other, this setting can save you a lot of button presses. You need to train yourself to be aware of and use the wrap-around feature.
- **Off (No Wrap).** The focus point selection stops at the edge of the focus zone array. If you're set in your ways or don't often need to zip from one side to the other, the default setting will cater to your habits.

a11 Focus Point Display

Options: Manual Focus Mode: On (default), Off; Dynamic-area AF Assist: On (default), Off; AF-C In-focus display: On, Off (default); 3D-tracking Focus Point Color: White (default), Red

My preference: Manual Focus Mode: On; Dynamic-area AF assist: On; AF-C In-focus Display: On; 3D-tracking Focus Point Color: White

How do you want the focus points displayed in the viewfinder? This entry gives you three toggle controls and a color choice during 3D-tracking. Your focus point options include:

- **Manual Focus mode.** When you're using manual focus instead of autofocus, the camera still monitors how well your image is in focus, using the active focus point. Here, you can choose how it is displayed.
    - **On.** Active point illumination is always shown when using manual focus. Select this option if you like to know what focus point is being used.
    - **Off.** Active point illumination is enabled during manual focus only during focus point selection as you move the point around the frame with the multi selector directional buttons or sub-selector.
- **Dynamic-area AF assist.** Can provide optional position information when using Dynamic-area AF.
    - **On.** Both the focus point selected *and* the surrounding focus points when using Dynamic-area AF. You might want to choose On as a reminder that the cluster of points around the main focus point are active. This setting has an important benefit: it clearly reminds you that you are using Dynamic-area AF, and displays the coverage of the Small, Medium, and Large variations.
    - **Off.** Only the selected focus point is shown. Once you become accustomed to using that AF-area mode and think you don't need to know how large the focus area is, you can turn the display Off and slightly declutter your screen.
- **AF-C In-focus Display.** The camera can let you know when focus is achieved when using AF-C focus.
    - **On.** The focus point will be displayed in green when the subject is in focus. Seeing focus points turn green can be a comforting confirmation.
    - **Off.** The focus point is always displayed in red or yellow, whether the subject is in focus or not. Because focus can change rapidly and repeatedly when working with AF-C, the default setting is Off, which many prefer to keep visual distractions to a minimum when shooting fast-moving subjects.
- **3D-tracking Focus Point Color.** You can specify whether a white or red box will be shown around the tracked subject when using 3D-tracking. If you've chosen On for AF-C in-focus display (above), the indicator will switch to green when focus is achieved.
- **Focus Point Border Width.** Choose widths from 1 to 3.

a12 Built-in AF-Assist Illuminator

Options: On (default), Off

My preference: Off

There is a green LED on the left front panel (as you hold the camera). It can illuminate to provide additional lighting to improve autofocus when using the AF-S focus mode. The illuminator is effective over a very narrow range (Nikon says 3'4" to 9'10") and its anemic burst of light can be obstructed by any lens hood you have mounted, or even a stray finger. If a Profoto A10's continuous LED light is configured to act as an AF-assist illuminator, it will light up even if you select Off.

a13 Focus Peaking

Options: Focus Peaking Display: On, Off (default); Focus Peaking Sensitivity: 3 (High Sensitivity), 2 (standard) (default), 1 (Low Sensitivity); Focus Peaking Highlight Color: Red (default), Yellow, Blue, White

My preference: N/A

Focus peaking is a focusing aid available to provide colored highlights around the edges of objects as they come into sharp focus. The most important parameter is Focus Peaking Sensitivity, which you can set to Low Sensitivity, Standard, or High Sensitivity. The Low setting is the most precise; only a narrow focus plane is used, while at the High setting, the "depth of focus" is deeper, so that more of the subject is considered to be in focus. Standard uses a value somewhere in between. You'd want to use Low Sensitivity and a magnified view for critical focus, and High Sensitivity for speed, especially if you're using a smaller f/stop that is more forgiving of slight focus errors.

You can choose from among red, yellow, blue, or white as your contrasting color. If your subject has a predominant color, you should select a peaking color that contrasts. For example, you might want to use yellow as your peaking tone when photographing red roses. I explained how to use focus peaking and showed you what it looks like in action in Chapter 3.

a14 Maximum Aperture Lv During Manual Focus (Z9 Only)

Options: On, Off (default)

My preference: (N/A)

On tells the camera to always use the maximum aperture for the shooting display in Manual focus mode.

a14/a15 Focus Point Selection Speed (Z8/Z9)

Options: Low, Normal (default), High

My preference: Normal

You can select how quickly you can manually move the selected focus point around the frame. With up to 493 selectable focus points, changing your current point's position can be cumbersome, and you'll rarely, if ever, want to use the Low speed option. Normal actually works quite well in most situations. The High speed option can be useful when you're working with AF-area modes that use the largest number of individual points, such as Single-point AF.

a16 Manual Focus Ring in AF Mode

Options: On (default), Off

My preference: On

Autofocus generally kicks in when you press the shutter release halfway. Many lenses allow you to press the shutter release halfway down to autofocus (or press your AF-ON button), and then fine-tune focus by rotating the lens's focus ring. If at any time you want to refocus automatically, release the shutter button or AF-ON button, and press again. Override AF by rotating the focus ring, then press the shutter release down all the way to take the picture. Or, you can lift your finger from the release button and then half-press it again to activate AF again.

Normally, that's a good thing. However, sometimes you might want to turn off the manual refocus option to avoid accidentally disturbing focus set by the AF system. This setting adds that capability to compatible lenses that have a control ring in addition to a focusing ring. When set to Off with such lenses, the lens focus ring can't be used to manually focus in AF mode. Of course, you can disable the control ring on lenses that have only one or two rings by choosing Control Ring in Custom Setting f2 Custom Controls, and selecting None as its behavior, instead. But if a lens has three rings, this entry is the only way to disable the manual focus function.

Note: This entry appears *only* when a compatible lens is mounted on the camera. For example, it's not shown at all when I am using my Nikon 14-30mm f/4 S lens, but is available when my Nikon 24-120mm f/4 S optic is mounted.

b. Metering/Exposure

The yellow-coded Metering/Exposure Custom Settings (see Figure 7.5) let you define four different parameters that affect exposure metering.

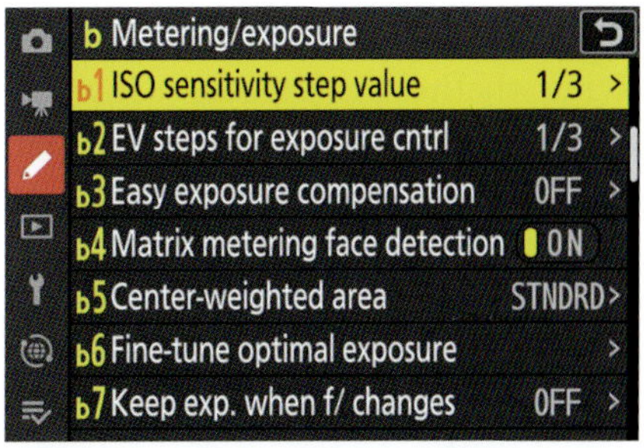

Figure 7.5 The first page of the Metering/Exposure menu

b1 ISO Sensitivity Step Value

Options: 1/3 Step (default), Full Step

My preference: 1/3 Step

This setting tells the camera the size of the "jumps" it should use when making ISO sensitivity adjustments—either one-third (the default) or one stop. Choose the 1/3-stop setting when you want the finest increments between ISO settings. For example, the camera will use values such as 64, 80, 100, 125, 160, 200, 250, 320... and so forth, giving you (and the autoexposure system) maximum flexibility.

With full-stop increments, you will have larger and more noticeable changes between settings. The camera will offer ISO settings such as 64, 100, 200, 400, and 800, instead. These coarser adjustments are useful when you want more dramatic changes between different exposures.

b2 EV Steps for Exposure Control

Options: 1/3 EV Steps (default), 1/2 EV Steps, 1 EV Steps

My preference: 1/3 EV Steps

This setting tells the camera the size of the "jumps" it should use when making exposure adjustments—one-third stop, one-half stop, or one full stop. The increment you specify here applies to f/stops, shutter speeds, autoexposure bracketing, and EV changes—with one exception. If you specify the 1 EV option, exposure compensation will use 1/3 stop instead.

Choose the 1/3-stop setting when you want the finest increments between shutter speeds and/or f/stops. For example, the camera will use shutter speeds such as 1/60th, 1/80th, 1/100th, 1/125th, and 1/160th second, and f/stops such as f/5.6, f/6.3, f/7.1, and f/8, giving you (and the autoexposure system) corresponding flexibility.

As with ISO settings, using 1/2-stop or full-stop increments, you will have larger and more noticeable changes between settings. Using the full-stop settings as an example, the camera will apply shutter speeds such as 1/60th, 1/125th, 1/250th, and 1/500th second, and f/stops including f/5.6, f/8, f/11, and f/16. These coarser adjustments are useful when you want more dramatic changes between different exposures. I sometimes use the 1 EV setting when I am experimenting with manual HDR exposures and want large jumps between shots.

b3 Easy Exposure Compensation

Options: On (Auto Reset), On, Off (default)

My preference: Off

This setting potentially simplifies dialing in EV (exposure value compensation) adjustments by specifying whether the Exposure Compensation button must be pressed while adding or extracting EV compensation. Because of the possibility of confusion or error, I tend to leave this setting turned off, which is the default. Your choices are as follows:

- **On (Auto Reset).** This setting allows you to add or subtract exposure by rotating the sub-command dial when in Program (P) or Shutter-priority (S) exposure modes, or by rotating the main command dial when using Aperture-priority (A) mode. Rotating either dial has no effect in Manual (M) exposure mode. (If you've reversed the behavior of the command dials using Custom Setting f5, the "opposite" command dial must be used to make the changes.) Any adjustments you've made are canceled when the camera is shut off, or the standby timer expires, and the exposure meters go back to sleep. **Note:** However, if you've activated an EV change *not* using the command dials, but by pressing the EV button located to the southeast of the shutter release, or a dial defined to perform exposure compensation, the reset *does not occur* when you power off and on again.

  That's a useful mode, because most of us have made an EV adjustment and then forgotten about it, only to expose a whole series of improperly exposed photos. You can still have "sticky" EV settings when Easy Exposure Compensation is turned on: just hold down the Exposure

Compensation button when you make your changes. You can also increase the Power Off Delay interval (using Custom Setting c3, described shortly) to a longer period so your adjustment will remain in force for a longer period of time.

- **On.** This setting brings the Easy Compensation mode into conformance with the camera's behavior when the Exposure Compensation button is pressed: in either case, any EV modifications you make will remain until you countermand them. As I have mentioned several times, forgetting to "turn off" EV changes after you've moved on to a different shooting environment is a primary cause of over- and underexposure among those of us who are forgetful or who ignore the flashing EV warnings.
- **Off.** With this default setting, you must always press the Exposure Compensation button while rotating the main command dial to add or subtract exposure. Use this choice when you don't want any EV changes unless you deliberately make them by pressing the button.

b4 Matrix Metering Face Detection

Options: On (default), Off

My preference: Off

Face detection has become so accurate and useful that the ability to adjust exposure expressly to take into account faces contained within the frame is a highly desirable *optional* feature. This entry allows you to enable such adjustments when you are using Matrix metering. The ability of Matrix metering to calculate exposure from a detailed array of segments within the frame allows the Z9 and Z8 to measure the light reflected from faces and optimize exposure based on them.

This setting is especially useful when shooting portrait-type images or other people pictures in which humans fill most of the frame. However, scenes in which people make up a smaller component of the image area can end up being improperly exposed when exposure priority is given to humans. I leave this setting Off most of the time, because Matrix metering generally does an excellent job with a wide variety of scenes. I turn it on primarily when shooting candid portraits under varying lighting conditions.

b5 Center-Weighted Area

Options: Small, Standard, Average

My preference: Standard

In many ways, Center-weighted metering is a hold-over from the early days of through-the-lens (TTL) exposure metering. The earliest cameras with this feature calculated exposure using the average of the entire frame. Center-weighting was developed to give additional priority to the area of the image where the most important subject matter was likely to appear. In the Z9 and Z8, a "fuzzy" central circle is used to calculate 75 percent of the total exposure, with the remainder of the frame used to account for the rest. Nikon recommends using Center-weighted metering for bright, contrasty scenes and when using circular polarizers.

Your choices with this entry include Small (with an 8mm circle); Standard (the default), with a 12mm circle; and Average, which is the same as the old-time full-frame averaging systems. I've found that changing the size really has very little effect most of the time. By default, the camera will show a translucent gray circle in the display that represents the size of the center-weighted area in display configurations 1–3 (which cycle through when you press the DISP button). You can disable/enable the circle using the Custom Monitor/Viewfinder Shooting Display entries (d20/d21 and d19/d20 for the Z9/Z8, respectively), as described later in this chapter.

b6 Fine-Tune Optimal Exposure

Options: Default (none), Plus or minus one stop in 1/6-stop increments for: Matrix metering, Center-weighted metering, Spot metering, Highlight-weighted metering

My preference: N/A

This setting is a powerful adjustment that allows you to dial in a specific amount of exposure compensation that will be applied, invisibly, to every photo you take using each of the metering modes. No more can you complain, "My camera always underexposes by 1/3 stop!" If that is actually the case, and the phenomenon is consistent, you can use this custom menu adjustment to compensate.

Exposure compensation is usually a better idea (does your camera *really* underexpose that consistently?), but this setting does allow you to "recalibrate" your camera yourself. However, you have no indication that fine-tuning has been made: any exposure compensation you add/subtract here is not reflected in the Z9 or Z8's live view display. You'll need to remember what you've done. After all, you someday might discover that your camera is consistently *over*exposing images by 1/3 stop, not realizing that your Custom Setting b6 adjustment is the culprit.

In practice, it's rare that the camera will *consistently* provide the wrong exposure in any of the four metering modes, especially Matrix metering, which can alter exposure dramatically based on an internal database of typical scenes. Fine-tune optimal exposure may be most useful for Spot metering, if you always take a reading off the same type of subject, such as a human face or 18 percent gray card. Should you find that the gray card readings, for example, always differ from what you would prefer, go ahead and fine-tune optimal exposure for Spot metering, and use that to read your gray cards. To use this feature:

1. **Select fine-tuning.** Choose Custom Setting b6: Fine-tune Optimal Exposure from the Custom Settings menu.
2. **Consider yourself warned.** In the screen that appears, choose Yes after carefully reading the warning that Nikon insists on showing you every time this option is activated.
3. **Select metering mode to correct.** Choose Matrix, Center-weighted, Spot, or Highlight-weighted metering in the screen that follows by highlighting your choice and pressing the multi selector right button. (See Figure 7.6, left.)

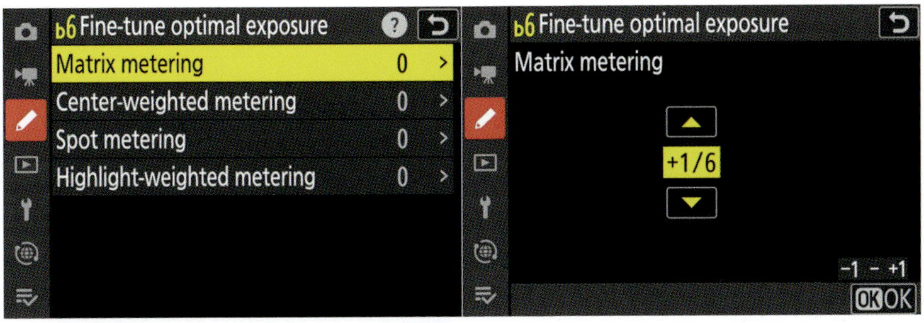

Figure 7.6 You can fine-tune any of four metering modes (left). Increments of 1/6 stop are available (right).

4. **Specify amount of correction.** Press the up/down buttons to dial in the exposure compensation you want to apply. You can specify compensation up to +/– one stop, in increments of 1/6 stop, half as large a change as conventional exposure compensation. Compensation of up to one full stop (plus or minus) can be entered. This is truly *fine-tuning.* (See Figure 7.6, right.)
5. **Confirm your change.** Press OK when finished. You can repeat the action to fine-tune the other exposure modes if necessary.

b7 Keep Exposure When f/stop Changes

Options: Shutter Speed, ISO Sensitivity, Exposure Maintenance Off (default)

My preference: N/A

This entry is a clever failsafe that protects you when you want to use a particular aperture, but the camera is unable to achieve the correct exposure because the f/stop you specified is not available. The situations in which you might encounter this include:

- **Variable aperture lens.** Say you're working with the Nikkor 24-200mm f/4-6.3 VR lens and had been taking photos in Aperture-priority at the 24mm zoom position and specified f/4. When you zoom to 200mm the maximum aperture becomes f/6.3 and your image would ordinarily be underexposed by 1 1/3 stop.
- **You change lenses.** You had been shooting with the S Nikkor 24-70mm f/2.8 lens at a selected f/2.8 aperture. Then, you switch to the S Nikkor 24-120mm f/4 optic. Your image would be a full stop underexposed.
- **Macro shooting.** A lens's effective aperture changes when shooting close-ups, and the adjustment can be dramatic at very close distances. When using extension tubes your S 105mm f/2.8 VR lens would have an effective maximum aperture of f/5.6 at a 1:1 reproduction ratio.

This setting allows you to tell the camera what to do if it is unable to provide optimum exposure at the designated aperture. The default setting is Off (no correction), but you can select to correct using either shutter speed or ISO sensitivity, and the Z9 or Z8 will adjust the exposure using the shutter speed or ISO setting, respectively.

c. Timers/AE Lock

This category (see Figure 7.7) is a mixed bag of settings, covering how the shutter release and AE-L buttons interact (c1) and entries that adjust delay times (c2 and c3).

c1 Shutter-Release Button AE-L

Options: Off (default), On (half press), On (burst mode)

My preference: On when using back-button focus, as described in Chapter 5

This is another of Nikon's easily confusing options for controlling how and when autofocus and exposure are activated and locked. The intent is to allow you to separate autofocus and autoexposure activation and locking.

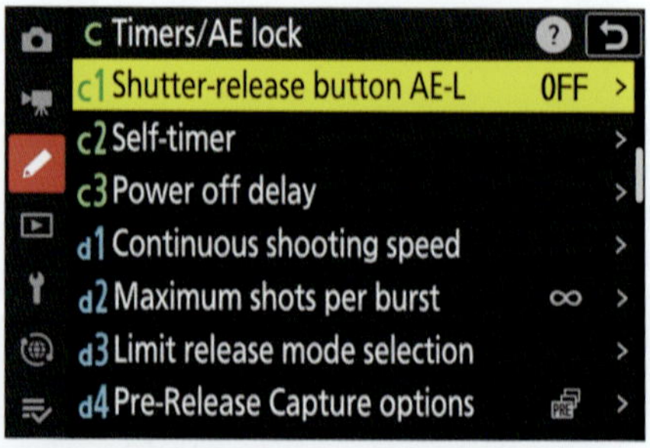

Figure 7.7 The Timers/AE Lock settings.

- **Off.** Exposure is locked *only* when the button assigned to AE-L/AF-L is pressed. This is the default. The shutter release does not lock exposure.
- **On (half press).** Exposure locks when either the shutter release button is depressed *halfway,* or the designated AE-L/AF-L button is held down. If you always want exposure locked when the shutter release is pressed halfway, use this option. That makes the most sense when you are using back-button focus (BBF). You want to be able to lock the exposure (alone) while activating autofocus separately with the AF-ON button when using back-button focus.
- **On (burst mode).** Exposure locks when the shutter release button is pressed down all the way. You'd do this during continuous shooting, when you press the shutter release and hold it down while your series of shots is captured. This option locks the exposure for the first image, ensuring that all the other images in the sequence are given the same exposure.

LOCKED EXPOSURE VS LOCKED SETTINGS

Locking the amount of exposure does not mean you are locking the *settings* your camera uses. When using Shutter-priority, Aperture-priority, or Programmed Auto modes, exposure is locked, but you can still rotate the main command dial to change to a different shutter speed (in S mode), or sub-command dial to switch to a different aperture (in A mode). In P mode, the main dial will provide different combinations of both shutter speed and aperture. The camera will adjust the other setting to provide the same overall exposure.

c2 Self-Timer

Options: Self-timer Delay (default: 10 sec.), Number of Shots (default: 1), Interval Between Shots (default: 0.5 sec.)

My preference: N/A

This setting lets you choose the length of the self-timer shutter release delay. Your options include:

- **Self-timer Delay.** The default value is 10 seconds. You can also choose 2, 5, 10, or 20 seconds. If I have the camera mounted on a tripod or other support and am too lazy to attach the MC-30A cable release (I have three, one for each camera bag, so I *always* have one available), I can set a 2-second delay that is sufficient to let the camera stop vibrating after I've pressed the shutter release. I use a longer delay time if I am racing to get into the picture myself and am not sure I can make it in 10 seconds. The lamp on the front of the camera will blink when the countdown begins, and then illuminate steadily for the final two seconds.
- **Number of Shots.** After the timer finishes counting down, you can take from 1 to 9 different shots. This is a godsend when shooting photos of groups, especially if you want to appear in the photo itself. You'll always want to shoot several pictures to ensure that everyone's eyes are open and there are smiling expressions on each face. Instead of racing back and forth to trigger the self-timer multiple times, you can select the number of shots taken after a single countdown. For small groups, I always take at least as many shots as there are people in the group—plus one. That gives everybody a chance to close their eyes.
- **Interval Between Shots.** If you've selected 2 to 9 as your number of shots to be snapped off, you can use this option to space out the different exposures. Your choices are 0.5, 1, 2, or 3 seconds. Use a short interval when you want to capture everyone saying "Cheese!" The 3-second option is helpful if you're using flash, as 3 seconds is generally long enough to allow the flash to recycle and have enough juice for the next photo.

c3 Power Off Delay

Options: Separate settings for Playback, Menus, Picture Review, Standby Timer

My preference: Playback (20 seconds); Menus (1 minute); Picture Review (4 seconds); Standby Timer (10 minutes for sports, weddings, other events with frequent shooting)

You can adjust the amount of time the viewfinder or LCD monitor displays remain on when no other operations are being performed. The delays you can adjust include:

- **Playback.** This parameter controls how long until the displays are turned off. The default is 10 seconds. This setting is *not* the same as the Picture Review that occurs when you press the Playback button.
- **Menus.** Menus will display for up to 1 minute by default, then disappear if there is no user activity. The default value is usually fine.
- **Picture Review.** Determines how long an image is displayed after you press the Playback button, or when displayed automatically because Picture Review in the Playback menu is set to On. The default is four seconds

- **Standby Timer.** The camera displays, sensor, exposure meters, and GPS (if enabled on the Z9) will remain active until this timer expires. The default is 30 seconds, and the display will warn you by dimming a few seconds before putting the camera to sleep. This is generally the most critical of the four; keep in mind that your sensor remains energized the whole time and uses a lot more juice than cameras that rely on an optical viewfinder.

  You'll rarely need or want to have playback, menus, or picture review active for long periods. But sports shooters, wildlife photographers, and some others prefer a longer delay because they can keep their camera always "at the ready" with no delay to interfere with taking an action shot that unexpectedly presents itself. Extra battery consumption is just part of the price paid.

  For example, when I am shooting football, a standby timer of 20 seconds is plenty, because the players lining up for the snap is my signal to get ready to shoot. But for basketball or soccer, I typically set the standby timer for 30 minutes, because action is virtually continuous. My camera has plenty of power, and I carry two sets of spare batteries. I rarely shoot much more than 1,000 to 1,200 shots at any sports event, so that's often sufficient juice even with the standby timer set for 30 minutes or No Limit.

Some exceptions to be aware of:

- **Resetting the Standby Timer.** Tapping the shutter release (or another button) will extend the Standby Timer's active period. You'll receive a warning when the display dims just before the Standby Timer expires.
- ***i* menu extension.** If you happen to set the Standby Timer to 10 seconds, the Z9 or Z8 will extend the active display to 20 seconds if the *i* menu is in use.
- **Picture Review override.** The camera will always override the review display when the shutter button is partially or fully depressed, so you'll never miss a shot because a previous image was on the screen.
- **Self-timer extension.** All four timers extend by 60 seconds when you're using the self-timer.
- **Video recording.** You should set the Standby Timer to Unlimited when using your camera as a Web cam or when recording to an external device through the Z9 or Z8's HDMI port.

d. Shooting/Display

This menu section offers a variety of sometimes unrelated shooting and display options not found elsewhere, but which are not frequently changed, making them suitable for a Custom Settings entry. Figure 7.8 shows only the first seven entries of the Z9's Shooting/Display menu.

NOTE The numbering of the Z8's counterpart Shooting/Display menu is slightly different, as I'll point out in the sections which follow. Nikon did not include the Limit Release Mode and Exposure Delay Mode entries on the Z8, causing the disparity.

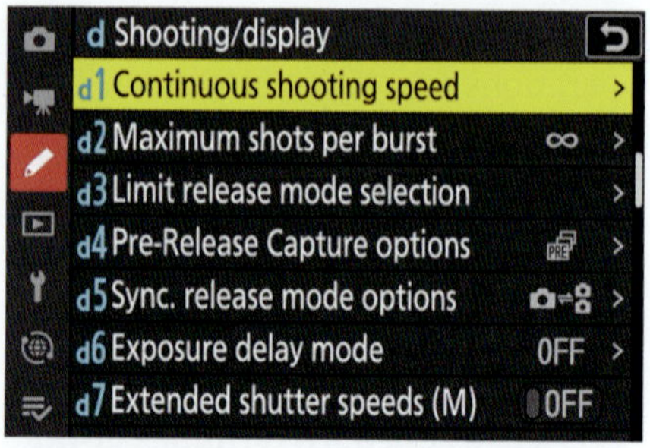

Figure 7.8 A mixed bag of entries is found in the Shooting/Display submenu.

d1 Continuous Shooting Speed

Options: Continuous H (10 to 20 fps, default: 20 fps); Continuous L (1 to 10 fps, default: 5 fps)

My preference: Continuous H: 12 fps; Continuous L: 1 fps

You can specify the frames-per-second shooting rate for both continuous high- and low-speed shooting that are available when the camera is set to the Continuous H or L modes. Faster rates are better for sports action, but you have many other choices available.

Choose one of these firing speed ranges for Continuous H/L from among those available that is suitable for the kind of shooting environment you're in:

- **Normal continuous shooting.** I set the Continuous L value on my camera to the 1 fps rate most of the time, so that I can take multiple shots quickly without needing to press the shutter release repeatedly. A one-second rate isn't so fast that I end up taking a bunch of shots that I don't want, but it is fast enough that I can shoot a series.
- **Multiple exposures.** Your ideal shooting speed may vary, depending on the type of multiple exposure you're looking for. A setting of 1 fps is slow enough to allow you to reframe your image to place your multiple images exactly where you want them in the frame. When I am shooting a concert and want to capture multiple images of a performer's movement, I might select a 5 fps rate, and then zoom or move my camera to offset the individual images.
- **Bracketing.** When I'm using bracketing, I generally have the camera set to shoot a bracketed set of at least three pictures: under, normal, and overexposure. With the camera set to 3 fps, I can press the shutter once and take all three bracketed shots, with basically the same framing, within about one second.
- **Unlimited Shooting.** If you select 12 fps for your Continuous H setting, you can enjoy virtually unlimited continuous shooting without worrying about any slowdown from a full buffer—even if you're shooting RAW files at the Lossless compressed NEF setting.
- **HDR bracketing.** On the other hand, if you're bracketing to combine individual images in an image editor to produce a high dynamic range photo, you'll want the exposures to be captured as quickly as possible. That will minimize any differences between the images, so they can be more easily aligned as they are merged. Use a high frame rate in this case.
- **Slower action sequences.** For some types of action, such as long-distance running, golf, swimming, or routine baseball plays, a rate of 2 fps might be sufficient. You can make this more reasonable speed available by defining it here as the continuous low-speed frame rate. You won't have as many individual shots to sort through, which can easily be the case at the maximum 20 fps frame rate.
- **Faster action sequences.** You can specify higher frame rates, up to 20 fps, when you want to grab more images in a brief burst. However, in most cases, if you need the highest rates you'll use the quick-release mode, which allows additional frame rates C30, C60, or C120 (30, 60, or 120 frames per second).

d2 Maximum Shots Per Burst

Options: 1–200 shots, Infinity (default)

My preference: Infinity

When you have a camera with an electronic shutter that can shoot silently at very high frame rates, it's easy to get carried away. I've taken as many as 7,200 shots in a single day at an airshow, which was a thrilling experience (both from a photographic and observer viewpoint), but it was less exciting to spend hours wading through so many images to find the keepers among the near-misses.

At most Image Size/Quality settings, your Z9 or Z8 can shoot continuously for hundreds of shots without filling its buffer or even producing a slow-down of the shooting rate. If you'd rather put an upper limit on the number of images in a continuous burst, you can do that here. The default value is Infinity—although it's likely your memory cards will fill or the entropic heat-death of the universe will occur first. You can also choose a less vague number between 1 and 200.

I generally leave this setting at the default, but, in addition to laziness and dwindling memory card space, there are other reasons why a lower value would be useful. Say you wanted to illustrate an event sequence—such as a golfer's swing over a period of two seconds—and wanted to end up with a 4 × 4 array of 16 individual images. Theoretically, you could set the maximum burst to 16 shots, choose a frame rate of 8 frames per second, and end up with exactly that. In practice, however, it would be smarter to apply a fudge factor and capture 18–20 frames (or more) and use 16 shots from the middle of the sequence. Why? Because the action you are illustrating is unlikely to take exactly two seconds, and, as it happens, your camera's stated 8 fps frame rate is closer to 7.5 fps in real life.

d3 Limit Release Mode Selection (Z9 Only)

Options: Enable/Disable Single-frame, Continuous L, Continuous H, C30, C60, C120, or Self-timer

My preference: Enable all

This entry lets Nikon Z9 owners disable little-used release modes from quick-release mode availability. The Z9's release mode dial itself has five physical positions: Single-frame, Continuous L, Continuous H, Self-timer, and quick-release modes. You can choose any of them by pressing the release mode dial lock release and rotating the dial to the desired position. That can be slow or difficult to do, especially when it's dark.

It often makes more sense to leave the Z9's dial in the quick-release position. You can then select Single-frame, Continuous L, Continuous H, C30, C60, C120, or Self-timer by holding down the release mode button and rotating the main command dial. Each of the available modes will cycle through and appear on both the control panel and rear LCD monitor. Spinning the sub-command dial allows adjustment of the Continuous L and H frame rates and Self-timer intervals.

If it happens that you don't often use a particular release mode, you can disable its quick-release availability. Say you never use the C30, C60, or C120 high-speed modes (or use just one of them). You can remove the check mark next to that release option in this menu entry and speed up release mode selection. All the release modes (except for C30, C60, and C120) will still be available using the physical release mode dial. So, you could, if you wanted to, enable *only* Single-frame and Continuous H and switch back and forth between them rapidly.

d3/d4 Pre-Release Capture Options (Z8/Z9)

Options: Pre-release Burst: Off (default), 0.3, 0.5, 1.0 seconds; Post-release Burst: 1, 2, 3 seconds, Max (default)

My preference: Pre-release Burst: 1 second; Post-release Burst: Max

As I noted earlier, the Z8 and Z9 use slightly different menu numbers. The Z8 lacks the Limit Release Mode Selection option described above, and assigns d3 to this entry. Both cameras, fortunately, have the cool new pre-release capture options.

Indeed, your Nikon's pre-release capture feature is one capability for which the term "game-changer" is not hyperbole. It gives you the ability to capture images that took place up to a full second *before* you pressed the shutter release. In effect, you can partially nullify the limitations of human reaction times and capture bursts of lightning and other spontaneous events without a specialized light/sound trigger, and capture decisive sports action or unpredictable wildlife movement with ease. If you're like me, you've spent a lot of time waiting for a butterfly to alight, only to end up with photos of blossoms where a rare specimen *used to be*. Or, you've tried, without success, to capture an osprey at the moment it dives and snares a fish.

Your Nikon's pre-release capture options make such pictures easy. When the shutter release is pressed halfway, the camera will immediately begin capturing images in its buffer, just as if you were taking a picture. However, this stream of images remains in the buffer and is not written to your memory card. The images cycle through the buffer, which retains up to the most recent one second's worth. You can keep half-pressing the shutter release for up to 30 seconds. When you press the shutter button down all the way during that span, the camera transports the most recent one second's worth of images (or just 1/3 or 1/2 second's worth as you specify), to the memory card. It continues to grab images for a few additional seconds.

This feature works only when the Z9 or Z8 is set to the C15 (Z9 only), C30, C60, or C120 release modes, which can capture from 10 to 120 frames *before* the shutter release is pressed down all the way, along with additional action that happens up to around four seconds *after* you trigger the sequence. You can set your pre-release options ahead of time; the Z9 or Z8's time-travel features remain dormant until you specifically switch to C15 (Z9 only), C30, C60, or C120 release modes. Note that high-speed images are always captured in JPEG (or HEIF) Normal format. Here's how to get set up:

1. **Access the d4/d3 Pre-release Capture Options entry.** When you navigate to this entry, you'll be shown two sets of options: Pre-release burst and Post-release burst.
2. **Choose pre-release duration.** The Pre-release burst screen, shown at left in Figure 7.9, is Off by default. To enable pre-release capture, choose 0.3 seconds (actually about a third of a second), 0.5 seconds, or 1.0 seconds. That will determine both the duration of your pre-buffering, as well as the number of images captured before the shutter release is pressed down all the way:
    - **C15/C30:** 0.3s: 10 images; 0.5s: 15 images; 1.0s: 30 images. Each will be 45MP full-frame images.
    - **C60:** 0.3s: 20 images; 0.5s: 30 images; 1.0s: 60 images. Each will be 19.4MP DX-crop images.
    - **C120:** 0.3s: 40 images; 0.5s: 60 images; 1.0s: 120 images. Each will be 11MP full-frame down-sampled images.

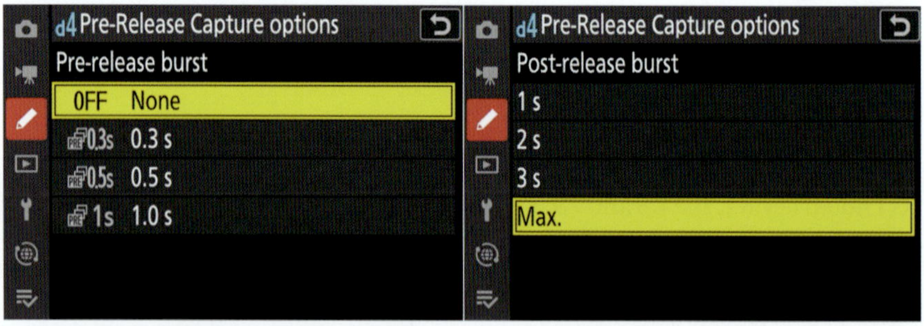

Figure 7.9 Set Pre-release burst (left) and Post-release burst (right).

3. **Choose post-release burst.** The camera can continue to capture moments that occur after the shutter release is pressed (see Figure 7.9, right). Depending on how important the post-shot sequence is, you can choose 1, 2, or 3 seconds, or Max (in which case capture will continue until the buffer fills, which is usually about four seconds, or you release the shutter button). For events that happen in a split second, such as a lightning burst, you sometimes won't care much about post-event images (but keep in mind that multiple bolts of lightning can happen in rapid succession).
4. **Access high-speed capture modes (Z9 only).** Press the release mode dial lock release button on the left shoulder of the Z9, and rotate the release mode dial all the way to the right past the self-timer label to the quick-release mode icon. The Z8 does not require this extra step.
5. **Choose capture speed.** Hold down the release mode button and rotate the main command dial to select C15, C30, C60, or C120 high-speed frame capture modes, as seen at left in Figure 7.10.
6. **Confirm pre-release mode.** Check the upper right edge of the LCD monitor, as shown in Figure 7.10, right, or at the bottom of the viewfinder to see the PRE icon displayed. You have activated pre-release capture.
7. **Capture images.** Press and hold the shutter release halfway to begin capturing images to the buffer. A green dot will appear in the PRE icon to show that images are being buffered. If you hold down the shutter release halfway for more than roughly 30 seconds, a ! warning appears in the PRE icon and pre-release capture is cancelled. To resume, lift your finger from the shutter release and press it halfway again.

   Note: If the time between when you press the shutter halfway and then all the way down to direct images to the memory card is less than the specified pre-release burst, you won't get a full set of images. In other words, if you have set a 1-second pre-release burst but press the shutter release all the way less than one second after buffering begins, you'll save only the frames already accumulated, plus any captured during the post-release burst.

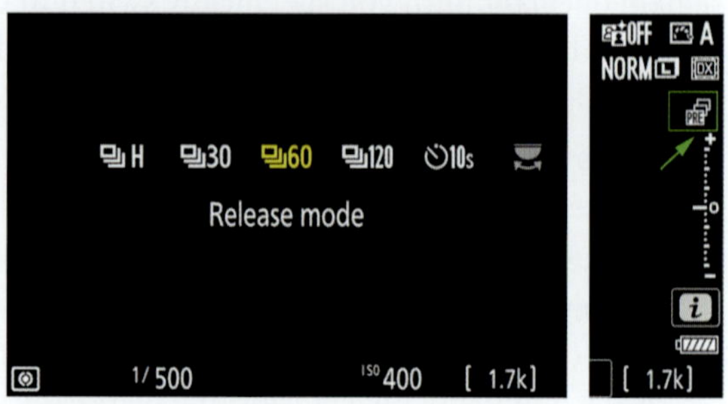

Figure 7.10 Choose capture speed (left). Pre-release indicator (right).

TIPS

- For moving subjects (rather than lightning, for example) you might want to use a focal length slightly wider than necessary to frame your image tightly. Give yourself some extra room to account for sudden, erratic movement when your subject takes flight, or performs some other action. This works particularly well at the C30 setting, because you'll have 45MP images that can be cropped to re-frame your image.
- Choose your AF-area mode carefully. You will probably want to use Wide-area AF (L) with subject detection appropriate for your subject matter.
- You're going to capture a lot of images even if you don't buffer a lot of extra frames. Take advantage of the Series Playback options (described in Chapter 8). You can set your camera to move between the first images of bursts using the sub-selector, display the burst in real time for a few seconds, and specify that only the first image in a burst appear in thumbnail views. These will help you review and access your bursts more efficiently.

d4/d5 Sync. Release Mode Options (Z8/Z9)

Options: Sync (default), No Sync

My preference: Sync

If you own multiple compatible Nikon cameras equipped with optional WR-R10 or WR-11a wireless remote controllers, you can configure them such that they all fire at the same time. One camera acts as a master that controls the shutter release of the additional cameras. Sports photographers love this capability, because they can install remote cameras, say, above a basketball rim, and then position themselves along the baseline to shoot action in the paint. One click of the master camera produces shots from both angles simultaneously. (This is basically how I cover basketball games, except for the part about having a second, remote-controlled camera mounted high above the rim.)

This is a rather esoteric feature, available only to those who own, say, two or more Nikon Z-series, D850, D500, D5, or D6 cameras. Synchronized release is also available with some other models, including the D4 and D4s equipped with the optional WT-5/5A wireless transmitter. It can also be used with earlier D8xx- and D7xxx-series cameras with the UT-1 Communication Unit. You can use this entry to activate or deactivate the feature, but it's probably a better idea to use Custom Setting f2 and assign Sync. Release Selection to a function button.

d5/d6 Exposure Delay Mode (Z8/Z9)

Options: 3, 2, 1, 0.5, 0.2 seconds, Off (default)

My preference: Off

This is a marginally useful feature. (It can actually be mildly annoying if you forget to turn it off.) It's used to force the camera to snap a picture about 0.2, 0.5, 1, 2, or 3 seconds (your choice) after you've pressed the shutter release button all the way, like a limited-delay self-timer.

It's useful when you are using shutter speeds of about 1/8th to 1/60th second hand-held and want to minimize the effects of the vibration that results when you depress the shutter button. It can also be used when the camera is mounted on a tripod, although the self-timer function, set to a two-second delay, is more useful in that scenario. When switched On, the camera will pause while you steady your steely grip, taking the picture about one second later. When turned Off, the picture is taken when the shutter release is pressed, as normal.

One interesting side-effect of this mode is that it separates the normally invisible pre-flash produced by any camera's external flash that's connected with the delay. That can have an unwanted side-effect. For example, if you're shooting living subjects (human or animal), and set the delay for one second, your subject may be startled by the initial flash and close their eyes just before the main flash fires 1,000 milliseconds later. Longer delays can produce incorrect exposures if you happen to accidentally (or intentionally) reframe or pan during the interval between when the pre-flash fires (and the camera calculates exposure) and the moment when the shutter opens/flash fires to take the actual picture.

Z8 users can substitute the self-timer's 2- or 5-second delays, and use the longer 10- or 20-second timers if needed.

d6/d7 Extended Shutter Speeds (M) (Z8/Z9)

Options: Off (default), On (Allows exposures of 60, 90, 120, 180, 240, 300, 480, 600, 720, and 900 seconds)

My preference: Off

Extra-long shutter speeds, up to 900 seconds, are available in Manual exposure mode if you activate the feature here. Once you've done that, the next shutter speed shown after 30 seconds is 60 seconds, followed by 90 seconds and on up to 900 seconds (15 minutes). The Bulb and Time settings are still available, but moved to the very end, which can be inconvenient if you need to access one of them while this setting is enabled.

The extended shutter speed and time remaining will be displayed on the top LCD control panel to the right of the exposure mode. At the (conventional) shutter speeds between 1 second and 30 seconds, the actual exposure time will differ slightly (a 30-second exposure will last 32 seconds), but will match again if you set a speed between 60 and 900 seconds.

d7/d8 Limit Selectable Image Area (Z8/Z9)

Options: All Available (default), Individually Disable DX, 1:1, or 16:9 Formats

My preference: FX, DX, and 16:9 only enabled

This is the first entry on the next group of menu entries (see Figure 7.11). Your camera may provide you with more image area formats than you ever need—but it also gives you the ability to make any of them (except the full-frame FX choice) invisible.

Disabling or enabling one or more image area options is easy. Highlight any format (except FX, which cannot be

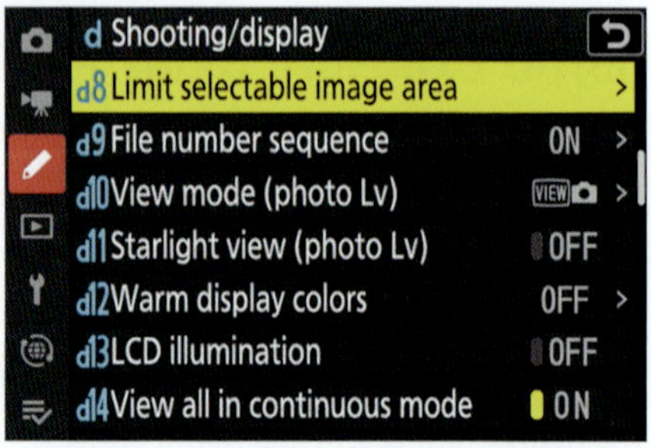

Figure 7.11 The next group of Shooting/Display entries.

disabled) and press the right multi selector button or press OK to mark or unmark your choice. You must press MENU to confirm. I don't use the 1:1 image area much, so I disable it. I sometimes shoot in DX mode for sports to capture more compact 19.5MP images with the DX format's 1.5X field-of-view crop. When I am taking stills to use for movie storyboards, I prefer to shoot them using the same high-definition 16:9 proportions that the movie will be captured in, so I keep that available.

The image areas you specify can be selected using the Image Area entry of the Photo Shooting and Video Record menus. If you mount a Nikon F-mount DX (APS-C type) lens on the Z9/Z8 using an FTZ adapter, the camera *automatically* switches to DX mode; indeed, the Image Area options are not available. Unfortunately, that means you can't manually change to FX mode for those lenses (some of them do cover the full frame at certain focal lengths). But when working with both Z-mount and F-mount full-frame lenses, you can choose one of the cropped image areas; the camera will enlarge the DX crop to fill the display and add black bars at top, bottom, or sides (as appropriate) to provide a visual reference for the other crops. (That's a distinct advantage this mirrorless model has over its dSLR siblings, which must use a mask to show the image area when using the optical viewfinder.)

d8/d9 File Number Sequence (Z8/Z9)

Options: On (default), Off, Reset

My preference: On

The camera will automatically apply a file number to each picture you take, using consecutive numbering for all your photos over a long period of time, spanning many different memory cards, starting over from scratch when you insert a new card or when you manually reset the numbers. Numbers are applied from 0001 to 9999, at which time the camera "rolls over" to 0001 again.

The camera keeps track of the last number used in its internal memory and, if File Number Sequence is turned On, will apply a number that's one higher, or a number that's one higher than the largest number in the current folder on the inserted memory card. You can also start over each time a new folder has been created on the memory card or reset the current counter back to 0001 at any time. Here's how it works:

- **On.** At this default setting, the camera will use the number stored in its internal memory any time a new folder is created, a new memory card is inserted, or an existing memory card is formatted. If the card is not blank and contains images, then the next number will be one greater than the highest number on the card *or* in internal memory (whichever is higher).
- **Off.** If you're using a blank/reformatted memory card, or a new folder is created, the next photo taken will be numbered 0001. File number sequences will be reset every time you use or format a card, or a new folder is created (which happens when an existing folder on the card contains 5,000 shots).
- **Reset.** The camera assigns a file number that's one larger than the largest file number in the current folder, unless the folder is empty, in which case numbering is reset to 0001. At this setting, new or reformatted memory cards will always have 0001 as the first file number.

HOW MANY SHOTS, REALLY?

The file numbers produced by the camera don't provide information about the actual number of times the electronic shutter has been tripped—called *actuations*. For that data, you'll need a third-party software solution, such as the free Opanda iExif (www.opanda.com) for Windows or the non-free ($39.95) GraphicConverter for Macintosh (www.lemkesoft.com). These utilities can be used to extract the true number of actuations from the Exif information embedded in a JPEG file.

d9/d10 View Mode (Photo Live View) (Z8/Z9)

Options: Show effects of settings: Always, Only when flash not used; Adjust for ease of viewing: Auto, Custom

My preference: On, except when using studio flash

This entry provides control over when the display reflects how your current settings of white balance, Picture Controls, and exposure compensation will affect your image when the photo is actually taken. It's a good way to preview the "look" of your image as it is adjusted by your selected settings. In Manual exposure mode, you will even be able to preview how your *exposure* will change the image; the displays will actually lighten or darken to reflect exposure changes. Sounds like a good idea, right?

However, there are times when you *don't* want to see the effects of the settings you've made in the display. For example, when you are using flash in Manual exposure mode, the camera has no way of knowing exactly how much light will be illuminating your scene. You'll especially want to change this setting to Off when working with "dumb" studio strobes connected using the Z9's old-school PC/X connector, hidden under the flash sync/ten-pin remote terminal cover on the front of the camera (or connected to a Nikon AS-15 Sync Terminal adapter attached to the hot shoe).

After all, that f/16 aperture you've selected may be ideal for a shot exposed by your studio strobes, but the camera will show you a preview based on the ambient light, rather than the flash. The result? Your display image is very, very dim.

However, in all other cases, at the default Show Effects of Settings > Always setting, the display reflects the *relative* effects of any white balance, Picture Control, or exposure compensation settings you've made. In that mode, this allows for a reasonable representation of what the photo will look like and enables you to evaluate whether the current settings will provide the effects you want.

STILLS ONLY

This setting has no effect in video mode; the effects of your camera settings *always* are reflected in what you see in the display when capturing movies.

The Always option can be especially helpful when you're using any of the Picture Controls, because you can preview the exact rendition that the selected effect and its overrides will provide. It's also very useful when you're setting some exposure compensation, as you can visually determine how much lighter or darker each adjustment makes the image. And when you're trying to achieve correct color balance, it's useful to be able to preview the effect of your white balance setting.

If you'd like to preview the image *without* the effect of settings visible, you can disable the feature, and the display will no longer accurately depict what your photo will look like when it's taken. So, for most users, Always is the most suitable option. Unfortunately, this setting has caused more than a few minutes of head-scratching among new users who switch to Manual exposure mode and find themselves with a completely black (or utterly white) screen. The black screen, especially, may fool you into thinking your camera has malfunctioned. Here is an overview of your options for this setting:

- **Always.** The camera always adjusts the display. A VIEW indicator with a camera icon next to it appears when adjustments are active. The exact behavior differs, depending on your shooting mode:
  - **Manual exposure mode.** As you make manual adjustments to shutter speed, f/stop, or ISO, the screen will darken or brighten to reflect your exposure fine-tuning. White balance and the effects of any Picture Controls you select will also be reflected in the display.

    Note: Even when using Manual exposure, the camera will continue to calculate what the correct exposure *should* be, and if it decides an appropriate exposure is not possible at the current settings, the aperture or shutter speed readouts or the plus/minus exposure bar will blink. When that happens, the display no longer represents the final image.
  - **Manual exposure mode + ISO Auto.** You'll recall that in Manual exposure mode, when ISO Auto is enabled, two things happen. First, if your manual settings don't allow an appropriate exposure, the camera will increase or decrease the ISO sensitivity to produce a correct exposure. In that case, the screen won't darken/brighten until you exceed the ability to make an adjustment (based on your current ISO Auto parameters, set as described in Chapter 6). When those limits are reached, the display will adjust to account for the over or under exposure.

    Second, when ISO Auto is active in Manual exposure mode, you can apply exposure compensation, and the display will brighten or darken to reflect your EV changes. If ISO Auto is disabled, exposure compensation has no effect in Manual exposure mode.
  - **Auto exposure modes.** Exposure changes you apply using exposure compensation will be reflected in the display image, along with White Balance and Picture Control effects. The exposure changes resulting from automatic adjustments made in Aperture-priority, Shutter-priority, or Programmed Auto modes won't result in any changes in the display. However, if any of the automatic modes are unable to provide an appropriate exposure (as shown by blinking indicators), the display may not represent the actual image you'll capture.

- **Only When Flash is not Used.** The alternative to Always is to tell the camera to adjust the display for ease of viewing *only* when a compatible Speedlight is not attached and powered up. Ease of Viewing overrides the adjustments the Z8 or Z9 would ordinarily make as described above, so if you choose this option, the display will *not* reflect exposure, exposure compensation, White Balance, or Picture Control effects *when a compatible flash is in use.*
- **Adjust for ease of viewing.** You can disable the on-screen adjustments when needed, say, when you're using a studio flash connected to your camera through the PC/X terminal. A VIEW indicator with an icon representing the profile of an eyeball (VIEW ▷) is visible when adjustments are active. Unfortunately, using this option disables the useful live histogram display. There are two options for this setting:
  - **Auto.** The display adjustments are made only during what Nikon calls "long periods of use."
  - **Custom.** You can individually adjust which of your camera settings are applied to the preview image, while leaving the others disabled.
    - **White Balance.** Select either Preview Current Setting, Auto, or Choose Color Temperature. The latter allows you to specify a specific Kelvin value to use.
    - **Set Picture Control.** Choose Preview Current Setting, or Adjust for Ease of Viewing (which *does not* apply the Picture Control to the preview image).
    - **Brighten Shadows.** Select Off (shadows reflect the effects of your settings), or Brighten shadows by factors of +1 to +3 stops.

d10/d11 Starlight View (Photo Live View) (Z8/Z9)

Options: Off (default), On

My preference: Off

Under many circumstances, your Z8 or Z9 may be able to see better at night than you can, especially if your eyes have not yet adjusted to the darkness. This entry can make viewing under low-light conditions easier, by reducing the frame rate of the display and increasing the exposure. The display will be noisier and slower, but easier to view, and the autofocus system will always use contrast detection confirmation. Unfortunately, because the brightness is boosted, you must use the live histogram or exposure metering bar to judge exposure, as the visual representation will no longer be accurate.

d11/d12 Warm Display Colors (Z8/Z9)

Options: Warm Display Color Options: Mode 1, Mode 2, Off; Warm Color Display Brightness: +/– 3

My preference: N/A

Many devices—probably including your smartphone or e-reader—have an option or setting that switches to a warmer illumination for the screen at night or under darker conditions, offering comfortable viewing with your night-adapted vision and, perhaps, making it easier to fall asleep. Your camera offers a similar feature (although much more pronounced), especially useful for astrophotography and other night shooting.

Your options include:

- **Warm Display Color Options.** Choose from:
    - **Mode 1.** The menu display information changes to red on black (as shown in Figure 7.12) and the viewfinder and rear LCD monitor display overlays are reduced in intensity and tinted red.
    - **Mode 2.** The menu display information takes on the red/black color scheme, along with the icons and overlays. The live view image of your subject and playback views are not affected.
    - **Off.** Warm colors are not applied.
- **Warm Color Display Brightness.** As you can see from the figure, the display is quite dim. This option lets you increase or decrease brightness using the up/down directional controls.

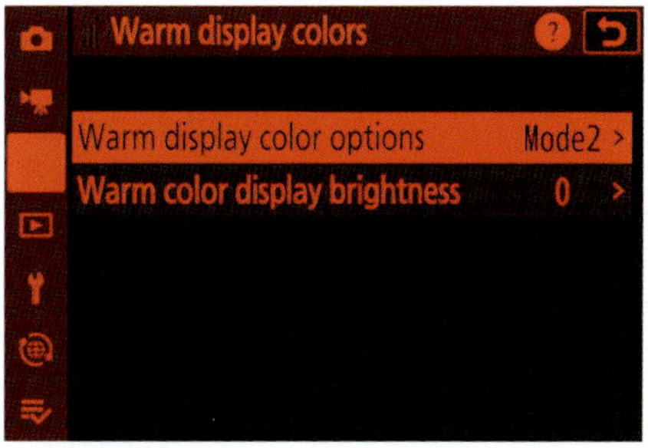

Figure 7.12 The warm display options help preserve your night vision.

d12/d13 LCD Illumination (Z8/Z9)

Options: On, Off (default)

My preference: On (for night photography)

Your Nikon Z9 or Z8 has the capability of back-illuminating the top LCD panel and either 11 (Z8) or 15 (Z9) buttons on the top and back surfaces of the camera. If you choose Off (the default), the backlights are turned on *only* when you rotate the power switch clockwise all the way to the "light bulb" position. If you choose On, the backlights will be illuminated any time the Standby Timer is active (in other words, while you are actively shooting). They will extinguish when the Standby Timer runs out, or when you press the shutter-release button. You can re-light them by releasing or tapping the shutter release button. I do a great deal of night photography and enable the hands-free mode so I don't need to carry around a mini flashlight. Table 7.1 shows which buttons are illuminated.

d13/d14 View All in Continuous Mode (Z8/Z9)

Options: On (default), Off

My preference: On

This setting lets you specify whether the viewfinder displays the scene at all times during burst shooting with all continuous release modes. If you select Off, the viewfinder turns black during continuous exposures.

TABLE 7.1 Illuminated Buttons

Z8 ILLUMINATED BUTTONS	Z9 ILLUMINATED BUTTONS
LEFT SIDE OF CAMERA	
Release Mode button	Release Mode button
Bracket button	Bracket button
White Balance button	Flash button
MODE button	MODE button
Protect/F3 button	Protect/F4 button
Delete/Format button	Delete/Format button
RIGHT SIDE OF CAMERA	
i button	*i* button
MENU button	MENU button
Playback button	Playback button
Zoom In button	Zoom In button
Zoom Out button	Zoom Out button
LOWER EDGE OF CAMERA	
	Vertical *i* button
	White Balance button
	QUAL button
	Voice Memo button

d14/d15 Release Timing Indicator (Z8/Z9)

Options: Indicator Type: Type A, Type B (default), Type C, Off; Type A Auto Restore Delay: 1/6 s to 1/200 s

My preference: Type B, 1/6 s

This is the first entry in the next group of Shooting/Display options. (See Figure 7.13.) This entry allows you to enable a visual indicator in the viewfinder that shows you that the Z8 or Z9 is taking pictures. It's a useful solution to a "feature has become a bug" problem: the nifty silent photography features of your camera's electronic shutter mean that it's not always easy to see whether you're actually capturing images.

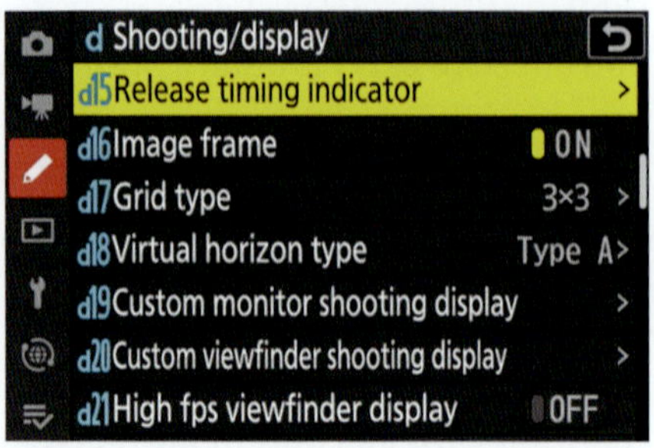

Figure 7.13 The next group of Shooting/Display entries.

I always use the Camera Sounds entry in the Setup menu (as described in Chapter 9) to silence my Z8 and Z9 when doing street photography, shooting performances, meetings and religious services, and in other situations where noises can be undesirable. While there are various indicators in the display that demonstrate your camera is capturing images, it's nice to have a prominent visual cue as a constant reminder. You can choose any of three Types, plus Off if you want no visual prompt, plus a slow-shutter speed blackout prompt. (See Figure 7.14, left.) They are:

- **Type A.** The display goes black for a moment, taking you back to the thrilling days of SLR yesteryear.
- **Type B.** A line appears at the top, bottom, left, and right edges of the display. This is the default.
- **Type C.** Lines appear only at the left and right of the display. This is a least intrusive indicator, and also the easiest to miss if you're not alert.
- **Off.** No indicator appears.
- **Type A Auto Restore Delay.** If you select Type B or Type C, you can tell the camera to use the Type A display blackout mode anyway when the shutter speed is equal to or slower than the value you specify here. The available range is 1/200 to 1/6 second. Set to the speed below which the blackout provides a useful reminder without being intrusive. Typically that will be relatively slow shutter speeds. (See Figure 7.14, right.)

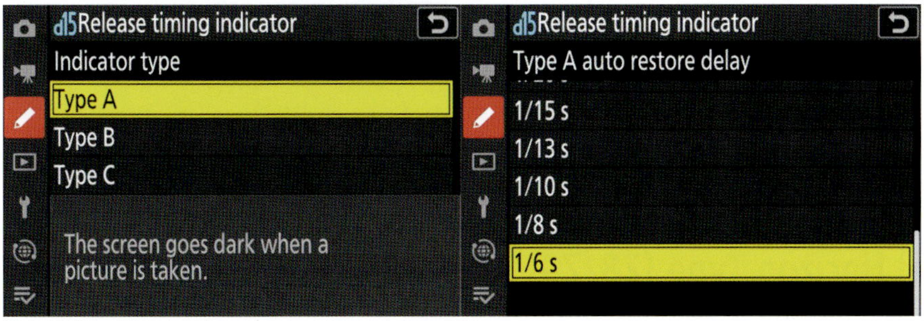

Figure 7.14 Choose indicator type (left) and delay (right).

d15/d16 Image Frame (Z8/Z9)

Options: On (default), Off

My preference: On

This feature tells the camera to display a faint line around the edge of the image area. It's an essential tool for framing your image when shooting in very dark areas, such as outdoors at night or in dark theaters or auditoriums. Under these conditions, you may not be able to discern the edge of the image frame from the surrounding dark area of the display. In addition, both cameras have a Setup menu command that allows reducing the size of the viewfinder display to make it more easily seen by those wearing glasses and Viewfinder Display Size. When enabled, you'll clearly see where your scene ends and the non-image area begins.

d16/d17 Grid Type (Z8/Z9)

Options: 3 × 3 (default), 4 × 4, 5:4, 1:1, 16:9

My preference: 3 × 3

The camera can display five different types of guidelines that can be overlaid on the viewfinder and rear LCD monitor image as you cycle through the available displays with the DISP button. The guides offer some help when you want to align vertical or horizontal lines, particularly for architectural or scenic photography, and in visually arranging your compositions in the frame to allow cropping in post-production. The latter offers extra flexibility compared to choosing a fixed aspect ratio using the Image Area option in the Photo Shooting menu (which also crops any RAW files you capture). You're not locked into the composition you worked with when the image was captured. You can select a Rule of Thirds grid, or Nikon's traditional Rule of Quarters layout, plus centered 5:4, 1:1, and 16:9 overlays. (See Figure 7.15.) You might want the 5:4 guide when you plan to produce a lot of 8 × 10 prints or the 16:9 overlay for storyboard images that will be used to plan your next video shoot.

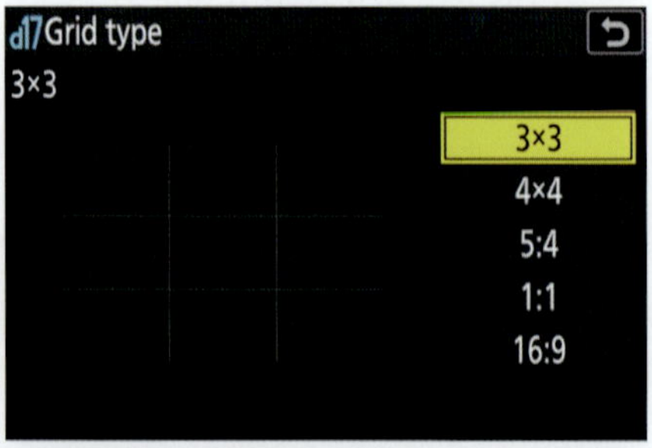

Figure 7.15 Grid types.

Note: This setting does not enable/disable grid display; it only specifies what type of overlay will be used. To activate a grid, you have to include that as an option in one of your display layouts using the Custom Monitor Shooting Display and Custom Viewfinder Shooting Display entries discussed shortly.

d17/d18 Virtual Horizon Type (Z8/Z9)

Options: Type A (default), Type B

My preference: Type B

Your Z8/Z9 can overlay a virtual "horizon" guide on the viewfinder and rear LCD monitor to show approximately how far the camera's position varies from level, in terms of rotation around the axis of the lens and upward/downward tilt. There are two types of indicators, Type A and Type B, shown at left in Figure 7.16. Neither are 100 percent accurate, but can provide a useful guide, especially when shooting scenics and architecture.

Type A features pairs of lines, the inner lines showing the degree of pitch, and the outer lines representing rotation. When the camera is level, the lines will turn green and line up at the horizontal center of the screen (see Figure 7.16, top center). When the camera is tilted up, the inner indicators rise above the longer rotational indicators, and sink below it when the camera is tilted down (see Figure 7.16, top right).

The Type B guides consist of indicators at the bottom of the display (for rotation) and right side (for pitch/tilt), as seen in Figure 7.16, bottom center. The indicators show the current orientation when the camera is rotated or tilted (Figure 7.16, bottom right).

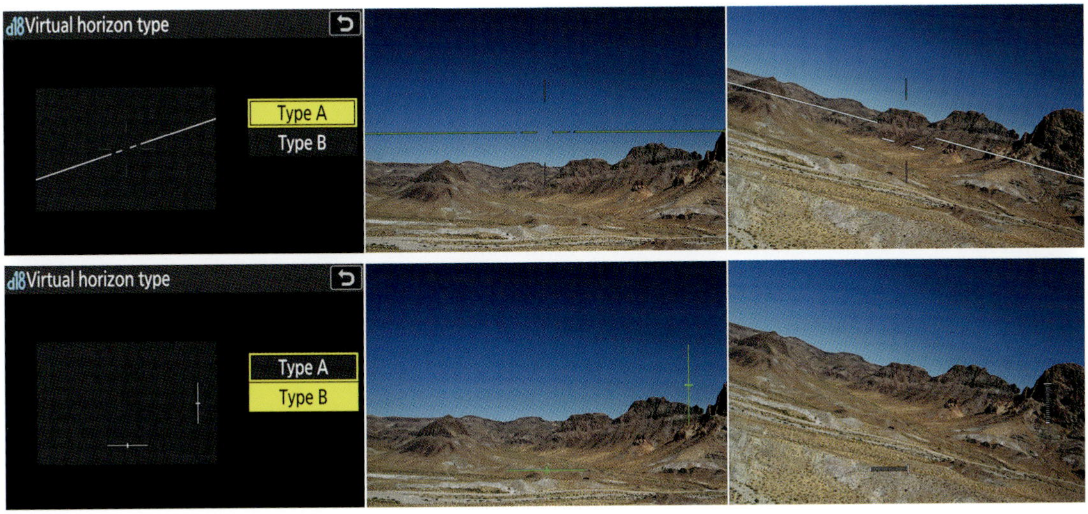

Figure 7.16 Two types of virtual horizons (left). Display when the camera is level (center) and rotated/tilted (right).

d18/d19 Half-press to cancel zoom (MF)

Options: On, Off

Half press of shutter release cancels zoom.

d19/d20 Custom Monitor Shooting Display (Z8/Z9)

Options: Display 1, Display 2, Display 3, Display 4, Display 5

My preference: Varies

The preview image seen in the optical viewfinder of conventional dSLR cameras can display only a limited amount of information that can be shown, and it differs significantly from what you see on the same camera's rear LCD live view. Mirrorless cameras like the Nikon Z8 and Z9, in contrast, can show virtually identical views on both displays, the amount and types of information available is virtually unlimited.

The bad news is that your display can easily become too cluttered for easy viewing and composition. Fortunately, Nikon has given you the ability to create up to five different customized screens for *each* type of display, so you can tailor your view to show only and exactly what you want to see. This entry is used to set up configurations for your rear LCD monitor. There are eight sets of information to choose from, which you can enable by placing a check mark next to the label/icon representing that information:

- **Minimum.** If none of the label/icons are checked, the display will show only the focus point, shutter speed, aperture, ISO, and exposure bar as appropriate.
- **Simple.** P, A, S, or M shooting modes, metering mode battery status, and the shots remaining indicator are added to the minimum display.

- **Detailed Shooting Info.** In addition to the minimum display, you'll see release mode, focus mode, focus area, white balance information, Active D-Lighting, Picture Controls, Image Quality/Size indicators, and the current Image Area.
- **Touch Controls.** An icon for enabling/disabling touch AF controls and the *i* menu icon are added to the minimum display.
- **Virtual Horizon.** Only the minimum information and the virtual horizon indicators are shown.
- **Histogram.** A live histogram is added to the minimum.
- **Framing grid.** The grid you specified using the Grid Type entry will be shown along with the minimum information.
- **Center indicator.** A cross-hair appears in the exact center of the frame, added to the minimum display.
- **Center-weighted area.** The part of the frame emphasized by center-weighted metering is shown as a faint circle of the size you have chosen.

To customize your LCD display you just need to follow a few simple steps:

1. **Access this menu entry.** The screen shown at left in Figure 7.17 appears.
2. **Apply customization.** Highlight the numbered Display choice you want to customize, and press the multi selector right button. The screen shown in Figure 7.17, right, pops up.
3. **Enable/disable sets.** Highlight any of the eight information sets and press the multi selector right button to enable or disable that set. When finished, press MENU to confirm and exit to the previous screen.
4. **Enable/display Displays.** The camera will cycle among the available Displays when you press the DISP button. You can have as few as one or as many as five Displays enabled at one time. Highlight a particular Display 2–5 and press the multi selector right button to enable or disable it. Display 1 cannot be disabled, and will always be available.
5. **Exit.** Press MENU to confirm and exit.

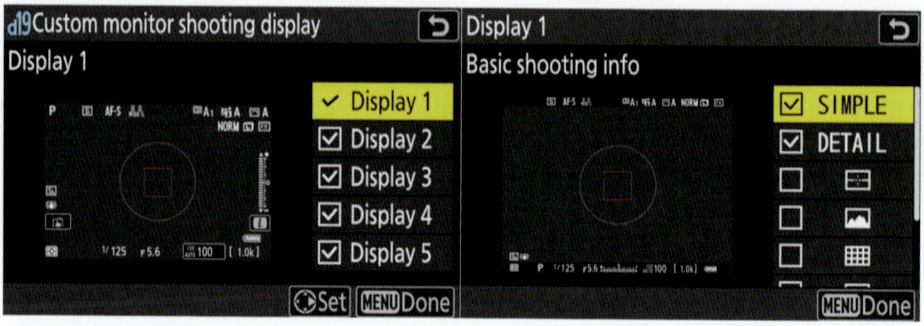

Figure 7.17 Choose which Displays to enable (left), and specify the types of information shown (right).

d20/d21 Custom Viewfinder Shooting Display (Z8/Z9)

Options: Display 1, Display 2, Display 3, Display 4

My preference: Varies

Use this entry to customize your viewfinder displays. It operates similarly to the Custom Monitor Shooting Display entry, but Touch Controls are not one of the available sets, and it offers only four different Display variations.

d21/d22 High Frames per Second Viewfinder Shooting Display (Z8/Z9)

Options: On, Off (default)

My preference: Off

Fast-moving objects may appear somewhat jerky on your electronic viewfinder. This option lets you switch from the default 60 Hz refresh rate for the EVF to a smoother-looking 120 Hz. Sports photographers who spend a lot of time capturing action shots may prefer to use this, at the expense of battery life. Those of us, pros or otherwise, who do a lot of that type of photography always have plenty of spare batteries on hand and know how to time the reloading step, so the extra drain is unlikely to be an issue.

e. Bracketing/Flash

There are lots of useful settings in this submenu (see Figure 7.18) that deal with bracketing and electronic flash (hence the cleverly concocted name). I provided a thorough description of using bracketing in Chapter 2, and a complete rundown of flash options in Chapter 4. In this section, I'll offer a recap of the settings at your disposal.

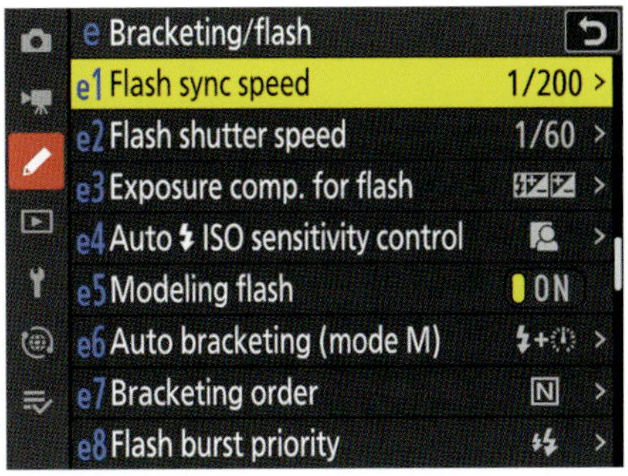

Figure 7.18 Bracketing and flash options are available in this menu.

e1 Flash Sync Speed

Options: 1/250 s (Auto FP), 1/200 s (Auto FP), 1/200 s–1/60 s (default 1/200 s)

My preference: 1/200 s (Auto FP)

As you learned in Chapter 4, the sensor must be fully energized when the external flash fires; otherwise, you'll capture an image of one edge or the other of the electronic shutter's virtual "curtain" in your photo. Ordinarily, the fastest shutter speed during which the sensor is completely energized for an instant is 1/250th or 1/200th second. However, there are exceptions when you can use faster shutter speeds with certain flash units (such as the Nikon SB-5000, SB-910, SB-700, and SB-R200) for automatic FP (focal plane) synchronization. This is called Auto FP *high-speed sync* (usually abbreviated HSS). The HSS feature allows you to use higher shutter speeds to supply fill flash, say, outdoors, where a shutter speed of 1/500th second might be needed to enable a wider aperture for reduced depth-of-field.

There are also situations in which you might want to set flash sync speed to *less* than 1/200th second, say, because you *want* ambient light to produce secondary ghost images in your frame. (I described all these sync issues in Chapter 4.) To address your choice of flash sync speeds, you can choose from the following settings:

- **1/250 s (Auto FP)/1/200 s (Auto FP).** At these two settings, you may use individual shutter speeds up to 1/250th or 1/200th second with any Nikon flash and compatible third party units. However, you can also use *faster* shutter speeds with flash units compatible with high-speed sync (such as those mentioned above, plus some third-party flashes). If one of those units is mounted and powered up:
    - **P or A mode:** The camera selects the shutter speed in both Program and Aperture-priority modes. With an HSS-compatible flash attached, the camera is free to select a shutter speed as fast as 1/8000th second.
    - **S or M mode:** In these modes, *you* select the shutter speed, and you can select one as fast as 1/8000th second in high-speed sync mode.

  I tend to stick with the 1/200s (Auto FP) setting because the faster 1/250th s (Auto FP) setting sometimes causes banding, and I sometimes use flash units that don't sync properly at 1/250th second even when HSS is not being used.
- **1/200 s–1/60 s.** You can specify a shutter speed from 1/200th second to 1/60th second to be used as the synchronization speed for flash units.

e2 Flash Shutter Speed

Options: 1/60 second (default) to 30 seconds

My preference: 1/30 second

This setting determines the *slowest* shutter speed that is available for electronic flash synchronization in the PASM exposure modes when you're not using a "slow sync" mode (described in Chapter 9). As you may know, when you're using flash, the flash itself typically provides virtually all of the illumination that makes the main exposure, and the shutter speed determines how much, if any, of the ambient light contributes to that second, non-flash exposure. Indeed, if the camera or subject is moving, you can end up with two distinct exposures in the same frame: the sharply defined flash exposure and a second, blurry "ghost" picture created by the ambient light.

If you *don't* want that second exposure, you should use the highest shutter speed that will synchronize with your flash. This setting prevents Program or Aperture-priority modes (which both select the shutter speed for you) from inadvertently selecting a "too-slow" shutter speed. You can select a value from 30 s to 1/60 s, and the camera will *avoid* using speeds slower than the one you specify with electronic flash (unless you've selected slow sync, slow rear-curtain sync, or red-eye reduction with slow sync, as described in Chapter 4). The "slow-sync" modes do permit the ambient light to contribute to the exposure (say, to allow the background to register in night shots, or to use the ghost image as a special effect). For brighter backgrounds, you'll need to put the camera on a tripod or other support to avoid the blurry ghosts that can occur from camera shake, even if the subject is stationary.

If you are able to hold the camera steady, a value of 1/30 s is a good compromise; if you have shaky hands, use 1/60 s. Those with extraordinarily solid grips, a tripod, or a lens with vibration reduction can try the 1/15 s setting (or slower when using a tripod). Remember that this setting only determines the *slowest* shutter speed that will be chosen by the camera, not the default shutter speed.

e3 Exposure Compensation for Flash

Options: Entire Frame (default), Background Only

My preference: Background Only

Use this to specify how the camera modifies the flash level when you apply exposure compensation. Keep in mind that your camera has separate ambient light exposure compensation and flash exposure compensation settings. They enable you to adjust one or the other, or both if you are using flash. The camera will attempt to balance ambient and flash exposure compensation, but when you add or subtract compensation when the flash is attached and powered up *both* change. This setting affects only *exposure compensation* (the ambient kind) when you are also using flash. It determines how ambient exposure compensation is applied when some of the illumination will also come from a flash unit:

- **Entire Frame.** When you apply ambient exposure compensation (press the EV button on top of the camera to the right of the ISO button and rotate the main command dial), both ambient *and* flash exposure compensation are adjusted over the entire frame. That balances the exposure for the two elements. While this works in many situations, you may find that with backgrounds and subject matter that differ widely in brightness, your results may be less than optimum.
- **Background Only.** When this option is selected *only* ambient exposure compensation is changed when you apply it; flash exposure compensation is unaffected. So, exposure compensation is applied only to the background areas of your image, which are typically illuminated by ambient light. Flash exposure compensation is not affected but can be set separately. I prefer to use this setting and control each type of exposure compensation myself.

e4 Auto Flash ISO Sensitivity Control

Options: Subject and Background (default), Subject Only

My preference: Subject and Background

This setting allows you to customize how Auto ISO sensitivity control makes its adjustments. If you choose Subject and Background, the exposure meter will take into account both your subject matter and the background—the entire scene, in other words—when automatically changing ISO sensitivity. Choose Subject Only and the Z8/Z9 will adjust automatic ISO sensitivity based only on what it deems to be the primary subject, as determined by the focus plane and metering data.

e5 Modeling Flash

Options: On (default), Off

My preference: On

Certain compatible external flash units (like the SB-5000, SB-500, SB-700, SB-800 and SB-910/SB-900) have the capability of simulating a modeling lamp, which gives you the limited capability of previewing how your flash illumination is going to look in the finished photo. The modeling flash is not a perfect substitute for a real incandescent or fluorescent modeling lamp, but it does help you see how your subject is illuminated and spot any potential problems with shadows.

While your flash may have a button that can trigger the modeling light, this option uses a button on the camera, which is usually more convenient. When this feature is activated, pressing the button you have defined as the Preview (depth-of-field) button on the camera briefly triggers the modeling flash for your preview. (You can define a Preview button using Custom Setting f2: Custom Controls, as described later in this chapter.)

Selecting Off disables the feature. You'll generally want to leave it On, except when you anticipate using the depth-of-field preview button for depth-of-field purposes (imagine that) and do *not* want the modeling flash to fire when the flash unit is charged and ready. Some external flash units, such as the SB-5000 and SB-910, have their own modeling flash buttons.

e6 Auto Bracketing (Mode M)

Options: Flash/Speed (default), Flash/Speed/Aperture, Flash/Aperture, Flash/ISO Sensitivity, Flash Only

My preference: Flash/Speed

When you are using Manual exposure mode and Auto ISO Sensitivity Control is set to Off in the Photo Shooting menu, the camera allows you to specify what exposure parameters—flash output, shutter speed, ISO, and aperture—are used to create the bracketed images. Here are your options and reasons to select each of them. Remember that these apply *only* when you are bracketing in Manual exposure mode and Auto ISO sensitivity is disabled. If Auto ISO is active, this entry is ignored.

- **Flash/Speed.** If you've selected AE Bracketing in Auto Bracketing Set in the Photo Shooting menu, the camera will adjust only the shutter speed during bracketed exposures. If you selected AE & Flash Bracketing instead, the camera will also adjust the flash output level when flash is used. The aperture will remain the same, making this a good choice for HDR photos or other subjects where you want to keep the same amount of depth-of-field in successive shots.
- **Flash/Speed/Aperture.** The camera can use both shutter speed and aperture when AE Bracketing is selected, plus flash output level if AE & Flash Bracketing was selected and flash is used. This gives the camera the maximum amount of flexibility in choosing exposure parameter combinations. That's especially helpful when shooting bracket sequences of 7 or 9 shots (and/or with large increments, say, 3 stops, between shots). That's because such extreme adjustments in exposure may be difficult to achieve with only one or two parameters available—particularly when ambient light only is being bracketed. (The flash is able to adjust its output over a very wide range.)

- **Flash/Aperture.** The camera varies aperture only if AE Bracketing is specified, or aperture and flash output if AE & Flash Bracketing is selected in the Photo Shooting menu. Your selected shutter speed remains the same, so you would want to use this if retaining the same shutter speed is important (say, when shooting sports).
- **Flash/ISO Sensitivity.** The camera will adjust ISO sensitivity alone if AE Bracketing has been specified. If AE & Flash Bracketing are enabled, both ISO sensitivity and flash level will be adjusted.
- **Flash Only.** The camera varies the flash output only when AE & Flash Bracketing is active. No ambient light bracketing is done.

e7 Bracketing Order

Options: MTR > Under > Over (default), Under > MTR > Over

My preference: Under > MTR > Over, which orders frames by increasing exposure

Use this setting to define the sequence in which bracketing is carried out. Your choices are the default: MTR > Under > Over (metered exposure, followed by the version receiving less exposure, and finishing with the picture receiving the most exposure) and Under > MTR > Over, which orders the exposures from least exposed to most exposed (for both ambient and flash exposures). The same order is applied to white balance bracketing, too, but the values are Normal > More Yellow > More Blue and More Yellow > Normal > More Blue. (Nikon actually calls "yellow" by the term "amber," but I've found "yellow" easier to understand.)

This order works well if you are shooting at least three images in your sequence. If you set bracketing to just two exposures, the specified order is used, but one of the three is omitted. You'll find lots more about bracketing in Chapter 4. When doing ADL bracketing, this setting has no effect.

e8 Flash Burst Priority

Options: Prioritize Frame Advance Rate, Prioritize Precise Flash Control (default)

My preference: Prioritize Frame Advance Rate

Now that some flash units can recycle quickly enough to allow using strobes during continuous shooting, this option has become necessary. It allows you to lock flash exposure to the value calculated for the *first frame* in a continuous burst, rather than calculate exposure for each individual frame (which is the default). The problem with the more precise flash exposure mode is that the Speedlight will need to issue a monitor pre-flash before each shot, potentially slowing the frame rate.

I recommend doing some tests and evaluating whether your flash is able to recycle fast enough at the distances and frame rates you use most frequently. When you're satisfied that locking exposure at the first calculated value won't produce a string of underexposed images, you can safely select Prioritize Frame Advance Rate.

f. Controls

You can modify the way various control buttons and dials perform when shooting still photos by using the options in this submenu. You can even modify the twelve adjustments that appear in the *i* menu. The first seven Controls entries are shown in Figure 7.19. Note that you can also make some control adjustments for Video mode, and I'll cover those in the section that follows this one.

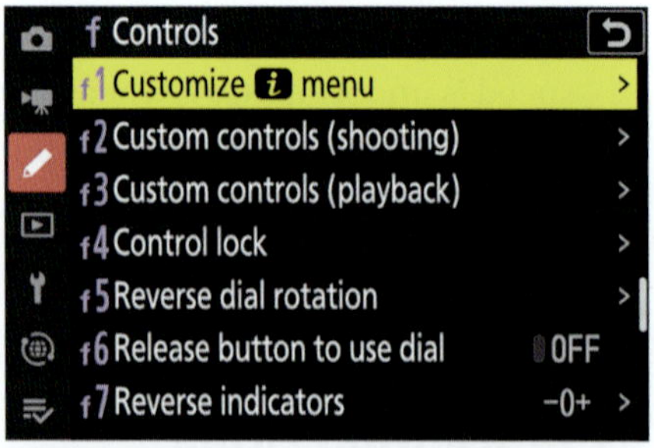

Figure 7.19 Modify the behavior of the camera's controls with these menu options.

f1 Customize *i* Menu

Options: Allows defining functions available from the *i* menu. Includes different functions that you can use to replace or add to those provided in the default version of the *i* menu.

My preference: Varies

The quick-access *i* menu can be a valuable tool for jumping directly to the controls that make frequently used adjustments. The bad news is that the 12 default entries on the *i* menu may not be ones you use often. The good news is that if you would rather have some other tools available in the *i* menu, there's a good chance you can replace your own "useless" *i* menu entries with those that are more to your liking. These 12 entries occupy the *i* menu by default. You can choose to keep these, move them, or replace them with other functions:

Set Picture Control	White Balance	Image Quality	Image Size	AF-area Mode/ Subject Detection	Focus Mode
Metering (Z9) Tone Mode (Z8)	Vibration Reduction	Shooting Menu Bank	Custom Controls (Shooting)	Airplane Mode	View Memory Card Information

Depending on your shooting habits, many of these are likely candidates for replacement with other functions. Indeed, many of the default entries in the bottom row of the *i* menu may have you wondering why Nikon put them there. Indeed, several of the default *i* menu functions are already available using other direct controls that duplicate their behavior. Others may be functions that you use so rarely that you don't need quick access to them through the *i* menu. They include:

Duplicates:

- **Shooting Menu Bank.** Available from the Fn1 button on both the Z8 and Z9.
- **Set Picture Control.** Already assigned to Fn4 (Z9) or Fn3 (Z8).
- **White Balance.** Both cameras have a WB button.
- **Image Quality.** The Z9 already has a QUAL button.

Other candidates:

- **Tone Mode (Z8).** This function switches between SDR (standard dynamic range), and HLG (for high dynamic range video). If you don't use the non-standard tone modes or shoot little video at all, you can replace this entry with a more useful function of your choice.

- **Vibration Reduction.** Unless you frequently fiddle with your VR settings, you can do without this function, as well.
- **Shooting Menu Bank.** How often do you switch Shooting Menu banks?
- **Custom Controls.** This one does nothing but provide a shortcut to the Custom Settings f2 screen.
- **Airplane Mode.** Use of your camera's Airplane Mode isn't necessarily limited to when you're airborne. Turning it on is a quick way of disabling your camera's power-sucking Wi-Fi features. However, few of us need to use this feature often enough to justify a slot in the *i* menu.
- **View Memory Card Information.** This is an informational tool only, and does nothing but show you which memory card will be used as the destination for your files. It's especially ripe for replacement.

Below is a list of functions you can assign to the 12 *i* menu slots. The default *i* menu functions are in boldface, and the functions that are duplicates of behaviors already assigned to a control are marked with a Button label. They are likely to be the best candidates to replace a function you don't use regularly:

- **Shooting Menu Bank (*i* menu default) (Button)**
- Select Custom Settings Bank
- Choose Image Area
- **Tone Mode (*i* menu default—Z8 only)**
- **Image Quality (*i* menu default) (Button—Z9)**
- **Image Size (*i* menu default)**
- **View Memory Card Info (*i* menu default)**
- Exposure Compensation
- ISO Sensitivity Settings
- **White Balance (*i* menu default) (Button)**
- **Set Picture Control (*i* menu default) (Button)**
- Set Picture Control (HLG) (Z8 only)
- Color Space
- Active D-Lighting
- Long Exposure NR
- High ISO NR
- Skin Softening
- Portrait Impression Balance
- **Metering (*i* menu default—Z9 only)**
- **Flash Mode (*i* menu default)**
- Flash Compensation
- Wireless Options/ Flash Mode
- Group Flash Options
- Test Flash
- Flash Info
- Radio Remote Flash Info
- **Focus Mode (*i* menu default)**
- **AF-area Mode/Subject Detection (*i* menu default)**
- **Vibration Reduction (*i* menu default)**
- Auto Bracketing
- Multiple Exposure
- HDR Overlay
- Interval Timer Shooting
- Time-lapse Video
- Focus Shift Shooting
- Focus Tracking with Lock-on
- Silent Mode
- Pre-release Capture Options
- Release Mode (Z8 only)
- **Custom Controls (Shooting) (*i* menu default)**
- Exposure Delay Mode (Z9 Only)
- View Mode (Photo Lv)
- Split-screen Display Zoom
- Focus Peaking
- Monitor/Viewfinder Brightness
- **Airplane Mode (*i* menu default)**
- Warm Display Colors
- MB-N12 Info (Z8 only)
- Auto Capture

I don't use the Airplane Mode function very often, so I replaced it with Multiple Exposure. It was easy to do:

1. Choose Custom Setting f1: Customize *i* menu.
2. Highlight the Airplane mode icon in the bottom row and press OK. (See Figure 7.20, left.)
3. Choose replacement. From the screen that appears, scroll to Multiple Exposure. Press OK to select and confirm. (See Figure 7.20, center.)
4. You'll be returned to the Customize *i* menu screen, with your changes made in the menu, as shown in Figure 7.20, right.

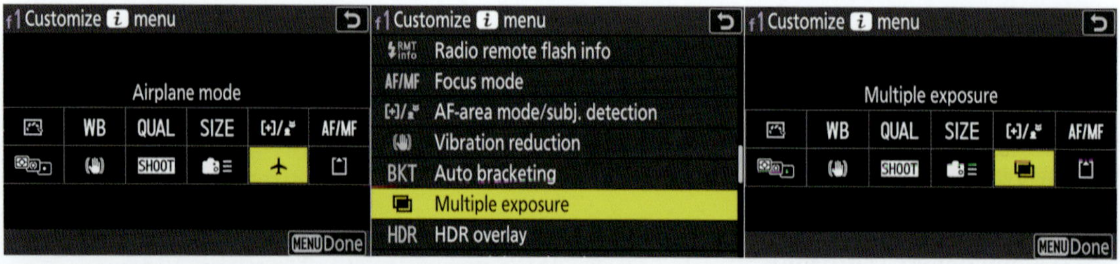

Figure 7.20 Replacing Airplane mode with Multiple Exposure in the *i* menu.

f2 Custom Controls (Shooting)

Options: Allows defining functions for camera/lens controls

My preference: Varies

Your Nikon Z8 and Z9 have a large number of controls that can be programmed to perform various functions in still photography shooting mode. (Different behaviors can be assigned for use when the camera is in Video Recording mode or Playback mode.) The number and location of the controls are shown in Table 7.2. The programmable controls include function buttons, the sub-selector (when pressed inward), and a few others that are only available if you own a certain piece of gear, such as the MB-N12 grip for the Z8 or a lens that has the M-Set (Memory Set), Lens Fn, or Lens Fn2 buttons. Keep in mind that command dials and lens control rings can also be assigned functions.

There are a total of more than 75 *different* still photography actions that can be programmed (plus None—no action), augmenting or *replacing* the button's original function. As this book was being written, Nikon changed the number of functions no less than three times through firmware updates, and I expect there will be more by the time this guide hits the shelves. After revising an "assignable functions" table showing which behaviors can be assigned to which controls multiple times, I decided that providing online access to Nikon's latest information would be more valuable than a printed table that would quickly become outdated. You can find my updates and other bonus content for this book at https://rockynook.com/nikon-z8-z9/.

When redefining your camera's operating features, you should always consider the side-effects of choosing your own non-standard control configuration. Your custom settings can be a boon, or if you don't remember the assignments you've made as you work, a hindrance.

To apply a definition, highlight the button name on the screen shown at left in Figure 7.21.

TABLE 7.2 Programmable Controls

Z9 CONTROLS	LOCATION	Z8 CONTROLS	CAMERA LOCATION
Fn1	Front	Fn1	Front
Fn2	Front	Fn2	Front
Fn3	Front	Fn3	Back Left
Fn4/Protect	Back Left	—	—
Fn (Vertical)	Right Edge	Fn (MB-N12)	Right Edge
ISO (Vertical)	Right Edge	—	—
AF-ON	Back Upper Right	AF-ON	Back Upper Right
AF-ON (Vertical)	Right Lower Edge	AF-ON (MB-N12)	Right Lower Edge
ISO	Top	ISO	Top
DISP	Back Upper Right	DISP	Back Upper Right
Sub-selector center	Back Upper Right	Sub-selector center	Back Upper Right
Sub-selector center (Vertical)	Right Lower Edge	Sub-selector center (MB-N12)	Right Lower Edge
OK	Direction Pad Center	OK	Direction Pad Center
Audio Memo	Back Bottom	—	—
QUAL	Back Bottom	—	—
WB	Back Bottom	WB	Top Left
Playback	Back Lower Right	Playback	Back Lower Right
Exposure Compensation	Top Right	Exposure Compensation	Top Right
M-Set	Lens	M-Set	Lens
L-Fn	Lens	L-Fn	Lens
L-Fn2	Lens	L-Fn2	Lens
Movie/Video	Top Right	Movie/Video	Top Right
Command Dials	Front/Back	Command Dials	Front/Back
Flash	Top Left	—	—
Bracketing	Top Left	Bracketing	Top Left
Lens Fn	On Lens	Lens Fn	On Lens
Lens Fn2	On Lens	Lens Fn2	On Lens
Lens Fn Ring (Counterclockwise)	On Lens	Lens Fn Ring (Counterclockwise)	On Lens
Lens Fn Ring (Clockwise)	On Lens	Lens Fn Ring (Clockwise)	On Lens
Lens Control Ring	On Lens	Lens Control Ring	On Lens
ISO (Vertical)	Right Lower Edge	—	—

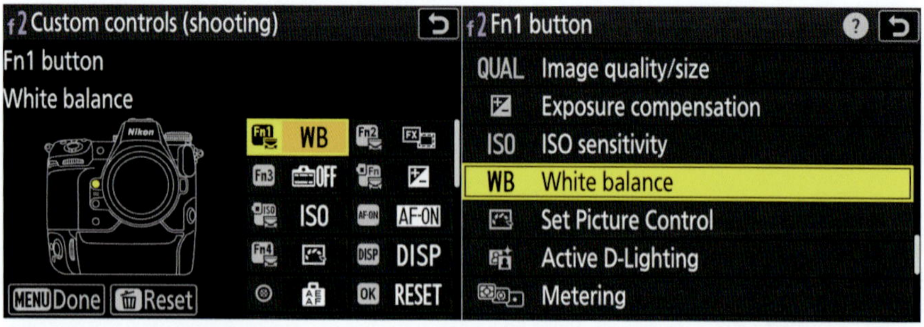

Figure 7.21 Highlight a control (left) and press OK to summon a list of possible definitions (right).

Then scroll through the list of available options, as shown at right in Figure 7.21. Some choices in the scrolling list are behaviors that require nothing more than a button press to activate. Nikon inserts a "Press" header at the start of the listing for those behaviors. For example, if a button is defined as Preview or Matrix Metering, you simply press and hold the button to activate the depth-of-field preview, or to switch from your current mode to Matrix Metering. When you release the defined button, the preview stops or the camera returns to your previous metering mode.

The other behaviors follow a header that reads "Press+Command Dials." Those options include those listed from "Choose Image Area" to "Choose Non-CPU Lens Number." Behaviors that do use the command dials produce a screen that displays the options for that behavior, plus an icon prompt representing a main or sub-command dial (or both). For instance, you'd press and hold the defined button and rotate the main command dial to change the flash sync mode, and the sub-command dial to add/subtract flash exposure compensation.

The definitions you assign to your controls are highly personal and should be implemented to reflect the features you will most need to have available at the press of a button or spin of a dial. Remember that once you re-assign a control from its default value, you must remember it in order to avoid becoming hopelessly confused. You'll no longer be able to loan your camera to someone else without risking confusing *them* as well.

- **Quickly switch to an alternate focus mode or AF-area mode.** You might use Auto-area AF most of the time to let the camera select a focus point for you, yet quickly switch to Single Point mode while you hold down the defined button. You can then move the focus point around within the frame with the directional controls. The Focus mode/AF-area mode behavior allows you to press a defined button and then rotate the main command dial to choose a focus mode, and the AF-area mode with the sub-command dial.
- **Switch metering modes.** If you use Matrix metering mode most of the time and want to be able to use Spot metering when appropriate, just assign a button to that function.
- **Disable/enable flash.** You can leave your external flash attached and powered up yet disable it quickly at the press of a defined button. That would allow you to intermingle photos taken by ambient light, and those in which flash illumination is added, on the fly.
- **Bracketing burst.** This option adds some versatility to exposure, flash, or ADL bracketing by telling the camera to take all the exposures in a bracketed set in one burst. You must have activated a bracketing program, as described in Chapter 4. Perhaps you've been shooting bracketed sequences in Single-shot mode (rather than continuous mode) and decide you want to capture

an entire set at once. Define a key for the Bracketing Burst function and hold it down. Then, each time you press the shutter release an entire burst will be captured. If the release mode has already been set for a continuous mode or white balance bracketing has been selected, the camera will capture all the exposures in the set while the shutter release is held down.

- **Add a RAW image while shooting only JPEGs.** When the +RAW behavior is specified, pressing the defined key tells the camera to shoot an additional RAW image even if the current Image Quality setting is JPEG (only) while the button is held down. That will allow you to capture a RAW image if you think you might need one later, say, to adjust color balance for a picture taken under tricky illumination.
- **Activate the framing grid.** Even if you don't use the alignment grid often, you can define a key to produce it at the press of a button.
- **FAQs (Frequently Accessed Quickly).** Have a menu entry you need to access quickly—and often? The Fn2 button can be defined to jump to the top item in your My Menu list (as described in Chapter 13), which can be that most-used entry. Or, you can define the Fn2 button to produce the My Menu list, which you can populate with your own personal most-used items.
- **Choose Image Area.** If you're shooting in FX mode and decide you want to switch to one of the crop modes (perhaps you're shooting sports and need some extra "reach"), a defined button+command dial definition can invoke the image area of your choice. Note that you can enable/disable any of the crop modes (but not FX mode) so that rotating the command dial switches among as many or as few modes as you want. I only enable DX mode when shooting sports, so I can switch quickly from FX to DX and back again.
- **Other frequently used settings.** Other button+command dial definitions can let you switch exposure modes, change white balance, access multiple exposure options, or control HDR settings quickly, too.

f3 Custom Controls (Playback)

Options: Allows defining functions camera/lens controls for Playback mode

My preference: Varies

You can define a set of functions that will be enabled in Playback mode different from the ones summoned in Photo Shooting or Video Recording modes. The definable buttons more or less correspond to the controls listed in Table 7.2, but a set of behaviors especially useful during playback are available. These include:

- Protect
- Delete (Z9 only)
- Zoom On/Off
- Filtered Playback
- Filtered Playback (Select Criteria)
- Start Series Playback
- Voice Memo
- Select for Upload to Computer
- Select for Upload (FTP)
- View Histograms
- Choose Slot and Folder
- Cycle Info Display (DISP)
- Resume Shooting
- Apply Rating
- None

Selection of a control to re-define and specification of the preferred function can be done as described under Custom Controls (Shooting).

f4 Control Lock

Options: Shutter Speed Lock, Aperture Lock, Focus-point lock (default: Off for all three)

My preference: Varies

There are times when you'll want to lock the shutter speed at a particular value when using Shutter-priority or Manual exposure modes and times when you want to lock down a particular f/stop when using Aperture-priority or Manual exposure modes. Or, you may wish to lock in a particular focus plane, perhaps for a macro series. You can use this entry to lock the shutter speed, aperture, or focus point (or a combination of the three) so it can't be changed. I use this most in the studio when I use Manual exposure and studio lights. Once I've set the exposure for a series of shots, I lock my Shutter Speed/Aperture Lock button and freeze the settings, so I don't have to worry about accidentally rotating a command dial.

If you think accessing this menu entry to lock in a setting is needlessly complex, you're right. It makes a lot more sense to define a physical button to provide this function, as described earlier under f2: Custom Controls (Shooting). I assigned the function to the Fn1 button. To lock the shutter speed and/or aperture, I first set either or both to the value I want. Then, I press the Fn1 button and rotate the main command dial to lock/unlock shutter speed and the sub-command dial to lock/unlock aperture. An L symbol appears next to the locked setting on the control panel and viewfinder/LCD monitor displays.

Note that when the camera is set to Shutter-priority, you are able to enable/disable only the Shutter Speed Lock and focus-point functions. When set to Aperture-priority, only aperture lock and focus point are accessible. In Manual exposure mode, you can adjust all three, and in Program mode, only focus point can be locked. **Note:** Focus-point lock does not keep the 3D-tracking autofocus-area mode from adjusting focus. Only the starting position of the focus point is locked.

f5 Reverse Dial Rotation

Options: Reverse Rotation Direction of Main and Sub-command Dials: Exposure Compensation: Checked, Unchecked (default); Shutter speed/Aperture: Checked, Unchecked (default)

My preference: Varies

This menu entry can swap the rotational direction of the command dials (including the command dial used for vertical shooting with the Z9 or Z8 equipped with the MB-N12 vertical grip. This is most useful if you're coming to the Nikon world from another vendor's product that uses the opposite operational scheme. Keep in mind that redefining basic controls in this way can prove confusing if someone other than yourself uses your camera, or if you find yourself working with other Nikon cameras that have retained the normal command dial behavior. The reason that the dials are set for their default directions is to match the direction of rotation of the aperture ring/sub-command dial (when changing the aperture). Turning any of them to the left decreases exposure, while rotating to the right increases exposure. You can reverse dial direction for Exposure Compensation, Shutter Speed/Aperture settings, or both.

f6 Release Button to Use Dial

Options: On, Off (default)

My preference: Off

Normally, any button used in conjunction with a command dial, such as the Exposure Compensation or ISO buttons, must be held down while the command dial or sub-command dial is rotated. That is the behavior when this entry is set to Off, the default, and is usually the best choice for most of us.

If you choose On, you just need to press the button once. You can then release it and rotate a command dial to make your setting, and continue to make adjustments until you press the button a second time—or until the Standby timer expires or you press the shutter release. I recommend leaving this option set to Off, instead. Holding down a button is not inconvenient, and it's too easy to forget to make that second button press when you're in a hurry to capture the decisive moment. The button/command dial combinations affected by this entry include the Exposure Compensation, ISO, Auto Bracketing, Release Mode, MODE, WB, and Focus Mode buttons, plus the Fn4, QUAL, and Flash button on the Z9.

f7 Reverse Indicators

Options: Direction of exposure indicators: –0+ (default), +0–

My preference: –0+

By default, the exposure indicators at the bottom of the display have the negative values shown at the left of the zero point, and positive values to the right (–0+). That's the orientation used by vendors of other cameras, such as Canon, and by Nikon since the introduction of the Nikon D4 dSLR. This setting allows you to reverse the direction (+0–). You might want to do this if you're coming to a system that uses the reverse orientation, have been using older Nikon cameras for a loooong time, or, for some reason, you own and use quite a few old manual focus AI and AI-S Nikkor lenses. (Older Nikon lenses have the smallest aperture on the ring to the left, and the largest to the right, so rotating the aperture ring to the right increases exposure; to the left decreases exposure.) My oldest camera still in frequent use is a Nikon D3200, and it uses the current scheme, so I've gone with the flow.

f8 Reverse Ring for Focus

Options: On, Off (default)

My preference: Off

This is the first of the second seven entries of the Controls menu. (See Figure 7.22.) It is another setting for grizzled veterans who refuse to update to the 21st Century, or those coming to Nikon from some other platforms. You can reverse the direction of rotation for the focus or control rings on Z-mount lenses during manual focus to match the

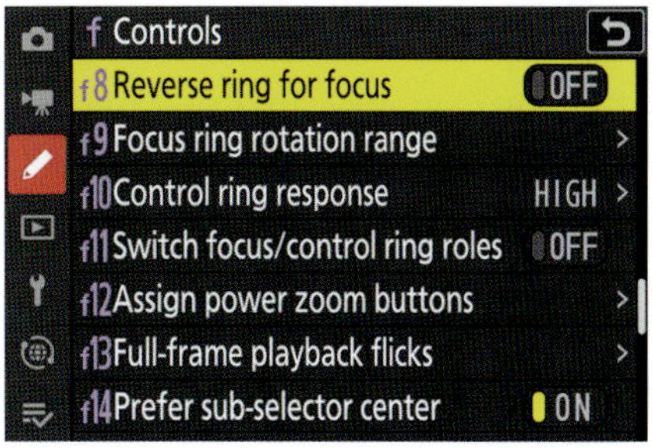

Figure 7.22 The next seven entries in the Controls menu.

direction of older Nikon optics. This setting does not affect non-autofocus Z-mount lenses, such as the S Nikkor 58mm f/0.95 Noct lens, or F-mount lenses attached using an FTZ adapter. In addition, the left-/right-pointing triangles that appear in the viewfinder as a manual focus aid do not switch directions to match.

f9 Focus Ring Rotation Range

Options: Non-linear(default), 90, 120, 150, 180, 210, 240, 270, 300, 330, 360, 540, 720 degrees, Max

My preference: Non-linear for still photography

One of the perks of the focus-by-wire electronics of the typical Z-mount lens is that you can adjust how dramatically focus changes with a given twist of the focus ring. Tweaking the manual focus response can be useful for sports photography, for example, and an absolute necessity for some types of videography. It's possible only because compatible lenses use an electronic system to transfer focus ring rotation to a variable-speed motor that actually does the focusing, rather than a fixed mechanical linkage used in traditional lenses.

At the default setting, rotating the focus mechanism responds in a non-linear manner. If you rotate the ring quickly, the focus plane is adjusted by a large amount. Slower rotation produces adjustments in smaller increments. Ordinarily, that's exactly what you'd want for still photography; if a major focus change is needed (something that can be frequent with action shooting), you want it to happen quickly. But fine-tuning, say, for macro photography, is better suited to smaller changes to the focus plane.

In some circumstances, non-linear focus is less desirable, and this entry allows you to define exactly how you'd like the focus ring to respond. A fixed speed can be specified over a particular rotational range with compatible lenses. The "fastest" focus parameter is 90 degrees; a lens will adjust focus from the minimum distance to maximum (or vice versa) with a mere 90 degrees of rotation. If you start with the lens focused at some midpoint, the amount of rotation will be even less.

You can choose fixed arcs from 90 to 360 degrees in 30 degree increments, plus 540 and 720 degrees, and a setting labeled Max (which requires focusing from the minimum to infinity over the maximum distance available at the current lens settings).

This linear focus characteristic is particularly useful for movie-making, since any manual focus changes you make *while capturing video* can be seen in the footage. It's essential if you're using pull- or push-focus techniques, which use selective focus with a wide aperture to draw the viewer's attention from, say, an object in the foreground to something in the background. The change can be subtle if done slowly, or dramatic, if performed quickly, but in either case the focus adjustment needs to be smooth rather than jerky.

This setting may not work with all lenses, although Nikon has periodically issued firmware updates to bring additional optics into the fold. If your lens is not compatible, this entry will be grayed out and focus will be fixed at non-linear.

f10 Control Ring Response

Options: High (default), Low

My preference: Low

Adjusting the responsiveness of a lens ring isn't exclusively the province of manual focus adjustments. The "bonus" control ring introduced with Nikon's Z-mount optics, and available on selected lenses, can be assigned roles such as aperture and power aperture setting, exposure compensation, and ISO sensitivity adjustments using f2 Custom Controls (Shooting) as described earlier in this chapter. The response isn't quite as granular as focus ring rotation range: you can choose the default, High (for fast response), or Low to make the ring less sensitive to smaller rotations. I happen to like the more measured response and set my cameras to Low. **Note:** This setting does not apply if the control ring behavior is set to focus.

f11 Switch Focus/Control Ring Roles

Options: On, Off (default)

My preference: Off

If your lens includes both a focus ring and control ring you may find it more convenient to use the innermost or outermost rings for either focus or the custom behavior. This setting allows you to reverse the functions with compatible lenses. Set to Off, the focus ring focuses, and the control ring performs its defined function. Select On, and the two rings trade functions.

f12 Assign Power Zoom Buttons (Z9 Only)

Options: Use Zoom In/Zoom Out buttons: On, Off (default); Power zoom speed: –3 (slower) to +3 (faster)

My preference: N/A

The good news is that Nikon is making power zoom (PZ) lenses available in Z mount. The bad news is that the first such lens introduced is an APS-C optic, the Nikkor Z DX 12-28mm f/3.5 PZ VR. It's targeted at vloggers and content creators with a focal length range that covers an 18mm (equivalent) wide angle view that, as Nikon asserts, "lets you record yourself within the scene from arm's length."

The lens can be used on the Z9, of course, for both video capture and stills using its 18-42mm equivalent zoom range in APS-C crop mode, and, as you might guess, it would be most useful for video shooting that can best take advantage of its power zoom features. This entry allows you to assign the zoom in/zoom out functions to the Zoom in and Zoom Out buttons, and specify a power zooming speed. As I write this, the Z8 does not sport this entry in its Custom Settings menu, but it's likely to have been added by the time this book is published.

The lens's internal linear motor is used to adjust focal lengths, and zooming can be controlled via the camera buttons, plus additional options, including the optional ML-L7 Bluetooth Remote, the SnapBridge app, or when using NX Tether Software and the optional MC-N10 Remote Grip.

f12/f13 Full Frame Playback Flicks (Z8/Z9)

Options: Flick Up, Flick Down, Flick Advance Direction

My preference: N/A

This setting lets you customize how your Z8/Z9 behaves when you use a finger to flick up, down, or side to side on the rear LCD screen during Playback. When Touch Controls is enabled in the Setup Menu, the screen can be used to perform a variety of functions. They include initiating focus and specifying a focus spot, navigating menus, entering text, and performing functions during image review playback. The flick features for Playback, shown in Figure 7.23, include:

- **Flick Up.** An upward motion on the screen can be assigned different functions:
  - **Rating.** One specific rating will be given to the currently displayed image. You'll need to decide which rating will be given when you activate this option. Select from zero to five stars, or a mark that indicates the image is a candidate for deletion. This is a convenient choice if you have a large number of images to which you want to assign a particular star rating or, more commonly, to mark some for deletion.
  - **Select for Upload to Computer.** The current image will be assigned for transfer using all methods, including FTP.
  - **Select for Upload (FTP).** The current image will be assigned for transfer using FTP.
  - **Protect.** The flicked image will be marked as Protected. A second flick will unprotect it.
  - **Voice memo.** The voice memo recorded for the displayed image using the Record Voice Memo option of the Playback version of the *i* menu will be played back.
  - **None.** Upward flicks are ignored.
- **Flick Down.** Downward flicks on the screen can be assigned one of the exact same functions available for the Flick Up gesture. In general, you'll want to choose a complementary behavior, say to assign one rating using a flick up, and a different rating for a flick down. I set my cameras so that an upward swipe protects that image, while a downward swipe marks it for later deletion, as sort of a thumbs up/thumbs down procedure.
- **Flick Advance Direction.** Use this option to change from the default left/right gesture to advance to the next image during playback to the reverse (right to left). **Note:** The *labels* in the menu entry both read Left-Right; it is only the *arrows* separating the two words that flip direction.

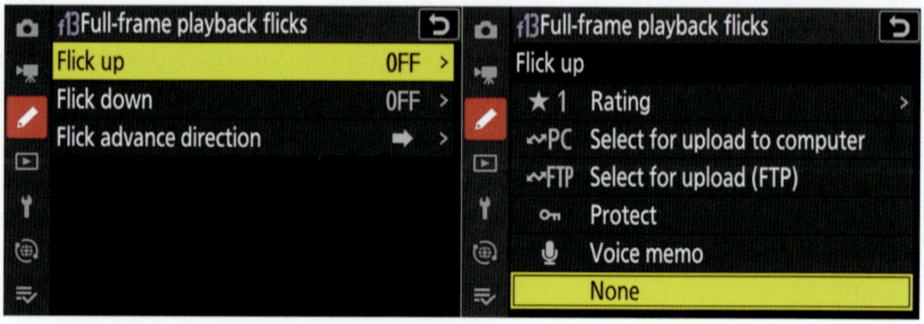

Figure 7.23 Playback flick options, left. Choices for Flick Up (and Down), right.

f13/f14 Prefer Sub-Selector Center (Z8/Z9)

Options: On (default), Off

My preference: Off

I've been guilty of not using the sub-selector joystick/button as often as I could, because, as a clumsy person, I found I was often unintentionally moving the focus point when I meant to be pressing the selector perpendicularly inward to summon its button behavior (the default is AE/AF lock). Nikon provided a kind of fix for that problem by adding this entry. At the new default setting, On, pressing the sub-selector inward disables focus point movement, so you don't have to worry that accidental slight shifts of your thumb off-center will cause the focus point to stray.

You can choose Off to restore the original behavior if you're coordinated enough to be able to press (to invoke the button function) while adroitly (and intentionally) moving the focus point simultaneously. Nikon even has some advice for those with finger skills: Assign AF-area mode to the sub-selector button, and you'll be able to temporarily switch AF-area modes and reposition the focus point at the same time.

g. Video

Here you can set separately for movie shooting some of the options available for still shooting. The first seven entries in this menu are shown in Figure 7.24.

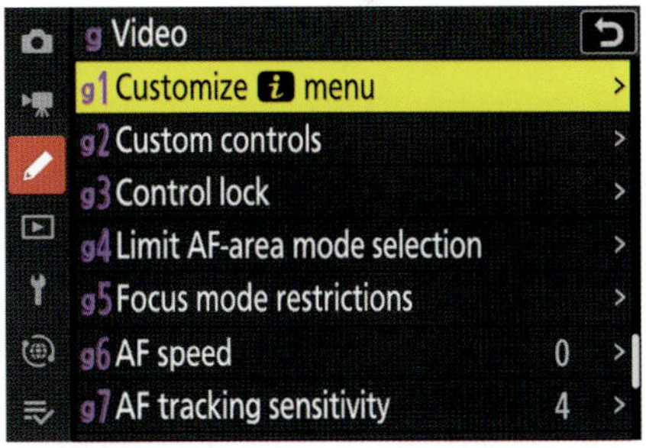

Figure 7.24 The first seven entries of the Custom Settings Video options.

g1 Customize *i* Menu

Options: Allows defining functions available from the Video Recording version of the *i* menu. Includes different functions that you can use to replace or add to those provided in the default version of the *i* menu.

My preference: Varies

The Video Recording version of the Customize *i* menu entry can be a valuable tool for quick access to video-oriented commands. That's especially true since there are several entries, including Set Picture Control, Airplane mode, and Destination that are ripe for replacement with functions you use more often. These 12 entries occupy the *i* menu by default. You can choose to keep these, move them, or replace them with other functions:

- Set Picture Control
- White Balance
- Frame Size/Rate
- Microphone Sensitivity
- AF-area mode/Subject Detection
- Focus Mode
- Electronic VR
- Vibration Reduction
- Shooting Menu Bank
- Custom Controls (Shooting)
- Airplane mode (Z8) Video Info (Z9)
- Destination

As I noted earlier, several of the default *i* menu functions are already available using other direct controls that duplicate their behavior: Shooting Menu Bank, Set Picture Control, and White Balance.

g2 Custom Controls

Options: Allows defining functions for camera/lens controls

My preference: Varies

The programmable controls available for defining functions used when in Video Recording mode are more or less the same as those for still photography, with a few exceptions. For example, the sub-selector button, and AF-ON and OK buttons cannot be defined for button+dial functions. The actual behaviors you can assign to those controls include some that are different from those available in Photo Shooting mode, or are used in different ways. Among the video-oriented options available for assignment are Hi-Res Zoom, Power Zoom, Pattern Tone Range, Microphone Sensitivity, and Power Aperture.

The latter comes in two varieties: Power Aperture (Open) and Power Aperture (Closed). The function can be assigned to open/close the aperture when the Fn1 and Fn2 buttons are pressed, or to perform that function when the Lens Fn Ring is rotated clockwise or counterclockwise. Note that the ability to change frame size and frame rate cannot be assigned to one of these controls; fast access is available only from the *i* menu.

g3 Control Lock

Options: Shutter Speed Lock; Aperture Lock, Focus-point lock (default: Off for all three)

My preference: Varies

As I noted earlier, you may want to lock the shutter speed at a particular value when using Shutter-priority or Manual exposure modes. That's especially true for video shooting, as faster shutter speeds (those more than twice the frame rate) can produce unwanted visual effects, such as "judder" (explained in Chapter 12). You may also want to lock down a particular f/stop when using Aperture-priority or Manual exposure modes, as unwanted changes in aperture cause changes in depth-of-field, which can be visibly jarring in video. You can use this entry to lock the shutter speed, aperture, or focus point (or a combination of the three) so it can't be changed.

Note that when the camera is set to Shutter-priority, you are able to enable/disable only the Focus-point lock function. When set to Aperture-priority, only aperture lock and focus point are accessible. In Manual exposure mode, you can adjust all three, and in Program mode, only focus point can be locked. **Note:** Focus-point lock does not keep the 3D-tracking autofocus-area mode from adjusting focus. Only the starting position of the focus point is locked.

g4 Limit AF-Area Mode Selection

Options: Single-point AF, Wide-area AF (Small, Large, C1, C2), Subject-tracking AF, Auto-area AF (Default is all available)

My preference: N/A

- This entry is the equivalent of Custom Setting a8, used for still photography. It functions exactly as its counterpart described earlier, except in Video Recording mode Pinpoint AF and Dynamic-area AF options aren't available and 3D-tracking AF is replaced by Subject Tracking AF for video.

- Single-point AF-area mode is always available and cannot be disabled. However, you can highlight any of the others and press the multi selector right button to remove the check box next to that mode's label to disable it. You can thus enable Single-point AF, plus any combination of the other AF-area modes. I explained this feature in Chapter 3.

g5 Focus Mode Restrictions

Options: Single AF, Continuous AF, Full-time AF, Manual Focus, No restrictions (default)

My preference: No restrictions

Like its still photography counterpart, this entry allows you to lock in one particular focus mode so that it can't be changed accidentally or intentionally. You can choose to set the camera so that your choice of Single AF (AF-S), Continuous AF (AF-C), Full-time AF (AF-F) (available only for video shooting), and Manual focus (MF) are mandatory for a given session. Most of the time you'll want to use the default, No Restrictions. You might want to use this in a critical situation where it's important to avoid switching focus mode, or when your camera may be used/handled by someone else and you don't want them messing with your setting.

g6 AF Speed

Options: Autofocusing speed (+/–5) (default 0); When to Apply: Always (default), Only While Recording

My preference: Varies

The speed with which the camera autofocuses takes on a different significance when you're shooting movies, because any AF changes are recorded within the movie itself. You may want focus to change slowly as a scene unfolds and people or objects move within the frame, or the frame itself is recomposed. Or, during action sequences, you might prefer to have AF keep pace with subject and camera changes and focus rapidly. This entry lets you speed up or slow down focus speed in Movie mode, using a slider moved via the touch screen or multi selector directional buttons. The When to Apply option can be set to Always (in which case the camera's autofocus will refocus constantly at the speed you select) or Only While Recording (so the focus speed is changed only when you're actually capturing video). When using AF-F (full-time autofocus) you might prefer normal focusing speed (which is equivalent to +5—as fast as possible) as you compose your shot, and then have the camera switch automatically to a preferred slower speed once you start recording. (See Figure 7.25.)

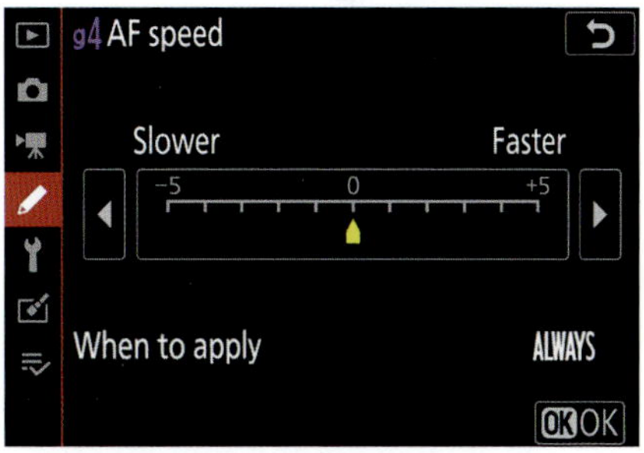

Figure 7.25 Setting AF Speed.

g7 AF Tracking Sensitivity

Options: 7 (Low) to 1 (High); 4 (default)

My preference: Varies

This is roughly the movie equivalent of Custom Setting a3: Focus Tracking with Lock-on for still photography. It specifies how quickly the AF system responds when the subject either exits the frame or something else intervenes—the referee at a football game is the classic example.

A setting of 7 (Low) causes the camera to ignore the intervening subject matter for a significant period of time. Use this setting when shooting subjects, such as sports, in which focus interruptions are likely to be frequent and significant. You can also choose a setting of 1 (High), which tells the camera to wait only a moment before refocusing. The middle value, 4, the default, offers an intermediate delay before the camera refocuses on the new subject.

g8 High-Res Zoom Speed

Options: Slower, Faster, Standard (Z8); Slower (–5) to Faster (+5) (Z9)

My preference: Depends on speed of subject

This function is the first in the next group of video settings (see Figure 7.26). It is available only if you've used Custom Setting g2: Custom Controls to assign the Hi-Res Zoom function to the Fn1, Fn2, or Lens Fn ring (in both clockwise or counterclockwise directions). Once enabled, you can use this entry to specify how quickly zooming occurs, from Slower, Faster, or Standard options. You'll want to experiment to see just how rapid zooming takes place and adjust this entry to account for the speed of movement of your subject.

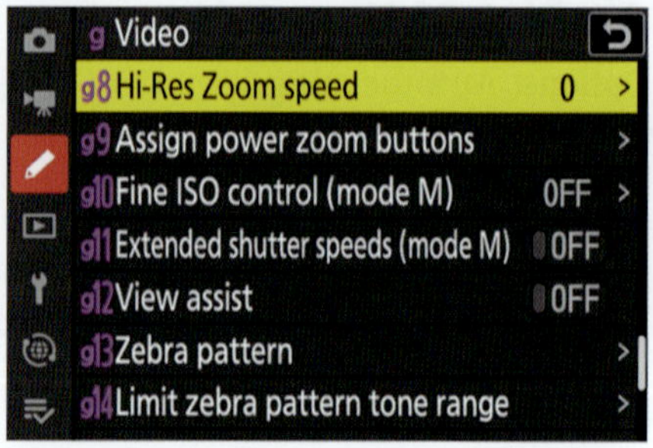

Figure 7.26 The next group of video settings.

g9 Assign Power Zoom Buttons

Options: Use Zoom In/Zoom Out buttons: On, Off (default); Power zoom speed: –3 (slower) to +3 (faster)

My preference: N/A

The good news is that Nikon is making power zoom (PZ) lenses available in Z mount. The bad news is that the first such lens introduced is an APS-C optic, the Nikkor Z DX 12-28mm f/3.5 PZ VR. It's targeted at vloggers and content creators with a focal length range that covers an 18mm (equivalent) wide angle view that, as Nikon asserts, "lets you record yourself within the scene from arm's length."

The lens can be used on the Z9, of course, for both video capture and stills using its 18-42mm equivalent zoom range in APS-C crop mode, and, as you might guess, it would be most useful for video shooting that can best take advantage of its power zoom features. This entry allows you to assign the zoom in/zoom out functions to the Zoom in/Zoom out buttons, and specify a power zooming speed. As I write this, the Z8 does not sport this entry in its Custom Settings menu, but it's likely to have been added by the time this book is published.

The lens's internal linear motor is used to adjust focal lengths, and zooming can be controlled via the camera buttons, plus additional options, including the optional ML-L7 Bluetooth Remote, the SnapBridge app, or when using NX Tether Software and the optional MC-N10 Remote Grip.

g10 Fine ISO Control (Mode M)

Options: On (1/6 EV), Off

My preference: Off

If you need very fine control over ISO sensitivity, you can change the settings increment from the camera's default value of 1/3 stop to a more granular 1/6 stop.

g11 Extended Shutter Speeds (Mode M)

Options: Off (default), On

My preference: Off

As I've already mentioned, the optimum shutter speeds for video recording can vary, depending on the frame rate you're using; anything *shorter* than about twice the frame rate produces an undesirable look. In addition, *longer* shutter speeds are locked out to prevent blurring/distortion that I'll describe shortly. Your Z8/Z9 automatically limits the available slow shutter speeds whenever you are in Video Recording mode. This setting allows a partial override of those limits.

- **Off (default).** At this setting, the slowest shutter speed you can use roughly corresponds to the frame rate, from 1/125th second at 120p down to 1/25th second at 24p.
- **On.** The slowest shutter speed available for 60/50p, 30/25p, and 24p changes to 1/2 second. At those speeds, the camera will include repeated copies of the same frame to fill out a full-second's worth of video. That is, at 60p and a shutter speed of 1/60th second you'd end up with 60 individual images for each second of elapsed time. But at 60p and a 1/4-second exposure time, the camera would fill out each second with 14 copies of the original frame (15 in all).

  Keep in mind that slow shutter speeds may also produce blurring from subject movement as well as camera movement. Mounting the Z8/Z9 and/or VR/electronic VR can counter camera shake, but have no effect on the movement of your subject. Nikon says that the main reason for using these slow shutter speeds is to reduce the need to increase the ISO setting to capture very dark subjects.

g12 View Assist

Options: On (default), Off

My preference: Off

This setting provides a more natural-looking live preview of your video when you're using the high dynamic range video options HLG or N-log. The colors are simplified and increased from the flat recorded appearance to a high contrast representation. You'll need to activate this *only* when you are using HLG or N-log *and* review your videos on your Z8/Z9's display.

g13 Zebra Pattern

Options: Pattern Tone Range: Highlights, Mid-tones, Off (default); Pattern: Pattern 1 (forward diagonal lines), Pattern 2 (back-leaning diagonal lines); Highlight Threshold: 255, 250 (default), 245, 240, 235, 230, 225, 220, 215, 210, 205, 200, 195, 190, 185, 180, 175, 170, 165, 160, 155, 150, 145, 140, 135, 130, 125, 120; Mid-tone Value: 0 to 255; Range: +5 to+20

My preference: N/A

Video has its own version of the still photography's Highlights display ("blinkies"), commonly known as Zebra display, because it uses contrasting stripes to represent blown highlights. It warns you when the brightest areas of your image may be overexposed when capturing video—but does so *before* you begin capture. Instead of solid flashing indicators, the camera displays one of two striped "zebra" patterns in the affected areas. The zebra stripes jump out at you and make it easy to identify exactly which highlights may be overexposed. You can then adjust exposure or lighting to bring the highlights under control.

This menu entry allows you to specify a number of parameters:

- **Pattern tone range:** Here you choose whether you want the Zebra display to indicate high values for either highlights or mid-tones. Or, you can choose Off to disable the Zebra display. The Highlights choice is useful for checking for overexposure. Use mid-tones instead to insure that the middle tonal values of your scene are within the range you specify. If they are "off" you can adjust the lighting. The actual limits for highlights or mid-tones are set below.

  Note: I used Custom Setting g2 Custom Controls to assign the Pattern Tone Range function to Fn4 (on my Z9) and Fn3 (on my Z8). I can then turn the Zebra display on or off by pressing that button while shooting video.
- **Pattern:** Choose from Zebra pattern 1 (forward-tilting diagonal lines) or Pattern 2 (back-leaning lines).
- **Highlight threshold:** Set a brightness value above which the Zebra pattern will appear. You can choose 28 values from 255 to 120. The default is 250, but a more common setting is 235 for average facial tones. (More on that shortly.)
- **Mid-tone range:** You can choose brightness values from 0 (black) to 255 (white) to specify the tone you want to reside in the middle of your selected range. Then, choose an acceptable range deviation, between +5 to +20 of your value setting.

So, exactly how bright *is* too bright? A value of 255 indicates pure white, so any Zebra pattern visible when using this setting indicates that your image is extremely overexposed. Any details in the highlights are gone and cannot be retrieved. Settings from 213 to 235 can be used to make sure facial tones are not overexposed. As a general rule of thumb, Caucasian skin generally falls in the 235 range, with darker skin tones registering as low as 213, and very fair skin or lighter areas of your subject edging closer to 248. Once you've decided the approximate range of tones that you want to make sure do *not* blow out, you can set the Zebra pattern sensitivity appropriately and receive the flashing striped warning on the LCD. (See Figure 7.27.) The pattern does not appear in your final image, of course—it's just an aid to keep you from blowing it, so to speak.

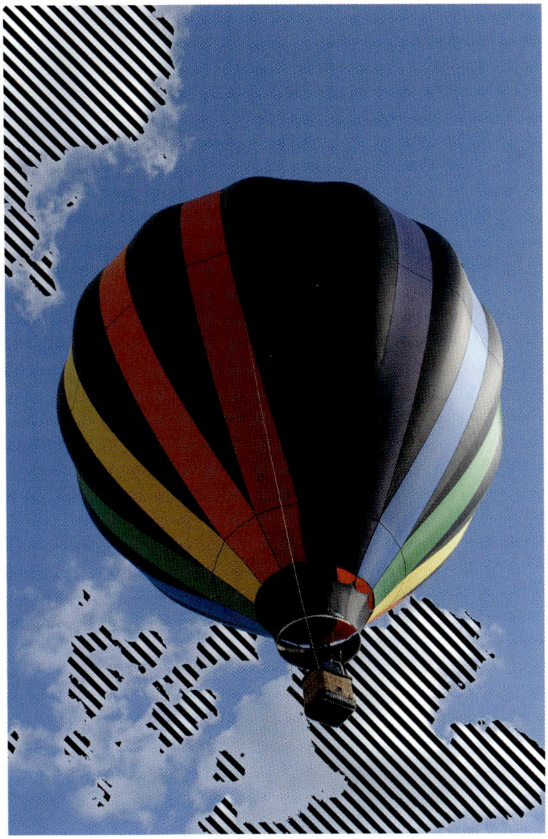

Figure 7.27 The flashing stripes show an area is overexposed.

Zebra patterns are a much more useful tool than "blinkies," because you are given an alert *before* you take the picture and can actually specify exactly how bright *too bright* is. The feature is not new: it has long been used in video equipment, dating back before the digital age. Veteran videographers will note that Nikon uses a section of the 0–255 brightness value scale, rather than the traditional IRE measure of a video signal level, in which numbers from 70 to 100/100+ are used. The Zebra feature has been a staple of professional video shooting for a long time, as you might guess from the moniker assigned to the unit used to specify brightness: IRE, a measure of video signal level, which stands for *Institute of Radio Engineers.*

g14 Limit Zebra Pattern Tone Range

Options: Highlights, Mid-tones, No Restrictions (default)

My preference: N/A

This setting provides a way to limit activation of Pattern Tone Range, although it's only useful when you've defined a custom button to turn the Zebra display on or off, as I recommended above. If you select Highlights or Mid-tones, the Zebra display is enabled *only* if you've selected Highlights or Mid-tones (respectively) under the Pattern Tone Range option of Custom Setting g12/g13. Choose No Restrictions (the default), and the Zebra display will always be turned on or off when the button is pressed.

g15 Grid Type

Options: 3 × 3 (default), 4 × 4, 4:3, 2:35:1, 1:85:1, 1:1, 90%

My preference: N/A

This is the first entry in the next batch of settings (see Figure 7.28). The display grids available for video recording have an additional function beyond simple compositional aspects. Movies can be shot or edited to produce specific aspect ratios, depending on the intent of the production. Your Nikon Z9/Z8's grids can be used as *marker frames* to remind you of those proportions while you're recording, so you can keep the important subject matter within those boundaries.

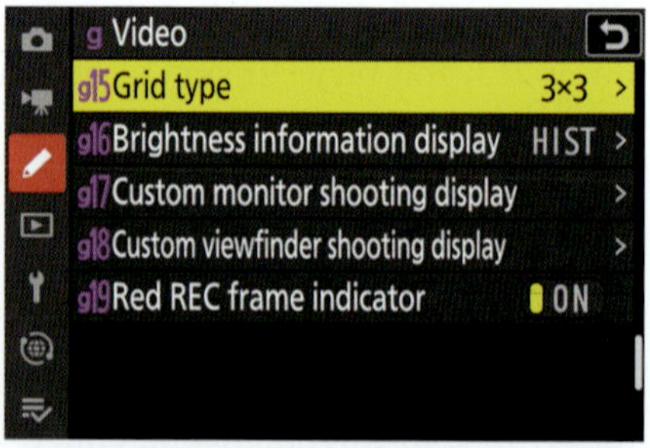

Figure 7.28 The final five entries.

They are a popular tool for videographers because they allow viewing the area outside the actual frame that will be captured (the "look-around area") so you can monitor moving subjects before they enter the frame. In professional productions, it's useful to look at the region outside the captured frame to detect when boom microphones, careless crew members, or other objects threaten to intrude on the frame. It's common to shoot movies knowing in advance that they will be cropped down eventually for display in a slightly different format. The director simply makes sure that the important parts of the frame are included in the "safety zone" that will never be cropped out. For example, you wouldn't want to put two characters who are talking to each other at opposite ends of the entire frame but would instead locate them in the safety zone so both would be visible.

The marker frames available with the Z9 and Z8 are shown in Figure 7.29. Here's an overview of how they are used:

- **No grids.** Keep in mind that when grids are not displayed, the image you see in the viewfinder and rear LCD *is already cropped* for you when the camera is in Video Recording mode. You will view the area captured when shooting Full HD and 4K video in 16:9 format, at 1920 × 1080 and 3840 × 2160 resolutions. This is a popular widescreen format, also applied to 8K video, and is used for movies and television. Its panoramic view is excellent for documentaries, sports action, or any scenes with lots of detail, and was used in some *Avengers* movies.

  It was established by the Society of Motion Picture and Television Engineers. **Note:** The Digital Cinema Initiatives standards organization has defined additional resolution/aspect ratio specifications that you don't need to worry about, in general.

- **3 × 3, 4 × 4, 1:1, and 4:3.** The first two most often used to help you determine whether horizontal and vertical lines are skewed and can also be used as a Rule of Thirds or Rule of Quarters guide for composition. The latter two are specific aspect ratios you might want to incorporate into your compositions. Some filmmakers, like Wes Anderson, still use the 4:3 aspect ratio to provide an "old-timey" look.

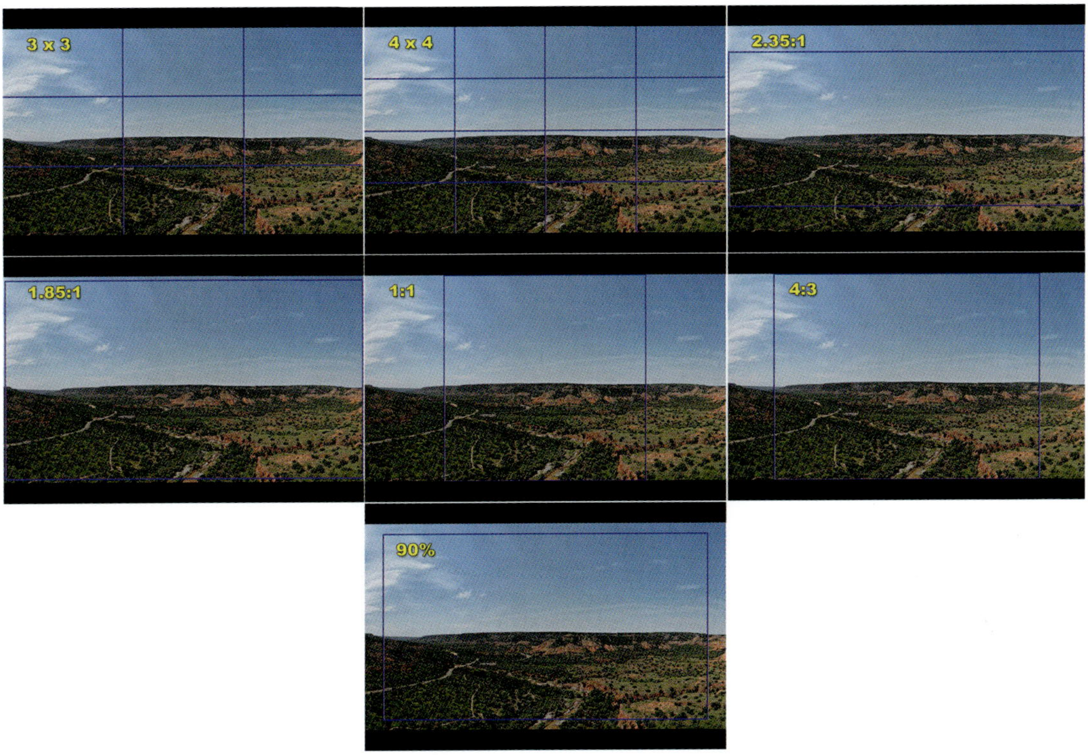

Figure 7.29 The seven grids available for video recording.

- **1:85:1.** This aspect ratio, wider than 4:3 but not as panoramic as 16:9, it's often used for drama, romantic comedies, and other films where the emphasis is on the actors rather than their surroundings, like *Forrest Gump* and *The Godfather* trilogy.
- **2:35:1.** These proportions, along with the more common 2:39:1, are called CinemaScope format (or, often, just "Scope"), an extremely wide aspect ratio used in *Star Wars.*
- **90 Percent.** It's common to shoot movies knowing in advance that they will be cropped down eventually for display in a slightly different format. The director simply makes sure that the important parts of the frame are included in the "safety zone" that will never be cropped out. For example, you wouldn't want to put two characters who are talking to each other at opposite ends of the entire frame but would instead locate them in the safety zone so both would be visible. Your camera provides a 90 percent safety zone to represent the area that will always be shown when the movie is viewed on a standard HDTV.

Note: This setting does not enable/disable grid display; it only specifies what type of overlay will be used. To activate a grid, you have to include that as an option in one of your display layouts using the Custom Monitor Shooting Display and Custom Viewfinder Shooting Display entries discussed shortly.

g16 Brightness Information Display

Options: Histogram, Waveform Monitor, Waveform Monitor (Large)

My preference: N/A

This is a super-techie option for serious videographers who want to replace the histogram with a waveform monitor display (small or large) (see Figure 7.30). The waveform display provides luminance information showing how bright areas are, with horizontal grid lines at the 25, 50, and 75 percent levels. Total black is represented at the bottom of the graph and total white at the top.

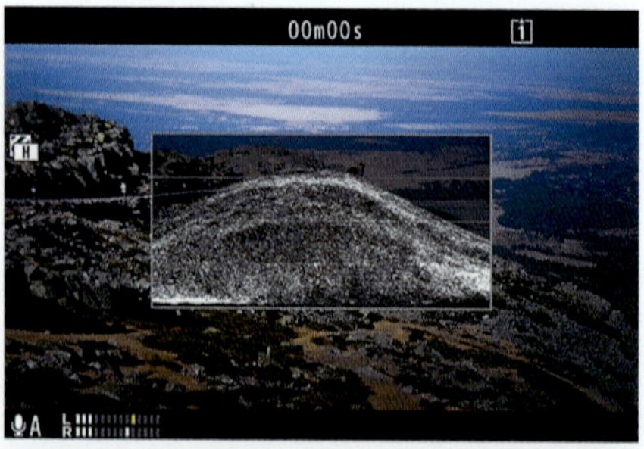

Figure 7.30 Waveform monitor display (Large).

g17 Half-press to Cancel Zoom

Options: Off (default), On

A half-press of the shutter release cancels manual focus zooming.

g18 Custom Monitor Shooting Display

Options: Display 1, Display 2, Display 3, Display 4

My preference: Varies

This entry provides only four different displays (instead of five), the Histogram option is labeled Brightness, instead and there is no Center-weighted display available. You can set up your displays as described earlier.

g19 Custom Viewfinder Shooting Display

Options: Display 1, Display 2, Display 3

My preference: Varies

This is the video version of the still photo Custom Viewfinder Shooting Display (d18/20) described above. It offers three display options, rather than four, and the same entries as its g16/g17 counterpart just described.

g18/g19 Red REC Frame Indicator

Options: On (default), Off

My preference: On

By default, your Z8/Z9 displays a transparent red frame around the edge of the display while video recording is underway, reminding you that your camera is "live" and recording, much like the tally light found on professional video cameras and monitors. An important difference is that actual tally lights are visible to those in front of the camera, too, so that subjects are aware they are being recorded. Nikon's Recording Frame Indicator is not intrusive, so I keep it enabled at all times.

Playback Menu

8

The blue-coded Playback menu has 12 entries where you select options related to the display, review, transfer, and printing of the photos you've taken. Figure 8.1 shows the first seven entries. Note that some entries, such as Delete, are *functions*, rather than settings, and do not have a default value, as such.

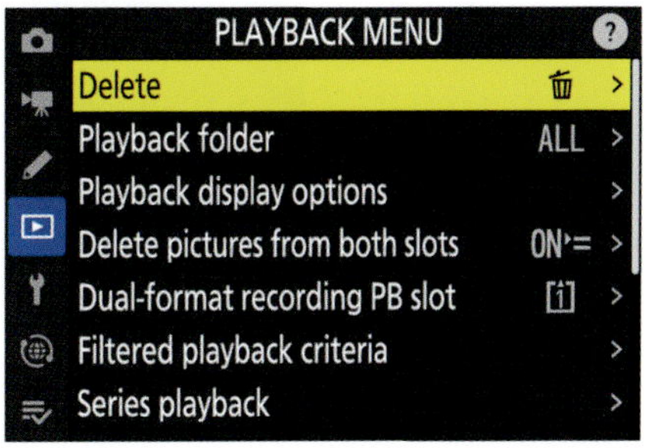

Figure 8.1 The first seven Playback menu entries.

- Delete
- Playback Folder
- Playback Display Options
- Delete Pictures from Both Slots
- Dual-Format Recording PB Slot
- Filtered Playback Criteria
- Series Playback
- Picture Review
- After Delete
- After Burst, Show
- Auto-Rotate Pictures
- Copy Image(s)

Delete

Options: Selected Pictures, Candidates for Deletion, Pictures Shot on Selected Dates, All Pictures

My preference: N/A

Choose this menu entry and you'll be given four choices, shown in Figure 8.2, upper left: Selected Pictures (to choose individual images to delete); Candidates for Deletion (to remove images rated using the Delete option); Pictures Shot on Selected Dates (to remove all photos taken on a particular day); or All Pictures (to remove all images in the folder currently selected for playback).

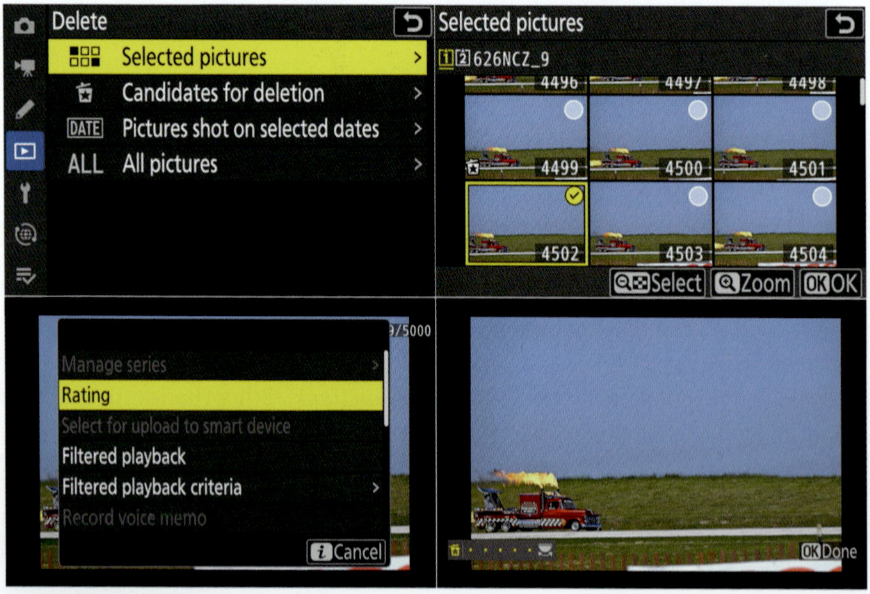

Figure 8.2 Select pictures to delete (top). Assign Delete rating using the Playback version of the *i* menu (bottom).

To select images use one of these options:

- **Selected Pictures.** A selection screen, like the one shown at upper right in Figure 8.2 appears. Scroll through the thumbnails of the images displayed using the multi selector's directional buttons. Hold down the Zoom In button to enlarge the highlighted thumbnail to full-screen view. Press the Zoom Out button to mark a highlighted image for deletion, or to unmark one that has already been marked. A yellow checkmark is overlaid on the upper-right corner of a thumbnail when an image is marked for removal. When finished marking, press OK to delete. Choose Yes from the screen that appears, or No to cancel.
- **Candidates for Deletion.** This option deletes images that you have already marked for deletion using the Rating feature of the Playback version of the *i* menu. You cannot select images here. Instead, in Playback mode, press the *i* button and choose Rating from the screen that appears. (Figure 8.2, lower left.) Then rotate the main command dial and select the Trash can icon (Figure 8.2, lower right).
- **Pictures Shot on Selected Dates.** A list of dates on which pictures were taken appears. Press the right multi selector button to checkmark a date, or to unmark a date that has been selected. Once you've highlighted one or more dates, if you're sure you want to delete all those images, press the Zoom Out button to confirm, then press OK, and give the camera the go-ahead to continue on the confirmation screen that pops up.
- **All Pictures.** Choose your Slot and press OK, then select Yes or No to delete the images.

Using this menu to delete images will have no effect on images that have been marked with an overlaid key icon when protected using the Protect option available from the *i* menu that appears when you press the *i* button during Playback. Keep in mind that deleting images in this way is slower than just wiping out the whole card with the Format command, so using Format is generally much faster than choosing Delete: All Pictures, and also is a safer way of returning your memory card to a fresh, blank state.

Playback Folder

Options: NCZ_9/NCZ_8, All (default), Current

My preference: N/A

Your camera will create folders on your memory card to store the images that it creates. It assigns the first folder a number, like 100NCZ_9, and when that folder is filled, a new folder is automatically created numbered one higher, such as 101NCZ_9. A folder is completely full when it contains 5,000 images, or a picture numbered 9999. If you use the same memory card in another camera, that camera will also create its own folder. Thus, you can end up with several folders on the same memory card, until you eventually reformat the card and folder creation starts anew.

This menu item allows you to choose which folders are accessed when displaying images using the Playback facility. Your choices are as follows:

- **NCZ_9 (or NCZ_8).** Only the folders on your memory card created by the camera will be used, and those created by other cameras ignored. Images in all the camera's folders will be displayed. This is the default folder name. You can rename these folders using the Storage Folder > Rename entry in the Photo Shooting menu. Personally, I feel that the space between NCZ and the 9 or 8 in the folder name is a waste of good ASCII, and described some alternatives in Chapter 5.
- **All (default).** All folders containing images that the camera can read will be accessed, regardless of which camera created them. You might want to use this setting if you swap memory cards among several cameras and want to be able to review all the photos (especially when considering reformatting the memory card). You will be able to view images even if they were created by a non-Nikon camera if those images conform to the Design Rule for Camera File system (DCF) specifications.
- **Current.** The camera will display only images in the current folder. For example, if you have been shooting heavily at an event and have already accumulated more than 5,000 shots in one folder (or an image has been stored that's numbered 9999) and the camera has created a new folder for the overflow, you'd use this setting to view only the most recent photos, which reside in the current folder. You can change the current folder to any other folder on your memory card using the Active Folder option in the Photo Shooting menu, described later in this chapter.

Playback Display Options

Options: Basic photo info: Focus Point; Mark First Shot in Series; Additional photo info: Exposure Info, Highlights, RGB Histogram, Shooting Data, Overview, None (Image only), File Info; Detailed photo info: Basic Shooting Data, Flash Data, Picture Control/HLG Data, Other Shooting Data, Copyright Info, Location Data, IPTC Data

My preference: N/A

You'll recall from Chapter 7 that a great deal of information, available on multiple screens, can be cycled through by pressing the DISP button when previewing images, and that you could select which items are shown. This menu item helps you reduce/increase the Playback screen clutter by specifying which information and screens will be available. To activate or deactivate an info option, scroll to that option and press the right multi selector button to add a checkmark to the box next to that item. Press the right button to unmark an item that has previously been checked. If no boxes are checked, only the default view—the image with basic information shown at the bottom of the frame—is displayed. Shooting data may require multiple pages, which you can scroll through using the multi selector up and down buttons. Your additional info options include:

- **Focus Point.** Activate this option to display the active focus point(s) with red highlighting.
- **Mark First Shot in Series.** You can have a marker inserted for the first image captured during a continuous shooting sequence. An icon, representing a stack of images and the number of shots in the sequence will appear in the upper-right corner of the first image when played back.
- **Exposure Info.** Shows only frame number and basic exposure information, including release mode, shutter speed, aperture, exposure compensation, and ISO sensitivity.
- **Highlights.** When enabled, overexposed highlight areas in your image will blink with a black border during picture review. That's your cue to consider using exposure compensation to reduce exposure, unless a minus EV setting will cause loss of shadow detail that you want to preserve. You can read more about correcting exposure in Chapter 2.
- **RGB Histogram.** Displays both luminance (brightness) and RGB histograms on a screen that can be displayed using the up/down multi selector buttons. I explained the use of histograms in Chapter 2.
- **Shooting Data.** Activates the pages of shooting data shown.
- **Overview.** Activates the overview screen. You must scroll down the list to access this option.
- **None.** A screen with the image only and no photo information will be displayed.
- **File Info.** Displays information about the image file, including file and folder name.
- **Basic Shooting Data.** Shows a screen with the full range of information, including exposure data, lens settings, white balance settings, focus/autofocus modes, etc.
- **Flash Data.** Displays flash type, modes, and flash compensation information.
- **Picture Control/HLG Data.** Shows any Picture Control settings in effect for the image, and HLG Quality settings for video.

- **Other Shooting Data.** Includes noise reduction, Active D-Lighting, HDR strength, Vignette control, any retouching that has been done, and image comments.
- **Copyright Info.** Displays copyright data, if recorded.
- **Location Data.** If location data, including latitude, longitude, altitude, and Universal Coordinated Time (UTC) are embedded in the file, it will be shown on this screen.
- **IPTC Data.** If you've enabled and specified IPTC information, it will be displayed here.

Delete Pictures From Both Slots

Options: Yes (Confirmation Required)(default), Yes, No

My preference: Yes (Confirmation Required)

This entry lets you choose whether or not to retain additional copies of an image when deleting pictures using the Playback menu entry described above. As you learned in Chapter 5, your camera is able to store multiple copies of the same image in different locations, depending on the role you've selected for the second card slot. If you've set the second slot to function as an Overflow destination when your first card fills up, only one copy of each picture will exist, so this entry has no bearing.

However, if you've specified Backup, RAW Slot 1-JPEG Slot 2, or JPEG Shot 1-JPEG Shot 2 (with a different Image Size for the additional JPEG image), then you'll end up with duplicates of the same image. I recommend sticking with the default setting, so that when you decide to trash a particular image, the camera will remind you that a copy is stored on the other card and ask for confirmation. Choose Yes, and the copy will always be removed forthwith; No, and it will be retained as a backup in case you change your mind or have made an error.

Dual-Format Recording PB Slot

Options: Slot 1 (default)/Slot 2 (Z9), CFexpress/XQD (default) / SD Card Slot (Z8)

My preference: Slot containing JPEG images

Your camera has two memory card slots (Slot 1, Slot 2). Both Z9 slots accept CFexpress/XQD cards only, while the Z8 has one for CFexpress/XQD memory cards, and one for SD cards. With the Z8, you can define *either* of these two as the primary slot, making the other the secondary slot, using the Primary Slot Selection and Secondary Slot Selection settings in the Photo Shooting menu (discussed in Chapter 5). That's because the Z8's two slots each accept a different type of memory card.

You can specify how the memory card in each slot is used. You can tell the camera to use the second slot for *overflow* once the first slot card fills; copy each shot to *both* for backup; or to save RAW images on one card and the JPEG versions on the other card.

This entry comes into play only when you are shooting in RAW+JPEG mode and have chosen RAW Primary—JPEG Secondary in the Secondary Slot Function entry for the Z8, or the Z9's RAW Slot 1—JPEG Slot 2 entry instead. That specifies which of the two versions of your dual-format images should be displayed during Playback. You can elect to have the version stored in the CFexpress/XQD slot displayed, or the version stored in the SD card slot (on the Z8) or second slot on the Z9.

Filtered Playback Criteria

Options: Protect; Picture Type (Photos, Videos); Rating (Zero to five stars, Not Rated, Candidate for Deletion), Select for Upload to Computer/FTP; Voice Memo; Retouched Pictures

My preference: N/A

Ordinarily, your camera will show you all the available images in the active folder during Playback. You can choose several types of filters to weed through your images so that only the ones meeting your criteria are shown. A white border appears around the image to remind you that only the filtered images are being displayed. In addition to this menu entry, filtered playback and setting filtered playback parameters are also available from the Playback version of the *i* menu. This entry is used to specify which filters will be used when you initiate filtered playback. The filters available include:

- **Protected images.** You must protect images individually or in groups.
- **Picture Type.** Choose Photos or Videos.
- **Rating.** You can select any combination of zero to five stars, unrated images, and pictures marked as candidates for deletion.
- **Uploads.** You can view those selected for upload to your computer. You can select pictures for transfer in the Playback version of the *i* menu. You can view only photos that have previously been uploaded to a computer or FTP server, those that have not yet been uploaded, or both types.
- **Voice memo.** View images that have been tagged with a recorded voice memo using the Playback version of the *i* menu. Voice memos can be listened to using the *i* menu during review.
- **Retouched pictures.** Review all images that have been retouched using the Playback version of the *i* menu.

Because you can select any combination of the listed parameters, you can do things like review only protected still photos with four- or five-star ratings, if that's what you want. This is a handy way of sorting through a lot of images quickly, if you've taken the time to protect them or assign a rating. To search for images using the filters you've specified, just follow these steps:

1. Press the Playback button to display an image.
2. Press the *i* button to display the *i* menu.
3. Select Filtered Playback from the menu.
4. Press OK to display the filtered images.

Series Playback

Options: Sub-selector Displays First Shot: On (default), Off; Auto Series Playback: On, Off (default); List Series as Single Thumbnails: On, Off (default)

My preference: All three On

This entry provides some shortcuts that can be helpful when reviewing images during playback. There are three options:

- **Sub-selector Displays First Shot.** By default this setting is On, and pressing the sub-selector joystick left or right jumps ahead or back to the first shot in each continuous sequence. If you want to advance/retreat one frame at a time, use the directional pad's left/right buttons instead. Change this setting to Off, and the sub-selector and directional pad buttons both move only one frame at a time.
- **Auto Series Playback/Playback Options.** This setting is Off by default, and after you've finished a continuous sequence, you can start reviewing your images manually. If you'd rather have the camera display the individual pictures in sequence automatically, turn this option On. When you press Playback to view the first image in a series, after about three seconds the camera will begin showing the remaining images one after another. Playback Options include Loop Playback, Wait Before Playback, and Auto Series Playback Speed.
- **List Series as a Single Thumbnail.** Do yourself a favor and activate this option. It will save time when trying to find an individual scene or sequence using thumbnails. When enabled, only the first shot in a continuous sequence will be displayed as a thumbnail with a "stack" overlay indicating there are other images in the series.

Picture Review

Options: On, On (Monitor Only), Off (default)

My preference: N/A

This is the first of the remaining entries in the Playback menu. (See Figure 8.3.) There are certain shooting situations in which it's useful to have the picture you've just shot pop up on the monitor automatically for review. Perhaps you're fine-tuning exposure or autofocus and want to be able to see whether your most recent image is acceptable. Or, maybe you're the nervous type and just want confirmation that you actually took a picture. Image review has saved my bacon a few times when I accidentally made an inappropriate setting (such as specifying ISO 25600 when it really wasn't needed or desirable).

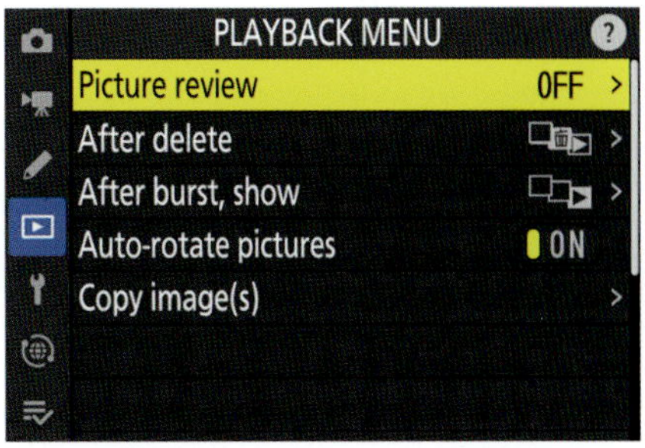

Figure 8.3 The last five entries in the Playback menu.

A lot of the time, however, it's a better idea to *not* automatically review your shots to conserve battery power (the LCD monitor and EVF are two of the major juice drains) or to speed up or simplify operations. For example, if you've just fired off a burst of eight shots during a football game, do you *really* need to have every frame display as the camera clears its buffer and stores the photos on your memory card? This menu operation allows you to choose which mode to use. You can elect to have the review image always appear, appear on the LCD monitor only, or never appear. Unfortunately, Nikon neglected to give us an On (Viewfinder Only) option for image review, but I'm going to give you several workarounds.

- **On.** Image review is automatic after every shot is taken, and your image will appear in the viewfinder or on the LCD monitor (depending on which you are using).
- **On (Monitor Only).** Image review is displayed *only* on the rear-panel LCD monitor, and then only if you are *not* currently looking through the viewfinder; to see image review, move the camera away from your eye.
- **Off.** Images are displayed only when you press the Playback button. Nikon, in its wisdom, has made this the default setting.

QUENCH THAT MONITOR!

When I am shooting concerts and performances where the audience area is darkened, I don't want the LCD monitor lighting up after every shot and annoying people. Even so, I may want to review my images and would like them to appear immediately—just not on the monitor. There are several ways to activate that behavior.

- If you select ON with this menu entry, if your Limit Monitor Mode Selection option (in the Setup menu and described in Chapter 9) is set to activate Automatic Selection Display Switch, as long as you keep your eye up to the viewfinder, the image preview will not appear on the monitor.
- A better choice is to disable Automatic Selection and enable just Viewfinder Only or Monitor Only options. Then you can manually toggle between the viewfinder and monitor using the VF/Monitor button on the left side of the camera's pentaprism. Your image review will appear *only* on the currently selected screen.
- If you absolutely want to prevent having your image review appear on the monitor, visit the Limit Monitor Mode Selection entry and disable everything but Viewfinder Only.
- A compromise is to use the Monitor Brightness entry in the Setup menu and set Manual Brightness to –5. This produces a very dark screen, which is unlikely to annoy those around you. It also makes it difficult to judge exposure from the monitor alone. (*That's what the histogram is for!*)

After Delete

Options: Show Next (default), Show Previous, Continue as Before

My preference: Show Next

When you've deleted an image, you probably will want to do one of three things: display the next picture (in the order shot); show the *previous* picture; or show either the next *or* previous picture, depending on which way you were scrolling during picture review. You can select which action to take:

- **Show Next.** It's likely that you'll want to look at the picture taken after the one you just deleted, so Nikon makes this the default action.
- **Show Previous.** I use this setting a lot when shooting sports with a continuous shooting setting. After the sequence is taken, I press the Playback button to see the last picture in the series and sometimes discover that the whole sequence missed the boat. I sometimes go ahead and press the Trash button twice to delete the offending image, then continue moving backward to delete the five or six or eleven other pictures in the wasted sequence. You'll often find yourself with time on your hands at football games and feel the urge to delete a stinker series of shots to save you time reviewing back at the computer (plus freeing up a little space on your card).
- **Continue as Before.** This setting makes a lot of sense: if you were scrolling backward or forward and deleting photos as you go, you might want to continue in the same direction weeding out bad shots. Use this setting to set your camera to behave that way.

After Burst, Show

Options: First Picture in Burst, Last Picture in Burst (default)

My preference: Last Picture in Burst

This menu choice allows you to determine which image is shown after a continuous series of shots are captured, when Image Review is turned off. In practice, the camera will *not* display any images on the LCD monitor while you are shooting a burst, allowing the camera to capture frames and store them on your memory card at maximum speed. However, when the burst is complete, one image will then be shown on the screen—either the first image of the series or the last image captured. I prefer to view the final image; if it's okay in terms of exposure and focus, I can assume the others in the series are similar and move on to initiate another burst immediately if I want. Select First Picture in Burst, instead, if you want to see the initial shot and then, perhaps, continue checking subsequent photos.

Auto Image Rotation

Options: On (default), Off

My preference: Off

When you rotate the camera to photograph vertical subjects in portrait (tall), rather than landscape (wide) orientation, you probably don't want to view them tilted onto their sides later, either on the monitor and viewfinder or within your image viewing/editing application on your computer. The camera has a directional sensor built in that can detect whether it was rotated when the photo was taken and hide this information in the image file itself.

The orientation data is applied in two different ways. It can be used by the camera to automatically rotate images when they are displayed on the monitor and viewfinder (when On is enabled), or you can ignore the data and let the images display in non-rotated fashion when Off is selected (so you have to rotate the camera to view them in their proper orientation). As mentioned earlier, your image-editing application can also use the embedded file data to automatically rotate images on your computer screen.

This menu choice deals only with whether the image should be rotated when displayed on the *camera LCD monitor* or *in the electronic viewfinder.* (If you de-activate this option, your image-editing software can still read the embedded rotation data and properly display your images.) When Rotate Tall is turned off, the camera does not rotate pictures taken in vertical orientation. The image is large on your display, but you must rotate the camera to view it upright. When Rotate Tall is turned on, the camera rotates pictures taken in vertical orientation on the monitor screen so you don't have to turn the camera to view them comfortably. However, this orientation also means that the longest dimension of the image is shown using the shortest dimension of the monitor, so the picture displayed (but not the image itself) is reduced in size.

So, turn this feature On if you'd rather not turn your camera to view vertical shots in their natural orientation, and don't mind the smaller image. Turn the feature Off if, as I do, you'd rather see a larger image and are willing to rotate the camera to do so. Rotating the camera is no big deal, and worth the trouble in order to see the largest possible review image on the display.

Copy Image(s)

Options: Select Source, Select Picture(s), Select Destination Folder, Copy Picture(s)?

My preference: N/A

The ability to work with two memory cards simultaneously ranks as one of my favorite features in any camera that offers dual slots. One of the best uses for two cards is to make back-up images while traveling, or at any other time that your computer isn't easily accessible.

Here are some examples of what I do:

- **Shoot to two cards simultaneously.** This gives you an instant backup in case pictures on your primary card become corrupt or erased. Ideally, your two cards should be equal in storage size.
- **Make a copy.** Use this Copy Image(s) facility to make a copy of images you shot on one card to your second card. Instead of shooting on two cards at once (which does slow down the camera a bit), use only one card when you take photos, then make a backup onto a second card at the end of the day. You can copy all or only some of the photos you've shot.
- **Make copies to distribute.** Z8 owners, because their cameras can work with cheap SD cards, have an option that's not quite as feasible for Z9 users. I bought a bunch of 16GB SD memory cards for $4 each, and I find it's quick and easy to make multiple copies of photos, not for backup, but for distribution either on the spot, say, to provide models I've hired with some raw (not RAW) images or to send by snail mail to colleagues, friends, or family. Such small cards won't hold many images, but in many cases, that's enough space. No computer required!
- **Leave your laptop or external storage at home.** Since I've begun using Nikon cameras with dual memory card slots, I leave my hard disk/personal storage device with its built-in reader or my laptop at home more often. If I am going to be gone for only a day or two, it's easier to just make copies in the camera, and not bother with another external device.

To copy images from one card to another, just follow these steps (which are available only when two memory cards are present in the camera):

1. **Access copy menus.** Choose Copy Images(s) from the Playback menu. There are four choices that may be available to you: Select Source, Select Picture(s), Select Destination Folder, and Copy Picture(s)?. They are shown at upper left in Figure 8.4.
   - If you have images on only one card, all other choices will be grayed out, and the card containing images will be selected automatically.
   - If there are images on both cards already, you can choose Select Source to specify which card slot as the source to copy from.
   - If you have already marked some images previously, then all four choices will be available.
2. **Select Source.** If you have images on both cards and want to choose images from the non-default slot that is pre-selected, highlight Select Source and press the right button on the multi selector. Choose the desired slot and press the right button again to return to the previous menu. (See Figure 8.4, upper right.)
3. **Select Pictures.** Highlight Select Picture(s) and press the right button. The screen shown at left center in Figure 8.4 appears. You can now choose from:
   - **All Pictures in Slot.** If you select this, all the images on the card will be selected and you'll be returned to the previous menu. (See Figure 8.4 center left.)
   - **Images in a folder in that slot.** If more than one folder resides on that card, all will be shown. Select a folder and press the right button, and the screen shown at center right in Figure 8.4 appears. You can again choose Select All Pictures or Select Protected Pictures (which you have previously marked). The top choice in the list, Deselect All, automatically unselects previously selected images (if any) and takes you to the Deselect All/Select screen that allows you to highlight individual images and checkmark them with the OK button.

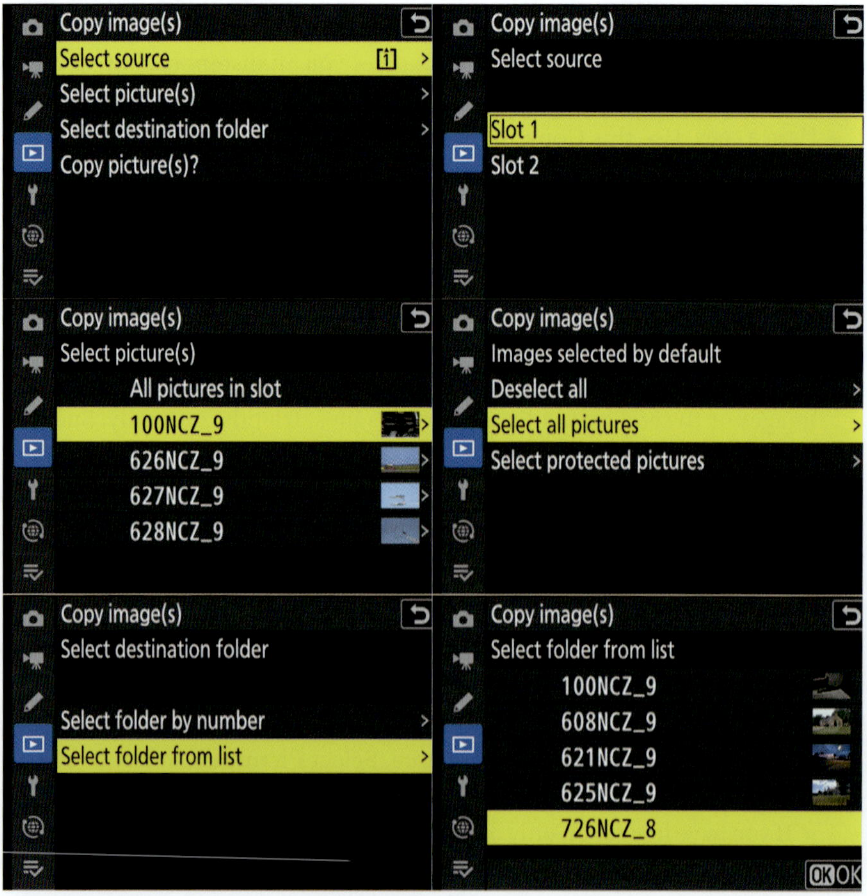

Figure 8.4 These six screens allow you to select a source slot, specific images, destination folder, and initiate copying.

4. **Select destination folder.** When finished selecting images, press OK to return to the Copy Image(s) screen. There, you can optionally choose Select Destination Folder and select a folder by number, or from a list of existing folders on the target card. If you do not specify a destination folder the camera will create one for you on the destination memory card. (See Figure 8.4, lower left and right.)
5. **Start copying.** If you do not want to choose a specific destination, select Copy Pictures(s)?. You'll see a confirmation screen that displays the number of images that will be copied. Highlight Yes, press OK, and a progress screen with a green progress bar appears while the copying is underway. You'll see a Copy Complete message when the task is finished. Press OK, and then the MENU button twice to back out of the menus; or just tap the shutter-release button.

TIP The Copy command will ask for confirmation before overwriting images on the destination card that have the same name as the source images. You can choose Replace Existing Image, Replace All, Skip, or Cancel the rest of the copying operation.

9 The Setup Menu

We're not done covering the menu options yet. There are three more menus to deal with. These include the Setup menu, which deals with adjustments that are generally outside the actual shooting experience, such as formatting a memory card, adjusting the time, or checking your battery; the Network menu, used to connect your camera to smart devices and computers; and the My Menu system, which can help you set up a customized menu that contains only the entries you want, or your most recently accessed entries.

Setup Menu Options

There is a long list of entries in the orange-brown coded Setup menu. The first page of entries is shown in Figure 9.1. All the Setup menu options let you make additional adjustments on how your camera *behaves* before or during your shooting session, as differentiated from the Photo Shooting menu, which adjusts how the pictures are actually taken. Your choices include:

- Format Memory Card
- Language
- Time Zone and Date
- Monitor Brightness
- Monitor Color Balance
- Viewfinder Brightness
- Viewfinder Color Balance
- Viewfinder Display Size (Photo LV)
- Limit Monitor Mode Selection
- Auto Rotate Info Display
- AF Fine-Tuning Options
- Non-CPU Lens Data
- Distance Units (Z9 Only)
- Save Focus Position
- Save Zoom Position (PZ lenses) (Z9 Only)
- Auto Temperature Cutout
- Sensor Shield Behavior at Power Off
- Clean Image Sensor
- Image Dust Off Reference Photo
- Pixel Mapping
- Image Comment
- Copyright Information
- IPTC
- Voice Memo Options
- Camera Sounds
- Silent Mode
- Touch Controls
- HDMI
- USB Connection Priority
- Location Data (Built-in) (Z9)/Location Data (Z8)
- Wireless Remote (WR) Options
- Assign remote (WR) Fn Button
- Conformity Marking
- Battery Info
- USB Power Delivery
- Energy Saving (Photo Mode)
- Slot Empty Release Lock
- Save/Load Menu Settings
- Reset All Settings
- Firmware Version

Format Memory Card

Options: Choose memory card to format

My preference: N/A

I recommend using this menu entry to reformat your memory card after each shoot. Although you can move files from the memory card to your computer, creating a blank card, or delete files using the Playback menu's Delete feature, both of those options can leave behind stray files (such as those that have been marked as Protected). Format removes those files completely and beyond retrieval (unless you use a special utility program) and establishes a spanking-new fresh file system on the card. All the file allocation table (FAT or exFAT) pointers (which tell the camera and your computer's operating system where all the images reside) are reset, efficiently pointing where they are supposed to on a blank card.

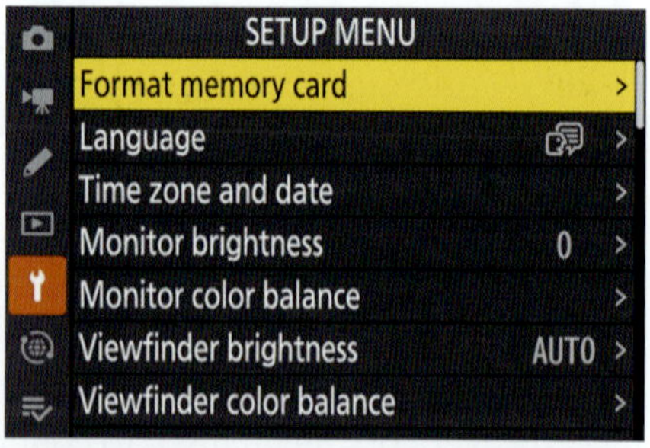

Figure 9.1 The Setup menu allows you to adjust how the camera behaves.

When you access this memory entry, or press the ISO and Trash buttons for more than two seconds, a dialog box will pop up allowing you to select which memory card to format. With compatible CFexpress cards, a dialog asking whether you want a Full Format or Quick Format will display. The latter is fastest and will be fine most of the time. If you feel your memory card has slowed down and it takes longer to read or write to the card, the Full Format option will eliminate any fragmentation and lock out defective sectors. **Note:** Formatting in a computer with the memory card inserted in a card reader *will not* produce the kind of file system your camera can use.

Language

Options: In the Americas: English, Spanish, French, Portuguese

My preference: English, of course, but steadily improving in Spanish

Nikon's thrown us a curveball in the language option department. Instead of the couple dozen languages offered in many previous Nikon cameras, camera bodies sold in North and South America now offer only the official languages commonly used on those continents. The change was either done "for user convenience" (which is rarely true) or to prevent gray market imports from one area of the world to another.

If you'd like to see your menus and prompts in German, Japanese, or some other language, you'll need to buy a camera built for Europe or Asia, respectively. As far as I know, Nikon does not offer the ability to install firmware updates from other areas to a camera intended for a different locale. Fortunately, I haven't heard any reports of anyone trying this and munging their camera. This change won't impact a large number of us, but for expats who want to use their native tongue, it's an inconvenience, at best.

Time Zone and Date

Options: Time Zone, Date and Time, Date Format, Daylight Saving Time (default: Off)

My preference: N/A

Use this menu entry to adjust the internal clock. Your options include:

- **Time Zone.** You can choose your local time zone. I sometimes forget to change the time zone when I travel (especially when going to Europe), so my pictures are all time-stamped incorrectly. I like to use the time stamp to recall exactly when a photo was taken, so keeping this setting correct is important.
- **Date and Time.** Use this setting to enter the exact year, month, day, hour, minute, and second.
- **Date Format.** Choose from Y/M/D (year/month/day), M/D/Y (month/day/year), or D/M/Y (day/month/year) formats.
- **Daylight Saving Time.** Use this to turn daylight saving time On or Off. Because the date on which DST goes into effect each year has been changed from time to time, if you turn this feature on you may need to monitor your camera to make sure DST has been implemented correctly.

Monitor Brightness

Options: Lo 2, Lo 1, –5 to +5 (default: 0), Hi 1, Hi 2

My preference: N/A

Choose this menu option and a screen appears allowing you to specify brightness (see Figure 9.2, left). Use the multi selector up/down keys to adjust the brightness to a comfortable viewing level. Under the lighting conditions that exist when you make this adjustment, you should be able to see all 10 swatches from black to white. If the two left-end swatches blend together, the brightness has been set too low. If the two whitest swatches on the right end of the strip blend together, the brightness is too high. Brighter settings use more battery power but can allow you to view an image on the monitor outdoors in bright sunlight. You can adjust brightness plus/minus 5, with additional Lo 1, Lo 2, Hi 1, and Hi 2 settings available if you happen to need an extremely dim or bright screen.

When you have the brightness you want, press OK to lock it in and return to the menu. Although the Z9/Z8 cameras have great viewfinders, you'll still find yourself using the monitor for both preview and review functions. I often tilt the LCD upward when shooting from low perspectives, so I don't

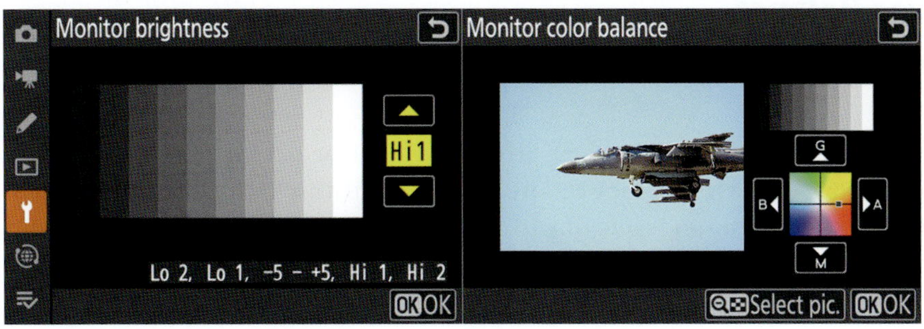

Figure 9.2 Choose to adjust monitor brightness (left) or monitor color balance (right).

have to crouch or kneel or tilt it forward when I am holding the camera overhead for a periscope view. **Note:** This feature cannot be used if Viewfinder Only is selected for monitor mode, or when your eye is placed next to the viewfinder.

Monitor Color Balance

Options: Choose reference picture; Adjust color balance (default: A–B:0, G–M:0)

My preference: N/A

This entry allows you to adjust the color balance of the LCD monitor using an image residing on your memory card as a reference. (See Figure 9.2, right.) By default, the large thumbnail image will be the last photograph taken, or, if you are using Playback mode, the last photograph viewed. You can also press the Zoom Out button to select a different reference image on your memory card from a thumbnail list.

Use the multi selector directional buttons to bias the monitor hue along the blue/amber (left/right buttons) and/or green/magenta (up/down buttons) axes. The grayscale tone strip above helps you judge the neutrality of your selected balance settings. Press OK to confirm your adjustment. Changing the monitor color balance has *no* effect on the color balance of the photos you take, but will affect how you evaluate images, as the colors will be different. **Note:** This feature cannot be used if Viewfinder Only is selected for monitor mode, or when your eye is placed next to the viewfinder.

Viewfinder Brightness

Options: Auto (default); Manual: Lo 2, Lo 1, –5 to +8 (default: 0), Hi 1, Hi 2

My preference: N/A

You can also adjust the brightness for the electronic viewfinder. Unlike the monitor brightness adjustment, the Viewfinder option includes an Auto setting that will modify brightness based on ambient light conditions. In Manual mode, while peering through the viewfinder at the grayscale patches, you can brighten/darken the display using a plus/minus 8 range, plus Lo 2, Lo 1, Hi 1, and Hi 2. Use the multi selector up/down keys to adjust the brightness to a comfortable viewing level. When you have the brightness you want, press OK to lock it in and return to the menu. **Note:** This feature cannot be used if Monitor Only is selected for monitor mode.

Viewfinder Color Balance

Options: Adjust color balance (default: A–B:0, G–M:0)

My preference: N/A

Viewfinder color balance is adjusted using the same procedure described above for Monitor Color Balance, while looking through the viewfinder window. **Note:** This feature cannot be used if Monitor Only is selected for monitor mode, and changing from the default color balance will affect your evaluation of your images.

Viewfinder Display Size (Photo Lv)

Options: Standard (default), Small

My preference: Standard

This is the first entry in the next group of Setup menu options. (See Figure 9.3.) The distance your eye can be from the viewfinder and still see the entire frame is called the *eyepoint*, and is 21mm for the Nikon Z9 and Z8. Most users will be able to view the whole frame comfortably using the Standard setting with the factory eyecup, but may have problems if they wear glasses or use one of those fancy third-party flexible eyecups. You can use this entry to slightly decrease the size of the viewfinder display, which may make it easier to view the corners of the frame.

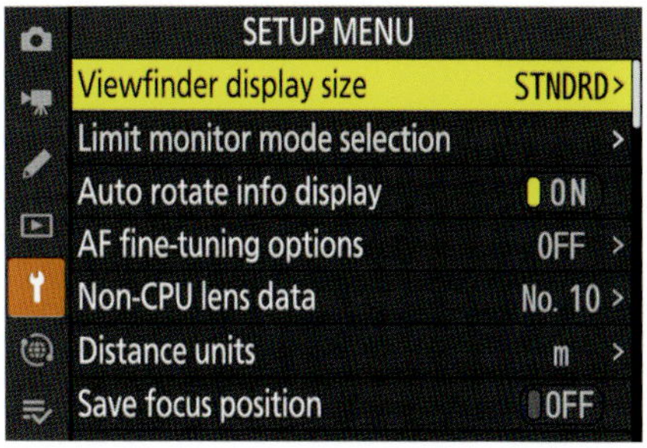

Figure 9.3 The second group of Setup menu options.

I was a sports photographer for many years, and Nikon had a "high eyepoint" sports finder prism replacement for my film cameras that extended the eyepoint to 25mm. Nevertheless, I've spent my whole career shooting without my glasses and relying on the diopter adjustment knob and prefer to stick with that.

Limit Monitor Mode Selection

Options: Automatic Display Switch, Viewfinder Only, Monitor Only, Prioritize Viewfinder 1, Prioritize Viewfinder 2 (default: All enabled)

My preference: Enable All

One of my favorite features is the ability to use the electronic viewfinder for tasks that, on a digital SLR, require looking at the LCD monitor. For example, I can keep the camera up to my eye and make menu adjustments and review images I've shot in Playback mode—even under the brightest daylight conditions.

This menu item lets you choose which monitor viewing modes are available when you press the monitor mode button (located on the left side of the camera's "pentaprism" hump). Pressing the button repeatedly cycles among the options you've enabled. At least one *must* be enabled (you cannot disable all of them). Your options are as follows:

- **Automatic Display Switch.** The active display always switches from the monitor to the viewfinder when you place your eye up to the viewfinder (or when anything else comes in proximity to the sensor located above the viewfinder window). When you remove your eye from the EVF, the display switches to the LCD monitor. This is often the most convenient mode. However, you may encounter unwanted switching if something other than your eye comes within roughly two inches of the viewfinder sensor. For example, if you've swiveled the monitor and are using the touch screen, a finger may switch the display. Artifacts on the eye sensor, including dirt and moisture, and swiveling the display can disable monitor switching.

- **Viewfinder Only.** The monitor is disabled, and the viewfinder is used exclusively for shooting, navigating menus, or image playback. This is my preferred mode in dark venues—especially concerts—where an illuminated LCD can distract or annoy others. I can access most camera features with the menus and viewfinder, so, for example, I don't need to fumble with my fingers to locate the ISO or Exposure Compensation direct-access buttons. I also use Viewfinder Only outdoors when the monitor washes out or is difficult to view.
- **Monitor Only.** The viewfinder is disabled, and display is directed to the LCD monitor only. This is my choice when I'm composing and shooting using the monitor—say, for macro photography or other scenes shot with the camera at waist level or lower or mounted on a tripod. I don't want the eye sensor to switch to the EVF as I work, so I switch to the Monitor Only setting.
- **Prioritize Viewfinder 1/2.** With these options, when you're shooting pictures, the display is directed to the viewfinder exclusively; it turns on when you move your eye to the EVF and turns off when you remove your eye. Versions 1 and 2 behave slightly differently:
    - **Prioritize Viewfinder 1.** The viewfinder is active only when your eye is up to the viewfinder. You can toggle the rear LCD on or off by pressing the MENU or Playback buttons.
    - **Prioritize Viewfinder 2.** The viewfinder is active when your eye is detected at the viewfinder. In addition, the viewfinder will become active for a few seconds when the camera is first turned on, when the shutter release is pressed halfway, or when the AF-ON button is pressed. It will turn off again after a few seconds if your eye is not at the viewfinder. You can toggle the rear LCD on or off by pressing the MENU or Playback buttons.

  The two Prioritize modes save more than a little power, especially if there are intervals when you are not taking photos at all, but don't want to turn off the camera. (The image sensor and the electronic viewfinder can always be active when the camera is powered up, in contrast to digital SLRs that are, effectively, in a low-power mode until you start using the exposure meters, autofocus mechanism, or LCD monitor.)

  When you're reviewing images in Playback mode, while capturing movies, or when menus are displayed, the monitor *will* turn on when you remove your eye from the viewfinder.

Auto Rotate Information Display

Options: On (default), Off

My preference: On

Your camera's viewfinder and rear LCD shooting displays can rotate 90 degrees automatically when you change from a landscape to a portrait shooting stance. All the indicators and text labels will rotate, too, making it easier to view your readouts. This is an especially cool tool for owners of the Z9, which has a built-in vertical grip, and for Z8 users who have the MB-N12 vertical grip, as your shooting display will shift as you change the orientation of the camera and your hands. Unfortunately, only the shooting displays (including the *i* menu) rotate. The conventional menus remain in their fixed landscape mode.

AF Fine-Tuning Options

Options: AF Fine-Tune On/Off (default: Off), Fine-tune and Save Lens, Default, List Saved Values, Choose Value for Current Lens

My preference: N/A

Troubled by lenses that don't focus exactly where they should, producing back-focus or front-focus problems? If your problems are *consistent* and not periodic, there is no need to send your lens and/or camera into Nikon for servicing. The camera allows you to fine-tune focus for up to 40 different lenses and adjust focus for both wide and telephoto ends of the zoom range for zoom lenses. Best of all, it works perfectly with both Z-mount and F-mount lenses (using an FTZ adapter).

You may never need to use this feature, particularly with Z-mount S-series lenses, which use fast stepper motors that are extremely accurate. However, if you are working with older F-mount lenses and an FTZ adapter, slight focus errors are more common, often stemming from sensor/mount alignment variations.

To fine-tune your lenses, first perform some tests to see just how much fine-tuning is required, using one of the many available third-party alignment charts. The only problem I've run into is that with some lenses, particularly short focal length lenses, using large negative values (0 to –20) to move the focal point closer to the camera sometimes results in being unable to focus to infinity. If you run into that, you may be better off sending the lens to Nikon so they can recalibrate the focus for you. As you commence the tuning process, the camera will automatically recognize any CPU-equipped Nikon lens, both F-mount and Z-mount, and report the serial number of the Z lens. It may or may not be able to identify non-Nikon lenses, and I recommend using the third-party vendor's focus adjustment system (using their proprietary USB dock) to make changes.

This menu option has five choices, shown at upper left in Figure 9.4:

- **AF Fine-Tune (On/Off).** Enable/disable application of your AF fine-tuning changes.
- **Fine-tune and Save Lens.** View or enter an adjustment for the lens currently mounted on your camera. You can select values from 0 to +20 to move the focal point farther from the lens, and 0 to –20 to move the focal point closer to the sensor. If a zoom lens is mounted, you can set a value for both the wide-angle and tele ends of its range. (See Figure 9.4, upper right.) Both the original values and new settings are shown, so you can quickly return to the default if you want.

  Press OK to save your new values. You can elect to overwrite the value already in place for the lens, or save your settings under a new name, as shown in Figure 9.4, center left and right. Although the settings are called "Lens Number," you can actually apply a more detailed alphanumeric description.
- **Default.** Set the default value to be applied to lenses that haven't been recalibrated. You'd use this if your camera has a certain amount of front- or back-focus problems with *all* lenses. Use with caution, as it affects every CPU lens that you use.

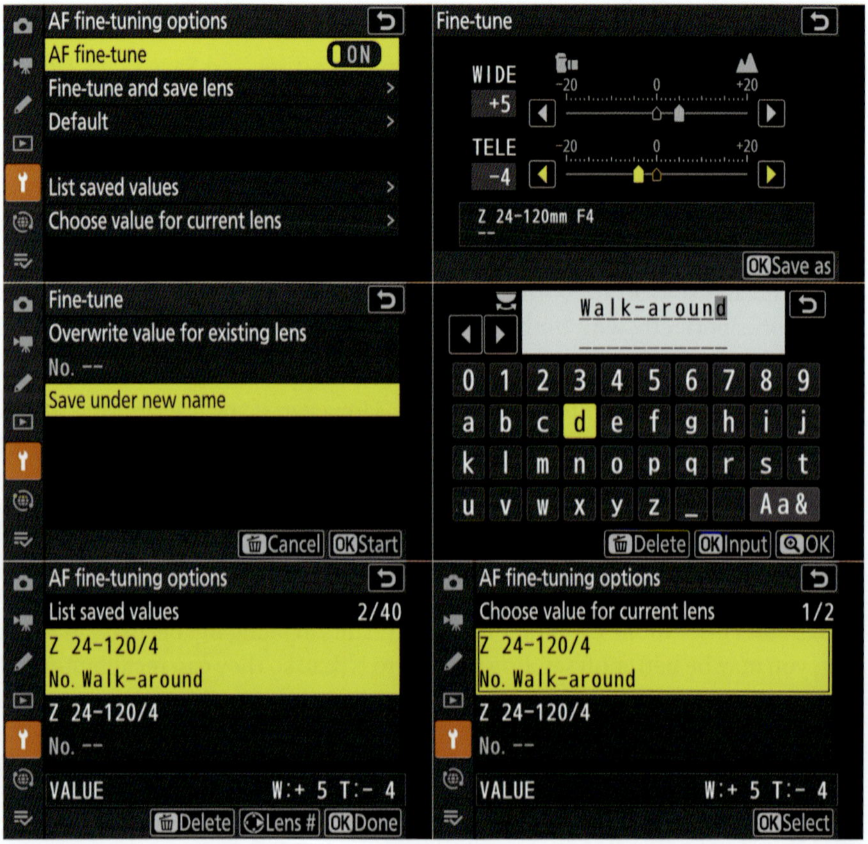

Figure 9.4 The autofocus of lenses can be adjusted here.

- **List Saved Values.** View, label, and delete tuning values you've saved. (See Figure 9.4, lower left.) Highlight a value and press the right directional button to view more information (including the serial number of a Z-mount lens), and press the right button a second time if you want to rename the setting. You can delete a value by highlighting it and pressing the Trash button.
- **Choose Value for Current Lens.** If more than one value setting is available for a current lens you can choose which to apply. (See Figure 9.4, lower right.)

Non-CPU Lens Data

Options: Lens Number, Focal Length (mm), Maximum Aperture, Lens Name

My preference: N/A

This is an odd entry, as it contributes absolutely nothing to the operation of your camera, other than enabling it to embed the focal length and maximum aperture available of some older manual focus lenses in the EXIF data embedded in your image file. I use this option more than most, because I own some 15 older manual focus lenses I picked up in the '60s and early '70s and still use for their unique characteristics. (My old Nikkor-P 105mm f/2.5 looks really cool on a Nikon Df or Zf.)

One of the best accessories is an FTZ adapter, which makes it easy to mount Nikon F-mount lenses to the camera. It gives you four types of functionality in PSAM modes:

- **AF-S, AF-P, and AF-I lenses, plus AF-S/AF-I teleconverters.** These retain all their features, including autofocus and autoexposure.
- **AF and AF-D lenses.** You must focus these optics manually, but with AF-D lenses the electronic rangefinder will assist in determining correct focus. Peaking Highlights (described in Chapter 12) works with either type. You can adjust the aperture electronically and use Aperture-priority autoexposure.
- **AI-P and all lenses with a CPU chip.** You get manual focus only (with Peaking Highlights) and Aperture-priority exposure.
- **AI, AI-S, and Series-E lenses.** These lenses offer manual focus and manual exposure only, but you can still use this menu entry to specify the maximum aperture and focal length of the lens (zoom focal length ranges are not supported). That information will be included in the EXIF metadata but *not* the actual aperture used to take the photo. You may also be able to mount and use non-AI F-mount lenses (pre-1977) but may have mechanical interference problems.

For AI, AI-S, and Series-E lenses, you'll need to specify lens focal length data and maximum aperture. The camera allows defining up to 20 different lenses, and you can choose any of them with a quick trip to this menu entry (or to the equivalent menu item in My Menu, described later in this chapter), or using a button defined for this feature, as described for Custom Setting f2 in Chapter 7.

To enter this information, follow these steps. Note that you can configure the lens's information even if the lens is not mounted on the camera. (The camera has no way of knowing which of these lenses are attached.)

1. Choose Non-CPU lens data from the Setup menu.
2. Highlight Lens Number and press the multi selector left/right buttons to choose a number. If you are defining several lenses, I recommend numbering them in order of increasing focal length, or, if you prefer, in order of frequency of use.
3. Scroll down to Focal Length (mm) and use the multi selector left/right buttons to choose a focal length between 0.1mm and 9000mm.
4. Scroll down to Maximum Aperture and use the multi selector left/right buttons to choose a maximum f/stop.
5. Scroll to Lens Name and select an alphanumeric label of your choice.
6. Choose Done. You can now select a registered lens number from this menu entry, or by choosing the lens number with a button you define for the function.

Distance Units

Options: Meters, Feet (default)

My preference: N/A

This entry defines the distance units (meters or feet) used by the camera for certain distance display functions, including the focus distance indicator for manual focus. However, the Photo Shooting Menu > Auto Capture > Advanced > Distance parameter's Near and Far displays are shown in meters only.

Save Focus Position

Options: On, Off (default)

My preference: Off

The current focus point position is, by default, not a "sticky" setting. That is, when you turn the camera off, the user-specified placement of the focus point within the frame is discarded and returns to the default location when the camera is powered up again. That can be inconvenient if you're shooting the same or similar subject matter over and over, particularly if the camera is mounted on a tripod. It's common to turn the camera off if you won't be taking any photos for several minutes, for example, when you're photographing wildlife and have the focus point centered, say, over a bird's nest in a nearby tree. Activate this feature and you can turn the camera off to save battery power as needed and have the selected focus point restored when you turn the camera on again. If some conditions change, such as zoom setting, the focus point may be different when the camera is powered up again.

Save Zoom Position (PZ Lenses)

Options: On, Off (default)

My preference: N/A

This is the first entry in the next group of Setup menu options. (See Figure 9.5.) As you learned in Chapter 7, Custom Settings f12 and g9 allow choosing to use the Zoom In and Zoom Out buttons to control a Nikon lens equipped with power zoom. Other buttons can be defined instead using Custom Setting f2 and g2.

This entry tells the camera whether the current zoom position is saved when the camera is turned off, and then restored when powered up again.

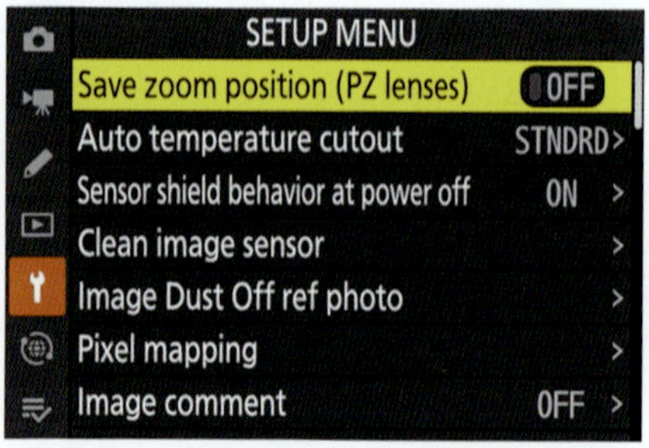

Figure 9.5 The next group of Setup menu entries.

Auto Temperature Cutout

Options: Standard (default), High

My preference: Standard

This entry helps you manage your camera's behavior as it begins to heat up during heavy use. Mirrorless cameras like the Nikon Z9 and Z8 tend to run quite a bit hotter than your grandfather's dSLR, generally because their image sensors are energized continually as you make settings and preview your image on the display. The viewfinder and rear LCD themselves produce additional heat, and some activities, particularly 4K or 8K video captured at higher frame rates generate even higher temperatures. Ambient temperature needs to be taken into account, too, even if you're not shooting in Death Valley.

To avoid damaging the sensor and other components (including your fingers), the camera will turn off automatically when its internal temperature rises beyond recommended levels. High temperatures tend to increase visual noise, too, so you have an additional reason for avoiding running hot. You have your choice of two settings:

- **Standard.** At this default setting, you'll get plenty of warning when the Z9/Z8 reaches significant heat thresholds. A thermometer icon appears on the display, followed by a more urgent warning with an exclamation point, and then a count-down timer indicating when the camera will shut off.
- **High.** This setting gives you an additional amount of time, adding a HIGH thermometer before the countdown begins. Be aware that the camera can become hot to the touch; if you're shooting video it's likely that the Z9/Z8 will be mounted on a tripod. That's a good thing, as long as you know that touching the camera body can be painful or dangerous.

Sensor Shield Behavior at Power Off

Options: Sensor shield closes, Sensor shield stays open (default)

My preference: Sensor shield closes

Your camera's all-electronic shutter has made an additional feature possible: better protection for your sensor. Traditional shutters must be kept light in weight to allow their rapid and precise motion. While many mirrorless cameras have provided an option for closing the shutter when the camera is powered down, the shutter itself really didn't provide much protection against dust or even slight physical contact. Worse, there was nothing to protect the shutter itself, and replacing the mechanism could be costly.

Since your Z9/Z8 has no physical shutter, Nikon has included a more rugged apparatus in the form of a shutter-like sensor shield. This entry lets you specify whether to have the shield descend to cover the sensor when the camera is powered down, or to remain open. I prefer to have it closed, particularly when changing lenses, and leave it open only to clean the sensor.

Clean Image Sensor

Options: Start; Automatic Cleaning: Clean at Shutdown (default), Cleaning Off

My preference: Automatic Cleaning (Clean at Shutdown)

This entry gives you some control over the automatic sensor cleaning feature, which removes dust through a vibration cycle that shakes the sensor until dust, presumably, falls off. If you happen to take a picture and notice an artifact in an area that contains little detail (such as the sky or a blank wall), you can access this menu choice, place the camera with its base downward, and choose Clean Now. A Cleaning Sensor message now appears, and the dust you noticed has probably been shaken off.

You can also tell the camera when you'd like it to perform automatic cleaning without specific instructions from you. Select from:

- **Clean Now.** Triggers the dust-shaking cycle immediately. For best results, remove the lens and point the camera downward so the dust can fall outside the camera body.
- **Automatic Cleaning: Clean at Shutdown.** This removes any dust that may have accumulated since the camera has been turned on, say, from dust infiltration while changing lenses.
- **Automatic Cleaning: Cleaning Off.** No automatic dust removal will be performed. Use this to preserve battery power, or if you prefer to use automatic dust removal only when you explicitly want to apply it.

Image Dust Off Ref Photo

Options: Start, Clean Sensor and Then Start

My preference: N/A

This menu choice lets you "take a picture" of any dust or other particles that may be adhering to your sensor. The camera will then append information about the location of this dust to your photos, so that the Image Dust Off option in NX Studio can be used to mask the dust in the RAW image.

To use this feature, select Image Dust Off Ref Photo, choose either Start or Clean Sensor and Then Start, and then press OK. If directed to do so, the camera will first perform a self-cleaning operation by applying ultrasonic vibration to the top layer of the sensor. I recommend doing this—you might as well capture your reference photo with a sensor that is as clean as possible. However, the new reference data you capture cannot be used to correct images taken before your most recent cleaning.

A screen will appear asking you to take a photo of a bright featureless white object 10cm (about four inches) from the lens. Nikon recommends using a lens with a focal length of at least 50mm. If you're using a zoom lens, zoom to the longest focal length. If autofocus is enabled, focus will be set to infinity automatically; you should manually focus to infinity if AF is not active. Note that the dust-off information can be applied to *all* your images, not just those taken with the lens used to capture the reference photo.

Point the camera at a solid-white card and press the shutter release. If the reference object is too dark or light, you may be asked to try again with a different object. An image with the extension .ndf will be created and can be used by Nikon NX Studio as a reference photo if the "dust-off" picture is placed in the same folder as an image to be processed for dust removal.

Pixel Mapping

Options: Start

My preference: N/A

Even with the most sophisticated manufacturing techniques and quality control measures, producing a sensor with absolutely no defects among 50 million individual photosites is quite a challenge. Sometimes a pixel "dies" and becomes permanently dark or, worse, becomes stuck or "hot" so that it will be displayed as a bright spot in areas that should be dark or even black. Pixel mapping provides a way to detect those defective pixels and automatically map them, so they no longer contribute to your images. Instead, information from surrounding pixels will be used to determine how that photosite appears in your image.

If you notice what appears to be a bad pixel, compare several different shots to see if it appears in the same place. Keep in mind that some "bad" pixels can be caused by overheating and will return to normal once your camera has been powered down for a short period. If you need to permanently correct for a bad pixel, just follow these steps:

1. Select Pixel Mapping from the Setup menu. This entry may not be available if the camera is already overheated or its battery is not fully charged.
2. Press the right directional button and choose Start.
3. The control panel will display a buSY message. Do not operate the camera, turn it off, or disconnect from external power while pixel mapping is underway!
4. When the operation is complete, turn off the camera.

Image Comment

Options: Attach Comment, Input Comment

My preference: N/A

The Image Comment is your opportunity to add a copyright notice, personal information about yourself (including contact info), or even a description of where the image was taken (e.g., Browns Super Bowl 2025), although text entry is a bit too clumsy (even when using the touch screen) for doing a lot of individual annotation of your photos. (But you still might want to change the comment each time, say, you change cities during your travels.) The embedded comments can be read by many software programs, including Nikon NX Studio.

The standard text-entry screen can be used to enter your comment, with up to 36 characters available. For the copyright symbol, embed a lowercase "c" within opening and closing parentheses: (c). You can input the comment, turn attachment of the comment On or Off using the Attach Comment entry, and press the Zoom In button or tap OK on the LCD monitor when you're finished working with comments. If your fingers are too fat for typing on the touch screen or you find typing with a cursor too tedious, you can enter your comment in Nikon NX Studio and upload it to the camera through a USB cable.

Copyright Information

Options: Attach Copyright Information, Artist, Copyright

My preference: N/A

This is the first entry within the next group of Setup menu options. (See Figure 9.6.) This is an expansion of the Image Comment capability, allowing you to specify the name of the "artist" (photographer), and enter copyright information. Use the standard Nikon text-entry screen described earlier. Highlight the Attach Copyright Information option and press the right multi selector button, which toggles it On or Off to control whether your copyright data is embedded in each photo as taken. The touch screen comes in useful for this input, as well.

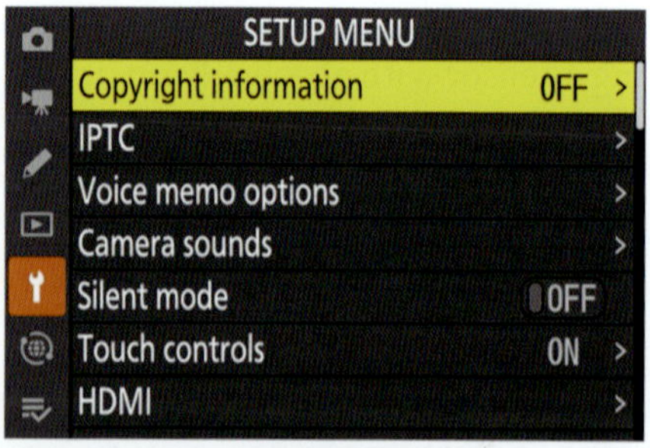

Figure 9.6 More Setup menu entries.

IPTC

Options: Edit/Save, Delete, Auto Embed During Shooting, Load/Save

My preference: N/A

Photojournalists, especially, will want to create IPTC (International Press Telecommunications Council) entries, a standardized metadata format that can be embedded in each image you take automatically. You can include caption, event ID, headline, object name, city, state, country, category, supplemental categories, byline, byline title, writer/editor, credit, and source for each available slot. The information from a given slot can be copied to your memory card, and you can select one of the listings to be automatically embedded into your image files during a particular shoot. Many major publications and news agencies require including IPTC data with submissions, so you should become familiar with the process.

You can create your IPTC entries ahead of time, or on the fly as you begin your shoot. The data can be added directly from your camera's text-entry screens (which can be tedious even with a touch screen), or typed up on your computer. Nikon's NX Mobile Air software for iOS and Android can speed things up by filling in IPTC fields using your device's voice-to-text capabilities. The app also allows you to add voice memos. Creating an IPTC data set ahead of time is often your best option. Nikon offers a free downloadable Windows/macOS program IPTC Preset Manager.

When you access this entry in the camera, you'll first see a screen similar to the one shown in Figure 9.7, upper left, with options for editing/saving IPTC data, deleting existing data sets, enabling/disabling automatic embedding of IPTC data as you shoot, and loading/saving data with a memory card. There are ten slots available, numbered IPTC-P-1 to IPTC-P-10. (See Figure 9.7, upper right.) Select a slot, and a scrollable list of available fields appears (Figure 9.7, lower left and right). You can enter the information using the standard Z9/Z8 text-entry screen, and then save it on your memory card.

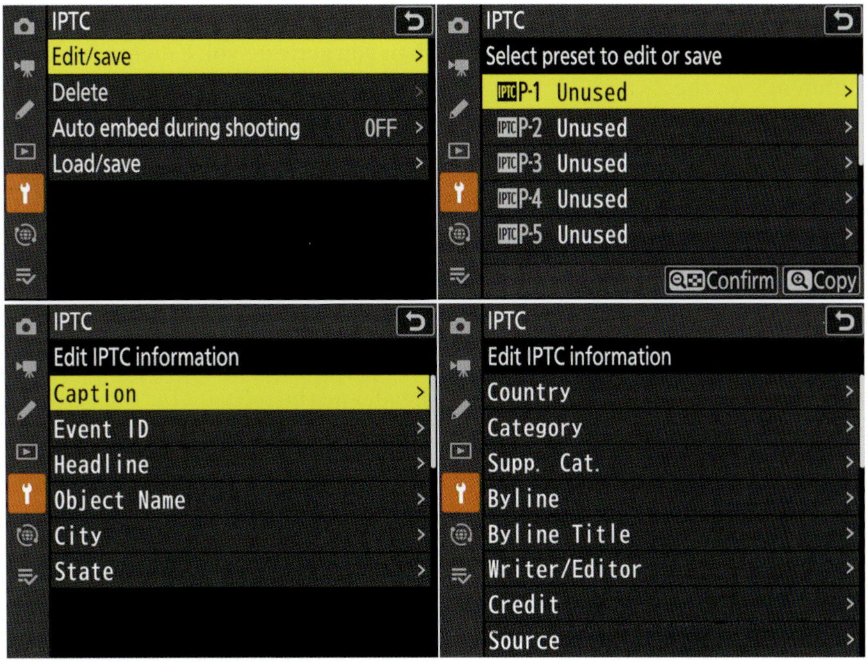

Figure 9.7 Adding IPTC data sets to your images' EXIF metadata.

The Caption field can contain up to 2,000 characters, Event ID can have 64 characters. The other eleven fields have a maximum length of 256 characters.

To embed one of the ten entries in each image's EXIF metadata, choose, Auto Embed During Shooting and select the entry you want to apply. All the data fields you have populated will be added, along with copyright information you may have specified as described above.

Voice Memo Options

Options: Voice memo control, Audio output (playback)

My preference: N/A

Voice memos are an annotation feature. You can use it to optionally accompany each image you shoot with a voice recording of up to 60 seconds in length, which is stored as a separate WAV (waveform audio file format) file on your memory card. The memo will have the same name (other than extension) as the image file, and, if you have a memory card inserted in both slots, will always be recorded to the card in the primary slot, or, if Overflow is active, the WAV file will be recorded on the memory card where the original image is stored.

Before you start recording voice memos, you'll want to set up the available options.

Voice Memo Control

This setting determines what happens when you activate voice memo recording. The feature works differently on the Z9 and Z8:

- **Z9.** To begin a voice memo, in Playback mode with the image you want to annotate visible, press the Voice Memo button located on the lower-left edge of the back of the Z9. (You can also record a voice memo using the *i* menu, as described next.)
- **Z8.** To record a voice memo, press Playback and view the image to be annotated. Then press the *i* button and select Record Voice Memo. Then press OK to begin recording.

This sub-entry lets you specify how the voice recording is ended. If you choose Press and Hold, the Voice Memo button (Z9) or OK button (Z8) must be held down; recording ceases when the button is released. Select Press to Start/Stop instead, and the relevant button can be pressed once to begin and a second time to stop recording.

Once recording has commenced, you can speak for up to 60 seconds. A microphone icon appears in the display as an indicator. Only one memo is allowed per image; if a picture already has a voice memo, it must be deleted before a new one can be recorded.

Audio Output (Playback)

This choice routes the audio output, enabling you to play back your voice memos using the speaker on the camera (located just under the viewfinder window on the Z9 and on the top-right panel of the Z8), or to the HDMI or audio-video output ports:

- **Speaker/headphones.** If you choose this option, you can use the up/down multi selector directional buttons to increase or decrease the playback volume.
- **HDMI/audio-video output.** Select this choice if you've connected your camera to an HDTV through the HDMI port, or to a monitor using the video port. The sound will be played back through the external device's speakers.
- **Off.** Voice memos are not played back at all.

Basic voice memo recording is fairly easy. You cannot add memos to video clips or Image Dust Off exposures. Once you've set up all the options, including enabling the feature and choosing maximum recording length, the basic steps are these:

- **Interrupt a recording.** Don't worry about missing a shot if an opportunity comes up while you're recording a voice memo. Pressing the shutter release halfway ends a recording automatically. So does pressing the MENU button, Playback button, or turning the camera off.
- **Play back a memo.** Review the image in playback mode, either as a full-frame image or a highlighted thumbnail. Images with voice memos available have a musical note icon superimposed in the upper-right corner of the full-frame image. Press the Voice Memo button to start playback (on the Z9) or, with the Z8, press the *i* menu button and choose Play Voice Memo. Playback will stop when the entire voice memo has been played or the Voice Memo button is pressed a second time.

- **Delete a memo.** Press the Trash button. A screen will pop up offering the choice of deleting both the image and sound recording, or of deleting only the sound. Use the up/down buttons to choose, then press the Trash button a second time to delete. Press the Play button to exit without deleting either.

Camera Sounds

Options: Shutter: Shutter Sound, Volume, Type; Beep: On/Off, Volume, Pitch

My preference: Shutter and Beep Off

Thanks to its electronic shutter, your Z9 and Z8 can be a remarkably silent beast. Those of us who shoot concerts, events, street work, or stealth photography like to keep it that way. I'm usually happy monitoring a visual indicator in the viewfinder to remind me (and confirm) that I'm actually taking pictures. However, if you like that reassuring synthetic shutter click or prefer a helpful beep when focus is attained, your camera has a range of options for fine-tuning your audio feedback. When you select this entry, the screen shown in Figure 9.8 appears (Z9 only) with six options controlling both shutter noises and the camera's periodic chirps. The Z8 has only four of these, as described below. These are separate from the camera's Silent mode, discussed shortly.

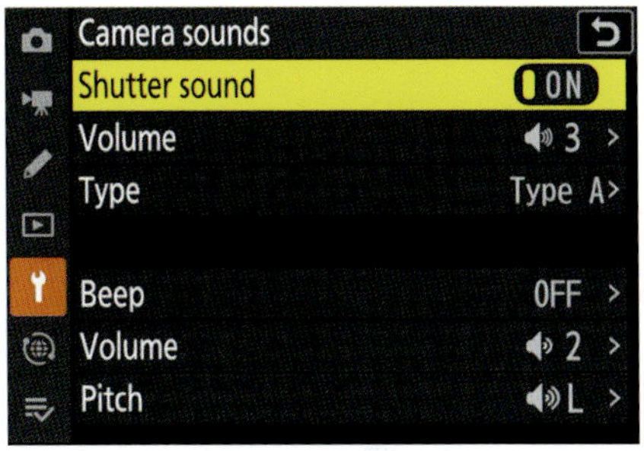

Figure 9.8 Specifying camera sounds.

Shutter Sounds

Z9 owners have three different types of separate control of your shutter sounds:

- **Shutter Sound.** Use this setting to turn shutter sounds on or off.
- **Volume.** The default value is right in the middle at 3, but you can go from soft (1) to loud (5), depending on your needs and the ambient environment.
- **Type.** There are five different types of shutter sounds, labeled Type A to Type E.

Beep Options

The internal beeper provides a (usually) superfluous chirp to signify various functions, such as the countdown of the self-timer, the termination of time-lapse recording, or autofocus confirmation in AF-S mode (unless you've selected release-priority in Custom Setting a2). You can (and probably should) switch it off if you want to avoid the beep because it's annoying, impolite, distracting (at a concert or museum), or undesired for any other reason. Note that the beeper is automatically squelched if you've activated Silent Photography in the Photo Shooting menu.

Choose this menu entry, and select one of the following:

- **Beep On/Off.** Enable or disable the beeper.
- **Volume.** Select values of 1 (soft) through 3 (loud). A quarter-note icon appears in the control panel and the shooting information display.
- **Pitch.** Select High for a high-pitched beep, or Low for a deeper tone.

Silent Mode

Options: On, Off (default)

My preference: Off

This is an additional quiet mode that reduces some sounds even further. It overrides the Camera Sounds options set earlier; when enabled, both the shutter and beep sounds are turned off. The Z9/Z8's built-in speaker is muted, and the camera enters a slightly crippled mode in which your continuous shooting rate may drop, and aperture and focus may be slower as they operate more quietly. Electronic flash is disabled and long exposure noise reduction is turned off. An SL icon appears at the lower left of the display. On mutes the speaker and reduces aperture and focus sounds, reducing performance. You'll still hear a click when the standby timer expires and the sensor vibration reduction locks in its present position.

I rarely have need of totally silent operation (which is virtually impossible to achieve, anyway), so I generally leave this setting turned off.

Touch Controls

Options: Enable (default), Disable, Playback Only, Glove mode

My preference: N/A

This entry allows you to specify when touch controls are available. Your choices include:

- **Enable.** Touch control is available for both menu functions and image review/playback, plus for specifying a focus point and taking a picture using the Touch Shutter/Touch AF feature.
- **Playback Only.** Touch control is not available for navigating menus, but can be used when reviewing images.
- **Disable.** No touch controls are available.
- **Glove mode.** Sensitivity of the touch screen is increased to improve performance when wearing gloves.

HDMI

Options: Output Resolution (default: Auto), Output Range (default: Auto), Output Shooting Information (default: On), Mirror Camera Information Display (default: On)

My preference: N/A

This entry deals with the High-Definition Multimedia Interface (HDMI) video connection. The port allows you to play back your images on HDTV, HD monitors using an HDMI cable, and direct video output to external video recorders, such as the Atomos Ninja V and Ninja Ultra. I use HDMI playback for slide shows, too, and captured most of the screenshot images in this book using the HDMI output and a $25 4K video capture device with OBS (Open Broadcaster Software) Studio. Before you link up your equipment, you'll want to choose from the following options:

- **Output Resolution.** Select Auto and the camera will sense the correct output resolution to use. It will try to determine whether the external device supports the frame size/rate currently enabled in the camera. If not, it will try lower resolutions and slower frame rates. Auto will be applied (even if you select another resolution) when the HDMI port is used to display the image during video capture and video playback. The available resolutions all use progressive scanning; 1080i is not available in Auto mode.

  You can also choose specific resolutions, including 4320p (8K), 2160p (4K), 1080p (Full HD), and 720p (Standard HD). These are all progressive scan. You can also select 1080i if your device accepts only interlaced scanning. However, in that case, footage captured at 120p, 60p, 30p, or 24p are output at 60i, and 100p, 50p, or 25p are output at 50i.

  A couple caveats for advanced videographers: First, 10-bit video is output at 10 bits only to HDMI recorders that support it. In addition, regardless of the resolution you select here, when the Video File Type selected in the Video Recording menu is N-RAW 12-bit (NEV) or ProRes RAW HQ 12-bit (MOV), the output resolution will be 1920 × 1080. Finally, 8K video, or 4K video captured at 120p/100p will not be output at HDMI if there is a memory card in the camera and either 4320p (progressive) or 2160p (progressive) is specified as the Output Resolution.
- **Output Range.** Choose Auto (the default, and the best choice under most circumstances), Limited Range, or Full Range. In most cases, the camera will be able to determine the output range of your HDMI device. If not, you can choose a range:
  - **Limited Range.** This setting uses values of 16 to 235, clipping off the darkest (0–16) and brightest (235–255) portions of the image. Use Limited Range if you're plagued with reduced detail in the shadows of your image.
  - **Full Range.** This may be your choice if shadows are washed out or excessively bright. It accepts video signals with the full range from 0 to 255.
- **Output Shooting Information.** Choose On, and the icons and shooting information shown on the electronic viewfinder or LCD monitor will be included in the output to the external device. Select Off and the information will be stripped out.
- **Mirror Camera Information Display.** When directing output to an external device, you may want to also have it shown on the rear LCD monitor (the default), especially if the external device is a monitor not physically attached to the camera. If you're using a recorder/display mounted on the camera or its cage, you can save some battery power by choosing Off for this item.

Additional HDMI settings are available in the Video Recording menu, described in Chapter 6. They include External Recording Control (HDMI) for devices that support control from the camera.

USB Connection Priority

Options: Upload (default), Shooting

My preference: Upload

This is the first in the next group of Setup menu options. (See Figure 9.9.) This entry determines the mode the Z9/Z8 enters when the camera is connected to a computer over a USB cable. Ostensibly, it seemingly determines whether the rear LCD monitor display is effectively blanked while the camera is connected to a computer with a USB cable. (Tethering software may override this, however.) In practice, this setting can affect upload speeds. With the default Upload setting, the LCD screen displays only a message "The camera is in upload priority mode," and the transfer speed will be optimized. Pressing the shutter release halfway reactivates the screen. If you choose Shooting instead, the LCD display functions normally, but transfer speeds slow down.

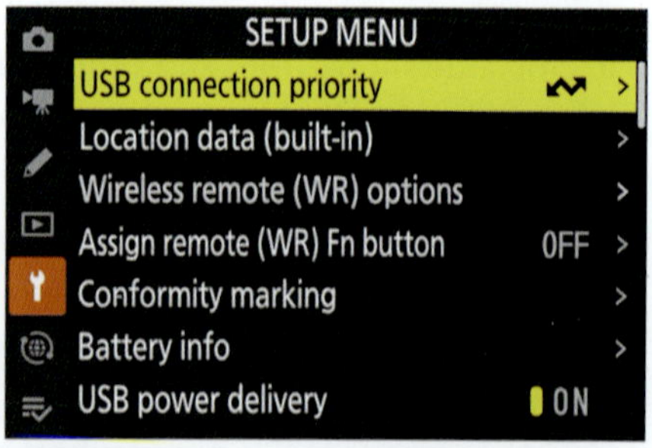

Figure 9.9 The next group of Setup menu entries.

Location Data (Built-in) (Z9)/Location Data (Z8)

Options: Record Location Data (Z9 Only): Off (default), On; Standby Timer: On (default), Off; Set Clock from Satellite: Off (default), On; Create Log (Z9 Only): Off (default), Log Location Data, Log Interval, Log Length; Log List (Z9 Only); Position

My preference: N/A

One significant difference between the Nikon Z9 and Z8 is that the Z9, unlike the Z8, has a built-in GNSS (Global Navigation Satellite System) receiver, more commonly known as GPS, and can embed location information within the camera's EXIF metadata. That doesn't mean that Z8 owners are left out in the cold; their cameras can collect GPS information from a smartphone though a SnapBridge connection or, preferably from an external GPS receiver connected to the Z8 through the 10-pin port on the front. Indeed, I have successfully used Nikon's own GP-1a unit, which the company has unfortunately discontinued. There are also third-party units available, including the Downtech Eco ProFessional, which attaches to the front of the camera and has a 10-pin pass-through terminal so you can still connect the Nikon MC-30a remote trigger release. The Micnova GPS-N clips onto the Z8's accessory shoe and connects to the camera with a 10-pin cable.

This menu entry is always visible in the Z9's Setup menu, but appears on the Z8 only when connected to a GPS receiver. Figure 9.10, left, shows the Z9 version; the Z8 lacks the Record Location Data, Create Log, and Log List entries. When GPS is active, it will be stored within each still photo, but only the initial position of video clips is included.

Your options include:

- **Record Location Data (Z9 Only).** Since the Z9's receiver is built in, you'll need to use this option to turn it On to capture GPS data, or, to save power, Off.
- **Standby Timer.** The GPS system drains the battery somewhat, and this option lets you specify whether it is active all the time, or whether GPS shuts down when the Standby Timer expires. Here are your choices:
    - **On.** The GPS receiver is active anytime the camera is active, until the Standby Timer runs out. Then the GPS will stop collecting data. That saves battery power, but the GPS may need to reacquire satellites when you resume using the camera. That takes time, and you may end up taking photos with no accurate GPS data captured and recorded.
    - **Off.** The camera continuously tries to capture GPS data, even after the Standby Timer expires. Over the course of a long shooting session the power usage can be significant. The plus side is that the GPS can effectively remain active and ready to go.
- **Set Clock From Satellite.** Choose On to allow the camera to update its internal clock from information provided by the GPS device when attached. Off disables this updating feature. You might want to avoid updating the clock if you're traveling and want all the basic date/time information embedded in your image files to reflect the settings back home, rather than the date and time where your pictures are taken. However, this can cause some problems. Even if you choose to not update your camera's clock, if the GPS device is active when shooting, the local date and time will be embedded in the GPS portion of the EXIF data, not the camera's Date and Time setting. It's usually a better idea to sync your camera's clock with the GPS time.

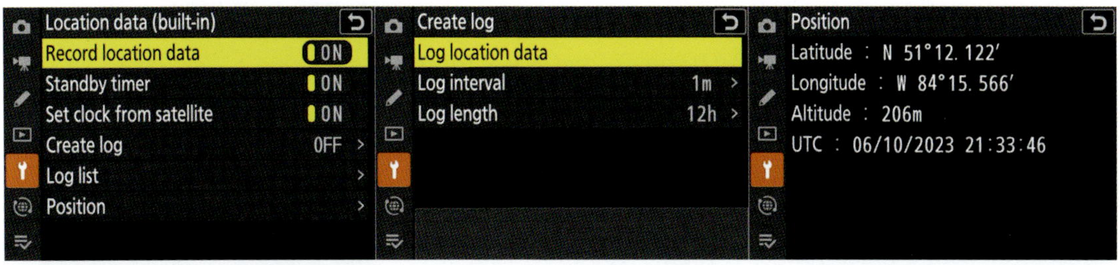

Figure 9.10 Location Data options (left); Creating a log (center); Position data (right).

- **Create Log (Z9 Only).** Although GPS data will be embedded in each image while the receiver is active and connected, you might want to create a log during a trip. You can specify the interval between each recorded position, with 15 and 30 seconds and 1-, 2-, or 5-minute spacing available. The Log Length determines how long the camera records your travels. You can select from 6, 12, or 24 hours, but can close a log earlier if you want. The camera continues to record data even when the camera is powered down and connected to satellites. (See Figure 9.10, center.) A Log in Progress and Time Remaining indicator appears on Location Data display when recording. All saved logs are stored in NMEA (National Marine Electronics Association) format, which can be read by a number of different applications. The file name begins with N, includes the year, month, day, and log number (Nyymmddx), with a .log extension in the DCIM > NIKON > GNSS folder on the card.
- **Log List (Z9 Only).** This shows a list of data recorded and saved on your current memory card.
- **Position.** This is an information display, rather than a selectable option. It appears when the GPS is connected and receiving satellite positioning data. It shows the latitude, longitude, altitude, and Coordinated Universal Time (UTC) values. (See Figure 9.10, right.)

Wireless Remote (WR) Options

Options: LED Lamp: On (default), Off; Link Mode: Pairing (default), PIN
My preference: N/A

This option, which is grayed out unless the WR-R10 or WR-R11a transmitter is plugged into the 10-pin port on the camera, allows you to make several settings for the Nikon WR-10/11a radio remote control. The system consists of the WR-R10/R11a receiver, shown at top in Figure 9.11, which is attached to the camera, and the WR-T10 transmitter (see Figure 9.11, bottom). The set, which allows triggering cameras and compatible electronic flash units (such as the SB-5000), has a practical range of about 66 feet, and costs about $200. (If you use one WR-R10/11a receiver as an intermediate master and a second on the camera, range extends to 164 feet.) A single transmitter can be used to control multiple cameras that have a receiver installed.

The system is also compatible with the WR-1, a sophisticated transceiver with a much longer (roughly 400 foot) range, 15 channels, and additional features such as more sophisticated camera group controls (to fire multiple cameras simultaneously). It also costs a great deal more, at around $470.

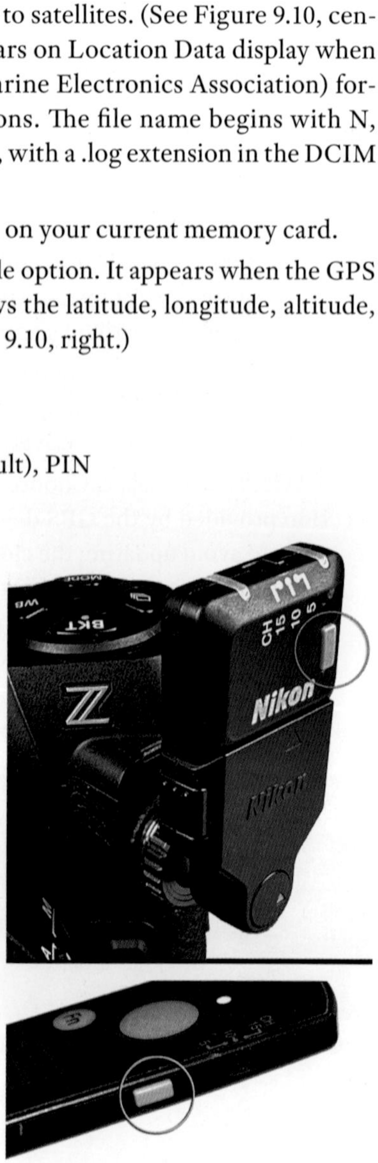

Figure 9.11 Press the Pairing buttons on the WR-R10/11a receiver (top) and WR-T10 transmitter (bottom) simultaneously.

TIP While useful as a remote control, my favorite feature of the WR-10 radio control system is the ability to use the transmitter's function button to activate some other feature, such as autoexposure/autofocus lock. I'll explain those options in the next section.

To use the WR-R10/WR-11a, insert the receiver into the 10-pin port on the front of the camera. Make sure the transmitter and receiver are using the same channel (15, 10, or 5), and then pair them by pressing the gray pairing buttons indicated by green circles in Figure 9.11, simultaneously. The LEDs on top of the receiver will alternate red and green to show that pairing has taken place; thereafter, the receiver's green LED will flash to indicate there is a connection. **Note:** If you have the older WR-R10, make sure its firmware is at least version 3.00. It is displayed in the Setup > Firmware entry (prefixed with a W) when attached to the camera. If you have the older firmware, you'll have to send your WR-R10 to Nikon for the update.

This menu entry has two options, which most camera owners may never need to use:

- **LED Lamp.** You can enable or disable this lamp. I sometimes turn the blinking lamp off when I am working in dark environments and don't want to distract others around me—or make them aware that I am taking stealth photos with a remote control. Disabling the LEDs also saves power, but you'll have no operational feedback when they're off.
- **Link Mode.** You can choose whether the transmitter and receiver are linked using pairing (the usual procedure) or through a PIN, which is possible when working with the Nikon SB-5000 flash (or any radio-controlled flash Nikon may introduce after this book is written). If you're using the WR-1 transceiver, you must use pairing as the link mode. Your choices:
  - **Pairing.** The camera will link only to devices *it has already been paired with.* That's good news, because it means you don't have to worry about signal interference with other nearby devices, which can happen at sporting events.
  - **PIN.** This is a better choice when more devices are involved. You can choose your own four-digit PIN and link, say, several flashes that share that PIN. It's easier to ensure that you and other photographers in the vicinity are using different PINS.

Assign Remote (WR) Fn Button

Options: AF-ON, AF Lock Only, AE Lock (Reset on Release), AE Lock Only, AE/AF Lock, FV Lock, Flash Disable/Enable, Switch FX/DX, Photo Flicker Reduction, Preview, Recall Shooting Functions, High Frequency Flicker Reduction, + RAW, View Mode (Photo Lv), None (default)

My preference: AF-ON

Radio remote control is cool, but I *really* like the WR-10 system's ability to trigger any of nine different features, using the transmitter's Fn button. I most often use the button to start autofocus using the AF-ON behavior. You might love the ability to tell the camera to add a RAW picture to the JPEG image you've specified for that one picture, then switch back to JPEG-only mode.

Select Assign Remote (WR) Fn button, and then choose from: AF-ON, AF Lock Only, AE Lock (Reset on Release), AE Lock Only, AE/AF Lock, FV Lock, Flash Disable/Enable, Switch FX/DX, Photo Flicker Reduction, Preview, Recall Shooting Functions, High Frequency Flicker Reduction, + RAW, View Mode (Photo Lv), None (default).

Conformity Marking

Options: Display only. No selections.

My preference: N/A

This entry does nothing but display the various international standards with which the camera complies. It's included here because Nikon can easily update the listing during a firmware upgrade. The alternative might be to print new labels (like the one with the serial number of the camera located behind the tilting LCD monitor on the camera) each time a change is made.

Battery Info

Options: None. This screen is purely informational.

My preference: N/A

When invoked, you can see the following information (if the MB-N12 is mounted and contains two batteries, the data for both will be displayed):

- **Charge.** The current battery level, shown as a percentage from 100 to 0 percent.
- **No. of shots.** This shows the number of actuations with the current battery since it was last recharged. This number can be larger than the number of photos taken, because other functions, such as white balance presetting, can cause the shutter to be tripped.
- **Battery Age.** Eventually, a battery will no longer accept a charge as well as it did when it was new and must be replaced. This indicator shows when a battery is considered new (0); has begun to degrade slightly (1,2,3); or has reached the end of its charging life and is ready for replacement (4). Batteries charged at temperatures lower than 41 degrees F may display an impaired charging life temporarily, but return to their true "health" when recharged above 68 degrees F.

USB Power Delivery

Options: Enable (default), Disable

My preference: N/A

Allows you to specify whether power supplied by external sources through the USB Type-C port (with the Z9) or the lower USB Type-C Power Delivery port on the Z8 can be used to power the camera, thereby limiting the drain on the camera's battery. A USB Power Delivery icon appears at the left side of the shooting display when the camera is being powered from an external source. A battery must be installed in the camera even if the external power is being used to operate it. Your options are as follows:

- **Enable.** The camera can be operated through a power source connected via the USB port. Power will be drawn *only* while the camera is on, except if a Bluetooth upload is in progress or the camera is storing an image on a memory card when the camera is turned off.
- **Disable.** When power is supplied to the USB port, charging of the battery will take place, but the camera cannot be operated using the external source's juice.

Energy Saving (Photo Mode)

Options: Off (default), On

My preference: N/A

This entry is the first in the last page of the Setup menu. (See Figure 9.12.) It is an additional power-saving option that sets the shooting displays to a slower refresh rate and turns off the display roughly 15 seconds before the Standby Timer that you set using Custom Setting c3: Power Off Delay elapses. This setting is overridden if your Standby Timer has been set for No Limit or a delay of less than 30 seconds. It also does not take effect if the camera is connected to another device using the HDMI port, when attached to an AC adapter or power from the USP Type-C port, or if the camera is connected to a computer and exchanging data.

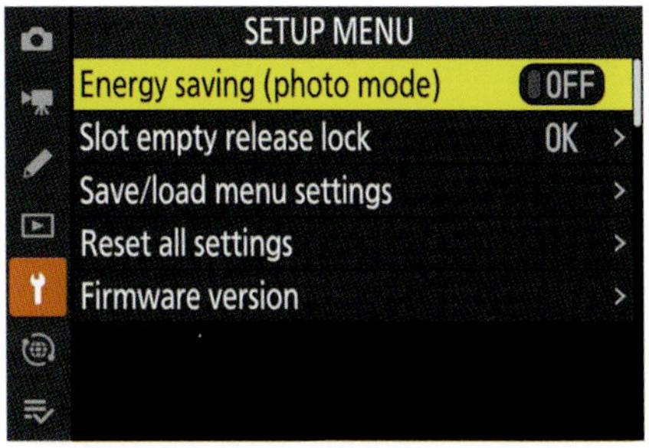

Figure 9.12 The last page of the Setup menu.

When enabled, energy is saved and your battery life is extended, but the display refresh rate may be reduced. Disable this setting, and battery life will not be extended. The display screen may still dim a few seconds before the standby timer expires.

Slot Empty Release Lock

Options: Release Locked (LOCK), Enable Release (OK)(default)

My preference: Release Locked

This option gives you the ability to snap off "pictures" without a memory card installed—or to lock the shutter release if that is the case. It is sometimes called play mode, because you can experiment with your camera's features or even hand your camera to a friend to let them fool around, without any danger of pictures actually being taken.

Back in our film days, we'd sometimes finish a roll, rewind the film back into its cassette surreptitiously, and then hand the camera to a child to take a few pictures—without actually wasting any film. It's hard to waste digital film, but "shoot without card" mode is still appreciated by some, especially camera vendors who want to be able to demo a camera at a store or trade show, but don't want to have to equip each and every demonstrator model with a memory card. Choose Enable Release to activate "play" mode or Release Locked to disable it.

The pictures you actually "take" are displayed on the LCD monitor with the legend "Demo" superimposed on the screen, and they are, of course, not saved. Note that if you are using the optional Camera Control Pro 2 software to record photos from a USB-tethered camera directly to a computer, no memory card is required to unlock the shutter even if Release Locked has been selected.

Save/Load Menu Settings

Options: Save Menu Settings, Load Menu Settings

My preference: N/A

You can store many camera settings to your memory card in a file named NCSETxxx.bin, with the xxx representing the camera model (you can't load settings for your Nikon Z8 into your Nikon Z9, for example). Settings can be reloaded to the same model later using this menu item. This is a good way to archive your favorite camera settings for the Playback menu, all Photo/Video Recording Shooting menus, Custom Settings menu, the Setup menu settings, and all My Menu items. You can restore your settings if you've messed them up or save multiple sets of settings to multiple memory cards. If you own more than one camera, this is a handy way to share settings between them. You can save only one group of settings at a time to a particular card (always in the Primary/Slot 1 location). If you want to save multiple settings, simply use multiple memory cards. Note that storing/restoration is an all-or-nothing proposition. When you select Save Settings, all your current settings are stored on the memory card; choose Load Settings, and the current settings are replaced with the values stored on the memory card. The following settings are *not* saved, with a few exceptions noted:

- **Playback menu.** Playback Folder and Slide Show.
- **Photo Shooting menu.** Storage Folder, HDR Overlay, Multiple Exposure, Interval Timer Shooting, Time-lapse Movie, and Focus Shift Shooting settings.
- **Video Recording menu.** Storage Folder.
- **Custom Settings menu.** All saved.
- **Setup menu.** Date and Time, Monitor Brightness, Monitor Color Balance, Viewfinder Brightness, Viewfinder Color Balance, AF Fine-tuning, Save Focus Position, GPS Position, Battery Info.
- **My Menu/Recent Settings.** All My Menu entries, All recent settings, Active tab are all saved.

Reset All Settings

Options: Reset, Do Not Reset

My preference: N/A

This entry resets all settings, including Copyright Information, and other user-generated settings, except Language and Time Zone and Date. You should save your current settings to a memory card before using this entry, just to be safe. This command requires use of a confirmation screen to make sure you don't remove your settings accidentally. After the reset, you'll be instructed to turn the camera off. The next time the camera is powered up, the default settings will be in place.

Firmware Version

Options: Display current settings, Update, Remove Firmware Files

My preference: N/A

You can see the current firmware release in use in the menu listing. If a new firmware update is in the top-level of a memory card, additional options appear allowing you to proceed with an update, and, after the update, to erase the firmware file from the memory card.

Network Menu

10

Given that the focus of this book is on still photography and not Information Technology, this chapter is for reference only, and is not intended to serve as a how-to. Nikon has included an 85-page Connection Guide in the manual provided for the Z8, and an expanded 109-page networking manual that covers LAN topics in its Z9 guidebook. Both provide detailed step-by-step instructions for connecting your camera to smart devices, computers, and FTP servers, and duplicating that material is beyond the scope of this book. We won't be going down the IT rabbit hole in this book.

Although the Z9 and Z8 are aimed at advanced photographers, it's unlikely that the majority of you will be using the most advanced connection technology Nikon has to offer. For example, Nikon's optional, but very pricey (about $750), WT-7/WT-7A transmitter has both wireless and Ethernet connections and can upload photos and videos to a computer, your smart device, or FTP server, plus control the camera remotely, or view/capture pictures (but *not* videos) wirelessly with a browser on your computer or smart device.

But for those who need these advanced capabilities, it's comforting to know that Nikon has carefully considered your needs and is attempting to provide the features you need. At the time I write this, some capabilities, particularly FTP connectivity, need some (ahem) fine-tuning. But others, such as wireless connections through the camera and SnapBridge, have overcome most of the previous obstacles and can now be accessed more easily by following the instructions Nikon provides in the connection guide sections of its manuals. Your wireless options alone are these:

- **Camera to smart device using Bluetooth LE.** In this mode, you'll use SnapBridge and the Bluetooth LE capabilities built into both the smart device and the camera. Bluetooth LE is a more efficient low-energy protocol that allows wireless connectivity to remain active even when the camera is technically powered off.
- **Camera to smart device using the camera's built-in Wi-Fi hot spot.** SnapBridge will link the two devices with your smart device logging in to the Wi-Fi access point built into the camera.
- **Camera to computer using a wireless router.** Your camera will connect to your computer's access point supplied by your home/office router.
- **Camera to computer using the camera's built-in Wi-Fi hot spot.** Your computer will connect to the camera's built-in Wi-Fi access point directly, without need for an external network.

Once you're connected, you can perform a variety of functions, including controlling your camera using SnapBridge—when connected to a smart device—or Camera Control 2 (or other tethering software, such as Lightroom)—when connected to a computer. I've found that most users end up working with SnapBridge-to-camera links most of the time, because they can do the following:

- **Auto uploads.** You can use SnapBridge to automatically upload JPEG images (but not RAW files) from your camera to your smart device.
- **Upload selected photos.** During image review, you can press the *i* button and choose Select to Send to Smart Device/Deselect to choose specific images to transfer to your smart device. You can also use the Select to Send to Smart Device entry in the Playback menu. Up to 1,000 photos can be marked for upload in one session.
- **Resize images.** Obviously uploading full-resolution images to your smart device would be slow and use a lot of storage space on your device. SnapBridge defaults to low-resolution 2-megapixel images (which should be fine for smart device display or sharing on social media), and the app lets you specify a different upload size.
- **Add credits.** The app also lets you choose to embed comments and copyright information entered in the Setup menu (as described in Chapter 9) or entered using the SnapBridge app itself.
- **Multiple devices.** If you own multiple phones and tablets, you can pair the camera with as many as five different devices. However, the camera can connect to only one at a time. You can manually switch between devices using the connection options described shortly.
- **Remote control.** You can trigger the shutter using your smart device (as long as the camera is on), giving you wireless remote control without the need of purchasing an accessory.
- **Imprint photos.** You can overlay comments or the time the photo was taken.

The complete Network menu is shown in Figure 10.1.

- Airplane Mode
- Wired LAN (Z9 Only)
- Connect to Smart Device
- Connect to Computer
- Connect to FTP Server
- Connect to Other Cameras
- ATOMOS AirGlu BT Options
- USB (Z9)/USB Connection (Z8)
- Start via LAN
- Router Frequency Band
- MAC Address
- Wireless Transmitter (WT-7)

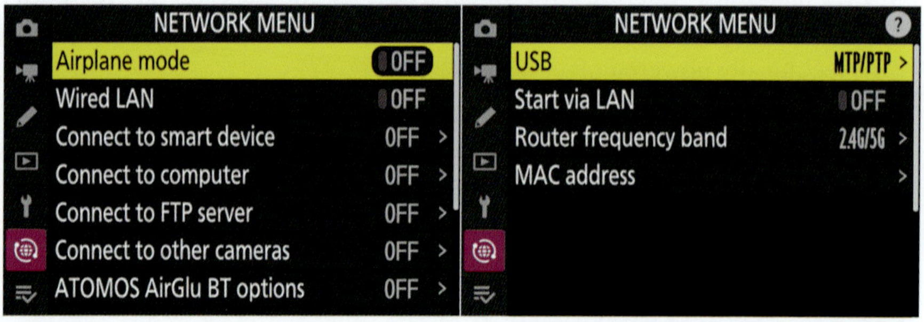

Figure 10.1 The Network menu.

Airplane Mode

Options: Off (default), On

My preference: On

Like the Airplane mode on your smartphone or tablet, this option turns off Wi-Fi and Bluetooth capabilities. I enable the feature any time I am not planning to use Bluetooth or Wi-Fi, because it saves a lot of power.

Wired LAN (Z9 Only)

Options: Off (default), On

My preference: Off

Although initially developed in the '70s, Ethernet saw its first use in local area networks (LANs) in the early 1980s and quickly supplanted other technologies used for wired communication between computers. Today, most of us rely almost entirely on wireless communication between our home/office routers or hotspots and our devices, but Ethernet is still heavily used in professional/business environments. To meet the needs of those users, the Z9 is equipped with a physical Ethernet port located on the side of the camera. The Z8 has no such connection built-in, but a USB-C-to-Ethernet adapter can be attached to make this entry available.

You must select On to enable a direct connection to an Ethernet network, using an Ethernet cable plugged into the LAN connection on the left side of the camera. You will then connect to the network using a network profile, a process that is essentially the same for this wired connection as it is for a direct wireless link-up, described under the Connect to Computer entry below.

Connect to Smart Device

Options: Pairing (Bluetooth), Select Pictures for Upload, Wi-Fi Connection (AP mode), Wi-Fi Connection (STA mode), Upload While Off, Location Data (Smart Device)

My preference: N/A

Use this entry to set up your SnapBridge or Wi-Fi connection to your smartphone, tablet, or computer. Connecting your camera to your smart device (phone or tablet) is generally done using the SnapBridge application on the device (although there are other apps that perform some of the same functions). The Nikon SnapBridge app supports *only* camera-to-smart-device communications. Your first step in using SnapBridge is to download and install the SnapBridge app onto your smart device from the Google Play store or the Apple iTunes store. You'll find step-by-step instructions for making the connection with SnapBridge in Nikon's PDF manual.

Nikon has split Wi-Fi connection into two types. The original mode has been renamed "Wi-Fi (AP mode), for Access Point, which uses the camera's built-in access point. A new "Station" option, Wi-Fi (STA mode) has been added to allow connecting the camera to a smart device on an existing network using a wireless LAN access point.

Connect to Computer

Options: Network Settings: Create Profile, Copy to/from Card, End Current Connection; Connection Type: Picture Transfer, Camera Control; Options: Adjust upload settings

My preference: N/A

You have a choice of how you connect your Z9/Z8 to your computer. You can link your camera to your computer using an Ethernet cabled connection (if you have the Z9 or a USB-C-to-Ethernet adapter attached to the Z8), or with a wireless link to your local area network with a direct wireless connection from the camera to the computer (Access-point mode) or by linking to your home/office network's wireless router (Infrastructure mode).

In most cases, your Nikon camera's Bluetooth and Wi-Fi capabilities, coupled with SnapBridge, will supply all the connectivity you'll ever need. Some photographers, particularly those who shoot in a studio or at events, like to take the next step and shoot tethered, in which images captured by the camera show up almost instantaneously on a computer. Such transfers are most useful for quick edits, demonstrations, client previews, and evaluating images as they are taken. In most cases, *wireless* tethering is not especially practical, because the transfer takes too long.

Instead, photographers who need this capability generally use cables to link their cameras to the computer, and work with software specifically designed for tethering, such as Adobe Lightroom, Nikon Camera Control 2, Capture One Pro, or Helicon Remote.

If you need a wireless connection other than SnapBridge, you have several options. Nikon offers a free utility called the Wireless Transmitter Utility (see Figure 10.2), which Nikon says "allows users to connect the camera to networks via wired or wireless LANs. Wired Ethernet connections are available with D6-, D5-, and D4-series cameras, the WT-7 and WT-4 wireless transmitters, and the UT-1 communications unit; and wireless connections with cameras featuring built-in wireless LAN or with a WT-7, WT-6, WT-5, or WT-4 wireless transmitter." Ack! This is the IT rabbit hole I'm trying to skirt around.

In (only slightly) less technical terms, it can use the camera's built-in Wi-Fi to connect wirelessly to a computer in "Access Point Mode" with the camera serving as a wireless LAN access point. When connected in this way, the camera's Wi-Fi hot spot substitutes for an internet connection (that is, the computer cannot communicate with the camera and the internet simultaneously). As such, it's an option when working outdoors or in other locations that don't have a stand-alone router/wireless network.

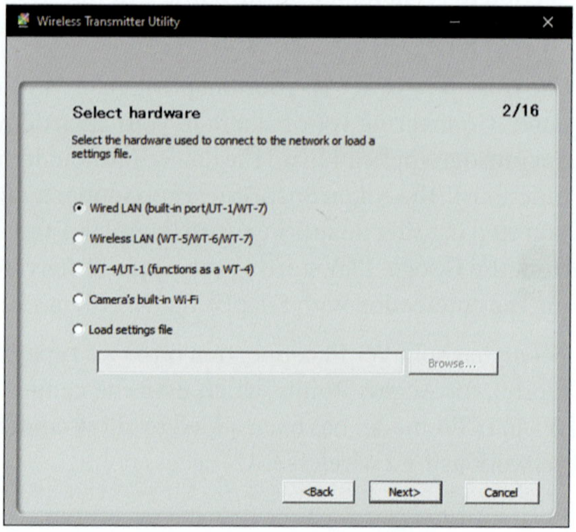

Figure 10.2 Using the Wireless Transmitter Utility.

As I noted earlier, I'm devoting all the available space in this book to photography topics and tips, rather than diverting pages to IT topics. That's because if you need these advanced capabilities you probably already know all about IP and MAC addresses, SSIDs, and other stuff and don't need an explanation from me.

Instead, I'm going to provide just an overview that will give you an idea of what's involved, and I'm not going to discuss the pricey WT-7/WT-7A wireless transmitter at all, as most readers won't need a separate $750 component to connect to computers, FTP servers, or other devices over Ethernet or wireless networks. For Access-Point mode, to create a new host profile, visit the Connect to Computer entry in the Network menu, then follow these steps:

1. **Choose Connection Type.** At the screen that appears, shown at upper left in Figure 10.3, press the right button and choose Picture Transfer or Camera Control, as shown in Figure 10.3, upper center and press OK.
2. **Select Create Profile.** The Connection Wizard will allow you to choose a name for this network profile. Press OK to enter one using the standard text-entry screen, or press the Zoom In button to accept the default name supplied. (See Figure 10.3, lower left.)
3. **Select Wireless Type.** Next, select the type of wireless connection you want. (See Figure 10.3, lower center.)
   - **Direct connection.** If you choose Direct Connection to Computer, you'll be shown the SSID of your camera and asked to connect your computer to that access point. (Figure 10.3, lower right.)
   - **Wi-Fi Connection.** Instead of using your computer to connect to the camera's built-in access point, you can do the reverse, and have the camera log into your computer's Wi-Fi network. The camera will then search and present a list of available networks (Figure 10.4, upper left). In most cases, you can allow the camera to obtain an IP address automatically (Figure 10.4, upper right). You'll be notified when the IP address has been set and asked to start the Wireless Transmitter Utility on your camera and then select your own Z9 or Z8 (Figure 10.4, lower left and right). Infrastructure mode allows the computer to continue to connect to the internet while communicating with your camera.

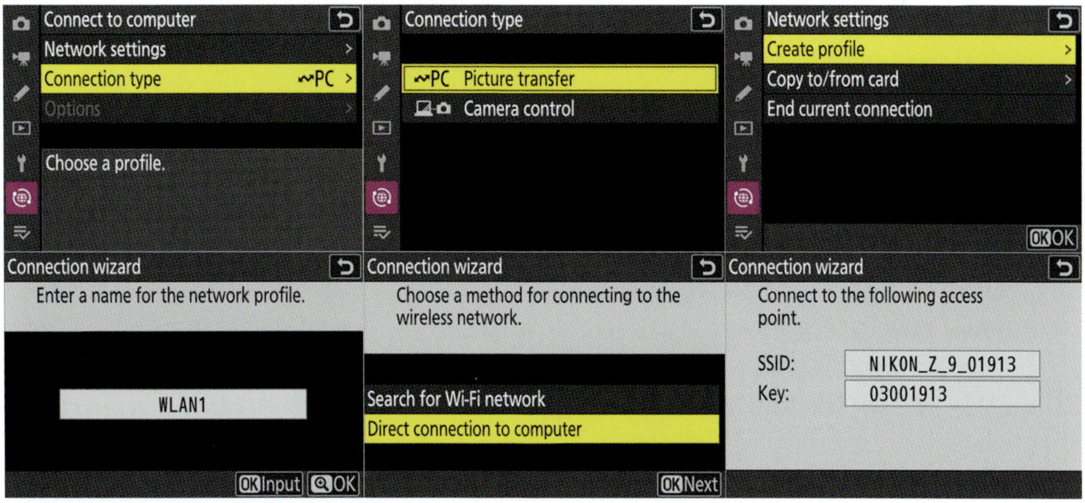

Figure 10.3 Connecting using Access-Point mode.

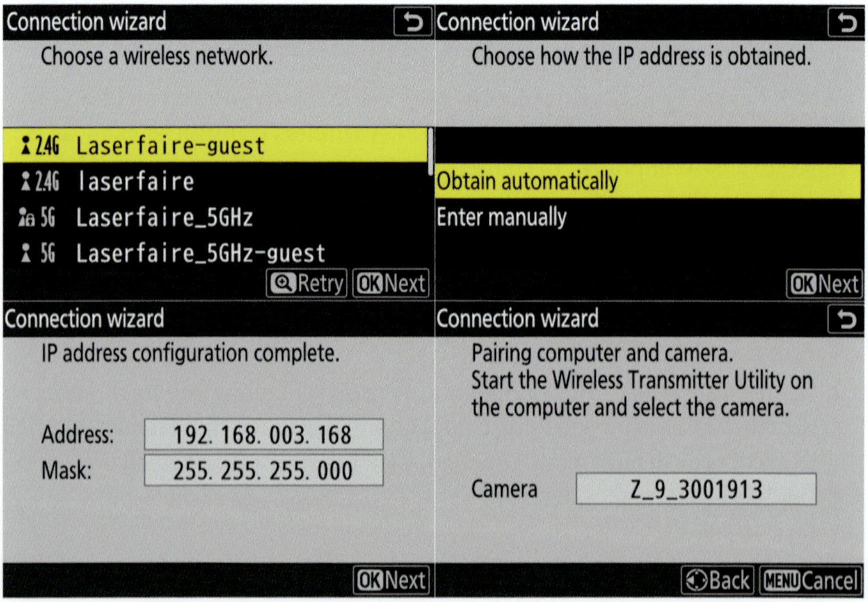

Figure 10.4 Making a Wi-Fi connection using Infrastructure mode.

Here's a summary of the options available with this entry, and the Connect to FTP Server entry below:

- **Create Profile.** Runs a connection wizard which will search for an existing Wi-Fi network, or allow you to connect directly to the computer using your camera's built-in network.
- **Copy to/from Card.** You can copy network settings you've previously stored on a memory card, or copy your current network settings to a card, if it is not password-protected.
- **End Current Connection.** This disconnects the current camera-to-computer connection.
- **Connection Type.** You can choose Picture Transfer, which allows uploading photos to your computer, either as they are taken or as you select them for transfer. Alternatively, you can opt for Camera Control to allow you to operate your camera and take photos using either Camera Control Pro 2 (an extra-cost option), or the free NX Tether software.
- **Options.** Here you can specify upload options:
  - **Auto Upload.** Choose On to mark each new still photo for upload. (Videos cannot be auto uploaded.)
  - **Delete After Upload.** Select On to delete photos from the memory card once the upload is completed. Files already marked for transfer will not be deleted. This is a dangerous option. Use it with care.
  - **Upload RAW+ JPEG As.** Here you can choose to upload only the JPEG or both RAW and JPEG if you are shooting both.
  - **JPEG+ JPEG Slot Selection.** If you've specified storing JPEG files on both cards, you can choose which slot to use when uploading.

- **Upload RAW Video As.** N-RAW 12-bit (NEV) and ProRes RAW HQ 12-bit (MOV) files also create an MP4 copy of the video. Here you can choose whether to transfer both or only the MP4 version.
- **Overwrite if Same Name.** Choose whether or not to overwrite.
- **Protect if Marked for Upload.** Add/delete protection.
- **Upload Marking.** Designate uploads.
- **Upload Folder.** This marks all still photos in a folder you select for upload, *even if they have already been uploaded.*
- **Deselect All?** This removes the upload marker from all images, including those currently being uploaded.
- **Keep Connection.** Keep or end the current connection.
- **Manage Root Certificate.** Modify root certificate.

You can instruct your camera to automatically upload new still photos (but not videos) to your smart device or computer when the camera and device are linked. If they are not connected, the camera will mark a maximum of 1,000 photos and upload them the next time a wireless connection is made.

Connect to FTP Server

Options: Network Settings, Options, Choose a Profile (Information only)

My preference: N/A

Any previous FTP connection profiles you've created will be shown here, or you can create a new one and specify the options listed above. You can connect to an FTP server using access points or infrastructure mode. If you want to avoid manually entering SSID, encryption keys, IP addresses, etc., the Connection Wizard and Easy Connect option (which uses either Push-Button WPS or PIN-entry WPS) are available to help you create a profile and establish a connection. You can now select a specific FTP port number, and choose to upload in HEIF format.

Connect to Other Cameras

Options: Synchronized Release (On, Off), Network Settings, Master/Remote, Group Settings, Group Name, Synchronize Date and Time, Overwrite Copyright Information, Remote Camera List

My preference: N/A

Some features that professional photojournalists need boggle the mind of those of us with more modest requirements. Nikon is not out to disappoint its most demanding customers and offers considerably advanced features. One of these is this capability to connect multiple Z9 and Z8 cameras in order to synchronize their clocks (for applications when matching the date and time a picture was taken is essential). The other is the ability to synchronize up to 10 remote Z9 or Z8 cameras in the same group simultaneously.

Synchronized release is done by creating host profiles for each camera using Network Settings screen similar to the ones shown earlier. The cameras are ordinarily connected using a wireless LAN, whereupon each Z9 or Z8 captures images when triggered by the master camera, then saves them to their own memory cards. The Standby timer does not expire automatically in synchronized release mode. If you're using Z9 cameras, they can also be connected using a wired Ethernet connection.

The master camera will display a Remote Camera List which shows each of the group's cameras and their IP addresses, along with status, such as Connected, Busy (controlled by a different master camera), Off , or Error. The time for the most recent shot will be shown. The master camera can also edit the settings of each remote camera and temporarily suspend connections. The available options for this entry are shown in Figure 10.5.

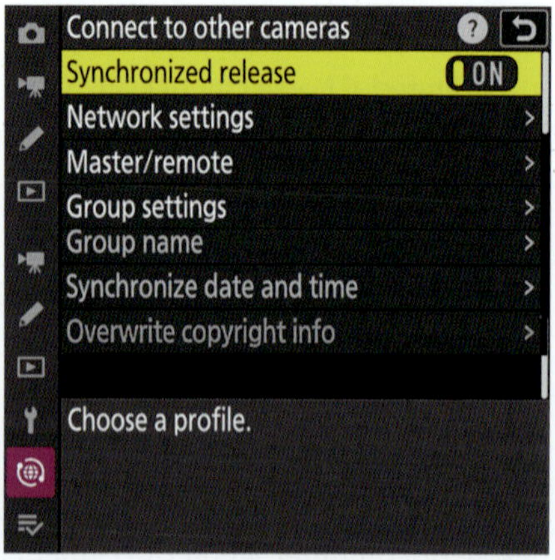

Figure 10.5 Synchronized release options.

ATOMOS AirGlu BT Options

Options: Connect to Atomos AirGlu BT, Save Atomos AirGlu BT, Delete Atomos AirGlu BT Pairing Info, Camera

My preference: N/A

As discussed in Chapter 12, professional video editing uses time codes to synchronize footage captured from multiple sources or sessions. Atomos uses its own time code synchronization with its UltraSync accessory to share the data between devices including its Ninja V monitor, cameras, audio recorders, and smartphones over Bluetooth. This entry allows pairing your Z9/Z8 with these devices using Bluetooth. Nikon has added support for for the MC-N10 remote grip. Using this entry you can:

- Make a Bluetooth connection to a paired UltraSync Blue device.
- Create and save the initial pairing of the Z9/Z8 with the UltraSync Blue device.
- End the connection and remove pairing information.
- Specify a name the UltraSync Blue device will apply to your camera.

USB (Z9)/USB Data Connection (Z8)

Options: MTP/PTP, iPhone, USB-LAN (Z8 Only)

My preference: N/A

This setting allows you to choose the protocol used for image transfer when your camera is connected to your computer using a USB cable. If you want to transfer images directly from the Z9 or Z8 to your computer over USB, you'll first need to set USB Connection Priority in the Setup menu, as described in Chapter 9. That entry determines whether the camera disables shooting information and switches to upload mode when a USB connection is live.

Then, you'll need to use this entry to determine the protocol used for transfer. Your choices are:

- **MTP/PTP.** The acronyms stand for Media Transfer Protocol (in which the connected device appears as a mass storage/disk drive on the computer) and Picture Transfer Protocol (in which the device *does not* appear as a disk drive). This choice actually enables only PTP; if you connect your camera to your computer and use the File Manager you'll *see* the Z9 or Z8 shown with a drive icon, but clicking on it shows no files. To transfer your pictures, you'll need to use a software application that works with PTP. You can also use connection applications like Nikon Camera Control Pro to operate your camera over the USB connection. The free Nikon NX Tether can be used to take photos remotely and transfer them to an application such as NX Studio.
- **iPhone.** This option allows you to connect your iPhone to your computer using the Nikon application NX MobilAir and a Lightning-to-USB cable needed for iPhones introduced before the iPhone 15.
- **USB-LAN (Z8 Only).** Allows a wired Ethernet connection using a USB-C-to-Ethernet dongle with the Z8.

Start via LAN

Options: On, Off (default)

My preference: N/A

This entry allows activating a camera connected to an Ethernet network.

Router Frequency Band

Options: 2.4 GHz/5 GHz, 2.4 GHz, 5 GHz

My preference: N/A

If you have a home network, you're probably familiar with the two frequency bands used by your wireless router and access point. Most routers have both 2.4 GHz and a faster 5 GHz band which can be used individually or combined for access by devices that can take advantage of dual-band operation. This entry lets you specify which band your camera uses—or both, if that is your preference.

MAC Address

Options: On, Off (default)

My preference: N/A

Displays the MAC address of your camera. This is the Media Access Control identifier (it has nothing to do with Mac computers), which is a unique serial number that only your device—such as your Z9 or Z8 camera—uses when connected to a network.

Wireless Transmitter (WT-7)

Options: Network Settings, Current Settings, Reset Connection Settings

My preference: N/A

This entry allows you to configure wireless local area network (LAN) settings. You'll find instructions for setting up this expensive accessory in the manual furnished with the WT-7 transmitter. Note that the latest firmware (Version 1.5 or later) and most recent version of the Wireless Transmitter Utility Version 1.11.0 (or later) must be used.

Retouch and My Menus

11

We're not done covering the menu options yet. There are two more menus to deal with: the Retouch menu, available only from the Playback version of the *i* menu, and the My Menu system, which can help you set up a customized menu that contains only the entries you want, or, alternatively, a list of your most recently accessed entries.

Retouch Menu

The Retouch menu contains the post-processing options you can apply to your images after you've taken a photo. When reviewing an image in Playback mode, press the *i* button and *i* menu choices available during playback appear, as seen at left in Figure 11.1. (Like the other menus in this book, I've edited the figure to show more entries than can actually appear on your screen at once, for clarity.) Highlight Retouch and press the multi selector right button to view your options, shown in expanded mode at right in Figure 11.1.

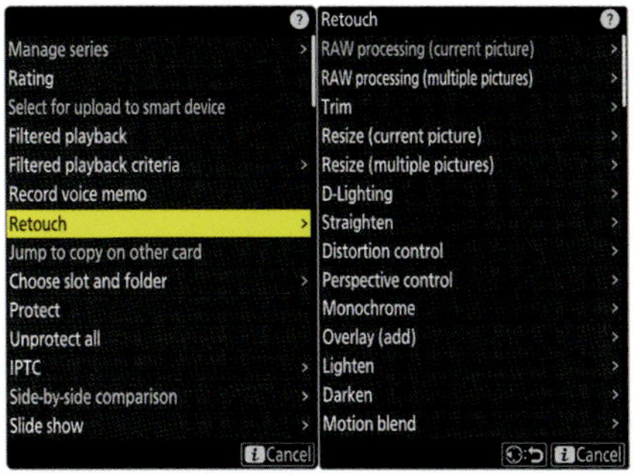

Figure 11.1 The Retouch menu allows simple in-camera editing.

They include:

- RAW Processing (current picture)
- RAW Processing (multiple pictures)
- Trim
- Resize (current picture)
- Resize (multiple pictures)
- D-Lighting
- Straighten
- Distortion Control
- Perspective Control
- Monochrome
- Overlay (add)
- Lighten
- Darken
- Motion Blend

The Retouch menu is most useful when you want to create a modified copy of an image on the spot, for immediate printing or e-mailing without first importing into your computer for more extensive editing. You can also use it to create a JPEG version of an image in the camera when you are shooting RAW-only photos. You can retouch images that have already been processed by the Retouch menu, except for copies created with the Image Overlay option. You may notice some quality loss when applying more than one retouch option. "The Customize Retouch Options" entry at the top of the list allows you to specify which retouching options are available.

To retouch a photo:

1. **Choose image retouching option.** From the Retouch menu, select the option you want from those available and press the multi selector right button. **Note:** If you elect to work on an image that has been captured in dual RAW+JPEG format, *only* the RAW image will be retouched. If you have an image on your memory card that was recorded by a different model, your camera may not be able to display or retouch the image.
2. **Manipulate image.** Work with the options available from that particular Retouch menu feature and press OK to create the modified copy, or Playback to cancel your changes. Keep in mind that if the delay for Menus that you've specified in Custom Setting c3: Power Off Delay expires, the camera will exit the menu screen and any unsaved changes canceled. You may want to select a longer power-off delay for Menus.
3. **View copy.** A retouched JPEG image will be the same size and quality as the original, except for copies created using the RAW Processing, Trim, and Resize options. Resized or Cropped copies created from NEF and TIFF images are always saved as JPEG Fine images. During review, retouched copies are overlaid with a paint brush icon in their upper-left corner.

DOUBLE DUTY

Once you've retouched an image using one of the Retouch menu's entries, you can apply most of the remaining options to the manipulated copy (except for those produced by Trim Movie). Any that are not available will be grayed out. That said, it's probably not a good idea to retouch a retouched copy, as you'll lose some image quality each time.

RAW Processing (Current Picture)/(Multiple Pictures)

Options: Image Quality, Image Size, White Balance, Exposure Compensation, Set Picture Control, High ISO NR, Color Space, Vignette Control, Active D-Lighting, Diffraction Compensation, Portrait Impression Balance (Z8 Only); (Multiple Pictures Only): Select Picture(s), Select Date, Select Folder, Choose Destination

My preference: N/A

The RAW Processing feature creates a JPEG version of any image saved in RAW. When I am out of my office I sometimes need a reduced resolution JPEG to transfer to my iPhone to send or upload. This entry not only lets you create that JPEG from any RAW file in your camera, it allows you to adjust the image quality and size and apply many useful corrections, including white balance adjustments, exposure compensation, and noise reduction.

Nikon gives you two versions of the tool, one is labeled (Current Picture), which lets you quickly create the JPEG from any one image. The other is labeled (Multiple Pictures) and can be used to apply the same settings to a group of RAW files as you create your JPEG version.

Just follow these steps:

1. **Choose RAW image(s).** If you choose the (Current Picture) version, you can begin processing the image immediately. With the (Multiple Pictures) version, you'll be taken to the standard Z9/Z8 image selection routine, which allows you to:
   - **Select pictures** by viewing thumbnails and pressing the Zoom In button to view individual thumbnails of NEF files full screen, or the Zoom Out button to select/unselect a thumbnail. Press OK to confirm and exit.
   - **Select Date** by specifying the slot containing your RAW images and then selecting from a list showing all dates on which you took photos with that card. Press OK to confirm and exit.
   - **Select Folder** by choosing card slot and folder name and OK to confirm and exit.
   - **Choose Destination.** Select a memory card slot for your JPEG versions, and press the multi selector left button to confirm and exit.

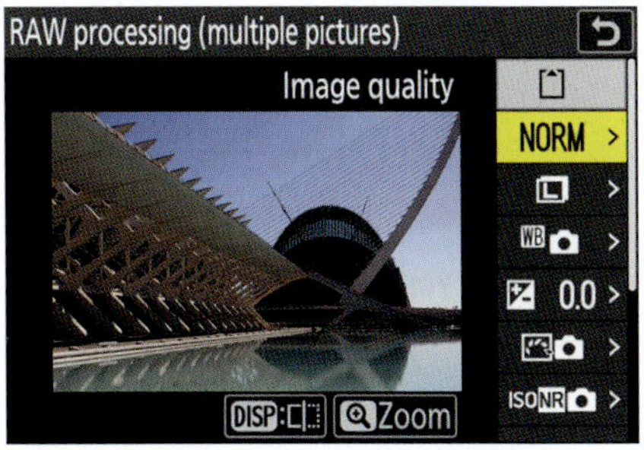

Figure 11.2 Adjust the parameters and then save your JPEG copy from a RAW original file.

2. **Select attributes.** In the RAW processing screen, you can use the multi selector up/down keys to select from these attributes of the RAW image information to apply to the JPEG copies made of your selected image(s): Choose Image Quality (Fine, Normal, or Basic, plus * versions of each), Image Size (Large, Medium, or Small), White Balance, Exposure Compensation, Set Picture Control, High ISO Noise Reduction, Color Space, Vignette Control, D-Lighting, Diffraction Compensation, and (for the Z8 only) Portrait Impression Balance.
3. **Examine image.** Press the Zoom In button to magnify the image temporarily while the button is held down. Press the DISP button to toggle between views of the original and the processed image.
4. **Change your mind?** Press the Playback button if you change your mind, to exit from the processing screen.
5. **Execute.** When all parameters are set, highlight EXE (for Execute) at the top of the settings list and press OK. The camera will create a JPEG file for each of the selected images with the settings you've specified, and show an Image Saved message on the monitor when finished.

Trim

Options: Various sizes

My preference: N/A

This option creates copies in specific sizes based on the final size you select, chosen from among 1:1, 3:2, 4:3, 5:4, 16:9, 4:5, 3:4, 2:3, and 9:16 aspect ratios (proportions). You can use this feature to create smaller versions of a picture for e-mailing without the need to first transfer the image to your own computer. Just follow these steps:

1. **Select your photo.** In Playback mode, choose Trim from the Retouch menu.
2. **Choose your aspect ratio.** Rotate the main command dial to change from 3:2, 4:3, 5:4, 16:9 (and their inverses), plus 1:1 aspect ratios. These proportions happen to correspond to the proportions of common print sizes, including the two most popular sizes: 4 × 6 inches (3:2) and 8 × 10 inches (5:4).
3. **Crop in on your photo.** Press the Zoom In/Zoom Out buttons to choose a crop for your picture. The pixel dimensions of the cropped image at the selected proportions will be displayed in the upper-left corner (see Figure 11.3) as you zoom. The trim sizes vary depending on the Image Size and Aspect Ratio selected. The current framed size is outlined in yellow.
4. **Move cropped area within the image.** Use the multi selector left/right and up/down buttons to relocate the yellow cropping border within the frame.
5. **Save the cropped image.** Press OK to save a copy of the image using the current crop and size or press the Playback button to exit without creating a copy. Copies created from JPEG Fine, Normal, or Standard have the same Image Quality setting as the original; copies made from RAW files or any RAW+JPEG setting will use JPEG Fine compression. Note that you may not be able to zoom in on a cropped image during Playback once it has been saved.

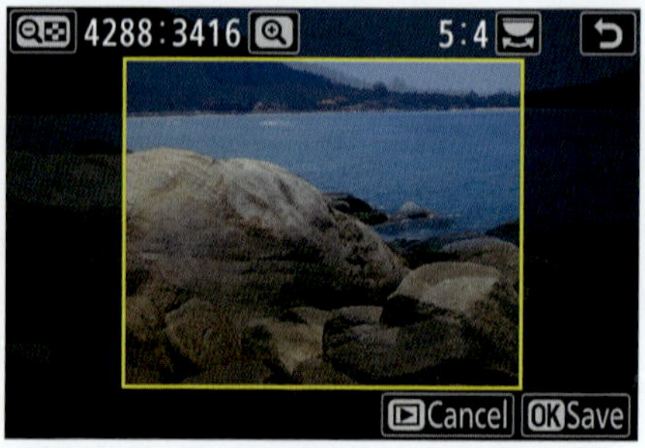

Figure 11.3 The Trim feature of the Retouch menu allows in-camera cropping.

Resize (Current Picture)/(Multiple Pictures)

Options: Choose Destination, Choose Size; Select Image (Multiple Pictures): Select Picture(s), Select Date, Select Folder, Choose Destination, Choose Size

My preference: N/A

This is another pair of options for resizing the current photo or multiple photos that you select. It can be applied while viewing a single image in full-size mode (just press the *i* button while viewing a photo) or accessed from the Retouch menu (especially useful if you'd like to select and resize multiple images). You might want smaller images to post on a website or send by e-mail.

Just follow these steps:

1. **Select Pictures.** Choose one or multiple images from the Retouch menu.
2. **Choose destination.** Select the memory card slot containing the image(s).
3. **Choose size.** Next, select the size for the finished copy, from 2304 × 1536 (3.5MB), 1920 × 1280 (2.5MB), 1280 × 856 (1.1MB), or 960 × 640 (0.6 megabytes).
4. **Confirm.** Press OK to create your copy, the *i* button to cancel, or the left directional button to back out of the Size screen. Note that, as with Trim, you may not be able to zoom in on a resized image during Playback once it has been saved.

D-Lighting

Options: High, Normal, Low

My preference: N/A

D-Lighting is the term for Nikon's shadow enhancement processing applied after an image has already been captured, as opposed to Active D-Lighting, which is performed at the time the picture is captured. Thus, this option brightens the shadows of pictures during picture review. Once you've selected your photo for modification, press the multi selector's up/down directional controls to choose from High, Normal, or Low corrections. (See Figure 11.4.) Press the Zoom In button to magnify the image. Press the DISP button to toggle between the unaltered version and your adjusted version. When you're happy with the corrected image on the right, compared to the original on the left, press OK to save the copy to your memory card.

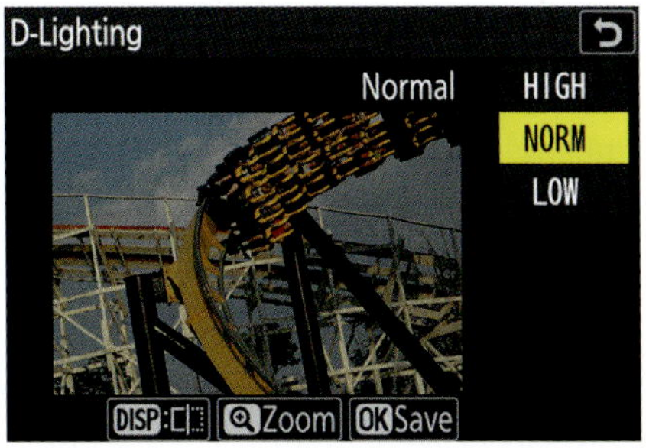

Figure 11.4 An image with dark shadows can be improved with post-shot D-Lighting.

Straighten

Options: Rotation

My preference: N/A

Use this to create a corrected copy of a crooked image, rotated by up to five degrees in either direction, in increments of one-quarter of a degree (–20 to +20). Use the down directional button to rotate clockwise, and the up directional button to rotate counterclockwise. The amount of your correction will be visible on the display. You can zoom in on the image or press the DISP button to toggle between the original and corrected versions. Press OK to make a corrected copy, or the Playback button to exit without saving a copy. Note that you will lose some picture information during this process, as the camera must trim the edges of the rotated image to produce the rectangular final image.

Distortion Control

Options: Auto, Manual

My preference: N/A

This option produces a copy with reduced barrel distortion (a bowing out effect) or pincushion distortion (an inward-bending effect), both of these forms of *peripheral distortion* are most noticeable at the edges of a photo. If the camera detects distortion, you can select Auto to let the camera make this correction. You can use Manual to make the fix yourself visually. Use the down directional button to reduce barrel distortion (bowing outward of lines at the edges) and the up directional button to reduce pincushion distortion (which produces lines bowing inward). In both cases, some of the edges of the photo will be cropped out of your image. The DISP button toggles between original and corrected versions. Press OK to make a corrected copy, or the Playback button to exit without saving a copy. Note that Auto cannot be used with images exposed using the Auto Distortion Control feature in the Photo Shooting menu.

Perspective Control

Options: Adjust tilt

My preference: N/A

This option lets you adjust the perspective of an image, reducing the falling-back effect produced when the camera is tilted to take in the top of a tall subject, such as a building, or to one side to include a longer structure or object. Choose which orientation you want to correct for (see Figure 11.5, left). Use the multi selector buttons up/down to "tilt" the image in various directions and visually correct the distortion. (Figure 11.5, right.) You can zoom in on the image, or press the DISP button to toggle between the original image and the corrected image.

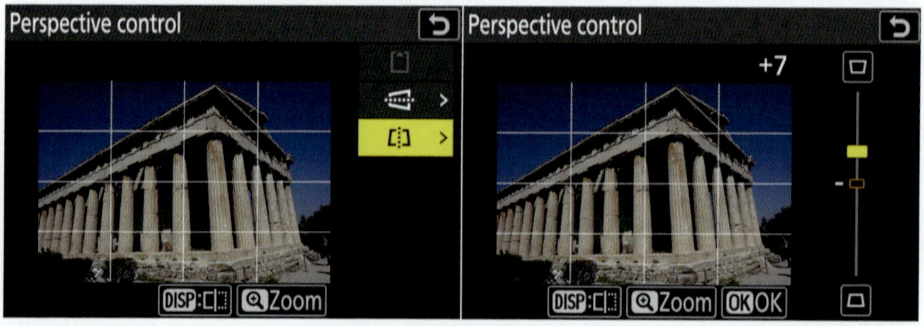

Figure 11.5 Perspective Control lets you fix "falling-back" distortion when photographing tall subjects.

Monochrome

Options: Black-and-white, Sepia, Cyanotype

My preference: N/A

This Retouch choice allows you to produce a copy of the selected photo as a black-and-white image, sepia-toned image, or cyanotype (blue-and-white). You can fine-tune the color saturation of the previewed Sepia or Cyanotype version by pressing the multi selector up button to increase color richness, and the down button to decrease saturation. When satisfied, press OK to create the monochrome duplicate, which will be assigned its own filename. Cancel by pressing the Playback button. As always, the DISP button toggles between original image and processed version.

Overlay (Add)

Options: Combine two RAW photos, Add, Lighten, Darken

My preference: N/A

This feature allows you to combine two RAW photos (only RAW files can be used) in a composite image that Nikon claims is better than a "double exposure" created in an image-editing application, because the overlays are made using RAW data. To produce this composite image, follow these steps:

1. **Choose images.** Select the two images from the standard selection screen, pressing the Zoom Out button to mark/unmark thumbnails. Press OK to continue.
2. **Adjust balance.** Press the multi selector up and down buttons to adjust the percentage of each image to be used in the final version, starting from the default 50/50 to your desired proportions. The up button increases the strength of the first picture selected, while the down button increases the strength of the second photo.
3. When you're ready to store your composite copy, press the OK button. The combined image is stored in JPEG * format on the memory card and displayed full frame for your review.

Lighten/Darken

Options: Select Slot, Select Pictures, Select Consecutive Pictures in a Range, or Select All Pictures in Folder; Apply Photoshop-style Lighten or Darken Merge

My preference: N/A

This pair of options aren't used to darken or lighten an individual picture. Instead, they are used to perform a Photoshop-style merger in which the camera compares the pixels in each photo and uses only the brightest or darkest for the final version.

Motion Blend

Options: Select Slot, Select Pictures

My preference: N/A

This option allows you to select a series of RAW (NEF) pictures in a continuous burst, locate moving subjects, and overlay them in a single JPEG image. From 5 pictures (the minimum) to 20 (the maximum) can be selected. Press OK to execute processing. This feature only works if the background of each image is substantially the same and the subject is actually moving in some way.

Using My Menu

The last menu in the main menu screen has two versions: Recent Settings and My Menu. The default mode is Recent Settings, which simply shows an ever-changing roster of the 20 menu items you used most recently. You'll probably find it more useful to activate the My Menu option instead, which contains only those menu items that you deposit there extracted from the Playback, Photo Shooting, Video Recording, Custom Settings, Setup, and Retouch menus, based on your own decisions on which you use most. Remember that the camera always returns to the last menu and menu entry accessed when you press the MENU button. So, you can set up My Menu (see Figure 11.6) to include just the items accessed most frequently, and (as long as you haven't used another menu) jump to those items instantly by pressing the MENU button.

Switching back and forth is easy. The My Menu and Recent Settings menus each has a menu choice called Choose Tab. Highlight that entry and press the right multi selector button to view a screen that allows you to activate either the My Menu or Recent Settings menu. Press OK to confirm.

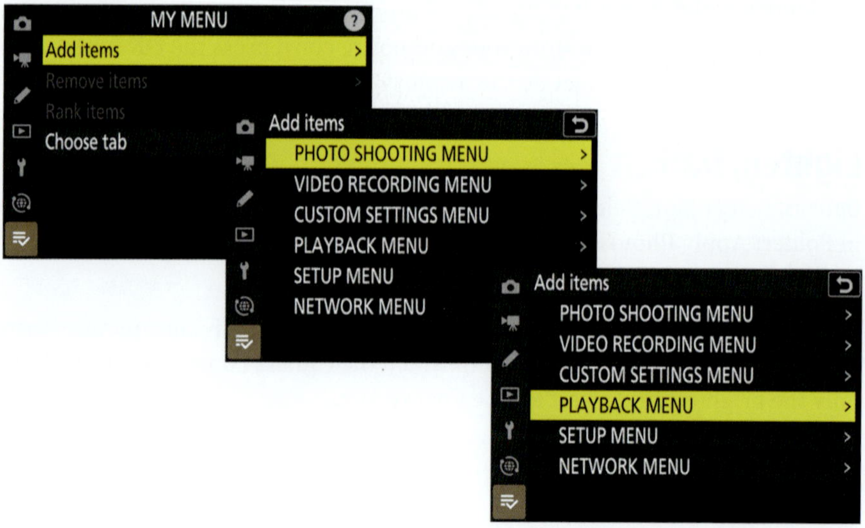

Figure 11.6 You can include your favorite menu items in the fast-access My Menu.

I tend to include frequently used functions that aren't available using direct-access buttons in My Menu. For example, I include High ISO NR, Long Exp. NR, and Battery Info there, because I may want to turn noise reduction on or off, or check the status of my battery during shooting. I *don't* include ISO or WB changes in My Menu, even though they are available in the menu system, because I can quickly change those values by pressing dedicated buttons and rotating the main and sub-command dials.

You can add or subtract entries on My Menu at any time, and re-order (or rank) the entries so the ones you access most often are shown at the top of the list. Here's all you need to know to work with My Menu. To add entries to My Menu:

1. Select My Menu and choose Add Items.
2. A list of the available menus will appear (Photo Shooting, Video Recording, Custom Settings, Playback, Setup, and Network menus). Highlight one and press the multi selector's right button.
3. Within the selected menu, choose the menu item you want to add and press OK.
4. The label Choose Position appears at the top of the My Menu screen. Use the up/down buttons to select a rank among the entries and press OK to confirm and add the new item.
5. Repeat steps 1–4 if you want to add more entries to My Menu.

To reorder the menu listings:

1. Within the My Menu screen, choose Rank Items.
2. Use the up/down buttons to select the item to be moved and press OK.
3. Use the up/down buttons to relocate the selected item and press OK.
4. Repeat steps 2–3 to move additional entries.

To remove entries from the list, you can simply press the Trash button while an item is highlighted in the My Menu screen. To remove multiple items, follow these steps:

1. Within the My Menu screen, choose Remove Items.
2. A list with checkboxes next to the menu items appears. Scroll down to an item you want to remove and press the multi selector right button to mark its box. If you change your mind, highlight the item and press the right button again to unmark the box.
3. When finished, highlight Done and press the OK button.
4. Press OK to confirm the deletion.

Introduction to Video

12

Your Nikon Z9/Z8 is bristling with professional-level video features capable of interfacing with equally high-end recorders and other accessories. Pro videographers are actually capturing footage for feature films with these cameras. Fortunately, for the rest of us, shooting movies with the Nikon Z9/Z8 can be as easy as flipping a switch—the Photo/Video mode switch located to the right of the viewfinder. If you're looking for no-fuss, casual video, after you've selected Video mode, press the red Video button located on top of the camera, just southwest of the shutter-release button. Capture will start; press the Video button again to stop recording. That's all there is to grabbing good video clips.

So, although explaining how to use the full range of sophisticated movie-making features is beyond the scope of this book, I am going to introduce the basics so you'll know what you need to master if you want to go beyond "good" to "excellent." I listed and briefly described the options in the Video Recording menu in Chapter 6.

Both the Nikon Z9 and Z8 can capture video at up to 8K resolution, create slow-motion movies, and record both standard dynamic range and high-dynamic range video. The Z9 can record continuously for more than two hours (barring heat build-up, which can be especially problematic with 8K video). The Z8's smaller body is less efficient at dissipating heat, and can record for about 90 minutes. Table 12.1 lists the key specifications for both cameras.

TECH ALERT #1

Two terms you are likely to encounter, but don't really need to be concerned about (unless you're an advanced videographer) are encoding and bit transfer rate.

- **Encoding.** If you're sending "clean" video output to the HDMI port, while it is not compressed, it is *encoded* using a procedure called *chroma subsampling,* which does reduce the amount of information that needs to be transferred. Chroma subsampling takes advantage of the fact that human beings don't detect changes in color (chroma) as easily as they do for brightness (luma). The designation 4:2:2 simply indicates that the full amount of brightness information is passed along ("4") while the two chroma values are sampled at half that rate ("2:2"). Subsampling in this way reduces the bandwidth of the otherwise uncompressed video signal by as much as one-third with no visual difference.
- **Transfer bit rate.** This is the speed the camera outputs its video to your memory card or external recorder. High transfer rates require fast memory cards; an external recorder should be able to suck up video as quickly as your camera can deliver it.

Other terms you'll run into in the table below and early parts of this chapter will be explained in more detail later on.

TABLE 12.1 Video Specifications

FILE TYPE	RESOLUTION	FORMAT	BIT DEPTH	TONE	CHROMA SUBSAMPLING
N-Raw	8.3K 60/50p, 30/25p, 24p 4.1K 120/100p, 60/50p, 30/25p, 24p 5.4K (DX) 60/50p, 30/25p, 24p 4K (2.3X) 120/100p	NEV	12 bit	Standard Dynamic Range (SDR) N-Log	—
ProRes RAW HQ	4.1K 60/50p, 30/25p, 24p 5.4K (DX) 30/25p, 24p 4K (2.3X) 60/50p	MOV	12 bit	Standard Dynamic Range (SDR) N-Log	—
ProRes 422 HQ	4K 60/50p, 30/25p, 24p 1080 120/100p, 60/50p	MOV	10 bit	Standard Dynamic Range (SDR) N-Log	4:2:2
H.265	8K 30/25p, 24p 4K 120/100p, 60/50p, 30/25p, 24p 1080 120/100p	MOV	10 bit/8 bit	Standard Dynamic Range (SDR) High Dynamic Range/ Hybrid Log Gamma (HLG) N-Log	4:2:0
H.264	1080 60/50p, 30/25p, 24p 30/25p 4X slow-motion 24p 5X slow-motion	MP4	8 bit	Standard Dynamic Range (SDR)	4:2:0

Quick Start Checklist

The following is a list of things to keep in mind as you improve your video-capture skills and take your video work to the next level. Some of these items are recaps of information you learned about still photo shooting; others are of special concern for video capture. Even if you decide to just skim through this chapter for now and come back for more after you've explored video capture, you should at least read this section before you begin your epic documentary or feature production.

- **Stills photos in Video mode?** Unfortunately, when the Photo/Video switch is set to capture movies, you cannot press the shutter release down all the way to take a still photo, whether the camera is actively capturing video or in standby mode. Other Z models do allow taking as many as 50 shots per video clip during recording and can capture images in standby mode as well, so, unless the Z9/Z8's electronic shutter precludes this feature, it may be added in the future with a firmware update. You can, however, pause a video during playback and extract an individual frame from H.265 8-bit (MOV) and H.264 8-bit (MP4) videos, as I'll describe shortly.
- **No flash.** You cannot use flash when the selector switch is set to the Video position.

- **Two-for-one.** When shooting N-RAW, the camera will save two video files: the RAW file with a .NEV extension, plus a much smaller 8-bit MP4 proxy file that can be used for faster and easier editing. The RAW footage, synchronized using time codes (as explained later), replaces the proxy when editing is finished.
- **Exposure compensation.** When shooting movies, exposure compensation is available in plus/minus 3 EV steps in 1/3 EV increments. (Remember that still photos offer plus/minus 5 EV steps.)
- **ISO fine-tuning and limitations.** Custom Setting g9/g10 (Z8/Z9): Fine ISO Control (Mode M) allows using 1/6 EV increments when setting ISO sensitivity in Manual exposure mode. The Z9/Z8 use a base ISO of 64 in Standard Dynamic Range (SDR) video modes. When shooting non-log HDR video in HLG mode, the lowest ISO available is ISO 400. In addition, ISO Auto is enabled at all times, except in manual exposure mode.
- **Use the right card.** You'll want to use a fast CFexpress card if possible. If you insist on using a slower card the recording may stop after a minute or two, given that 8K and 4K video can require bit rates of up to 400 Mbps. In addition, some cards impose length restrictions, as described next.
- **Length restrictions.** Videos can be no longer than 125 minutes and their length may be limited by the available storage of your memory card. Other restrictions apply to cards formatted using the FAT32 file system, which allows files no larger than 4GB. These will generally be cards with capacities of 32GB or less:
    - **RAW file types.** Cards formatted with FAT32 cannot be used to record RAW video under any circumstances.
    - **ProRes 422 HQ 10-bit (MOV).** If a card has been formatted using FAT32, recording will end completely when the file reaches 4GB in size. The length of the 4GB video will be determined by the frame size/frame rate (higher resolutions require more storage space per frame).
    - **Other non-RAW file types.** When a video reaches 4GB in size, recording will continue, saving additional footage across a maximum of eight files, each no larger than 4GB.
- **Internal recording of 8K video.** Other cameras may require using an external recorder for high-resolution or fast-frame-rate video. The Z9/Z8 can capture 8K RAW video internally.
- **Carry extra cards.** You're probably used to shooting still photographs. It's easy to estimate how much of your memory card's capacity you've already consumed, and how much is left, based on the shots remaining indicator on the LCD monitor and viewfinder displays. Video usage is a bit of a different animal. While the camera does show how much space you have remaining for a clip as you shoot, you really need to monitor the amount of time remaining on the current Destination card, as displayed on the top-right corner of the monitor and electronic viewfinder. The best practice is to carry along many more cards than you think you need.
- **Add an external mic.** For the best sound quality, and to avoid picking up the sound of the autofocus or zoom motor, get an external stereo mic. I'll have more advice about capturing sound and describe specific types of microphones later in this chapter.

- **Minimize zooming.** While it's great to be able to use the zoom for filling the frame with a distant subject, think twice before zooming. Unless you are using an external mic, the sound of the zoom ring rotating will be picked up and it will be audible when you play a movie. Any more than the occasional minor zoom will be very distracting to friends who watch your videos.
- **Use a fully charged battery.** A fresh battery will allow about 170 minutes of capture at normal (non-winter) temperatures with the Z9, or 85 minutes with the Z8, but that can be shorter if there are many focus adjustments.
- **Disable Standby Timer.** Be sure to set Custom Setting c3: Power Off Delay > Standby Timer to No Limit, so your camera doesn't power down while you are shooting when you are recording a video via an HDMI connection to an external device.
- **Keep it cool.** Nikon claims the Z9 is able to capture 8K video with a 30/25p frame rate for more than two hours in environments with an ambient temperature of 73.4F/23C without overheating. While the Z8 doesn't handle heat quite as well, it should be good for up to an hour under those conditions.

  However, RAW video at 60/50p and many resolutions and faster frame rates can cause overheating with higher ambient temperatures, so you'll want to watch for heat build-up with both cameras. Video quality can suffer terribly when the imaging sensor gets hot, so keep the Z9/Z8 in a cool place. When shooting on hot days especially, the sensor can get hot quicker than usual; when there's a risk of overheating, the camera will stop recording and it will shut down about five seconds later. Give it time to cool down before using it again.

PROTECT YOURSELF AND YOUR CAMERA

By default, the Z9/Z8 will display two warning icons in the upper-left corner of the display, each representing an increasing temperature level. Once the second level has been reached, a countdown timer will appear that indicates when the camera will be powered down automatically. You can visit the Auto Temperature Cutout entry of the Setup menu and change the default Standard setting to High, which will allow additional time before shutdown. However, the camera and memory cards will become quite hot and image quality is reduced.

- **Just press the Video button.** You don't have to hold it down. Press it again to stop recording.

Lean, Mean, Video Machine

The Z9 and Z8 are the best video cameras ever offered by the company that introduced the first movie-making capabilities in an interchangeable-lens still camera—the Nikon D90—in 2008. And how far we've come since then! The D90 captured monaural movies using manual focus at a fixed 24 frames per second for up to five whole minutes at 1280 × 720p (standard HD) resolution. If you dropped down to coarse 640 × 424 and 320 × 216 frame sizes, you could shoot a clip as long as 20 minutes. Your camera is packed with features that owners of many dedicated video camcorders only dreamed about a few years ago.

Capturing Video

In the Video Recording menus (see Figure 12.1), you can make the following choices, also described in the Chapter 6 reference that includes a description of the various options each entry offers. I won't repeat that information here. Many of these entries are like those for still photography in the Photo Shooting menu.

Here are your options:

- **Shooting Menu Bank.** The Z9 and Z8 share the same Shooting menu bank between the Photo Shooting menu and Video Recording menu. Changes you make in one are reflected in the other.
- **Extended Menu Banks.** These are also shared.
- **Storage Folder.** Rename, select, or choose a folder from the list of available folders, just as described in Chapter 5.

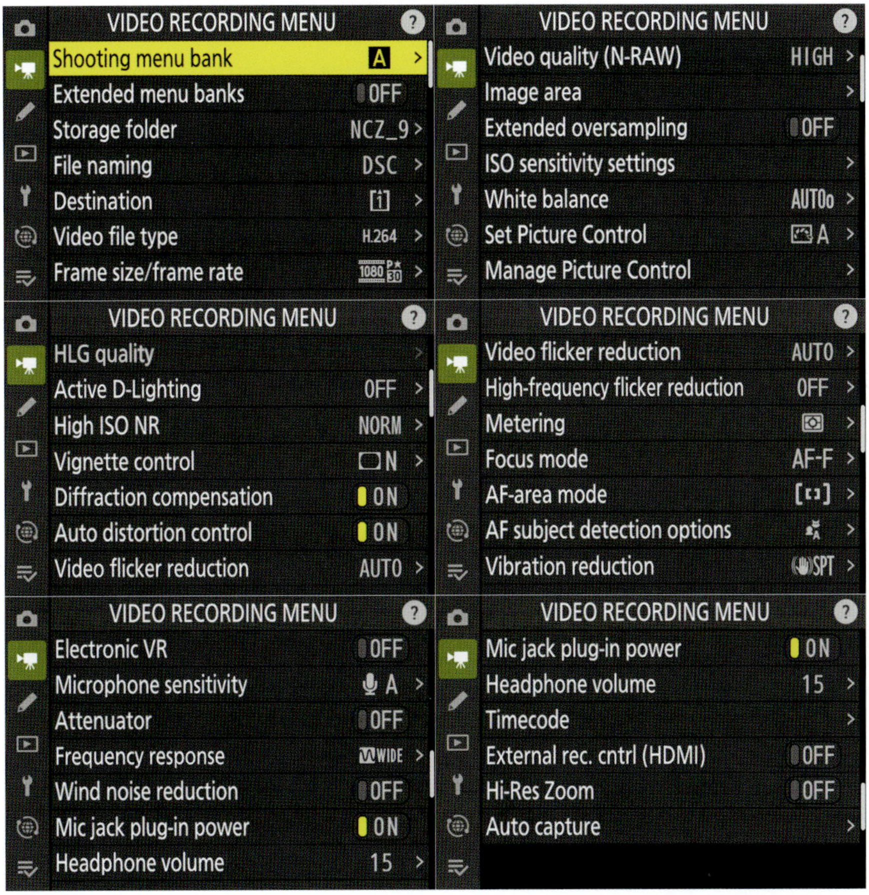

Figure 12.1 Video Recording menus.

- **File Naming.** I recommend using a different substitution in Video mode for the default DSC characters in filenames created for movie files. I use NZ9/NZ8 for still photos and MOV for video files. The limitations and instructions are the same as for the File Naming entry in the Photo Shooting menu, as described in Chapter 5.
- **Destination.** You can select which of the two memory card slots will be used to store video. You can select a different card to be used for video than the one specified with the slot function entries of the Photo Shooting menu. The amount of time available for storing video is displayed when you choose the destination.
- **Video File Type.** Here you can select different video formats and resolutions for conventional movies, with additional settings for slow-motion video. The 100/50/25 fps frame rates are used for PAL video systems overseas, while the others are compatible with the NTSC system used in the USA, Japan, and some other areas. (See the sidebar.)

  The "container" type is MOV for all video file types except H.264 8-bit, which uses MP4. I'll explain the difference between the two later; video-editing software can convert back and forth between either one.
- **Frame Size/Frame Rate.** Choose from among 8K (FX): 50/60p, 30/25p, 24p; 4K (FX): 100/120p, 50/60p, 30/25p, 24p; 5.4K (DX): 50/60p, 30/25p, 24p; 3.8K (2.3X): 100/120p; 1920 × 1080: 100/120p, 50/60p, 30/25p, 24p; 1920 × 1080 (Slow-Motion): 30/25p, 24p.

  These options are the frame resolutions (8K, 4K, 5.4K, 3.8K (2.3X crop), and Full HD [1920 × 1080]) and frame rates (100/120p, 50/60p, 30/25p, 24p, plus two slow-motion settings) available with the various video file types shown under the Video File Type entry above. The particular sizes and rates available vary, depending on the file type.

WHAT FRAME RATE?

Even intermediate movie shooters can be confused by the choice between 24 fps and 30/25, 60/50, or 120/100 fps, especially since those are only nominal figures (with the camera, the 24 fps setting yields 23.976 frames per second; 30 fps gives you 29.97 actual "frames" per second; 60 fps yields 59.94, while 120p yields 119.88 fps). The difference lies in the two "worlds" of motion images—film and video. The standard frame rate for motion picture film is 24 fps, while the video rate, at least in the United States, Japan, and other places using the NTSC standard, is 30 fps (60 interlaced *fields* per second). Most computer video-editing software can handle either type and convert between them. The choice between 24 fps and 30 fps is determined by what you plan to do with your video. Your camera can also shoot at 25/50/100 fps for use with PAL systems, which don't use NTSC standards.

The short explanation is that, for technical reasons I won't go into here, shooting at 24 fps gives your movie a "film" look, excellent for showing fine detail. (I'll have more to say about that later in this chapter.)

However, if your clip has moving subjects, or you pan the camera, 24 fps can produce a jerky effect called "judder." A 30/60/120 fps rate produces a home-video look that some feel is less desirable, but which is smoother and less jittery when displayed on an electronic monitor. I suggest you try both and use the frame rate that best suits your tastes and video-editing software.

- **Video Quality (N-RAW).** Select High Quality or Normal Quality for N-RAW capture. Your choice affects the sharpness/detail in your image and the maximum bit rate that can be sustained and length of the movies you can record. If you have fast memory cards and will be displaying your video at larger sizes, you'll want to use High Quality, which is my preference.
- **Image Area.** This parameter determines image area used when capturing video. Your Z9/Z8 provides three variations, which crop 16:9 (HDTV) proportioned areas from the full-frame still photography view: FX, DX, and 2.3X (see Figure 12.2). The availability of each depends on what video file type you're using, as shown in Table 12.2.

TABLE 12.2 Image Areas by Video File Type

FILE TYPES	LENS TYPE/ CROP	FRAME SIZE/ RATES	LENS TYPE/ CROP	FRAME SIZE/ RATES
NON-RAW				
ProRes 422 HQ 10-bit (MOV)	FX	4K 60/50p, 30/25p, 24p 1080 120/100p, 60/50p	DX	4K 60/50p, 30/35p, 24p 1080 120/100p, 60/50p
H.265 10-bit/ 8 bit (MOV)	FX	8K 30/25p, 24p 4K 120/100p, 60/50p, 30/25p, 24p 1080 120/100p, 60/50p, 30/25p, 24p	DX	8K 30/25p, 24p 4K 120/100p, 60/50p, 30/25p, 24p 1080 120/100p, 60/50p, 30/25p, 24p
H.264 8-bit (MP4)	FX	1080 60/50p, 30/25p, 24p	DX	1080 60/50p, 30/25p, 24p
RAW				
N-RAW 12-bit (NEV)	FX	FX: 8.3K 60/50p, 30/25p, 24p 4.1K 120/100p, 60/50p, 30/25p, 24p DX: 5.4K 60/50p, 30/25p, 24p 2.3X: 120/100p	DX	DX: 5.4K 60/50p, 30/25p, 24p 2.3X: 120/100p
ProRes RAW HQ 12-bit (MOV)	FX	FX: 4.1K 60/50p, 30/25p, 24p DX: 5.4K 30/25p, 24p 2.3X: 60/50p	DX	DX: 30/25p, 24p 2.3X: 60/50p

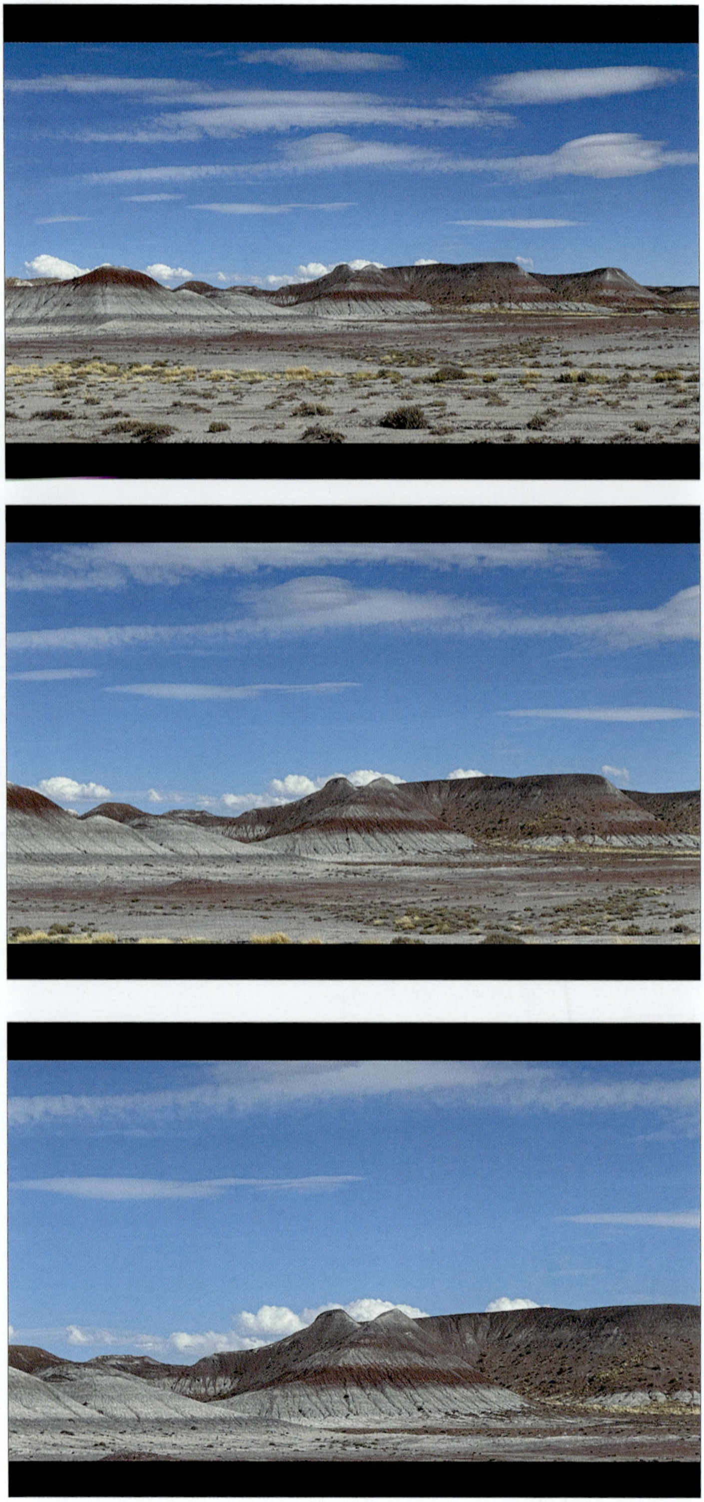

Figure 12.2 FX-based (top), DX-based (center), and 2.3X-cropped-based (bottom) movie formats.

Fortunately, the Z9/Z8 don't use a mask to mark off the cropped area. Instead, they helpfully enlarge the captured portion to fill the frame, as seen in Figure 12.2.

USING DX LENSES

If you use an FTZ adapter (either the original or Mark II model) to mount a lens that the camera recognizes as a DX/APS-C lens, the camera will switch to DX-based movie format automatically (without the need to specify FX or DX with the Image Area entry, which is grayed out, in any case). (**Reminder:** Image sizes are determined by the frame size/rate with the RAW file types.)

As in still photo mode, you cannot force the camera to use the DX lens as if it were a full-frame optic. Remember that the camera may or may not detect APS-C (DX) lenses from third-party manufacturers.

When Electronic VR is selected using the *i* button menu or Video Recording menu, the camera provides a slight additional crop (to allow adjusting the frame to compensate for camera movement). Slow-motion movies are always cropped, as I'll explain shortly.

- **Extended Oversampling.** Oversampling is the process of using the full resolution of a sensor, and then scaling it down to a lower resolution, which can result in better image quality. This entry adds the ability to capture 2:1 oversampled 4K video from 8K capture, improving video quality while increasing battery drain. Just keep in mind that very, very fast media is needed to capture all this information.
- **ISO Sensitivity Settings (for Videos).** Like the ISO settings in the Photo Shooting menu, as explained in Chapter 5, this setting allows you to select a fixed ISO setting for Manual exposure mode, from ISO 64 to ISO 25600, plus Hi 0.3, Hi 0.7, Hi 1.0, and Hi 2.0. That allows you greater control over the ISO used. If you've enabled Custom Setting g9/g10 (Z8/Z9): Fine ISO Control (Mode M), increments of 1/6 EV are used instead of the default 1/3 EV.

  When shooting movies in P, A, or S exposure modes, Auto ISO sensitivity is always used. However, in Manual exposure mode Auto ISO can be turned off, or assigned a *maximum* ISO that can be selected automatically, from ISO 64 to Hi 2.0.
- **White Balance.** Here you can select the white balance used to shoot movies. You can choose:
  - **Same As Photo Settings.** The camera will use whatever white balance setting you've specified in the Photo Shooting menu.
  - **Any of the other white balance options.** The selection will apply *only* to video. The white balance of movie clips isn't easy to adjust, so you will usually want to set a specific white balance in this menu entry or opt for Auto white balance. I usually keep this setting the same as selected for still photos.

- **Set Picture Control.** You can specify Same as Photo Settings, or independently specify a Picture Control to be used only when shooting movies. The procedures for selecting and modifying a Picture Control in this menu entry is otherwise the same as described in Chapter 7.

  However, of special note here is the Flat Picture Control (available in both still and movie modes), which produces a dull, washed-out rendition. Why would you want that? Flat captures a wider dynamic range than other Picture Control modes, including Standard, giving you a better "raw" video image to fine-tune in your video-editing software, using your program's video color-grading functions. Grading is used to adjust contrast, color, saturation, detail, black level, and white point, and is especially powerful when used with relatively flat images, like those produced by the Flat Picture Control, or with N-log gamma. As I've mentioned, I'll explain N-log in more detail later.
- **Manage Picture Control.** This entry includes the Save/Edit, Rename, Delete, and Load/Save options that operate the same as the corresponding control in the Photo Shooting menu, described in Chapter 5. You can make a copy of a Picture Control, save an edited copy, rename or remove a style, or retrieve a Picture Control from a memory card.
- **HLG Quality.** This entry is available when Video File Type is set to H.265 10-bit (MOV), and HLG Tone mode has been selected. You can then make adjustments to the only Picture Control available for HLG video (all others are grayed out and unavailable). You'll find step-by-step instructions for fine-tuning the HLG quality options in Chapter 6.
- **Active D-Lighting.** You can choose Same as Photo Settings, Extra High, High, Normal, Low, or Off.
- **High ISO NR.** Video Recording doesn't involve *long* exposures, so the Video Recording menu includes only a High ISO Noise Reduction entry. You can set it to High, Normal, Low, or Off. See the entry for this feature under Photo Shooting menu, earlier in Chapter 5.
- **Vignette Control/Diffraction Compensation/Auto Distortion Control.** These three all operate the same as for still photo shooting and were described in Chapter 5.
- **Skin Softening (Z8 Only).** You can choose Same as Photo Settings, High, Low, Normal, or Off, which is the default. The camera can detect and process up to three subjects to produce a more flattering look.
- **Portrait Impression Balance (Z8 Only).** Three separate profiles that specify magenta/amber color bias (greens and blues are not affected) and set a brightness level to be used when shooting portraits can be created.
- **Video Flicker Reduction/High-Frequency Flicker Reduction.** For the former, choose Auto, or select either 50Hz or 60Hz, as described in Chapter 5. The High Frequency version for shutter speed fine-tuning can be turned on or off.

- **Metering.** Only Matrix, Center-weighted, and Highlight-weighted metering, as described in Chapter 4, are available. Spot metering is not available in Video mode.
- **Focus Mode.** In addition to AF-S, AF-C, and Manual focus, Full-time AF (AF-F) is available in Video mode. Unlike AF-S or AF-C, the AF-F autofocus mode doesn't need to be activated by pressing the shutter release or AF-ON button; AF-F functions as its name suggests: it is active at all times when you're in Video mode. While power consumption is greater, there is less of a lag in achieving sharp focus once you begin video capture.
- **AF-Area Mode.** Only Single-point AF, Wide-area AF (Small, Large, C1, C2), Subject-tracking AF, and Auto-area AF are available. Pinpoint AF is not available in Video mode.
- **AF Subject Detection Options.** You can set the priority for the type of subject the camera will look for during autofocus, including Auto (the default), People, Animal, Birds (on the Z9 only at present), Vehicle, or Airplanes. Subject detection can also be turned off.
- **Vibration Reduction.** This menu entry controls the camera's built-in body image stabilization. You can choose Same as Photo Settings, On (Normal), Sport, or Off.
- **Electronic VR.** As I said earlier in this chapter and in Chapter 5, this electronic form of image stabilization does not shift the sensor's carrier mechanism, as IBIS does. Instead, the electronic version crops the video frame slightly, and shifts the entire frame up, down, left, right, or diagonally enough to counter some camera movement in those directions.

  This feature is not available when shooting 8K video, with 120/100p frame rates, or when Hi-Res Zoom is enabled. Electronic VR is Off with N-RAW 12-bit (NEV) or ProRes RAW HQ 12-bit (MOV) video file types, with frame rates 1920 × 1080 100/120p, or when shooting Slo-Mo. A "waving hand" indicator appears at the right side of the display when Electronic VR is active. Keep in mind that, because of the cropping, the angle of view is reduced slightly, producing a slight focal length "multiplier" effect.
- **Microphone Sensitivity.** This entry has three options that control the built-in microphone or any external microphone you attach. You can choose Auto Sensitivity, Manual Sensitivity to set recording levels yourself (with a handy volume meter on screen showing the current ambient sound levels), or turn the microphone off entirely if you're planning to record silent video, use another sound recording source, or add sound in post-production. (See Figure 12.3.)

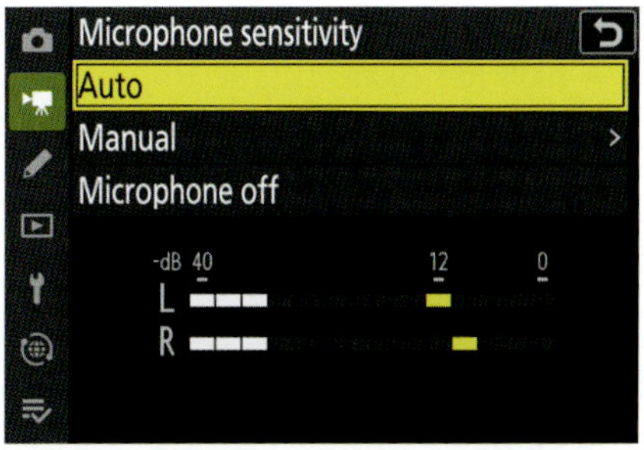

Figure 12.3 Adjusting microphone sensitivity.

- **Attenuator.** Enable this feature to minimize audio distortion from background sounds when capturing video in loud environments.
- **Frequency Response.** Select from Wide Range frequency response to record a broad range of sounds, or Vocal Range to optimize audio recording for vocals.
- **Wind Noise Reduction.** Wind blowing across your microphone can be distracting. This setting reduces wind noise (and may also affect other sounds; so, use it carefully) for the built-in microphones *only.* Your external microphone, like the Nikon ME-1, may have its own wind noise reduction filter on/off switch.
- **Mic Jack Plug-in Power.** If your microphone does not need to draw power from the camera, you can set this entry to Off and prevent possible noise produced by the power supply.
- **Headphone Volume.** You can set a volume from 1 to 30; the default is 15.
- **Timecode.** As I've noted in several places in this book, including Chapter 6, advanced video editing and other software-oriented topics, such as Photoshop, are generally beyond the scope of this book. In any case, using timecodes is a fairly advanced procedure, and those who use them don't need instruction from me.

  However, the ability to embed timecodes in video is a new and highly useful feature for Nikon interchangeable-lens cameras. As I said in Chapter 6, where all the timecode options are described, they provide precise *hour:minute:second:frame* markers that allow identifying and synchronizing frames and audio. The time code system includes a provision for "dropping" frames to ensure that the fractional frame rate of captured video (remember that a 24 fps setting actually yields 23.976 frames per second while 30 fps capture gives you 29.97 actual "frames" per second) can be matched up with actual time spans.
- **External Recording Control (HDMI).** This is the first entry on the last page of the Video Recording menu. Use it to allow your camera's controls to stop and start recording on a compatible external recorder.
- **High-Res Zoom.** This setting uses your camera's extra resolution to provide a high-quality digital zoom effect—even to prime lenses, which have a fixed focal length. When active, you can zoom in and out by pressing the Fn1 or Fn2 buttons, or by rotating the lens control ring. I provided step-by-step instructions for using this feature in Chapter 6.
- **Auto Capture (Z9 only).** In this mode, the camera will constantly evaluate a scene, and then record a video only when a subject is found in the frame at a pre-defined range of distances and moving in a particular direction you specify. The video version uses the same options found in the still photography version, as described in Chapter 5. You can define up to five sets of conditions with appropriate settings for a variety of situations.

Slow-Motion Videos

Slow-motion video is a cool feature that allows you to reduce the apparent playback speed of your movies by 4X or 5X, so you can analyze movement, or apply the effect to your next video involving fast-moving superheroes or those intrepid *Baywatch* lifeguards. It's available only when you have selected "H.264 8-bit (MP4)" from the "Video File Type" setting. At the time this book was written, this feature had yet to be added to the Z8.

In the Frame Size/Frame Rate entry of the Video Recording menu, you have the option of scrolling down to select 1920 × 1080 settings at either 30/25p × 4 (slow-mo) or 24p × 5 (slow-mo) (both NTSC). Video intended for use in PAL countries can select 25p × 4 and 24p × 5 instead.

In slow-motion mode, the camera records Normal Quality video, at 120/100 frames per second (NTSC/PAL) for up to no more than three minutes. When 120/100 fps video is viewed at 30/25 frames per second, the clip takes four times as long to play back; at 24 fps, the clip requires 5X the normal time. As a result, a three-minute clip will stretch to fill 12 minutes when shot at 30/25 fps, or 15 minutes at 24 fps. You can analyze your golf swing or add a slo-mo effect to your movies. While the three-minute capture rate may seem like a limitation, how often do you really want to watch 12 to 15 minutes of slow-motion "action?"

Shooting Your Video

By this time, you're ready to capture some video. To shoot your movies, follow these steps:

1. **Plug in the microphone (optional).** If you want to use an external monaural or stereo microphone with a 3.5mm stereo mini plug, attach it to the microphone jack on the left side of the camera.
2. **Choose an exposure mode.** Select Program, Shutter-priority, Aperture-priority, or Manual exposure, and either Matrix, Center-weighted, or Highlight-weighted metering.
3. **Adjust exposure.** The adjustments you can make depend on the exposure mode you select.
   - **Program/Shutter-priority.** Adjust only exposure compensation by pressing the EV button on top of the camera and rotating the main command dial. The screen image will brighten and darken as you make adjustments. Shutter speed and ISO sensitivity are selected for you by the camera.
   - **Aperture-priority.** You can change the f/stop by rotating the sub-command dial and adjust exposure compensation with the EV button and the main command dial. Shutter speed and ISO sensitivity are selected for you by the camera.
   - **Manual exposure.** The main command dial changes the shutter speed, and the sub-command dial adjusts the aperture. Press the ISO button and rotate the main command dial to change the ISO sensitivity.
4. **Enable movie recording.** Activate movie recording by rotating the Photo/Video switch to the Video position.

5. **Choose a focus and AF-area mode.** Select from autofocus or manual focus using camera settings. Then choose AF-S or AF-F. Select an AF-area mode.
6. **Set audio level.** Use the Microphone Sensitivity entry in the Video Recording menu to specify audio recording level, using Auto Sensitivity to allow the camera to set the volume, or Manual Sensitivity to adjust using an audio meter. You can also turn off audio to record a silent movie, say, if you plan to add a voice-over track, music, or other audio in post-production using your video-editing software.
7. **Start/Stop recording.** Press the red-dotted movie recording button to lock in focus and begin capture. Press again to stop recording. The LCD monitor display as you're capturing video looks like Figure 12.4, with a rectangular red border indicating that recording is underway. The viewfinder display has the same information, arranged slightly differently, and not overlaid on the image area. You can press the DISP button to increase or decrease the amount of information overlaid on the screen during movie recording.

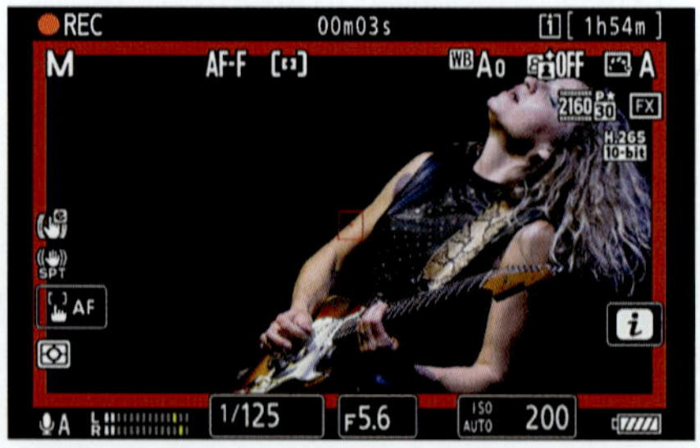

Figure 12.4 The LCD monitor display during movie capture.

8. **No flash.** You can't use electronic flash during movie recording, but you *can* use the built-in LED movie light on the Nikon SB-500 unit.

Using the *i* button Menu

The *i* button, which is so useful in Photo mode, also offers real-time adjustment of parameters and controls while you capture your video. These are not only important for fine-tuning your movies as you capture them but allow for some special tools that veteran videographers will know and love, but which may be new to still photographers. Here's a description of the useful options that pop up when you press the *i* button. (See Figure 12.5.) Many of these are also available in the Video Recording menu, as explained in Chapter 6.

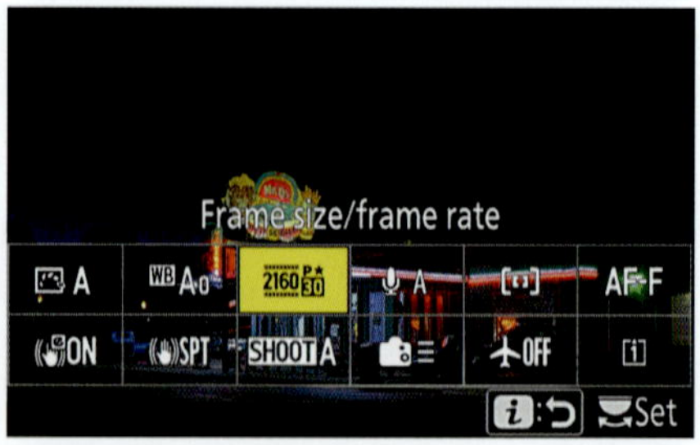

Figure 12.5 *i* button options.

The Set Picture Control, White Balance, and Vibration Reduction entries have pairs of options that are separately adjusted using the main command dial and sub-command dial. A yellow camera icon with arrows appears to the far right of the display to remind you. All the other entries can be adjusted by rotating either command dial, except for Custom Controls and Airplane Mode (press OK instead).

Here are your options:

- **Set Picture Control.** You can use any of the Picture Controls described in Chapter 5 in Video mode and specify them here.
- **White Balance.** Set your white balance for movie shooting here, using the main command dial for the primary settings and sub-command dial for any options available.
- **Frame Size/Frame Rate.** Select your frame rate here.
- **Microphone Sensitivity.** It's useful to be able to use the *i* menu while shooting video to adjust the sensitivity of your microphone on the fly. As this adjustment controls both the built-in and optional external stereo microphones, you might find yourself needing to make your mic more sensitive or less sensitive as the ambient sound conditions change. For example, if you were capturing a clip with only background sound (no vocals) and someone started using a jackhammer a block away, you might want to reduce microphone sensitivity to minimize the clamor.
- **AF-area Mode/Subject Detection.** Choose from among the available AF-area modes with the main command dial, and adjust subject detection with the sub-command dial.
- **Focus Mode.** Choose AF-S, AF-C, AF-F, or MF.
- **Electronic VR.** Turn it on or off.
- **Vibration Reduction.** You can turn in-body image stabilization off, or choose between Normal and Sport modes.
- **Shooting Menu Bank.** Quickly switch among the shared Shooting Menu banks A–D.
- **Custom Controls.** The command dials do nothing when this setting is highlighted. Press OK to access the Custom Controls setting screen.
- **Airplane Mode.** Press OK or tap the icon to turn airplane mode on or off. Again, the dials perform no function here.
- **Destination.** Quickly switch from one memory card slot to the other with either command dial, and view how much recording time is available on each card.

As I described in Chapter 7, there is a Custom Setting g1: Customize *i* button menu entry that allows you to swap out and change Video mode *i* menu items. You'll probably want to do so, because Nikon's choice of which features to include in the video *i* menu don't make a lot of sense to me. I think you'll find there are other functions that you need much more. My top candidates for replacement are the Custom Controls and Airplane mode options, which access rarely used features. If you don't frequently use Picture Controls, you can dispense with that one, too.

As in Photo mode, the *i* button has additional features during Playback, when you can use available options to trim videos, grab an individual frame as a still photo, apply ratings, and perform other functions. I'll explain these later in this chapter.

Stop That!

You might think that setting your camera to a faster shutter speed will help give you sharper video frames. But the choice of a shutter speed for movie making is a bit more complicated than that. First, you can't select the shutter speed at all for your movies when you're using Auto, P, S, or A exposure modes. You can select a shutter speed only if you switch to Manual exposure. Here's how it works:

- **Program and Shutter-priority modes.** The camera selects the shutter speed (such as 1/30th second) and ISO sensitivity appropriate for your lighting conditions. Your only exposure adjustment option is to press the EV button and add/subtract exposure compensation. As you might guess, P and S modes are not the best choices for those who want to shoot creatively.
- **Aperture-priority mode.** This is the mode to use when you want to put selective focus to work by choosing an aperture that will provide more, or less, depth-of-field. In A mode, you can select any f/stop available with your lens, and the camera will choose a shutter speed and ISO setting to suit. Generally, if you choose a large aperture, the camera will lower the ISO sensitivity as much as it can, to allow sticking with a shutter speed of 1/30th second. It will then select shorter shutter speeds, if necessary, under very bright illumination. My camera has jumped up to 1/200th second outdoors under bright daylight when I try to shoot at f/1.8 or f/1.4. In A mode, you can still add or subtract exposure compensation.
- **Manual exposure mode.** In this mode, you have control of aperture, shutter speed (from 1/25th second all the way up to 1/32000th second), and ISO—even if your settings result in video that is completely washed out, or entirely black. Because video capture is in the range of 24 to 120 frames per second, you can't select a shutter speed that is longer than the frame interval. That is, if your video mode is 1920 × 1080 at 30 fps, you can't choose a shutter speed longer than 1/30th second; at 120p, the longest shutter speed available is 1/125th second. Thanks to the Z9/Z8's ability to activate Auto ISO in manual mode, you can enable semi-manual/semi-automatic exposure, as I'll describe in the ISO Control in Video Mode section that follows.

So, how do you select an appropriate shutter speed? As you might guess, it's almost always best to leave the shutter speed at 1/30th second and allow the overall exposure to be adjusted by varying the aperture and/or ISO sensitivity. We don't normally stare at a video frame for longer than 1/30th or 1/24th second, so while the shakiness of the *camera* can be disruptive (and often corrected by VR), if there is a bit of blur in our *subjects* from movement, we tend not to notice. Each frame flashes by in the blink of an eye, so to speak, so a shutter speed of 1/30th second works a lot better in video than it does when shooting stills.

Higher shutter speeds introduce problems of their own. If you shoot a video frame using a shutter speed of 1/200th second, the actual moment in time that's captured represents only about 12 percent of the 1/30th second of elapsed time in that frame. Yet, when played back, that frame occupies the full 1/30th of a second, with 88 percent of that time filled by stretching the original image to fill it. The result is often a choppy/jumpy image, and one that may appear to be *too* sharp.

The reason for that is more social imprinting than scientific: we've all grown up accustomed to seeing the look of Hollywood productions that, by convention, were shot using a shutter speed that's half the reciprocal of the frame rate (that is, 1/48th second for a 24 fps movie). Video cameras use a rotary shutter (achieving that 1/48th-second exposure by using a 180-degree shutter "angle"), but the effect on our visual expectations is the same. For the most "film-like" appearance, use 24 fps and 1/60th-second shutter speed.

Faster shutter speeds do have some specialized uses for motion analysis, especially where individual frames are studied. The rest of the time, 1/30th or 1/60th of a second will suffice. If the reason you needed a higher shutter speed was to obtain the correct exposure, use a slower ISO setting, or a neutral-density filter to cut down on the amount of light passing through the lens.

A good rule of thumb when shooting progressive video (as opposed to interlaced video, which is not offered by the Z9 or Z8) is to use 1/60th second or slower when shooting at 24 fps; 1/60th second or slower at 30 fps; 1/125th second or slower at 60 fps; and 1/250th second or slower at 120 fps.

ISO Control in Video Mode

As I've pointed out several times earlier in the chapter, the Z9 and Z8 implement the ISO sensitivity setting slightly differently in video mode. In P, A, and S modes, Auto ISO is mandatory; you can't specify a particular ISO setting, and pressing the camera's ISO button does nothing. Your exposure adjustment options include only aperture, shutter speed, and exposure compensation through plus/minus EV settings.

If you need or want more control over ISO, say, because you want to avoid high ISO noise, switching to manual exposure is your best bet. You can lock in a specific ISO value if you like, or use Auto ISO to provide a sort of semi-manual/semi-automatic exposure mode.

Just navigate to the ISO Sensitivity Settings entry in the Video Recording menu, and access the Auto ISO Control (Mode M) option. When enabled, in manual exposure mode the camera will attempt to adjust the ISO setting to provide the correct exposure based on the current shutter speed, aperture, and exposure compensation values you've specified. That means you can select a suitable shutter speed, and an f/stop, and the camera will effectively provide you with autoexposure in Manual exposure mode. The Maximum Sensitivity option within the same entry lets you tell the camera not to use an ISO higher than the value you specify, from ISO 200 to Hi 2.0.

Viewing Your Videos

Once you've finished recording your movies, they are available for review. Film clips show up during picture review, the same as still photos, but they are differentiated by a movie camera icon overlay and "Play" prompt. Press the multi selector center button to start playback. During playback, you can perform the following functions:

- **Pause.** Press the multi selector down button to pause the clip during playback. Press the multi selector center button to resume playback.
- **Rewind/Advance.** Press the left/right multi selector buttons to rewind or advance (respectively). Press once for 2X speed, twice for 8X speed, or three times for 16X speed. Hold down the left/right buttons to move to the end or beginning of the clip.
- **Start Slo-Mo playback.** Press the down button while the movie is paused to play back in slow motion.
- **Skip 10 seconds.** Rotate the sub-command dial to skip ahead or back in 10-second increments.
- **Change volume.** Press the Zoom In and Zoom Out buttons to increase/decrease volume.
- **Trim movie/Save frame.** Press the *i* button and follow the steps in the next section.
- **Exit Playback.** Press the multi selector up button or the Playback button to exit playback.
- **Return to shooting mode.** Press the Video button to return to shooting mode.
- **View menus.** Press the MENU button to interrupt playback to access menus.

Trimming Your Videos

In-camera editing is limited to trimming the beginning or end from a clip, and the clip must be at least two seconds long. For more advanced editing, you'll need an application capable of editing movie clips. Google "Movie Editor" to locate any of the hundreds of free video editors available, or use a commercial product like iMovie, Corel Video Studio, Adobe Premiere Elements, or Pinnacle Studio. These will let you combine several clips into one movie, add titles, special effects, and transitions between scenes.

In-camera trimming can be done using the tools available during Playback. To do in-camera trimming, follow these steps:

1. **Start movie clip.** Use the Playback button to start image review and press the multi selector center button to start playback when you see a clip you want to edit. It will begin playing.
2. **View movie to start point.** To remove video from the beginning of a clip, play the movie until you reach the first frame you want to keep, and then press the down button to pause. The movie progress bar at the bottom left of the screen will show the current position in the movie with a yellow highlight marker. You can move the marker back and forth frame by frame while the video is paused by pressing the left/right buttons or rotating the main or sub-command dials. (See Figure 12.6, upper left.)

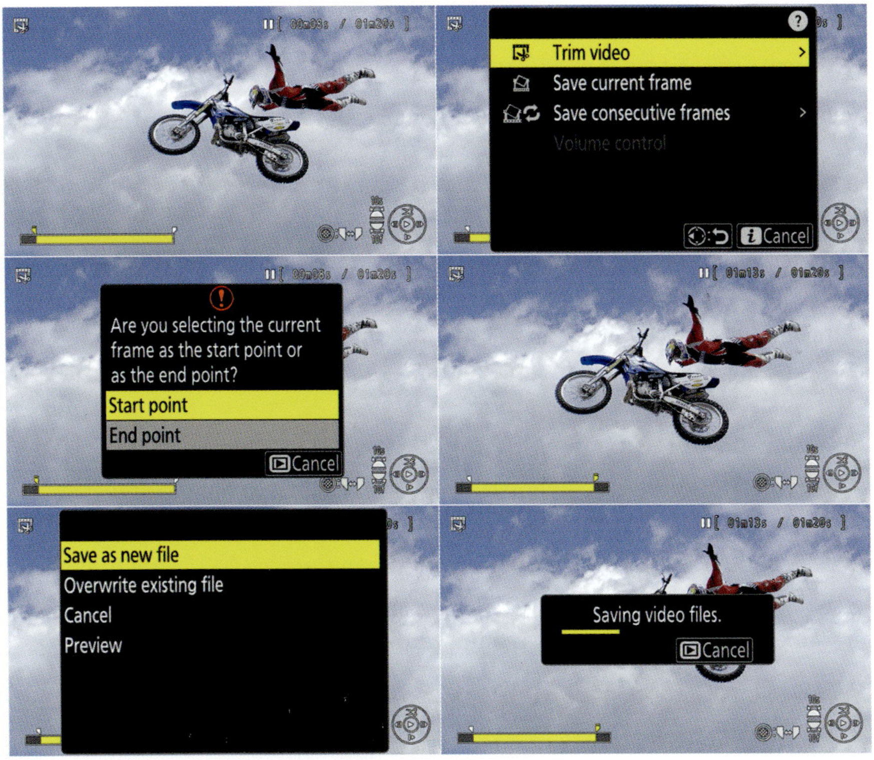

Figure 12.6 Editing a movie clip.

3. **Mark start.** Press the up button. The screen shown at upper right in the figure appears. Highlight Trim Video and press the right button. Press the right button again to confirm as the start point. (See Figure 12.6, center left.)
4. **Switch to end point.** Press the sub-selector button to move the yellow marker to the end of the clip, as seen in Figure 12.6, center right. Adjust the marker's position with the left/right buttons or command dials, as in Step 2. When satisfied, press the up button.
5. **Save edited clip.** The screen shown at lower left appears. You can save the edited clip as a new file, or overwrite the existing file. It's usually a good idea to retain the original in case you want to re-edit the clip later.
6. **File saved.** A progress bar indicates your edited movie is being saved. (See Figure 12.6, lower right.)

Saving Stills from a Video

You can store any single frame or a series of frames from one of your movies as a JPEG still, using the resolution of the current video format. The feature is available during Playback as an *i* menu option, as described above. Just follow these steps:

1. **Pause at desired frame.** As with the video-trimming feature, pause your movie at the frame you want to save by pressing the down button.
2. **Choose single or multiple frames.** Press the *i* button and highlight either Save Current Frame or Save Consecutive Frames.
3. **Save single frame or continue for multiple.** Press the right button to save the current frame and finish, or to move on to choosing how many consecutive frames you want to capture. (Figure 12.7, upper left.)
4. **Single frame saved.** Press the up button to save a still copy of the selected frame.
5. **Specify destination.** If storing multiple frames, choose where you want the images stored. (Figure 12.7, upper right.)
6. **Select length of capture.** You can capture all consecutive frames in the next 1, 2, 5, or 10 seconds of your video. (Figure 12.7, lower left.) Press the right button to continue.
7. **Frames stored.** Your frames will be saved to your memory card. (Figure 12.7, lower right.)

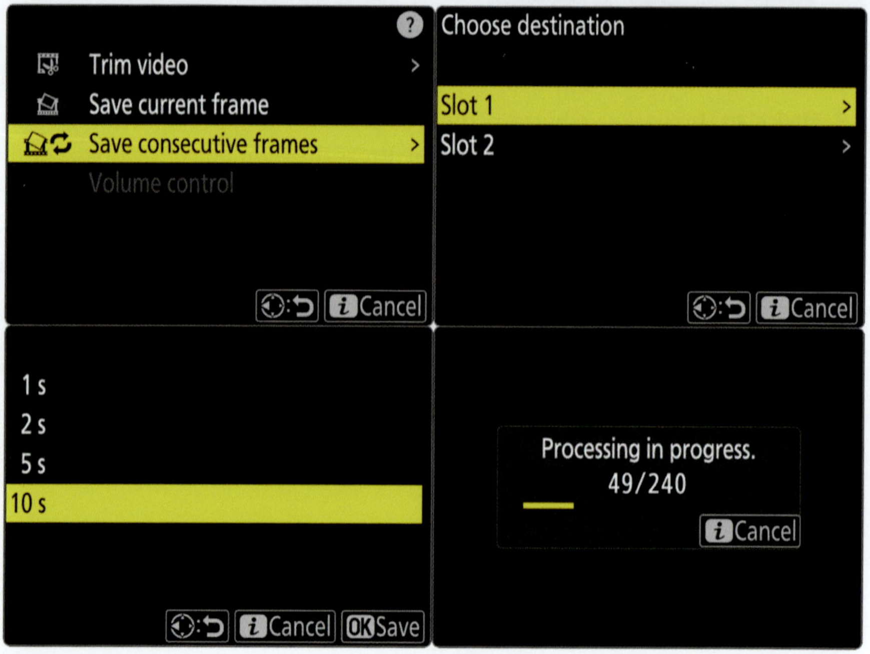

Figure 12.7 Capturing single or multiple frames from video.

Upping Your Video Game

Feature films have been shot entirely or in part using Nikon still cameras. Indeed, the Emmy-winning Showtime television series *Dexter* included many scenes captured with a Nikon camera. The Z9 and Z8 really up the ante by incorporating video capabilities that have been enhanced or simply not available with previous Nikon still cameras.

Two varieties of RAW recording, the availability of N-log recording, and HLG options are stellar examples, bringing advanced capture and color/tonal-correcting capabilities to cameras that can capture 8K, 4K, and Full HD–quality video while outperforming the typical modestly priced digital video camcorder—especially when you consider the range of lenses and other helpful accessories available for it that are not possible with more limited video-only devices.

Using an External Recorder

If you're truly becoming an advanced videographer, you'll probably be working with the camera's ability to output "clean" non-compressed HDMI video to an external monitor or video recorder, including the Atomos Shogun lineup, which includes versions that are quite affordable, at least in terms of professional video gear. You can choose models both with and without an external LCD monitor, and capture to solid-state drives (SSD), a laptop's internal or connected hard drive, or to CFast memory cards (the latter chiefly as a nod to those still using the "fast" version of Compact Flash cards). Such equipment allows very high transfer rates and is certainly your best choice if you're shooting 4K video.

Probably the best of the lot is the Atomos Ninja lineup, which launched with the original Ninja V shown in Figure 12.8, and followed by the V+ and most recent Ninja and Ninja Ultra models. They are all extremely portable, roughly 13-ounce units with a 5.2-inch screen and price tags that are currently among the lowest for this type of device. Add a battery, HDMI cable, and a 2.5-inch solid-state drive, and you're ready to go.

The Ninja monitor-recorders have HDMI input and output jacks on their left edges, as shown in the figure, which allows you to daisy-chain an even larger monitor or other device. A power button, headphone jack, microphone/audio input, and remote jack reside on the other edge. The touch screen enables you to view your video and access the monitor/recorder's menus and controls, which is convenient (except outdoors in cold weather when you're wearing gloves and might wish you had a few buttons to press instead). The only other "defect" of the unit is the noise produced by its fan; even when you're using an external microphone, the fan noise may be picked up in a quiet room.

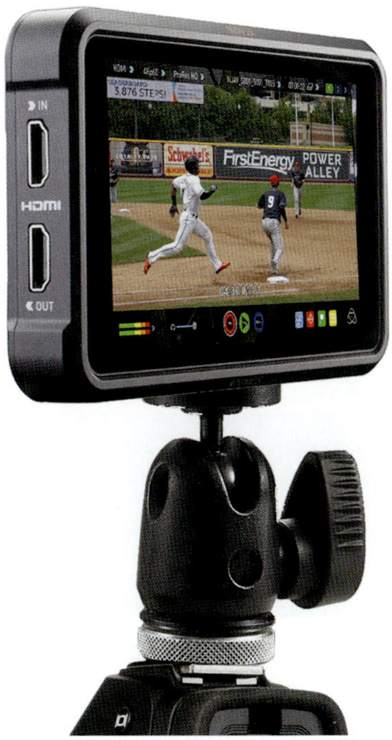

Figure 12.8 The Atomos Ninja V monitor/recorder.

Why use an external monitor/recorder when your camera has its own nifty monitor and can store quite a lot of video on its memory cards? From a monitor standpoint, an external unit's screen is larger, easier to see, and offers more flexibility in positioning. The screen tilts up or down; mounted on a ballhead like the one in the figure, you can adjust an external screen to any angle, including reversing it to point in the same direction as the lens, so vloggers can monitor themselves as they record or stream their video blog.

External monitor-recorders are especially adept at displaying and storing video captured at high resolutions, fast frame rates, and demanding transfer speeds using a variety of compression schemes. RAW video isn't actually compressed, and is even more demanding. While the Z9/Z8 can capture and store their full range of video types internally, an external recorder can be especially useful for those who do a great deal of videography.

The HDMI port accepts a full-size HDMI, which can be connected to the monitor, recorder, or other device of your choice. I use HDMI playback for slide shows, too, and captured most of the screenshot images in this book using the HDMI output and a $25 4K video capture device with OBS (Open Broadcaster Software) Studio. Before you link up your equipment, you'll want to choose from the following options, described in detail in Chapter 9 (see Figure 12.9, left):

- **Output Resolution.** Select Auto and the camera will sense the correct output resolution to use. You can also choose specific resolutions, including 4320p (8K), 2160p (4K), 1080p (Full HD), and 720p (Standard HD), as shown in Figure 12.9, center. These are all progressive scan. You can also select 1080i if your device accepts only interlaced scanning. However, in that case, footage captured at 120p, 60p, 30p, or 24p are output at 60i, and 100p, 50p, or 25p are output at 50i.

  As noted in Chapter 9, 10-bit video is output at 10 bits only to HDMI recorders that support it. In addition, Regardless of the resolution you select here, when the Video File Type selected in the Video Recording menu is N-RAW 12-bit (NEV) or ProRes RAW HQ 12-bit (MOV), the output resolution will be 1920 × 1080. Finally, 8K video, or 4K video captured at 120p/100p will not be output at HDMI if there is a memory card in the camera and either 4320p (progressive) or 2160p (progressive) is specified as the Output Resolution.

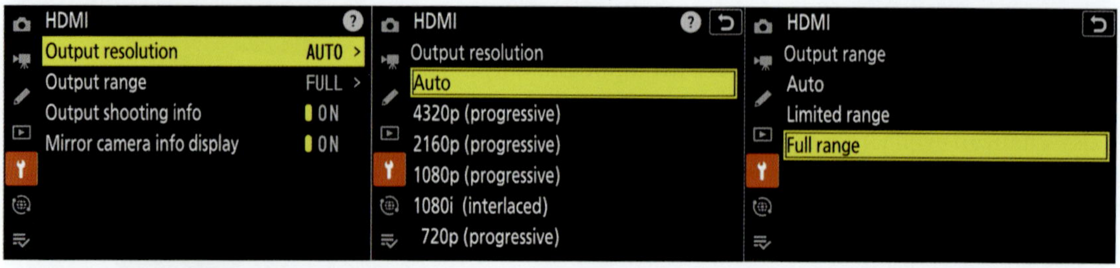

Figure 12.9 Choose output resolution and range.

- **Output Range.** Choose Auto (the default, and the best choice under most circumstances), Limited Range, or Full Range. In most cases, the camera will be able to determine the output range of your HDMI device. If not, you can choose a range, as described in Chapter 9. (See Figure 12.9, right.)
- **Output Shooting Information.** Choose On, and the icons and shooting information shown on the electronic viewfinder or LCD monitor will be included in the output to the external device if you want that display included, say, to illustrate operation of the camera. Select Off and the information will be stripped out, leaving you with a clean recording.
- **Mirror Camera Information Display.** When directing output to an external device, you may want to also have it shown on the rear LCD monitor (the default), especially if the external device is a monitor not physically attached to the camera. If you're using a recorder/display mounted on the camera or its cage, you can save some battery power by choosing Off for this item.

Additional HDMI settings are available in the Video Recording menu, described in Chapter 6. They include External Recording Control (HDMI) for devices that support control from the camera.

Tonal Grading

If you've been taking photos for a while, you're probably familiar with all the fixes and tweaks you can do with your still images within image editors like Photoshop. It's relatively easy to adjust color tones, contrast, sharpness, and other parameters prior to displaying or printing your photo. Videos are a little trickier, because any given video typically consists of *thousands* of individual photos, captured at 24 frames per second (or faster), with the possibility that each and every frame within a particular sequence might need fixes or creative adjustments.

Tonal control is one of the key parameters that determine the quality of your video, at least in terms of the dynamic range—the amount of detail in the deepest shadows and brightest highlights. The Z9 and Z8 can produce video with an excellent scale of tones, but for more serious productions there are several tools that allow extending the dynamic range using a post-processing tool called color grading.

TECH ALERT #2

Color grading is a highly technical aspect of video making, at least in terms of the amount of knowledge you need to possess to correctly judge what changing one of the parameters will do to your video. The rest of this section provides an overview with a quick description of the process, so you'll have a starting point when you start to explore advanced video techniques. It's not intended to be a complete guide to using N-log or HLG.

One way of increasing the range of tones in video is to shoot relatively low-contrast footage in order to capture the largest dynamic range possible, and then fine-tune the rendition later using editing software. Nikon offers several dynamic-range-enhancing features, including an N-log output option that provides low-contrast capture, which can then be manipulated using the *color grading* available in advanced video processing software.

There are three basic capture modes that affect dynamic range:

- **Standard Dynamic Range.** When choosing a video file type in the Video Recording menu, SDR (Standard Dynamic Range) is one of two options available for N-RAW 12-bit (NEV), ProRes RAW HQ 12-bit (MOV), ProRes 422 HQ 10-bit (MOV), and H.265 10-bit (MOV). This mode provides, as its name suggests, the basic "standard" range of tones, unless you modify that range using a Picture Control, most frequently the Flat picture control. Your footage will have relatively low contrast as shot, but can be adjusted somewhat with advanced video-editing software.
- **N-Log.** The video file types listed above can also be captured using Nikon's proprietary logarithmic (non-linear) gamma algorithms. I'll explain gamma in more detail shortly. N-Log video can be displayed using something called a lookup table (LUT), which translates a value from one environment to one more suited to another environment. They're used to convert from one color space to another or, in this case, to translate tones captured using N-Log into colors/tones that can be handled by a monitor or other device. I'll describe LUTs in more detail shortly.
- **HLG (Hybrid Log Gamma).** This is a high dynamic range recording method developed specifically for television video by a consortium of the British BBC and Japanese NHK broadcast organizations. HLG video, which also makes use of lookup tables, is available only when your video file type is H.265 10-bit (MOV).

Gamma, Gamma, Ding Dong

Grading is necessary thanks to our evolutionary heritage: humans don't see differences in tones in a linear manner. An absolutely smooth progression of pixels from absolute black to pure white (with 0 representing black and 256 representing white) would not look like a continuous gradient to our eyes. We'd be unable to detect differences in shadows and highlights that have the same change in tonal values as midtones. So, everything from computer monitors to printers use a correction factor (gamma) to cancel out the differences in the way we see tones.

This correction takes the form of a curve, called a *gamma curve*. If you remember your geometry, the x and y axes on a graph are used to define the shape of a curve, and in the case of gamma curves, the values use logarithmic units (ack!) to define the slope. That's where the term N-log, HLG (hybrid log gamma), and other mind-numbing jargon comes from. The whole shebang is needed to reconcile the ability of sensors to capture, video systems to display, and printers to output a range of tones in a linear way with the actual tones we perceive non-linearly. Gamma correction and gamma compression are used to help make sure that what we get is what we see. While gamma correction between computer platforms (that is, between Macs and PCs) may be different, the actual gamma values defined by video standards like NTSC and PAL are fixed and well-known.

N-log

As I noted above, the digital images we work with are always adjusted using a gamma curve, which changes the relative brightness/darkness of highlights, midtones, and shadows so they more closely resemble how the human eye sees them. You probably have worked with gamma curves if you calibrated your computer monitor or printer. There's really no need to have a deep understanding of the math involved in order to optimize the look of your images or video. And Nikon doesn't ask you to. But it does offer tools like N-log to let you improve their appearance.

TECH ALERT #3

In a camera, changes in sensor sensitivity or exposure are indicated using ISO settings, shutter speeds, or f/stops (for example, f/2 provides twice as much light as f/2.8 which, in turn, provides twice as much light as f/4). Unfortunately, that constant doubling is an inefficient way of storing information; the numbers quickly become too large to fit into the number of bits available to store them.

A much more efficient way to store the same visual information is to use logarithms instead. Those of us who never got much beyond algebra in math class will be happy to know that logarithms can simply be thought of as the flip side of linear visual information. Instead of doubling the number of pixels for each brightness increment, a log scale just increases the same amount for each step. That lets you specify many more brightness levels within the same storage space. Gamma curves/correction are a way of converting captured linear information into a more efficient logarithmic curve.

N-log is a logarithmic gamma curve that is used when the video will be processed after shooting and captures a much larger range of tones (roughly up to 14 stops!) than standard gamma curves. Indeed, the tones captured using N-log can't be displayed in all their glory on a standard TV or monitor, which are generally adjusted for the broadcast television BT-709 standard. Instead, the unprocessed video will look darker and lower in contrast because all those tonal values have been squeezed into the BT-709 (also called REC-709) range. You can enable Custom Setting g11/g12 (Z8/Z9): View Assist to adjust the *appearance* during preview of video recorded using N-Log or HLG (described next); while the colors are simplified and contrast increased, the actual recorded video is not changed.

To enable correcting brightness, saturation, and hue as you work with the expanded dynamic range during editing, you need a lookup table (LUT), as mentioned earlier. The LUT is an array of preselected values that map the colors contained in the original captured input to the desired colors of the final video. N-log creates a 3D LUT that assigns each RGB value to a single combined value in the table. You can use this LUT to perform color grading with software including Adobe Premier Pro CC, Apple Final Cut Pro X, and BlackMagic Design DaVinci Resolve 18.

Video signals normally encompass brightness levels from 0 percent to 110 percent (you read that right: modern video cameras can record detail in highlights that are actually brighter than was possible when the video age began; the old scale was retained, reminiscent of Nigel Tufnel's 11 setting on his amp). However, even 110 percent provides too much of a limitation; cameras can capture detail in highlights that are even brighter than *that*. So, a log gamma curve (in this case one called N-log) is used to *compress* all that image detail to fit into the space allowed for conventional video signals.

Post-processing and grading in a video editor allows working with all that information and produces a finished video that contains the filmmaker's selection of tonal values in a form that can be displayed comfortably. The full dynamic range can be used to produce the finished movie. You might find that useful when exposing for highlights while avoiding blowing out the sky, or for capturing detail in shadows without losing mid tones and highlights. N-log gives you even better results than using the Flat Picture control, which was also introduced with exactly this application in mind.

RESTRICTIONS

While capturing N-log, Picture Controls, Active D-Lighting, and High ISO NR are disabled. Maximum ISO Sensitivity can only be set in the range ISO 1600–25600, and the lowest value for ISO Sensitivity (Mode M) is ISO 800. You may see some noise or flicker in the LCD monitor. Finally, you'll need to visit the Timecode entry of the Video Recording menu and select On (With HDMI Output) to direct time-codes to the recorder.

HLG/HDR

A new wrinkle in the Nikon toolkit is the addition of HLG (Hybrid-Log Gamma) output, which produces a type of HDR footage used for broadcast video. Note that HDR in video terms is *not* the same thing as HDR for stills (which requires multiple exposures combined into one final image). HLG video is produced by extending the dynamic range of the original captured frames.

One problem with the original implementation of HDR video is that it could only be displayed on an HDR-capable television. So, two of the biggest gorillas in the broadcast industry, BBC and NHK, developed Hybrid-Log Gamma, which produces video that can show HDR content on non-HDR displays. Direct the same video to a 4K television with HLG/HDR support, and it will play back with the increased contrast, brighter highlights, and larger color gamut possible with high dynamic range video.

Refocusing on Focus

Although I explained autofocus and manual focus options in Chapter 5, there are some special considerations for focus when capturing video. The availability of usable AF when capturing movies, thanks to the on-sensor phase-detection autofocus (PDAF), is extremely important. The camera now more quickly and reliably is able to gauge subject distance, tracking and refocusing on subjects reliably; you really don't want inaccurate focus in video clips, where inconsistent focus is quite obvious when the movie is viewed.

Your three autofocus modes work extremely well. AF-S focuses once and is useful for non-moving subjects; AF-C refocuses only while you're holding down the shutter release or AF-ON button. That's particularly useful when you want to retain focus on a particular subject but refocus at your command as needed when the subject moves. AF-F (Full-time AF) is available if you need to refocus constantly as you capture. Use Custom Setting g6: AF Speed to control whether the camera refocuses quickly to follow a moving subject or refocuses more slowly to switch from one subject to another. Custom Setting g7: AF Tracking Sensitivity can enable/disable the ability to switch quickly when a different subject intervenes between the camera and the original subject. Both these fine-tuning behaviors can be used creatively to concentrate/deconcentrate attention on a particular subject or area of the frame.

Manual focus, with help from Custom Setting a13: Focus Peaking, is an option, particularly for those who want to "pull" or "push" focus, a creative technique for redirecting the viewer's attention from one subject to another, located in the foreground or background. The only complications are that the focus isn't particularly linear, so a certain degree of rotation of the focus/control ring doesn't necessarily result in the same amount of adjustment of the focus. I discussed this problem and its solutions in Chapter 3 in the section Using the Control/Focus Ring.

Shooting Better Video

Producing good-quality video is more complicated than just buying good equipment and learning how to use it. There are techniques that make for gripping storytelling and a visual language the average person is very accustomed to seeing, but also unaware of. After all, by comparison we're used to watching the best productions that television, video, and motion pictures can offer. Whether it's fair or not, our efforts are compared to what we're used to seeing produced by experts. While this book can't make you a professional videographer, there is some advice I can give you that will help you improve your results. There are many different things to consider when planning a video shoot, and when possible, a shooting script and storyboard can help you produce a higher-quality video.

Lens Craft

A discussion of why lens selection is important when shooting movies may be useful at this point. In the video world, not all lenses are created equal. The two most important considerations are depth-of-field, or the beneficial lack thereof, and zooming. I'll address each of these separately.

Depth-of-Field and Video

Have you wondered why professional videographers have gone nuts over still cameras that can also shoot video? The producers of *Saturday Night Live* could afford to have their director of photography use the niftiest, most-expensive high-resolution video cameras to shoot the opening sequences of the program. Instead, they opt for a digital still camera. One thing that makes digital still cameras so attractive for video is that they have relatively large sensors, which provides improved low-light performance and results in the oddly attractive reduced depth-of-field, compared with many professional video cameras.

But wait! you say. No matter what size sensor is used to capture a video frame, isn't the number of pixels in that frame the same? That's true—the final resolution of a full HD 1080p video image is exactly 1920 × 1080 pixels. For standard HD (720p) the resolution is 1280 × 720 pixels (which the camera does not offer), and for ultra HD/4K (2160p), the resolution is 3840 × 2160 pixels. The final resolution, at least for the most common 1080p resolution, is the same, whether you're capturing that frame with a point-and-shoot camera, a professional video camera, or a digital SLR. But that's only the *final* resolution. The number of pixels used to *originally* capture each video frame varies by sensor size.

For example, your camera does *not* use only its central 1920 × 1080 pixels to capture a full HD video frame. If it did that, you'd have to contend with a huge "crop" factor. That doesn't happen! Instead, when the camera is set for *FX-based movie format*, it captures a video frame using an area that stretches across nearly the full width of the sensor, measuring 7680 × 4320 pixels, using the *proportions* of a 16:9 area of its sensor (rather than the full 8256 × 5504 FX resolution of the sensor). That's true for *all* HD formats: standard HD (720p), full HD (1080p), ultra HD (4K, 2160p), and 8K (4320p). Your wide-angle and telephoto lenses retain roughly their same fields of view, and you can frame and compose your video through the viewfinder normally, with only the top and bottom of the frame cropped off to account for the wider video aspect ratio. (See Figure 12.10.)

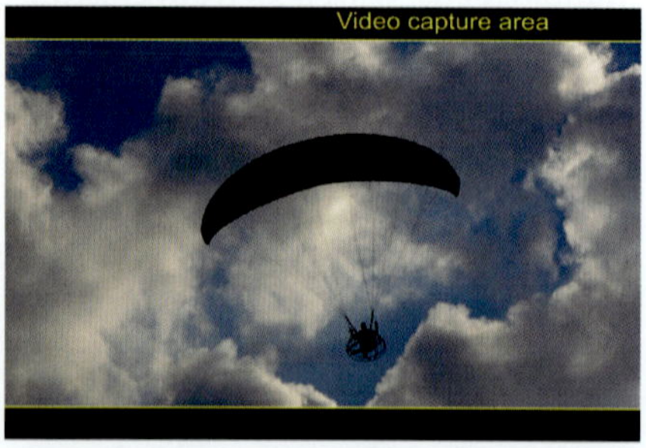

Figure 12.10 The cropped video capture area for HD movies.

A larger sensor calls for the use of longer focal lengths to produce the same field of view, so, in effect, a larger sensor like the full-frame FX sensor used in the camera has reduced depth-of-field. And *that's* what makes cameras like the Z9/Z8 attractive from a creative standpoint. Less depth-of-field means greater control over the range of what's in focus. Your Z9/Z8, with its larger sensor, has a distinct advantage over even DX models like the Nikon Z fc or Z50, is miles ahead of consumer camcorders in this regard, and even does a better job than many professional video cameras. (Some professional video cameras do use large sensors.) Figure 12.11 compares some typical sensor sizes.

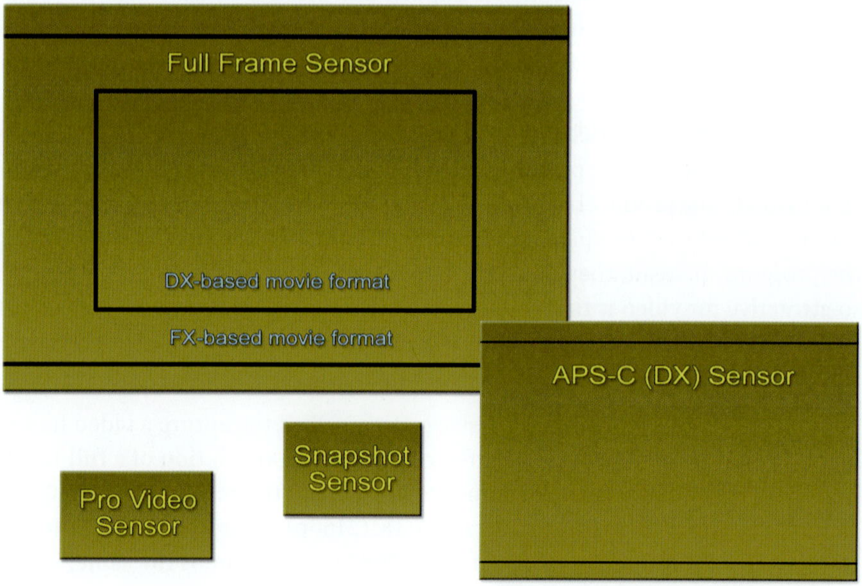

Figure 12.11 Relative size of full frame, APS-C, snapshot, and pro-video sensors.

Zooming and Video

When shooting still photos, a zoom is a zoom is a zoom. The key considerations for a zoom lens used only for still photography are the maximum aperture available at each focal length ("How *fast* is this lens?), the zoom range ("How far can I zoom in or out?"), and its sharpness at any given f/stop ("Do I lose sharpness when I shoot wide open?").

When shooting video, the priorities may change, and there are two additional parameters to consider. The first two I listed, lens speed and zoom range, have roughly the same importance in both still and video photography. Zoom range gains a bit of importance in videography, because you can always/usually move closer to shoot a still photograph, but when you're zooming during a shot most of us don't have that option (or the funds to buy/rent a dolly to smoothly move the camera during capture).

Oddly enough, overall sharpness may have slightly less importance under certain conditions when shooting video. That's because the image changes in some way many times per second (24/30/60/120 times per second), so any given frame doesn't hang around long enough for our eyes to pick out every single detail. You want a sharp image, of course, but your standards don't need to be quite as high when shooting video. Before purchasing any new lens that will be used for video, I recommend checking out discussions in online forums to see what videographers think of those optics. You'll find valuable information about the considerations listed below, as well as the pros and cons of other features, such as the ability to "de-click" the aperture (for silent f/stop changes) or accuracy of the aperture settings (videographers may prefer "T-stops," which represent actual light transmission, over f/stops).

Your Nikon Z9 or Z8 adds another wrinkle to video zooming considerations: both cameras offer a digital high-resolution zoom feature, as described in Chapter 6. The Hi-Res Zoom applies a digital zoom effect to any lens, even if a non-zooming prime lens is mounted on the camera. You'll need to assign the zoom in/zoom out behaviors to the Fn1 and Fn2 buttons, or the lens control ring, using Custom Setting g2: Custom Controls. Zoom speed can be set to Slower, Standard, or Faster (on the Z8) or a sliding scale from –5 to +5 (on the Z9) using Custom Setting g8. Image Area must be set to FX (so it won't work with DX lenses), and the video file type must be ProRes 422 HQ 10-bit (MOV), H.265 10-bit (MOV), H.265 8-bit (MOV), or H.264 (MP4). The Frame Size/Frame Rate can be either 4K (3840 × 2160) at 30/25p or 24p, or 1920 × 1080 at 120/100p, 60/50p, 30/25p, or 24p.

Here are the most important considerations for video shooters:

- **Zoom lens maximum aperture.** The speed of the lens matters in several ways. A zoom with a relatively large maximum aperture lets you shoot in lower light levels, and a big f/stop allows you to minimize depth-of-field for selective focus. Keep in mind that the maximum aperture may change during zooming. A lens that offers an f/3.5 maximum aperture at its widest focal length may provide only f/5.6 worth of light at the telephoto position.

- **Zoom range.** Use of zoom during actual capture should not be an everyday thing unless you're shooting a kung-fu movie. However, there are effective uses for a zoom shot, particularly if it's a "long" one from extreme wide angle to extreme close-up (or vice versa). Most of the time, you'll use the zoom range to adjust the perspective *between* shots, and a longer zoom range can mean less trotting back and forth to adjust the field of view. Zoom range also comes into play when you're working with selective focus (longer focal lengths have less depth-of-field) or want to expand or compress the apparent distance between foreground and background subjects. A longer range gives you more flexibility.
- **Linearity.** Interchangeable lenses may have some drawbacks, as many photographers who have been using the video features of their interchangeable-lens digital cameras have discovered. That's because, unless a lens is optimized for video recording, zooming with a particular lens may not necessarily be linear. Rotating the zoom collar manually at a constant speed doesn't always produce a smooth zoom. There may be "jumps" as the elements of the lens shift around during the zoom.

  Focus may be linear or non-linear, as well. By default, if you rotate the ring of Z-mount lenses quickly, the focus plane is adjusted by a large amount. Slower rotation produces adjustments in smaller increments. As I noted in Chapter 7, because Nikon Z-mount autofocus lenses use focus by wire, it's much easier to design them to focus in a linear manner when that's desirable. Using Custom Setting f9: Focus Ring Rotation Range, you can switch from the default non-linear response to fixed focus behavior over a rotational range from 90 to 720 degrees.

  Linear focus characteristics are useful for movie-making, since any focus changes made *while capturing video* can be seen in the footage. It's essential if you're using selective focus with pull- or push-focus techniques. In either case, the focus adjustment needs to be smooth rather than jerky.

Keeping Things Stable and on the Level

Camera shake's enough of a problem with still photography, but it becomes even more of a nuisance when you're shooting video. The image-stabilization feature found in many Nikon lenses (and some third-party optics) can help minimize this. That's why Nikon's VR-capable zoom lenses (described in the downloadable PDF bonus Chapter 13) make an excellent choice for Video Recording if you're planning on going for the hand-held cinema verité look.

The camera also has an *electronic VR* option, which I've described several times in this book. It's not available with N-RAW or ProRes RAW, 8K video, or 120/100 fps rates, and Hi-Res Zoom is disabled. To recap, electronic vibration reduction reduces the frame size by about 10 percent (in FX mode only; in DX mode the camera has the pixels outside the APS-C frame to play with) and uses the extra image area to realign the frames to counteract any camera motion.

Just realize that while hand-held camera shots—even image stabilized—may be perfect if you're shooting a documentary or video that intentionally mimics traditional home movie making, in other contexts it can be disconcerting or annoying. And even VR can't work miracles. As I'll point out soon the next section, it's the camera movement itself that is distracting—not necessarily any blur in our subject matter.

If you want your video to look professional, putting the camera on a tripod will give you smoother, steadier video clips to work with. It will be easier to intercut shots taken from different angles (or even at different times) if everything was shot on a tripod. Cutting from a tripod shot to a hand-held shot, or even from one hand-held shot to another one that has noticeably more (or less) camera movement can call attention to what otherwise might have been a smooth cut or transition.

Remember that telephoto lenses and telephoto zoom focal lengths magnify any camera shake, even with VR, so when you're using a longer focal length, that tripod becomes an even better idea. Tripods are essential if you want to pan from side to side during a shot, dolly in and out, or track from side to side (say, you want to shoot with the camera in your kid's coaster wagon). A tripod and (for panning) a fluid head built especially for smooth video movements can add a lot of production value to your movies.

ROLL ON, SHUTTER

Another side-effect to watch out for occurs when panning or capturing moving subjects, caused by the *rolling shutter.* Because your camera captures all the horizontal lines one at a time, the last line in a frame is captured a fraction of a second after the first line. So, if the subject or camera is moving from side to side, a vertical subject will appear to lean in the direction opposite the camera's movement, causing what is termed a "Jell-O effect." There's no way to eliminate this defect, but you should be aware of it when shooting. You may be able to minimize capturing moving subjects or edit offending clips out of your finished video.

Shooting Script

A shooting script is nothing more than a coordinated plan that covers both audio and video and provides order and structure for your video when you're in planned, storytelling mode. A detailed script will cover what types of shots you're going after, what dialogue you're going to use, audio effects, transitions, and graphics. A good script needn't constrain you: as the director you are free to make changes on the spot during actual capture. But, before you change the route to your final destination, it's good to know where you were headed, and how you originally planned to get there.

When putting together your shooting script, plan for lots and lots of different shots, even if you don't think you'll need them. Only amateurish videos consist of a bunch of long, tedious shots. You'll want to vary the pace of your production by cutting among lots of different views, angles, and perspectives, so jot down your ideas for these variations when you put together your script.

If you're shooting a documentary rather than telling a story that's already been completely mapped out, the idea of using a shooting script needs to be applied more flexibly. Documentary filmmakers often have no shooting script at all. They go out, do their interviews, capture video of people, places, and events as they find them, and allow the structure of the story to take shape as they learn more about the subject of their documentary. In such cases, the movie is typically "created" during editing, as bits and pieces are assembled into the finished piece.

Storyboards

A storyboard makes a great adjunct to a detailed shooting script. It is a series of panels providing visuals of what each scene should look like. While the ones produced by Hollywood are generally of very high quality, there's nothing that says drawing skills are important for this step. Stick figures work just fine if that's the best you can do. The storyboard just helps you visualize locations, placement of actors, props, and furniture, and helps everyone involved get an idea of what you're trying to show. It also helps show how you want to frame or compose a shot. You can even shoot a series of still photos and transform them into a "storyboard" if you want, such as in Figure 12.12.

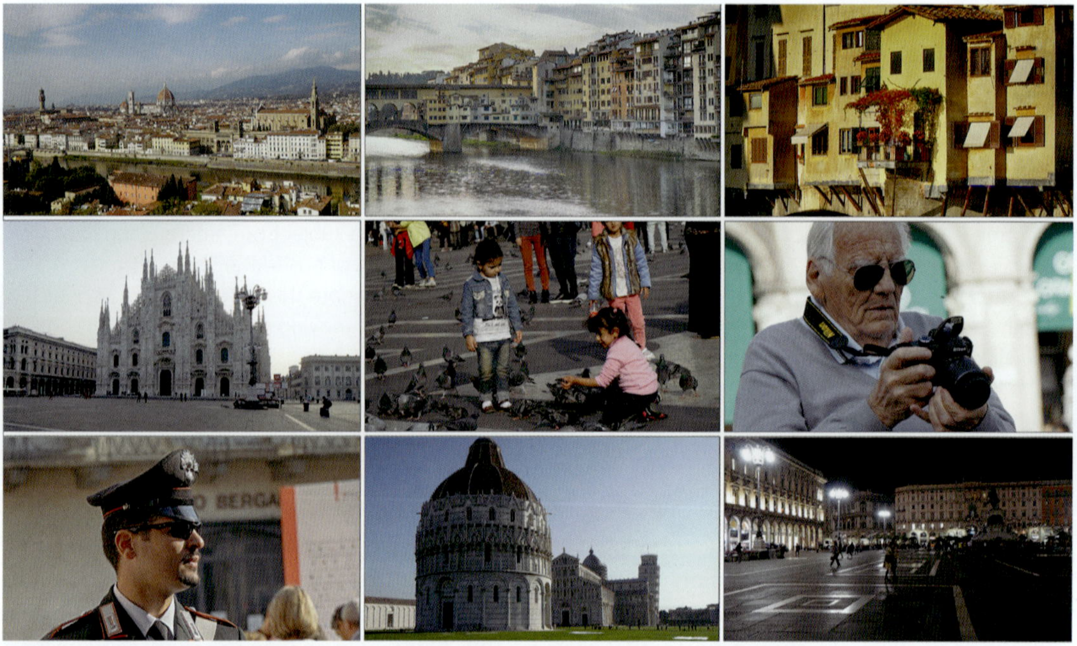

Figure 12.12 A storyboard is a series of simple sketches or photos to help visualize a segment of video.

Storytelling in Video

Today's audience is used to fast-paced, short-scene storytelling. To produce interesting video for such viewers, it's important to view video storytelling as a kind of shorthand code for the more leisurely efforts print media offers. Audio and video should always be advancing the story. While it's okay to let the camera linger from time to time, it should only be for a compelling reason and only briefly. Above all, look for movement in your scene as you shoot. You're not taking still photographs!

It only takes a second or two for an establishing shot to impart the necessary information. For example, many of the scenes for a video documenting a model being photographed in a rock 'n' roll music setting might be close-ups and talking heads, but an establishing shot showing the studio where the video was captured helps set the scene.

Provide variety too. If you put your shooting script together correctly, you'll be changing camera angles and perspectives often and never leave a static scene on the screen for a long period of time. (You can record a static scene for a reasonably long period and then edit in other shots that cut away and back to the longer scene with close-ups that show each person talking.)

When editing, keep transitions basic! I can't stress this one enough. Watch a television program or movie. The action "jumps" from one scene or person to the next. Fancy transitions that involve exotic "wipes," dissolves, or cross fades take too long for the average viewer and make your video ponderous.

Composition

In movie shooting, several factors restrict your composition, and impose requirements you just don't always have in still photography (although other rules of good composition do apply). Here are some of the key differences to keep in mind when composing movie frames:

- **Horizontal compositions only.** Some subjects, such as basketball players and tall buildings, just lend themselves to vertical compositions. But movies are shown in horizontal format only. So, if you're interviewing a local basketball star, you can end up with a worst-case situation like the one shown in Figure 12.13. If you want to show how tall your subject is, it's often impractical to move back far enough to show him full-length. You really can't capture a vertical composition. Tricks like getting down on the floor and shooting up at your subject can exaggerate the perspective but aren't a perfect solution.

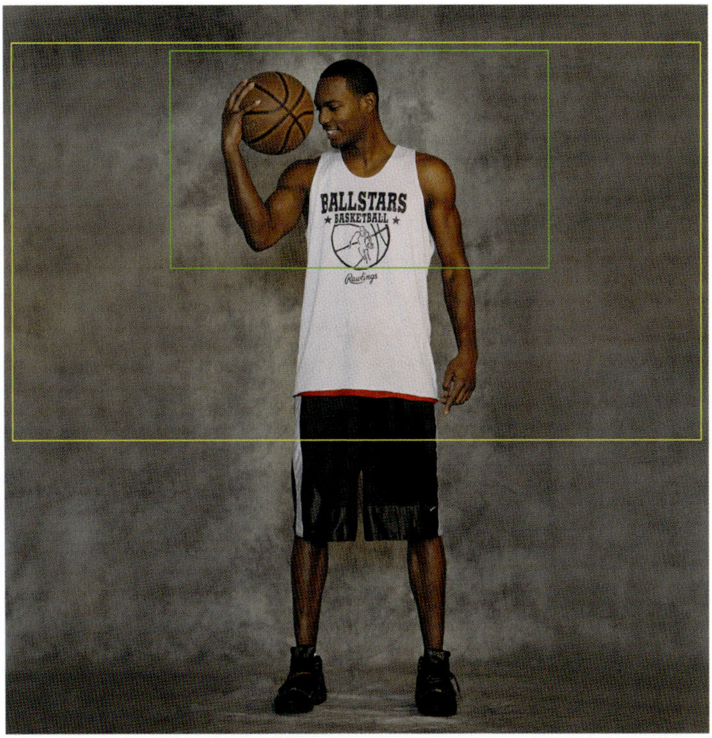

Figure 12.13 Video Recording requires you to fit all your subjects into a horizontally oriented frame.

- **Wasted space at the sides.** Moving in to frame the basketball player as outlined by the yellow box in Figure 12.13 means that you're still forced to leave a lot of empty space on either side. (Of course, you can fill that space with other people and/or interesting stuff, but that defeats your intent of concentrating on your main subject.) So, when faced with some types of subjects in a horizontal frame, you can be creative, or move in *really* tight. For example, if I was willing to give up the "height" aspect of my composition, I could have framed the shot as shown by the green box in the figure and wasted less of the image area at either side.
- **Seamless (or seamed) transitions.** Unless you're telling a picture story with a photo essay, still pictures often stand alone. But with movies, each of your compositions must relate to the shot that preceded it, and the one that follows. It can be jarring to jump from a long shot to a tight close-up unless the director—you—is very creative. Another common error is the "jump cut" in which successive shots vary only slightly in camera angle, making it appear that the main subject has "jumped" from one place to another. (Although everyone from French New Wave director Jean-Luc Goddard to Guy Ritchie—Madonna's ex—have used jump cuts effectively in their films.) The rule of thumb is to vary the camera angle by at least 30 degrees between shots to make it appear to be seamless. Unless you prefer that your images flaunt convention and appear to be "seamy."
- **The time dimension.** Unlike still photography, with motion pictures there's a lot more emphasis on using a series of images to build on each other to tell a story. Static shots where the camera is mounted on a tripod and everything is shot from the same distance are a recipe for dull videos. Watch a television program sometime and notice how often camera shots change distances and directions. Viewers are used to this variety and have come to expect it. Professional video productions are often done with multiple cameras shooting from different angles and positions. But many professional productions are shot with just one camera and careful planning, and you can do just fine with your camera.

Here's a look at the different types of commonly used compositional tools:

- **Establishing shot.** Much as it sounds, this type of composition, as shown in Figure 12.14, upper left, establishes the scene and tells the viewer where the action is taking place. Let's say you're shooting a video of your offspring's move to college; the establishing shot could be a wide shot of the campus with a sign welcoming you to the school in the foreground. Another example would be for a child's birthday party; the establishing shot could be the front of the house decorated with birthday signs and streamers or a shot of the dining room table decked out with party favors and a candle-covered birthday cake. In the example, I wanted to show the studio where the video was shot.
- **Medium shot.** This shot is composed from about waist to head room (some space above the subject's head). It's useful for providing variety from a series of close-ups and makes for a useful first look at a speaker. A medium shot is used to bring the viewer into a scene without shocking them. It can be used to introduce a character and provide context via their surroundings. (See Figure 12.14, upper right.)

- **Close-up.** The close-up, usually described as "from shirt pocket to head room," provides a good composition for someone talking directly to the camera. Although it's common to have your talking head centered in the shot, that's not a requirement. In Figure 12.14, center left, the subject was offset to the right. This would allow other images, especially graphics or titles, to be superimposed in the frame in a "real" (professional) production. But the compositional technique can be used with camera videos, too, even if special effects are not going to be added. A close-up generally shows the full face with a little head room at the top and down to the shoulders at the bottom of the frame.
- **Extreme close-up.** When I went through broadcast training, this shot was described as the "big talking face" shot and we were actively discouraged from employing it. Styles and tastes change over the years and now the big talking face is much more commonly used (maybe people are better looking these days?) and so this view may be appropriate. Just remember, your camera

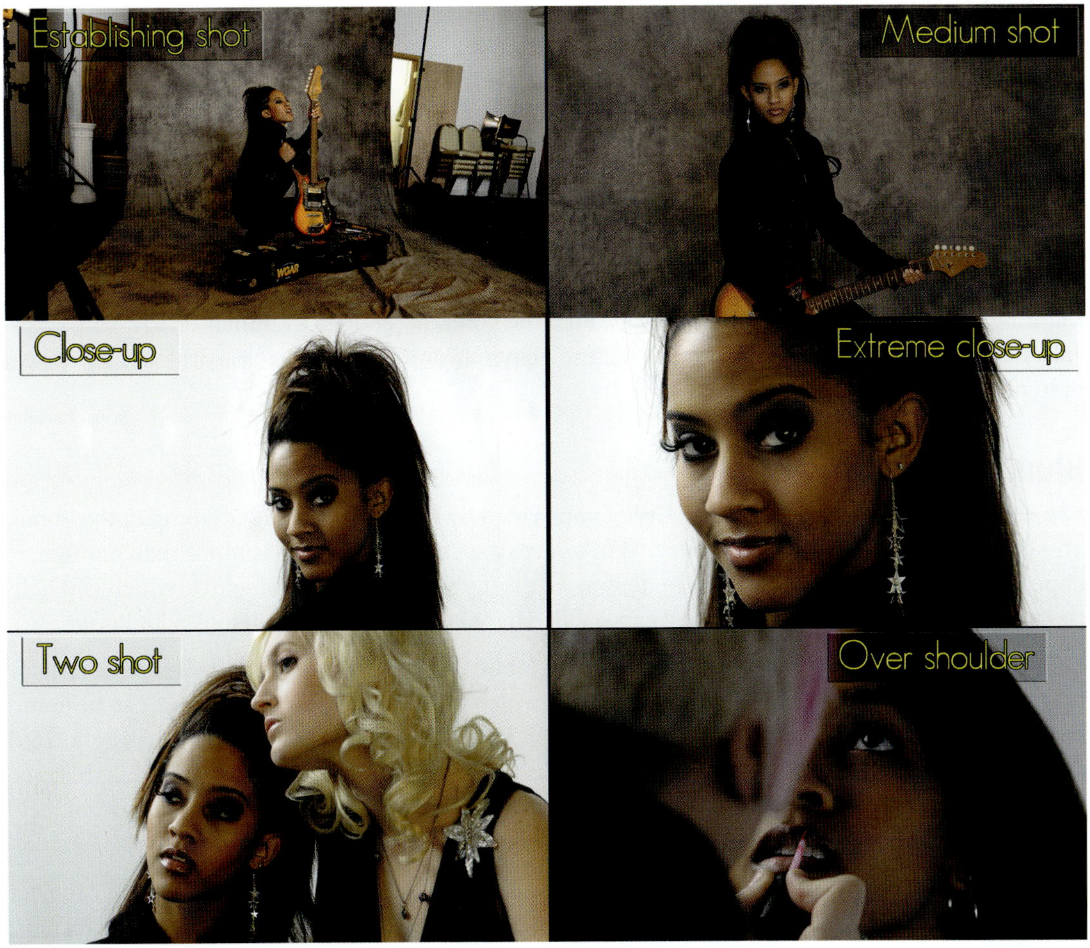

Figure 12.14 Use a full range of shot types.

is capable of shooting in high-definition video and you may be playing the video on a high-def TV; be careful that you use this composition on a face that can stand up to high definition. (See Figure 12.14, center right.) An extreme close-up is a very tight shot that cuts off everything above the top of the head and below the chin (or even closer!). Be careful using this shot since many of us look better from a distance!

- **Two shot.** A two shot shows a pair of subjects in one frame. They can be side by side or one in the foreground and one in the background. (See Figure 12.14, lower left.) This does not have to be a head-to-ground composition. Subjects can be standing or seated. A "three shot" is the same principle except that three people are in the frame. This version can be framed at various distances such as medium or close-up.
- **Over-shoulder shot.** Long a composition of interview programs, the "over-shoulder shot" uses the rear of one person's head and shoulder to serve as a frame for the other person. This puts the viewer's perspective as that of the person facing away from the camera. (See Figure 12.14, lower right.) An "over-shoulder" shot is a popular shot for interview programs. It helps make the viewers feel like they're the one asking the questions.

Lighting for Video

Much like in still photography, how you handle light pretty much can make or break your videography. Lighting for video can be more complicated than lighting for still photography, since both subject and camera movement are often part of the process.

Lighting for video presents several concerns. First off, you want enough illumination to create a useable video. Beyond that, you want to use light to help tell your story or increase drama. Let's take a better look at both.

Illumination

You can significantly improve the quality of your video by increasing the light falling in the scene. This is true indoors or out, by the way. While it may seem like sunlight is more than enough, it depends on how much contrast you're dealing with. If your subject is in shadow (which can help them from squinting) or wearing a ball cap, a video light can help make them look a lot better.

Lighting choices for amateur videographers are a lot better these days than they were a decade or two ago. An inexpensive incandescent video light, which will easily fit in a camera bag, can be found for $15 or $20. You can even get a good-quality LED video light for less than $100. Work lights sold at many home improvement stores can also serve as video lights since you can set the white balance to correct for any color casts. You'll need to mount these lights on a tripod or other support, or, perhaps, to a bracket that fastens to the tripod socket on the bottom of the camera.

Much of the challenge depends upon whether you're just trying to add some fill-light on your subject versus trying to boost the light on an entire scene. A small video light will do just fine for the former; it won't handle the latter. Fortunately, the versatility of the camera comes in quite handy here. Since the camera shoots video in Auto ISO mode, it can compensate for lower lighting levels and still produce a decent image. For best results though, better lighting is necessary.

Creative Lighting

While ramping up the light intensity will produce better technical quality in your video, it won't necessarily improve the artistic quality of it. Whether we're outdoors or indoors, we're used to seeing light come from above. Videographers need to consider how they position their lights to provide even illumination while up high enough to angle shadows down low and out of sight of the camera.

When lighting for video, there are several factors to consider. One is the quality of the light. It can either be hard (direct) light or soft (diffused) light. Hard light is good for showing detail but can also be very harsh and unforgiving. "Softening" the light, but diffusing it somehow, can reduce the intensity of the light but make for a kinder, gentler light as well.

While mixing light sources isn't always a good idea, one approach is to combine window light with supplemental lighting. Position your subject with the window to one side and bring in either a supplemental light or a reflector to the other side for reasonably even lighting.

Lighting Styles

Some lighting styles are more heavily used than others. Some forms are used for special effects, while others are designed to be invisible. At its most basic, lighting just illuminates the scene, but when used properly it can also create drama. Let's look at some types of lighting styles:

- **Three-point lighting.** This is a basic lighting setup for one person. A main light illuminates the strong side of a person's face, while a fill light lights up the other side. A third light is then positioned above and behind the subject to light the back of the head and shoulders. (See Figure 12.15, left.)
- **Flat lighting.** Use this type of lighting to provide illumination and nothing more. It calls for a variety of lights and diffusers set to raise the light level in a space enough for good video reproduction, but not to create a mood or emphasize a scene or individual. With flat lighting, you're trying to create even lighting levels throughout the video space and minimize any shadows. Generally, the lights are placed up high and angled downward (or possibly pointed straight up to bounce off a white ceiling). (See Figure 12.15, right.)

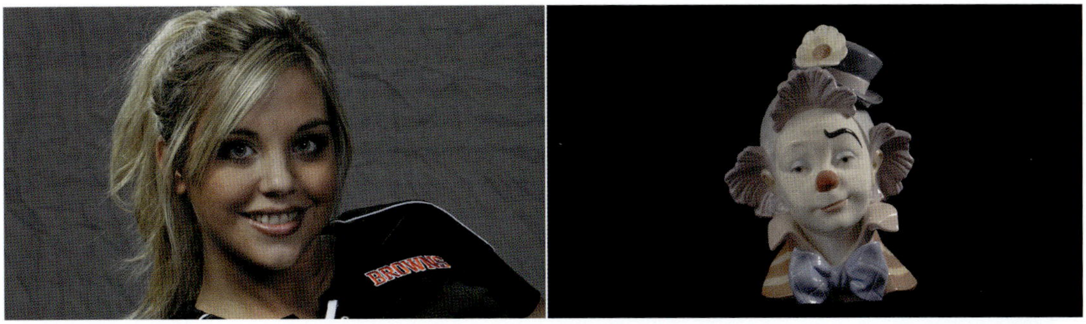

Figure 12.15 With three-point lighting (left) two lights are placed in front and to the side of the subject and another light is directed on the background to provide separation. Flat lighting (right) was bounced off a white ceiling and walls to fill in shadows as much as possible. It is a flexible lighting approach since the subject can change positions without needing a change in light direction.

- **"Ghoul lighting."** This is the style of lighting used for old horror movies. The idea is to position the light down low, pointed upward. It's such an unnatural style of lighting that it makes its targets seem weird and "ghoulish."
- **Outdoor lighting.** While shooting outdoors may seem easier because the sun provides more light, it also presents its own problems. As a rule of thumb, keep the sun behind you when you're shooting video outdoors, except when shooting faces (anything from a medium shot and closer) since the viewer won't want to see a squinting subject. When shooting another human this way, put the sun behind her and use a video light to balance light levels between the foreground and background. If the sun is simply too bright, position the subject in the shade and use the video light for your main illumination. Using reflectors (white board panels or aluminum foil–covered cardboard panels are cheap options) can also help balance light effectively.

Audio

When it comes to making a successful video, audio quality is one of those things that separates the professionals from the amateurs. We're used to watching top-quality productions on television and in the movies, yet the average person has no idea how much effort goes in to producing what seems to be "natural" sound. Much of the sound you hear in such productions is recorded on carefully controlled sound stages and "sweetened" with a variety of sound effects and other recordings of "natural" sound. Google "Foley artist" some time and you'll discover this part of a production is, indeed, a rich and complex art form.

Tips for Better Audio

Since recording high-quality audio is such a challenge, it's a good idea to do everything possible to maximize recording quality. Your Z9/Z8 has a stereo microphone located on each side of the viewfinder housing (what we called a pentaprism in the SLR days). Audio is recorded in 16-bit stereo with a 48 kHz sampling rate, with the sound quality basically limited by the quality of your microphone. While the Z9/Z8's microphone is good, you'll get better quality from a dedicated external mic. Here are some specific ideas for improving the quality of the audio your camera records:

- **Get the camera and its microphone close to the speaker.** The farther the microphone is from the audio source, the less effective it will be in picking up that sound. While having to position the camera and its built-in microphone closer to the subject affects your lens choices and lens perspective options, it will make the most of your audio source. Of course, if you're using a very wide-angle lens, getting too close to your subject can have unflattering results, so don't take this advice too far. It's important to think carefully about what sounds you want to capture. If you're shooting video of an acoustic combo that's not using a PA system, you'll want the microphone close to them, but not so close that, say, only the lead singer or instrumentalist is picked up, while the players at either side fade off into the background.

- **Use an external microphone.** You'll recall the description of the external microphone port in Chapter 1. As noted, this port accepts a stereo mini-plug from a standard external microphone, allowing you to achieve considerably higher audio quality for your movies than is possible with the built-in microphones (which are disabled when an external mic is plugged in). An external microphone reduces the amount of camera-induced noise that is picked up and recorded on your audio track. (The action of the lens as it focuses can be audible when the built-in microphones are active.)

  The external microphone port can provide plug-in power for microphones that can take their power from this sort of outlet rather than from a battery in the microphone. Nikon provides optional compatible microphones such as the ME-1 (see Figure 12.16); you also may find suitable microphones from companies such as Shure and Audio-Technica. If you are on a quest for superior audio quality, you can even obtain a portable mixer that can plug into this jack, such as the affordable Rolls MX124, letting you use multiple high-quality microphones (up to four) to record your soundtrack.

  An exciting new option designed specifically for still cameras is the Beachtek DXA-SLR Ultra HDSLR Audio Adapter. It's more expensive, but has even more professional sound options and clips right onto the bottom of your camera using the tripod-mounting socket.

  One advantage that a sound-mixing device like the DXA-SLR Ultra HDSLR offers over the stock camera is that it adds an additional headphone output jack to your camera, so you can monitor the sound actually being captured by the recorder (you can also listen to your soundtrack through the headphones during playback, which is *way* better than using the built-in speaker). The adapter has two balanced XLR microphone inputs and can also accept line input (from another audio source) and provides cool features like AGC (automatic gain control), built-in limiting, and VU meters you can use to monitor sound input.

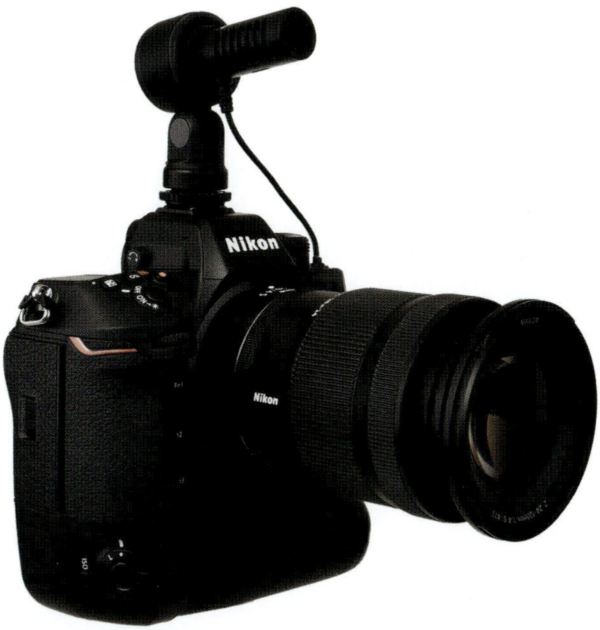

Figure 12.16 Nikon ME-1 external stereo microphone.

- **Hide the microphone.** Combine the first few tips by using an external mic, and getting it as close to your subject as possible. If you're capturing a single person, you can always use a lapel microphone (described in the next section). But if you want a single mic to capture sound from multiple sources, your best bet may be to hide it somewhere in the shot. Put it behind a vase, using duct tape to fasten the microphone, and fix the mic cable out of sight (if you're not using a wireless microphone).
- **Turn off any sound makers you can.** Little things like fans and air handling units aren't obvious to the human ear but will be picked up by the microphone. Turn off any machinery or devices that you can, plus make sure cell phones are set to silent mode. Also, do what you can to minimize sounds such as wind, radio, television, or people talking in the background.
- **Make sure to record some "natural" sound.** If you're shooting video at an event of some kind, make sure you get some background sound that you can add to your audio as desired in post-production.
- **Consider recording audio separately.** Lip-syncing is probably beyond most of the people you're going to be shooting, but there's nothing that says you can't record narration separately and add it later. It's relatively easy if you learn how to use simple software video-editing programs like iMovie (for the Macintosh) or Windows Movie Maker (for Windows PCs). Any time the speaker is off-camera, you can work with separately recorded narration rather than recording the speaker on-camera. This can produce much cleaner sound.

External Microphones

The single-most important thing you can do to improve your audio quality is to use an external microphone. The internal stereo microphones mounted on the front of the camera will do a decent job, but they have some significant drawbacks, partially spelled out in the previous section:

- **Camera noise.** There are plenty of noise sources emanating from the camera, including your own breathing and rustling around as the camera shifts in your hand. Manual zooming is bound to affect your sound, and your fingers will fall directly in front of the built-in mics as you change focal lengths. An external microphone isolates the sound recording from camera noise.
- **Distance.** Anytime your camera is located more than 6 to 8 feet from your subjects or sound source, the audio will suffer. An external unit allows you to place the mic right next to your subject.
- **Improved quality.** Obviously, Nikon didn't have room for a super-expensive, super-high-quality microphone on your compact mirrorless camera. Not all owners would appreciate the bulk or be willing to pay the premium, especially if they didn't plan to shoot much video themselves. An external microphone will almost always be of better quality.
- **Directionality.** The internal microphone generally records only sounds directly in front of it. An external microphone can be either of the directional type or omnidirectional, depending on whether you want to "shotgun" your sound or record more ambient sound.

You can choose from several different types of microphones, each of which has its own advantages and disadvantages. If you're serious about movie making, you might want to own more than one. Common configurations include:

- **Shotgun microphones.** These can be mounted directly on your camera, although, if the mic uses an accessory shoe mount, you'll need the optional adapter to convert the camera's shoe to a standard hot shoe. I prefer to use a bracket, which further isolates the microphone from any camera noise. One thing to keep in mind is that while the shotgun mic will generally ignore any sound coming from *behind* it, it will pick up any sound it is pointed at, even *behind* your subject. You may be capturing video and audio of someone you're interviewing in a restaurant, and not realize you're picking up the lunchtime conversation of the diners seated in the table behind your subject. Outdoors, you may record your speaker, as well as the traffic on a busy street or freeway in the background.
- **Lapel microphones.** Also called *lavalieres*, these microphones attach to the subject's clothing and pick up their voice with the best quality. You'll need a long enough cord or a wireless mic. These are especially good for video interviews, so whether you're producing a documentary or grilling relatives for a family history, you'll want one of these.
- **Hand-held microphones.** If you're capturing a singer crooning a tune or want your subject to mimic famed faux newscaster Wally Ballou, a hand-held mic may be your best choice. They serve much the same purpose as a lapel microphone, and they're more intrusive—but that may be the point. A hand-held microphone can make a great prop for your fake newscast! The speaker can talk right into the microphone, point it at another person, or use it to record ambient sound. If your narrator is not going to appear on-camera, one of these can be an inexpensive way to improve sound.
- **Wired and wireless external microphones.** This option is the most expensive, but you get a receiver and a transmitter (both battery-powered, so you'll need to make sure you have enough batteries). The transmitter is connected to the microphone, and the receiver is connected to your camera. In addition to being less klutzy and enabling you to avoid having wires on view in your scene, wireless mics, such as the Nikon ME-W1, let you record sounds that are physically located some distance from your camera. Of course, you need to keep in mind the range of your device and be aware of possible signal interference from other electronic components in the vicinity.

WIND NOISE REDUCTION

Always use the **wind screen** provided with an external microphone (especially the popular fuzzy "dead-cat" covering) to reduce the effect of noise produced by even light breezes blowing over the microphone. Many mics, such as the Nikon ME-1, include a low-cut filter to further reduce wind noise. However, these can also affect other sounds. You can disable the low-cut filters for the ME-1 by changing a switch on the back from L-cut (low cutoff) to Flat. Other external mics also have their own low-cut filter switch.

Special Features

The Z9 and Z8 also have two audio frequency response ranges (Wide and Vocal Range) and an Attenuator—both settings found near the bottom of the Video Recording menu, so you can tailor your microphone capture to your subject matter (for ambient sound or voice recording). Audio levels can be adjusted while recording, and the internal microphones have improved wind noise reduction.

Bonus Content Reminder

This edition of *David Busch's Nikon Z9/Z8 Guide to Digital Still Photography* covers firmware Version 5.0 (for the Z9) and Version 2.01 (for the Z8). As I noted in the introduction, future updates will be incorporated into bonus content available for download for free from the Rocky Nook website at:

https://rockynook.com/nikon-z8-z9/

Don't forget that in addition to descriptions of firmware enhancements, you'll find several extra chapters with useful information that couldn't be squeezed into the printed version of this book. Instead, they are integrated into ebook editions and offered as no-cost PDF downloads for other readers. Your bonus chapters include:

- **Chapter 13: Focus on Lenses.** A comprehensive guide that covers choosing and using lenses and descriptions of most Z-mount lenses and the most popular F-mount optics that could be used with one of the FTZ adapters.
- **Chapter 14: Protection, Prevention, and Troubleshooting.** Shows you how to keep your camera safe, diagnose problems, fix some common ills, and, importantly, learn how to avoid them in the future.

Firmware Updates

A

Both the Nikon Z9 and Z8 have been notable for the impressive firmware enhancements that have been released since each was introduced. The Z9 alone has had multiple small updates with bug fixes and no less than four major whole-number upgrades extending to the Version 5.0 current when this book was written. This book has been updated for the Z8's latest firmware, Version 2.01.

In refreshing this guide from its initial printing and incorporating all the changes into the main body of the book, it wasn't possible to include *everything*. That's why this Appendix has been added to provide last-minute coverage of the amazing Pixel Shift shooting feature. Nikon first offered it on the retro-styled Zf, and extended it to the Nikon Z8 with the 2.0 firmware release. By the time this book is printed, it may be available on the Z9, as well.

As I noted in the Introduction, I intend to support future firmware updates in a timely manner though free online downloadable PDF supplements on the Rocky Nook website. As Nikon continues to release firmware fixes and enhancements for these cameras, you can find them here:

https://rockynook.com/nikon-z8-z9/

In addition, purchasers of the printed version of this book can download several bonus chapters with useful information. They include Chapter 13, which is a comprehensive guide that covers choosing and using lenses and descriptions of most Z-mount lenses and the most popular F-mount optics that could be used with one of the FTZ adapters. The bonus Chapter 14, "Protection, Prevention, and Troubleshooting" shows you how to keep your camera safe, diagnose problems, fix some common ills, and, importantly, learn how to avoid them in the future.

Pixel Shift Shooting

Options: Pixel Shift Shooting Mode, Number of Shots, Delay, Interval Until Next Shot

My preference: N/A

If your camera's 45MP resolution isn't enough, Nikon has added an amazing Pixel Shift shooting capability to the Z8 that can mimic the amount of detail you might expect from a sensor with a whopping 180 megapixels! The limitations: the camera takes 8, 16, or 32 separate pictures that are merged in the free Nikon Studio NX software, and they must be captured with the camera rock-steady on a tripod, and I strongly recommend using a remote release. While this feature is not available for the Z9 as I write this, it's possible Nikon will be adding it in the future.

The secret behind the pixel-shift process is that your camera doesn't actually have 45MP of resolution in the first place. It does have 45MP worth of pixels, but each pixel can only detect one color—red, green, or blue. When you capture a conventional picture, about one quarter are sensitive *only* to blue light, another quarter detect only red light, and *half* (twice as many) are sensitive to green light. Even though each pixel captures only one of the three RGB colors, by examining the values of surrounding pixels, the camera can make a pretty good guess as to the actual color of a particular pixel through an interpolation process called *demosaicing*. The algorithms may tell the camera that a pixel captured by a green-sensitive photosite is probably red or blue instead. This works fairly well, but, as you might think, isn't perfect.

Figure A.1 shows a small section of a Bayer array, named after Kodak scientist Dr. Bryce Bayer, who patented the technology in 1976. He specified using twice as many green elements as red or blue to simulate human vision, which, in daylight, combines two different types of cells in the retina that are most sensitive to green light. At left, I've superimposed the array's red, green, and blue microfilters over a representation of the photosensitive layer beneath, which is colored gray for the illustration. At right in the figure, I show how the pixels are arranged: every other pixel is green, and the remaining pixels are red or blue, alternating rows.

While each pixel detects only one of the primary colors in ordinary shooting, the pixel-shift process fixes this deficiency by capturing *multiple* images, shifting the sensor slightly between shots so that each photosite has the opportunity to read each of the primary colors in turn. You can choose whether to take 4, 8, 16, or 32 different shots; with the larger number of shots determining the amount of shift between individual images and type of image processing performed using Nikon NX Studio:

- **4 shots.** The camera captures four separate exposures which can be processed using Nikon NX Studio to produce a picture with improved color reproduction.
- **8 shots.** A total of 8 shots are taken and processed by NX Studio to produce a photo with improved color and reduced noise.
- **16 shots.** The camera captures 16 images that can be processed to create a higher resolution version with improved color reproduction.
- **32 shots.** Combining the 32 shots captured in this mode gives you a higher resolution image with improved color and reduced noise.

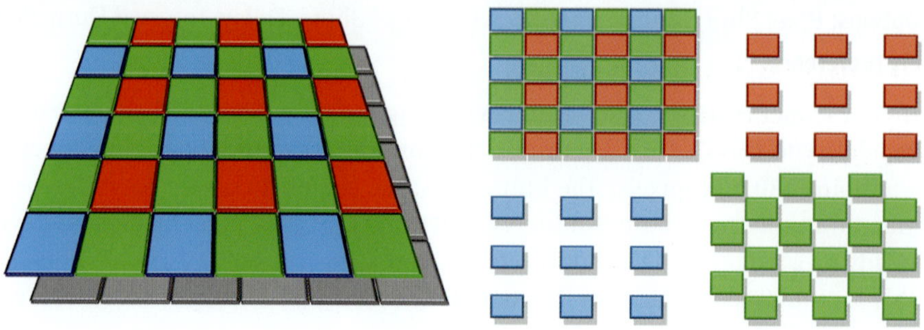

Figure A.1 A section of a Bayer array (left) and relative distribution of the red, green, and blue filters (right).

In practice, the camera starts with the first shot, which produces the standard image that results from non-shift mode. Then, the sensor shifts to grab additional images to capture information such that all colors are captured by every photosite. The result is a higher degree of detail without the need to "guess" which colors each pixel represents. With up to 32 shots captured, that's a huge amount of information, prodigious enough that the camera cannot process it internally (and you wouldn't want to wait that long between shots even if it could). So, the NX Studio's software interprets these multiple shots for you, to produce a single image in which every pixel reflects the actual color of your subject. You get more detail and potentially more accurate color at the cost of a little post-processing.

Capturing Your Images

Pixel shift works *only* with non-moving, static subjects, and neither the camera nor subject matter can move *at all* during the sequence of exposures. For that reason, you'll get the best results shooting indoors, as there are many factors outdoors that can cause subject/camera movement, even when a tripod is used. For example, you'd need to pay special attention to foliage; if there is any breeze at all, the leaves on trees will move. Using a high shutter speed may help somewhat, but, like MPG, your actual results may vary considerably between different sets of shots when working outdoors.

The plane of focus must not change, either, so you should use manual focus. The exposure itself should be constant, so I recommend manual exposure when using ambient lighting, as long as the illumination itself remains constant. Outdoors, swiftly moving clouds can cause changes in lighting, and indoors you'll find that fluorescent and other non-incandescent sources flicker slightly. I've found that Nikon's electronic flash units work well, even in automatic exposure mode, and can provide consistent illumination between shots (if you set the interval between them appropriately, as described below).

To capture a pixel-shift image, just follow these steps:

1. **Steady your camera.** Mount your camera on a rock-solid tripod. If possible, use only the legs of the tripod to achieve the shooting elevation you want, and avoid raising the center column. Lock all the tripod's positional controls. If you're using a lightweight tripod, suspend your camera bag or another weight from the center column to steady it. In my tests I discovered that even almost imperceptible movement (which can be produced simply by pressing the camera's shutter release too vigorously) can ruin a series. The tip-off: a slight amount of blurring in the first shot of a series, or a "ghost" image from ambient light when using flash, compared to the additional exposures, taken after short delay.
2. **Connect the camera to a remote release device or cable.** You'll want to eliminate any camera shake caused by pressing the shutter release manually.
3. **Update pixel map.** Nikon recommends using the Pixel Mapping feature (described in Chapter 9) to disable any defective pixels before using Pixel Shift.
4. **Power.** Make sure you have a fully charged battery or have connected the camera to an external power source.
5. **Shoot RAW.** NX Studio processes RAW files.

6. **Set exposure and focus manually.** Manually focus to get the sharpest possible image. Your extra resolution is wasted if you haven't focused properly. (Take a test shot, if you want.)
7. **Check your lighting.** Indoors, I use incandescent light or flash instead of fluorescent illumination; the flickering fluorescent lighting causes can produce banding in your image. Keep in mind that softer lighting (such as that produced by umbrellas, soft boxes, diffusers, or bounce lighting) reduces glare but may mask that extra detail you're looking for. More contrasty illumination (generally, direct lighting) can emphasize detail—and also any defects in your subject matter.
8. **Access Pixel Shift feature.** Navigate to the Pixel Shift Shooting entry of the Photo Shooting menu (see Figure A.2, upper left). Select Pixel Shift Shooting Mode and specify On (Series) or On (Single Photo). (See Figure A.2, upper right.)
9. **Number of shots.** Choose 4, 8, 16, or 32 shots, as shown center left in the figure. I recommend starting with four-shot sequences to help you master the pixel-shift feature. The exposures are made quickly, and the files are smaller and are combined faster in Nikon NX Studio. You'll rapidly see how and where your technique can be improved.

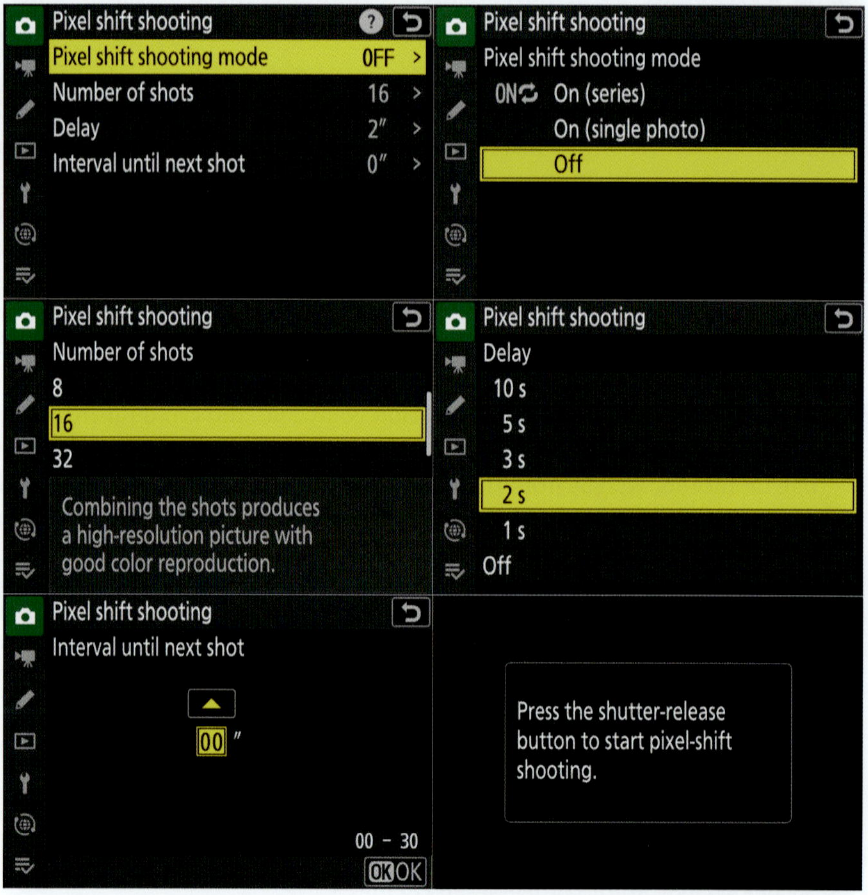

Figure A.2 Choose Pixel Shift parameters.

10. **Delay.** You can select an optional delay of from 1 to 10 seconds before capture begins. Select a longer pause if you plan to use flash. Just set the time for the amount of time it takes for your flash to recycle; you can err on the side of caution if using battery-powered units, which may have varying recycle times. (Figure A.2, center right.)
11. **Interval between shots.** Use the up/down controls to choose the amount of delay between shots, from 0 to 30 seconds. This default setting of zero will capture all the images continuously, one after another. This is usually your best choice, because it minimizes the chance of even slight movement of your subject between shots. (Figure A.2, lower left.)
12. **Trigger the shutter to take your images.** When you've finished making settings, the message shown at lower right in Figure A.2 appears. Don't touch the camera between shots.

Processing Your Pixel-Shift Exposures

Once you've captured your images, transfer them to your computer and launch the Nikon NX Studio software (which you can download from the Nikon website in your country). Then, just follow these steps:

1. **Navigate to image folder.** In the Folders panel (seen at lower left in Figure A.3), browse to your images using the directory/folder tree.
2. **Click Picture Shift Merge icon.** I've highlighted it with a green box at upper right in the figure. (The green box does *not* appear on your screen.)

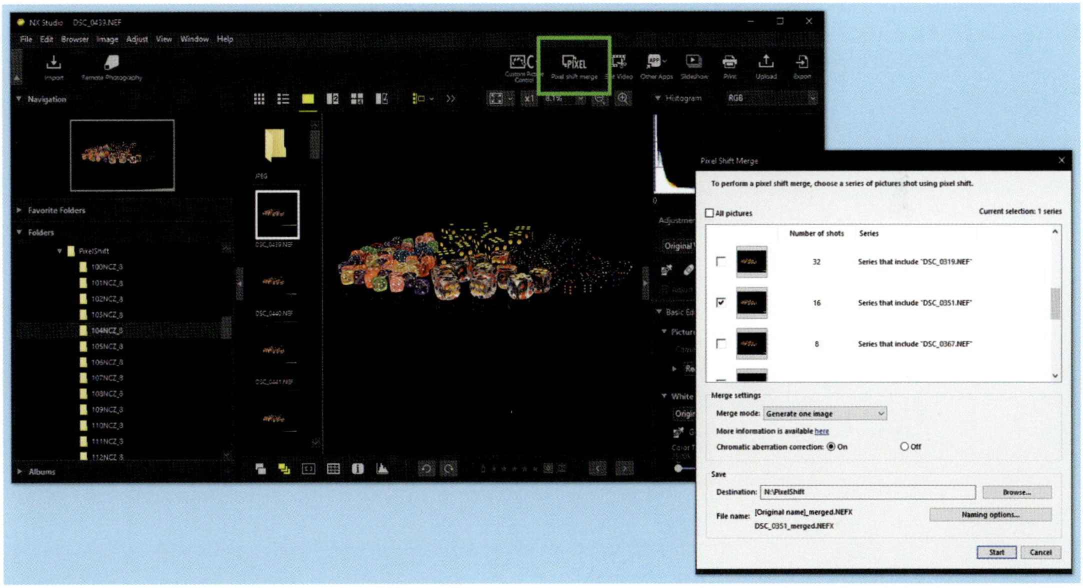

Figure A.3 Processing the RAW files in Nikon NX Studio.

3. **Choose sequence.** A dialog box, shown at right in the figure, will appear showing the sequences available. For example, if you selected 32 as your number of shots, you can select 32-, 16-, 8-, or 4-shot sequences. If you choose more than one, all will be merged when you proceed.
4. **Select Merge Mode.** Here you choose the number of images to be generated. The number depends on the number of shots available for merger. For example, if you chose 32 Shots, you can generate 2 images from 16 shots each; 4 images from 8 shots each; or 8 images from 4 shots apiece.
5. **Enable/Disable Chromatic Aberration Correction.** You can specify additional processing to reduce chromatic aberration effects if you want.
6. **Destination.** Specify or browse to a destination folder for your merged images.
7. **File Name.** NX Studio will create an .NEFX file (which can be later opened and modified using NX Studio), and give it a name that incorporates the original file name appended with "_merged." You can select a different name structure here.
8. **Begin.** Click Start to initiate processing.

You'll end up with a 180-megapixel image like the one shown at top in Figure A.4. It's difficult to show the difference on the printed page, but at the bottom of the figure you can see the original image at left and the increased resolution version at right.

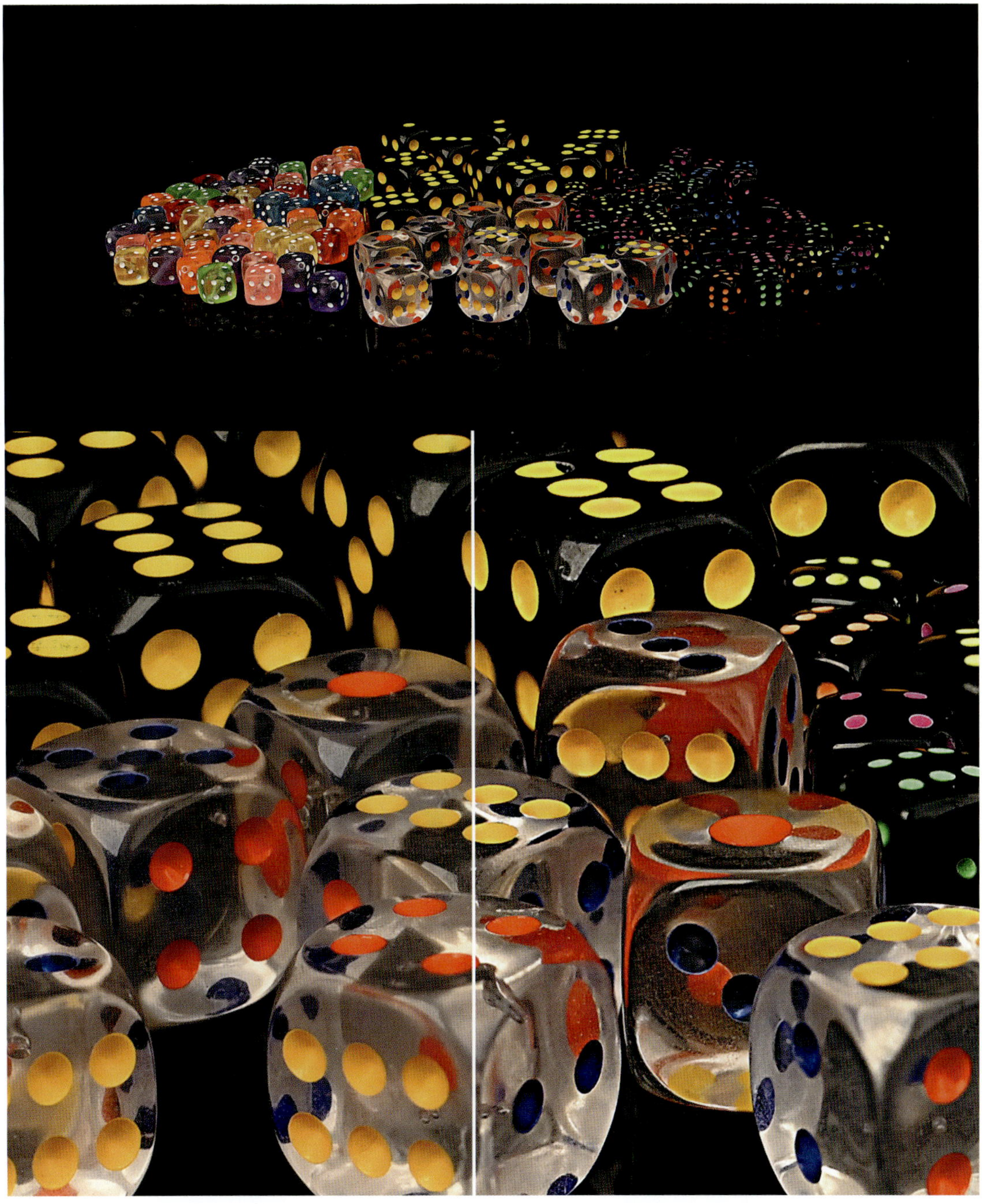

Figure A.4 The final composite image (top); an enlargement of the original image (lower left); and the pixel-shift version (lower right).

Index

C

D

G

H

I

J

K

L

O

P

W

X

Y

Z